conversation • help • activity • movement • participation • success

CHAMPS

A Proactive & Positive Approach
to Classroom Management

Second
EDITION

Randy Sprick, Ph.D.

With Contributions by:
Keba Baldwin
Mike Booher
Maureen Gale
Mickey Garrison
Amalio Nieves
Billie Jo Rodriguez

SECOND EDITION
Published in the United States by
Pacific Northwest Publishing
2451 Willamette St.
Eugene, Oregon 97405
www.pacificnwpublish.com

10 9 8 7 6   5 4 3 2 1

ISBN: 978-1-59909-030-6

Cover and interior design: Hannah Bontrager
Illustrations: Anna-Maria Crum and Tom Zillis
Indexing: Potomac Indexers

Additional graphics provided by Clipart.com. © 2009 Jupiterimages Corporation.

DEDICATION

To the trainers

I would like to dedicate this second edition of CHAMPS to the amazing *Safe & Civil Schools* trainers. This caring, dedicated, knowledgeable, articulate, and funny group of professionals has made CHAMPS come alive for many thousands of teachers over the last ten years. As of 2009, this group includes:

Keba Baldwin	Debbie Jackson
Dave Benson	Kim Marcum
Mike Booher	Bob McLaughlin
Lana Fry	Donna Meers
Laura Hamilton	Amalio Nieves
Phyllis Hamilton	Carolyn Novelly
Andrea Hanford	Linda Phillips
Dana Harader	Marcie Polin
Jane Harris	Susan Schilt
Suzanne Hays	Tricia McKale Skyles
Marilyn Hefferan	Jim Whitaker
Tricia Huder	Elizabeth Winford
Susan Isaacs	

In particular, I would like to acknowledge Laura Hamilton, Dana Harader, Susan Isaacs, Laura McCollough, Donna Meers, Ray Roth, Don Talley, Mike Waford, Jim Whitaker, and the other trainers and coaches from Kentucky who participated in the original Model Schools Project. This group worked with a pre-publication version of the original CHAMPS book and demonstrated to me the results that could be achieved with the material. That project and the subsequent Kentucky Instructional Discipline (KIDs) project would not have been possible without the leadership and expertise of Laura McCollough with the Kentucky State Department of Education.

Thanks to all of you for demonstrating how CHAMPS can assist teachers in making their classrooms places where students are highly motivated to behave responsibly and achieve academically.

I would also like to dedicate this book to the staff of Mt. Vernon Elementary School in Springfield, Oregon. Mt. Vernon was one of the original field-test schools for the first edition. I visited the school recently and was thrilled to see the entire staff still successfully and enthusiastically implementing the CHAMPS approach with students who were happily working hard, behaving responsibly, and having fun. In the first edition, three staff members were thanked specifically for their helpful feedback. Eleven years later, Melva Schumacher, Pat Gagnon, and Dianne Yonker are still positive, inspirational educators who are implementing the CHAMPS approach daily. Also, a special thanks to Principal Debbie Egan for getting it going and Principal Jim Keegan for keeping it thriving. Wow!

Randy Sprick
January 2009

Acknowledgments

I extend my thanks to Paula Rich for her extensive and skillful help in writing and editing this second edition. I would also like to thank Sara Ferris, Marilyn Sprick, and Matt Sprick for their skills, talents, and opinions throughout the editorial and publishing processes. To Keba Baldwin, Amalio Nieves, Shelley Jones, Mike Booher, Laura Hamilton, and Maureen Gale, thank you for providing valuable feedback on the content of this revision. Billie Jo Rodriguez provided great help with research citations and content suggestions. Thanks to Anna-Maria Crum and Tom Zillis for the artwork, and to Hannah Bontrager for the cover and Hannah and Natalie Conaway for the interior design and layout.

AUTHOR

Randy Sprick, Ph.D.

Randall S. Sprick, Ph.D., has worked as a paraprofessional, teacher, and teacher trainer at the elementary and secondary levels. Author of a number of widely read books on behavior and classroom management, Dr. Sprick is director of *Safe & Civil Schools*, a consulting company that provides inservice programs throughout the country. Each year, he conducts workshops for more than 20,000 teachers and administrators. He and his trainers work with numerous large and small school districts on longitudinal projects to improve student behavior and motivation. Dr. Sprick was the recipient of the 2007 Council for Exceptional Children (CEC) Wallin Lifetime Achievement Award.

CONTRIBUTORS

Keba Baldwin

Keba Baldwin has worked as a middle school science teacher, high school biology teacher, athletic director, coach, and district program coordinator of local, state, and federal programming. He has led school districts in developing policies and procedures to create safe, civil, and productive environments. Over the past years, he has worked on dropout prevention, safe schools programming, health and physical education, and character education. Mr. Baldwin was awarded Teacher of the Year status in 2000 at Githens Middle School, Durham, North Carolina.

Mike Booher

Mike Booher, M.Ed., has worked as a school psychologist, lead school psychologist, and supervisor of psychological services for Guilford County Schools. He has developed school intervention and assistance teams, crisis intervention services, professional development activities for teachers and parents, and ADHD interventions. He also coordinated the Responsible Discipline Program (RDP), a schoolwide discipline and classroom management program based on Foundations and CHAMPS. For much of his career, Mr. Booher worked with school crisis and suicide intervention teams. He served as a co-trainer for the district's suicide intervention training and as a co-leader of one of the district's two crisis teams. In addition, Mr. Booher has taught at several universities and served as a clinical instructor for the School Psychological Program at the University of North Carolina at Chapel Hill.

Maureen Gale

Maureen Gale, M.Ed., has been a special education teacher, staffing coordinator and behavior specialist. She has worked with students in grades K–12 at school sites and a psychiatric hospital, and as a special educator at the American International Schools in Uruguay, Japan, and South Africa. Ms. Gale is currently a District Behavior Coach for Orange County Public Schools (OCPS) in Florida. As a member of the OCPS Behavior Intervention Team, she works with schools to build capacity and establish site-based teams that provide a continuum of schoolwide, classroom, and individual student behavior support. Ms. Gale has conducted CHAMPS training for eight years. She is the author of *Survive & Thrive*, a laminated reference card for special education teachers (DayOne Publishing) and co-author of the *Survival Guide for the First-Year Special Education Teacher* (Council for Exceptional Children).

Mickey Garrison

Mickey Garrison, Ph.D., has been a teacher, administrator, and consultant. She is currently the school improvement director for a joint venture among the Oregon Department of Education, Oregon's Education Service Districts, Oregon's K–12 system, and higher education. Under Dr. Garrison's leadership, districts are advancing school improvement from being an event to becoming an integral part of how their schools operate. The professional development designed and created by Dr. Garrison for the DATA Project (www.oregondataproject.org) has received national attention from the Data Quality Campaign and the Gates Foundation. As a consultant, Dr. Garrison specializes in training school teams to increase student achievement and improve behavior. She has coordinated numerous statewide and school district change initiatives. Dr. Garrison is currently developing training materials that support difficult-to-reach students in grades K–10.

Amalio Nieves

Amalio Nieves, M.S., has served more than 25 years as a teacher, curriculum specialist, prevention coordinator, and teacher trainer at the elementary and secondary levels. Mr. Nieves is coordinator for Broward Schools' Office of Prevention, dedicated to empowering youth through substance abuse and violence prevention strategies. Each year, he conducts workshops for thousands of teachers and administrators. Mr. Nieves is a trainer for *Safe and Civil Schools* and works with numerous districts to improve student behavior and motivation. He is executive producer for the Telly Award–winning show *Reality Avenue* and was instrumental in developing and implementing Florida's first anti-bullying policy.

Billie Jo Rodriguez

Billie Jo Rodriguez, M.S., is a doctoral candidate in School Psychology at the University of Oregon. She has experience working with individual students, school teams, and districts on a variety of social behavior issues, including function-based assessment and support plan development, staff training, consultation for students with significant behavior challenges, and implementation of Positive Behavior Supports. Ms. Rodriguez has also worked to support schools in integrating academic and social behavior supports for elementary students identified as at-risk for developing long-term social or academic skill deficits.

NEW IN THIS EDITION

W hen CHAMPs first came out in 1998, I knew it could be useful to individual teachers. However, I never imagined the impact that it would have on entire schools and, more recently, on entire districts that have adopted CHAMPs as their building or district model for classroom management. I also never imagined that this approach would create a new lexicon. I have been amused to see implementation sites where CHAMP has become a verb: "I CHAMPed that activity and student behavior improved." Or "I need to re-CHAMP independent work because student behavior has gotten a bit sloppy."

I also never dreamed that people would adopt procedures and extend the concepts where my information was unclear, inconsistent, or nonexistent. For example, people often asked, "What does the 's' in the CHAMPs acronym stand for?" My lame answer was always, "Nothing, but CHAMPs sounds better than CHAMP." Most of the changes in this edition are based on the questions, concerns, and (most importantly) additions and exemplars provided by great teachers who have implemented these procedures over the last eleven years. For example, we have changed the lowercase "s" in CHAMPs to a capital "S" that stands for Success so that teachers can communicate to students the idea that if they strive to exhibit the expectations of the CHAMP acronym, it will lead to Success.

For any teachers who have the first edition but are unable to purchase the second, rest assured that the content is still basically the same—the first edition is still sound. The information in both editions is based on the research literature surrounding what effective teachers do to implement PBS (Positive Behavior Support) strategies in their classrooms. In the last ten years, there has been more and more confirmation that the types of strategies suggested in CHAMPS are what effective teachers use in their classrooms.

In this second edition, I have spruced up the design, added more tools, and revised the forms to be more user friendly. Following is a delineation of the major changes:

MORE WAYS TO CREATE VISUAL DISPLAYS

One change specifically related to the CHAMPS acronym is the use of visual representations to communicate expectations. I provide a broader range of examples of how teachers use visual displays to communicate expectations, and I have greatly expanded the range and usefulness of the CHAMPS icons used to create pictorial displays of these expectations. The first edition included 33 icons at the back of book, and they were not clearly labeled. The second edition features 66 icon subjects, or expectations, such as "CONVERSATION: Talk quietly with your small group" or "PARTICIPATION: Listening and Taking Notes." There are six versions of each icon subject: two that are aimed at primary-level teachers and students, one aimed at intermediate and middle school levels, a graphic version (as opposed to illustrated), a "sentence strip" text-based version, and a text-based version that uses a road sign theme. All 396 icons (66 icon subjects times 6 versions each) are clearly labeled. They are provided in electronic format on the CD included with the book.

CHOICE OF ACRONYM

I have added some acronyms to Chapter 4: Expectations. Some early childhood implementers of CHAMPS feel that acronym is too complex for very young children. So, in addition to the CHAMPS acronym, I suggest two simplified versions: TEAM (Talking, Effort, Activity, Movement) and MAC (Movement, Activity, Conversation). I also offer a more adult acronym: ACHIEVE (Activity, Conversation, Help, Integrity, Effort, Value, Efficiency). This range of acronyms reflects the way I approach things in CHAMPS—I give a range of examples and let the teacher (or the staff collectively for schoolwide implementation) decide what to use or adapt. In Chapter 4, I describe the origin of these acronyms and their use.

REORGANIZATION OF THE CONTENT

I have reorganized the content in this second edition to make it more user friendly and immediately applicable. For example, in the first edition, Module 7 (Correction Procedures) was packed with information, but the organization was confusing to some readers. So I have organized the content more sequentially into five sections: Structure, Teach, Observe, Interact Positively, and Correct Fluently (STOIC).

S **Structure** (organize) your classroom to prompt responsible student behavior. The way a setting is structured has a huge impact on the behavior and attitude of people in that setting.

T **Teach** your expectations regarding how to behave responsibly (i.e., be successful) within the structure that you have created. Sports coaches provide a great example of teaching behavior and re-teaching as needed to help each individual achieve full potential.

O **Observe** whether students are meeting expectations (monitor!). In the short run, this means circulate and visually scan the classroom. In the long run, this means collect and analyze meaningful data on student progress.

I **Interact** positively with students. Provide frequent noncontingent attention to build relationships. Provide frequent, age-appropriate positive feedback to acknowledge students' efforts to be successful.

C **Correct** misbehavior fluently. This means briefly, calmly, consistently, immediately, and (as much as possible) privately.

The first section of this book discusses how to **structure** the classroom for success. It contains a chapter on developing a clear vision for your class, a chapter on organizing your classroom, and a chapter on constructing your Classroom Management and Discipline Plan, including information on classroom rules and consequences for rule violations. The second section is about **teaching** your expectations—it, of course, includes information about teaching CHAMPS expectations during the first month of school. The third section covers information on **observing**: scanning the classroom and collecting data to use in making decisions about your management plan. The fourth section is about **interacting** positively with students, and the final section is about **correcting** misbehavior fluently.

> " *Many real-world examples of tools and strategies from people in the field are included.* "

I've also made the following changes in this edition:

- The term *Module* is replaced with the more traditional term *Chapter*.

- Academic references appear within the text to more directly demonstrate our evidence base and compatibility with the research literature.

- The chapter on teaching behavioral expectations includes new information on voice levels.

- More information is provided on managing homework and increasing the percentage of students who return homework.

- New reproducible reinforcement certificates, awards, and badges can be used for classwide and individual student rewards.

- Many real-world examples of tools and strategies from people in the field—with acknowledgements— are included.

- A new appendix offers suggestions for CHAMPS implementation by first-year teachers.

- A new appendix covers considerations for schoolwide implementation of the CHAMPS model.

TABLE OF CONTENTS

HOW TO USE
THIS BOOK

BEGINNING IN THE SPRING OR SUMMER

Ideally, you will be able to read the book and work through the tasks before school begins. Chapter 1: Vision, Chapter 2: Organization, Chapter 3: Management Plan, and Chapter 4: Expectations guide you through preparatory steps for starting the school year right. These steps include creating an organized classroom, establishing goals and your Guidelines for Success, constructing an effective Classroom Management and Discipline Plan, and developing expectations. As you read each task, think about whether your current classroom management plan addresses the issues raised in the book. Would implementing some or all of the suggestions have a positive effect on the behavior and motivation of your students? Chapter 5: Launch details how to implement all those plans in the crucial first month of school.

You should also at least read through Chapter 6: Observe, Chapter 7: Motivation, and Chapter 8: Classwide Motivation to get a complete picture of how the CHAMPS approach can work for you. Unless you are lucky enough to have a roomful of perfectly behaved and motivated children, you will undoubtedly want to make use of some or all of the strategies described in those chapters for observing students, collecting data, providing feedback, and increasing motivation. Skim through Chapter 9: Correcting to prepare yourself for dealing with any chronic or severe misbehavior that arises.

If you have only limited time before the school year begins, we suggest you work through Chapters 4 and 5. Then, as time permits, read through and consider the suggestions in Chapter 3. Also, as soon as you can, read through Chapters 7 and 8 to develop strategies for when and how you will provide frequent positive feedback to your students to keep them highly motivated. Monitor and revise your management plan as necessary throughout the school year.

BEGINNING IN THE FALL

The best time to have an impact on student behavior is the first day of school. However, if it's not possible to have a plan in place at that time, the first day of second semester is a good time to make needed changes. Skim through Chapters 1 through 8 to identify any suggestions that may be of immediate benefit to your classes. Then work through the chapters again in more detail as you have time. Plan to work through all of the chapters during the summer to be completely prepared for the first day of school next fall.

BEGINNING IN WINTER

If you begin the book somewhere in the middle of second semester, plan to read Chapter 4 on teaching expectations with clarity and Chapter 7 on providing frequent positive feedback. In addition, use the Table of Contents to identify tasks and suggestions that can help you address specific problems. Plan to work through the complete book over the summer, as suggested above.

REPRODUCIBLE FORMS

The Print from CD icon indicates that a blank version of a form shown in this book is available on the accompanying CD.

The CD also contains six versions of icons (visual representations of different expectations for each CHAMPS category—see example below) that can be used to teach CHAMPS expectations. See pp. 178–184 for more details on how these icons can be used. Appendix D lists all materials provided on the CD.

VERSION 1 Primary (B/W)	VERSION 2 Primary (Color)	VERSION 3 Intermediate	VERSION 4 Graphic	VERSION 5 Sentence Strip	VERSION 6 Road Sign
				CONVERSATION Talk quietly with anyone in your group	TALK QUIETLY WITH ANYONE IN YOUR GROUP
				PARTICIPATION Listening/ Answering/ Asking Questions/Sharing	LISTEN, ANSWER, ASK QUESTIONS, AND/OR SHARE

Permission is given to administrators and educators who purchase the book to reproduce any form labeled "Reproducible Form" and any CHAMPS icon solely for the purpose of classroom management and teaching CHAMPS expectations.

As the owner of this book, you have the right to reproduce as many copies of these icons as you need each year for your own classroom. Further reproduction of the icons and forms is strictly prohibited.

The reproducible forms on the CD are provided in PDF format. They can be printed and filled out by hand. They are also enabled so they can be filled out on your computer and saved electronically when opened in Adobe Reader version 6 or above. See the Readme file on the CD for more detailed instructions on how to fill out forms using Adobe Reader.

Figure I.1 *Decision Chart*

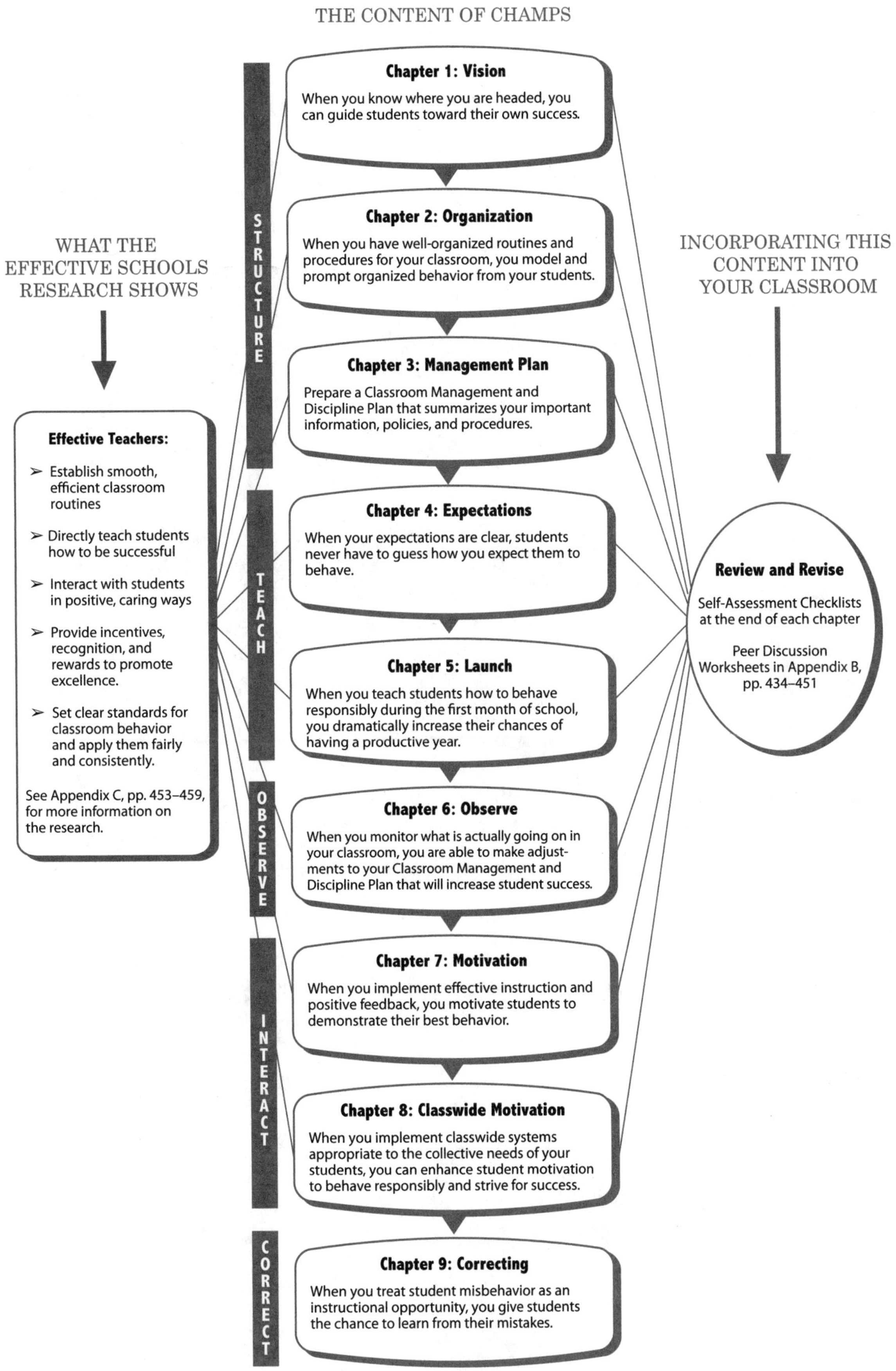

THE CONTENT OF CHAMPS

Chapter 1: Vision

When you know where you are headed, you can guide students toward their own success.

Chapter 2: Organization

When you have well-organized routines and procedures for your classroom, you model and prompt organized behavior from your students.

Chapter 3: Management Plan

Prepare a Classroom Management and Discipline Plan that summarizes your important information, policies, and procedures.

Chapter 4: Expectations

When your expectations are clear, students never have to guess how you expect them to behave.

Chapter 5: Launch

When you teach students how to behave responsibly during the first month of school, you dramatically increase their chances of having a productive year.

Chapter 6: Observe

When you monitor what is actually going on in your classroom, you are able to make adjustments to your Classroom Management and Discipline Plan that will increase student success.

Chapter 7: Motivation

When you implement effective instruction and positive feedback, you motivate students to demonstrate their best behavior.

Chapter 8: Classwide Motivation

When you implement classwide systems appropriate to the collective needs of your students, you can enhance student motivation to behave responsibly and strive for success.

Chapter 9: Correcting

When you treat student misbehavior as an instructional opportunity, you give students the chance to learn from their mistakes.

STRUCTURE

TEACH

OBSERVE

INTERACT

CORRECT

WHAT THE EFFECTIVE SCHOOLS RESEARCH SHOWS

Effective Teachers:

➢ Establish smooth, efficient classroom routines

➢ Directly teach students how to be successful

➢ Interact with students in positive, caring ways

➢ Provide incentives, recognition, and rewards to promote excellence.

➢ Set clear standards for classroom behavior and apply them fairly and consistently.

See Appendix C, pp. 453–459, for more information on the research.

INCORPORATING THIS CONTENT INTO YOUR CLASSROOM

Review and Revise

Self-Assessment Checklists at the end of each chapter

Peer Discussion Worksheets in Appendix B, pp. 434–451

INTRODUCTION

*T*his book was conceived and written to help teachers manage student behavior and increase student motivation so they can focus their time and energy on instruction and student success. Discipline problems in school have always been and continue to be a leading frustration for teachers and a drain on instructional time.

Half of new teachers will leave the profession within a few years. Two of the most common reasons given for leaving are discipline problems and lack of administrative support for dealing with discipline. Inexperienced and unskilled teachers are often frustrated and sometimes even terrified by students who misbehave and challenge authority. Models for positive behavior management such as CHAMPS can give these teachers the knowledge and skills to be confident and successful in dealing with difficult students. CHAMPS can also provide experienced teachers with a framework for evaluating and strengthening their classroom management and discipline plans.

> " *Half of new teachers will leave the profession within a few years.* "

There are many obvious and direct links between academic achievement and student behavior. One disruptive student can negatively affect the learning of all the other students in a class. If students are actively or passively resistant, a seemingly simple transition like moving to lab stations, which should take no more than two minutes, can take as long as ten minutes, wasting large amounts of instructional time. A student who is unmotivated will be less engaged in her work and learn less than if she is excited about the content.

If examples of misbehavior or apathy like these occur every day in every class, you are losing huge amounts of instructional time. By implementing effective management techniques, you can simultaneously increase student engagement and improve academic achievement (Brophy, 1996, 1980; Brophy & Good, 1986; Christenson, Reschly, Appleton, Berman-Young, Spanjers, & Varro, 2008; Gettinger & Ball, 2008; Luiselli, Putnam, Handler, & Feinberg, 2005; Scheuermann & Hall, 2008; Smith, 2000; Sprick, Booher, & Garrison, 2009).

Why bother with a positive approach to discipline?

The educational environment has changed greatly in the last 50 years. The accepted norm for disciplining problem students used to be punishment, and if the students continued to misbehave, suspension or expulsion. These measures did not necessarily change behavior, but they were easy solutions—and the problem disappeared. There were plenty of jobs on farms or in factories for those without a high school education. In 1900, high school graduation rates were only 6 percent.

More than 100 years later, graduation rates are about 71 percent. Schools are under tremendous pressure to successfully educate all students, including those who, years ago, would have left school because of academic or behavioral problems. Effective ways to motivate and encourage positive behavior are vital to serving these students. We need to do business differently. We cannot punish students into being motivated. We cannot punish students into wanting to stay in school.

Therefore, a proactive and positive approach like CHAMPS is essential. With these strategies you can guide students toward a successful school career, leading in turn to potential success in work and in life.

THE CHAMPS APPROACH

CHAMPS is designed to help you, the classroom teacher, develop (or fine tune) an effective classroom management plan that is proactive, positive, and instructional. In the last thirty years, a large and varied body of research literature has identified consistent and reliable findings concerning how effective teachers manage student behavior and enhance student motivation. The techniques included in this approach have been derived from that literature.

Unlike programs that have set procedures, the CHAMPS model guides the teacher in how to make effective decisions about managing behavior. For example, one of the tasks in Chapter 2: Organization is about physical setting. Rather than implying that only one physical setting is correct, we specify what factors should be taken into account when designing the seating arrangement in the classroom. One of the most important factors is the teacher's ability to move quickly and directly from any part of the room to any other part. This is important because it allows you to supervise by physically circulating throughout the room and to reach and speak quietly with any student in the room—to praise, correct misbehavior, or answer a question.

> " *The CHAMPS model guides the teacher in how to make effective decisions about managing behavior.* "

A second factor to consider is student conversation. How much talking will be allowed? Some physical arrangements are more conducive to conversation than others. After reviewing the factors to consider, we show different classroom arrangements and delineate the pros and cons of each. However, the teacher always makes the decisions: "How can I arrange my room to meet my needs and the needs of my students?"

> *Students should be treated with dignity and respect. Belittling or ridicule has no place in the effective teacher's repertoire of behavior support practices.*

In CHAMPS, we provide the information you need to make an informed decision—we don't tell you what to do. If you talk about CHAMPS with colleagues, we encourage you to talk about the CHAMPS approach, or even the CHAMPS model. We try to avoid calling it the CHAMPS program because is it not a canned program, but rather a way of thinking about how to prevent misbehavior and encourage responsible behavior.

CHAMPS, while not a program, does have one absolute rule: Students should be treated with dignity and respect. Belittling or ridicule has no place in the effective teacher's repertoire of behavior support practices.

The CHAMPS approach is based on the following principles or beliefs:

S Structure your classroom for success. The way the classroom is organized (physical setting, schedule, routines and procedures, quality of instruction, and so on) has a huge impact on student behavior; therefore, effective teachers carefully structure their classrooms in ways that prompt responsible student behavior (Baer, 1998; Evans & Lowell, 1979; Gettinger & Ball, 2008; Good & Brophy, 2000; Scheuermann & Hall, 2008; Udvari-Solner, 1996; Walker & Bullis, 1990; Weinstein, 1977).

T Teach behavioral expectations to students. Effective teachers overtly teach students how to behave responsibly and respectfully (in other words, to be successful) in every classroom situation—teacher-directed instruction, independent seatwork, cooperative groups, tests, and all major transitions (Brophy & Good, 1986; Emmer, Evertson, & Anderson, 1980; Evertson, Emmer, & Worsham, 2003; Lewis & Sugai, 1999; Sprick, Garrison, & Howard, 1998).

O Observe and supervise. Effective teachers monitor student behavior by physically circulating whenever possible and visually scanning all parts of the classroom frequently. In addition, effective teachers use meaningful data to observe student behavior, particularly chronic misbehavior, in objective ways and to monitor trends across time (Alberto & Troutman, 2006; Evertson et al., 2003; Scheuermann & Hall, 2008; Shores, Gunter, & Jack, 1993; Sprick & Garrison, 2008).

I Interact positively with students. When students are behaving responsibly, they receive attention and specific descriptive feedback on their behavior. Teachers should focus more time, attention, and energy on acknowledging responsible behavior than on responding to misbehavior—what we call a high ratio of positive to negative interactions (Brophy & Good, 1986; Martella, Nelson, & Marchand-Martella, 2003; Rosenshine, 1971; Sprick, 2006).

C Correct fluently. Teachers should preplan their responses to misbehavior to ensure that they respond in a brief, calm, and consistent manner, increasing the chances that the flow of instruction is maintained (Brophy & Good, 1986; Lewis & Sugai, 1999). In addition, with chronic and severe misbehavior, the teacher should think about the function of the misbehavior (Why is the student misbehaving?) and build a plan that ensures that the student learns and exhibits appropriate behavior (Alberto & Troutman, 2006; Crone & Horner, 2003; O'Neill et al., 1997; Sprick, Knight, Reinke, & McKale, 2007).

The acronym STOIC is an easy way to remember these five principles: Structure, Teach, Observe, Interact positively, Correct fluently. These are also the five sections of the book you have in your hand. At first glance, some people may think the word *stoic* implies someone who is cold and unfeeling. However, Encarta World English Dictionary gives us a definition of the adjective *stoic* as "tending to remain unemotional, especially showing admirable patience and endurance in the face of adversity." Thus, a stoic teacher is one who is unrattled by student misbehavior and who implements research-based strategies (as found in CHAMPS) with patience and endurance.

> *Teachers can help every student exhibit behavior that will make that student feel like a champion.*

We called this approach CHAMPS for two reasons.

First, we believe that by using effective management practices, teachers can help every student exhibit behavior that will make that student feel like a champion.

Second, the acronym CHAMPS reflects the categories, or types, of expectations that you, as a teacher, need to clarify for students about every major activity and transition that occurs in your classroom. If you identify and then teach students precisely what your expectations are for each classroom activity and transition, you will significantly reduce the amount of misbehavior and increase the amount of learning that takes place in your classroom. Following are brief descriptions of the types of expectations that need to be clarified:

C *Conversation*   Can students talk to each other?

H *Help*   How do students get their questions answered? How do they get your attention?

A *Activity*   What is the task or objective? What is the end product?

M *Movement*   Can students move about?

P *Participation*   What does the expected student behavior look and sound like? How do students show they are fully participating?

S *Success*   If students follow the CHAMPS expectations, they will be successful.

Where Does CHAMPS Fit in RTI?   %%%

Response to Intervention (RTI) is a framework for ensuring that a student who is experiencing behavioral or academic problems does not go unnoticed and that once noticed, the difficulties are addressed by school personnel. This process of problem identification matches the problem-solving processes and intervention to the intensity of the needs of the student. Within an RTI framework, CHAMPS represents a major component in a school or district's efforts to work toward universal prevention and early-stage problem-solving. Chapters 1 through 8 are designed to help you set up a classroom in which the vast majority of students can thrive behaviorally and academically. Chapter 9 addresses how to set up early-stage and chronic problem analysis and intervention. A three-tier approach to RTI may be organized as follows:

Tier 1: Universal prevention and early-stage problem-solving

Tier 2: Targeted problem-solving

Tier 3: Intensive problem-solving

In such a model, CHAMPS can serve as the staff development model for the Tier 1 prevention and intervention for meeting the social, emotional, and behavioral needs of all students.

POSITIVE BEHAVIOR SUPPORT AND CHAMPS

PBS (Positive Behavior Support) has become a popular label used in the field of behavior management. Traditional behavioral management views the individual as the problem and seeks to "fix" him or her by quickly eliminating the challenging behavior. Positive behavioral support and functional analysis view systems, settings, and lack of skill as parts of the problem and work to change those. PBS approaches are characterized as long-term strategies to reduce inappropriate behavior, teach more appropriate behavior, and provide contextual supports necessary for successful outcomes (Carr et al., 2002; Horner, Dunlap, et al., 1990; Warger, 1999).

So PBS is a broad, generic term for any set of procedures or techniques designed to help improve behavior. PBS can involve procedures at the schoolwide level, the classroom level, and the individual student level.

The most essential feature is that more time, effort, staff development, and financial resources should be placed on proactive, positive, and instructional approaches than on reactive and exclusionary approaches (Carr et al., 2002; Horner, Sugai, Todd, &

(continued on p. 10)

Cultural Competence
by Keba Baldwin and Amalio Nieves

Imagine...

Your family, including your seven-year-old daughter and ten-year-old son, has moved to another country. You have a basic knowledge of the language, but people talk quickly and use unfamiliar words—even simple conversations are difficult to follow.

Your family looks different. Everywhere you go, you are noticed. The dress, food, and customs are unfamiliar. Even the way people walk and greet one another is different.

The school your children will attend doesn't look like your old school. In this new place, the classes are huge and the teaching methods are different. What do your children need to fit in? What do your children need to thrive in this new environment?

To help your children adjust, you might hope the teachers learn a little about your culture, and what your children need to learn to be successful in theirs. You may hope the teachers ask, "What can we help these children learn so they can be successful?"

When cultures are different, what must we do to help all children be successful? Culture encompasses the beliefs, customs, practices, and social behavior of a particular nation or people. If we wish schools to welcome all students, staff members need to develop cultural competence—an awareness of and respect for different cultures. With cultural competence, teachers can help students successfully bridge two worlds.

Teaching students to transition from their home culture to their school culture requires the same skillful classroom management we need to afford to all students:

Structure your classroom for success.

Teach students how to be successful in your classroom.

Observe student behavior.

Interact positively.

Correct fluently.

By following the acronym STOIC, you can educate students about the behaviors and attitudes needed for the classroom—even those that may be different from behaviors and attitudes at home. Skillfully and respectfully guiding students toward successful classroom behavior does not devalue other beliefs, customs, practices, and social behavior. If classroom behaviors are new or different for the student, it is simply "the way we do it at school."

Know the Differences

Know where your students are coming from—literally, economically, and culturally. Values, beliefs, and behaviors may not be the same as yours. Let's look at a few examples of differences and culturally competent responses.

Value placed on education. You may work with students whose family members have dropped out of school for generations and been "all right." For these students, the long-term goal and benefits of graduation need to be taught across time. In the interim, these students may need immediate and tangible goals.

Dual rules. Students grow up with a set of rules that allows them to function in their homes and communities—sometimes these rules may be very different from the school's rules of conduct. Be aware of and respect this duality. Let students know that you understand that there are different rules outside school. Nonetheless, when in school, students need to follow school rules. For example, a family may encourage their children to hit anyone who hits or wrongs them. So, even though a no-hitting rule seems obvious, you will need to overtly teach some students that hitting is against school rules and teach them alternative ways of solving conflict.

Voice. Some children may expect adults to yell at them before they will do anything because that is what they are used to at home. In some cultures, the only way to be heard and respected is to talk loudly and above everyone else. If a student equates yelling with adult authority, you may need to teach some students that a soft voice deserves respect as well. In other cultures, a loud voice may convey anger. If you have a loud voice, you may need to teach some students that your loud voice does not mean anger.

Eye contact. In some cultures, children are disrespectful when they make eye contact with an adult. Yet in mainstream American culture, children may be chastised for not making direct eye contact. If students' use of eye contact is different from what you are used to, accept this. Across time and once students are thriving, you may wish to teach students that some teachers and employers may expect eye contact when they talk with their students or employees.

Competition. In some cultures, it is inappropriate to try to be better than others—to want a better grade, to want to be the best, to win a race. If students are more motivated by progress of the group than by competition, use more whole-class praise and consider whole-class reward ideas (Chapter 8).

Family involvement. Child-rearing practices vary from culture to culture. How families feel about needing and accepting help from others may be different from the school's expectations. In some cultures, families take an active role in their child's school life by assisting with homework, attending meetings, and volunteering. In other cultures, families believe it is not their place to interfere or intervene in the educational process. The educator is the expert. Concurrently, some families may also appear to distance themselves from school because of past negative experiences with their own schooling, fear or misunderstanding of the educational system, job schedules, and/or limited proficiency in English. If families stay away from school, it does not mean they are not interested or involved in their child's schooling. If there is little contact between the school and home, provide information to the home regarding the student's progress and continue to be welcoming.

Whether cultural differences are subtle or obvious, it isn't easy to spend the school day in one world and the rest of the day in another. ELL students have the challenge of learning a new language and must sometimes face the added difficulty of relocating from a different part of the world for complex reasons. What added stresses do these families face?

continued

Be aware of differences. Be respectful of the differences. Then teach your students how to behave successfully in your classroom, and you will demonstrate cultural competence.

Steps to Success

Below are examples of actions you can take to increase your success with culturally diverse students. Adjust these suggestions for the grade level and maturity of your students.

Take the time at the beginning of the year to get to know your students and their culture.
On the first day of school, as students wait for class to begin, have them complete a survey. Ask age-appropriate questions such as:

- How many siblings do you have?
- What are your responsibilities around the house?
- What do you like to do after school?
- What are your free-time activities?
- How much time do you spend on homework each night?
- Who do you spend your free time with?

You may find that some students are responsible for younger siblings. You may find that a student spends most of his time caring for a sick grandmother. Other students may work to help support the family. These circumstances can affect a student's school performance.

For young students with limited reading and writing skills, conduct interviews and ask questions in an informal, friendly way. You can also get this kind of information from the family if you meet with them before school starts. See Chapter 1, Task 7, for more information on family contacts.

Being aware of difficulties or differences does not mean lowering expectations. Continue making efforts to get to know your students and the variables that may affect their schooling throughout the year. Whether at the beginning of the year or later in the year, awareness allows respect and under-standing as you encourage and support students in their efforts to be successful.

Invite (but do not require) each family to write a short essay introducing their child to you.
This can be a powerful way to assess the level of support students get at home, the value the family places on committing to an assignment, the family's perception of the student, and their level of writing and language skills. (*Thanks to Tricia Huder for this suggestion.*)

Ask children about their names. Do their names have meaning? Show respect by learning how to pronounce names correctly. If a name is difficult, tell students it may take a while for you to learn it. Your efforts communicate that you care enough to learn their names.

Create a culture jar. Have students write something about their culture on a card and put it in the jar for sharing time. Use their ideas for decorating your classroom and creating special lessons.

Be prepared to teach soft skills. Soft skills include how to handle disagreements between teacher and student and between students, how to respond to authority without shutting down, how to keep voice levels low, and how to show respect for others. You can help your students learn these valuable lifelong skills through direct instruction—by modeling, explaining, and practicing. Primary-level students in high-risk schools must be overtly taught many social skills. Experienced teachers in high-risk schools say you should be prepared to teach these skills every hour of every day.

The teaching of rules, soft skills, and awareness and respect of cultural differences must begin on DAY ONE of the school year.

When you work in a diverse community, it is important to make an honest assessment. Are you suited to working with students from different cultures? Are you willing to learn from your students so they in turn can learn from you? Teaching in a school that serves a community very different from your own is not for everyone. A negative or even a helpless attitude can make a lasting negative impact on students. On the other hand, a respectful, supportive attitude can have a lasting positive impact.

To be an effective teacher of all students, including culturally diverse students, analyze your teaching style. Work through the ideas on effective instruction throughout CHAMPS. By striving to implement fast-paced, engaging lessons with frequent opportunities to respond, you will actively engage students of all cultural backgrounds.

Teach high expectations. Help students set goals and work toward them. You may be the first person to tell students they can attain goals. See Chapters 8 and 9 for specific suggestions on implementing goal setting as a strategy.

Let students know that you recognize when they are striving toward your Guidelines for Success and following school rules. Reward them for their efforts.

By skillfully implementing CHAMPS, you can guide students toward successful behavior in your class-room. By accepting cultural differences without judgment when implementing CHAMPS, you will demonstrate cultural competence.

Suggestions for Additional Reading

Resources

A Framework for Understanding Poverty by Ruby Payne (1995). Available from aha! Process, Inc. (www.ahaprocess.com).

Never Work Harder Than Your Students and Other Principles of Great Teaching by Robyn R. Jackson (2009). Available from ACSD (www.acsd.org).

Other People's Children: Cultural Conflict in the Classroom (2nd ed.) by Lisa Delpit (2006). Available from New Press (www.thenewpress.com).

Lewis-Palmer, 2005; Koegel, Koegel, & Dunlap, 1996; Sprick & Booher, 2006; Sprick, Knight, et al., 2007). The CHAMPS approach is an example of how to implement PBS procedures in the classroom.

Is CHAMPS "evidence based?"

Yes! First, CHAMPS is entirely compatible with more than 30 years of research on how effective teachers manage their classrooms in ways that enhance academic achievement. Second, *Safe and Civil Schools* has many examples of district-based studies where CHAMPS has been implemented with remarkable results. Improvements include marked reductions in classroom disruptions, office referrals, and in-school and out-of school suspensions, along with corresponding increases in teachers' perceptions of efficacy and student motivation and behavior.

For information on efficacy data, contact *Safe & Civil Schools* or go to www.safe andcivilschools.com. For more information on how CHAMPS is compatible with the research, see Appendix C.

CHAMPS is organized into five sections and nine chapters. Each chapter focuses on one important aspect of effective classroom management. Within each chapter, we present specific tasks that will help you address that chapter's content. We also offer detailed suggestions about how to accomplish the tasks themselves. Each chapter also includes a self-assessment tool that you can use to keep track of which tasks (or which parts of the tasks) you have completed and which you still need to address.

Appendix B: Schoolwide Implementation of CHAMPS provides information on how to implement CHAMPS schoolwide. It includes suggested discussion questions and professional development activities that can be used by two or more teachers or (even better) an entire faculty working together in a formal or informal study group. These questions and activities are designed to prompt group members to examine their beliefs and practices in a supportive environment and to use each other as resources in their professional development efforts.

When implemented well, CHAMPS has the potential to improve student behavior in ways that increase school connectedness, improve academic achievement, keep at-risk students in school, and improve teachers' senses of efficacy and accomplishment.

CHAPTER DESCRIPTIONS

SECTION 1: STRUCTURE YOUR CLASSROOM FOR SUCCESS

Chapter 1: Vision includes seven tasks that help you understand the basic principles of behavior and motivation that set the stage for the remainder of this book. After working through Chapter 1, you should have a clear understanding of how behavior is learned and the role that you (and your management plan) can play in shaping student behavior in positive and successful directions.

Chapter 2: Organization includes six tasks with suggestions and examples of how you can manipulate variables such as schedule, physical setting, using an attention signal, beginning and ending routines, procedures for managing student work, and strategies for getting students to be academically engaged during independent work periods. By manipulating these variables, you can create momentum in your classroom that draws students into functioning in a unified manner that is mature, responsible, and productive.

Chapter 3: Management Plan includes five tasks that lay the groundwork for implementing an effective classroom management plan, including a set of classroom rules that addresses the most likely misbehaviors. Once you develop the rules, either on your own or with help from your students, you determine a system of appropriate consequences. Your cohesive set of rules and consequences will help your administrator know your system and will be of great help to substitute teachers on days when you cannot be in the classroom. Feedback from administrators and substitutes has been very positive about this summary of the teacher's management plan. Chapter 3 also includes examples of different types of corrective consequences that you can implement in your classroom.

SECTION 2: TEACH EXPECTATIONS

Chapter 4: Expectations includes three tasks that help you clarify and then directly teach your expectations for all classroom activities and transitions. The CHAMPS acronym stands for the expected behaviors that you will teach your students for each major instructional activity and transition: Conversation, Help, Activity, Movement, and Participation. By directly teaching these expectations, the classroom teacher functions like an effective athletic coach who, before teaching the team content (the plays and patterns of the game), begins the first practice by teaching expectations for the players' behavior during practice and games.

Chapter 5: Launch includes five tasks that pull everything together from the first four chapters. This chapter provides tips on how to implement your management plan on the first day of school and how to run the first month of school in a way that firmly establishes the consistency of your vision, organization, discipline plan, and daily expectations.

SECTION 3: OBSERVE STUDENT BEHAVIOR

Chapter 6: Observe has specific suggestions on how to monitor behavior by physically circulating and visually scanning. By actively observing (supervising) student behavior, you influence students to use their best behavior because they do not want to get caught misbehaving and, even more importantly, when you build good relationships with your students, they do not want to disappoint you. This chapter also includes a variety of data collection suggestions so you can occasionally observe more objectively. Data collection can assist you in spotting trends across time, which in turn may help you adjust your management plan to further improve student behavior.

SECTION 4: INTERACT POSITIVELY

Chapter 7: Motivation provides four tasks that you can manipulate to build positive relationships with and provide positive feedback to students. By consciously paying attention to your ratio of positive interactions to negative interactions—that is, working to give each student more attention when the student is behaving well than when the student is misbehaving— you can reduce the probability of falling into the Criticism Trap. Understanding and acting on what motivates your students will enable you to help them succeed.

Chapter 8: Classwide Motivation includes a menu of systems that can be used as needed to increase student motivation. The menu includes goal-setting plans suitable for classes in which the majority of students are already highly motivated as well as reward-based systems for classes that need an extrinsic boost. This chapter also has samples of reward-based systems that can be used with one or two individuals who need additional support in getting motivated.

SECTION 5: CORRECT FLUENTLY

Chapter 9: Correcting acknowledges that no matter how well you plan and implement, chronic behavior problems will emerge. This chapter includes information on how to evaluate the implementation of your classroom management plan and make adjustments. In addition, this chapter includes a process for analyzing and improving the quality of the professional relationship you have with a student who is misbehaving or unmotivated. For those really difficult behaviors, you will learn how misbehaviors serve a function such as getting attention or escape for the student. You will also learn how you can reduce those misbehaviors by implementing a function-based intervention plan. Four major categories of misbehavior are addressed: awareness, ability, attention-seeking, and purposeful/habitual. Sample intervention plans are suggested for each.

ADDITIONAL MATERIALS

Appendix A: Tips on Professionalism for the First-Year Teacher provides suggestions for CHAMPS implementation by new teachers.

Appendix B: Schoolwide Implementation of CHAMPS covers considerations for schoolwide implementation of the CHAMPS model. It includes Peer Discussion Worksheets to guide study groups through each chapter.

Appendix C: Is CHAMPS Evidence Based? explores how CHAMPS incorporates best practices recommended by the research literature.

Appendix D: Guide to CHAMPS Icons and Reproducible Forms previews the CHAMPS icons and reproducible forms provided on the CD.

STOIC

Section One

The way the classroom is structured greatly influences student behavior, their level of motivation, and their attitude toward school. This section includes information on how to develop a clear vision for student behavior, how to organize your routines and procedures, and how to develop a systematic Classroom Management and Discipline Plan.

Structure Your Classroom for Success

Teach Expectations

Observe Student Behavior

Interact Positively

Correct Fluently

Imagine...

You make a reservation at a restaurant. When you arrive at the appointed time, you see a large number of people waiting to get in. It takes you ten minutes to squeeze through the throng of frustrated people to get to the maître d' —who is so frantically busy he does not even hear your polite statements that you have a reservation. After ten minutes of this treatment, you raise your voice and demand that he pay attention to you. When he finally checks his book, he politely but distractedly acknowledges that you did have a reservation, but it was for 15 minutes ago and he cannot possibly seat you now. You angrily state that you arrived 20 minutes ago and have been trying to get his attention ever since, but he ignored you. He looks apologetic, but shrugs in a "What else can I do?" gesture of helplessness. You are finally seated, but you are so agitated you do not even notice that the food and waitstaff are actually very good.

Now imagine the same scenario, but on arriving you find that the management is so organized you easily get through to the maître d', who greets you politely and shows you immediately to your table. You find the service, food, and price to be fantastic. Notice how the degree of organization has affected not just your behavior, but your attitude toward the setting.

Develop a
Clear
Vision for
Your Class

Vision

When you know where you are headed, you can guide students to their own success.

Introduction

*T*o effectively manage and motivate a class (or classes) of students, you need a clear vision of your ideal classroom—what it should look like, what it should sound like, what it should feel like to a class member or a visitor, and what you want your students to accomplish. Once you have a clear idea of what you want for your classroom, you can design procedures that will ensure that you achieve those goals.

In this chapter, seven tasks are presented to help you clarify your vision for your classroom. The first two will help you understand some fundamental principles of behavior management and motivation. The next two will help you define what you want your students to accomplish and what they will need to do to be successful. And the final three tasks describe strategies you can use to accomplish your vision.

By attending to all seven of these tasks, you can create a clear vision for the look, sound, feel, goals, and accomplishments of your class and the foundation for an effective management plan that will help achieve your vision.

At the end of the chapter is a Self-Assessment Checklist designed to help you determine which (or which parts) of the tasks you have done or are in the process of doing, and which tasks you still need to do. Use this Self-Assessment Checklist to develop an implementation plan. Identify, in detail, how you plan to apply the information from this chapter.

CHAPTER 1 TASKS

Task 1
Understand How to Shape Behavior

Task 2
Understand Motivation

Task 3
Identify Long-Range Classroom Goals

Task 4
Develop Guidelines for Success

Task 5
Maintain Positive Expectations

Task 6
Implement Effective Instructional Practices

Task 7
Initiate and Maintain Family Contacts

The seven tasks presented and explained in this chapter are:

Task 1: Understand How to Shape Behavior • Develop an understanding of fundamental behavior management principles so that you can make effective decisions and take appropriate actions to help your students learn to behave responsibly.

Task 2: Understand Motivation • A person's level of motivation on any given task is a product of both how much the person wants the rewards that accompany success and how much he or she expects to be successful.

Task 3: Identify Long-Range Classroom Goals • Identify several major goals—instructional and behavioral—that you want to accomplish with all your students by the end of the year.

Task 4: Develop Guidelines for Success • Develop and actively share with your students guidelines that describe basic attitudes, traits, and behaviors that will help students be successful in your classroom and throughout their lives.

Task 5: Maintain Positive Expectations • Ensure that you have and that you convey high positive expectations for the success of all your students.

Task 6: Implement Effective Instructional Practices • Implement effective instructional practices to keep students interested and academically engaged.

Task 7: Initiate and Maintain Family Contacts • Build positive relationships with your students' families by making initial contact with them at the beginning of the year and maintaining regular contact throughout the year.

Task 1: Understand How to Shape Behavior

Develop an understanding of fundamental behavior management principles so that you can make effective decisions and take appropriate actions to help students learn to behave responsibly.

Every school seems to have its angry, argumentative, unmotivated students. Frustrated teachers throw up their hands and declare these students lost causes. Teachers conclude, "They'll never change!" The students often enter a downward spiral fueled by low expectations, constant criticism, and academic failure.

Certainly, some tendencies and personality traits seem to be present from birth, but *most human behavior is learned*—which means it can also be unlearned, or shaped into a more desirable form.

Picture Rosa, a responsible and successful fifth-grade student. Imagine that one day, the rewards she receives and values for being a model student evaporate. Instead, she starts getting failing grades, and teachers are critical of her work. The other students laugh at her work and her class participation. They either ridicule her as stupid or ignore her altogether. No one notices when she stays on task, works hard, and is respectful to others. Her parents show no interest in her schoolwork.

If this continues day after day, at home and at school, Rosa will probably stop trying to succeed. She may even respond with anger and hostility. If her angry response is rewarded by attention from others, she may find that acting in an antagonistic and aggressive manner gives her a sense of satisfaction or self-preservation. If this were to continue for months or years, Rosa would develop into a very different student from the successful fifth-grader she once was.

Now picture a student, Malik, who is always argumentative and angry, and as a result is a low achiever. Imagine that school personnel create a setting in which he starts experiencing success and good grades, he receives peer recognition for his positive behavior, and he no longer gets so much attention or status for his anger and hostility. If done well, an environment like this can create a powerful positive change in Malik. Behavior can be taught and changed (Alberto & Troutman, 2006; Baer, Wolf, & Risley, 1968; Cooper, Heron, & Heward, 2007; Langland, Lewis-Palmer, & Sugai, 1998).

> "Exposing all students to the best circumstances can foster positive behavior and high levels of motivation in both good and bad students.

When a student frequently behaves irresponsibly, it's likely that the student hasn't experienced the benefits of responsible behavior enough, or even at all. It's also likely that this student has learned that irresponsible behavior is a more effective or efficient way of getting his needs met. He may find that he gets power, control, and perhaps even admiration from peers as a result of misbehavior (Gresham, 1998; Horner, Vaughn, Day, & Ard, 1996; Lalli et al., 1999; O'Neill et al., 1997; Scheuermann & Hall, 2008; Sprick, Booher, & Garrison, 2009).

If a good student will probably experience behavior changes due to repeated exposure to bad circumstances, a bad student repeatedly exposed to good circumstances has the same probability of experiencing behavior changes. The behavior management principles below provide the framework for the rest of this book—that is, exposing all students to the best circumstances can foster positive behavior and high levels of motivation in both good and bad students. *Behavior can be changed.*

BEHAVIOR MANAGEMENT PRINCIPLES

The focus of Chapter 1 is creating a vision of your ideal classroom. Because there will undoubtedly be times when your students behave irresponsibly, your classroom vision should include something about how you will help students learn to behave more responsibly. You can do this by developing an understanding of and skill in using fundamental behavior management principles. Specifically, as a teacher, you need to know why and how to:

- *Structure* your class to promote responsible student behavior.

- Effectively *acknowledge* responsible student behavior.

- Effectively *respond* to irresponsible student behavior.

An overview of the most important principles of behavior management is presented in the following pages. Chapters 2 through 9 provide more detailed information about the principles and specific actions that you can take.

The principles of behavior management are grounded in the assumption that people are constantly engaged in learning and that every life experience adds to a person's knowledge base. Every experience influences a person's subsequent actions, both consciously and unconsciously. And in general, behaviors that are rewarded over time are maintained, while those that are not rewarded are typically extinguished. For example, a job seeker who has submitted scores of résumés without any resulting interviews may decide to write a new résumé. He sends out the new résumé and gets multiple interviews. He has learned that the new résumé brings better results, and in the future he will likely use the new résumé instead of the old one. Similarly, if someone goes to a movie that a friend recommends and finds it to be a poor movie and a waste of money, that person will be less likely to trust the friend's movie recommendations in the future.

> *Behaviors that are rewarded over time are maintained, while those that are not rewarded are typically extinguished.*

Scenarios such as these are repeated in each person's life many times each day, in uncountable and interwoven combinations, to create a rich fabric of experiences and learning. Simply put, a person's behavior is influenced by events and conditions he or she experiences. Some experiences encourage that person to engage in certain behaviors, and others discourage that person from engaging in certain behaviors. Figure 1.1 shows a graphic representation of the three main variables that affect behavior.

Figure 1.1 *Variables That Affect Behavior*

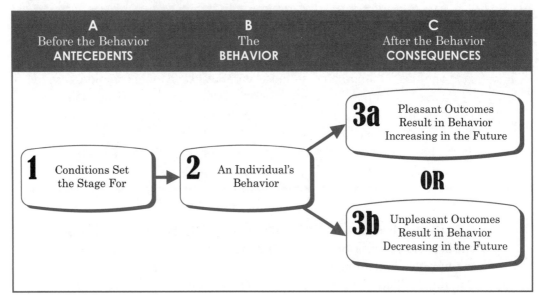

The three variables are:

1. **Conditions** What is prompting or enabling the behavior?

2. **The Behavior** What is the person doing?

3. **Consequences** What is encouraging and sustaining or discouraging the behavior? If consequences resulting from a particular behavior are perceived as pleasant, that behavior will increase or occur more frequently. If consequences resulting from a particular behavior are perceived as unpleasant, that behavior will decrease or occur less frequently.

Readers with behavioral training will recognize this as a simple model of behavioral theory expressed in commonsense and pragmatic terms. This model provides a useful structure for helping teachers understand basic behavior management principles.

To effectively apply the fundamental principles of behavior management to your classroom, you should keep in mind two essential underlying concepts. These concepts have very important implications for teachers about where they should focus their time and energy in terms of managing student behavior. The two concepts are:

- Effective teachers spend more time promoting responsible behavior than responding to irresponsible behavior (Beaman & Wheldall, 2000; Brophy & Good, 1986; Thompson, Becker, & Armstrong, 1968; Walker, Ramsey, & Gresham, 2004).

Because the vocabulary typically associated with behavioral theory is so often mis-understood or misused (or both), less technical vocabulary and more commonsense examples are used throughout this book. In addition, although the fundamentals of school-based behavior management are based on a large and comprehensive body of research findings, only that information most useful to teachers is included. As a result, what is presented here reflects a simple understanding of very complex principles.

- Effective teachers recognize that misbehavior (especially any chronic misbehavior) occurs for a reason, and they take that reason into account when determining a response to the misbehavior (Alberto & Troutman, 2006; Cooper et al., 2007; Scheuermann & Hall, 2008).

PROMOTING RESPONSIBLE BEHAVIOR

You will prevent most misbehavior from ever occurring when you focus the majority of your time and energy on these three major categories of teacher-based actions for promoting responsible behavior:

Conditions. Use effective instruction and set up conditions for students to be successful by prompting responsible behavior and discouraging irresponsible behavior. Specific actions include but are by no means limited to the following:

- Make sure students understand what the behavioral expectations are.
- Make sure students know how to meet the behavioral expectations.
- Arrange the physical space so that it is more conducive to responsible behavior than to irresponsible behavior.
- Design a fast-paced schedule and provide interesting lessons.
- Run efficient transitions between activities.
- Interact respectfully and positively with all students.
- Show an interest in student work.

Implement pleasant consequences. Ensure that students experience appropriate positive feedback when they engage in responsible behavior. Specific actions include the following:

- Give verbal praise.

- Write positive notes.

- Encourage students to praise themselves.

- Contact parents regarding students' responsible behavior.

- Occasionally reward individuals or the whole class with a special activity.

Eliminate unpleasant consequences. Ensure that students do not experience negative results from exhibiting responsible behavior. Specific actions include the following:

- Avoid embarrassing students with praise.

- Ensure that no student is the target of laughter for making a mistake during class participation.

- Ensure that no student ever feels like a geek for behaving responsibly.

- Ensure that no one is ridiculed as a teacher's pet for behaving responsibly.

MISBEHAVIOR OCCURS FOR A REASON

It is often difficult to understand why a student behaves irresponsibly, especially when the consequences of that behavior seem highly unpleasant. However, whenever a student or group of students exhibits irresponsible behavior on an *ongoing basis*, the behavior is occurring for a reason—it is not completely random (Carr, 1993; Gresham, Watson, & Skinner, 2001; Johnston & Pennypacker, 1993; Skinner, 1953). Therefore, the first thing you need to do is determine the reason for the misbehavior. Likely possibilities are:

- The student doesn't know exactly what you expect.

- The student doesn't know how to exhibit the responsible behavior.

- The student is unaware that he or she engaged in the misbehavior.

- The student is experiencing some pleasant outcome from exhibiting the misbehavior (for example, she likes the attention she gets from adults or peers).

- The student is successfully avoiding some unpleasant outcome by exhibiting the misbehavior (for example, he is getting out of assigned work).

Once you have a reasonable idea why a chronic misbehavior is occurring, you can take actions to reduce and eventually eliminate it. Again, there are three major categories of teacher-based actions for you to consider.

Conditions. Modify any conditions that may be perpetuating the misbehavior. Specific actions include but are by no means limited to the following:

- Provide lessons to teach the student how to behave responsibly.

- Assign different seats to two students who talk when they sit together.

- Modify work that is too difficult for the student who is not completing assignments.

- Pace lessons more quickly so students are less likely to get off task.

- Provide something for students to do when they complete classwork.

Eliminate pleasant consequences. Remove any pleasant outcomes that might be resulting from the misbehavior. Examples include the following:

- Ignore misbehavior that is designed to get attention.

- Respond calmly to a student who likes to make adults angry.

- Ensure that a student is not excused from assigned work as a result of the misbehavior.

Implement unpleasant consequences. Implement corrective consequences that will make exhibiting the misbehavior more unpleasant for the student. Examples include the following:

- Use a system of demerits (three demerits result in an after-school detention, for example).

- Take away fifteen seconds of recess (or other fun or choice activity) for each infraction.

- Use a classroom point system and institute point fines for particular infractions.

- Contact the student's parents about problem behavior.

CHAPTER 1 TASKS

| 1 • Shape Behavior | 2 • Understand Motivation | 3 • Long-Range Classroom Goals | 4 • Guidelines for Success |

Taking Action to Improve Irresponsible Behavior

Our case study involves a seventh-grade student who is chronically argumentative with staff, and has been since he entered the middle school. This student has been continually sent out of class and regularly assigned to detention. His parents must be called frequently, and he is often confrontational and argumentative with an increasing angry and frustrated school staff.

First, identify what the student gains from his behavior. There are several possibilities to consider. For example, getting lots of attention from adults (direct, angry engagement) may give this student a sense of power. Or, he may be getting lots of attention from his peers for appearing strong and powerful enough to fight with teachers. Following are the main types of action that school personnel might take to influence this student's behavior. Note that the specific procedures included for each category should be used as a menu. Not all of the procedures will be implemented. Staff select one or two from each category to implement with the argumentative student, depending on the exact nature of the situation.

Modify conditions (organization, schedule, physical structure, and so on) to encourage more responsible behavior and discourage the irresponsible behavior. Staff select one or two actions from the following:

- Give the student a high-status job (to be performed daily) that will increase his sense of power and purpose in the school.

- Because the student seems to behave better during teacher-directed instruction, consider arranging for a greater percentage of his daily schedule to be teacher-directed instruction.

- To mitigate the possibility that the student is misbehaving because he is frustrated by academic difficulties, arrange for him to receive private tutorial assistance in his most difficult subjects.

- Assign the student a different place to sit in the room.

- Tell all staff to make an effort to give the student very clear directions.

- Remind staff to avoid power struggles with the student.

continued ≫

Implement procedures designed to encourage responsible behavior. Staff select one or two actions from the following:

- Tell all staff that whenever the student exhibits responsible behavior, they should give him specific praise.

- Ask all staff members to make an effort to give the student frequent, unconditional, positive adult attention.

- Remind all staff to privately praise the student when he follows directions without arguing.

Remove any aversive aspects of exhibiting responsible behavior. Staff select one or two actions from the following:

- Modify the student's academic assignments so that he can succeed.

- Correct the student before he makes an error (for example, privately say to the student, "This is the type of work period where you need to try to stay calm and work with me without arguing. Let's have a good day today.")

- Teach particularly difficult assignments to the student prior to presenting the assignment to the class.

- Prearrange times during the day when the student can privately ask teachers questions or get assistance so he does not have to do so in front of his peers.

- Remind staff to avoid publicly praising the student for following directions.

Remove any positive aspects of exhibiting irresponsible behavior. Staff select one or two actions from the following:

- Remind staff to avoid engaging in arguments with the student. Provide training as necessary.

- Train other students to ignore situations in which the student begins to argue.

- Train staff to maintain instructional momentum so the student doesn't get attention from peers when he attempts to argue.

Case Study

(continued)

(continued)

Implement effective corrective consequences designed to reduce irresponsible behavior. Have all staff respond to the student's arguing with the following procedures:

- Give the student a warning when he begins to argue. ("This is an example of arguing.")

- Calmly implement a corrective consequence when the student continues to argue after the warning.

- Ignore any further attempts by the student to engage in arguing.

- Redirect the student to the activity he should be engaged in.

- Keep accurate records of the number of times and the duration of each arguing incident.

Implementing an intervention plan that includes procedures from some or all of these categories increases the probability that the staff will be successful in helping this student learn to behave more responsibly. An intervention plan may not be effective if staff does nothing to remove the positive aspects of exhibiting the irresponsible behavior, such as the peer and teacher attention the student receives. If getting peer and teacher attention is more valuable to him than anything he gains from the intervention steps taken, the student's behavior will not improve.

take note

Whether you are starting CHAMPS at the beginning of the year or during it, understanding that you, the teacher, can change student behavior—shaping students toward those behaviors that will allow them to succeed—is essential to understanding the CHAMPS approach. Most of the suggestions in the rest of the book assume that you understand the basics of behavior management that have been presented here.

Task 2: Understand Motivation

A person's level of motivation on any given task is a product of both how much the person wants the rewards that accompany success and how much he or she expects to be successful.

The word *motivate* can be defined as "to provide an incentive, to move to action, to drive forward." Understanding motivation will enhance your efforts to implement effective motivational procedures with your students—that is, to move them to do their best academically and exhibit responsible and successful behavior. When you implement effective instruction as presented in this chapter along with positive feedback (discussed in Chapter 7), you motivate students to demonstrate their best behavior. The concepts presented here can help you maintain the motivation of students who already follow the rules and do their best on assignments, increase the motivation of students who do nothing or only enough to get by, and motivate responsibility in students who tend to misbehave.

The first concept to understand is this: behavior that is repeated is motivated—behavior does not reoccur when there is no motivation (Katzell & Thompson, 1990). This concept is always true, regardless of what an individual may think or say about his own behavior. For example, a person may repeatedly complain about his job and even say that he is unmotivated to work, but if he goes to work regularly, he shows that he is in fact motivated in some way to work. Similarly, a person may say she is motivated to paint as a hobby, but if she never gets out her paints and brushes, she is not truly motivated to paint. This does not mean that the man will never lose his motivation to go to work or that the woman will never regain her motivation to paint, but their current behavior belies their words.

The importance of this concept is that teachers must realize that the student who repeatedly misbehaves is, at the moment, more motivated to misbehave than to behave. Likewise, the student who does nothing is more motivated to do nothing than to work. It means that you, as the teacher, need to increase these students' motivation to behave responsibly and complete assignments. This book is designed to help you do that.

A second important concept is this: Most people are motivated to engage in a particular behavior by a complex mix of intrinsic and extrinsic factors. A person is intrinsically motivated when the pleasant consequences of a behavior are natural, or directly related to the essential nature of that behavior. Thus, a person who is intrinsically motivated to read reads because he likes to learn new things, enjoys a good story, and finds curling up with a book relaxing. The person who is intrinsically

take note

If your efforts to increase students' motivation to engage in desired behaviors are not effective, you will also need to work at decreasing their motivation to engage in the undesired behaviors. See Chapter 9 for suggestions on how to do this.

motivated to ski does so because she finds the speed exhilarating, the fresh air pleasant, and the feeling of exhaustion at the end of a challenging day gratifying.

Extrinsic motivation occurs when someone engages in a behavior because of pleasant consequences that are not directly related to the essential nature of the behavior. For example, babies tend to utter "mama" and "dada" more frequently than other sounds because of the reactions (smiles, tickles, praise) these sounds elicit from the most significant people in their lives. A college student continues to attend and write papers for a class that she does not like because she wants a certain grade and because doing well in the class will move her toward her desired goal of a degree. A six-year-old child makes his bed to get lavish praise from his mom and dad regarding how responsible, hardworking, and helpful he is.

Though some people believe that the only valid kind of motivation is intrinsic motivation and that teachers should not give students praise and rewards of any kind (Cameron, Banko, & Pierce, 2001), this book does not adhere to that principle. This mistaken belief is addressed in more detail in Chapter 8, but it is enough to say that the line between intrinsic and extrinsic motivation is not as distinct as it may seem. Motivation for most behaviors is usually a mix of intrinsic and extrinsic factors. Although the person who reads a lot may do so for the intrinsic rewards of the task, he may also enjoy the compliments he gets for his wide knowledge. The frequent skier may find that in addition to the exhilaration of skiing itself, she also enjoys having others comment on her skill. The baby learning to talk makes "mama" and "dada" sounds because he enjoys making noise, not just because of the reactions of his parents. The college student who attends class and writes papers does so not only because of the grades, but also because sometimes the class is genuinely interesting.

Keep It Real

Keba Baldwin, Safe Schools Coordinator in Onslow County, North Carolina, notes that when working with students from diverse backgrounds, we must appeal to what is "real" to students to motivate them. This means to connect with the lives of the children where they are right now. Some students from very difficult life circumstances may not see a way out of their current situation. Teachers must discover what is real with students (which may be culturally different from the teacher's background) and use these connections to "pull out the student's potential." Connecting to what is real to the student will help develop intrinsic and extrinsic motivation. If you don't connect to their reality and what they currently know and believe, you will not connect enough to motivate them to strive for success. St. Thomas Aquinas stated this as: "When you want to convert someone to your view, you go over to where he is standing, take him by the hand, and guide him."

So if motivation is usually both intrinsic and extrinsic, this means that when you have students who are unmotivated to work or to behave responsibly, you need to try to enhance both their intrinsic (make a science lesson more engaging, for example) and extrinsic (write an encouraging note on returned homework) motivation. The key implication of this concept is that in the early stages of learning something new or when learning something difficult, some students (particularly those who have experienced frequent past failure) are not likely to be intrinsically motivated to engage in the behaviors necessary to learn. As the student becomes more proficient, plan to fade the use of extrinsic motivators in favor of more natural consequences. If you do not fade the extrinsic rewards, the behavior is unlikely to be sustained because the teacher will not always be around to provide the extrinsic incentives (Skinner, 1982). You can find suggestions for both intrinsic and extrinsic motivators in this chapter and in Chapters 7 and 8.

> *As the student becomes more proficient, plan to fade the use of extrinsic motivators in favor of more natural consequences.*

A third important concept has to do with the relationship between a person's intrinsic motivation to engage in a task and that person's proficiency at that task. A skilled woodworker is more likely to find spending time in a workshop rewarding than the person who has never learned to use tools. Similarly, the skilled musician is more likely to find daily practice intrinsically reinforcing than the person who has played for only three weeks. In addition, an individual who has experienced success at learning many different skills in the past is more likely to be motivated to try learning something new in the future than someone who has experienced repeated failure (Howell & Nolet, 2000; Jacobsen, Lowery, & Ducette, 1986). The student who has had a lot of academic success is more likely to feel excited about the challenge of a tough course than the student who has failed at academic pursuits in the past.

A further refinement of the concept is the Expectancy times Value theory of motivation. First used by Feather (1982), this theory explains a person's motivation on any given task as a function of the formula:

$$Expectancy \ x \ Value = Motivation$$

In this formula, *Expectancy* is defined as the degree to which an individual expects to be successful at the task and *Value* is defined as the degree to which an individual values the rewards that accompany that success. The power of this theory is its recognition that a person's level of motivation on any given task is a product of both how much the person wants the rewards that accompany success and how much he or she expects to be successful.

Note that the value factor in the formula can include extrinsic rewards (such as money, time, stickers, awards, and grades) or intrinsic rewards (such as sense of accomplishment, enjoyment of the task, and pride in a job well done). Regardless of the type of value involved, if the expectancy of success is low, motivation will be low.

Let's say that expectancy and value are each calibrated on a scale of 0 to 10, with 0 representing the lowest possible rate and 10 representing the highest possible rate. When a value rate and an expectancy rate for any given task are multiplied together, they equal a number between 0 and 100, which represents the percent of motivation a person has for that task. A key implication of the theory is that if the rate for either expectancy or value is zero, the other factor's rate won't matter—the resulting motivation rate will always be zero (see Table 1.1).

EXPECTANCY RATE	X VALUE RATE	= MOTIVATION
10	x 10	= 100
10	x 0	= 0
0	x 10	= 0

Table 1.1 *Expectancy times Value Equation*

Notice that the expectancy factor is just as important as the value factor in determining motivation. Many teachers, when trying to ascertain why a student is unmotivated to behave responsibly or complete assignments, tend to ascribe the lack of motivation to issues involving the value component of the formula only.

> *Nothing seems to motivate him. He doesn't care about getting good grades. He takes no pride in his accomplishments. He doesn't care about free time or stickers or positive notes home. I tried to put him on a point contract where he could earn time to play a game with a friend or computer time, but he said he didn't really care about games or computers. I guess there's nothing else I can do.*

What these explanations fail to take into account is that if the student does not *believe* that he can succeed at behaving responsibly or completing assignments (he has a low expectancy rate), his motivation will be very low or nonexistent as a result.

Another aspect of the theory is that the rates for both expectancy and value are defined by what a *student* believes, not what you, the teacher, believe. You may know that the student is absolutely capable of being successful if he would simply try. However, if the student has a low expectation of success, his motivation will also be low.

Whenever a student has no motivation to do something (complete work, participate in class discussions, behave more responsibly), you should try to determine whether the lack of motivation stems from a lack of value (intrinsic and extrinsic), a lack of expectancy, or a lack of both. If a student has no motivation to complete academic tasks, for example, one of the first things to do is determine whether or not the student is capable of being successful at the tasks. If she is not, you may need to modify the tasks so that she will be able to succeed. The modification of academic tasks is outside the scope of this program, but there are people in your district who can help with strategies for modifying instruction to bring success within your student's reach.

The Expectancy times Value theory can be a particularly useful way for teachers to think about behavior and motivation. To develop your understanding of this theory, periodically take the time to analyze activities you are motivated to do and those you are not motivated to do. When thinking about something you are highly motivated to do, identify the value you place on engaging in and completing the activity, and the expectancy of success you have before engaging in it. When you think about an activity that you are not motivated to do, see if you can determine what is low—the expectancy rate, the value rate, or both. Try to identify any activities that offer rewards you value but that you avoid doing because your expectancy of success is low. Analyzing your own motivation (or lack of motivation) will help you develop a deeper understanding of your students' motivation. As you work through subsequent chapters and analyze your students' motivations, keep the following concepts in mind:

- Your students' behavior will let you know what they are motivated and not motivated to do. You will have to work on increasing their motivation to engage in positive behavior and possibly on decreasing their motivation to engage in negative behavior.

- Use procedures that address both intrinsic and extrinsic motivation and that are naturally related to the desired outcomes when trying to increase positive student behavior (Haring, Roger, Lee, Breen, & Gaylord-Ross, 1986; Scheuermann & Hall, 2008; Skinner, 1982; Stokes & Baer, 1977).

- Students' motivation to engage in any behavior is related to the degree to which they value the rewards of engaging in that behavior and their expectation of succeeding at it.

Task 3: Identify Long-Range Classroom Goals

Identify several major goals—instructional and behavioral—that you want to accomplish with all of your students by the end of the year.

Without a destination in mind, you may arrive at a place you don't want to be. Although this is a seemingly obvious statement, it illustrates why it is so important to determine, before school begins, what you hope to accomplish with your students by the end of the school year. If you envision your goals, you are more likely to achieve them—and not end up achieving other, undesirable goals! Identify four to seven major goals that summarize why being in your classroom will be a worthwhile experience for your students. Specifically, identify what your students should know or be able to do differently at the end of the year that they didn't know or were unable to do on the first day of school.

Long-range goals can be instructional or academic, behavioral or social, or a mixture. Instructional goals focus on what students will be able to do differently as a result of the academic content you teach. Behavioral goals focus on the attitudes or traits you hope to instill in your students. Your goals may be predominantly behavioral or predominantly academic—it is entirely up to you.

take note

Take the time to think about and then write down your long-range goals for your class. You may want to post your goals in the classroom.

Long-range goals help you plan and make decisions on a daily basis throughout the year. For example, if one of your goals is for students to learn how to plan long-range projects and bring them to completion, you should devote instructional time to several long-range projects over the course of the year. On the other hand, if planning and completing long-range projects isn't a goal, you would plan for students to engage in more short daily activities and spend less time and energy on long-range projects.

Your goals should also help you make decisions about the behaviors and attitudes you want to emphasize with students. If one of your goals is that students will "learn to study independently and stay on task," you need to make an effort throughout the year to discuss, model, and provide feedback about students' on-task behavior. A teacher who does not have this goal may emphasize another behavior with her students.

Sharing your goals with your students and their families at the beginning of the year lets them know what you feel is important for students to learn, both academically and behaviorally, and how you hope to guide students toward accomplishments. Detailed information about how to share goals with students and their families is discussed in Chapter 7.

take note

If you are starting CHAMPS during the school year, implementing Task 3 may be a relatively low priority simply because it requires time for reflection and careful planning—time that you may not have during the school year. However, before the next school year begins, give careful thought to what your long-range goals for that year will be.

Keeping your long-range goals in mind can be particularly important as you move further into the school year. We all know how easy it is for teachers to get so busy and so immersed in daily details that they lose sight of the big picture—the set of skills, knowledge, and behaviors they want their students to have by the end of the year. With long-range goals in mind, you can keep your eyes on the prize and periodically ask yourself whether what you are doing on a daily basis is aiding (or hindering) your efforts to help students reach these goals.

To develop your own long-range goals, start by considering the suggestions that follow:

- Ask yourself what you want students to know and be able to do at the end of the year that they may not be able to do now. What knowledge, processes, attitudes, behaviors, and traits do you hope to instill in your students? What do you want students to remember about their year with you?

- Find out the building-, district-, and state-level goals for the grade level or subject you teach. Your goals should probably reflect some of these.

- Talk to other teachers at your grade level or above about the goals they have for their students. If you teach third grade, for example, ask fourth-grade teachers what skills, knowledge, and behaviors they think new fourth-grade students need to be successful.

Following are examples of major long-range goals for different grade levels and subject areas. You may want to post your goals in the classroom.

for example

take note

Kindergarten
All students will:
- Treat everyone with courtesy and respect.
- Learn to listen and follow directions.
- Learn to cooperate with others.
- Learn to stay on task and finish assignments and activities.
- Develop basic decoding and comprehension skills (for example, alphabet letter names and sounds, blending, segmenting, and rhyming).
- Develop basic math concepts (for example, numbers 1–20 and shapes).
(*This example was provided by Shelley Jones, Hoover Elementary, Salem, Oregon.*)

These samples are included to prompt your thinking. You should not necessarily adopt them as your own long-range goals.

First Grade

All students will:

- Develop basic decoding and comprehension skills and a love of good books.
- Learn to work independently and finish assigned tasks.
- Develop basic math concepts, including mastering single-digit addition and subtraction facts.
- Learn to work cooperatively in groups.
- Learn to listen and follow directions.
- Treat everyone with courtesy and respect.

Fourth Grade

All students will:

- Master all basic addition, subtraction, multiplication, and division facts and be able to use those facts accurately when doing computation and problem solving.
- Learn to work cooperatively in groups and sometimes take the leadership role.
- Develop writing skills that allow them to communicate in both narrative and expository styles.
- Learn to plan long-range projects and bring them to completion (including two major reports and two major projects).
- Learn to speak in front of their peers with confidence and style.
- Learn to stay focused on written tasks and bring them to completion.

Eighth Grade U.S. History

All students will:

- Memorize 10 key events in U.S. history (including the year the Constitution was ratified, the beginning and ending years of the Civil War, and the year the U.S. entered World War II) and be able to place those events on a timeline.
- Be able to describe and apply five essential concepts of the U.S. Constitution (including the three branches of government and the First Amendment right of free speech).
- Be able to learn something new about U.S. history and analyze that event using the timeline events and constitutional concepts noted above.
- Learn to take notes from lectures, films, and readings and use those notes to analyze and synthesize information on tests and projects.
- Learn to study independently and stay on-task during class and when working on homework.

Task 4: Develop Guidelines for Success

Develop and plan to actively share with your students guidelines that describe basic attitudes, traits, and behaviors that will help students be successful in your classroom and throughout their lives.

In addition to academics, teachers need to provide their students with specific information about attitudes, traits, and behaviors that will help them succeed in school and throughout their lives. Sadly, some students and families believe that school success is possible only for those from an educated or a rich family. Others believe that school success depends on the color of a person's skin or their ethnicity. Part of your responsibility as a teacher is to let your students know that they can succeed in school and to give them guidelines to follow that will help them succeed.

Goals and Guidelines for Success
Rules
Routines and Procedures

One way to keep these concepts clear in your mind is to compare them to driving a car.

Goals and Guidelines for Success are analogous to driving safely and courteously or driving defensively. They are values and goals to strive toward. They are always with you, consciously or subconsciously, and can always stand evaluation and improvement.

Classroom rules and the schoolwide code of conduct are like the enforceable rules of driving—stay under the speed limit, stop at stop signs, and keep in your lane. (Information on developing classroom rules is presented in Chapter 3.)

Classroom routines and procedures, such as where to hand in papers, how to line up for lunch, and how to behave during independent work, can be compared to routines and procedures such as adjusting your seat, keeping your keys in the same place so you can find them, and purchasing fuel. (Information on classroom routines is presented in Chapter 2, and Chapter 4 discusses how to clarify details of expectations.)

Your Guidelines for Success should reflect broad and—for want of a better word—noble ideals. They should represent what you really hope students will learn from you—not the academic content, but the attitudes or actions that will help them succeed in your class, in the classes they will have in the future, in their extracurricular activities, and in life in general. Try to imagine your students as young adults looking back on their elementary or middle school years and thinking, "I remember that my ___ grade teacher really taught me the importance of _____."

Having Guidelines for Success is important regardless of the socioeconomic status and learning abilities of the students you teach. Having them is especially critical when your school or class has many high-needs students. High-needs students often lack the knowledge of or motivation to exhibit traits that educators want, need, and expect students to have, such as staying focused on a task or choosing a hard task over a more entertaining one because of the long-term benefits. They can especially benefit from direct teaching of attitudes and traits that will help them succeed (Fairbanks, Sugai, Guardino, & Lathrop, 2007; Gersten & Brengelman, 1996; Gresham, 2002; Howell & Nolet, 2000; Lloyd, Forness, & Kavale, 1998; Scheuermann & Hall, 2008; Walker, Seversen, Feil, Stiller, & Golly, 1998). In addition, having these guidelines has been shown to benefit all students and may decrease the number of other supports your students need (Fairbanks & Sugai, 2007).

Some of your guidelines may overlap with or be taken directly from your long-range goals, but in general, they should be traits that will help students achieve the long-range goals. For example, if you have a goal about students becoming more proficient writers, ask yourself what attitudes or traits will help your students become proficient writers. Figure 1.2 shows a sample of one school's Guidelines for Success.

Optimally, Guidelines for Success are developed and used on a schoolwide basis (Sprick, Garrison, & Howard, 2002). That is, an entire staff creates and agrees to use the same guidelines. Sprick, Howard, Wise, Marcum, and Haykin (1998) provide suggestions for how to involve staff, students, and parents in developing schoolwide Guidelines for Success. Every teacher in the school should use the school's guidelines. However, a teacher may add one or two guidelines that he wishes to emphasize within his own classroom.

If there are no schoolwide Guidelines for Success, consider developing them just for your classroom. When developing your own Guidelines for Success (or Standards for Success, Goals to Strive Toward, or whatever you choose to call them), frame them as brief phrases that describe the attitudes, traits, and characteristics you hope to instill in your students. Plan to have no more than five, because you

Guidelines for Success

✗ Be responsible.

✗ Always try.

✗ Do your best.

✗ Cooperate with others.

✗ Treat everyone with respect (including yourself).

Figure 1.2 *Sample Guidelines for Success*

More Than 10 Years of CHAMPS

As part of the CHAMPS field testing in 1997, Mt. Vernon Elementary in Springfield, Oregon, developed schoolwide Guidelines for Success. The author visited the school in 2009, and their Guidelines (and all other aspects of the CHAMPS approach) are alive and well. Staff talk with students about the Guidelines in all school settings. Because of the consistent use and consistent language, they are successful in maintaining a schoolwide positive approach to behavior management based on their central focus of:

Be Respectful

Be Responsible

Be Safe

Excel

want students to remember them and easily use them as guiding principles for their behavior. If you can use an acronym or rhyme to make them catchy and easier to remember, consider doing so. Guidelines for Success are different from classroom rules. Rules pertain to specific and observable behaviors, and they generally have consequences associated with failing to follow them, whereas Guidelines for Success function more like values, goals, and principles.

Developing guidelines is just the first step. If students are truly going to learn to exhibit these attitudes, traits, and behaviors, you need to make the guidelines a vibrant part of your classroom. Post the guidelines in a prominent place in your classroom where everyone can see them. Teach them to students at the beginning of the year. As with your long-range goals, share your Guidelines for Success with students' families. Keep guidelines alive by using them frequently in the classroom. For example, you can use them to prompt motivation and to pump up your students to strive for excellence. You should also use the guidelines as a basis for providing both positive and corrective feedback to students about their behavior. "Hakeem, when you pick up litter in the classroom without being asked, it is a great example of being responsible." "Fiona, you need to work quietly. The guideline about treating everyone with respect means you do not disturb others when they are trying to work."

Guidelines for Success can be used as the basis for celebrations of progress (such as class awards at the end of the week), in the context of your classroom's monthly themes (October is Be Responsible Month), and as part of writing assignments and class discussions. (More specific information on how to use the guidelines to elicit motivation is provided in Chapters 7 and 8.)

CHAPTER 1 TASKS

Remember, when students do not receive information about or modeling of these kinds of attitudes, traits, and behaviors at home, the emphasis that school personnel place on their guidelines may provide critical lifelong lessons. If you find that some of your students have less of a context for understanding and operating from your guidelines, plan to provide more instruction on how students can implement them and be prepared to give students more encouragement and pep talks about their benefits.

Below is an example of an individual teacher's guidelines from an orchestra class in Jacksonville, Florida.

take note

Whether you are starting CHAMPS at the beginning of or during the school year, take the time to implement this task. Guidelines for Success give your students critical information about how they can meet expectations and accomplish goals—and this is valuable at any point in the year.

Mrs. Griffin's Orchestra Guidelines

Play With Passion
Take Responsibility for Your Actions
Do Your Best
Respect Yourself and One Another
Be Inspired—"Imagine the Possibilities"

This example shows how a kindergarten teacher from Hoover Elementary School in Salem, Oregon, used the basic guidelines suggested in Figure 1.2 and adapted them to fit her style.

Mrs. Jones's Guidelines for Success

I have identified these basic attitudes, traits, and/or behaviors that are important in order for my students to succeed in my classroom and in their lives.

- Be responsible. (Finish what you start.)

- Always try. (Try, try again.)

- Do your best. (Work hard. This is your job.)

- Cooperate with others. (Be kind. Take turns.)

- Treat everyone with dignity and respect, including yourself. (Remember to say "Please," "Thank you," "Excuse me.")

On the following two pages are examples of schoolwide Guidelines for Success from elementary and middle schools in Fayette County Schools in Lexington, Kentucky (see Figures 1.3 and 1.4).

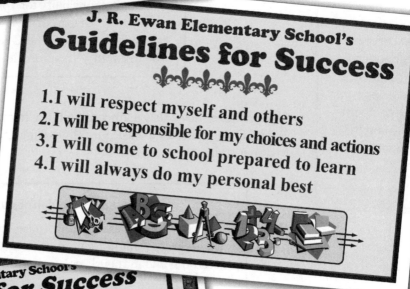

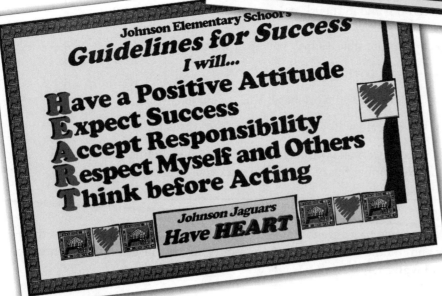

Figure 1.3 *Sample Guidelines for Success from Elementary Schools in Fayette County Schools, Lexington, Kentucky.*

CHAPTER 1 TASKS

1 • Shape Behavior | 2 • Understand Motivation | 3 • Long-Range Classroom Goals | 4 • Guidelines for Success

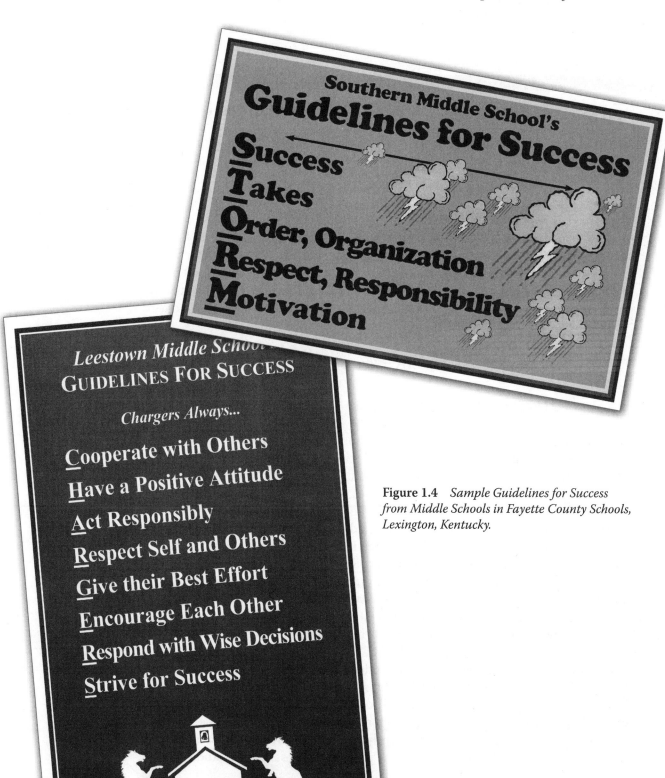

Figure 1.4 *Sample Guidelines for Success from Middle Schools in Fayette County Schools, Lexington, Kentucky.*

Task 5: Maintain Positive Expectations

Ensure that you have, and that you convey, high positive expectations for the success of all your students.

Research has repeatedly demonstrated what common sense tells us: When a teacher has low expectations for students, they achieve less than if the teacher has high expectations (Brophy & Good, 1986; Fuchs, Fuchs, & Hamlett, 1989). In other words, your vision of student achievement and performance has a significant impact on the reality of your students' achievement and performance. Therefore, to be an effective teacher, you must have and convey high expectations for all your students in regard to both academic achievement and their ability to behave responsibly.

low expectations = low achievement

high expectations = set the stage for high achievement

You should not wear rose-colored glasses or ignore the difficulties your students may have. Rather, you must foster high, albeit realistic, expectations for your students if you want them to accomplish what they are capable of accomplishing. To understand the difference, consider the following examples. Imagine that you have a student in your class who is permanently confined to a wheelchair due to a birth defect. Though it would be unrealistic to ignore the student's disability and pretend that she is not different from the other students, it is both realistic and important for you to expect her to thrive and be successful academically in your classroom. It would be unrealistic to expect this student to get out of her chair and run with other students in physical education class. However, you can and should expect her to participate actively and successfully in physical education class if you get information on how to adapt the class to her needs.

> *You should not wear rose-colored glasses or ignore the difficulties your students may have.*

For a more subtle example, imagine a student with a reputation for chronic and long-standing behavior problems. He is placed in your class at the beginning of a new school year. To think that this student will never misbehave is unrealistic. However, it is important for you to expect that he will be able to learn to behave independently and responsibly in your classroom. This task is all about believing in the potential success of every student.

The first step in ensuring that you have positive expectations for all students is to honestly and objectively consider the kinds of things you think to yourself and say to others about students. Whether or not you make disparaging remarks directly to students, you communicate low expectations when you let yourself think or talk about students in unproductive ways. Statements that indicate you may have low expectations for your students include:

- *This student can really press my buttons.*

- *That kid is ADHD, so he can't do it.*

- *What can you expect from a student like this?*

- *I just wish this student would move to a different school.*

- *I guess that kind of thing is expected with a student from that kind of a home.*

If you find that you have such thoughts or make such statements to others, realize that you need to stop. Try to identify specific alternate phrases that you can use. When you begin to think or speak negatively, force yourself to substitute a more positive way of thinking or speaking.

Even if you start the year with high expectations and positive feelings about your students, it can be difficult to sustain this mindset. It's easy to get so busy that you don't notice the negative thoughts and statements creeping in. Perhaps a particularly trying student or class wears you out and your expectations are inadvertently lowered. To alert yourself to possible negative changes, periodically make an honest evaluation of your attitude toward your students. Mark your calendar now with times during the year when you will thoroughly examine your thoughts and statements about students. (This suggestion appears in the Self-Assessment Checklist at the end of this chapter.)

In addition, once school is in session, make a point of monitoring the statements you actually make to students themselves. At various times throughout the year, be honestly self-critical about whether you have been using statements such as the following:

- To a small group: *You students have to work with me because you can't work by yourself.*

- *Are you that stupid that you can't figure it out?*

- *I am not even going to bother to answer that question.*

- *Stop asking such stupid questions.*

- *Why don't you just grow up?*

- *You can't do that. It is too difficult for you. You better do this instead.*

- *Why would you do something like that? Use your head.*

Remarks like these are not only damaging to students, they are unprofessional and unacceptable. All teachers need to make a commitment to never use this kind of language with students.

A college professor was once asked, "But what do you do about the kid you just don't like?" He wisely and calmly responded, "You can't dislike kids on company time." The point is that although you do not have to personally like every student (you can even dislike some on your own time), during the hours you are being paid, you must maintain high expectations for every student's success. The way you treat your students at school should have little to do with how much you like or dislike them, just as the quality of care your physician provides does not depend on her like or dislike of you. When you are feeling frustrated with a student or students, think before you speak. It is fine to address a misbehavior or problem with a statement such as, "Jill, you must quit making noise when people around you are trying to work." However, calling the student names or otherwise passing judgment about the student will in no way help make the situation better and will probably damage any trust the student has in you.

Implementing one or more of the following suggestions can help you to keep a positive attitude and high expectations for your students.

 ### *Take care of yourself.*

You are more likely to maintain a positive mindset when you are in good health. Design a wellness program for yourself to ensure you are getting adequate rest and exercise and that you have activities and interests outside of your career.

 ### *Maintain a positive but realistic vision of students behaving successfully.*

When problems occur, remind yourself of the vision of students behaving successfully. This is especially important if you are dealing with students who repeatedly behave poorly. Set aside a minute or two each day to visualize those students being successful.

 ### *Evaluate your behavior management plan.*

Periodically ask yourself what is going well and what needs improvement in your behavior management plan. When you identify something that needs improvement, take steps to do something differently. Remember that even though you may not be able to control student behavior directly, you can modify various aspects of your classroom (seating arrangements, schedules, the way you interact with a student), which in turn may have a positive effect on student behavior.

take note

Whether you are starting CHAMPS at the beginning of or during the school year, take the time to carefully consider Task 5. If you have low expectations for your students' behavior, they will live up to (or, perhaps more accurately, down to) your expectations. In order to successfully implement CHAMPS, you must have and communicate high expectations for the success of every student.

Don't take it personally.

If a student misbehaves, try to remain objective. You are not the cause of the problem, but you do offer the best hope of positively reaching the student. Remind yourself that you are a professional and that you can, eventually, solve any problem. It may also help to remember that you are probably not the student's only target—he or she probably treats most adults disrespectfully.

 Make an overt effort to interact positively with each student.

All students should feel that you notice and have positive regard for them. Say "hello" to them and show an interest in their interests. When you try to make contact with every student as an individual, they know that you value them—and that reduces the likelihood that they will misbehave.

 Consult with colleagues.

If an individual student or group becomes particularly challenging, discuss your concerns with fellow staff members. Be careful not to communicate low expectations, but do describe the kinds of problems the student is having. Collegial problem solving is a powerful mechanism for getting ideas about ways to help students.

 Implement the tasks described in this program.

All of the tasks presented in the nine chapters of this book are designed to help you develop an effective and comprehensive approach to managing student behavior. Keep trying different strategies until you find something that works for you.

It isn't enough to simply avoid having or communicating negative expectations about students. You also need to make a conscious effort to actively communicate high positive expectations to your students:

- Share your Guidelines for Success and tell students that you know they can achieve those guidelines.

- Remind students frequently that they are capable of achieving your classroom goals and any goal they set their minds to.

- Remember to treat all students with dignity and respect.

- Interact with students in a friendly manner.

Task 6: Implement Effective Instructional Practices

Implement effective instructional practices to keep students interested and academically engaged.

> "When students are successful, their sense of accomplishment can be so satisfying that they are more motivated to behave responsibly."

Effective instructional practices are an absolutely integral part of behavior management practices (Gettinger & Ball, 2008; Scheuermann & Hall, 2008). A teacher who implements dull instruction, presents unclear tasks, or assigns work that is consistently beyond the ability of some of the students is likely to have some students who appear unmotivated, disruptive, or hostile. This is true even if he or she does everything else right in terms of behavior management. Effective instruction can prevent a great deal of misbehavior if only because students who are highly engaged in meaningful tasks do not have time to misbehave. When students are successful, their sense of accomplishment can be so satisfying that they are more motivated to behave responsibly. Educators intuitively understand the link between effective instructional strategies and high academic achievement; a strong connection also exists between academic failure and disruptive behavior problems in students. Research has shown a clear link between inferior instruction and poor student behavior (Brophy & Good, 1986; Martella et al., 2003).

When evaluating a student's (or a group's) behavior problem, teachers should ask themselves whether it might be, at least in part, an instructional problem. It is outside the scope of this program to provide comprehensive inservice on effective instructional practices—the topic is far too broad and complex. However, this task includes descriptions of some elements of effective instruction that can significantly influence student behavior (Gersten & Baker, 2000; Good & Brophy, 2000; Howell & Nolet, 2000; Hudson & Miller, 2006; Kame'enui & Simmons, 1990; Sprick, Knight, et al., 2007; Watkins & Slocum, 2004). Below are lists of these strategies followed by explanatory text to clarify each bulleted item.

One key element of effective instruction is the teacher's style of presentation. A teacher should:

- Be clear about what students are to learn and explain why the task or behavior will be useful to students.

- Relate new tasks to previously learned skills.

- Give students a vision of what they will be able to do eventually.

- Rally the enthusiasm and energy of students, particularly when asking them to do something difficult or challenging.

Other effective practices include the following:

- Actively involve students in lessons—provide Opportunities to Respond (see p. 48).

- Have clear objectives and evaluate student progress.

- Ensure high rates of student success.

- Provide students with immediate performance feedback.

TUNE UP YOUR TEACHING STYLE

Teacher behavior can be a decisive factor in the behavior of students. Students are more likely to pay attention to a teacher who is dynamic, direct, humorous, and enthusiastic in class than to a teacher who talks in a monotone or is confusing or boring. Think back to your favorite teachers in high school and college. How did you feel about their classes? Chances are they were interesting, exciting people who challenged their students. Now think back to your boring teachers. How did you feel about their classes?

A motivational sports coach does more than simply teach his players the necessary skills of the game. The effective coach is passionate about the game and about encouraging his players to learn, even from their mistakes. Think about the motivational speeches an effective coach gives to his team before a big game and during halftime, and to individual players during the game. After the team has won, he might say, "You did great, but don't get overconfident. Next week we face the Cougars, and they may be even tougher than the team we just beat." If the team has lost, he might say, "Yes, we lost, but you played a great game. We can learn from the mistakes we made. We just need to work even harder next week." The words and actions of the effective coach are designed to inspire the players and motivate them to do their best.

> *Every teacher can and should strive to make his or her presentations as interesting as possible to students.*

Although some teachers will naturally be better presenters than others, every teacher can and should strive to make his or her presentations as interesting as possible to students. Make sure you vary the tone of your voice and avoid being monotone. (Remember Ben Stein as the teacher in *Ferris Bueller's Day Off*? You don't want to be compared to him.) Vary the intensity of your presentation—sometimes act excited, sometimes act calm and relaxed. Use humor—try to make at least some part of every lesson fun or funny.

Following are four specific strategies you can use alone or in combination as part of your presentation style to increase students' intrinsic motivation. By presenting tasks and behaviors in a manner that generates student enthusiasm, you can drive students forward to succeed.

Be clear about what students are to learn and explain why the task or behavior will be useful to students.

Most students find it easier to begin and complete an assignment when it has un-ambiguous directions and clear parameters (Ellis & Worthington, 1994; Gersten & Baker, 2000; Hudson & Miller, 2006; Kame'enui & Simmons, 1990; Rosenshine, 1986). Be very direct about the key concepts students need to understand—the more direct your communication, the better. Most people are more motivated to work on a task that has a clear and important purpose than on a task that seems like meaning-less busywork. Therefore, whenever possible, tell your students why you want them to work on the tasks you assign. For example, when presenting a new math skill, you might emphasize how the skill will help them solve certain types of problems. Or, when presenting an important historical event, you might emphasize how the event is relevant to the current events in the country you are studying. If you are trying to get your class to work harder toward one of your Guidelines for Success, you can stress how following the guideline will help them individually to be more successful and will make the classroom a better place for everyone.

Obviously, your explanations about why lessons are useful need to be age-appropri-ate. With kindergarten and first-grade students, it may be sufficient to say an activ-ity will be fun or interesting. With eighth-grade students you need to communicate more precisely what the expected outcome will be and how the task will be useful. It is not necessary to provide this kind of explanation for everything you ask students to do, but you should plan on doing it fairly frequently.

 Relate new tasks to previously learned skills.

Whenever you introduce a new skill or topic, tell students how the new skill relates to previously learned skills (Gersten & Baker; 2000; Hudson & Miller, 2006; Kame'enui & Carnine, 1998; Kame'enui & Simmons, 1990, 1999). Students should not feel that you are presenting hundreds of unconnected, random skills and concepts. They need to understand that what you ask them to do at any particular time relates to what they worked on in the past and will be working on in the future. In this way, stu-dents can see how what they have already mastered is useful in understanding new skills or concepts. When you combine this strategy with the previous suggestion (be clear about what students are to learn), you will ensure that students have a sense of continuity about their learning. Relating new tasks to previously learned skills is important for all students, but is especially important for students from diverse backgrounds or English language learners.

Although clear expectations and explicit instruction are important for all students, they can be espe-cially important for students from diverse backgrounds or English language learners. These students don't always have the contextual background that other students may have, so you cannot assume they will know why something is important (Gersten & Baker, 2000; Gersten & Jimenez, 2002; Rhodes, Ochoa, & Ortiz, 2005).

Give students a vision of what they will eventually be able to do.

Students should be aware of the long-term benefits of full and active participation in your class. That is, they should know what new skills they will be able to do at the end of the year if they follow your directions and work hard at the tasks you assign. The benefits may involve academic skills, study skills, social skills, or a mix of all three. Your long-range classroom goals (see Chapter 1, Task 3) may provide examples of skills that students will be learning. For example, with younger students, you might show them the kinds of books they will be able to read and understand, demonstrate the types of math problems they will be able to complete, and explain how they will learn to keep their attention focused on their work for longer and longer periods of time. With seventh-grade history students, you might share how they will be able to understand current events in new ways and how they will learn to take useful notes and study for tests.

 Rally the enthusiasm and energy of students, particularly when asking them to do something difficult or challenging.

Remember, many students will not be easily motivated to do something new or something difficult. In this situation, you should make a point of emulating a really masterful coach. Don't be afraid to give some variation of a "win one for the Gipper" speech (this cliché comes from an old Ronald Reagan movie in which the coach gives an impassioned speech to a football team before an especially challenging game).

for example

The following hypothetical speech might be given two days before a unit test in science: "Class, in two days we have the unit test in science. This is a tough unit, but I know that you can do it—you can get these important concepts. I want you to do three things in the next two days that will really help you get a good score on the test. First, work to pay attention in class. We are going to review the essential information you need to understand, so keep your attention focused. Second, any time you don't understand something we are reviewing, ask about it. There are no stupid questions. If you aren't sure how to ask a question, just ask me to give more information or to explain the idea again in a different way. Third, decide right now how much you are going to study tonight and how much you are going to study tomorrow night for this test. How many minutes are you going to study? Decide—right now! Now, add fifteen minutes to that number. If you were thinking that you would study zero minutes, add 15 minutes, so you will study at least fifteen minutes tonight and fifteen minutes tomorrow night. If you planned to study 30 minutes each night, make it 45 minutes. Remember, the more you study, the more you learn—and the more you learn, the better you will do on the test!"

ACTIVELY INVOLVE STUDENTS

Don't talk too much! When you speak for more than a few minutes without getting students involved in some way, the less motivated students will tend to tune you out. Ask questions and encourage oral responses. Research has shown that giving students lots of opportunities to respond to a teacher's instructional questions, statements, and gestures decreases problem behavior and increases academic achievement (Brophy & Good, 1986; Engelmann & Becker, 1978; Gunter, Coutinho, & Cade, 2002; Lewis, Hudson, Richter, & Johnson, 2004). Oral responses provide important immediate feedback to teachers. If students quickly and eagerly answer most questions correctly, you know they are learning the material. Oral responses also create opportunities for positive feedback to students ("Great answer, Dan." "You really understand the story, Lisa.") and keep students on task. Fast-paced lessons can give your students many Opportunities to Respond (OTRs). To increase your OTR rate, try some of these strategies.

- Break complex problems into smaller chunks and have students provide answers to each small part of the problem.

- Ask drill-and-practice questions from note cards and have students provide brief choral or individual answers.

- Provide a question and have the students write the answer on a small whiteboard. They can hold it up to show you when they have the answer.

- Mix brief, fast-paced, teacher-directed review of previous material into every lesson.

- Ask a question and then draw students' names from a jar. Once the question has been answered, place the names back in the jar.

Mix individual student responses with classroom choral responses. Craft questions that have the appropriate level of difficulty for the students in the class—problems that are not too easy and provide academic challenge.

According to the Council for Exceptional Children, the optimal rate of OTRs is four to six per minute of instruction on new material with 80% accuracy, and nine to twelve per minute of instruction on drill-and-practice material with 90% accuracy. To learn more about OTRs, see Tool 6 in Chapter 6. Other strategies for getting students involved in lessons, even during teacher-directed lessons, are:

- Give students tasks to work on in pairs.

- Present mini tasks for students to work on independently.

- Give mini quizzes.

- Set up role-plays.

- Present guided practice of tasks students will work on later.

HAVE CLEAR OBJECTIVES

You should always know exactly what you want your students to know or be able to do as a result of the lessons you teach and the tasks you assign. Think about classes you have taken in which the teacher's classroom lessons had nothing to do with her tests and assignments. Preparing for tests probably became guesswork, and going to class seemed like a waste of time. Most people would get pretty discouraged by this situation.

> "
> *Plan your lessons by first thinking about how you will evaluate students' mastery of the content.*
> "

Plan your lessons by first thinking about how you will evaluate students' mastery of the content. For example, before you begin a two-week science unit, create the test students will take at the end of the unit (or review it, if you are using a published test that goes with your textbook). By creating or looking at the test first, you will know the key vocabulary words, concepts, and operations that you need to directly teach during instruction. You can then make sure that any tasks you assign will help students practice those vocabulary words, concepts, and operations. For those who question this as "teaching to the test," consider that a test should cover the material you want students to learn, and so should your instruction. In fact, a clear and consistent match between instruction and evaluation is a hallmark of effective teaching (Fuchs, Fuchs, Dailey, & Power, 1985; Fuchs & Fuchs, 1986; Gresham, 2002; Howell & Nolet, 2000; Hudson & Miller, 2006; Shinn & Bamonto, 1998; Sprick, 2006; Ysseldyke & Christenson, 1988).

ENSURE HIGH RATES OF SUCCESS

Students learn faster when they get predominantly correct answers on both oral and written tasks. While it is true that students should be challenged with difficult tasks, it's also true that students will get discouraged over time when they are constantly presented with tasks that are too difficult. When tasks are too difficult, students make many errors, probably learn a lot of incorrect information along the way, and become more likely to engage in misbehavior (Berliner, 1978; Fisher et al., 1978; Martella et al., 2003; Rosenshine, 1997). Try to provide clear enough instruction and frequent enough practice opportunities to ensure that students will get approximately 90 percent correct on most tasks.

In situations where you know that students are likely to make many errors, you should plan to provide more teacher-directed instruction— whether you are working with students in small groups (while the other students work independently) or with the whole class. Consider the following example involving a whole-class math lesson.

Your original plans call for about 15 minutes of teacher-directed instruction and 30 minutes of independent work time for students to work on the assignment. During the teacher presentation portion you realize that many students are confused and do not seem to understand the assignment. If you stick with your plan, many students are likely to make lots of errors, and some will become discouraged. Several students may seek your help during the independent work period. Because many students are confused, a better approach would be to change your plan.

Instead of giving 30 minutes of independent work, you might say, "Class, since this is such a difficult assignment, I am going to walk you through the first ten problems. Anyone who wants to work ahead may do so, but I invite anyone who is still confused to do the problems with me. Watch me do problem 1, then copy what I have done."

PROVIDE IMMEDIATE FEEDBACK

When students practice a task, they need to receive information on the parts of the task they are doing correctly and the parts they are doing incorrectly—as quickly as possible (Gettinger & Ball, 2008; Good & Brophy, 2000; Hudson & Miller, 2006; Kame'enui & Simmons, 1990). If you have students do an assignment on a new math concept, but you take a week or more to return their corrected papers, they will learn little.

A student needs to know about her mistakes as soon as possible if she is going to learn from those mistakes. During an oral class exercise, you should provide this kind of performance information to students immediately. Likewise, feedback about

A reasonable goal to set for yourself is to be a slightly better presenter every year. Pick one or two of the suggestions in this task to focus on this year. Ask colleagues and administration to visit your classroom to observe and help you with your presentation style. Record your teaching on audio or video and then analyze your instructional style and look for improvements you can make.

correct and incorrect responses during guided practice in class should be immediate. When you assign written tasks that are to be done independently, be sure to correct the papers within one or two days and then go over the corrected papers when you return them. "Class, look at the papers I just handed back. Quite a few people had trouble with question number 5. Let's look at why you had trouble. When you do a problem like this, keep in mind that . . ."

Sincere, age-appropriate praise provides students with personal, immediate feedback as well as positive interactions with the teacher. Increased positive interactions between teachers and students have been shown to decrease misbehavior and lead to increases in on-task behavior (Beaman & Wheldall, 2000; Brophy & Good, 1986; Thomas, Becker, & Armstrong, 1968; Walker, Ramsey, & Gresham, 2004). Teachers generous in their praise typically experience less off-task or disruptive behavior from their students. A high rate of Opportunities to Respond and praise go hand in hand—OTRs provide lots of opportunities to praise correct academic responses and appropriate manners of response.

take note

More students than ever live in one-parent households, in foster care, with grandparents, and in other circumstances. It is often inaccurate to refer to "the student's parents," and it is cumbersome to continually refer to "the student's parent(s), grandparent(s), or guardian(s)." Therefore, in most cases the term "student's family" will be used when referring to a student's primary caregivers.

Task 7: Initiate and Maintain Family Contacts

Build positive relationships with your students' families by making initial contact with them at the beginning of the year and maintaining regular contact throughout the year.

There is no question that when school personnel and families work together to help meet the educational needs of students, the probability of effectively educating those students increases tremendously (Esler, Godber, & Christensen, 2008; Freer & Watson, 1999; Gortmaker, Warnes, & Sheridan, 2004; Henderson & Mapp, 2002; Keith et al., 1998; Rones & Hoagwood, 2000; Sheridan, Kratochwill, & Bergan, 1996). Part of your classroom vision should be to have your class be a place where you, your students, and your students' families work collaboratively to ensure student success. Building the positive relationships necessary to work collaboratively with families, however, is not always easy. First of all, it requires communication, which takes time—and time can be a problem for both teachers and families.

Making the effort to communicate with your students' families sends a powerful message that you want to include them in what happens at school. In addition, such efforts increase the probability that an individual student's family will be receptive should you need to inform them about and enlist their assistance in solving the student's behavioral or academic problem (Christenson & Godber, 2001; Miller & Kraft, 2008; Phelan, Yu, & Davison, 1994). (Specific information on how to work with families when behavior problems occur appears in Chapter 3.) Develop a specific plan for making initial contact with students' families at the beginning of the school year and maintaining contact with them throughout the year. A family contact plan increases the likelihood of communicating efficiently and effectively with your students' families.

Family contacts are especially important when you have a large number of high-needs students. Unfortunately, the families of high-needs students may be more likely to feel alienated from the school, and many of those students may come from troubled homes. Because it's also possible that contacts will be more difficult to achieve with families of high-needs students, remember that the greater the needs of your students, the greater the need for you to establish and maintain contact with their families.

> *The greater the needs of your students, the greater the need for you to establish and maintain contact with their families.*

Many schools have websites that allow you to post class information and assignments. Students and families can find teachers' e-mail addresses and phone numbers as well as general schoolwide information. In some schools, e-mail is the most common form of communication between families and teachers. However, you can't be sure that all of your students' families have access to a computer or even the knowledge to send e-mail. Electronic communication also tends to be impersonal. If you choose to take advantage of your school's website, be sure to also send home on paper all information and messages you post online.

take note

If the families of some (or many) of your students are not English speakers or have limited English, you face an additional challenge. Check with building or district personnel for information about getting assistance in communicating with families in their language. For example, a translator could help with written communications, or an interpreter could be present for telephone calls and at-school events like conferences and Open House. If your school is very diverse and there are many different primary languages, it may not be feasible to make adaptation arrangements for all of the languages. However, if half of your students come from Spanish-speaking homes, for example, arranging for important information to be translated into Spanish demonstrates to families the value you place on communicating with them.

CHAPTER 1 TASKS

The more personal you can make both initial and ongoing contacts, the more effective you can be in building friendly and productive relationships with your students' families. Face-to-face contacts are more personal than phone calls, phone calls are more personal than notes, and notes are more personal than form letters. More-personal contacts generally require more time than less-personal contacts. Thus, although it is critical for teachers to establish and maintain contact with their students' families, each teacher will have to determine the nature and amount of contact that is realistically possible for him or her. Obviously, a middle school teacher who sees 150 students every day will not be able to have as many, or as personal, contacts with families as a special education teacher who has 12 students.

INITIAL CONTACT

take note

See "Cultural Competence" (Introduction, pp. 6–9) for suggestions on working effectively with students and families whose backgrounds are different from yours.

Your initial contact with a student's family is their first impression of you, so it's important to make the contact friendly and inviting, yet also highly professional. When possible, try to establish initial contact with families before the first day of school. If that is not possible, make initial contact within the first two weeks of school.

The purpose of an initial contact is twofold: to begin establishing a productive relationship with the students' families, and to give the students and their families important information about yourself and your vision for the upcoming school year. Provide the following information during an initial contact:

- A welcome indicating that you are looking forward to an exciting and productive year.

- Your teaching background ("I have taught for fifteen years, with the last three years at the middle school level").

- A statement that you are looking forward to working with the student and getting to know the family.

- A statement stressing that you anticipate a very good year.

- Your major goals (academic and behavioral) for the year.

- When and how the family can contact you when they have questions or want to share helpful information about the student.

- When and how you will maintain ongoing communication with them ("I will be sending home a classroom newsletter every other week, starting next Friday").

- (Optional) A copy of your classroom rules, with a slip to be signed by the student and a family member to indicate that they have discussed the rules.

- (Optional for middle school teachers) A syllabus that orients students to some of the detailed expectations for the class, such as homework schedules, routines, and so on.

- Invite comments or questions and give families a chance to tell you how you can contact them.

Following are descriptions of four possible strategies for making initial contact with students' families, along with brief discussions of their relative pros and cons. As you read through them, consider whether one (or some combination) of the strategies might work for you. It's also possible that you already have or will need to develop a strategy that better meets your needs.

FACE-TO-FACE CONTACT PRIOR TO THE FIRST DAY OF SCHOOL

Some schools hold an Open House a day or so before school starts so that students and families can meet their teachers and see their classrooms. If there is any possibility of implementing this wonderful idea at your school, you may wish to encourage it. Families of students who are most likely to have trouble— those with a past history of behavioral or academic problems, for example—can especially benefit from attending an Open House. Consider phoning those families to personally invite them to the event. In addition, you should prepare a letter that contains the important initial contact information (see Figure 1.5) and give it to those students and families who attend the Open House. Of course, you will want to be sure that students and families who do not attend also receive the letter in some other manner.

> *Families of students who are most likely to have trouble can especially benefit from attending an Open House.*

If you like the idea of face-to-face family contact before school starts but your school doesn't hold an Open House, consider possible alternatives. For example, you might contact the families of students who have had problems in the past (such as a student who is painfully shy or has a history of acting out) and invite those students and families to meet you at school before the first day. Your building principal or counselor can probably let you know which students and families from your class would most benefit from a welcoming contact, if you are not sure.

Figure 1.5 *Sample First-Day Letter Home*

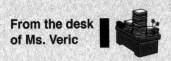

From the desk of Ms. Veric

Dear Families,

Hi! My name is Ms. Emily Veric and I am your child's teacher this year. I am looking forward to a very exciting and productive year. I have been a teacher for six years, but this will be my first year teaching fourth grade. As the year goes on, I am looking forward to meeting you and getting to know you and your student.

I want you and your student to know that my major goals for this year are that all students in my class will:

- Develop skills in written expression so they can communicate in both narrative and expository styles.
- Master all basic addition, subtraction, multiplication, and division facts and correctly apply those facts when doing computation and problem-solving.
- Learn to work cooperatively in groups and sometimes take the leadership role.
- Learn to plan long-range projects and bring them to completion, including two major reports and two major projects.
- Speak in front of groups with confidence and style.
- Stay focused on written tasks and bring those tasks to completion.

I will be sending home a classroom newsletter every other week, starting next Friday. In that letter, I will tell you about my Guidelines for Success and my classroom rules. This letter will also be posted on the school website. To read it online, go to www.ourschool.edu and click on the link for "Mrs. Veric's Class."

If you want to speak with me for any reason, please don't hesitate to give me a call. The best time to call is between 3:00 and 4:00 on Monday, Tuesday, Thursday, or Friday at 555-1234. Or call any time between 8:00 and 4:00 and leave a message, and I will get back to you. You may also send me an e-mail through the school website.

Please feel free to let me know any information that may help me to be successful with your child, and let me know the best way (and time) to reach you.

Good-bye for now, and let your child know that we will have a great year in Room 17.

Sincerely,

Ms. Veric

Ms. Veric
4th Grade Teacher

ABC School • Anytown, USA 55555 • (555) 555-1234

PHONE CONTACT PRIOR TO THE FIRST DAY OF SCHOOL

If you know who will be in your class, another option is to telephone each student's family. Most families will appreciate this effort to contact them directly. If you prepare an outline of the information you want the students and their families to have, you should be able to make the calls brief while still conveying all the important information they need. (Just make sure that you don't sound like an automated recording by the time you get to the last calls.) However, if families take this opportunity to share information about their student with you, this kind of contact can end up taking ten minutes or so per student. As with face-to-face contact, if contacting all families by telephone is not feasible, you might consider contacting only the families of those students who have experienced academic or behavioral difficulty in the past.

> " You might consider contacting only the families of those students who have experienced academic or behavioral difficulty in the past. "

LETTER SENT HOME (ON THE FIRST DAY OF SCHOOL)

A letter sent home with students on the first day of school may be the most common and least time-consuming strategy. However, it also tends to be the least personal. One major drawback is that if no one in the family speaks or reads English, a letter alone will be an ineffective method of communicating and may even make the family defensive. Also, when you send a letter home on the first day of school, it may get lost in a blizzard of other first-day papers, such as bus schedules, immunization information, and lunch menus. Figure 1.5 shows a letter to families by a fourth-grade teacher.

VIDEO ON CD OR DVD SENT HOME OR POSTED ONLINE

Many families today have a computer or DVD player at home. Another way to make initial contact with your students' families is to make a CD or DVD introducing you and your classroom and send copies home with students during the first week or two of school. A video may give students' families a better sense of who you are and create a greater level of comfort and trust than a letter would. A disadvantage is that it may put a student whose family does not have a computer or DVD player in an uncomfortable or embarrassing position. If your school has a website that allows videos to be posted, you could also make your video available online.

If you don't have access to a digital video camera, you can use the video function included on many cell phones and then make copies on CD or DVD. Teachers can pair up and help each other make their videos. As one teacher operates the camera, the other can greet her students' families, talk about her major goals for the year, and even give a brief tour of the classroom. ("And over here is the science learning center. When students are done with their work, this is one of five centers they can choose to spend time in. Of course, they will have to clean up the center after they work here, but we will be working on how to use and take care of the centers during the first two weeks of school.") Once the first person has finished, the teachers can change roles. If you prepare an outline in advance, filming a video like this should take no longer than writing a letter.

To make sure that each student has the opportunity to take a CD or DVD home during the first two weeks of school, you will probably need seven to ten copies. The time, expense, and technological know-how required to make multiple copies of the video may be a major disadvantage of this strategy. Check with your district's media department to see if they can help you. If there are many non-English-speaking families in your class, you should also look into having a couple of CDs with a voice-over translation.

If you use a video, you will still want to have a letter that goes over your classroom rules and your major goals for the class that the family can sign and return. The letter also provides a backup form of communication for any students who do not have a way to play the CD or DVD at home.

take note

If you are starting CHAMPS during the school year, making initial contact with families will probably be a relatively low priority. However, you should put time and energy into maintaining as much positive contact as you can to build relationships with your students' families. Before the beginning of the next school year, make sure that you have a specific plan for establishing and maintaining contact with families.

ONGOING CONTACT

In addition to making initial contact with your students' families at the beginning of the year, you also need to maintain contact with them during the year. If families feel that you are really making an effort to keep them informed, they are more likely to work with you should their student have a behavioral or academic problem. The key here is to come up with a way of maintaining communication without burning yourself out.

Some teachers provide families with an outline of their CHAMPS expectations for the class, as shown in Figure 1.6 on the next page. When CHAMPS is implemented schoolwide, such a letter can be sent to all families (See Appendix B for more details).

Plan to provide positive feedback to families when their child is doing well. Some contact opportunities will arise from regularly scheduled school events such as parent-teacher conferences, Open House, and Back-to-School Night. Other ways of keeping families informed of major class priorities, activities, and issues include having a weekly, biweekly, or monthly class newsletter or newspaper, or sending families a letter on a regular basis. The school website has already been mentioned. It can be a quick, easy way to get information to lots of people. But again, the Internet is inaccessible for some and impersonal.

Use a class list and some form of coding to keep track of your ongoing contacts with families. For example, you might write "9/22, Ph" and "10/4, Conf" next to a student's

Figure 1.6 *Sample CHAMPS Letter Home*

ABC School • Anytown, USA 55555 • (555) 555-1234

Dear Family,

I want to introduce you to my approach to classroom management and discipline issues. The approach is called CHAMPS: A Proactive and Positive Approach to Classroom Management.

Within this approach, the focus is on prevention and on teaching expectations to students. In my classroom, I make every effort to structure for success by creating meaningful activities with frequent variety to engage student interest.

In addition, I directly teach students how to behave responsibly in each major activity and transition. That is where CHAMPS comes in. CHAMPS stands for Conversation, Help, Activity, Movement, Participation, and Success. When students follow the CHAMP expectations, it leads to Success. I encourage you to ask your child if he or she knows about CHAMPS. Ask when and how students in the class can talk, get help, and get out of their seats. Ask how students in my class demonstrate that they are actively participating. If your child doesn't know, encourage him or her to ask me—it will give me a chance to review with students how they can be successful in my classroom.

When students are meeting my CHAMPS expectations, I let them know that they are doing a good job by praising them and occasionally letting the class choose a special game or activity.

When a student misbehaves, I try to correct the mistake by telling the student that behavior is unacceptable. I then give the student a chance to do it the right way. If the misbehavior continues, I may impose consequences such as 30 seconds off recess per infraction or a brief in-class timeout. If the problem occurs more than a few times, I will let you know so that we can work as partners to help your child behave responsibly and experience success in my classroom.

If you have questions about any of this, please let me know. By working together, families and teachers can communicate high expectations and ensure a successful experience for all students.

Sincerely,

Mr. Chang

Mr. Chang

CHAPTER 1 TASKS

1 • Shape Behavior | 2 • Understand Motivation | 3 • Long-Range Classroom Goals | 4 • Guidelines for Success

> *Emphasis on the positive will demonstrate to the family that you have the student's best interests at heart.*

name to indicate that you made a phone contact on September 22 and had a face-to-face conference at school on October 4. A written method like this lets you monitor how often and in what ways you have contacted each student's family. It also allows you to see at a glance whether there are any families you have not contacted. Try to have contacts about each student's positive behavior outnumber those for any negative behavior. This emphasis on the positive will demonstrate to the family that you have the student's best interests at heart and that you want to work with the family to help the student be successful in your classroom.

When family contact is necessary because of some problem a student is having, it's important to pre-think what you want to say and how you are going to say it. This preparation will reduce the chances that you will be misunderstood or inadvertently say something insensitive. Suggestions for handling this type of situation and reproducible templates for making notes prior to contacting a family are provided in Chapter 3.

Conclusion

This chapter covered seven tasks designed to help you clarify your vision for your classroom. After reviewing some fundamental principles of behavior management and motivation, you define what you want your students to accomplish and what they will need to do to be successful. The final three tasks describe strategies you can use to accomplish your vision. When you have completed all these tasks, you will have a clear vision for the look, sound, feel, goals, and accomplishments of your class and the foundation for an effective management plan that will help achieve your vision.

Use the Self-Assessment Checklist shown on the following pages to keep track of the tasks you've completed and those that require further work. A fillable version of the Self-Assessment Checklist is available on the CD.

Print from CD

Develop
a Clear Vision
for
Your Class

Chapter 1: Vision

Use the worksheet on the following pages to identify which (or which parts) of the tasks described in this chapter you have completed. For any item that has not been completed, note what needs to be done to complete it. Then translate your notes onto your planning calendar in the form of specific actions that you can take (e.g., August 17: finish Guidelines for Success, write orientation letter for parents.)

✓	TASK	NOTES & IMPLEMENTATION *Ideas*
	TASK 1: UNDERSTAND HOW TO SHAPE BEHAVIOR	
	I have sufficient knowledge of fundamental behavior management principles to effectively help my students learn to behave more responsibly. Specifically:	
☐	1. I know why and how to promote responsible behavior. • I will set up conditions that prompt responsible behavior. • I will ensure that students experience positive results for engaging in responsible behavior. • I will ensure that students do not experience negative results from exhibiting responsible behavior.	
☐	2. I know why and how to deal with misbehavior. • I recognize that all misbehavior occurs for a reason and will take that reason into account when designing an intervention. • I will identify and then modify any conditions that may be perpetuating the misbehavior. • I will identify and then eliminate any positive consequences that may be resulting from the misbehavior. • I will implement appropriate corrective consequences calmly and consistently when necessary.	

✓	TASK	NOTES & IMPLEMENTATION *Ideas*

✓	TASK	NOTES & IMPLEMENTATION *Ideas*
	TASK 2: UNDERSTAND MOTIVATION	
☐	I will work on increasing students' motivation to engage in positive behavior and on decreasing motivation to engage in negative behavior.	
☐	I will use procedures that foster both intrinsic and extrinsic motivation when trying to increase positive student behavior.	
☐	I understand that students' motivation to engage in any behavior is related to the degree to which they value the rewards of engaging in that behavior and their expectation of succeeding at it.	
☐	I understand the concept of Expectancy times Value. Any time a student seems unmotivated, I will investigate whether it is a problem of low expectancy, low value, or a combination of both. I will use that information in designing a plan to help improve that student's motivation.	
	TASK 3: IDENTIFY LONG-RANGE CLASSROOM GOALS	
☐	I have developed and written down four to seven major goals (instructional and/or behavioral) that I want to accomplish with all my students by the end of the school year.	
☐	I have identified specific ways in which I will use these goals to guide lesson planning and decision making throughout the year.	
☐	I have a specific plan for letting my students and their families know what the long-range classroom goals are.	

61

Print from CD

SELF-ASSESSMENT CHECKLIST pg. 3

✓	TASK	NOTES & IMPLEMENTATION *Ideas*
TASK 4: DEVELOP GUIDELINES FOR SUCCESS		
☐	I have identified three to six basic attitudes, traits, and/or behaviors that are important for my students to succeed in my classroom and in their lives. From them I have created a set of Guidelines for Success (or Guiding Principles, Goals etc.).	
☐	I have posted the Guidelines for Success in my classroom.	
☐	I have identified specific ways in which I can and will make frequent use of the Guidelines for Success. For example: • I will use them as topics for class discussions about behavior or goals. • I will refer to them when providing positive or corrective feedback to students. • I will use them as monthly class themes, as part of class assignments, during classwide celebrations of progress, etc.	
TASK 5: MAINTAIN POSITIVE EXPECTATIONS		
☐	I understand the importance of having high expectations for all my students. I will make a conscious effort not to say anything (to students, their families, or others) that would suggest that I have low expectations for any student.	
☐	I have identified specific ways I can and will convey my high expectations to students, their families, and others.	
☐	I have noted in my planning calendar times during the year when I will objectively examine my expectations for, language about, and behavior toward my students.	

SELF-ASSESSMENT CHECKLIST pg. 4

✓	TASK	NOTES & IMPLEMENTATION *Ideas*
TASK 6: IMPLEMENT EFFECTIVE INSTRUCTIONAL PRACTICES		
☐	I have identified one or two aspects of my presentation style that I will work to improve over the course of this year.	
☐	I have made a plan for working on ways to actively involve students in lessons this year.	
☐	I have determined specific ways in which I ensure that my lessons involve clear objectives and that the content of the lessons is reflected in student evaluation instruments.	
☐	I have determined specific ways in which I ensure high rates of student success on tasks.	
☐	I am prepared to give students immediate performance feedback.	
TASK 7: INITIATE AND MAINTAIN FAMILY CONTACTS		
☐	I am committed to establishing positive relationships with my students' families as part of my classroom vision.	
☐	I have a specific plan for how I will make initial contact with my students' families at the beginning of the year.	
☐	I have a specific plan for how I will maintain ongoing contact with my student's families throughout the year.	

Create
Consistent
Organizational
Patterns

Organization

When you have well-organized routines and procedures for your classroom, you model and prompt organized behavior from your students.

Introduction

*I*magine you are a student in two different college classes. You have an equal interest in each subject, but the two professors have very different ways of organizing their classes. In one class, the professor always begins class right on time, uses class time to focus on essential concepts, and gives clear assignments with definite due dates. In the other class, the professor never begins class on time because he is always sorting through his notes or organizing his visuals. This professor often uses class time to chat about whatever is on his mind. His assignments are unclear, and you are never sure when they are due. Which class are you likely to appreciate the most? In which class are you most likely to strive for excellence? The organization—procedures and routines—within a classroom greatly influences the behavior and motivation of students (Babkie, 2006; Brophy & Good, 1986; Emmer, Evertson, & Worsham, 2003; Fairbanks et al., 2007; Scheuermann & Hall, 2008; Simonsen, Fairbanks, Briesch, Myers, & Sugai, 2008; Trussell, 2008).

The six tasks presented in this chapter are designed to help you organize your classroom to be efficient and to prompt responsible behavior from your students. If possible, complete the tasks before the school year begins so that you have solid organizational structures in place from the first day of school. In addition, once you have finished the tasks, the essential information should be included on your Classroom Management and Discipline Plan (see Chapter 3).

At the end of this chapter is a Self-Assessment Checklist designed to help you determine which (or which parts) of the tasks you have done or are in the process of doing, and which you still need to do.

CHAPTER 2 TASKS

Task 1
Arrange an Efficient Daily Schedule

Task 2
Create a Positive Physical Space

Task 3
Use an Attention Signal

Task 4
Design Effective Beginning and Ending Routines

Task 5
Manage Student Assignments

Task 6
Manage Independent Work Periods

The six tasks presented and explained in this chapter are:

Task 1: Arrange an Efficient Daily Schedule • Arrange or modify your daily schedule to maximize instructional time and responsible behavior and minimize wasted time and irresponsible behavior.

Task 2: Create a Positive Physical Space • Arrange the physical space in your classroom so that it promotes positive student-teacher interactions and reduces the possibility of disruptions.

Task 3: Use an Attention Signal • Decide on a signal you can use to get students' attention. Teach them to respond by focusing on you and maintaining complete silence.

Task 4: Design Effective Beginning and Ending Routines • Design efficient and effective procedures for beginning and ending the school day or class period.

Task 5: Manage Student Assignments • Design efficient and effective procedures for assigning, monitoring, and collecting student work.

Task 6: Manage Independent Work Periods • Design efficient and effective procedures for scheduling and monitoring independent work periods.

take note

If you are starting this chapter during the school year, it may be wise to address the tasks one at a time and implement them gradually so that you do not make too many changes to your classroom routine too quickly.

Task 1: Arrange an Efficient Daily Schedule

Arrange or modify your daily schedule to maximize instructional time and responsible behavior and minimize wasted time and irresponsible behavior.

How you schedule subjects across a day and how you schedule tasks within an activity can have a tremendous influence on student behavior (Brophy & Evertson, 1976; Brown, 1998; Trussell, 2008). For example, the middle school teacher who schedules independent work for the last half of the last period of the day will probably find that students engage in an inordinate amount of off-task behavior. An effective schedule provides enough variety that, at any given time, students won't find it difficult to keep their attention focused on the task at hand. An effective schedule also takes into consideration the maturity level of your students and the degree of skill that you, the teacher, have in presenting various tasks and activities.

The information in this task is designed to help you evaluate (and modify, if necessary) your schedule to ensure that it is more likely to prompt responsible student behavior than irresponsible behavior. This task gives specific scheduling suggestions and also identifies the times of day when students are most prone to irresponsible behavior. It includes suggestions for helping students handle those times in a more responsible manner.

Most teachers cannot control all aspects of their daily schedule. For instance, if the teachers at your grade level share students for reading instruction, you must schedule reading for the same time as the other teachers. You may have no choice about when your students go to music or physical education—you just have to accept those time slots. The scheduling issues and decisions suggested below will help you arrange those times that have not been predetermined by the schoolwide schedule.

To work through the information in this task, first write down your schedule of daily subjects. Most middle school teachers will have the subject schedule already established, but elementary teachers need to make decisions about when and how long each subject will be taught. Once the schedule of subjects is established, list the activities that typically occur within each subject, the amount of time spent on each activity, and whether the activity is teacher directed (lecture, discussion, question/answer), independent work (seatwork, lab activities), or a cooperative group task. In other words, outline a typical lesson plan for each subject. For example, if you teach math from 9:30 to 10:30, it may look something like this:

5 minutes Teacher-directed review of previous concepts

10 minutes Teacher-directed introduction of new concepts

10 minutes Teacher-directed guided practice, working on assignments

25 minutes Independent work or cooperative tasks (depending on task)

10 minutes Teacher-directed corrections or guided practice to help students identify errors or misunderstandings

If you teach in 90-minute blocks, pay particular attention to keeping each activity to a reasonable length of time. You should schedule more activities within the period instead of longer activities. For example:

2 minutes Independent warm-up exercise and attendance

6 minutes Teacher-directed review of previous concepts

12 minutes Teacher-directed introduction of new concepts

10 minutes Teacher-directed guided practice, working on assignments

15 minutes	Independent work
5 minutes	Teacher-directed correcting and clarifying
5 minutes	Introduction to cooperative exercise
15 minutes	Cooperative group task
5 minutes	Teacher-directed clarification
10 minutes	Independent work
5 minutes	Teacher-directed introduction to homework

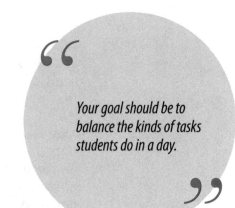

> *Your goal should be to balance the kinds of tasks students do in a day.*

Once you have written down your schedule of subjects and a sample schedule of activities within each subject, evaluate the variety of activities and times for each activity using the following guidelines:

- Make sure that you have a reasonable balance among the types of activities.

- Within each activity, avoid having any one type of task run too long.

- Schedule independent work and cooperative/peer group tasks so that they immediately follow teacher-directed tasks.

Make sure that you have a reasonable balance among the types of activities (teacher-directed instruction, independent seatwork, cooperative/peer group tasks) you use within and across subjects during the day (Beyda, Zentall, & Ferko, 2002; Emmer & Evertson, 1981; Miller, Gunter, Venn, Hummel, & Wiley, 2003; Pedota, 2007; Simonsen et al., 2008).

Your goal should be to balance the kinds of tasks students do in a day. You should especially watch for "too much of a good thing"—you may have a tendency to over-schedule one type of activity. For example, if you like having students work in cooperative groups and feel strongly that students learn a lot by working cooperatively, you may have inadvertently allotted a disproportionate amount of your daily schedule or class period for cooperative group tasks. Similarly, if you prefer teacher-directed activities (lectures, discussions, and demonstrations), you may tend to schedule an insufficient amount of independent work and cooperative group tasks.

Look at your daily schedule and estimate the approximate percentage of class time (not counting lunch, passing periods, and recesses) that students spend on the various types of tasks. Middle school teachers should think about one particular class over the course of a week. For example, you may find your activities look something like the following:

- 40% teacher-directed

- 35% independent work periods (and, as appropriate, lab activities or learning centers)

- 25% cooperative groups

There are no absolute rules for creating a balance of major instructional tasks. A technology class, for example, will have far more independent work and less teacher-directed instruction than a history class. To evaluate your schedule, look closely at what type of task takes up the highest percentage of your class time and honestly ask yourself if this might represent "too much of a good thing."

 Within each activity, avoid having any one type of task run too long.

Whenever students engage in one type of task for too long, behavior problems can result. Students tend to become inattentive when teacher-directed instruction is overly long. When students have to sit and do independent work for a long time, they may get bored and stop working.

There are no absolute rules about how long is too long or how much is too much (although any activity can be problematic if it runs longer than thirty minutes). In part, it depends on your skills and talents as a teacher. A teacher who designs clear, interesting, and fun independent assignments can successfully engage students in longer periods of independent work than a teacher who is not as talented in this regard. A teacher whose presentation style is dynamic, organized, and humorous can sustain student attention for longer periods of teacher-directed instruction than the teacher who is less skilled in presenting to the whole class. If you have found in the past that student behavior deteriorates as a task progresses (for example, they do well at the start of independent work, but get increasingly off task after about fifteen minutes), schedule shorter time periods for that particular type of task.

 Schedule independent work and cooperative/peer group tasks so that they immediately follow teacher-directed tasks.

Teacher-directed instruction is an excellent way to begin a class period, as it can generate positive energy and momentum and get everyone thinking about the same topic. On the other hand, beginning a class period with independent work can result in lower rates of on-task behavior. Starting the period by reviewing previous concepts, introducing some new concepts or skills, and then moving students into independent work or cooperative tasks allows you to clarify what students should be working on, creates a cohesive and clear expectation for on-task behavior, and has the power of instructional momentum (Emmer & Evertson, 1981; Good & Beckerman, 1978).

There are exceptions to this suggestion. For example, many teachers have students work on review exercises (independently or cooperatively) or a challenge problem as soon as they enter the classroom. During this time, the teacher takes attendance and deals with other housekeeping tasks. This strategy usually involves brief (two to five minutes) independent or cooperative activities and is a structured part of the daily routine (Ornstein & Lasley, 2004). Having work ready for students as they enter the classroom can be a very effective practice. Another exception may be a class in which students work mainly on extremely clear and highly motivating independent tasks—a computer lab class, for example. As you develop your daily schedule, remember that, in general, teacher-directed instruction is usually the best way to begin class. You should avoid starting class with a long period of independent work time.

> *In general, teacher-directed instruction is usually the best way to begin class.*

Implementing the preceding suggestions as you schedule daily subjects is one way to reduce the likelihood of irresponsible student behavior. Another way is to identify and proactively address the specific activities and tasks and the times of day when students typically exhibit the most misbehavior (Arlin, 1979; Babkie, 2006; Crone & Horner, 2003; Evertson et al., 2003; Mayer, 1995; Scheuermann & Hall, 2008; Sugai & Horner, 2002). For problematic times and activities, make a point of diligently teaching students what your expectations are and how to meet those expectations. Following are descriptions of times that are particularly troublesome for many teachers, along with some suggestions on how to mitigate the problems.

AFTER RECESS OR ENTRY INTO CLASS FROM HALL

Misbehavior tends to be common right after recess. You can decrease misbehavior by directly teaching students how to enter the classroom and settle down. The key here is to provide this instruction before every recess during the first couple of days of school. You should also plan for periodic re-teaching—especially after any long breaks such as winter and spring break. In addition, you should have a task or activity scheduled immediately after recess that helps students calm down and get mentally ready to pay attention to their work. For example, a primary teacher might have Sharing immediately after recess (rather than first thing in the morning) because it is largely teacher-directed but not overly intense. An intermediate teacher might schedule a five- to ten-minute discussion period on current events or a "What's New in My Life" sharing time.

THE LAST HOUR OF THE DAY

Students (and teachers!) tend to be tired by the end of the day. Students may be more easily distracted and more irritable than they were early in the day, so avoid scheduling too much independent work for the last hour. If you are a middle school teacher who has multiple sections of the same class, this may not seem feasible, but with a little creativity you can make easy modifications. Let's say you teach two classes of eighth-grade English—one first-period and one seventh-period class. Allowing the first-period class to spend thirty minutes working on a long-range assignment may be reasonable. If you allow the same thirty minutes in the seventh-period class, you will probably have high rates of off-task behavior. You would be better off to begin class with teacher-directed instruction, then have 15 minutes of independent work on students' projects, then have more teacher-directed instruction and guided practice during the last 20 minutes of class.

THE LAST FIVE MINUTES OF A CLASS PERIOD

This suggestion applies primarily to middle school teachers. Try to end each class period with a few minutes of teacher-directed instruction. If you schedule independent work time during the last part of the class, students may begin to think that once direct teaching is finished, they are free to do their work—or not. By scheduling the last activity as a teacher-directed task, you are making it clear that class time to work on assignments is indeed for the purpose of working on assignments. "Class, you have fifteen minutes to work on your assignment, and then I am going to end the class by bringing us all back together to find out if any parts of the assignment need clarification."

It is not very hard to arrange your schedule to end a subject with teacher-directed activities. Say you have students working—individually or in groups—on assignments during the second half of the class period. While they are working, you can monitor individual and group progress, noting common errors, misconceptions, and poor work habits. Then, as the period draws to a close, you can get everyone's attention and discuss the common errors and poor work habits. "Class, a few things you should keep in mind as you are working on a task like this are . . ."

> *Be careful to spend only a minimum amount of time on beginning and ending routines and transitions between activities.*

In addition to giving feedback about the current task, you can use the last few minutes of the period to review homework expectations or remind students about long-range projects and housekeeping details. "Class, do not forget that you should be done with your outline for the projects by Wednesday, and tomorrow is the last day to get your permission slips in for the field trip." Again, if you do not end the class with teacher-directed instruction, students may begin to act as if independent work time is free-choice time.

Instructional minutes are valuable. Be careful to spend only a minimum amount of time on beginning and ending routines and transitions between activities, but allow enough time so that they do not seem frantic or rushed. There is tremendous variability among teachers—some have no opening or closing rituals at all, whereas others spend so many minutes each day on opening and closing routines that they lose significant instructional time. Again, the key here is to have some balance—but in this case skewed to maximizing instructional minutes.

In summary, a well-designed schedule ensures that students experience a varied but balanced range of activities within subjects. If students are kept engaged with activities that are scheduled for reasonable lengths of time, responsible behavior will likely result. If students are required to engage in the same type of activity too often, or for too long, they may become bored, distracted, and even disruptive.

Task 2: Create a Positive Physical Space

Arrange the physical space in your classroom so that it promotes positive student-teacher interactions and reduces the possibility of disruptions.

Just as the daily schedule of activities can influence student behavior, so too can the physical organization of the classroom (Babkie, 2006; Scheuermann & Hall, 2008; Trussell, 2008). For example, if student desks are arranged in a way that makes it difficult for the teacher to circulate throughout the room, student behavior is likely to be less responsible than when the teacher can easily reach every student. In this task you will read about five specific aspects of a classroom's physical arrangement that you can address to increase the probability of responsible student behavior and reduce the probability of irresponsible student behavior. Well-designed physical space prevents a wide array of potential behavioral problems (Evans & Lowell, 1979; Simonsen et al., 2008; Weinstein, 1977).

Of course, you do not always have control over the physical arrangement of the space in which you teach. In some cases this is because you do not teach in your own classroom—for instance, you are a middle school teacher who teaches in a different classroom each period or an elementary music specialist who teaches students in their grade level classroom. In other cases, it may be because tables or workstations in your room are permanently attached to the floor—for example, you are a middle school English teacher whose students must work at lab stations because the science lab is the only classroom available during first period. It is also possible that you have less flexibility in arranging your physical environment because your classroom is small and you have large numbers of students.

If any of these scenarios apply to your situation, the suggestions that follow may be difficult to implement. Thus, the basic rule regarding physical arrangements is: Change what you can and make the best out of what you cannot change. For example, if you teach English in a science lab, you will probably have to put more energy into teaching your students to stay on task than you would if they worked at individual desks. You may also have to take the time to teach students not to play with the sinks and gas jets. In other words, manipulate those aspects of the physical space that you have some control over. If you have no control over the physical setting, try to address those issues that may arise from the less-than-desirable aspects of the situation. To whatever extent you can control the physical space in which you teach, consider the following suggestions.

 Arrange student desks to optimize the most common types of instructional tasks that you will use.

Following are descriptions of five common arrangements for individual student desks and their relative pros and cons. The arrangements are:

1. Desks in rows front to back

2. Desks in rows side to side

3. Desks clustered in fours

4. Desks in U-shape (version 1)

5. Desks in U-shape (version 2)

Remember, as you consider what classroom arrangement you want, whether it's one described here or another, you need to think about the instructional tasks students will be participating in and the level of classroom structure your students require.

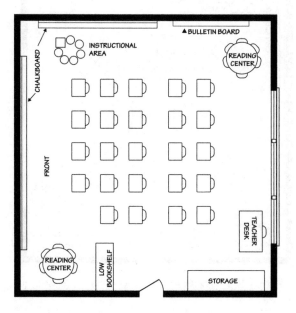

Figure 2.1 *Desks in Rows Front to Back*

1. DESKS IN ROWS FRONT TO BACK

This arrangement, shown in Figure 2.1:

- Is excellent when you schedule frequent whole-class instruction or when students must see the board for tasks.

- Allows for occasional cooperative learning activities. Students can be trained to move quickly from the rows into groups of four and back to the rows when the cooperative activity is completed.

- Allows students to interact, but the space between desks helps to keep off-task conversation down.

- Implies that student attention should be directed to the front of the room.

- Allows easy circulation among students.

2 DESKS IN ROWS SIDE TO SIDE

This arrangement, shown in Figure 2.2:

- Is excellent if you schedule frequent whole-class instruction or if students must see the board for tasks.

- Allows for occasional cooperative learning activities. Students can be trained to move quickly from the rows into groups of four and back to the rows when the cooperative activity is completed.

- Allows students to interact more easily than Desks in Rows Front to Back, which may result in more off-task conversation than desired.

- Implies that student attention should be directed to the front of the room.

- Maximizes available space in the room so that centers, work areas, and small group instruction can be located around the perimeter of the room.

- May hinder circulation among students because you must go all the way to one side of the room to get from one row to another. However, this problem can be alleviated by arranging one or two aisles running perpendicular to the rows.

3. DESKS IN CLUSTERS

This arrangement, shown in Figure 2.3:

- Allows easy access from any part of the room to any other part of the room, making it easy to circulate among students.

- Is excellent if you schedule frequent cooperative learning tasks.

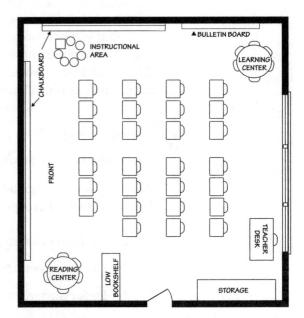

Figure 2.2   *Desks in Rows Side to Side*

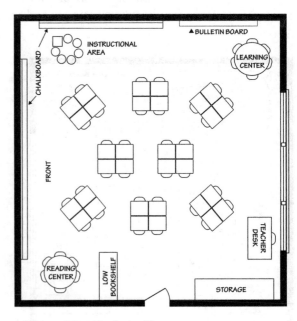

Figure 2.3   *Desks in Clusters*

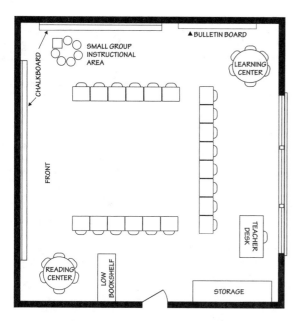

Figure 2.4 *Desks in U-Shape, Version 1*

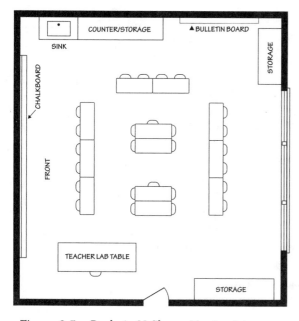

Figure 2.5 *Desks in U-Shape, Version 2*

• Can be problematic when you have students who need less stimulation and distraction. Being part of a cluster may make it more difficult for them to behave responsibly, but separating them may make them feel excluded.

• Requires students to turn sideways or completely around to see the board or teacher-directed instruction.

• May result in frequent off-task conversation during independent work periods and teacher-directed instruction.

• May prompt too much inappropriate student-to-student interaction for a class with high numbers of immature students.

4. DESKS IN U-SHAPE, VERSION 1

This arrangement, shown in Figure 2.4:

• Is excellent for whole-class discussions and teacher-directed instruction when you want students to participate with verbal responses.

• Is excellent for classroom circulation—you can quickly reach any student.

• Does not lend itself to cooperative group activities.

• Does not make good use of space (the area in the center of the U is largely unused). May not allow room for learning centers, small group instruction, and so on.

• Is probably not feasible when you have a large number of students (more than about 20).

• When used with a large class, may need two rows or some desks in the center of the U, as in figure 2.5. With two rows, make sure the inside U has access space to the outside U so you can easily interact with all students.

• Should provide access from the inside of the U to the outside so you and your students are able to cross the room easily.

5. DESKS IN U-SHAPE, VERSION 2

A science teacher shared this arrangement with us. This teacher looked at the suggested arrangements in CHAMPS, considered her own situation (she had tables, not individual desks), and developed a plan that worked for her class.

This arrangement, shown in Figure 2.5 on the previous page:

- Is excellent for whole-class discussions and teacher-directed instruction when you want students to participate with verbal responses.

- Is excellent for classroom circulation—you can quickly reach any student.

- Does not lend itself to cooperative group activities.

- May not allow room for learning centers, small group instruction, and so on.

- Is feasible for classes of up to 26 to 28 students.

- When used with a large class, may need two rows. With two rows, make sure the inside U has access space to the outside U so you can easily interact with all students.

- Should provide access from the inside of the U to the outside so you and your students are able to cross the room easily.

When you use a Desks in U-Shape arrangement with immature students, plan to use proximity management effectively and provide high rates of positive feedback.

 Make sure you have physical and visual access to all parts of the room.

One of the most effective behavior management strategies a teacher can implement is active supervision (Colvin, Sugai, Good, & Lee, 1997; DePry & Sugai, 2002; Gettinger & Ball, 2008; Schuldheisz & van der Mars, 2001). Active supervision includes moving around the room, interacting with students, correcting errors, and providing positive feedback. It requires that you circulate throughout the room as much and as unpredictably as possible. You are more likely to circulate when you can move about the room easily. Thus, regardless of how you arrange student desks, be absolutely certain that you can move easily from any part of the room to any other part of the room.

When students are working independently or in groups, your proximity will have a moderating effect on their behavior. As you circulate, you can provide corrective feedback to students who are off task, give positive feedback to students who are using the work time well, and answer the questions of students who need assistance. As you are helping one student, you may notice another student who is off task. You should be able to walk to the off-task student in a fairly direct route. If you have to walk all the way to the outside edges of the classroom and circle the room to reach the off-task student, you are more likely to find yourself frustrated and angry because you have to go out of your way to keep students engaged.

The physical arrangement should also allow you to visually scan all parts of the room from any other part of the room (Pedota, 2007; Shores et al., 1993). Be careful to avoid screens or bookcases that create spaces you cannot easily see. You will read about the importance of systematic supervision in Chapter 6—the physical arrangement of the room can make this easy or difficult.

 Minimize disruptions caused by high-traffic areas in the class.

There are a number of legitimate reasons why students need to move about the classroom during the day. Yet, whenever students are out of their seats there is a greater potential for misbehavior. Think of the reasons students need to leave their desks and where they need to go. Then arrange the room so that students who are moving about will be less likely to distract students who are working at their seats (Evertson et al., 2003; Jenson, Rhode, & Reavis, 1994). For example, you should keep student desks away from common high-traffic areas where students:

- Get supplies

- Sharpen their pencils

- Turn in their work

- Have small group instruction

- Use learning centers

If you must locate student desks near one or more of these high-traffic areas, you will need to directly teach students how to be in the area(s) without distracting other students.

 Devote some of your bulletin board or display space to student work.

Save the most prominent display space in your classroom for student work (Pedota, 2007; Trussell, 2008). When their work is prominently displayed, it demonstrates to students that you are proud of their accomplishments and that you want to show others what they've done. Artistic teachers sometimes feel that they must have every bit of wall space elaborately decorated. However, when you, the teacher, have done all the decorating, students may get the sense that they are just visitors in "your" room.

If needed, arrange for a timeout space in your classroom that is as unobtrusive as possible.

If you plan to send misbehaving students to a quiet space, you need to decide ahead of time where this area will be. When possible, avoid a location where the misbehaving student is on display to students working at their desks. You might also want to consider having the area screened off for privacy. For more information on using a timeout or problem-solving area, see Chapter 3.

In summary, the physical space in your classroom should be arranged to prompt responsible behavior from students (Jones & Jones, 2007; Simonsen et al., 2008; Trussell, 2008). Make sure that there is easy access from any one part of the room to any other part of the room so that you can circulate unpredictably among students and students can move about without disturbing others. In addition, desks and traffic patterns should be arranged in a manner that takes into account the major types of instructional activities you use and the level of structure needed in your classroom management plan. Finally, thinking ahead of time about where to display student work and whether or not you need an in-class timeout space will help you ensure that the physical space of your classroom is functional for both you and your students.

> "
> *The physical space in your classroom should be arranged to prompt responsible behavior from students.*
> "

Task 3: Use an Attention Signal

Decide on a signal you can use to get students' attention. Teach them to respond to the signal by focusing on you and maintaining complete silence.

Getting and holding students' undivided attention is an important management responsibility for all teachers. An orchestra conductor uses a signal, such as tapping his music stand with his baton, to get musicians to cease their individual warm-up activities and pay attention so that everyone can begin playing the music correctly. Like the conductor, you need a signal to get students to interrupt their individual efforts and focus on you so that you can give directions or provide instruction (Carnine, Silbert, Kame'enui, & Tarver, 2004; Scheuermann & Hall, 2008).

An attention signal is useful in many situations. Imagine a class of 28 students working in cooperative groups. As the teacher monitors the groups, she realizes that the students do not fully understand their assignment. Using a well-practiced signal, this teacher needs no more than five seconds to get students to cease their group conversations and pay attention to her. After briefly clarifying the directions and answering questions, she instructs the students to resume their small group work. Without a well-practiced signal, this teacher would likely spend several minutes repeatedly asking students to stop working. She might even yell over the noise of the groups. It is entirely possible that she would never get all the students to stop talking so that she could clarify the task.

Regardless of the grade level you teach, an attention signal is an important behavior management strategy that you should implement. Whatever level of structure your class requires, you need a way to get students to transition from potentially active and noisy activities into activities that demand that everyone's attention be focused on the same subject.

To implement this task, first identify what you will use as a signal. One commonly used and effective signal is to say in a firm (but not strident) voice, "Class, your attention please," while at the same time swinging your right arm in an arcing motion (from 9:00 to 12:00 on a clock face). Then, hold your hand in the 12:00 position. This prompts each student to stop talking, look at you, and raise his or her own hand—until all students are quiet and looking at you with their hands raised (see Figure 2.6)

This signal has several advantages. First of all, it can be given from any location in the room. Second, it can be used outside the classroom—in the hall or even on a field trip, for example. Third, it has both a visual (the sweeping motion and raised hand) and an auditory (the verbal statement) component. Students who don't hear the signal may see the sweeping arm motion and raised hand, and those who don't see it may hear it. An arcing motion is more likely to be seen peripherally by students, especially those who are not directly facing front, than a simple vertical raise of your hand. Another advantage of this signal (or something similar) is its ripple effect. Even a student who does not hear or see the teacher will find it hard to miss the raised hands of the other students.

Other commonly used signals may not have all the advantages mentioned above. For example, some teachers flick off the lights as a signal for attention. However, this signal requires that the teacher go to the light switch, and it cannot be used at all in the hall or on a field trip. A signal may be ineffective because it has to be repeated frequently before students pay attention. For example, you use a clapping rhythm that students echo back, but you find you have to use it three or four times in succession before all students stop what they are doing. If you already have a signal that works well for you, do not bother to change it. However, if you use a signal that has not worked well, you might want to consider using the signal described above.

Figure 2.6 *Attention Signal*

Some teachers use multiple signals for variety. As long as the different signals do not confuse the students, and as long as the signals are effective in getting the attention of all students, there is nothing wrong with this. It is largely a matter of teacher style.

In summary, regardless of the signal you decide to use, you must teach students what the signal is and how to respond to it from the first day of school. Information on when and how to teach your attention signal is provided in Chapter 5: Launch. For now, just be sure that you know what signal you will use to gain students' attention.

Task 4: Design Effective Beginning and Ending Routines

Design efficient and effective procedures for beginning and ending the school day or class period.

The activities and procedures you use to start and end each school day or class period have a significant influence on the climate of your classroom. Effective and efficient beginning and ending procedures create an inviting and supportive environment; they communicate that time is valuable and will not be wasted (Babkie, 2006; Emmer et al., 2003; Marshall, 2001). The resulting atmosphere, in turn, makes a difference in student behavior. Consider the following two middle school scenarios.

Beginning Routines: Teacher A vs. Teacher B

Teacher A begins the day by warmly greeting students as they enter the classroom. She has previously taught students that when they enter the room they are to immediately take their seats, get out any required materials listed on the board, and begin working on the challenge problem shown via the LCD projector or on the board. Students who do not have their materials do not interrupt the teacher while she is greeting students because, starting on the second day of school, she taught them specific procedures for dealing with this situation. When the bell rings, the students continue to work on the challenge problem while the teacher uses her seating chart to take attendance. Within one minute after the

Case Study »

(continued)

bell rings, Teacher A has taken attendance, secured the attention of the class, and started teaching. Six minutes later, and again four minutes after that, a student enters late, but Teacher A does not stop teaching. She has previously taught students her procedures for tardiness (both excused and unexcused), which are designed to ensure accurate record-keeping without disrupting class.

The situation is different in Teacher B's class. As students enter the class, Teacher B is seated at her desk trying to finish up last-minute preparations for the lesson. Some students take their seats, while others socialize in groups of two to five. When the bell rings, Teacher B looks up from her work and acknowledges the students by saying, "Quit talking and go sit down. It is time to begin class." After two minutes of nagging and cajoling by Teacher B, the students are finally in their seats and reasonably quiet. The teacher instructs students to get out their materials, then spends several minutes helping a couple of students who are not prepared (she lets them borrow books and pencils), all the while nagging them to be responsible. Five minutes after the bell rings, Teacher B finally begins teaching. One minute later, and again four minutes after that, a student enters late. Both times the teacher stops teaching to fill out the necessary paperwork and determine whether the tardiness is excused or unexcused.

Note that Teacher A spends only one minute on attendance, materials, and tardiness procedures, and even during that minute students are engaged in an instructional task. Teacher B spends seven minutes on attendance, materials, and tardiness. Students who arrived on time with all of their materials have been forced to sit and do nothing while the teacher deals with these procedures. In both scenarios, a couple of students did not have their materials and a couple of students arrived late—situations that happen occasionally with even the most effective teacher. The difference is that Teacher A has anticipated these common problems and has taught her students procedures for handling them. Her procedures do not usurp teacher time and attention and do not waste the time of the students who are punctual and prepared.

In this task, you will learn how to begin and end your school day or class period with a positive tone and maintain maximum time for instructional activities. We identify seven critical times and issues related to beginning and ending the day or class period, develop a goal statement for each that describes optimal outcomes related to that time or issue, and then provide suggested routines and procedures for achieving the goal. While elementary teachers will find useful suggestions for beginning and ending their school day and for beginning and ending each subject period, this task may be even more critical for middle school teachers who typically have five to seven different classes each day and for elementary specialists (music, PE, computer, art) who may have a new group every 30 minutes.

The seven critical times and issues are:

- Entering Class

- Opening Activities (Middle School)

- Opening Activities (Elementary Level)

- Dealing With Students Not Prepared With Materials

- Dealing With Students Returning After an Absence

- Procedures for End of Day or End of Class Period

- Dismissal

Keep in mind that these suggestions represent just one way of dealing with beginning and ending your day or class. If you already have efficient and effective beginning and ending routines (procedures that adequately address the goal statements), there is no reason to change what you do. If you do not have good routines established, read these suggestions or talk to colleagues (or both), then design beginning and ending procedures for your class that are time efficient and set a positive tone.

ENTERING CLASS

 Students feel welcome and immediately go to their seats and start on a productive task.

Greeting students as they enter your classroom helps them feel welcome and reduces classroom behavior problems. A brief greeting communicates to students that you are aware of them not just as students but as individuals and that you are interested in them—"Marguerite, how did things go at the choir concert last night?" In addition, greeting students as they enter provides a subtle but powerful message that you are aware of students and what they are doing from the minute they enter the classroom, not just after the bell rings.

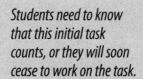

> *Students need to know that this initial task counts, or they will soon cease to work on the task.*

In general, you want to greet students at the door. If you are supervising the hall outside your room, you can greet them before they even enter your doorway. Although you can greet students inside the classroom (while seated at your desk, for instance), the effect is not quite as powerful as being at or near the door and greeting them immediately as they enter.

You should also have a task prepared that students can work on when they sit down. The purpose of the task is to keep students busy while they wait for the bell to ring and while you take care of any attendance and housekeeping tasks during the first minute or two of class. Having students work on a daily task like this communicates to them that you value instructional time and plan to use every minute as efficiently as possible.

Keep the task relatively short, requiring three to five minutes of work from students. It should be a review task that students can perform independently, but should also be instructionally relevant—not just busy work. For example, math teachers might give a short daily quiz on the previous night's homework assignment. Language arts teachers might have students work in their journals or do a power-writing exercise. A primary teacher may have students work on a handwriting exercise or a practice page of math facts.

When you finish taking attendance, give the students feedback on the correct responses for the task. Have them correct their own papers or trade with a neighbor. Then collect the papers so that later you can enter the score or a check mark in your grade book to indicate that students completed the task. Students need to know that this initial task counts, or they will soon cease to work on the task.

OPENING ACTIVITIES (MIDDLE SCHOOL)

If you are a middle school teacher, you should make sure that your procedures for opening activities accomplish the following three goals:

 GOAL 1 *Students are instructionally engaged while you take attendance.*

When the bell rings, and as students continue to work on the assigned task, use a seating chart—rather than an oral roll call—to determine who is present and who is absent. This allows students to continue to focus on their work while you take attendance. Sitting and doing nothing except for the split second needed to respond to roll call is a very boring way for a student to begin class. Some teachers use a seating chart that includes pictures of students, which is a great resource for a substitute teacher.

GOAL 2 *Your procedures for dealing with tardiness are effective.*

A procedure is effective when it does the following:

- Ensures that students who are tardy do not disrupt class or take your attention away from teaching.

- Allows you to keep accurate records of excused and unexcused tardies.

- Lets you assign consistent corrective consequences for unexcused tardiness.

One effective procedure for dealing with tardy students is to have a three-ring binder filled with forms similar to Reproducible Form 2.1, Record of Tardies. Place the binder on a table or shelf near the door to the classroom. Each day before students arrive, make sure that a new page is showing with the correct day and date filled in at the top. Attach a couple of paper clips to the page so that students with excused tardies can attach either the excuse slip from the attendance office or a note from the teacher who is excusing the tardy.

During the first week of school, teach your students the procedure to follow when they are tardy, whether it is excused or unexcused. Tell them they are to quietly enter the classroom without interrupting you or any students in the class. They are to go to the tardy notebook, put their name in the box for the appropriate period, indicate Excused or Unexcused, and attach the excuse, if they have one. Then they can quietly take their seat.

When a student enters late, do not stop what you are doing. Visually monitor to make sure that the tardy student goes to the notebook and writes something (you can check later to make sure that the student wrote his or her name). If the student does not go to the notebook, provide a verbal reminder: "Paul, before you sit down, put your name in the tardy notebook and indicate whether you have an excused or unexcused tardy. Now class, what I was saying was . . ."

Reproducible 2.1   *Record of Tardies*

Later in the period, when the class is engaged in independent work or cooperative groups, check the information on the tardy student(s) in the notebook. Record the information in your grade book and follow any schoolwide procedures for reporting unexcused tardies to the attendance office. With excused tardies, look at the note or slip to verify accuracy. If you need to talk to a student about being tardy, do it at this time, while the rest of the class is instructionally engaged. Note that following these procedures prevents the tardy student(s) from getting attention and interrupting your lesson.

There should be corrective consequences for unexcused tardies. Most middle schools have a schoolwide tardiness policy that is managed and implemented by the administration. For example, a school's policy for tardies per semester may be:

2 unexcused tardies » Family notification (notification occurs for each subsequent incident)

4 unexcused tardies » After-school detention

6 unexcused tardies » Half-day in-school suspension

If your school does not have a tardy policy, develop your own and inform students of it on the first day of school. A policy similar to the schoolwide example above can work for you as an individual teacher, although you probably cannot assign an in-school suspension without administrative approval.

GOAL 3 *Announcements and other housekeeping tasks do not take up too much time.*

You should begin instructional activities as quickly as possible after the beginning of the period. Try to spend no more than a minute or two on announcements and housekeeping. Activities that are not directly related to the subject of the class (such as general social skills training and school spirit discussions) should be reserved for advisory or homeroom periods.

OPENING ACTIVITIES (ELEMENTARY LEVEL)

If you are an elementary school teacher, you should make sure that your procedures for opening activities accomplish the following two goals.

 **GOAL 1** *Opening activities are efficient and orderly, and ease students into the school day.*

Effective elementary teachers vary widely in the way they deal with the beginning of the school day. This variation reflects, among other things, grade level and personal style. For example, some teachers include sharing as an opening activity, while others do not. Some teachers like to have students do class jobs and take time each morning to assign these jobs. Some teachers conduct calendar and weather activities, and others do not. Because there is no one correct way to start the day, consider the following when planning your opening activities:

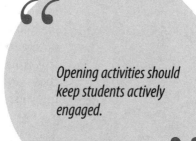

Opening activities should keep students actively engaged.

Opening activities should include the accurate recording of attendance, lunch count, and any other housekeeping duties.

Opening activities that take more than a few minutes should have an educational objective. For example, if you take five minutes each day to discuss the weather, it should be because one of your science objectives is that students master some basic concepts about weather. Otherwise, don't bother with this five-minute activity. Likewise, if you do a sharing activity, you should have some compelling reasons why you take class time for this activity each day.

Opening activities should keep students actively engaged (Ornstein & Lasley, 2004). If students are expected to sit and do nothing, you will have behavior problems. Think about your typical opening activities. Are students actively engaged and learning? If not, modify your opening exercises. For example, if you have sharing, you should structure the activity so it does not take too long. Because only one student talks at a time, the activity is largely passive. Students, particularly those at the primary level, will get restless if sharing goes on for more than about five minutes.

If your existing procedures for opening activities address the considerations above, there is no reason to change. If they don't, talk to other teachers about what they do first thing in the morning and how much time they take for their opening procedures.

 GOAL 2 *Students understand that school attendance and punctuality are important.*

Have a brief discussion every two weeks or so with your class about the importance of consistent attendance and punctuality. When punctuality and regular attendance are not high priorities for students' families, teachers can help students develop these values by regularly emphasizing the importance of coming to school and getting there on time. If either absenteeism or tardiness becomes a significant problem, one effective technique is to calculate and publicly chart the percentage of students who come to school or arrive on time each day (or both). Tracking students like this gives you an opportunity to talk to your class about the importance of attendance and punctuality. It can also put gentle pressure on students to push their family (if needed) to get them to school on time. If necessary and appropriate, you might also set up a small reward system. For example, when everyone is on time, the class gets a point. When the class collects ten points, the students get to go to recess five minutes early.

If the chronic tardiness involves only one or two students, do not use either of the preceding procedures. It is probably more effective in this case to ask your administrator for help in putting pressure on the family to get the student to school on time. You might also want to set up an individual contract and some form of reinforcement system with the student. However, be aware that putting pressure only on the student may put him in a very difficult position—a student cannot "make" his parents do anything. See *The Teacher's Encyclopedia of Behavior Management: 100 Problems/500 Plans* by Randy Sprick and Lisa Howard (Pacific Northwest Publishing, 1995) for ideas on setting up such a reinforcement system.

DEALING WITH STUDENTS NOT PREPARED WITH MATERIALS

GOAL *Your procedures deal effectively with students who do not have materials or who are not prepared to participate in the class.*

To be effective, a procedure does the following:

- Ensures that students can get needed materials in a way that does not disrupt or slow down instruction.

- Establishes reasonable penalties that reduce the likelihood that students will forget materials in the future.

- Reduces the amount of time and energy that you, the teacher, spend dealing with this problem.

First, be sure to clearly communicate to students exactly what materials you expect them to have each day in your class (two sharpened pencils, a binder for science class, lined notebook paper, the science textbook, for example). This information should be communicated verbally to students and in writing to students' families as part of a

Students from families living in poverty may not be able to purchase materials. Talk to your administrator and counselor about your school's processes for helping students get the supplies they need when their family is either unable or unwilling to provide them.

syllabus or notice that goes home on the first day of school. At the end of each class period during the first week of school, remind students what materials they should have when they return to class the next day.

Next, develop procedures that allow a student who lacks any of the necessary materials to get what she needs to participate in the lesson. The student should also receive a mild consequence designed to reduce the probability that she will forget materials again. For example, you might inform students that, when possible, they should try to borrow the missing material (such as a pencil or some paper) from another student without involving you or interrupting instruction. And explain that, because borrowing materials from the teacher wastes teaching time, they will owe a short amount of time after class. Assign something like thirty seconds after class for middle school students or a minute off recess for elementary school students.

If students need to go to their lockers to get missing materials, develop procedures that minimize the teaching time lost when you fill out hall passes. For example, you could inform students that if they have to return to their locker for materials after class has begun, it will count as a tardy. Tell them that you will give them a hall pass that they fill out and you sign. While the student is filling out the pass, continue with your other teaching responsibilities. Having the student fill out the pass reduces your involvement with this student from two or three minutes to only thirty seconds or so. Some secondary schools implement a schoolwide program titled *START on Time!* to address tardiness. One feature of this program is that teachers do not issue hall passes for the first ten minutes of class. *START on Time!*, by Randy Sprick (2003), is available from Pacific Northwest Publishing (www.pacificnwpublish.com).

take note

Never let more than one student at a time leave class to go back to the lockers.

Resource

If you ask other teachers in your building how they deal with students who do not have materials, you will probably hear about a wide variety of procedures. Some teachers just give away pencils and lend books without any penalty. "I don't make an issue of it. If they need a pencil, I give them one." Other teachers impose penalties. "I think students must learn to be responsible. If they don't have a pencil and I have to give them one, the student owes me a quarter or an after-school detention." There is no one right answer. The important thing is for you to decide in advance how you will deal with this very common occurrence. If you aren't sure whether your planned procedure is fair or appropriate, ask your building administrator for feedback. Some administrators, for example, may not want teachers to impose a choice-type penalty such as "a quarter or a detention—your choice."

It's important that you inform students during the first couple of days of school how you will respond if they do not have their materials. Then, a couple of days into the first week of school, start conducting periodic spot checks. "As you are working on the challenge problem on the overhead, I want to check that you came to class with the materials you need. Put your extra pencil, your notebook, and your science book on your desk. While you are working, I'll come around and check." If any students are missing one or more of the required materials, provide a gentle but firm reminder about the importance of being responsible for bringing materials every day.

> *After the first couple of weeks, conduct unpredictable, intermittent spot checks of materials.*

After the first couple of weeks, conduct unpredictable, intermittent spot checks of materials. Any students who do not have what they need should receive a minor corrective consequence—they lose a point from their participation grade, for example. Students who have all materials might receive a bonus point. If you plan to do this, be sure to inform students during the first week of school that you may conduct spot checks once or twice a week during the first few weeks of school. When a student does come unprepared to class, try not to get upset or frustrated; simply follow through consistently with your stated procedures. Remember that you should implement procedures that do not usurp too much of your time. If you start feeling frustrated because you spend too much time dealing with students who have forgotten materials, ask colleagues for ideas on how to streamline procedures so that you can keep your focus on instruction.

DEALING WITH STUDENTS RETURNING AFTER AN ABSENCE

GOAL *Students who have been absent can find out what assignments they missed and get any handouts and returned papers without consuming much of your time and energy.*

Set up two baskets for students to access. Keep the baskets in a permanent location—on a counter, a shelf, or your desk. One should be labeled "Absent—What You Missed" and the other, "Absent—Assignments In." Any time you give students an assignment, a handout (worksheets, reading materials, bulletins, or notices), or graded papers, put that same material in a folder for an absent student. The folder should have the date, the class period, and the student's name on it. Some teachers pair students in a buddy system. When one of the students is absent, it is the responsibility of his or her partner to copy any assignments, collect any handouts and graded papers, and put that material in a folder labeled with the student's name and the date. A folder should be prepared every day the student is absent and placed in the basket marked "Absent—What You Missed."

Teach students that when they return after an absence, they should collect their folder or folders from the basket. This way, they find out all the tasks they must do and get any handouts they need without interrupting you.

The basket marked "Absent—Assignments In" can be used in two ways. When a student returns on Tuesday from an absence on Monday, he turns in any assignment that was due on Monday to the "Absent—Assignments In" basket. At the same time, he picks up his folder from the "Absent—What You Missed" basket. When the student completes the work assigned on Monday (the day he was absent), he turns that work into the "Absent—Assignments In" basket also.

A system like this can save you lots of time and interruptions, but it will work only if you keep the baskets up to date by checking them daily and reminding students to use them when they return from being absent.

As a general rule, give students the same number of days to complete missed assignments as the number of days they were absent. Thus, the student who returns Tuesday from being absent on Monday has until Wednesday to turn in work that was assigned on Monday and due Tuesday. If the student does not return until Thursday, he has until the following Tuesday, or three school days following the day he returned, to turn in the missed assignments.

PROCEDURES FOR END OF DAY OR END OF CLASS PERIOD

 *Your procedures for wrapping up the day, class period, or activity will ensure that students don't leave the classroom before they organize their materials and complete any necessary clean-up tasks, and provide you with enough time to give students both positive and corrective feedback.*

Allow enough time at the conclusion of the day, class period, or activity to make sure it ends on a relaxed, positive note. How much time this entails will vary. For example, in a middle school math class, one minute will probably be sufficient. In a middle school art class, it may take up to ten minutes to get all supplies put away and the room ready for the next class. Elementary teachers may need five to ten minutes at the end of the day to help students get organized, make sure the room is clean, and make last-minute announcements.

At the beginning of the year, elementary teachers especially should plan to allow more time than they think is necessary for wrapping up. Remember that during the first week of school, you may have to take time to help students figure out which bus to take, where their family is going to pick them up, and so on. If the wrap-up and cleanup takes less time than you scheduled, you can always use the extra couple of minutes for a discussion, a song, or a word game.

When students finish organizing and cleaning up, give the class as a whole feedback on things they are doing well and also on the behaviors and skills that may require more effort on their part. This is especially important during the first six weeks of school, but is also useful intermittently throughout the school year.

> *Give the class as a whole feedback on things they are doing well and also on the behaviors and skills that may require more effort on their part.*

Class, I want to let you know that the way you have been using class time demonstrates a high level of responsibility. We should be very proud of how well we are all functioning as a group. One thing that a few people need to manage more effectively is remembering homework. Tomorrow, you have a math assignment and a science assignment due. Make a decision right now about when you are going to work on those assignments—this afternoon or this evening. I expect to see two completed homework assignments from each of you. (Bell rings.) Thanks for a good day today. Have a nice evening. You are all excused to go.

DISMISSAL

 GOAL *Students do not leave the classroom until you dismiss them. The bell is not a dismissal signal.*

On the first day of school and periodically thereafter, remind your students that they are not to leave their seats when the bell rings. Explain that the bell is a signal to you—you will excuse the class when they are reasonably quiet and when all wrap-up tasks are completed. If you let students bolt for the door when the bell rings, it sets a precedent that your instructional control ends when the bell rings. By reserving the right to excuse the class, you can make judgments about whether you should excuse the whole class at once or by rows or table clusters. As a general rule, primary students should be excused by rows, and older students can be excused as a class. However, let the older students know that if they rush out of the room or crowd the door, you will start excusing them by rows or clusters.

In summary, the beginning and ending of the day or class period play a major role in setting the climate of the classroom. Opening and dismissal routines that are welcoming, calm, efficient, and purposeful demonstrate to students that you are pleased to see them and that you care so much about class time that not a minute will be wasted.

Task 5: Manage Student Assignments

Design efficient and effective procedures for assigning,
monitoring, and collecting student work.

An all-too-common frustration for most teachers is dealing with students who do not complete assigned classwork or homework. Students who do not complete assignments often do not get the practice necessary to achieve mastery of essential instructional objectives. In addition, without seeing students' completed assignments, you may not have sufficient information to determine whether they have mastered the skills or whether they need more practice. Anything that you can do to increase the likelihood that students will complete assignments is worthwhile because you will significantly increase the rates of student learning and significantly decrease your level of frustration. In this task, you will read about procedures and routines for managing student assignments. Implementing well-designed and well-organized strategies for assigning, monitoring, and collecting student work can alleviate much of your potential frustration. Good strategies for managing assignments accomplish the following:

- They let students know that you put a high value on completing work.

- They prompt more responsible student behavior regarding assigned tasks.

- They help you effectively manage student assignments without taking unreasonable amounts of time.

There are four major areas related to managing student work for you to consider (see Figure 2.7). This task covers the kinds of decisions you should think about for each area as well as strategies you might implement.

ASSIGNING CLASSWORK AND HOMEWORK

One of the first things to consider in this task is implementing a system that allows students to easily find information about assignments. Students should have a specific place to look, such as the board or an assignment sheet, to find out what they are assigned. It is not enough to simply tell students the assignments or to write them on an overhead projector during the lessons. These methods do not create a permanent place for students to check to see what they need to do. When there is no set place where students can check their assignments, a student who forgets what the day's

Figure 2.7 *Four Major Areas to Consider for Managing Student Assignments*

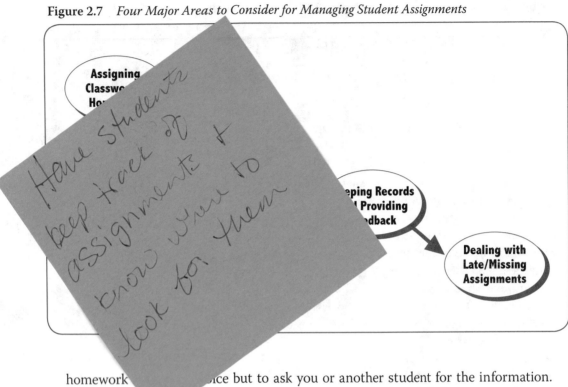

homework ... ice but to ask you or another student for the information. When assign... are written and left on the board or recorded on an assignment sheet, the stude...t can simply look at the board or assignment sheet.

You should also teach students to keep their own records of assigned homework so that when they get home, they know what they need to do. If your procedure is to write assignments on the board, teach students to copy the homework assignments onto a sheet of notebook paper and keep it in a consistent place in their notebook. If you give out a weekly assignment sheet, students should be taught to keep the assignment sheet in a consistent place in their notebooks. Be specific—tell students exactly how and where they should record the information. Show them a model and, especially at the beginning of the year, monitor whether they are following through. "Class, we have a

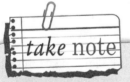

take note

With primary students in particular, strive to make homework a positive experience. For example, if students do not have support at home for getting homework done (perhaps no one speaks English in the home), you could suggest that students use the time before class begins in the morning to complete their homework—perhaps with older students available to assist the younger students.

couple of minutes before the bell. Open your notebooks to the page immediately after the divider for this class. I want to see that you have the Weekly Assignment Sheet in the correct place." See the end of this task for more information.

Figure 2.8   *Sample of Assignmen*

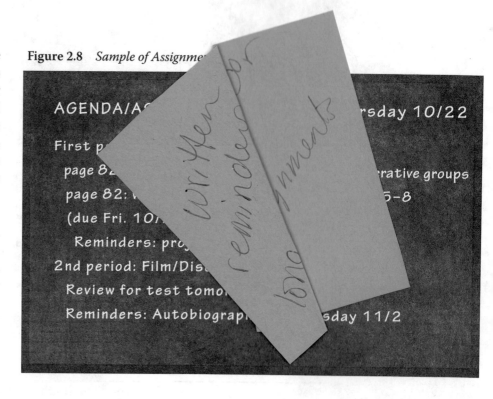

If you give both short-term daily assignments and long-term assignments (a term paper, for example), be sure to note both types of assignments on the board or assignment sheet. Daily reminders about a long-term task will help students remember to work on the task on an ongoing basis rather than put it off to the last minute. Written reminders can also prompt you to let students know what parts of a long-term assignment they should have done by certain points in time. "Remember that your projects are due in one week, so by Monday you should have your outline and your first draft completed."

Figure 2.8 shows how you might use board space for recording assignments. An alternative to using board space or assignment sheets is to use a flip chart. You can also put a large sheet of paper on the bulletin board and write each day's assignments on one page. Middle school teachers might use one page for each class period for a full week. Each day, you can flip over (or add) a new page for that day's assignments. This system has the additional advantage of providing easy access to information about previous assignments. When a student has been absent, he can simply go to the flip chart or bulletin board, find the pages for the days he was absent, and copy down what he needs to do.

Because a class with high risk factors is likely to have frequent student absences, having a permanent record of daily assignments is especially useful. Plan on keeping an ongoing record of assignments if you have determined that your students need a high-structure classroom management plan.

As part of your plan for assigning work, determine how you expect students to organize materials and monitor assignments. That is, when you give an assignment, where will students keep a record of it? One effective strategy used in many schools is to have students keep a three-ring binder with dividers for various subjects. If your school has adopted a particular schoolwide study skills curriculum, you should follow the organizational strategies suggested in that curriculum.

If your school does not have a study skills curriculum, you might want to suggest that your staff consider a schoolwide adoption of *Skills for School Success*, by Anita Archer and Mary Gleason, published by Curriculum Associates. This excellent curriculum teaches strategies for organization and studying that will enhance the academic achievement of all students. It emphasizes the effective use of a three-ring binder.

COLLECTING COMPLETED WORK

Another issue to consider is how students turn in completed homework and in-class work. Whenever possible, collect work personally from each student. "Class, put your homework on the upper right-hand corner of your desk. While you are working on the challenge problem on the overhead, I will come around and collect it." The biggest advantage to this procedure is that you know immediately which students have not completed the work (and students know you know). If a student does not have his or her homework, you can take that moment to emphasize that work completion is an important aspect of responsible behavior in your class. Do not listen to excuses, but let the student know that he or she will need to speak to you later. When you use this procedure, students should be doing something worthwhile while you collect their work. If they are doing nothing, it is a waste of potentially productive time.

This procedure is especially important for collecting homework. Students know they will have to face you when they don't have their homework. If you have worked at building relationships with your students, they will not want to disappoint you. You send a powerful message about responsibility when you stand right beside a student and provide positive feedback on the student's demonstration of responsibility or express disappointment at his or her lack of homework. See the last section of this task, Dealing with Late and Missing Assignments, for some ideas to increase work completion rates.

> "Whenever possible, collect work personally from each student."

By collecting work personally from each student, you put yourself in a position to give students immediate feedback—that is, intermittent positive feedback to students who completed their work and consistent corrective feedback to students who did not do their work. You should collect student work personally if you have determined that your students need a high-structure classroom management plan. On the other hand, the procedure has the disadvantage of being time and labor intensive for the teacher. If you require only a low- or medium-structure classroom management plan, you may prefer another procedure.

Procedures that are less time intensive include the following:

- Have students hand in their work by rows or tables.

- Have a student helper collect it.

- Have students put their work in a designated basket.

These procedures lack the interpersonal contact and immediate feedback advantages that you get from collecting work directly from each student. With these procedures, students don't actually see you handling their homework and class assignments, and until you grade the papers you don't know who has completed the assignment and who has not. Thus, any feedback (positive or corrective) is delayed until the next day or even longer. If you used one of these methods in the past and were unhappy with your students' rate of work completion, try experimenting with collecting work directly from students and see whether work completion improves.

 Consider having students check off completed tasks.

If you give students a daily or weekly assignment sheet or have them use an assignment notebook, consider adding check-off boxes so students can indicate that they have completed a task. Another option is to have students check off completed tasks on a wall chart (similar to Reproducible Form 2.2, Completed Assignments Checklist). If you use some kind of wall chart in an elementary classroom, you should include on it all the major daily tasks and plan on putting up a fresh copy (with student names on it) each day. In middle school, you can probably put up one sheet per class for the whole week. Note that an assignment check-off sheet like this is not an official record and does not take the place of or supersede your grade records. It is simply an opportunity for students to put closure on the task.

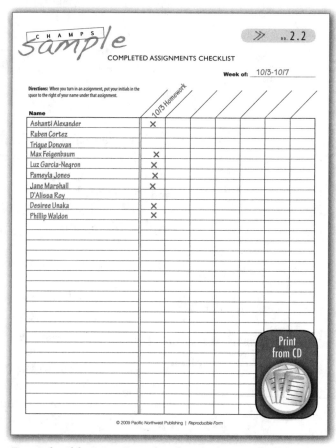

Once you have taught students how to use a check-off procedure, you can also teach them to self-reinforce in an age-appropriate manner. For example, with middle school students you might say, "When you check off your completed math assignment, tell yourself, 'I am choosing to be successful in this class because I am responsible for completing my work.'"

Reproducible 2.2 *Completed Assignments Checklist*

You might even consider posting the statement above the chart so students can read the statement as they check off each completed task. It is no accident that the major time-management systems used by adults include check-off boxes on the list of daily tasks so each one can be checked off when it's completed. Self-reinforcement and closure on tasks can be achieved using this simple but powerful idea of a check-off procedure.

KEEPING RECORDS AND PROVIDING FEEDBACK

An important yet often overlooked aspect of managing student assignments is providing regular feedback to students on their completed work and current grade status. Experienced teachers know that an accurate and complete grade book is an essential part of a well-run classroom. Grade book information is critical for monitoring and evaluating student performance. Many teachers with complete and comprehensive grade books, however, do not have procedures for keeping students informed of their current grade status. A student who isn't aware of his grade status in the middle of a term may not realize that he needs to improve.

If a student is falling behind by the second week of school, you should immediately inform the student and her family that she is not making adequate progress. In addition, you should have a standard policy to send notes or make phone calls (or both) to families of students who have more than a certain number of missing assignments (five, for example). Regular and gentle nagging will increase rates of work completion, and students need to learn that they are still accountable for completing assignments even when they are past due.

In primary classrooms, regularly informing students of their grade status may not be useful or appropriate, but intermediate and middle school teachers should definitely have a system for keeping students updated weekly on their current grade status. Descriptions of two such systems follow. Consider implementing the one that best fits your personal style.

1. ***Use a grade book software program on a computer and print out a weekly report for each student on each subject.***

   If you don't already keep your grade records using one of the many fine computer programs for grading, consider doing so. In addition to saving time when you have to figure grades at the end of the term, these program allow you to print out a grade record for every student each week. The printout shows any missing assignments or tests, the score possible and the score earned on each assignment, the total points accumulated, and the current grade.

2. Have students complete a Student Grade Record.

If you do not have access to a computer grading program, have each student keep his or her own records. You can design a form that includes the range of assignments and tests you anticipate during each grading period (see Reproducible 2.3).

Each time you hand something back to students, have them get out their record sheet and enter the score they received in the appropriate space (such as a 92% on Test 2). About once a week, have students total the points they have earned. As students are adding up their points, you can put a breakdown of the point range for each letter grade on the board or an overhead (see Figure 2.9).

The major disadvantage of using a student grade record rather than a computer-generated printout is that you have to depend on students to keep track of their forms and enter the scores each time you hand something back. This organizational dependence on the students can work, but it requires that you be very direct about your expectations and that you take class time to have students record their scores every time you hand back graded work.

EXTRA PROCEDURE FOR CLASSES NEEDING A BOOST

In addition to ensuring that all students receive regular and ongoing feedback about their current grade status, you may be able to increase rates of work completion by providing feedback to the class as a whole on the classwide percentage of completed work. For example, you might use a large wall chart (or an overhead transparency if wall space is not available) to record the daily percentage of homework handed in. Simply take the number of completed homework assignments and divide it by the number of students present that day to create a chart like the one shown in Figure 2.10.

Reproducible 2.3   *Student Grade Record*

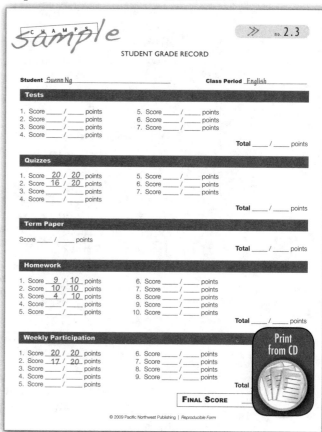

Figure 2.9   *Sample Point Range for Letter Grades*

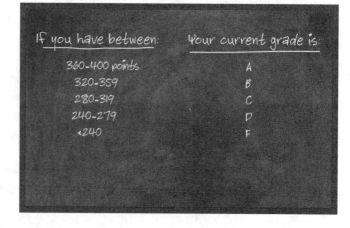

Figure 2.10 *Sample Homework Completion Chart*

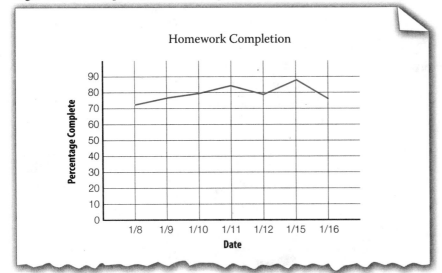

An advantage to using a charting procedure is that it provides a daily opportunity for you to discuss the importance of being responsible for completing homework. In addition, it may create a bit of peer pressure to complete work because each student's work completion, or lack thereof, affects the class percentage. If you wish, you can tie small-scale rewards to achieving certain goals. "When the class percentage is 92% or higher, the class earns the last five minutes of class as choice time.'"

DEALING WITH LATE AND MISSING ASSIGNMENTS

The last major consideration regarding managing student assignments is how to deal with late and missing assignments. Some teachers choose to have no penalty for late work (students can hand in anything, anytime, and there is no cost), while others do not allow students to turn in any assignment late (a late assignment equals zero points).

Figure 2.11 *Sample Late Assignments Policy*

Late Assignments Policy:

1) Any assignment that is turned in late will receive an immediate 10% penalty (for example, a 100-point lab will have 10 points deducted from whatever score you earn).

2) No assignment will be accepted beyond one week late.

3) I will inform the family of any student who has more than three late or missing assignments.

4) No more than four late assignments will be accepted during the quarter.

You should probably adopt some middle ground between these two extremes. When there is no penalty, some students turn in everything late, possibly even handing in all assignments on the last day of the term. If students are allowed to do this, it is unfair to you (you should not have to stay up all night at the end of every grading period) and it is unfair to the students (they can learn that they do not really have to pay attention to due dates). On the other hand, an extreme "If it's late, it's a zero" policy does not take into

Reproducible 2.4   *Zero Slip*

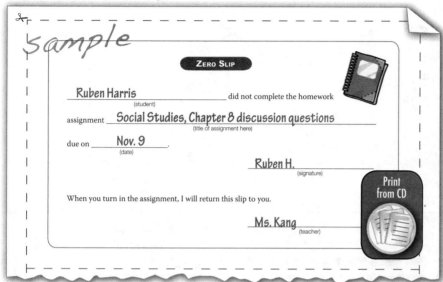

account that an occasional late assignment is likely for even the most responsible student. Figure 2.11 on the previous page shows a sample policy that might be implemented by a middle school science teacher.

One effective way to deal with students who do not complete their assignments by the due date is to have them fill out a Zero Slip (see Reproducible 2.4). By filling out the slip, they are acknowledging that they did not turn in their work. It eliminates the problem of a student saying "I did that assignment—could you have lost it when you were grading the papers?" You hold onto the Zero Slip. If students hand in the assignment later, you can give the slip back to them. The accumulation of Zero Slips will be a written, signed record of every missed assignment, and this can be powerful evidence to show at family conferences.

Reproducible 2.5 is a No Assignment form similar to one shared by a high school teacher. She requires students to complete the form when they don't submit homework or classwork by the established deadline. This teacher found that the excuses written by students came in handy during subsequent family conferences because some students blamed family members for their missing homework. Once students understood that the family would see these "no homework" forms when they came for a conference or when the teacher contacted the family about missing homework, it had a positive impact on the rate of homework completion.

In most classrooms, a large percentage of students' time is spent working on written tasks. The way you manage assignments and work periods has a big impact on how much responsibility students take for managing and completing their written tasks. If you effectively manage student assignments, students are more likely to complete

take note

Details of and criteria used in a late and missing work policy will reflect the decisions of individual teachers. Most importantly, develop a policy that works for you and inform students and their families about the policy at the beginning of the year or term.

Reproducible 2.5 *No Assignment Form (Source: Cristie Cantor, Shreveport, Louisiana.)*

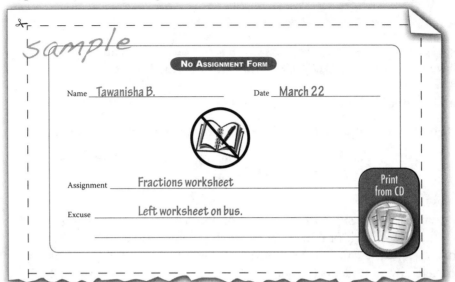

that work, thus giving them the practice they need on essential instructional objectives. In addition, when students complete their work, you can see whether they are achieving mastery of those objectives and can make judgments about whether additional instruction is necessary.

Task 6: Manage Independent Work Periods

Design efficient and effective procedures for scheduling and monitoring independent work periods.

The following suggestions focus on how to effectively set up independent work periods. In Chapters 4 and 5, we provide additional information on how to clarify and directly teach your behavioral expectations regarding independent work periods.

When students are expected to work without direct teacher supervision, off-task behavior can easily result. There is more potential for off-task behavior—which can lead to inappropriate horseplay and disrespectful interactions among students—when students are working independently than during any other type of activity. Your goal should be to keep students on task and actively engaged in their work. The following suggestions can help minimize off-task behavior during independent work periods.

Be sure that any independent work you assign can be done independently by students.

If you assign students tasks that they cannot complete, you set them up to fail. When students have to do work that is beyond their ability, they are likely to:

- Do the work, but fail because of excessive errors.

- Not do the work and fail because they didn't complete the assignment.

- Do the work, but deal with feeling and looking helpless because they ask for help day after day from you or peers.

Over time, many students slip into the second option because when they do nothing, at least they look tough or bored instead of stupid and helpless. Following are suggestions for steps you can take to ensure that the independent work you assign can be completed by all students (Babkie, 2006; Barbetta, Nornona, & Bicard, 2005; Gettinger & Hall, 2008; Howell & Nolet, 2000; Simonsen et al., 2008):

- Modify assignments to meet the needs of the lower-performing students in the class. For more information on modifying instruction for such students, see *Interventions: Evidence-Based Behavior Strategies for Individual Students* by Randall Sprick and Mickey Garrison, published by Pacific Northwest Publishing (2008).

- Provide alternative assignments for some of the students.

- Work together on the assignment with a few students in a small group while the rest of the class works independently (Ysseldyke, Thurlow, Wotruba, & Nania, 1990).

- Have students work in pairs or cooperative groups so they can help each other (Delquardri et al., 1986; Simmons, Fuchs, & Fuchs, 1995; Spencer, 2006). Do not overuse this strategy or your higher-performing students may get tired of helping others do their work.

- Use computer-assisted instruction (Clarfield & Stoner, 2005; Silver-Pacuilla & Fleischman, 2006).

- Provide students with guided notes (Sweeney et al., 1999).

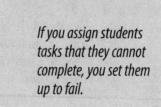

If you assign students tasks that they cannot complete, you set them up to fail.

CHAPTER 2 TASKS

1 • Arrange an Efficient Daily Schedule   2 • Create a Positive Physical Space   3 • Use an Attention Signal

Schedule independent work times in a way that maximizes on-task behavior.

The subject of scheduling to maximize on-task behavior and minimize off-task behavior was discussed in Task 1 of this chapter. The following information summarizes the suggestions in Task 1: Arrange an Efficient Daily Schedule on how to improve student engagement during independent work periods.

- Do not schedule long periods during which students are expected to stay on task while working independently. There is no magic rule about how long students can stay focused, but in general, having students work on the same task for more than thirty minutes without some change in routine will result in high rates of off-task behavior. Even thirty minutes can be too long for primary-grade students unless you have built up to that amount. See Chapter 5 (Task 4) for ideas on how to teach primary-age students to stay on task during independent work periods.

- Do not schedule independent work periods to immediately follow high-excitement times such as recess or assemblies.

- Do schedule independent work periods to follow some form of teacher-directed instruction.

- Arrange for the independent work periods that occur at the end of the day to be shorter than independent work periods that occur at the beginning of the day.

 Develop a clear vision of what student behavior should look and sound like during work times.

This suggestion is covered in detail in Chapter 4: Expectations. For now, remember that if you do not clarify and teach exactly what you want from students, some students are likely to assume that behaviors such as chatting in groups, moving about the room, and playing with toys are OK during independent work times. Once you have a vision of the behaviors you want students to exhibit (and correspondingly, the behaviors you do not want them to exhibit), teach students to meet those expectations (Barbetta, Norona, & Bicard, 2005; Emmer et al., 1980; Greenwood, Hops, Delquadri, & Guild, 1974; Lewis & Sugai, 1999; Marshall, 2001; Mayer, 1995; Simonsen et al., 2008).

Provide guided practice on tasks and assignments—that is, work with students in a teacher-directed activity for the first 10 to 50 percent of an assignment.

Guided practice is important because it increases the chance that students will have the skills or knowledge needed to successfully complete the task. Guided practice can also create "behavioral momentum." That is, when you guide students through the first part of a task, a portion of the task is already completed by the time you say, "Now do the rest of the assignment on your own (or in groups)." Without guided practice, when you say, "Get to work on your assignment," students are faced with a blank piece of paper. For many individuals, the hardest part of doing assigned tasks is getting started. Guided practice increases work completion because it ensures that students have started their work, and likely understand it, before the independent part of the class period begins (Council for Exceptional Children, 1987; Rosenshine, 1983).

for example

When teaching a math lesson, you might start by reviewing previously taught concepts, then introduce the day's new concept, then work through the first several exercises of the math assignment, and finally turn students loose to work on the remainder of the assignment independently or in groups. If there are 30 problems in the assignment, you might model and lead students through the first six.

"Watch me do the first two problems on the overhead and copy what I do." Then you demonstrate and explain.

"On the next two problems, I'll do the first half and you do the second half of the problem." You demonstrate the first part and let students do the second part. Correct the problems and answer student questions or re-teach based on student mistakes.

"Now do the next two problems on your own. Stop when you finish problem six so we can correct." Let all students do two problems while you monitor their performance. Then model or have individual students demonstrate the correct answer. Answer questions and provide any additional instructions.

If students are doing well, you can then assign the remaining problems as independent work. If many students are having problems, continue to work through the problems together until you are sure students understand the concepts and processes.

Develop a specific system that enables students to ask questions and get help during independent work periods (Scheuermann & Hall, 2008; Trussell, 2008).

When students have a question about how to do something, they may feel that they cannot continue with their work until the question is answered. If you have not structured a way for students to ask questions, get answers, and get help when necessary, you will have higher rates of off-task behavior. For those independent work periods in which you (or another adult—a co-teacher or paraprofessional) are available to answer questions, develop and teach your students to use a predetermined visual signal when they need assistance. You can have students put an upright book (not the book they need for the assignment) or a flag or sign on the corner of their desk.

Figure 2.12 shows how a sign can be used. One side of the sign says, "I'm fine." Another side says "Please help!" The third side says, "Make note of your question and keep working." Reproducible 2.6, Student Work Status Display, on the CD is a pre-made sign that you can print and fold for students to use. (This idea was originally suggested by Paine, Radicchi, Rosellini, Deutchman, & Darch, 1983.)

Another idea, shown in Figure 2.13, is to get two paper or plastic cups, one green and one red, and tape the open ends together. All students have a taped-together pair of cups on their desks. When a student is doing OK, the green cup is on top. When she needs help, she turns the cups over so that the red cup is on top.

Figure 2.12 *Flag as a Help Signal*

red cup

green cup

Figure 2.13 *Colored Cups as a Help Signal*

Another way students can indicate they need assistance is to write their name on the board, along with the question or problem number they need help with. If several students have a question about the same item, you can gather those students together and provide assistance at one time instead of helping each person individually. "Sandra, Mark, and Dani, please come to my desk so we can figure out problem number 5."

Note that none of these suggestions require students to raise their hands when they want help. This is deliberate. The problems with the traditional hand-raising procedure are:

> *Note that none of these suggestions require students to raise their hands when they want help.*

- It is physically difficult to keep a hand in the air for the three to five minutes it may take you to respond.

- The student is necessarily off-task while he or she is waiting for your help.

- Hand raising tends to draw more attention to a student, which may discourage some students from asking for help.

With the signals described above (or some variation), students can be trained to un-obtrusively put up their signal, mark the question or problem they need help with, and continue working on other problems.

For those independent work times when you are not available (for instance, you are working with a small reading group while other students work on independent assignments), you should devise strategies for students to ask and help each other. Be sure that students understand that this talking is permitted only to get needed help on assignments.

Conclusion

The tasks in this chapter guide you through organizing your classroom to be efficient and to prompt responsible behavior from your students. If you are able to complete the tasks before the school year begins, you will start off on the first day of school with solid organizational structures in place.

Use the Self-Assessment Checklist shown on the following pages to keep track of the tasks you've completed and those that require further work. A fillable version of the Self-Assessment Checklist is available on the CD.

Print from CD

Chapter 2:
Create
Consistent
Organizational
Patterns

Chapter 2: Organization

Use the worksheet on the following pages to identify which (or which parts) of the tasks described in this chapter you have completed. For any item that has not been completed, note what needs to be done to complete it. Then translate your notes onto your planning calendar in the form of specific actions that you can take (e.g., August 24: determine classroom arrangement, decide on attention signal.)

✓	TASK	NOTES & IMPLEMENTATION *Ideas*
	TASK 1: ARRANGE AN EFFICIENT DAILY SCHEDULE	
☐	I have arranged my daily schedule to include a reasonable balance of teacher-directed work, independent work, and cooperative group activities—within a given subject and/or across subjects during the day.	
☐	I have arranged my daily schedule so that no one type of activity (teacher-directed work, independent work, or cooperative group) runs for too long a period of time.	
☐	I have scheduled independent work and cooperative group activities to immediately follow teacher-directed tasks.	
☐	I have identified and taken steps to proactively address those times of the class or day when students are more likely to misbehave.	
	TASK 2: CREATE A POSITIVE PHYSICAL SPACE	
☐	I have arranged the desks in my classroom to optimize the most common types of instructional activities students engage in and to reflect the level of structure my students require.	
☐	My classroom is arranged so that I have physical and visual access to all parts of the room.	

✓	TASK	NOTES & IMPLEMENTATION *Ideas*
☐	My classroom is arranged so that disruptions caused by activity in high-traffic areas are kept to a minimum.	
☐	I have devoted some of my bulletin board/display space to student work.	
	TASK 3: USE AN ATTENTION SIGNAL	
☐	I have identified and will teach to students an attention signal that has both auditory and visual components.	
☐	I have a specific plan for how I will provide both positive and corrective feedback to students regarding how they respond to the signal.	
	TASK 4: DESIGN EFFECTIVE BEGINNING AND ENDING ROUTINES	
☐	I have identified how I will begin class and/or the school day in a way that makes students feel welcome and prompts them to go immediately to their seats to work on a productive task.	
☐	As a middle school teacher, I have determined how I will conduct opening activities to meet the following goals: • Students are instructionally engaged while I take attendance. • My procedures for dealing with tardiness ensure that tardy students do not disrupt class or take my attention • Announcements and housekeeping tasks do not take up too much time.	

106

Print from CD

✓	TASK	NOTES & IMPLEMENTATION *Ideas*
☐	As an elementary school teacher, I have determined how I will conduct opening activities to meet the following goals: • Opening activities are efficient and orderly, and ease students into the school day. • Students understand that school attendance and punctuality are important.	
☐	I have identified procedures for dealing with students who do not have necessary materials and/or are not prepared. These procedures: • Ensure the student(s) can get needed materials in a way that does not disrupt instruction. • Establish reasonable penalties to reduce the likelihood the student(s) will forget materials in the future. • Reduce the amount of time and energy I have to spend dealing with this issue.	
☐	I have identified how I will deal with students who return after an absence so that they can find out what assignments they missed and get any handouts or returned papers without involving much of my time and energy.	
☐	I have developed procedures for wrapping up at the end of the school day and/or class period. These procedures ensure that: • Students will not leave the classroom before they have organized their own materials and completed any necessary cleanup tasks. • I have enough time to set a positive tone for the class and give students both positive and corrective feedback.	
☐	I have developed dismissal procedures that ensure that students do not leave the classroom until I dismiss them (the bell is not a dismissal signal).	

✓	TASK	NOTES & IMPLEMENTATION *Ideas*
	TASK 5: MANAGE STUDENT ASSIGNMENTS	
☐	I have designed procedures for assigning classwork and homework that ensure that students can easily find information about the tasks they have been assigned to complete.	
☐	I have designed efficient and effective procedures for collecting student work.	
☐	I have designed efficient and effective procedures for keeping records of students' work and giving them feedback about their progress.	
☐	I have designed efficient and effective procedures for dealing with late and/or missing assignments.	
	TASK 6: MANAGE INDEPENDENT WORK PERIODS	
☐	As I set up my independent work periods, I will make sure that I do the following: • Only assign independent work that I know students can do independently. • Schedule independent work times in a way that maximizes on-task behavior (see Task 1: Daily Schedule). • Establish a clear vision of what student behavior should look and sound like during independent work times. • Arrange to provide guided practice on tasks and assignments that I expect students to do independently. • Develop a specific system for how students can ask questions and get help during independent work periods.	

Construct a Classroom Management and Discipline Plan

Management Plan

Prepare a Classroom Management and Discipline Plan that summarizes the important information, policies, and procedures you will use to motivate students and address student misbehavior.

Introduction

*B*y developing a Classroom Management and Discipline Plan before the school year begins, you set the stage to deal productively with the range of behaviors, both positive and negative, that students will exhibit in your classroom (Alberto & Troutman, 2006; Brown, 1998; Emmer et al., 1980; Emmer, Anderson, & Worsham, 2003; Marshall, 2001; Scheuermann & Hall, 2008; Trussell, 2008).

An effective management and discipline plan is not a canned program or a static entity. It is a framework that supports a variety of rituals, routines, rules, consequences, and motivational techniques you can use to ensure that students are academically engaged and emotionally thriving. Though your plan should be in place before the school year begins, you will adjust the initial plan you developed to meet the changing needs of the class as the year progresses. Your plan will be somewhat different on the first day of school, on the 20th day of school, on a day a new student comes to class, and on the last day of school.

Let's look at an example from the field of medicine to get a sense of this concept. If you are going into the hospital for surgery, you assume (and hope!) that the surgeon, the nurses, and the lab have a plan in place for how everything is going to work. Without a coordinated plan, the possibility of disaster is high—they may not have the blood type you need, the equipment may not be sterilized, or perhaps there won't be enough nurses to assist in the operation. However, even

CHAPTER 3 TASKS

Task 1
Determine the Level of Classroom Structure

Task 2
Develop and Display Classroom Rules

Task 3
Correct Rule Violations During the First Week of School

Task 4
Establish Corrective Consequences for Rule Violations

Task 5
Know When (and When Not) to Use Disciplinary Referral

with the most organized plan, adjustments need to be made during the course of the operation. They may need more plasma than originally anticipated, they may need immediate information from the lab about an abnormal growth, or they may find your organs are in a slightly atypical position. With the basic plan in place, it can be adjusted to meet the needs that arise during the course of the operation.

Your Classroom Management and Discipline Plan may be very tightly or very loosely structured. This notion of structure has nothing to do with being friendly or punitive, but simply refers to the degree of orchestration of student behavior. For example, in a highly structured classroom, dismissal may be very organized, with students excused in small groups for a calm, orderly, and quiet exit. In a low-structure management plan, the entire class may be excused at once, resulting in a slightly more chaotic feel. The low-structure approach requires greater maturity on the part of the class to ensure safe and responsible exiting.

The level of structure in your management plan should be based on two factors—your unique personal needs and the collective needs of the students. In Task 1, you will be encouraged to think about these two factors. What are your own unique needs—for example, your tolerance for noise and movement? If a fair amount of noise or quite a bit of movement is not bothersome to you (but remember, you will deal with it all day, every day, for the entire year), you may be able to have less structure in your management plan than the teacher with very low tolerance for noise and movement. Next, what are the collective needs of your students? The class that is collectively less mature and has more behavior problems has a greater need for a high-structure management plan—one that is more tightly orchestrated and directed by the teacher—than a class that is collectively mature, motivated, cooperative, and respectful. Also, a large class usually requires more structure than a small class—the class with thirty students needs greater structure than the class with only fifteen students.

> " *The class that is collectively less mature and has more behavior problems has a greater need for a high-structure management plan.* "

At the end of this chapter is a Self-Assessment Checklist designed to help you determine which (or which parts) of the tasks you have done or are in the process of doing, and which you still need to do.

The five tasks in this chapter are:

Task 1: Determine the Level of Classroom Structure • Determine whether you need to develop a low-, medium-, or high-structure management plan by taking into account your personal needs and the collective needs of your students.

Task 2: Develop and Display Classroom Rules • Develop a plan for designing and then posting three to six specific classroom rules that will be used as the basis for implementing consequences for misbehavior.

Task 3: Correct Rule Violations During the First Week of School • In the first few days of school, be prepared to respond to rule violations with corrective techniques that clarify your rules and expectations.

Task 4: Establish Corrective Consequences for Rule Violations • Once students fully understand your classroom procedures and your classroom rules, calmly implement consequences when rules are violated.

Task 5: Know When (and When Not) to Use Disciplinary Referral • Be sure you know what behavior warrants sending students to the office (according to your principal or vice principal's guidelines), and what situations you should handle in your own classroom. Also, be sure you know how to write a disciplinary referral.

In this chapter, you will be setting up the "discipline" part of your Classroom Management and Discipline Plan. The importance of positive consequences (praise, building personal connections with students, providing extrinsic incentives) is briefly mentioned in this chapter, but positive consequences are such an important part of your management plan that two full chapters are devoted to the topic—Chapters 7 and 8. Those chapters on the positive aspects of your management plan are as important as the content on structure, rules, and consequences discussed in this chapter.

Task 1: Determine the Level of Classroom Structure

Determine whether you need to develop a low-, medium-, or high-structure management plan by taking into account your personal needs and the collective needs of your students.

The level of structure in your management plan will be based on your personal style and on the collective needs of the students. In the first part of this task, you will be encouraged to reflect on your own style and your needs in the classroom. If you have a high need for structure (minimal background noise and very orderly movement, for example) you will be encouraged to have a highly orchestrated management plan even if your students can responsibly handle a less structured setting. On the other hand, if you personally have quite a bit of tolerance for noise and movement, you can reflect more on the needs of your students. You will think about your students' needs in the second part of this task as you fill out a form about the school in which you will be teaching and the class or classes you will have on the first day of school.

Bear in mind that it is always better to err on the side of high structure. In general, research has shown that classrooms with more structure typically promote increases in appropriate academic and social behaviors (Simonsen et al., 2008). If you personally like and need a highly structured classroom environment, it is all right to plan for that even if the students do not need high structure. However, if you would like a low-structure classroom but the students clearly have a need for a high-structure classroom, you need to develop a relatively highly structured management plan. It is not acceptable to have a low-structure plan if the result is chaotic, off-task, or disrespectful behavior from students.

> *Bear in mind that it is always better to err on the side of high structure.*

 Consider your needs.

Reflect on your personal style. Are there issues that you need to address in order to be comfortable in the classroom? For example, what is your tolerance for noise? A teacher with a high tolerance for noise needs to teach students appropriate noise levels, but is unlikely to be rattled by a classroom activity in which students are excitedly engaged in cooperative groups. On the other hand, a teacher with a low tolerance for noise may find that a cooperative group activity—with the voices of 30 students getting progressively louder—has a sense of chaos and may feel that the class is bordering on out-of-control. The difference here is not the behavior of the students but the perception of the teacher. The teacher who knows he has a low tolerance for background noise needs a management plan that directly teaches students to keep noise to a minimum. He must monitor and provide feedback to students about the level of noise that is acceptable. This is especially true during activities such as cooperative groups and independent work times such as lab activities.

Reflect on the questions shown in Figure 3.1. There are no right answers to these questions. Assign yourself a score on a scale between 0 and 20 for each question. Plan to be honest with yourself about yourself.

This survey is not a scientific instrument, but rather a good way to reflect on the type of classroom setting you need in order to thrive as a positive and energetic force. If you scored 20 or less on this survey, you may be fine in any type of setting. As long as your students can responsibly handle low structure, you can establish a management plan that has a slightly chaotic feel—but with very engaged and respectful students. If you scored 60 or more on this instrument, you probably need more structure, even if your students can handle a less structured setting. If noise, movement, interruptions, and multitasking make you nervous, structure your classroom to keep them to a minimum so you can stay calm and positive.

Figure 3.1 *Classroom Management and Discipline Planning Questionnaire (Teacher's Needs)*

Read each question, then assign yourself a score from 0 to 20, where 0 represents the answer on the left of the scale and 20 the answer on the right.

1	What is your tolerance for background noise?	I love to have conversations in crowded, noisy restaurants.	Christmas music in department stores drives me crazy after about 30 minutes.
		0 1 2 3 4 5 6 7 8 9 10 11 12 13 14 15 16 17 18 19 20	
2	What is your tolerance for individual voices (volume, pitch, whiny, mumbling, etc.)?	No style seems to bother me—even when there are several at once.	Some voices are like fingernails on a chalkboard.
		0 1 2 3 4 5 6 7 8 9 10 11 12 13 14 15 16 17 18 19 20	
3	What is your tolerance for interruption?	I would be fine working as a receptionist—managing phones, people, and equipment.	When the phone rings twice during dinner, I want to scream.
		0 1 2 3 4 5 6 7 8 9 10 11 12 13 14 15 16 17 18 19 20	
4	What is your tolerance for background movement?	I thrive on the hustle and bustle of downtown in a large city during the holiday season.	I prefer to relax by the side of a lake.
		0 1 2 3 4 5 6 7 8 9 10 11 12 13 14 15 16 17 18 19 20	
5	What is your ability to multitask without becoming flustered?	I love to do three things at once.	I do not like to talk to anyone while I am collating papers.
		0 1 2 3 4 5 6 7 8 9 10 11 12 13 14 15 16 17 18 19 20	
	Total your score →		

 Consider your student's needs.

The second consideration in determining the structure level of your management plan is the risk factors of your students. Reproducible 3.1 on p. 112 shows a set of risk factors you will use to evaluate your students. An example is the number of students in your class—you probably need a more structured management plan for a class of thirty students than a class of fifteen. If you have significant numbers of immature or emotionally needy children, the risk factors are probably high and so you need a more tightly structured plan. If your class is composed of predominantly mature and independent students, the risk factors are likely to be low, and a more loosely structured plan may be perfectly adequate.

If your class has high risk factors and you do not orchestrate activities and transitions tightly enough, student behavior tends to be problematic (Barbetta et al., 2005; Huston-Stein, Friedrich-Cofer, & Susman, 1977; Mayer, 1995; Martella et al., 2003). For example, beginning instruction quickly is a good idea regardless of a class's risk factors. In a class with high risk factors, however, student behavior may

Reproducible 3.1   *Management and Discipline Planning Questionnaire*

>> no. 3.1

C H A M P S
sample

MANAGEMENT & DISCIPLINE PLANNING QUESTIONNAIRE (2 of 2)

INTERPRETING YOUR RESULTS: Use the following scale to interpret your risk factors and determine the most appropriate level of structure for your classroom management plan.

If your total is:	Your risk factors are:
0 to 30	**Low:** Your students can probably be successful with a classroom management plan that involves **Low**, **Medium**, or **High** Structure.
31 to 60	**Medium:** For your students to be successful, your classroom management plan should involve **Medium** or **High** Structure.
61 to 120	**High:** For your students to be successful, your classroom management plan should involve **High** Structure.

FOR USE BEFORE SCHOOL YEAR BEGINS

>> no. 3.1

C H A M P S
sample

MANAGEMENT & DISCIPLINE PLANNING QUESTIONNAIRE (1 of 2)

For each question, circle the number under the statement that best answers the question. If you are unsure about or do not know the answer to a question, circle the middle choice. When you are done, add all the numbers circled and enter the total on the line provided (you should have a number between 0 and 120).

Class is at the high end of the medium-structure range. Start school year with high-structure plan, then evaluate after the first month or so.

Questions 1–6 relate to the population of the entire school.

1 How would you describe the overall behavior of students in your school?	Generally quite irresponsible. I frequently have to nag and/or assign consequences. **10**	Most students behave responsibly, but about 10% put me in the position where I have to nag and/or assign consequences. **(5)**	Generally responsible. I rarely find it necessary to nag and/or assign consequences. **0**
2 What percentage of students in your school qualify for free or reduced lunch?*	60% or more **(10)**	10% to 60% **5**	Less than 10% **0**
3 What percentage of students in your school typically move in and/or out of the school during the course of the school year?	50% or more **(10)**	10% to 50% **5**	Less than 10% **0**
4 How would you describe the overall attitude of students toward school?	A large percentage hate school and ridicule the students who are motivated. **10**	It's a mix, but most students feel OK about school. **(5)**	The vast majority of students like school and are highly motivated. **0**
5 How would you describe the overall nature of the interactions between students and adults in your school?	There are frequent confrontations that include sarcasm and/or disrespect. **10**	There is a mix, but most interactions are respectful and positive. **(5)**	The vast majority of interactions are respectful and positive. **0**
6 How would you describe the level of interest and support provided by the parents of students in your school?	Many parents are openly antagonistic, and many show no interest in school. **10**	Most parents are at least somewhat supportive of school. **(5)**	The majority of parents are interested, involved, and supportive of what goes on in school. **0**

Questions 7–11 relate to students in your class this year.
Middle school teachers: Evaluate your most difficult class.

7 What grade level do you teach?	K or 1 **20**	6, 7, or 8 **10**	Other **(0)**
8 How many students do you have in your class?	30 or more **10**	23 to 30 **(5)**	22 or fewer **0**
9 What is the reputation of this group of students from previous years (e.g., if you teach fifth grade, what was the reputation of these students as fourth graders)?	This is the class from hell. **10**	It's a mix, but most of the students work hard and cooperate. **(5)**	This group is very hard working and cooperative. **0**
10 How many students in your class have been identified as Severely Emotionally Disturbed (SED)? Note: This label varies from state to state (e.g., ED, EBD, BD, etc.).	Two or more **10**	One **(5)**	Zero **0**
11 Not including students identified as SED, how many students in your class have a reputation for chronic discipline problems?	Three or more **10**	One or two **(5)**	Zero **0**

	Total 60

* While poverty level tells you nothing about an individual student, the percentage of students from poverty has an influence on the teacher's initial decision about level of structure. Notice that this is weighted the same as Item 8, the number of students in the class.

Print from CD

be especially problematic if you do not orchestrate the beginning of class well. If students in such a class have nothing to do for the first two minutes of class because you are taking attendance and doing housekeeping activities, they are likely to talk, be out of their seats, and exhibit other misbehaviors. Their behavior, in turn, may make it difficult for you to begin teaching once you finish with the attendance and housekeeping procedures. If you begin instruction immediately after the bell rings and then take attendance after students start working on a task, you establish instructional momentum and increase the probability that students will behave appropriately.

> *After the year begins, the behavior of the students will dictate the need for structure.*

As you read through the subsequent chapters in this book, you will notice references to how various tasks might be implemented differently depending on whether your class has high risk factors or low risk factors. If your students have high risk factors, you should plan to implement all of the tasks in all nine chapters of the book. If your students have low risk factors, you may implement only those tasks you think might facilitate student engagement with academic tasks and avoid any procedures that might cut into instructional time. If your students have medium risk factors, plan to implement most of the tasks in this book (except those that seem unnecessary because students will be engaged and motivated without them), but don't worry about implementing the tasks in a highly structured fashion. To summarize, the greater the number of risk factors, the greater the pressure on you, the teacher, to orchestrate carefully and to implement all of the tasks.

Make a preliminary determination about the necessary level of structure before you begin designing your Classroom Management and Discipline Plan. To do so, work through the questionnaire in Reproducible 3.1. If you do not know the answer to any question, check with your building administrator for the needed information. After the year begins, you will not need the questionnaire because the behavior of the students will dictate the need for structure—the greater the number and intensity of the misbehaviors that occur, the greater the need for a highly structured management plan.

WHAT LEVEL OF STRUCTURE DO YOU NEED?

The Management and Discipline Planning Questionnaire (Reproducible 3.1) is designed to be completed before the school year begins to help you determine the risk factors for your class and the level of structure that is most appropriate for your Classroom Management and Discipline Plan. It can also be used throughout the year to increase your awareness of those aspects of your plan that you should review and revise to increase or decrease the level of structure in your classroom. You can also judge the appropriateness of your plan's level of structure by the frequency and intensity of misbehavior. Very little misbehavior means your structure is about right. Frequent misbehavior is an indication that you need to increase the structure of your management plan.

Use the scale on p. 2 of Reproducible 3.1 to interpret students' risk factors and determine the most appropriate level of structure for your Classroom Management and Discipline Plan. Once you have determined your structure level, plan to re-examine your organizational routines from Chapter 2 and see if you need to increase the level of orchestration. Also, review Chapter 8 to determine whether the class might benefit from a group-based motivation plan such as 100 Squares or a Lottery System.

> *Plan to evaluate students' need for structure at various times throughout the year.*

START THE YEAR WITH HIGH STRUCTURE

As we've already suggested, plan to err on the side of being too highly structured. This rule applies especially to the beginning of the year. By starting the school year highly structured, you increase the likelihood that students will engage in high levels of academic engagement and appropriate behavior later in the year (Emmer et al., 1980; Evertson & Emmer, 1982). In addition, you can easily move to less structure if you find your class to be highly responsible. For example, in your end-of-class routine, it is more structured to excuse students in small groups—by rows or table groups—than to simply say, "Class, you are excused. See you tomorrow." During the first two weeks of school, you excuse your class by small groups and find that they are a highly respectful and responsible group. You may then say, "Class, for the last two weeks I have been excusing you in groups. You are such a responsible class that, starting today, I will excuse the entire class at once. I know that you will handle this responsibly, with no racing to the door. Everyone will remember to respect everyone else's physical safety and to use quiet voices." Now imagine that, on the first day of school, you excused the entire class at the same time and they were loud and unruly. It will now be harder to enforce a more highly structured dismissal because the students will expect (and may even look forward to) a loud, unruly end to the day.

MAKE ADJUSTMENTS AS THE YEAR PROGRESSES

Plan to evaluate students' need for structure at various times throughout the year. For example, sometime during the fourth or fifth week of school and again after winter and spring break, evaluate how well students are meeting your expectations. If a significant number of students are not meeting expectations, you may need to move to a higher level of structure and organization (Barbetta et al., 2005; Simonsen et al., 2008). Recognize that during the last month of school, student behavior predictably deteriorates somewhat. Rather than relaxing your structure, it is probably better to increase your structure at that time (Sprick, 2006).

CHAPTER 3 TASKS

| 1 • Determine Classroom Structure | 2 • Develop Classroom Rules | 3 • Correct Rule Violations the First Week |

Task 2: Develop and Display Classroom Rules

Develop a plan for designing and then posting three to six specific classroom rules that will be used as the basis for implementing consequences for misbehavior.

Posted classroom rules should communicate to students that you have specific expectations. Therefore, your rules should be as specific as possible so that as you teach the rules, you can provide clear examples of what it means to follow the rule and what it means to break the rule (see Figure 3.2). You should also inform students that unacceptable behaviors (rule violations) will result in corrective consequences (Malone & Tietjens, 2000; McLeod, Fischer, & Hoover, 2003).

The rules should serve as the basis for implementing consequences for the most frequent misbehaviors—so ideally, if students follow the rules, the most likely misbehaviors will not occur. It follows then that before you develop your classroom rules, you need to identify the misbehaviors that you think are most likely to occur. Think about your grade level and the typical developmental level of students in your class. Also consider your schedule, your routines, your procedures for managing work, and so on. Once you have developed your rules, it's important to teach students what the rules are and how they can demonstrate that they are following those rules (Brophy & Good, 1986; Mendler & Curwin, 2007).

Classroom Rules

1. Come to class every day that you are not seriously ill.

2. Keep hands, feet, and objects to yourself.

3. Follow directions the first time they are given.

4. Stay on task during all work times.

Figure 3.2 *Sample Classroom Rules*

DECIDE WHO WILL HAVE INPUT INTO THE RULES

The first thing to decide is whether you are going to develop the rules yourself or whether you will work them out with your students. This decision is really a matter of style and expediency; both teacher-designed and student-designed rules have high correlations with teacher effectiveness (Emmer et al., 2003; Evertson et al., 2003). An advantage of student-developed rules is that the process itself may give students a greater sense of ownership in the classroom (Gathercoal, 1997; Martella et al.,

2003; Paine et al., 1983; Salend & Sylvestre, 2005). There are disadvantages to student-developed rules, however. Students tend to create too many rules and rules that are overly restrictive (Rhode, Jenson, & Reavis, 1992). When students develop rules, there will be no rules in place for the first day of school. It will be difficult to keep track of multiple sets of rules if you teach more than one class, and students may not make all the rules you feel you need to have an orderly classroom. If you don't know whether to use teacher-designed or student-designed rules and you have not involved students in rule development before, it is best to design the rules yourself. However, if you like the idea of involving students in rule development and have been successful with the practice in the past, you certainly should continue doing so.

Be aware that if you allow students to have input in developing classroom rules, you will have to guide the group in developing a manageable number of positively stated rules. Some groups of students will tend to develop a laundry list of negatively stated rules (Rhode et al., 1992). Thus, you may want to start by having the class brainstorm possibilities, then state each in positive terms (if possible) and select a set of three to six that are the most important. See below for additional guidelines for developing effective rules.

A typical set of classroom rules might include:

1. Come to class every day that you are not seriously ill.

2. Keep hands, feet, and objects to yourself.

3. Follow directions the first time they are given.

4. Stay on task during all work times.

> *If you have too many rules, students will not be able to keep track of them.*

You should have no more than six rules. If you have too many rules, students will not be able to keep track of them and you may have difficulty enforcing them (Babkie, 2006; Barbetta et al., 2005; Simonsen et al., 2008). Additionally, a long list of rules sets a negative and adversarial tone when you present the rules to the students. You do not have to have a rule for every possible misbehavior that might occur—only those that are the most likely to occur, such as off-task behavior, minor disruptions, and not having materials. Some guidelines to keep in mind when developing your rules are:

• Rules should be stated positively.

• Rules should be specific and refer to observable behaviors.

• Plan to teach your rules using positive and negative examples.

• Rules must be applicable throughout the entire class period.

• Rules should be posted in a prominent, visible location.

Rules should be stated positively.

Positively stated rules communicate both high expectations and an assumption of compliance. They set a more positive tone. In addition, clearly stating what you want students to do ensures that students know the expected behavior and sets the stage for student success (Barbetta et al., 2005; Colvin et al., 1993; Darch & Kame'enui, 2004; Walker et al., 1996). You cannot assume that when you tell students what not to do, they know what they should be doing instead. One or two of your rules may be difficult to state positively, but make sure that the majority of the rules state what you want students to do. Instead of saying, "No food or drinks in the computer lab," you could say, "Leave food and drinks outside the lab."

 Rules should be specific and refer to observable behaviors.

Develop rules that describe specific behaviors, not attitudes, traits, or conclusions. If a student breaks a rule, it should be clear to everyone that a rule has been broken because the rules will be enforced with the application of consequences (Barbetta et al., 2005). "Arrive on time with all of your materials" is specific and observable. "Be responsible" is not. "Stay on task during all work times" is observable. "Always do your best" is not. Nonspecific rules like "Be responsible" can have different interpretations to different people—it will create strife when you enforce a behavior you found to be irresponsible that your class did not.

Your classroom rules should be different from your Guidelines for Success. The Guidelines for Success are general, unspecific goals. For example, a statement such as "Do your best" is a goal you want students to strive toward, not a rule. "Do your best" is too broad, subjective, and open to interpretation to be a rule that has consequences tied to it. While you may have a discussion with a student about your perception that she is not doing her best, you are not going to impose penalties on her for not doing so. Rules must be specific because infractions of those rules have consequences. The rules are specific behavioral expectations that you enforce with reasonable consequences. The Guidelines for Success are the traits that you try to instill in students and encourage them to exhibit (see Chapter 1).

Some teachers like to link their rules and guidelines. For example, a teacher might use "Be Responsible," "Be Respectful," and "Do your Best" as the Guidelines for Success in the classroom, then link specific rules to each guideline. For example, being responsible in class includes rules like "stay on task" and "complete your work."

Plan to teach your rules using positive and negative examples.

The best way to help students understand your rules is to demonstrate specific examples of following and not following the rules. Through the use of both positive and negative examples, you teach students to understand your interpretation of the rule and how you will make judgments about whether a particular behavior follows or breaks a rule (Gresham, 1998; Kame'enui & Simmons, 1990; Sugai & Lewis, 1996). Students may not know what being irresponsible looks like. This may require teaching some behaviors that you feel are unnecessary, but it is better to over-teach than to under-teach. You might sit at a desk and show your students what not paying attention looks like, to contrast it with what paying attention looks like. This can help make an abstract concept concrete and more easily understood. Plan to teach your rules each day for at least the first five to ten days of school. More information on teaching rules to students will be provided in Chapter 5.

> *Posting the rules serves as a visual reminder of your expectations and creates a sense of permanence and importance.*

 Rules must be applicable throughout the class period.

The rules you post must apply throughout the entire class period. For example, "Keep hands, feet, and objects to yourself" applies throughout the entire class period. "Raise your hand before speaking" may apply only to teacher-directed instruction—you would not expect students to do this when working in cooperative groups. Therefore, "Raise your hand before speaking" should not be posted as a rule, but may be taught as one of the CHAMPS expectations specific to teacher-directed instruction. (CHAMPS expectations will be discussed Chapter 4.) Some rules that may not apply to the entire class period, such as "Arrive on time with all your materials," can be kept if no portion of the class period invalidates them. Although "Arrive on time with all your materials" focuses only on the beginning of class, it affects the entire class period. If you feel a rule like this is important to have posted, you should include it on your list.

 Rules should be posted in a prominent, visible location.

Posting the rules serves as a visual reminder of your expectations and creates a sense of permanence and importance—more so than simply telling the rules to students (Mayer, 1995; Scheuermann & Hall, 2008; Simonsen et al., 2008). Rules should also be included in your syllabus (Brophy, 1986a), but posting the rules allows you to point to them whenever they are discussed. Posting the rules also allows you to be brief in some of your reminders about minor violations. For example, if students are getting restless and off task during a teacher-directed portion of a lesson, you can give a quick reminder as you point to your rules, such as, "Class, remember Rule 5. Please stay focused on the lesson."

take note

Teachers of very young children may want to provide pictures or graphic images to go along with text-based rules.

When you have to speak to an individual student about a rule violation, point or refer to the rules as you speak to him or her. The act of orienting the student's attention to the rules reduces the sense of negative personalization—the sense that you are attacking the student—and implies that you are simply enforcing the classroom rules. In addition, the act of indicating the rules decreases any intense eye contact between you and the student. This make-eye-contact, break-eye-contact pattern can also reduce the possibility that the student will argue with you about the rules.

Subsequent tasks will provide suggestions on what to do when one or more students break a rule. Task 3 provides information on how to correct misbehavior in the first several days of school, and Task 4 provides information on when and how to apply corrective consequences for rule violations.

Task 3: Correct Rule Violations During the First Week of School

In the first few days of school, be prepared to respond to rule violations with corrective techniques that clarify your rules and expectations.

take note

In addition to correcting rule violations, you will also be making a concerted effort to provide positive feedback when students are following the rules. This will be discussed in detail in Chapter 7.

During the first week or so of school, plan to correct rule violations in an instructional manner—that is, correct the misbehavior by providing instruction about the rule and how to follow it (Darch & Kame'enui, 2004; Emmer et al., 1980, 2003; Evertson et al., 2003). The most effective error corrections are direct, brief, and explicit (Abramowitz, O'Leary, & Futtersak, 1988; McAllister, Stachowiak, Baer, & Conderman, 1969). Remember that your room is unique—a behavior that is unacceptable in your room may have been acceptable in the student's classroom last year. Therefore, you should view misbehavior, at least initially, as an honest error, not as an intentional or willful attempt to push the limits in your classroom. Correct these errors with informational corrections rather than corrective consequences. With older students, you may use these early-stage strategies for only a couple of days, then move on to using corrective consequences as described in Task 4: Establish Corrective Consequences for Rule Violations.

You should also use these informational corrective techniques for a student who enters your class midyear and for any entirely new behavior or situation that is not covered by your classroom rules.

Preplanning how you will respond to misbehavior will make your corrections more effective. Because it is not possible to preplan for every potential misbehavior you may encounter during the first week of school, the information in this task is designed to help you develop a repertoire of simple correction strategies to use with early-stage misbehaviors. The basic rule for early-stage misbehavior is to try the easiest correction first. In general, the easiest correction strategies involve simply giving the student information about what he or she should be doing at that moment. If you try a simple correction strategy and it solves the problem (the problem does not occur or occurs only rarely in the future), the problem is gone—end of discussion. If the misbehavior continues across a period of days or weeks, well past the first week of school, it is no longer an early-stage problem, and you need to look at the situation more systematically and analytically (see Task 4).

Following is a menu of correction strategies that are appropriate for addressing early-stage misbehaviors. If you take the time to familiarize yourself with these strategies, you will be prepared to respond effectively when faced with a rule violation during the first week of school or an early-stage misbehavior.

PRECORRECTION

Precorrection essentially means that you prompt the desired behavior (following the rules) during the first week or so of school to minimize problem behaviors (Colvin et al., 1993; Darch & Kame'enui, 2004). In other words, if you think the students are likely to violate a particular rule in a particular context such as cooperative groups, correct the behavior before the activity begins. Prompt the students about the appropriate behavior that you expect to see and set a high expectation—tell students you know they will make a special effort to follow the rule.

PROXIMITY

In the classroom, proximity involves simply moving toward the students who are engaged in misbehavior. The proximity correction strategy is based on a principle of human behavior that is used very effectively by the highway patrol—most people, even those who tend to exceed the speed limit, are more likely to obey the speed limit when a police officer is nearby. Students' misbehavior is likely to cease as you approach them because your proximity at that moment prompts them to stop exhibiting the misbehavior and start exhibiting the desired behavior. The more you move throughout your room in unpredictable ways, the better you can correct misbehavior through proximity (DePry & Sugai, 2002; Schuldheisz & van der Mars, 2001; Shores et al., 1993).

> *The more you move throughout your room in unpredictable ways, the better you can correct misbehavior through proximity.*

For example, if you are presenting a lesson and a couple of students begin talking to each other instead of listening to you, start walking over to that part of the room while continuing to present the lesson. If the students quit talking while you are on the way, continue the lesson from where you are, and then move to a different place in the room or back to the front. After a few minutes, make eye contact with the students who were talking. You may even want to compliment them for listening and participating (although in middle school this is inadvisable if you think it would embarrass them in front of peers).

GENTLE VERBAL REPRIMAND

To use a gentle verbal reprimand (correction), simply go over to the student or students engaged in misbehavior and quietly remind or tell them what they should be doing at that moment. For example, if the two students described in the previous scenario did not stop talking when you moved in their direction, you might quietly say to them, "Johanna, Alexander, if you have something to say, you need to raise your hand and wait to be called on." Effective verbal reprimands have the following features (Abramowitz, O'Leary, & Futtersak, 1988; Acker & O'Leary, 1988; McAllister et al., 1969; O'Leary & Becker, 1968; Winett & Vachon, 1974):

- They are short—one or two words or very short sentences.

- They cause only a very brief interruption in the lesson.

- They are given when you are physically near misbehaving students—not from across the room.

- Their tone and content are respectful.

- They are clear and unequivocal.

- They state the expected behavior, rather than accusing the student(s) of the misbehavior.

- They are given in a way that creates the illusion of privacy. You don't want to try to make it truly secret or the other students will try to hear what you are saying to the misbehaving student, but you also do not want to make it seem that you are putting the student on public display.

DISCUSSION

Sometimes you may need to talk with a student about a misbehavior in a way that is more detailed and lengthy than a reprimand. For example, if a student makes a disrespectful comment as you are presenting a lesson, you may want to have a talk with the student about the importance of treating others respectfully. Provide a gentle reprimand immediately and let the student know that the behavior is serious enough that you want to discuss it later—after class.

Discussions that occur at a neutral time usually work best. In fact, there are several reasons why having a discussion immediately after a misbehavior tends to be ineffective:

- You leave the rest of the class waiting.

- You give the misbehaving student too much immediate attention.

- The student is likely to be defensive.

- You are likely to be somewhat frustrated or angry.

It is far more effective to wait until later, when the class is engaged in independent work, or even after class, and then privately discuss the situation with the student. During your meeting, be sure to discuss with the student better ways to handle similar situations in the future.

FAMILY CONTACT

Communication between a student's family and school may increase the effectiveness of behavioral supports provided at school and promote the maintenance of positive behavior over time (Gortmaker et al., 2004; Sheridan et al., 1996). Parents often have additional insight into their child's behavior and can support the child's success at school (Rones & Hoagwood, 2000). Therefore, a very important and potentially effective correction procedure during the first week of school is family contact.

Reproducible 3.2 outlines the content you should cover in an early-stage family contact. A fillable version is provided on the CD. The sample shows a template that has been completed by a fifth-grade teacher.

When making contact with the family regarding misbehavior, keep the following suggestions in mind:

- Provide an objective description of the behavior, not a judgment about the student.

- Suggest that it would be useful for the family to discuss the behavior with the student and communicate the expectation that the student behave more responsibly in the future.

- Avoid implying that the student should be punished at home or that the family should "make" the student behave.

- Create a sense that you and the family can work as partners in helping the student reduce misbehavior and succeed in your class.

See "Cultural Competence" (Introduction, pp. 6–9) for suggestions on working effectively with students and families whose backgrounds are different from yours.

Reproducible 3.2 *Early-Stage Problems—Family Contact*

CHAMPS

EARLY-STAGE PROBLEMS—FAMILY CONTACT

1. **Introduce yourself and provide an appropriate greeting:**
   Hello, Mrs. Thompson? This is Mr. McLemore, Rasheed's teacher. How are you today? I'll bet that new baby is keeping you very busy. How is she doing? May I take just a moment of your time?

2. **Inform the family that you are calling about a problem:**
   I am calling because I wanted to speak with you about a problem that has been going on at school.

3. **Describe the problem (avoid labeling or passing judgment on the child):**
   For the last two days, Rasheed has not been doing his work in class. He sits at his desk and stares out the window, talks with his neighbor, and plays with his pencil. When I remind him to get to work, he will work if I am standing right there, but as soon as I go to do something else, he quits working again. Today he didn't finish any of his assignments.

4. **Describe why the behavior is a problem (keep the focus on the student, not on yourself or the other students). Emphasize that you know the student can be successful:**
   I am concerned because Rasheed is a very able student. I don't want him to develop the bad habit of wasting class time. To succeed at school, he will need to learn to keep his attention on his work.

5. **If appropriate, ask whether the family has any insight into why the behavior may be occurring. If they share with you, adjust the remainder of this call based on what you learn:**
   One of the reasons I am calling is to find out if you know of anything that might be bothering Rasheed or that could be distracting him from his classwork.

6. **Make suggestions about how the family might help the child:**
   I am not calling so that you will punish Rasheed. I am just concerned about him and hope you will talk to him about the problem. I know that he is capable of being successful in my class, but he has to keep his attention focused and do his work. Please tell him I called and that I look forward to seeing him tomorrow. I will call you in a few days to let you know how he is doing. Feel free to call me as well. The best time to reach me is between 3:30 and 4:00 any afternoon but Tuesday.

Date of this contact: September 27

Notes on the contact:
   Mrs. Thompson couldn't tell me any particular reason that Rasheed has been so inattentive the last two days. She said she would talk to him, find out if anything is wrong, and encourage him to pay attention to his work.

HUMOR

Humor can be a powerful and effective way to respond to misbehavior—especially with older students. For example, consider a situation in which a student makes a smart-aleck comment on the second day of school as the teacher is presenting a lesson. If the teacher is quick-witted enough, she might be able to respond to the student's comment in a way that will make the student himself laugh, and a tense moment will be diffused. However, please note that you should not use sarcasm or ridicule. The sensitive use of humor brings people closer together. Sarcasm or ridicule makes a student feel hostile and angry that you made a joke at his expense.

> *The sensitive use of humor brings people closer together.*

If you do use humor in response to a misbehavior, you should plan on talking to the student later to make sure that he understands that his behavior was not acceptable and that he knows you expect him to behave more responsibly in the future. In addition, you can check to see that you did not embarrass the student with your humorous comment.

---

for example

In a situation similar to the one in the previous paragraph, you might say something like:

"Thomas, today in class you made a comment, and then I made a joke out of what you said. First, I want to make sure that I did not embarrass you. Good, I'm glad I didn't. I owe it to all students to treat them as respectfully as I expect them to treat me. If I ever do anything that feels disrespectful to you, please come and talk to me about it. Now, I need to remind you to raise your hand when you have something to say in class and make an effort to see that your comments are respectful. I appreciate humor in the classroom, and I suspect that you will be someone who will not only contribute to our lessons, but also get us to see the humor in different situations as well. Thanks for taking the time to talk to me. I'm looking forward to seeing you in class tomorrow."

PRAISE STUDENTS WHO ARE BEHAVING RESPONSIBLY

Teacher praise that is contingent on appropriate student behavior has been shown to increase desired behaviors (both academic and pro-social) and decrease disruptive, problematic behavior (Chalk & Bizo, 2004; Gunter & Jack, 1993; Lewis & Sugai, 1999; Scheuermann & Hall, 2008; Simonsen et al., 2008; Sugai & Tindal, 1993, Sutherland, Wehby, & Copeland, 2000).

When one student is misbehaving, it can sometimes be effective to use specific, descriptive praise addressed to one or more students who are behaving responsibly at that same moment. "Gayle, Rashonda, and Jose Luis are doing a great job of following my direction to come to the rug for story time." When you use specific praise this way, the praise can serve as a prompt for the student who is not doing what you want her to be doing. This technique is most likely to be successful in the primary grades because young students typically enjoy positive teacher attention. Be careful with older students, though, because praise can actually backfire at the middle school level if the praised students are embarrassed. How to provide positive feedback is covered in detail in Chapter 7.

RESTITUTION

The goal of restitution is for a misbehaving student to learn that when her behavior causes damage, she needs to repair that damage. If a student writes on a desk, he should have to wash that desk. If a student is rude to a guest speaker, she should be required to apologize in writing, on the phone, or in person to the guest speaker. If you use the restitution strategy, try to make it clear to the student that what you are asking her to do, such as apologize to the guest speaker, is not a punishment but a reparation—an attempt to repair any damage her rudeness may have caused in terms of the guest speaker's feelings or his opinion of students in the school.

EMOTIONAL REACTION

Exhibiting an emotional reaction (such as anger) is a strategy that should be used very sparingly—not more than twice a year with any group of students—and not at all in the first five or six weeks with a new class. It is appropriate to use with a group, but not with individuals. For example, say that most of the students in a class start acting silly while a guest speaker is in the room. Usually this class is respectful and a pleasure to teach. It might not be bad to let the class know that you are angry and disappointed in them. If the class has never seen you angry before, it may have a bit of a shock effect and help improve the class's behavior in the future.

The reason you should avoid using this particular strategy with an individual student is because you may be dealing with someone who is seeking power through his misbehavior. Angering an adult can be a powerful motivating force for this kind of student, and your negative response may be very reinforcing to the student (Alberto & Troutman, 2006; Dreikurs, Grunwald, & Pepper, 1998). The reason you shouldn't use the procedure at the beginning of the school year is that showing students anger or frustration too early in the year may encourage the class to act up more in the future—they may think it is fun or funny to see you get angry. Finally, if you overuse the procedure (use it more than twice a year), it will lose any power it may have had. An emotional reaction will shock students only if they rarely see it. If students are used to seeing you get angry repeatedly, they are more likely to think, "There he goes again, blowing his stack over nothing."

GIVE POSITIVE FEEDBACK WHEN BEHAVIOR IMPROVES

Whichever correction strategy you use to respond to a misbehavior during the first week of school, be sure that when the students who engaged in the misbehavior begin to behave responsibly, you give them positive feedback. Students need to see that you notice positive behavior more than misbehavior (Mayer, 1995; Shores et al., 1993; Thomas et al., 1968; Walker et al., 2004). This is important because, generally, the behaviors that receive more attention increase while those that receive less attention decrease. Therefore, when you see a student re-engage in appropriate behavior, be sure to provide specific praise and acknowledgment for that behavior to increase the likelihood the student will engage in the expected behavior in the future. Also, remember that if one or more of these strategies does not solve the problem quickly, you will need to develop and implement an intervention plan based on a more thoughtful analysis of the misbehavior (Babkie, 2006; Sugai et al., 2000; Trussell, 2008). See Task 4: Establish Corrective Consequences for Rule Violations. Also note that Chapter 9: Correcting provides suggestions for handling any misbehavior that is not solved by your system of rules and consequences.

Task 4: Establish Corrective Consequences for Rule Violations

Once students fully understand your classroom procedures and your classroom rules, calmly implement consequences when rules are violated.

When you are sure that students understand your rules, you should plan to move from informative early-stage corrective techniques to consequences that impose a penalty for breaking a rule. If you do not plan in advance what your response will be, there is a high probability that you may inadvertently reinforce misbehavior by being emotional or by giving too much attention to the misbehaving students (Alberto & Troutman, 2006; Lovitt, 1978).

If you developed the classroom rules with your students, this step should involve student input as well. If you developed your rules by yourself, you can decide whether or not to involve students in determining consequences. Either way, give a lot of thought to what the consequence for each rule violation should be. Identify what should happen when a student does not arrive on time with all materials. Identify an appropriate consequence for tardiness, speaking out of turn, and so on (Ma & Willms, 2004).

The following suggestions can help you choose and implement effective corrective consequences that help the student learn that engaging in misbehavior has a cost associated with it. A menu of potential corrective consequences for rules violations begins on p. 129.

Plan to implement the corrective consequence consistently.

For corrective consequences to reduce or eliminate purposeful or habitual misbehavior, they must be implemented consistently (Acker & O'Leary, 1988; Alberto & Troutman, 2006; Scheuermann & Hall, 2008). When you implement a corrective consequence only some of the time, the consequence, no matter how severe, is not likely to change the behavior. In fact, it may even make things worse than if there were no consequence at all (Barbetta et al., 2005). Any time a student is able to violate a rule and not receive the designated consequence, he is likely to feel a great sense of satisfaction. Getting away with misbehavior can be great fun, and the student may find he likes to see how frequently he can engage in the behavior and not get caught.

> "When you don't implement consequences consistently, it becomes difficult for students to know what is and what is not acceptable behavior.

Teachers tend to implement corrective consequences based on an accumulation of misbehavior. Teacher emotion sometimes controls classroom consequences, but consequences should be controlled by a series of rules. Let's say a student gets away with a misbehavior five times—but the sixth time is the last straw for the teacher, and she finally gives the student a consequence. To the student, the consequence for the sixth time seems to happen out of the blue, only as a result of the teacher's emotion. While this is understandable behavior on the part of the teacher and can happen to anyone, it will not create a disciplined environment in your class. To reduce misbehavior over time, you need to define specific behaviors that are not acceptable and then implement corrective consequences for them every time, regardless of how you feel about the behavior at the moment.

When you don't implement consequences consistently, it becomes difficult for students to know what is and what is not acceptable behavior. If a student sometimes receives corrective consequences for a behavior and other times engages in the behavior without consequences from you, the line between acceptable and unacceptable behavior becomes blurred.

Your goal is to develop clear expectations of what behaviors are unacceptable so that you can be consistent with your students. If you are concerned about disruptions, specify the precise behaviors you consider disruptive and connect the concept of disruption to one of the positively stated rules. Also be sure to provide positive examples of nondisruptive behavior and class participation so the class knows exactly what you expect.

Make sure the corrective consequence fits the severity and frequency of the misbehavior.

When deciding what corrective consequence to implement, choose one that matches the severity of the problem (Simonsen et al., 2008; Wolfgang & Glickman, 1986). Choose a consequence that fits even the mildest example of the rule violation. All too often, teachers pick a consequence that is so harsh they are unwilling to implement it when the occasion arises.

"LaVona, stop that because I do not want to have to give you a detention." This statement is an indication of inconsistency. In this case, you are letting the student get away with it, but in some cases you may give a correction. You want a consequence that is mild enough that you will be comfortable implementing it every time the student exhibits an irresponsible behavior. When determining the severity of a consequence, err on the side of making consequences too mild, because you may not follow through if the consequence is too harsh.

Whatever corrective consequence you choose, plan to implement the consequence in the same way for all behavior within that category and with any student who violates that rule. In other words, if you have decided to deduct a point, all disruptive acts should result in the loss of one point. Do not create a situation in which some disruptive acts cost one point and some cost three. You will find yourself having to explain why you feel the acts are of different severities and deserve different penalties. If you decide to use time owed as a consequence for a student who tends to be disrespectful, have each infraction equal the same amount of time owed (for example, fifteen seconds owed after class). Do not issue fifteen seconds in some instances and several minutes in others.

> " *When you err on the side of mild consequences, you are much more likely to follow through than when the consequences are too harsh.* "

Again, when you err on the side of mild consequences, you are much more likely to follow through than when the consequences are too harsh. Also keep in mind that a student may exhibit the misbehavior several times. If the consequence is fairly severe—a detention, for example—you probably cannot assign three detentions to the same student in one class period. On the other hand, if the student is disruptive three times, you can impose fifteen seconds for each incident.

 Plan to implement the consequence unemotionally.

Some students have learned that there is a high probability they can make adults frustrated, hurt, or angry by misbehaving. For some students, this is virtually an invitation to misbehave as often as they can. If you get angry when correcting a student, your anger may reinforce the student's misbehavior (Alberto & Troutman,

2006). When a student is seeking a sense of power, seeing an adult frustrated or exasperated can be highly satisfying. For this student, getting an adult angry on a regular basis can provide a huge sense of power and control. You must strive to implement corrective consequences unemotionally so your reactions do not give any students the idea that they can have power over you by misbehaving (Dreikurs et al., 1998).

 Plan to interact with the student briefly, and without arguing, at the time of the misbehavior.

When any student breaks a rule, your interaction with that student at that time should be brief. Simply state the rule and the consequence (McAllister et al., 1969). A common mistake is to explain and justify. The student may ask you for such information, but resist explaining yourself. Any explanations should already be self-evident from your instruction or can be analyzed in a discussion with the student later. Sometime during the first few days of school, let the students know that if they ever want to speak to you about something they think is unfair, they can make an appointment to see you before or after school. Once you have made this clear, simply remind any student who tries to argue that he can make an appointment to see you, and then resume teaching. It is imperative that you don't let your students draw you into explaining your actions, your consequences, or your reasoning. Doing so transfers the power to them and lets them know that they can disrupt class by misbehaving and by making you explain yourself.

Although keeping interactions brief may be a difficult habit to develop, you will find that it allows you to keep your focus where it belongs—on teaching and providing positive feedback to all students who are meeting your expectations. Remember that the frequency of your positive feedback must far outweigh your negative feedback (Mayer, 1995; Shores et al., 1993; Thomas et al., 1968; Walker et al., 2004). Think about the consequence you plan to use for a targeted misbehavior. If you cannot imagine implementing that consequence without lengthy explanations or negotiations at the time of the misbehavior, you should consider a different consequence.

POTENTIAL CORRECTIVE CONSEQUENCES FOR RULE VIOLATIONS

The following pages contain descriptions of effective corrective consequences that can be implemented in a classroom setting. Each description includes a brief explanation of the consequence and how to use it. Remember, when using corrective consequences, be sure to assign them consistently and calmly, and keep the interaction with the student as brief as possible.

TIME OWED

When a student misbehaves and you have to intervene, some of your time is wasted. Therefore, a reasonable corrective consequence is to have the student lose time from an activity she values—recess or a fun activity, for example. Time owed is an appropriate and effective corrective consequence for misbehaviors that occur frequently (disruptions, talking during lessons, name calling, disrespectful behavior) and for behaviors that tend to involve duration (a student is out of his seat for a period of time, or a student takes an excessive amount of time to comply with a direction). For a duration type of misbehavior, the time a student owes should be equal to the time spent misbehaving.

Never use a corrective consequence that involves humiliation or ridicule of the student. Also avoid using academic tasks (such as extra math homework or an essay) as corrective consequences.

To use this corrective consequence, you will have to decide when the time owed will be paid back. The time should be deducted from an activity that the student values. For example, for an elementary student who likes recess, time owed from recess is an easy and logical choice. If your schedule does not include recesses, or if the misbehaving student prefers not to go to recess, possible alternatives are passing periods between classes or free-time activities. It is important that the payment of the time owed does not interfere with the student's time with another teacher. Thus, if keeping middle school students after class for more than one minute means that they won't be able to get to their next class on time, you should plan to keep any student for no more than one minute. Similarly, an elementary student should not be assigned to repay time owed during PE class if this reduces the time the student spends with the PE teacher.

Another decision you need to make is how much time will be owed for each infraction. As a general rule, keep the amount of time short enough that you will not hesitate to implement the consequence each time the student misbehaves. Also keep in mind the amount of time available for the penalty. Thus, elementary teachers might have students owe 30 seconds per infraction, while middle school teachers (who can't keep students after class for more than one minute) may use 10 seconds owed for each infraction. Although 10 seconds might sound almost silly, it is actually a pretty long time for an adolescent who wants to be in the hall talking with friends. And it allows you to assign the consequence for up to six infractions. Middle school teachers may need to establish a policy such as "Each infraction will cost 10 seconds of time owed, and if there are more than four infractions, the student will be assigned to Lunchtime Detention."

When dealing with behaviors that last for a period of time, establish a minute-by-minute correspondence between the behavior and the consequence so that the number of minutes owed corresponds directly to the number of minutes the student engages in the misbehavior.

Finally, decide what the student will do when repaying the time owed. As a general rule, have the student do nothing. If it is the student's first time paying this consequence, you may wish to use the time to discuss the misbehavior and ways the student can behave more responsibly in the future. Do not do this regularly, however, as the one-on-one interaction time with you may become reinforcing to the student and actually serve to perpetuate the misbehavior.

TIMEOUT (IN-CLASS)

Many people think that the purpose of timeout is to send the student to an aversive setting. That is not the case. The actual purpose of timeout is to remove a misbehaving student from the opportunity to earn positive reinforcement (Alberto & Troutman, 2006). That is, the goal is to communicate to the student that if he engages in the misbehavior, he will not get to participate in the interesting, productive, and enjoyable activities going on in the classroom. The obvious implication here is that instruction and classroom activities need to be interesting, productive, and enjoyable. Following are descriptions of four different types of timeouts that are appropriate for different logistical situations and different ages of students.

Timeout from a favorite object (primary level). When developing an intervention plan to correct a primary student with chronic misbehavior, ask the student if he would like to bring a favorite object, such as a stuffed animal, to class. Tell him that the stuffed animal is there to watch him work and follow the rules. Initially the object is placed on the student's desk. If the student misbehaves, the object is removed and placed on the teacher's desk facing away from the student. When the student begins behaving appropriately, the object is returned to the student's desk. Rhode et al. (1992) describe this as a Bumpy Bunny Timeout.

If you are concerned that the student may play with the object, explain to the student that playing with the object means that the object goes to timeout on your desk. Another option is to place the object near the student initially, on a bookshelf near his desk, for example. If the student misbehaves, take the object to a different part of the room and place it facing away from the student. When the student begins to behave responsibly again, return the object to the shelf near the student so that it can "watch" the student behaving responsibly.

Timeout from small group instruction (elementary level). If a student misbehaves during small group instruction, have the student push back her chair so that she is not physically part of the group. You should conduct the next minute or two of instruction in an especially fun and reinforcing manner so the student feels that she is missing out on the privilege of participating in something that is enjoyable and beneficial.

Timeout at desk (elementary level). If a student misbehaves, ask the student to put his head down on his desk and close his eyes for a short period of time—two minutes, for example. This form of timeout is very mild but can be effective for relatively minor problems such as disruptions during instructional periods or independent seatwork.

Timeout in class isolation area (elementary and middle school levels). In this option, you establish a timeout area in a low-traffic part of your classroom. The area can be as simple as a chair off to the side of the room or a screened-off area arranged so that you can see the student but he cannot see the majority of his classmates.

With all the above options, you should keep the timeout brief. Don't allow the student to take work to the timeout area. For primary students, a two- or three- minute timeout is best; for intermediate and middle school students, the optimal time is five minutes. When using this consequence, instruct the student to go to timeout each time she misbehaves. The timeout period should begin when the student is in the area, seated and quiet.

If you think the student is unlikely to go to timeout and she is old enough to understand the concept of time owed, establish the rule that when instructed to go to timeout, the student has one minute to get there and get settled. If it takes more than one minute for the student to go to timeout, she will owe time equivalent to that extra time—time owed will be deducted from recess or a fun activity. If the student is unlikely to understand time owed (as in the case of a kindergarten student or a student with cognitive deficits), plan to conduct a few practice sessions in which you model and have the student role-play going to timeout. If you conduct sessions like this, be sure the student knows he has not done anything wrong—you are just pretending so that he can learn how to go to timeout if it is necessary.

TIMEOUT (IN ANOTHER CLASS)

For students who are likely to misbehave during an in-class timeout (such as the student who clowns around to get a laugh from other students), it may be necessary to assign the student to timeout in another class. To do this, you need to find a teacher with a room near yours who has a class with fairly mature students. It could be a younger grade or an older grade, but should probably not be your exact grade level.

> *The student is less likely to show off for students in a different class, especially a class at a different grade level.*

If the student misbehaves in your room, she should be sent to the timeout teacher's room. This teacher should have a prearranged location for the student—perhaps a chair in a low-traffic area of the class—and should preteach his class to ignore the student when she enters. The timeout teacher should not be required to stop teaching his class or do problem-solving with the misbehaving student. The idea behind this procedure is simply that the student is less likely to show off for students in a different class, especially a class at a different grade level.

Unlike the in-class timeout options above, the student probably should have work to do so she does not get so bored that she begins to entertain herself by showing off for the other students. Both you and the timeout teacher must work out in advance how long the timeout period will last and how the student will transition from one room to the other.

RESTITUTION

Restitution, which was presented as a correction strategy for early-stage problems in Task 3, can also be effective with chronic purposeful misbehaviors when they involve damage to property or to social relationships (Rusch & Close, 1976). If a student engages in behavior that causes damage, a logical consequence is that the student has to repair the damage. For example, if a student plugs a washroom sink with paper towels so that water runs all over the floor, requiring the student to mop the floor is more logical than having the custodian clean up the mess. (You probably cannot have the student use chemicals such as disinfectants, but he can certainly use a mop and bucket.)

When this strategy is used with ongoing misbehavior, the "amount" of the restitution should increase with successive instances of misbehavior (Azrin & Foxx, 1971). Thus, when a student writes on a desk, you might have her wash the desk. If she does it a second time, have her wash all the desks in the class.

POSITIVE PRACTICE

If a student breaks a rule about a behavior that can easily be practiced correctly, positive practice (or overcorrection) is an appropriate corrective consequence. The major components of positive practice are rehearsal and attention to learning the task (Foxx & Bechtel, 1982). An obvious example is when a student runs in the halls, you ask him to go back and walk. A student who runs in the halls repeatedly might be required to spend time during recess or after school practicing walking in the halls.

RESPONSE COST—LOSS OF POINTS

Point systems are useful tools for promoting motivation and can also provide another corrective consequence option. If you use any kind of a point system in your class, establish a rule that certain infractions result in point "fines." More detailed information on how to use point systems as a management tool is provided in Chapter 8.

An example of a simple way to use a point system as a corrective consequence is to have the student start each day with twenty points. Every time you have to speak to him about the problem behavior, he loses a point. At the end of the day, you write the number of points he has remaining on a special note that he takes home. Each remaining point equals ten minutes of television or video game time (or some other privilege the student enjoys) at home. The less the student misbehaves, the more points he has at the end of the day and the more television time he gets. Obviously, this system depends on family cooperation. Also, because your main interaction with the system is to give the student attention when he has misbehaved, you will need to make a concerted effort to pay attention to the student when he is not misbehaving to ensure that he always gets more attention for following the rules than for violating them.

RESPONSE COST LOTTERY

Response cost lottery is a variation on a response cost consequence that can be used in situations where three or four students in class have challenging behaviors. You give those students, or even every student in the class, a certain number of tickets (ten, for example) at the beginning of each day, or each week for middle school level. Each time a student misbehaves, that student loses a ticket. At the end of the day or week, the students write their names on all their remaining tickets and place them in a container (hat, bowl, box) for a drawing. The name of the student on the drawn ticket gets a treat or a small reward. The more tickets a student has, the greater his or her chances of winning.

DETENTION

Detention is usually a schoolwide system. Students who have misbehaved are assigned a set amount of time (40 minutes, for example) they must spend in a non-stimulating setting. Most schools that use detention have their detention periods during lunch. When used as a schoolwide procedure, any teacher can assign any student to detention. Often, detention is structured so that students are required to do academic tasks during the detention period. One problem with detention is that students may find it reinforcing when they happen to have friends assigned to the same detention period. As with any corrective consequence you try, keep a written record of the detentions you assign. If you repeatedly assign the same student to detention across a period of weeks, this particular corrective consequence is not working for that student, and you should modify your correction plan to include a more effective consequence.

BEHAVIOR IMPROVEMENT FORM

If students have mastered basic academic skills, one consequence is to have the misbehaving student complete a Behavior Improvement Form so the student can reflect on her actions and avoid future problems. Reproducible 3.3 (Version 1) shows a very basic example of such a form. Reproducible 3.3 (Version 2) shows an example of a more complex form that can be used with older, more sophisticated students. Note that on the more sophisticated version of the form, the student is asked to describe how he thinks you, the teacher, would describe the incident. Reproducible 3.3 (Version 3) is a form specifically for classes and schools that use the CHAMPS acronym to guide behavior.

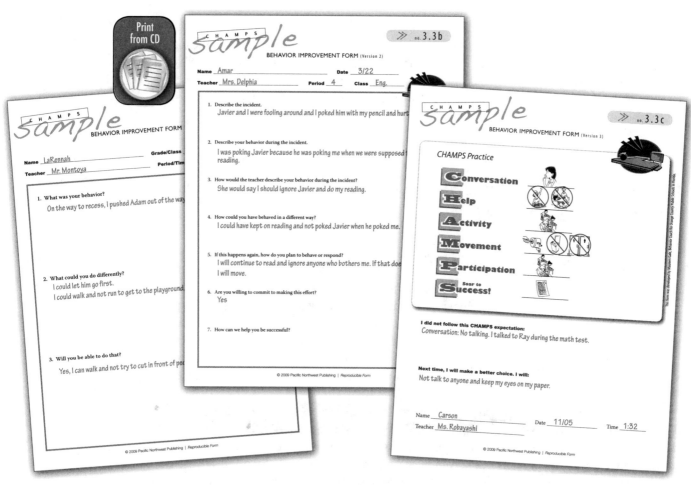

Reproducible 3.3 *Behavior Improvement Forms (left to right: Version 1, Version 2, and Version 3)*

DEMERITS

Demerits represent negative points that, when accumulated, result in the loss of a privilege or the imposition of a negative consequence. Demerits can be used to soften a predetermined consequence that might otherwise be overly harsh for a single example of a misbehavior. For example, if the consequence for talking in class is lunchtime detention (which seems rather harsh for a single instance), the teacher is likely to respond to that behavior inconsistently—sometimes ignoring the behavior, sometimes threatening ("If you keep talking, I am going to have to give you a detention"), and maybe finally giving the detention. The use of demerits allows the teacher to set up a more consistent policy. For example, a middle school teacher might tell students that each time he has to speak to a student about talking in class (or some other minor disruption), that student will get a demerit. If a student gets four demerits within one week, it equals a lunchtime detention. With this system, the teacher is more likely to intervene every time there is a disruptive behavior because the response for each single incident is reasonable, resulting in a more consistent policy.

Another way to use demerits, which may be especially useful for elementary teachers, is to establish a rule that all students who have no more than five demerits get to participate in a free-time activity at the end of the day, but those with six or more demerits do not get to participate. You could even up the ante by arranging to give a special treat to each student who has no more than one demerit.

PROGRESSIVE AND NONPROGRESSIVE CONSEQUENCES

DECIDE WHETHER YOUR CONSEQUENCES WILL BE IMPLEMENTED PROGRESSIVELY

When evaluating any disciplinary intervention, begin by asking yourself two questions. First, does the intervention treat children with dignity and respect? If the answer is no, reject the intervention immediately. In the case of progressive consequences, the answer is probably yes—it is entirely possible for a teacher to assign progressively more serious consequences and do it in a manner that is respectful.

Second, ask yourself, "Is the intervention working? Is it helping my efforts to motivate students to be responsible and actively engaged in instruction?" If the answer is yes, then you have a disciplinary plan. If it isn't broken, don't try to fix it! However, if you are using progressive consequences, the answer can easily be no. It is very difficult for a teacher to be consistent, day after day, in handing out progressive penalties, especially if that teacher is with the same children for the entire day. It's probably easier for a middle or high school teacher to implement a system of progressive consequences. For an elementary teacher, it can be almost impossible. Consider the following scenario.

Case Study

Johnny absentmindedly begins to tap his pencil on his desk. He is not doing this purposefully to cause trouble. It's a habit that he is virtually unaware of. However, his action is disruptive to the lesson. The teacher issues a warning and pulls Johnny's green card from the pocket. Johnny stops immediately. Twenty minutes later, he starts up again. The teacher, who genuinely likes Johnny, pulls his yellow card. Now he's lost his recess. But he does stop the misbehavior.

Case Study »

(continued)

Ten minutes go by—then Johnny starts up again. What does the teacher do now? Pull the orange card and call his parents? What if he taps his pencil another time? Would the teacher send him to the office?

At this point, the misbehavior is too trivial for the severity of the consequence, yet that is the progression. To be consistent, the teacher should pull the orange card—but she doesn't really want to send Johnny to the office for tapping his pencil four times. So instead, she looks him straight in the eye and says firmly, "Don't make me pull this card!"—a phrase that can only lead Johnny into thinking that he has the power to "make" his teacher do something she doesn't want to do. Or even worse, she says, "I really don't want to pull this card," leading Johnny to wonder what she does want to do and to continue the misbehavior just to find out.

The problem inherent in a progressive consequences system is that all misbehavior is addressed with the same increasingly severe penalties. However, misbehaviors are not equivalent. Tapping a pencil is not the same as pushing someone. If the government used such a system, we could easily end up in jail for parking tickets! Fortunately for most of us, the government doesn't consider parking tickets to be as serious as speeding tickets and DUIs, and so issues consequences on different levels for the different infractions.

What Are Progressive Consequences?

Many teachers use a classroom management plan in which each student has a set of colored cards contained in a pocket chart. The pocket chart is located in a prominent place in the classroom. When a student misbehaves, a card is pulled from his or her pocket. Each card is a different color, and the colors represent a progression of consequence. When the green card is pulled, it serves as a warning. When the yellow card is pulled, the student loses recess. When the orange card is pulled, there will be a parental contact. When the red card is pulled, the student is sent to the office.

MAKING PROGRESSIVE CONSEQUENCES WORK

To make a progressive consequences system work better, consider following the government's example—recognize that misbehavior can be minor or serious and respond appropriately.

Set up a parallel system for misbehaviors. On one side are the "speeding ticket" misbehaviors. Those are the ones that receive progressive consequences. On the other side are the "parking ticket" misbehaviors. These are treated with consequences that you hold on the same level for each infraction.

> Before you implement any system of consequences, it is important to clearly and explicitly teach your students what to expect.

For instance, tapping a pencil is a minor misbehavior. A teacher might simply choose to take time from the student. For instance, every time Johnny taps his pencil (or a similar minor disruption), he loses 15 seconds from time on the computer. If Johnny misbehaves 12 times, he is corrected 12 times but still has lost only three minutes of computer time. If you get 12 parking tickets, it does not bankrupt you, but it is annoying enough that you are more likely to put money in the meter next time you park. If the consequence is a small amount of time owed for each infraction, you are not escalating the punishment over some trivial offense—that means you can be calm and consistent in correcting the misbehavior every time it occurs.

In addition, if you plan to use a progressive system, consider implementing it so students can move back and forth (not just back) from green to red. For example, if the green card is pulled but then the student begins behaving appropriately, you can put the green card back into the pocket. A system like this can teach students how to recover from their mistakes and provides an additional way for you to acknowledge appropriate behaviors in addition to correcting rule violations.

Before you implement any system of consequences, it is important to clearly and explicitly teach your students what to expect—which misbehaviors merit progressive consequences (for example, pulling the next card), which merit nonprogressive consequences (for example, 15 seconds owed off recess), and what those consequences will be.

USING NONPROGRESSIVE CONSEQUENCES

Another option to consider implementing is a nonprogressive system that covers all misbehavior. In this system, as part of your pre-planning, you identify four categories. The first category is misbehavior that receives no consequences at all, just reminders. This might be the case in kindergarten, for instance. Your young pupils simply forget that they are not supposed to shout out an answer. No need to issue a consequence when a simple reminder will do—this was discussed in Task 3 about early-stage corrections.

The second category is misbehavior that receives minor consequences—like Johnny with his pencil. This category corresponds to parking tickets, and the consequences remain on the same level. Every time Johnny taps, he owes 15 seconds.

For most teachers, these two categories will take care of 90 to 95 percent of the misbehaviors that occur. The final two categories deal with the other 5 to 10 percent.

The third category is the more serious misbehavior that earns more serious consequences—examples include displays of disrespect and use of bad language. For these actions, you can devise a menu of consequences that all of your students know about and understand. When one of these misbehaviors occur, you select a consequence from the menu—for example, time owed, timeout, detention, parental contact, or parent conference. The fourth category is the misbehavior that violates your school's code of conduct or involves physical or emotional violence—for these you issue the ultimate consequence, such as office referral or parental notification. See the next task for more information on office referrals.

Once again, you must make sure that your students understand your system. Teach them exactly what consequences apply to which behaviors.

A nonprogressive consequences system allows some flexibility between classrooms. Not every teacher needs to use the same classifications, with one exception—consequences for category four misbehaviors (disciplinary referral to the office—discussed in Task 5) should be consistently implemented throughout the entire school.

Task 5: Know When (and When Not) to Use Disciplinary Referral

Be sure you know what behavior warrants sending students to the office according to your principal or vice principal's guidelines and what situations you should handle in your own classroom. Also be sure you know how to write a disciplinary referral.

Severe misbehavior may require the involvement of the school administrator in charge of discipline. This may be the principal, or in larger schools an assistant principal. Regardless of who this person is, as a teacher you must know his or her expectations regarding what types of behaviors you should handle on your own and what types warrant sending a student to the office—known as an ODR (office disciplinary referral).

If the administrator has clarified her expectations during an inservice and you feel you understand her position, you may disregard the suggestions below. However, if you are at all unclear, make an appointment with the administrator to discuss the following issues.

Find out precisely what types of behaviors you should refer the first time they occur. For example, should you refer physically dangerous acts? The answer will probably be yes, but what exactly is a physically dangerous act? You do not want to refer a student for a first-time infraction only to have the administrator ask, "What did you try before you resorted to ODR?"

Likewise, you should be clear on the broad categories of behaviors that can result in ODRs. Find out the administrator's recommendations about each of the following categories and examples. Should they be handled with an ODR the first time they occur, or should you handle them with your classroom-based consequences and parental contacts? There is no right answer to what warrants an ODR and what does not—the key is that both you and the administrator are in agreement.

---

for example

Physically dangerous acts
- One student hits another student.
- One student pushes a student in line, but no one is hurt.
- Two students are in a slugging fight.
- Two students are arguing, and one pushes the other.
- One student pulls a chair out from another student.
- A student is tipping over desks.
- A student is throwing books.

Insubordination
- A student makes a rude comment.
- A student directs an obscenity at the teacher.
- A student makes a disparaging remark about an assignment or about the teacher, but there is no obscenity.

Threats
- A student threatens to damage materials.
- A student threatens violence toward another student or an adult.
- A student threatens to bring a weapon.

Refusal to follow directions
- A student says, "I am not going to . . .," but actually complies.
- A student says, "I am not going to . . .," and does not comply.

Classroom disruption
- A student is tapping a pencil.
- A student is screaming.
- A student is telling jokes.
- A student is pounding on his desk.

Find out exactly what kind of referral form should be used in the event you do need to send a student to the office. Be sure to use objective language to describe the incident that led to the referral. The administrator needs an objective description in concrete terms that explains what you saw and heard that prompted you to refer the student. The referral form should not contain responses that are based on jargon, labels, or judgments, all of which are conclusions about, rather than observations of, events. Conclusions can be biased depending on whether you are having a good day, whether you like the student, or even whether you have unconscious prejudices about ethnicity, gender, age level, or other issues.

Figure 3.3 shows the differences between objective and nonobjective descriptions of the same event that resulted in an office referral.

OBJECTIVE DESCRIPTION	JARGON/LABEL/CONCLUSION (Nonobjective Description)
Kindra was pounding on her desk. When I asked her to stop, she loudly shouted, "You fat, ugly b___."	Kindra was obscene and obnoxious.
During a cooperative group activity, Allen and Alphonso were disagreeing. As I made my way to that part of the room, Allen got out of his seat, grabbed Alphonso by the shirt, and threw him to the floor. I was able to intervene at that point.	Allen attacked Alphonso.
James was out of his seat, pulling students' hair and knocking work off their desks. When I told him to go to his desk and sit down, he kept running around the room, refusing to go to his seat. I repeated the instruction three times.	James's ADHD is out of control, and I can't take it any more!

Figure 3.3   *Objective versus Nonobjective Descriptions*

Nonobjective responses tell very little about what actually took place. In some cases, as in James's example above, they tell more about the teacher than what the student actually did. The goal here is to ensure that you and the administrator are on exactly the same page. In some schools, teachers feel they are not supported by administrators regarding disciplinary issues, and the administrator feels that teachers should handle more behaviors on their own without involving administration. When teachers and administrators feel this way, the implication is that there is some miscommunication about the details of implementing ODR.

Reproducible 3.4 is a sample referral form taken from *Foundations: A Positive Approach to Schoolwide Discipline* (Sprick, Garrison, & Howard, 2002; available from Pacific Northwest Publishing).

Note that this referral form includes a place where the teacher can provide a referral for a moderate infraction—the student stays in the classroom but the referral form goes to the office. Ask your administrator if your school has provision for a referral in which the student is not removed from class, but administrative or counseling staff are given an incident report. The teacher can use this type of referral when a student's behavior may warrant a more serious, collaborative response, but is not so severe as to warrant removing the student for an ODR.

Conclusion

Your Classroom Management and Discipline Plan is the framework that supports a variety of rituals, routines, rules, consequences, and motivational techniques you can use to ensure that students are academically engaged and emotionally thriving. It may be highly or loosely structured to meet your needs and the needs of your class. It also outlines your classroom rules, corrective consequences for rule violations, and guidelines for using disciplinary referrals. Remember to adjust your initial plan to meet the changing needs of the class as the year progresses.

Use the Self-Assessment Checklist shown on the following pages to keep track of the tasks you've completed and those that require further work. A fillable version of the Self-Assessment Checklist is available on the CD.

Reproducible 3.4 *Behavior Incident Report Form*

C H A M P S

sample

no. **3.4**

BEHAVIOR INCIDENT REPORT FORM

Student _Jayden_   **Gender: F** ___ **M** _X_   **Grade Level** _3_

Date _12/4_   **Class Period** _2_   **Location** _Hall_

(If classroom, indicate subject of class)

Moderate (Paper goes to office)	**Severe** (Student goes to office)
❏ Chronic misbehavior (e.g., late to class, homework, classwork, disruption)	❏ Illegal (e.g., threats, weapons, drugs, assault)
☒ Not following direction (but eventually complies)	❏ Physically dangerous
❏ Disrespect to an adult (low grade)	❏ Not following direction (even when direction is written)
❏ Name-calling, put-downs, or mild behavior that might be gender or racially based	❏ Gross insubordination
❏ Other _____	❏ Gender, racial, or other gross teasing
_____	❏ Other _____
_____	_____
	_____

Description of problem/situation _Jayden was running in the hallway after first period. I asked him to stop and show me how he is supposed to behave in the halls between classes._

Action taken by referring adult:

❏ Use a one-liner (e.g., "That is not OK. Keep your hands to yourself.")

❏ Instructional/verbal correction (e.g., for minor disrespect)

❏ State that you will follow up (e.g., "We'll talk later.")

❏ Parental contact

☒ Have student demonstrate or practice the rule

❏ Off-limits or otherwise restrict activity

❏ Stay with supervisor

❏ Assigned school-based consequence (e.g., detention)

❏ Restitution

❏ Other _____

_____

Referring adult _Mr. Apo_

Action taken by administrator _____

_____

_____

_____

Print from CD

Construct Your Classroom Management and Discipline Plan

Chapter 3: Management Plan

Use the worksheet on the following pages to identify which (or which parts) of the tasks described in this chapter you have completed. For any item that has not been completed, note what needs to be done to complete it. Then translate your notes onto your planning calendar in the form of specific actions that you can take (e.g., September 5: post and teach classroom rules).

✔	TASK	NOTES & IMPLEMENTATION *Ideas*
	TASK 1: DETERMINE THE LEVEL OF CLASSROOM STRUCTURE	
☐	I have carefully considered all factors, especially the needs of my students, to determine whether my classroom management plan needs to involve high, medium, or low structure.	
☐	I have noted in my planning calendar times throughout the year to reevaluate the level of structure my classroom needs. Specifically: • During the fourth or fifth week of school, I will evaluate how well students are meeting my expectations. • Shortly after winter and spring vacations, I will evaluate how ...meeting my expectations.	

✔	TASK	
		NOTES & IMPLEMENTATION *Ideas*
	TASK 3: CORRECT RULE VIOLATIONS DURING THE FIRST WEEK OF SCHOOL	
☐	I have a repertoire of information-giving correction strategies to use with early-stage misbehaviors. These strategies include: • Proximity • Gentle verbal reprimands • Discussion • Family contact • Humor • Praise for students who are behaving responsibly • Restitution • Emotional reaction	
☐	When implementing any early-stage correction strategy, I am careful to always treat students with dignity and respect.	

TASK 4: ES...

☐	I am prepa... and will kee...	
☐	I have consi... the misbeha...	

✔	TASK	NOTES & IMPLEMENTATION *Ideas*
☐	I have a repertoire of corrective strategies such as: • Time owed • Timeout • Restitution • Positive practice • Response cost—loss of points • Response cost lottery • Detention • Demerits • Behavior improvement form	
☐	I understand the system of Progressive Consequences and, if I choose to use it, I know how to make it work.	
☐	I understand the concept of Nonprogressive Consequences.	
☐	I have developed a plan for applying consequences to rule violations.	
	TASK 5: KNOW WHEN (AND WHEN NOT) TO USE DISCIPLINARY REFERRAL	
☐	I know what behavior warrants sending students to the office according to my principal or assistant principal's guidelines, and what situations I should handle in my own classroom.	
☐	I know how to write an objective disciplinary referral.	

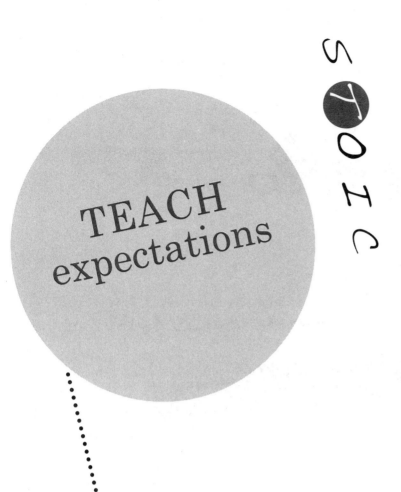

S T O I C

TEACH
expectations

Structure Your
Classroom for
Success

Teach
Expectations

Observe Student
Behavior

Interact Positively

Correct Fluently

Section *Two*

Once you have structured your classroom for success, the next step is to directly teach students how to behave successfully in your classroom (Barbetta et al., 2005; Evertson & Emmer, 1981, 1982; Moskowitz & Hayman, 1976; Simonsen et al., 2008). Teaching expected behavior involves far more than simply telling students what you expect on the first day of school. You will teach students to strive toward your vision and your Guidelines for Success. You will also teach them the details of how to function successfully in your classroom. The first chapter of this section, Chapter 4, introduces the CHAMPS acronym and guides you through clarifying and then teaching Conversation, Help, Activity, Movement, and Participation for all major instructional activities and transitions. Chapter 5 provides information on how to implement your management plan and how to teach expected behavior, practice those behaviors, and rehearse to mastery during the first month of school.

Section
Two

TEACH
expectations

Imagine...

You decide to participate in a team sport that you have never played before. At the first practice, the coach covers all the information about how she expects the team to function—from big-picture items like sportsmanship and teamwork to the types of plays and patterns the team will run on the field to the specifics of each position on the team. After presenting this massive amount of information, the coach informs the team that she will not be going over any of this information again—everyone is expected to know and operate from this information for the rest of the season. Even when the team does badly, the coach refuses to review or practice. She reasons, "I taught my expectations on the first day of practice. What is wrong with this team?"

Now imagine a coach who, at the first practice, covers some big-picture items like sportsmanship and teamwork, but at every practice refines and extends the details of those goals. At first, the coach mainly focuses on conditioning and one or two specific plays. As each new play is introduced in subsequent practices, the coach models the play, has the team practice, provides positive and corrective feedback, and then reruns the play until the team reaches mastery. Then the team practices previously taught plays to ensure that they are integrating new expectations with the basics. At every practice the coach provides more leadership, inspiration, and opportunities to practice to mastery all the skills that are required to make the best team possible.

Which team would you like to join?

Generate Clear Expectations

Expectations

When your expectations are clear, students never have to guess how you expect them to behave.

Introduction

School and teacher effectiveness literature has consistently shown that successful teachers are very clear with students about exactly how they expect students to behave (Brophy & Good, 1986; Colvin & Sugai, 1988; Emmer & Evertson, 1980, 1981, 1982; Emmer et al., 1980; Johnson, Stoner, & Green, 1996; McNamara, Evans, & Hill, 1986; Moskowitz & Hayman, 1976; Sharpe, Brown, & Crider, 1995; Simonsen et al., 2008). If a teacher doesn't know or doesn't communicate her behavioral expectations to students, the students have to guess at what constitutes responsible behavior. When students must guess how they are supposed to behave, the results are often behaviors such as these most common misbehaviors that occur in the typical classroom:

- Students talk too much, too loudly, or about the wrong things.

- Students demand attention by following the teacher around or by calling out to the teacher.

- Students do math when they should be working on science.

- Students socialize when they should be cleaning up.

- Students wander around the room or sharpen pencils when they are supposed to be listening to the teacher.

- Some students monopolize classroom discussions, and others don't participate at all.

- Some students disrupt lessons, and others sit and do nothing during work periods.

CHAPTER 4 TASKS

Task 1
Clarify CHAMPS Expectations for Instructional Activities

Task 2
Clarify CHAMPS Expectations for Transitions

Task 3
Prepare Lessons to Communicate Your Expectations

You can avoid most, if not all, of these problems by clearly defining for yourself and then communicating to your students how you expect them to behave during each and every classroom activity and transition (Brophy, 1987; Marshall, 2001; Mayer, 1995; Scheuermann & Hall, 2008). If you do not, your students won't know whether it is all right to sharpen their pencils during cooperative group times, to ask other students for help during a work period, or to ask you questions while you take attendance.

Be aware that your expectations for student behavior will be different for each major type of instructional activity and each major transition. For example, your expectations for conversation (whether students can talk or not) in cooperative group activities are probably very different from your expectations for conversation when you are giving a test.

> *Your expectations for student behavior will be different for each major type of instructional activity and each major transition.*

Why should I have to teach expectations? Students should just know how to behave in the classroom!

Teachers may mistakenly conclude that the teaching of expectations is not really necessary for three reasons. First, an experienced teacher may have such a clear vision of how her classroom should operate that she may not even realize that her room is a unique and idiosyncratic mix of rules, expectations, routines, policies, and procedures. She may, perhaps unconsciously, think that the way she does things is just the logical way all classrooms should operate, and she may not realize how complex her room actually is. "Why should I have to teach the obvious?" she reasons. What this teacher fails to realize is that her familiarity with this complex mix of procedures and routines is based on years of inventing and shaping it, teaching and living with it. However, this mix—this complex world of Room 19—is brand new to students. It's a world they have never experienced before, and they have no preconceived ideas about how to function in it.

The second reason is that teachers—both veteran and new teachers—think the older the students are, the more the students should know how to behave in the classroom. In other words, first graders may need instruction in behavior, but by the sixth grade, students should not need any. "These students have been in school for seven years. They should already know how to behave. Why should I have to teach them?" While at first glance this statement seems reasonable, the argument against this assumption is much the same as the one above—every classroom is unique. The more different classrooms the student has experienced, the broader the range of classroom structures the student has experienced. A sixth-grade student has probably experienced at least one teacher with a low tolerance for noise and movement and one with high tolerance, at least one teacher who lets students sharpen their pencils whenever they want and one who requires students to ask permission. In fact, the older a student gets, the less he or she knows about your unique mix of rules, expectations, routines, and procedures.

CHAPTER 4 TASKS

See "Cultural Competence" (Introduction, pp. 6–9) for suggestions on working effectively with students and families whose backgrounds are different from yours.

The third reason teachers may think that teaching expectations is unnecessary is that they feel many behavioral expectations should be taught at home. However, many teachers quickly learn that children do not necessarily learn the behaviors they need for the classroom at home. In her book *A Framework for Understanding Poverty*, Ruby Payne insists that educators must have a clear understanding of the hidden rules in any setting. These rules are the unspoken cues and habits of a group and do not necessarily coincide with expectations for students at schools. That is, in some communities there are street rules, and then there are school rules. Each set of rules allows students to be successful in that particular environment. Understanding these hidden rules will allow teachers to promote successful behaviors among students by directly teaching them all the behavioral expectations that are necessary for success in the classroom. This information is particularly crucial when working with students and families in poverty situations.

Remember that your classroom expectations are unique. Your classroom is no less complex than a basketball team. As coaches know, if you want a team to be successful, you have to teach and practice over and over to mastery. This chapter will help you recognize the complexity of your expectations and help you set up a plan to teach the individuals in your class to function successfully as a team.

No two teachers have exactly the same set of expectations for their classrooms. That is why the first two tasks in this chapter are designed to help you define your specific behavioral expectations for students during major classroom activities—teacher-directed instruction, independent seat work, class discussions, cooperative group work—and common transition times such as switching from one subject to another, getting textbooks open to a particular page, and trading papers for correction. The foundation for completing the tasks is the CHAMPS acronym, which reflects the major issues that affect student behavior. The issues incorporated in CHAMPS and the basic questions to be addressed for each issue are:

C	*Conversation*	Can students talk to each other?
H	*Help*	How do students get their questions answered? How do they get your attention?
A	*Activity*	What is the task or objective? What is the end product?
M	*Movement*	Can students move about?
P	*Participation*	What does the expected student behavior look and sound like? How do students show they are fully participating?
S	*Success*	If students follow the CHAMPS expectations, they will be successful.

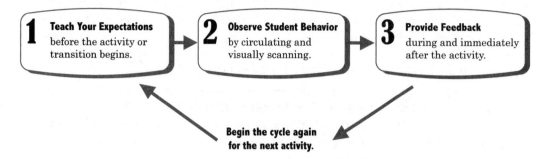

Figure 4.1   *Three-Step Process for Communicating Expectations*

Specifically defining your expectations is essential if you hope to have a positive and productive classroom. However, defining your expectations is not—in and of itself—sufficient to achieve that goal. You also must effectively communicate your expectations to your students (Brophy & Good, 1986; Simonsen et al., 2008; Sulzer-Azaroff & Mayer, 1991; Trussell, 2008). Thus, the third task in this chapter covers designing lessons to teach students the expectations you have defined. Teaching expectations is the first step in a three-step process for effectively communicating expectations to students:

1. Teach expectations.

2. Observe student behavior during activities and transitions.

3. Give students feedback about their implementation of the expectations.

This three-step process is summarized in Figure 4.1 above. Detailed information about how to apply this three-step communication process appears in Chapter 5: Launch. The three tasks described in this chapter are designed to ensure that you will be ready for the first day of school with clear expectations and lessons for teaching those expectations to students.

Even if you are starting this program partway into the school year, it is essential that you attend to the tasks in this chapter. Clarifying and teaching expectations is especially useful for any activities or transitions during which student behavior has been consistently problematic.

CHAPTER 4 TASKS

At the end of the chapter is a Self-Assessment Checklist designed to help you determine which (or which parts) of the tasks you have done or are in the process of doing, and which tasks you still need to do.

The three tasks presented and explained in this chapter are:

Task 1: Clarify CHAMPS Expectations for Instructional Activities • Define clear and consistent behavioral expectations for all regularly scheduled instructional activities, such as small group instruction and independent work periods.

Task 2: Clarify CHAMPS Expectations for Transitions • Define clear and consistent behavioral expectations for the common transitions (within and between activities) that occur during a typical school day.

Task 3: Prepare Lessons to Communicate Your Expectations • Develop a preliminary plan and prepare lessons for teaching your CHAMPS expectations to students.

Task 1: Clarify CHAMPS Expectations for Instructional Activities

Define clear and consistent behavioral expectations for all regularly scheduled instructional activities, such as small group instruction and independent work periods.

The first step in defining your behavioral expectations for classroom activities is to make a list of the major types of activities that your students will engage in on a daily (or regular) basis. Your list might include activities like:

- Opening/attendance routines
- Class meetings
- Teacher-directed instruction
- Tests/quizzes
- Small group instruction
- Centers/lab stations
- Independent work
- Peer tutoring sessions

- Sustained silent reading

- Cooperative groups

- Cushion activities (for students who have finished assigned work before the work period is over)

Try to identify all the specific activities and categories of activities for which you have different behavioral expectations. For example, you may have a single item on the list for teacher-directed instruction because your expectations for student

Special Considerations

The focus of this chapter is on student behavior in individual classrooms. However, two other related areas need to be addressed, preferably on a schoolwide basis: (1) Student behavior in the school's common areas and (2) schoolwide teaching of pro-social skills. Although these two important areas are not specifically covered in this book, following is some basic information along with suggested programs for addressing them.

Common Areas

Students need to know the behavioral expectations for common areas such as hallways, cafeteria, playground, bus waiting areas, buses, and assemblies. If your school has not clarified schoolwide expectations for common areas, ask your principal what you should teach your students about responsible behavior in these settings. For more information on defining and teaching behavioral expectations for common-area settings, you may want to preview one or more of these programs:

- *Stepping In: A Substitute's Guide to Behavior and Instruction* by R. S. Sprick and L. Howard (2009). Eugene, OR: Pacific Northwest Publishing.

- *Cafeteria Discipline: Positive Techniques for Lunchroom Supervision* (Video) by R. S. Sprick (1995). Eugene, OR: Pacific Northwest Publishing.

- *Foundations: Establishing Positive Discipline and Schoolwide Behavior Support* (CD-ROM; 2nd edition) by R. S. Sprick, M. Garrison, and L. Howard (2002). Eugene, OR: Pacific Northwest Publishing.

- *In the Driver's Seat: A Roadmap to Managing Student Behavior on the Bus* (CD-ROM and DVD program) by R.S. Sprick, L. Swartz, and A. Glang (2007). Eugene, OR: Pacific Northwest Publishing and Oregon Center for Applied Sciences.

- *On the Playground: A Guide to Playground Management* (CD-ROM) by R.S. Sprick, L. Swartz, and A. Glang (2005). Eugene, OR: Pacific Northwest Publishing and Oregon Center for Applied Sciences.

- *START on Time! Safe Transitions and Reduced Tardies* (CD-ROM) by R. S. Sprick (2003). Eugene, OR: Pacific Northwest Publishing.

behavior during teacher-directed instruction are the same regardless of subject matter. Or you may have one list item for teacher-directed instruction in math and reading (because behavioral expectations for both of them are the same), and another for teacher-directed instruction in science (because your expectations for science class are different from those for math and reading class). Middle school teachers likely have the same basic classroom activities for each subject area they teach (the same activities for all foreign language sections, for example), but different expectations for other classes they teach, such as a science class.

Social Skills and Bully Prevention

Sometimes when a teacher thinks a student has a behavior problem, it is in fact a skill problem. If many of the students in your school exhibit poor social skills, you may want to encourage your whole staff to review one or more of these programs for possible schoolwide implementation:

- *ASSIST Program: Affective/Social Skills: Instructional Strategies and Techniques* by P. Huggins (1990). Longmont, CO: Sopris West.

- *Antisocial Behavior In School: Strategies and Best Practices* by H.M. Walker, G. Colvin, and E. Ramsey (1995). Pacific Grove, CA: Brooks/Cole.

- *Got It! Seven Steps for Teaching Students to Get On Top of Their Problems* by L. Hartwig and G. Meredith (1994). Longmont, CO: Sopris West.

- *The One-Minute Skill Builder: Improving Student Social Skills* by S. L. Fister and K. A. Kemp (1995). Longmont, CO: Sopris West.

- *Second Step: Student Success Through Prevention* (2008). Seattle, WA: Committee For Children.

- *Second Step: A Violence Prevention Curriculum* (2002). Seattle, WA: Committee For Children.

- *Steps to Respect: A Bullying Prevention Program* (2005). Seattle, WA: Committee For Children.

- *The Tough Kid Bully Blockers Book: 15-Minute Lessons for Preventing and Reducing Bullying* by J. Bowen, P. Ashcraft, W. R. Jenson, and G. Rhode (2008). Eugene, OR: Pacific Northwest Publishing.

- *The Tough Kid Social Skills Book* by S. Sheridan (1995). Longmont, CO: Sopris West.

- *The Walker Social Skills Curriculum: The ACCEPTS Program* by H. M. Walker, S. McConnell, D. Holmes, B. Todis, J. Walker, and N. Golden (1988). Austin, TX: Pro-Ed.

- *The Walker Social Skills Curriculum: The ACCESS Program* by H. M. Walker, B. Todis, D. Holmes, and D. Horton (1988). Austin, TX: Pro-Ed.

Reproducible 4.1 is a CHAMPS Classroom Activities List form. Stop now. Print the form from the CD and use it to list each type of classroom activity that will occur in your classroom. Your list will probably look similar to the bulleted list above.

Once you identify your major classroom activities, use the CHAMPS acronym as your guide to the important issues. For each activity, define detailed behavioral expectations for students in terms of the following:

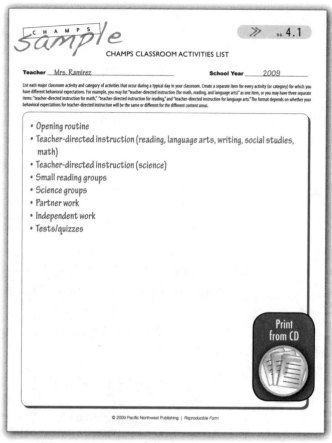

Reproducible 4.1 *CHAMPS Classroom Activities List*

C *Conversation* Under what circumstances, if any, can students talk to each other during the activity?

H *Help* How do students get their questions answered during the activity? How do they get your attention?

A *Activity* What is the activity? What is its intended objective or end product?

M *Movement* Under what circumstances, if any, can students move about during the activity? For example, can they sharpen a pencil?

P *Participation* What does appropriate student work behavior during the activity look and sound like? How do students demonstrate their full participation?

S *Success* Soar to Success!

Remember, details are important. The more specific you are in your own mind about what you expect from students, the more clearly you will communicate your expectations to your students. In addition, the more specific your expectations are, the more consistent you are likely to be in enforcing them (Barbetta et al., 2005).

Two examples of expectations you should carefully define within the Participation category are how to accept a compliment and how to accept a behavioral correction or reprimand. Think about how you will praise appropriate behavior and then identify a range of ways that students could respond responsibly, and one or two examples of responses you would prefer not to see or hear.

for example

Appropriate responses might include:
- Say nothing but nod your head or smile.
- Say "Thank you."
- Say nothing and just continue on with your work.

Unacceptable responses might include:
- Disagree.
- Misbehave immediately after being complimented.

In addition, plan to provide positive and negative examples of how to respond to a reprimand or correction. Often students do not realize that arguing about a minor misbehavior can get them into more trouble than just quietly accepting the reprimand. You could illustrate this with a baseball metaphor—good players don't argue with the umpire about every call.

VOICE LEVELS

One strategy that makes the whole CHAMPS process more efficient is to develop voice levels. This allows you to specify, as part of a clarifying conversation, the voice level students are expected to use during a particular activity.

Below is a sample way to define voice levels using a numbered scale:

0 = **No sound/No talking**
Examples: Taking a test, listening to a concert

1 = **Whisper** (no vocal cords)
Example: Asking another student a question during an independent work time in which conversation is allowed

2 = **Quiet conversational voice** (Only people near you can hear.)
Examples: Two or three students walking down the hall, four students working in a cooperative group

3 = **Presentational voice** (An entire class can hear you.)
Examples: A student giving a report, a teacher teaching a class

4 = **Outside voice** (You can be heard across a playing field.)
Example: Cheering at a football game

Of course, you should modify this list to suit your style. If you are going to use voice levels, plan to make and post a chart that students can easily see from anywhere in the room. Then as you transition into an activity, you can specify to students that the activity is an independent work period, for example, and your voice level expectation is 1. Students can look at your chart and know what is expected.

LEVEL OF STRUCTURE AND CHAMPS EXPECTATIONS FOR INSTRUCTIONAL ACTIVITIES

When defining your behavioral expectations, pay close attention to the level of structure your students need. The greater the level of structure your students require, the more precisely you need to design your expectations (Barbetta et al., 2005; Mayer, 1995; Scheuermann & Hall, 2008). The more precise your expectations, the lower the probability that students will make irresponsible behavioral choices. For example, with a class that needs high structure, you should have narrowly defined guidelines about when and how it is acceptable for students to sharpen their pencils (OK during independent work, but not OK during teacher-directed instruction, for example). However, for a class with low structure, it is probably perfectly reasonable to have a broad guideline that permits pencil sharpening at any time.

Also keep in mind that it's always easier to lessen highly structured procedures (gradually!) than to try to implement more structure in a low-structure class because students are making bad choices. So, if students need high structure, it is probably advisable not to allow student-to-student talking during work periods at the beginning of the year. However, two or three weeks into the year, after you've had a chance to see how the students behave, you might revise your expectations. "Class, starting today, if you have a question and I am not available, you can whisper to the person next to you, get the question answered, and then get right back to quiet, independent work."

Reproducible 4.2 on the CD is a template of a CHAMPS Classroom Activity Worksheet. Make multiple copies of this form. Then document your behavioral expectations by filling out one worksheet for each major type of activity you identified on the Classroom Activities List. The completed worksheets will provide the content for your lessons about your behavioral expectations. Specific information on teaching your expectations is covered in Task 3 of this chapter and in Chapter 5.

(continued on p. 165)

take note

On the following pages are several completed samples of the CHAMPS Classroom Activity Worksheet that show CHAMPS expectations for a variety of classroom activities (see Reproducible 4.2, Samples A–H). These completed samples are provided as models only— you should not necessarily use the expectations included on them.

Reproducible 4.2 *CHAMPS Classroom Activity Worksheet (Sample A)*

CHAMPS

sample

CHAMPS CLASSROOM ACTIVITY WORKSHEET

≫ no. 4.2

Activity *Independent seatwork while teacher is with small group*

Conversation

Can students engage in conversations with each other during this activity? *Yes*   Voice Level: *1*
If yes, about what? *Questions about work assignment*   With whom? *Other students at their tables*
How many students can be involved in a single conversation? *Two to four students*
How long can the conversation last? *About a minute*

Help

How do students get questions answered? How do students get your attention? *They should try to get answers without teacher help. If no one at the table can help, they can come and stand in the Question Box.*
If students have to wait for help, what should they do while they wait? *Stand quietly in the square*

Activity

What is the expected end product of this activity? (Note: This may vary from day to day.)
Students will complete seatwork packet. When done, they can go to book or science learning center.

Movement

Can students get out of their seats during the activity? *Yes*
If yes, acceptable reasons include: pencil sharpener *Yes*   restroom *Yes*
                                       drink *Yes*   hand in/pick up materials *Yes*
                                       other: *Go to the Question Box*
Do they need permission from you? *No*

Participation

What behaviors show that students are participating fully and responsibly? *Looking at paper. Writing or coloring. Talking with tablemate while looking at paper.*

What behaviors show that a student is not participating? *Talking without looking at paper. Staring out window. Wandering around room.*

Success!

© 2009 Pacific Northwest Publishing | *Reproducible Form*

Reproducible 4.2 *CHAMPS Classroom Activity Worksheet (Sample B)*

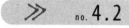

CHAMPS CLASSROOM ACTIVITY WORKSHEET

no. 4.2

Activity *Small group reading instruction*

 **Conversation**

Can students engage in conversations with each other during this activity? *No*   Voice Level: *0*
If yes, about what?   With whom?
How many students can be involved in a single conversation?
How long can the conversation last?

 Help

How do students get questions answered? How do students get your attention? *Raise their hands*

If students have to wait for help, what should they do while they wait? *Keep hand raised, wait quietly*

 **Activity**

What is the expected end product of this activity? (Note: This may vary from day to day.)
Working on tasks and activities presented by the teacher. Verbal and written responses to teacher-presented tasks.

Movement

Can students get out of their seats during the activity? *Yes*
If yes, acceptable reasons include: pencil sharpener *No*   restroom *Yes*
                                         drink *No*   hand in/pick up materials *No*
                                         other:
Do they need permission from you? *Yes, to leave group to use the restroom*

Participation

What behaviors show that students are participating fully and responsibly? *Looking at teacher. Raising hand with something to say. Answering questions. Looking at reader or presentation book. Writing on individual chalkboard.*

What behaviors show that a student is not participating? *Not answering questions. Talking to another student. Staring out window. Leaving circle without permission. Not following directions.*

 **Success!**

Reproducible 4.2 *CHAMPS Classroom Activity Worksheet (Sample C)*

CHAMPS

≫ no. 4.2

CHAMPS CLASSROOM ACTIVITY WORKSHEET

Activity <u>Teacher-directed instruction</u>

Conversation

Can students engage in conversations with each other during this activity? No   Voice Level: 0
If yes, about what?   With whom?
How many students can be involved in a single conversation?
How long can the conversation last?

Help

How do students get questions answered? How do students get your attention? Raise their hands

If students have to wait for help, what should they do while they wait? Keep hand raised, wait quietly

Activity

What is the expected end product of this activity? (Note: This may vary from day to day.)
Working on tasks and activities presented by the teacher. Verbal and written responses to teacher-presented tasks.

Movement

Can students get out of their seats during the activity? Yes
If yes, acceptable reasons include: pencil sharpener No   restroom Yes
                                           drink No   hand in/pick up materials Only if directed
                                           other: by teacher
Do they need permission from you? Must have permission for <u>any</u> leaving of seat

Participation

What behaviors show that students are participating fully and responsibly? Looking at teacher. Raising hand with something to say. Answering questions when called on or signaled to. Looking where teacher directs. Writing as directed by teacher.

What behaviors show that a student is not participating? Talking to another student. Getting out of seat without permission. Looking somewhere other than where directed. Not following teacher directions. Not raising hand. Not answering when signaled.

Success!

Reproducible 4.2 *CHAMPS Classroom Activity Worksheet (Sample D)*

CHAMPS CLASSROOM ACTIVITY WORKSHEET

Activity *Group activity*

**onversation**

Can students engage in conversations with each other during this activity? Yes   Voice Level: *Up to 2*
If yes, about what? *The assignment they're working on*   With whom? *Only students they are working with*
How many students can be involved in a single conversation? *Those assigned to activity with you*
How long can the conversation last? *Throughout activity*
until signal is given

elp

How do students get questions answered? How do students get your attention? *Put out Help sign*

If students have to wait for help, what should they do while they wait? *Students will continue working on the rest of the assignment.*

**ctivity**

What is the expected end product of this activity? (Note: This may vary from day to day.)
Students will complete as much of assignment as possible during time given. If finished before time is up, read quietly or finish prior assignments at your desk.

Movement

Can students get out of their seats during the activity? Yes
If yes, acceptable reasons include: pencil sharpener   Yes   restroom *No*
                            drink *No*   hand in/pick up materials *Yes, only relating*
                            other: *to the assignment*
Do they need permission from you? *Any movement must be assignment related.*

Participation

What behaviors show that students are participating fully and responsibly? *Looking at paper or others in group. Writing or doing what task requires. Talking only with those in group. Staying with group until finished.*

What behaviors show that a student is not participating? *Not working with group. Not writing or doing what task requires. Talking with others outside of group. Leaving group when not finished.*

**uccess!**

Reproducible 4.2 *CHAMPS Classroom Activity Worksheet (Sample E)*

Print from CD

 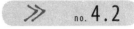

C H A M P S

sample

no. 4.2

CHAMPS CLASSROOM ACTIVITY WORKSHEET

Activity Oral written tests (such as spelling)

Conversation

Can students engage in conversations with each other during this activity? No   Voice Level: 0
If yes, about what?   With whom?
How many students can be involved in a single conversation?
How long can the conversation last?

Help

How do students get questions answered? How do students get your attention? Raise their hands

If students have to wait for help, what should they do while they wait? Keep hand raised, wait quietly

Activity

What is the expected end product of this activity? (Note: This may vary from day to day.)
Listening and writing answers to oral test. When finished with test, sit quietly.

Movement

Can students get out of their seats during the activity? No
If yes, acceptable reasons include: pencil sharpener   restroom
                                         drink   hand in/pick up materials
                                         other:
Do they need permission from you?

Participation

What behaviors show that students are participating fully and responsibly? Looking at paper. Writing or doing what task requires. Not talking. Not leaving seat for any reason.

What behaviors show that a student is not participating? Talking to another student. Getting out of seat. Not looking at paper. Not working on task.

Success!

Reproducible 4.2 *CHAMPS Classroom Activity Worksheet (Sample F)*

C H A M P S

sample

>> no. 4.2

CHAMPS CLASSROOM ACTIVITY WORKSHEET

Activity <u>Individual written tests</u>

Conversation

Can students engage in conversations with each other during this activity? No   Voice Level: *0*
If yes, about what?   With whom?
How many students can be involved in a single conversation?
How long can the conversation last?

Help

How do students get questions answered? How do students get your attention? *Put out Help sign if it's an individual test*
If students have to wait for help, what should they do while they wait? *Student will continue working on the rest of the test.*

Activity

What is the expected end product of this activity? (Note: This may vary from day to day.)
Working on written test. When finished with test, sit quietly and read.

Movement

Can students get out of their seats during the activity? No
If yes, acceptable reasons include: pencil sharpener   restroom
                                          drink   hand in/pick up materials
                                          other:
Do they need permission from you?

Participation

What behaviors show that students are participating fully and responsibly? *Looking at paper. Writing or doing what task requires. Not talking. Not leaving seat for any reason.*

What behaviors show that a student is not participating? *Talking to another student. Getting out of seat. Not looking at paper. Not working on task.*

Success!

Reproducible 4.2   *CHAMPS Classroom Activity Worksheet (Sample G)*

CHAMPS CLASSROOM ACTIVITY WORKSHEET

Activity _Peer tutoring_

 Conversation

Can students engage in conversations with each other during this activity? **Yes**   Voice Level: **1 only**
If yes, about what? **The assignment they're working on**   With whom? **Only student they're working with**
How many students can be involved in a single conversation? **Only two students**
How long can the conversation last?   **About 5 minutes**

Help

How do students get questions answered? How do students get your attention? **Put out Help sign and mark question for when the teacher gets to you**
If students have to wait for help, what should they do while they wait? **Students will continue working on the rest of the assignment.**

 **Activity**

What is the expected end product of this activity? (Note: This may vary from day to day.)
Helping another student do an assignment

Movement

Can students get out of their seats during the activity? **No**
If yes, acceptable reasons include: pencil sharpener   restroom
                                      drink   hand in/pick up materials
                                      other:
Do they need permission from you?

Participation

What behaviors show that students are participating fully and responsibly? **Looking at paper. Writing or doing what task requires. Talking only with peer. Not leaving seat until finished. Giving help so the other student understands how to do it.**

What behaviors show that a student is not participating? **Giving answers instead of help. Getting out of seat. Not looking at paper. Not working on task. Talking to others not involved in tutoring.**

 **Success!**

Reproducible 4.2   *CHAMPS Classroom Activity Worksheet (Sample H)*

Print from CD

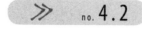 no. **4.2**

CHAMPS CLASSROOM ACTIVITY WORKSHEET

Activity _Individual seatwork_

onversation

Can students engage in conversations with each other during this activity? Yes   Voice Level: 1 only
If yes, about what? Questions about work assignment   With whom? Only students they sit next to
How many students can be involved in a single conversation? Only two students
How long can the conversation last? About a minute

Help

How do students get questions answered? How do students get your attention? Put out Help sign and mark question for when the teacher gets to you
If students have to wait for help, what should they do while they wait? Student will continue working on the rest of the assignment.

Activity

What is the expected end product of this activity? (Note: This may vary from day to day.)
Completing the assignment

ovement

Can students get out of their seats during the activity? Yes
If yes, acceptable reasons include: pencil sharpener Yes   restroom Yes, after signing out
                                        drink Yes, one at a time   hand in/pick up materials Yes
                                        other:
Do they need permission from you? Only for the restroom

Participation

What behaviors show that students are participating fully and responsibly? Looking at paper. Writing or doing what task requires. Talking only to help or get help.

What behaviors show that a student is not participating? Talking about anything besides the assignment. Talking during movement. Wandering around the room. Looking somewhere other than at work. Not doing task.

Success!

Task 2: CHAMPS Expectations for Transitions

Define clear and consistent behavioral expectations for the common transitions (within and between activities) that occur during a typical school day.

In addition to the classroom activities, there are transitions that take place during the school day. One type of transition is when students move from one task to another during an activity. For example, math lessons may start with teacher-directed instruction, then students get out their math books and work on several problems as a class, guided by the teacher. Or a transition may occur from one activity to another—for example, when moving from whole class instruction into cooperative groups. Transitions are often problematic in terms of student behavior (Barbetta et al., 2005; Huston-Stein et al., 1977; Martella et al., 2003). Poorly managed transitions are troublesome because of their potential for student misbehavior and because they end up consuming valuable instructional time (Arlin, 1979; Barbetta et al., 2005; Brophy & Good, 1986; Hofmeister & Lubke, 1990; Martella et al., 2003).

When you clearly define and communicate your expectations for transitions, you will have well-managed and efficient transitions.

As discussed in the previous task about classroom activities, the first step in defining behavioral expectations for transitions involves listing the major transitions that typically occur during your school day or class period. Use Reproducible 4.3, CHAMPS Transitions List, which can be printed from the CD.

Be sure to identify all the specific transitions and categories of transitions for which you will have different behavioral expectations. A list of transitions might include the following:

Reproducible 4.3 *CHAMPS Transitions List*

- Before the bell rings

- After the bell rings

- Getting out paper and pencils

- Getting a book out and opening to a particular page

- Moving to and from a small group location

- Students leaving and entering the classroom (for example, grade-level teachers grouping across classes for math instruction)

- Putting things away (clearing desks)

- Handing in work (for example, after an in-class assignment or quiz)

- Trading papers for corrections

- Cleaning up after project activities

- Leaving the classroom at the end of day (or class period)

- Moving as a class to a different and specific location (for example, library or playground)

- Handing things out (for example, an assignment sheet or art supplies)

- Handing things back (for example, graded papers)

- Opening and dismissal routines (expectations for these transitions were discussed in Chapter 2, Task 4)

Note: An elementary teacher who has the same group of students all day will probably have more variety in types of transitions throughout the day than does a middle school teacher.

Once you have your list of transitions, use the CHAMPS acronym as a guide for defining your behavioral expectations for the important issues. Make copies of the reproducible CHAMPS Transition Worksheet template (Reproducible 4.4—available as a fillable form on the CD) for all of the transitions on your list. Then, complete one worksheet for each type of transition.

Be thorough—remember, the more detailed you are, the more clearly you will be able to communicate your expectations to students and the more consistent you are likely to be in implementing your expectations. Information on teaching expectations to students is covered in Task 3 of this chapter and in Chapter 5.

take note

On the following pages are several completed samples of the CHAMPS Transition Worksheet that show CHAMPS expectations for a variety of transitions (see Reproducible 4.4, Samples A–I). These completed samples are provided as models only—you should not necessarily use the expectations included on them.

You will notice that some of the specific questions included with the CHAMPS acronym for transitions are slightly different from those included for classroom activities. In particular, the A for Activity needs to be much more detailed regarding the nature and type of transition than the A on the instructional worksheet. This is because of the unique nature of transitions.

C *Conversation* Can students talk to each other during the transition?

H *Help* How can students get your attention during the transition?

A *Activity* What is the objective of the transition, or what will be different after the transition—for example, a location change, different materials to work with? How long should the transition take?

M *Movement* Can students move about during the transition? If so, for what purposes?

P *Participation* What does the desired student behavior during the transition look and sound like?

S *Success* Soar to success!

LEVEL OF STRUCTURE AND CHAMPS EXPECTATIONS FOR TRANSITIONS

The more structure your class requires, the more specific and tightly orchestrated you need to make your expectations for transitions. For a low-structure class, you probably don't need to specify the routes for students to take to the small-group instruction area. On the other hand, for students who need high structure, you should include the expectation that students take the most direct route and that they keep their hands, feet, and objects to themselves so they do not disturb students who are working at their seats (Evertson et al., 2003; Jenson et al., 1994; Jones & Jones, 2007; Shores et al., 1993; Stichter, Lewis, Johnson, & Trussell, 2004).

Remember that structure is based on both students' needs and your needs. If you have a low tolerance for background noise and movement, you want transitions that are more quiet and orderly than those of a teacher who is less bothered by stimuli.

(continued on p. 177)

Reproducible 4.4   *CHAMPS Transition Worksheet (Sample A)*

Print from CD

>> no. **4.4**

C H A M P S
sample

CHAMPS TRANSITION WORKSHEET

Transition   *Getting a book out and opening to a particular page*
                (e.g., for guided practice on problems during a math lesson)

Conversation

Can students engage in conversations with each other during this transition? Yes   Voice Level: 1
If yes, clarify how (so that they keep their attention on completing the transition).

Only if you need to ask to look on with a neighbor because you do not have your book in the desk.
If you need to look on with a neighbor, you can whisper and quietly move a chair so you can both see.

Help

How do students get questions answered? How do students get your attention? *Raise hands*

Activity

Explain the transition. What will be different afterwards? (e.g., change in location, use of different materials, etc.).
Include time criteria (how long it should take).   *Teacher will tell and write on the board the book and the page number.*
Within ten seconds, all students will have the book open to the correct page and be waiting quietly. If a student
does not have the book, he or she can ask to look on with a neighbor.

Movement

If the transition itself does not involve getting out of seats, can students get out of their seat for any reason during
the transition?   *No*   If yes, what are acceptable reasons?

If the transition itself involves out-of-seat movement, can a student go elsewhere (e.g., to sharpen a pencil)?

Participation

What behaviors show that students are participating in the transition fully and responsibly? *As soon as the*
instruction is given, students will open the book quickly and quietly and wait for further instruction.

What behaviors show that a student is not participating appropriately in the transition?   *Asking, "What page?"*
Talking (other than asking quietly to share book). Wasting time (e.g., looking for book in messy desk or playing).

Success!

Reproducible 4.4   *CHAMPS Transition Worksheet (Sample B)*

C H A M P S

sample

>> no. **4.4**

CHAMPS TRANSITION WORKSHEET

Transition   *Moving to and from small reading groups*

 **C**onversation

Can students engage in conversations with each other during this transition? *No*   Voice Level: *0*
If yes, clarify how (so that they keep their attention on completing the transition).

 Help

How do students get questions answered? How do students get your attention? *Raise hands at their desks or from where they are seated for the small group*

 **A**ctivity

Explain the transition. What will be different afterwards? (e.g., change in location, use of different materials, etc.). Include time criteria (how long it should take). *Teacher will announce which group should come to the reading area. Students in that group should gather their reading materials, push in their chairs, and come quickly and quietly to the reading area. All students should be in the reading area within 30 seconds of the announcement.*

Movement

If the transition itself does not involve getting out of seats, can students get out of their seat for any reason during the transition? *Yes*   If yes, what are acceptable reasons? *To come to or leave the reading area*

If the transition itself involves out-of-seat movement, can a student go elsewhere (e.g., to sharpen a pencil)? *No*

Participation

What behaviors show that students are participating in the transition fully and responsibly? *As soon as the direction is given, students will go directly to the correct location (to reading area or back to seats) quickly and quietly.*

What behaviors show that a student is not participating appropriately in the transition? *Not moving immediately (e.g., continuing to work at desk). Talking or poking someone or knocking things off desks as they pass by. Running or making noise on the way.*

 **S**uccess!

Reproducible 4.4   *CHAMPS Transition Worksheet (Sample C)*

no. **4.4**

CHAMPS TRANSITION WORKSHEET

Transition   *Getting out supplies (paper/pencil, etc.)*

Can students engage in conversations with each other during this transition? No   Voice Level: 0
If yes, clarify how (so that they keep their attention on completing the transition).

How do students get questions answered? How do students get your attention? *Raise their hands*

Explain the transition. What will be different afterwards? (e.g., change in location, use of different materials, etc.).
Include time criteria (how long it should take). *Teacher will tell and write on the board what supplies are needed.*
Within 10 seconds, all students will have the supplies out and be waiting quietly.

Movement

If the transition itself does not involve getting out of seats, can students get out of their seat for any reason during
the transition? No   If yes, what are acceptable reasons?

If the transition itself involves out-of-seat movement, can a student go elsewhere (e.g., to sharpen a pencil)?

Participation

What behaviors show that students are participating in the transition fully and responsibly? *As soon as the*
instruction is given, students will get out supplies quickly and quietly and wait for further instruction to be given.
They will be prepared for this by making sure they have supplies in the morning.

What behaviors show that a student is not participating appropriately in the transition? *Asking, "What do we need?"*
Talking. Wasting time (looking for supplies in messy desk or playing).

Reproducible 4.4 *CHAMPS Transition Worksheet (Sample D)*

 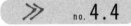

CHAMPS TRANSITION WORKSHEET

Transition <u>Movement of small group</u>

Can students engage in conversations with each other during this transition? Yes   Voice Level: 2 only
If yes, clarify how (so that they keep their attention on completing the transition).
Conversation is only for the purpose of saying "excuse me," "thank you," and "please."

Help

How do students get questions answered? How do students get your attention? Raise their hands

Activity

Explain the transition. What will be different afterwards? (e.g., change in location, use of different materials, etc.).
Include time criteria (how long it should take). Teacher will announce that it's group time (spelling, reading, etc.).
Those leaving will get their supplies out, push in their chairs, and go quickly and quietly to the small group area they
are assigned to. All students should be in their area within 30 seconds of the announcement.

If the transition itself does not involve getting out of seats, can students get out of their seat for any reason during
the transition? Yes   If yes, what are acceptable reasons? When told to go to groups

If the transition itself involves out-of-seat movement, can a student go elsewhere (e.g., to sharpen a pencil)?
No, only to go to group

Participation

What behaviors show that students are participating in the transition fully and responsibly? As soon as the
instruction is given, students will go quickly and quietly, then wait for further instruction to be given. They will walk
in single file. Talking is allowed only for reasons listed above.

What behaviors show that a student is not participating appropriately in the transition? Talking without a reason
listed above. Not going when told to. Not going straight to group by most direct route or route given. Being next to
someone instead of in front or behind when going.

Reproducible 4.4   *CHAMPS Transition Worksheet (Sample E)*

CHAMPS TRANSITION WORKSHEET

Transition   Handing out papers/supplies

Can students engage in conversations with each other during this transition?   **Yes**   Voice Level: *2 only*
If yes, clarify how (so that they keep their attention on completing the transition).
Conversation is only for the purpose of saying "excuse me," "thank you," and "please."

How do students get questions answered? How do students get your attention?   *Raise their hands*

Activity

Explain the transition. What will be different afterwards? (e.g., change in location, use of different materials, etc.).
Include time criteria (how long it should take).   *Teacher will hand papers to the person at the end of the row,*
and that person will pass them to the next person, and so on. Passing out papers should take no longer than 30
seconds.

Movement

If the transition itself does not involve getting out of seats, can students get out of their seat for any reason during
the transition? *No*   If yes, what are acceptable reasons?

If the transition itself involves out-of-seat movement, can a student go elsewhere (e.g., to sharpen a pencil)?

Participation

What behaviors show that students are participating in the transition fully and responsibly? *As soon as they are*
handed the papers, students will take one and pass the rest to the person next to them, making sure the papers
don't fall on the floor. Talking only for reasons listed above. Paying attention so everyone gets the papers quickly.

What behaviors show that a student is not participating appropriately in the transition? *Talking without reasons*
given above. Throwing papers to the next person. Getting up and passing papers to each person in your row. Not
paying attention, so others don't get the papers.

Reproducible 4.4   *CHAMPS Transition Worksheet (Sample F)*

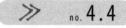

CHAMPS TRANSITION WORKSHEET

Transition Handing in papers (tests, etc.)

Can students engage in conversations with each other during this transition? Yes   Voice Level: 1 only
If yes, clarify how (so that they keep their attention on completing the transition).
Conversation is only for the purpose of saying "excuse me," "thank you," and "please."

How do students get questions answered? How do students get your attention?
Raise their hands

Activity

Explain the transition. What will be different afterwards? (e.g., change in location, use of different materials, etc.).
Include time criteria (how long it should take). *Students will pass their paper to the next person and so on in the
direction the teacher indicates. Last person at the back row will come forward, collecting papers from the other
rows, and give papers to teacher. Collecting papers should take no longer than 30 seconds.*

Movement

If the transition itself does not involve getting out of seats, can students get out of their seat for any reason during
the transition? Yes   If yes, what are acceptable reasons? *Only the last person in the back row to bring papers
forward*
If the transition itself involves out-of-seat movement, can a student go elsewhere (e.g., to sharpen a pencil)? No

Participation

What behaviors show that students are participating in the transition fully and responsibly? *Students will collect
and pass papers as directed to the people next to them, making sure the papers don't fall on the floor. Talking only
as above. Paying attention so everyone gets the papers in quickly.*

What behaviors show that a student is not participating appropriately in the transition? *Talking without a reason
given above. Throwing papers to the next person. Getting up and collecting papers from each person in your row. Not
paying attention, so others don't get their papers turned in.*

Reproducible 4.4 *CHAMPS Transition Worksheet (Sample G)*

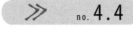no. **4.4**

CHAMPS TRANSITION WORKSHEET

Transition *Before bell*

onversation

Can students engage in conversations with each other during this transition?   Yes   Voice Level: 1 only
If yes, clarify how (so that they keep their attention on completing the transition).
Conversation is only for the purpose of saying "excuse me," "thank you," and "please."

Help

How do students get questions answered? How do students get your attention? *Put out Help sign and continue to work. I'll be able to help when I finish greeting your classmates. I will eventually assign a few helpers for this time.*

Activity

Explain the transition. What will be different afterwards? (e.g., change in location, use of different materials, etc.). Include time criteria (how long it should take). *Students come into the classroom quickly and quietly. They take care of housekeeping details and get the morning handout or check the overhead for the assignment. They get to work in their seats by the time the bell rings.*

Movement

If the transition itself does not involve getting out of seats, can students get out of their seat for any reason during the transition? Yes   If yes, what are acceptable reasons? *Sharpen pencils. Get silent reading book. Get paper. Turn in assignments. Check job chart. Put away backpack/coat.*
If the transition itself involves out-of-seat movement, can a student go elsewhere (e.g., to sharpen a pencil)?
Only with permission

Participation

What behaviors show that students are participating in the transition fully and responsibly? *Enter the classroom quietly. Empty and put away backpacks and make sure you have two sharpened pencils, silent reading book, and paper. Turn in homework. On Mondays, check the job chart for your assigned job. Put chairs down for your area. Get the morning handout or check the overhead for the assignment and get to work*
What behaviors show that a student is not participating appropriately in the transition?
Come in noisily. Leave supplies and homework in backpack. Don't get ready for day. Don't check job chart. Don't do morning work.

uccess!

Reproducible 4.4 *CHAMPS Transition Worksheet (Sample H)*

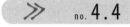
no. 4.4

CHAMPS TRANSITION WORKSHEET

Transition _Class travel_

onversation

Can students engage in conversations with each other during this transition? Yes   Voice Level: 1 only
If yes, clarify how (so that they keep their attention on completing the transition).
Conversation is only for the purpose of saying "excuse me," "thank you," and "please."

elp

How do students get questions answered? How do students get your attention? *Raise their hands*

ctivity

Explain the transition. What will be different afterwards? (e.g., change in location, use of different materials, etc.).
Include time criteria (how long it should take). *Teacher will announce where class is going and then have line leader and door holder go to the door. Rows will quietly line up when called on. Students will push in their chairs as they line up to go. All students will be lined up within 30 seconds.*

Movement

If the transition itself does not involve getting out of seats, can students get out of their seat for any reason during
the transition? Yes   If yes, what are acceptable reasons? *When called on to line up*

If the transition itself involves out-of-seat movement, can a student go elsewhere (e.g., to sharpen a pencil)?
No, only to line up

Participation

What behaviors show that students are participating in the transition fully and responsibly? *As soon as the instruction is given, students will line up quickly and quietly and wait for further instruction to be given. They will be face the back of the student in front of them. They will be in single file. Talking only for reasons listed above.*

What behaviors show that a student is not participating appropriately in the transition? *Talking without a reason listed above. Not lining up when told to. Not going straight to line by most direct route or route given. Being next to someone instead of in front or behind.*

uccess!

Reproducible 4.4   *CHAMPS Transition Worksheet (Sample I)*

Print
from CD

C H A M P S
sample

>> no. **4.4**

CHAMPS TRANSITION WORKSHEET

Transition   *Clean up at end of day*

Conversation

Can students engage in conversations with each other during this transition?   **Yes**   Voice Level: **2 only**
If yes, clarify how (so that they keep their attention on completing the transition).
Conversation is only for the purpose of saying "excuse me," "thank you," and "please."

Help

How do students get questions answered? How do students get your attention? **Raise their hands**

Activity

Explain the transition. What will be different afterwards? (e.g., change in location, use of different materials, etc.).
Include time criteria (how long it should take). *Students get out homework folders and place what they need to take
home on their desk. When called on by the teacher, students go as rows first to the coat rack, then to their mailbox
to collect their things. They put everything going home into their backpacks. They stack their chairs on their desks
and stand quietly until told by row to line up. Complete within 10 minutes, then teacher makes announcements.*

Movement

If the transition itself does not involve getting out of seats, can students get out of their seat for any reason during
the transition? **Yes**   If yes, what are acceptable reasons? *When directed by the teacher to do so*

If the transition itself involves out-of-seat movement, can a student go elsewhere (e.g., to sharpen a pencil)? **Yes**

Participation

What behaviors show that students are participating in the transition fully and responsibly? *Students get what they
need from their desks, follow teacher directions, put items to go home in their backpack, stack chairs in a quiet and
orderly manner, and wait quietly until told to line up.*

What behaviors show that a student is not participating appropriately in the transition? *Talking without a reason
given above. Putting papers from mailbox into desk. Not getting homework ready. Talking above level 2. Not being
careful when stacking chairs.*

Success!

Task 3: Prepare Lessons to Communicate Your Expectations

Develop a preliminary plan and prepare lessons for teaching your CHAMPS expectations to students.

In Tasks 1 and 2 you learned how important it is to define exactly how you expect students to behave during various classroom activities and transitions. But identifying expectations alone is not enough. If students are going to be able to meet your expectations, you need to communicate those expectations to students clearly and thoroughly (Brophy & Good, 1986; Simonsen et al., 2008; Sulzer-Azaroff & Mayer, 1991; Trussell, 2008). Effective communication of your expectations can be accomplished through the three-step process introduced earlier in this chapter.

As shown in Figure 4.1 on p. 150, the first step in the communication process is teaching your expectations to students. To teach effectively, you need to prepare lessons that communicate your expectations during the first week of school. The remainder of this chapter addresses this issue.

Your plan for how you will teach your CHAMPS expectations should be based on the complexity of the expectations you have defined, your own teaching style, the age and sophistication of your students, and the level of structure you plan to establish in your classroom. For example, in settings with mature and responsible students (a class that needs only a low-structure management plan), it may be sufficient to verbally describe your expectations on the first day of school and provide a simple list on a flip chart of the three or four major considerations. Then provide short verbal reviews on the second and third days, and thereafter use only occasional reminders. On the other hand, with students who need a more highly structured management plan, you should probably plan to teach your expectations—using visual displays, demonstrations, and perhaps even actual practice—every day for at least the first ten days of school. For primary-level students, especially kindergarten and first grade, you will probably extend this instruction on behavioral expectations for at least the first month and, if needed, throughout the first quarter of the year—a strategy also instrumental in addressing the needs of English Language Learners and special-needs students in your classroom.

When developing your teaching plan, you need to make decisions about how to organize the content and then how to display the expectations for the students. Following are examples of how to apply these concepts of lesson organization and use of visual displays for high-structure, medium-structure, and low-structure lessons.

take note

Detailed information on the second and third steps in the communication process—observing student behavior and giving students feedback on their implementation of expectations—is presented in Tasks 2 and 3 of Chapter 5.

take note

If your school is using CHAMPS as a schoolwide approach to managing students' behavior, follow the example below for high-structure lessons because that example suggests directly using the CHAMPS acronym with students. See Appendix B: Implementing CHAMPS Schoolwide.

USING THE CHAMPS ACRONYM

For classes (or teachers!) that can benefit from high structure, you should use the CHAMPS acronym as the basis for teaching your expectations and creating visual displays to communicate that information to students. The acronym is a useful way to communicate that there is consistency in what students have to know to behave responsibly. Although the specific expected behaviors may be different between, for example, cooperative groups and teacher-directed instruction, students learn that the headings (Conversation, Help, Movement, Participation) are the same from one activity or transition to another. Students also realize that you have definite thoughts about each classroom activity and transition. Without the acronym as an anchor, students may feel that there are just thousands of unconnected expectations. Another advantage to using the CHAMPS acronym is that the content is already neatly organized for you—all you have to do is use your CHAMPS worksheets. See the CHAMPS adaptations on pp. 180–181 for examples of how some teachers have adapted the CHAMPS acronym for younger and older students.

VISUAL DISPLAYS OF CHAMPS INFORMATION

Decide whether your visual displays will be text or picture based. The CD that accompanies this book includes 396 visuals for you to choose from—six different icons for 66 different CHAMPS expectations such as "CONVERSATION: Talk Quietly with Anyone in your Group" and "PARTICIPATION: Listening/Answering/Asking" (see the sample icons in Figure 4.2). The six different versions of the icons associated with each expectation are:

take note

As the owner of this book you have the right to reproduce as many copies of these icons as you need each year for your own classroom. Further reproduction of the icons and forms on the CD is strictly prohibited.

Version 1: Primary (B/W). Line drawings that young students (K–2) can color

Version 2: Primary (Color). Full-color illustrations aimed at young students (K–2). Note that thumbnails are shown in grayscale, but the images on the CD are in full color.)

Version 3: Intermediate. Grayscale drawings for older students (3–8)

Version 4: Graphic. Black and white graphic symbols

Version 5: Sentence strip. Text-only icons

Version 6: Road sign. Text-based street signs in different shapes and colors

VERSION 1 Primary (B/W)	VERSION 2 Primary (Color)	VERSION 3 Intermediate	VERSION 4 Graphic	VERSION 5 Sentence Strip	VERSION 6 Road Sign
				CONVERSATION Talk quietly with anyone in your group	TALK QUIETLY WITH ANYONE IN YOUR GROUP
				PARTICIPATION Listening/ Answering/ Asking Questions/Sharing	LISTEN, ANSWER, ASK QUESTIONS, AND/OR SHARE

Figure 4.2 *Samples of CHAMPS Icons*

Each of these 396 icons is available on the CD as a PDF file that you can size to meet your needs. A list of the available icons and thumbnails of all the different versions can be found in Appendix D. Note that Versions 1 and 2 are essentially the same. Version 1 icons are line drawings that students can color. Version 2 icons are full color but can be printed in either grayscale or full color, depending on your printing capability.

Once you have selected the icons that are appropriate for your class (artistic teachers may wish to design their own), determine how you will use them to create classroom displays. One of the easiest options is to create a poster-size version of each of your major instructional activities and major transitions (use the CHAMPS worksheets you filled out for Tasks 1 and 2 for guidance) and paste the icons in an appropriate place.

(continued on p. 182)

Adaptations of CHAMPS for Young Children

If you teach very young students (pre-kindergarten or kindergarten) or students with cognitive deficits, you may wish to simplify the CHAMPS acronym.

For example, Ray Roth and Suzanne Hayes implemented CHAMPS in a preschool setting. CHAMPS was shortened to MAC: Movement, Activity, and Conversation. Susan Schilt, of the Pinellas County Public Schools in Florida, used this concept to develop "Mr. MAC" posters. She used Boardmaker, a software program from Mayer-Johnson, to develop posters like the one shown in Figure 4.3.

Figure 4.3 *Sample Mr. MAC Poster*

Another example of adapting the CHAMPS concept for young children comes from the *Read Well* beginning reading curriculum by Marilyn Sprick and Shelley Jones. They developed TEAM: Talk, Effort, Ask, and Move. Figure 4.4 is an example of how this can be applied to independent work periods.

T	Talk	Talk quietly about reading and writing only to the person next to you.
E	Effort	Think about reading and writing. Do your personal best handwriting and spelling.
A	Ask	Put your question card up, but keep working.
M	Move	Stand or sit at your desk, in your personal space.

Figure 4.4   *Sample Expectations for Independent Work*

Adaptation of CHAMPS for Older Students

Another adaptation is ACHIEVE—Activity, Conversation, Help, Integrity, Effort, Value, Efficiency. Susan Banks and Leslie Salmon of the Adult Education Center in West Palm Beach, Florida, used this acronym with students whose ages range from 17 to 70. The ACHIEVE acronym is from *Discipline in the Secondary Classroom* (Sprick, 2006), which is essentially CHAMPS for grades 9–12.

Figure 4.5 *Sample ACHIEVE posters*

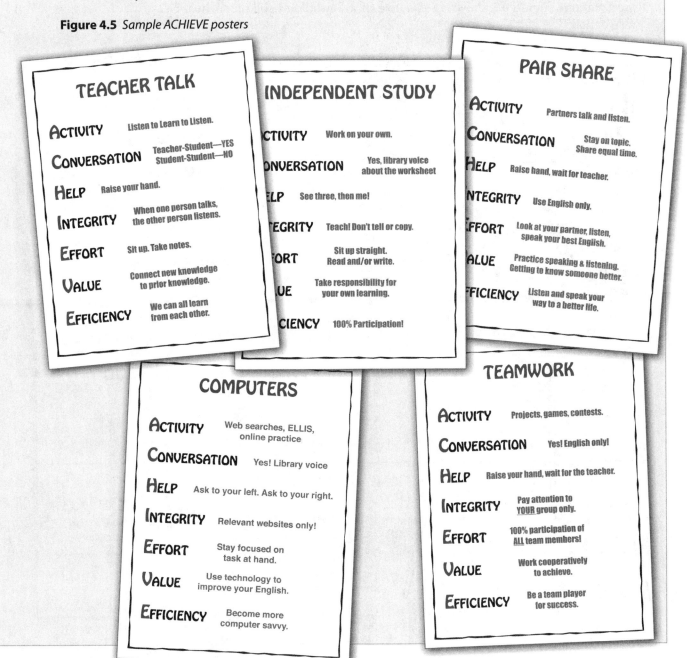

A chart stand, as shown in Figure 4.6, is a good way to display your expectations in poster form. Another way is to mount all the posters above your board space in the front of the room—this eliminates the need to flip to the correct poster each time you change activities. You might put the expectations on transparencies or standard paper for display with an overhead projector or a visual presenter such as those from ELMO Company.

You could also use a projector and load the icons into PowerPoint or Keynote presentations. Figure 4.7 shows an example of a PowerPoint slide for whole-class instruction.

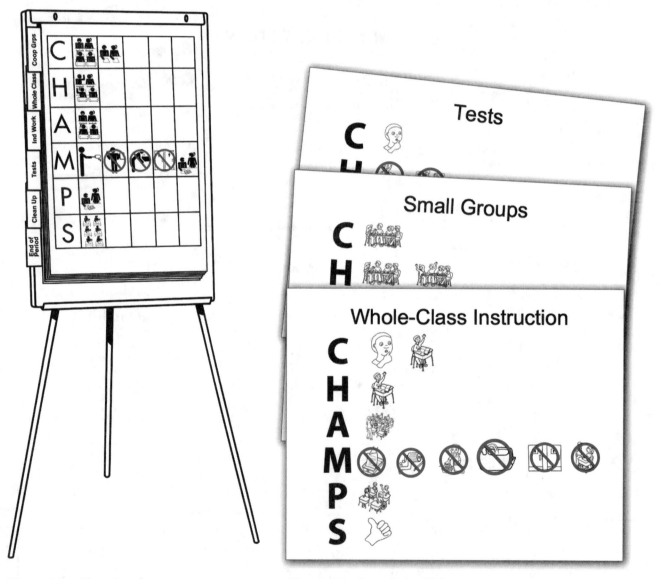

Figure 4.6   *Chart Stand*   **Figure 4.7**   *PowerPoint Slides*

CHAPTER 4 TASKS

Some teachers devote an entire bulletin board to a CHAMPS display, using push pins to display the relevant icons. Another example of how one teacher uses the icons with the CHAMPS acronym is shown in Figure 4.8. As you can see, the teacher has made a large chart that displays the CHAMPS acronym. Pockets are positioned next to each letter. Just before she begins a new activity or transition, she places the appropriate icons in the appropriate pockets on the chart. At the beginning of the year (and periodically thereafter), she explains what each icon means as she places it in the pocket. In Figure 4.8, the icons indicate that the activity is independent work. During this activity, students may talk quietly to a student nearby, a student who has a question should put up the "Please Help" flag, and it is OK to get out of seats to get a drink, turn in work, get supplies, or visit the restroom. The authors wish to thank Clerese Sprague from Hood River, Oregon, for sharing this wonderful idea with us.

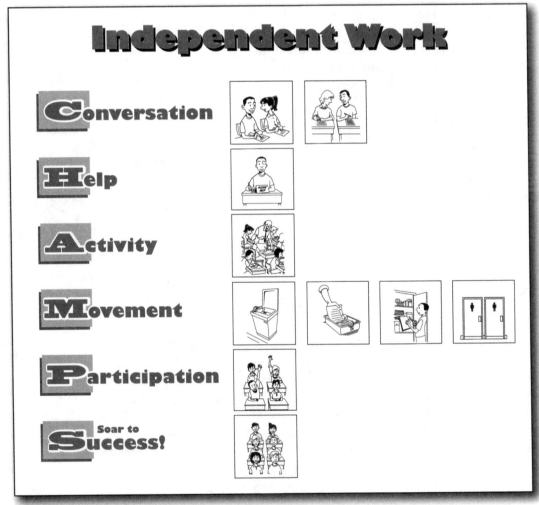

Figure 4.8   *CHAMPS Chart with Icons*

If you prefer to use text-based displays, the Version 5 icons are sentence strips that work well for pocket charts. They can even be printed as magnetic strips for use on a magnet board. Because the icons are in PDF format on the CD, you can electronically size them to fit your needs.

If you want to create your own text-based versions of your expectations, you can use Reproducible 4.5a: CHAMPS Expectations, a fillable form provided on the CD. This form is a version of a CHAMPS chart that allows you to fill in the activity or transition and then type in the content that you want for each part of the CHAMPS acronym. You can also cut and paste CHAMPS icons into these templates. The default print size is 8.5" x 11", but you can rescale to print at poster size if your computer and printer have that capability. Ask your school's technical experts for assistance with this, if needed.

The CD also contains fillable templates for the MAC and ACHIEVE acronyms (Reproducibles 4.5b and 4.5c, respectively). See Appendix D for more details.

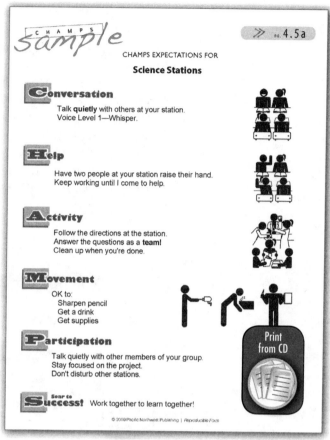

Reproducible 4.5a   *CHAMPS Expectations (Version 1)*

PREPARE LESSONS FOR TEACHING YOUR CHAMPS EXPECTATIONS

When developing your plan for teaching expectations—that is, deciding how detailed your lessons will be, anticipating how many days you will actively teach the expectations, and choosing how you will organize the content—it is better to overplan than to underplan. For high structure, plan to err on the side of more lessons and more detail than you think you might need because it is always easier to condense (or eliminate) some lessons you started with than to scramble to create new lessons once school has begun.

> *For high structure, plan to err on the side of more lessons and more detail than you think you might need.*

HIGH-STRUCTURE LESSONS

For high-structure lessons, plan to implement the following steps:

- Tell students the type of activity that is coming next.

- Tell students what you expect and show the CHAMPS expectations.

- Model the behaviors you expect to see, with particular emphasis on Participation.

- Have some students demonstrate the expectations.

- Model some things not to do.

- Model the correct way one more time.

- Verify that students understand the expectations: Model behavior, and have students identify whether you are exhibiting appropriate or inappropriate behavior.

- Review all the positive expectations and re-model the right way.

- Have students get started on the activity or transition.

Some aspects of behavioral expectations may be clearer to students if they are demonstrated. One way to do this is to model (act out) both positive and negative examples of what you expect (Gresham, 1998; Sugai & Lewis, 1996). For example, when teaching students what participation (the P from the CHAMPS acronym) should look and sound like during independent work periods, model the right way and the wrong way to participate in the activity. You can even ham it up a bit to make it more interesting for students. If you use modeling, it's a good idea to first provide a couple of positive models (the right ways to demonstrate participation), then give the negative models (the most probable wrong ways students might behave). Finally, briefly demonstrate the positive models again. By beginning and ending with positive models, you reduce the chance that students will mistakenly view the negative models as the right way to do things (Bandura, 1977; Kame'enui & Simmons, 1990).

With transitions and activities that are complex or potentially problematic, students will not really understand what is expected of them until they have experienced the transition or activity. One way of addressing this problem is to have the class practice the actual behavior. For example, washing hands and lining up for lunch tends to be a complex set of expectations for primary-age students. Therefore, sometime before lunch on the first day of school, have students actually practice the behavior. At the intermediate grade and middle school levels, you could have students practice getting out materials and heading a paper within a reasonable period of time (30 seconds, for example). Other expectations that can benefit from practice include entering the room in an orderly fashion from recess or at the beginning of class, appropriate noise level within cooperative groups, getting quiet when the attention signal is given, moving quickly and quietly to and from small groups or lab stations, moving desks into and out of cooperative group activities, and so on.

You may also wish to involve students when modeling expectations. Students at both the elementary and middle school levels enjoy participating in role-play situations in which student volunteers demonstrate (model) one or more aspects of the expectations. The advantage of involving students in role-play situations is that it gets them more actively involved in the lesson and gives them an opportunity to practice the expected behaviors you are teaching (McGinnis & Goldstein, 1994; Walker, Ramsey, & Gresham, 2004). Ask for a couple of volunteers and have them demonstrate a positive model of one or more aspects of your expectations. Then you can model some examples of the wrong way to behave and end by asking different students to demonstrate the positive expectation.

> *The answers students give (or fail to give) will help you determine whether you have adequately explained the essential information.*

For ELL students, consider setting up a buddy system that allows each student to comfortably model the expectations with a peer.

Regardless of exactly how you teach your expectations for a given activity or transition, you should ask students a few questions about the expectations before you start the activity or transition. The answers students give (or fail to give) will help you determine whether you have adequately explained the essential information. If students can answer your questions, you are probably ready to start the activity or transition. On the other hand, if students seem unsure of their answers or are unable to answer the questions at all, you should go over the information again more thoroughly. Plan on re-teaching the expectations until students know them.

Do not ask for volunteers to answer the questions. Students who do not know the answer are unlikely to volunteer, so you will not get accurate information about whether all students understand the expectations. A more effective approach is to ask the question first, give everyone time to think, and then assign one individual student to answer.

> *Everyone, get ready to answer a few questions. During the time we will be working in cooperative groups, can you get out of your seat for any reason? If so, what are the reasons?* (Pause for students to think.) *Jared, please answer.*

As you move into subsequent days of school, you may be able to reduce the amount of modeling substantially, but keep in mind that whenever you model the wrong way to do things, it should be sandwiched between modeling it the right way.

For classes that need high structure, you will probably want to teach expectations for at least the first ten days of school, then begin fading to every other day, then every third day. You will likely want to re-teach (some teachers say "re-CHAMP")

CHAPTER 4 TASKS

| 1 • Clarify CHAMPS Expectations for Instructional Activities | 2 • Clarify CHAMPS Expectations for Transitions |

the expectations at least every three to four weeks. You will also want to plan for re-teaching at times of the year (immediately after a long break or before a field trip, for example) that you know are likely to be more difficult for students (Mayer, 1995; Scheuermann & Hall, 2008).

MEDIUM-STRUCTURE LESSONS

For classes with a medium-structure management plan, you may choose not to go into the full details of implementing the CHAMPS acronym. A slightly less structured approach is to develop T-charts for your major instructional activities and transitions. They are called T-charts because they look like a capital T with "Looks Like" on one side of the T and "Sounds Like" on the other side (see Figure 4.9). An advantage of T-charts is their simplicity, but a disadvantage is that they do not provide specific information on the details of Conversation, Help, Activity, Movement, and Participation. However, for a medium-structure class, they may provide sufficient information. T-charts can be graphically displayed in all the same ways that CHAMPS charts can be displayed—posters, projected, bulletin board, and so on.

With medium-structure classes, you may be able to teach expectations more quickly and with fewer steps. For example, the following steps may be sufficient:

- Tell students the type of activity that is coming next.

- Tell students what you expect and show the T-chart.

- Model the behaviors you expect to see.

Figure 4.9 *T-chart of Expectations for Teacher-Directed Instruction and Discussions*

LOOKS LIKE	SOUNDS LIKE
Eyes on speaker, overhead, or your own notes	Only one voice at a time can be heard
Everyone looks as if they are listening to the speaker	Presentation voice is used when you are the speaker
Hands raised before speaking	Questions and comments from the speaker relate to the lesson
Notes being taken on essential points	No noise other than writing or turning a page of your notes if you are not the current speaker
Everyone in seat, except speaker	
If someone disagrees, he or she raises hand to become the speaker—there are no nonverbal expressions of disagreement	All verbal participation sounds respectful—even when you are disagreeing

- Have some students demonstrate the expectations.

- Review all the positive expectations and re-model the right way.

- Have students get started on the activity or transition.

In addition, with classes that can handle less structure, you may be able to phase out teaching expectations before activities and transitions as early as the second week of school, and simply review expectations at the beginning of the week for a few weeks.

For primary-level students, you can use pictures on each side of the T-chart in place of sentences.

LOW-STRUCTURE LESSONS

For classes with a low-structure management plan, you may not even need to prepare T-charts. It is possible that you need to delineate only three or four specific expectations for each major activity or transition. If this is the case, print the expectations for each activity and transition onto 8.5" x 11" paper in landscape format. Add a tabbed divider to each page that labels the activity or transition so you can quickly flip to the correct page. Put these pages into a tabletop display portfolio (available at art supply stores), as shown in Figure 4.10. These may also be known as presentation displays or easel binders. A notebook taped to stay upright like a tent will work, too (see Figure 4.11).

The advantage of a display portfolio or notebook is its simplicity. The disadvantage is that on an 8.5" x 11" paper you will be able to display only a few sentences that can be seen from across the room, so you can't incorporate as much information as you can with T-charts and CHAMPS posters.

If low-structure lessons work with your students, you may not even need to prepare any lessons—you can just have your CHAMPS worksheets handy as you show the expectations

Figure 4.10 *Display Portfolio*

Figure 4.11 *Notebook as a Flip Chart*

on the display portfolio. Then talk students through your expectations and explain what it takes to be successful in your classroom. Plan to do this for at least the first two or three days of school. If students are behaving well, you can fade out instruction on your expectations quickly. Decide whether or not the flip chart is still helpful to students. If it is, you can simply flip to the appropriate page of the folio (without instructing students) whenever you move from one transition to another.

Remember that structure is also about the teacher's needs, not just the needs of the students. If you are bothered by noise, lots of movement, and interruptions, you should probably implement the suggestions for high-structure lessons. Detailed CHAMPS lessons give students the specific information they need to meet your expectations for a calm, orderly classroom. A number of district-based CHAMPS trainers have said that when a teacher does not use the CHAMPS acronym for a high-structure class, the students are not as clear about the teacher's exact expectations.

Conclusion

In this chapter, you identified all your major instructional activities and for each one completed a CHAMPS worksheet to clarify for yourself exactly how you expect students to behave during each particular type of activity. You also identified the major transitions that take place regularly in your classroom and completed worksheets for them. Using this information, you then designed lessons and graphic displays to communicate your expectations to students. If you are creating a classroom with high structure, you will design lessons and displays using the CHAMPS acronym and CHAMPS displays in the form of posters, bulletin boards, or projections. If you plan to implement a less highly structured classroom, you may choose not to use the CHAMPS acronym with students and instead display your expectations via T-chart posters or display three- or four-sentence expectations on a tabletop display portfolio.

Use the Self-Assessment Checklist shown on the following pages to keep track of the tasks you've completed and those that require further work. A fillable version of the Self-Assessment Checklist is available on the CD.

Print from CD

Generate Clear Expectations

Chapter 4: Expectations

Use the worksheet on the following pages to identify which (or which parts) of the tasks described in this chapter you have completed. For any item that has not been completed, note what needs to be done to complete it. Then translate your notes onto your planning calendar in the form of specific actions that you can take (e.g., August 28: finish developing CHAMPS expectations for math class.)

✓	TASK	NOTES & IMPLEMENTATION *Ideas*
	TASK 1: CLARIFY CHAMPS EXPECTATIONS FOR INSTRUCTIONAL ACTIVITIES	
☐	I have made a list of the major instructional activities and/or categories of activities that take place during a typical day.	
☐	For each activity or category that I have listed, I have defined, specifically and in detail, my behavioral expectations for students. For each activity or category, I have considered the level of classroom structure my students need as I addressed the following issues/questions:	
	• **Conversation:** How much and what type of conversation among students is allowed?	
	• **Help:** How are students to request help? What should they do while they are waiting for help?	
	...activity, task, or assignment students will ...the expected end	

✓	TASK	NOTES & IMPLEMENTATION *Ideas*
	TASK 2: CLARIFY CHAMPS EXPECTATIONS FOR TRANSITIONS	

| ☐ | I have made a list of the common transitions and/or categories of transitions within and between activities that will take place during a typical day. |
| ☐ | For each transition or category listed, I have defined, specifically and in detail, my behavioral expectations for students. For each transition or category, I have considered the level of classroom structure my students need as I addressed the following issues/questions: |

• **Conversation:** How much and what type of conversation among students is allowed?

• **Help:** How are students to request help? What should they do while they are waiting for help?

• **Activity:** What is the transition? What is its purpose? What will be different after the transition is complete? How long should the transition take?

• **M**... ho... ab... res...

• **Pa**... resp... behi... tran...

✓	TASK	NOTES & IMPLEMENTATION *Ideas*

	TASK 3: PREPARE LESSONS TO COMMUNICATE YOUR EXPECTATIONS	
☐	Based on the needs of my students, I have developed a plan to teach my CHAMPS expectations for activities and transitions. In developing my plan, I considered whether and how to use the following:	
	• The CHAMPS acronym	
	• Visual displays	
	• Modeling and/or role-play demonstrations	
	• Practice by the class	
	• Verification of students' understanding of expectations	
☐	Based on my plan, I have prepared CHAMPS lessons that I will use at the beginning of the school year to communicate behavioral expectations to students.	

Launch

When you teach students how to behave responsibly during the first month of school, you dramatically increase their chances of having a productive year.

Introduction

*B*y following the suggestions presented so far in this book, you have created the potential for a wonderful classroom. You have developed your classroom vision and organization, and defined your CHAMPS expectations for student behavior.

This chapter offers suggestions for how you can implement all of the creative work you have done and make the first month of school a highly productive one, setting the stage for the rest of the year. The first month of school is an incredibly important time. It is essential to get students "on board" and behaving responsibly from the start because it can be very difficult (not impossible, but very difficult) to change negative behavior patterns later in the year. Research has shown that starting the year with an effective classroom management plan results in increased appropriate behavior and improved academic performance (Emmer et al., 1980; Evertson & Anderson, 1979; Evertson & Emmer, 1982; Kounin, 1970). Also, student-rated "best" teachers focused more on teaching expectations and establishing guidelines for appropriate behavior from the first day of school (Moskowitz & Hayman, 1976).

The information and strategies in this chapter are designed to ensure that during the first month of school you build positive relationships with students and communicate your expectations so clearly that you and your students are working productively as a team by the end of the first four weeks of school.

CHAPTER 5 TASKS

Task 1
Summarize Your Classroom Management and Discipline Plan

Task 2
Make Final Preparations for Day One

Task 3
Implement Your Plan on Day One

Task 4
Implement Your Plan on Days 2 Through 20 (The First Four Weeks)

Task 5
Prepare Your Students for Special Circumstances

The five tasks in this chapter are presented chronologically. They address final preparations you should make before school starts, what to do on the first day of school, procedures and considerations to deal with during the remainder of the first month, and preparations for special circumstances that may come up later.

Task 1 begins with the suggestion that you review your implementation of the most essential concepts from Chapters 1 through 4 to make sure you are ready for the first day of school. This task guides you through compiling information about your vision, classroom organization, and discipline plan to create a concise summary of your Classroom Management and Discipline Plan—a plan tailored to fit your personal style and the students' need for structure. You will then have a compact summary document for you, your administrator, and substitute teachers to use. If you have worked through Chapters 1 through 4 in detail, completing this template will be easy.

> *Give careful thought to the first impression students will form about you and your classroom.*

Task 2 describes a few ideas that may help the first day of school run more smoothly. These ideas include making it easy for students to find your classroom, planning for how you will get students into the room and settled down, and preparing to make effective use of the first ten minutes of class.

Task 3 provides specific how-to information for the first day of school. Most students are somewhat apprehensive about that first day. They have questions such as, "Where will I go? Will any of my friends be in my class? What will my teacher be like? Will the teacher be mean? Will I feel stupid? Will other students think my new clothes look awful?" Also, recognize that some students have had previous negative experiences in other classrooms. The more you can do to help students feel safe and comfortable, the greater the probability that students will feel a sense of appreciation and loyalty to you. It's also important to give careful thought to the first impression students will form about you and your classroom. Ideally, students should leave at the end of their first day (or class period) with an idea of what you and the class will be like, what you view as the major goals for the year, and what will be expected of them.

We also discuss in detail how to use the three-step process for communicating expectations on the first day of school. This information includes ideas on teaching the lessons you have developed about your expectations (Step 1), comprehensive suggestions for observing student behavior using circulating and visual scanning (Step 2), and specific strategies for providing feedback to students about how they are meeting expectations during and after each activity and transition (Step 3).

The fourth task in this chapter focuses on the process of communicating your behavioral expectations throughout the first month of school. You need to ensure that by the end of the first week, students have a thorough understanding of how to

CHAPTER 5 TASKS

| 1 • Summarize Your Plan | 2 • Make Final Preparations for Day 1 | 3 • Implement Your Plan on Day 1 |

behave during each type of classroom activity and transition. In addition, if you are an elementary teacher, you should have coordinated with specialists (media, music, physical education) so that your students know the behavioral expectations for these classes. During weeks two and three, continue to teach, monitor, and give feedback on your expectations. Eventually you will objectively verify student understanding of the expectations using a brief quiz or interviews with students. If you find that students do not fully understand what is expected of them, you will need to re-teach your CHAMPS expectations.

Task 5 addresses two issues related to communicating expectations:

- How to teach your CHAMPS expectations to new students—students who did not participate in your CHAMPS lessons during the first couple of weeks of school.

- How to design CHAMPS lessons for any special or unique activities (guest speakers and field trips, for example).

At the end of this chapter is a Self-Assessment Checklist designed to help you determine which (or which parts) of the tasks you have done or are in the process of doing, and which you still need to do.

The five tasks presented and explained in this chapter are:

Task 1: Summarize Your Classroom Management and Discipline Plan • Compile essential information about your vision, classroom organization, and discipline procedures into a concise document for use by you, your building administrator, and substitute teachers.

Task 2: Make Final Preparations for Day One • Make final preparations to ensure an orderly, respectful, and comfortable first day for you and your students.

Task 3: Implement Your Plan on Day One • Be prepared to implement strategies on the first day of school that will allow you to make a great impression on your students.

Task 4: Implement Your Plan on Days 2 Through 20 (The First Four Weeks) • During the first month of school, continue to implement the three-step process for communicating expectations and take the time to verify that students understand what is expected of them.

Task 5: Prepare Your Students for Special Circumstances • Be prepared to teach your CHAMPS expectations to any new students who enter your class and be prepared to develop and teach all students your expectations for any unique events that may occur.

Task 1: Summarize Your Classroom Management and Discipline Plan

Compile essential information regarding your vision, classroom organization, and discipline procedures into a concise document for use by you, your building administrator, and substitute teachers.

If you are fully prepared for the first day of school, you will be relaxed and ready to handle whatever takes place. In the previous chapters you identified the most essential preparation tasks, and in this task you will summarize that information. The process of summarizing your vision, organization, and procedures in writing helps ensure that you are clear on your own plan. It also creates a document to share with building administrators and substitute teachers. When you've completed the document, ask your administrator to review it to ensure that he or she is comfortable with and supportive of your ideas, particularly the types of corrective actions you will take regarding misbehavior. This completed Classroom Management and Discipline Plan can also be kept on file with the other information you leave for substitute teachers.

Reproducible 5.1 shows a completed Classroom Management and Discipline Plan. A fillable version of this form that you can complete is provided on the CD. Figure 5.1 is a template that includes bulleted highlights from the previous chapters to assist you in filling out your version of the Classroom Management and Discipline Plan. Consider copying Reproducible 5.1 from the CD onto your computer, then filling it out as you look at the reference template in Figure 5.1. Or if you prefer, you can print out the form and fill it in by hand. Special thanks to Mike Booher for the idea to provide Figure 5.1, the template with bulleted explanations.

take note

One part of this form has not yet been covered in the CHAMPS book—the section that asks about your Encouragement Procedures. If time permits, read Chapters 7 and 8 thoroughly. The content of those chapters relates to the "I" of the STOIC acronym: Interact Positively with Students. If you think a low-structure management plan is appropriate for your classroom, the concepts in Chapter 7: Motivation will probably be sufficient. If you anticipate using a medium- or high-structure plan, you should begin the year with one or more structured reinforcement systems.

Reproducible 5.1 *Classroom Management and Discipline Plan (p. 1 of 3)*

Print from CD

C H A M P S
sample

≫ no. **5.1**

CLASSROOM MANAGEMENT AND DISCIPLINE PLAN (1 of 3)

Teacher Mr. Kusche   **School Year** 00/00   **Room No.** 27   **Grade Level** 5

The level of structure I anticipate establishing is (check one): ☑ High ☐ Medium ☐ Low

Guidelines for Success	Posted Rules
I use the Schoolwide Guidelines—the ABCs.	Arrive on time with all your materials.
Always do your best.	Keep hands, feet, and objects to self.
Be respectful of yourself and others.	Follow directions the first time given.
Cooperate.	Stay focused during all instructional activities.
I have also added an extra Room 27 Guideline: ALWAYS TRY. PERSEVERE!!	

Attention Signal

Use a quiet voice to say, "Your attention please." Arcing hand raise, keep hand in air until class is quiet.

CHAMPS Expectations for Classroom Activities and Transitions

See my attached CHAMPS plans.

Encouragement Procedures (See Chapter 7, Motivation, and Chapter 8, Classwide Motivation.)

- Frequent greetings and friendly interactions.
- Descriptive verbal praise.
- Occasional intermittent rewards such as first to line up, sit at teacher desk, stickers, and giving the whole class a privilege such as playing music during a work period.
- I will strive for a 3:1 Ratio of Positive to Negative Interactions.
- I will use a Lottery Ticket system to acknowledge individual performance. I will fade this out in November if the class does not seem to need it.
- During the first month of school, I will use 100 Squares. I will use other systems on a temporary basis as needed (such as between Thanksgiving and Winter break). ➡

Reproducible 5.1   *Classroom Management and Discipline Plan (p. 2 of 3)*

C H A M P S
sample

Print from CD

≫   no. 5.1

CLASSROOM MANAGEMENT AND DISCIPLINE PLAN (2 of 3)

Correction Procedures for Misbehavior (both early-stage corrections and rule violation consequences)

Early-stage corrections include:

• Proximity
• Verbal reminders
• Discussion

Consequences for rule violations include:

• End of line for lunch, recess, or dismissal
• 15 seconds time owed
• In-class timeout (head down at desk or go to timeout area)
• Family contact

Beginning and Ending Routines

1. Routine for how students will enter the room: I greet students at the door and shake hands as they enter. Students go directly to seats and begin working on our Morning Starter on the board, which they can work on individually or quietly with their table partners. If a student is high energy or upset, I ask that he or she speak with me while others are entering. I let that student enter after he or she is calm.

2. Routine for how students will be instructionally engaged while attendance is taken and for how opening business is conducted: I take attendance using a seating chart while students continue to work on the Morning Starter. After taking attendance, we discuss the Morning Starter, go over the schedule for the day, take care of announcements, and discuss the weather. Within 5 minutes of the bell, we get started with Language Arts.

3. Routine for dealing with tardy students: Any students who are late go to the folder by the pencil sharpener and fill out the Tardy Slip that indicates if it is an excused or unexcused tardy, then take their seats and join the class activity. I wait until the class is engaged in independent work, then go to the tardy folder. If the tardy was unexcused, I go and talk with the student.

4. Routine for dealing with students who come to class without necessary materials:
   If students do not have a pencil, they may quietly get up and borrow a pencil from the can on my desk that contains sharpened golf pencils and pencil stubs. I also keep notebook paper there if a student needs it. If borrowing becomes habitual, I plan to talk with the student and the student's family.

5. Routine for dealing with students returning after an absence: If a student is absent on a Monday, he or she goes to the "Absent—What you missed!" basket and gets the Weekly Assignment Sheet that lists all assignments due that week. When students complete missing work, they turn that work into the "Completed Assignments" basket. The due date for work after absences is equal to the number of days absent (e.g., if they missed Mon. & Tues. and return on Wed., they have until Fri. to get the work in to receive full credit).

6. Routine for wrapping up at end of day/class: I schedule five minutes at the end of the day to: (a) Make sure the class is reasonably clean and litter is picked up. (b) Make sure that students are clear on homework assignments due in coming days. (c) Provide positive feedback on what went well today. (d) Set goals for improvement for tomorrow. If time permits, I have volunteers share, "Something I learned today is . . . ."

7. Routine for dismissal:
   Students know that the ringing bell is for me, not for them. After the bell rings and the class is calm and quiet, I excuse them by table groups. I tell them, "I look forward to seeing you tomorrow," as they exit.   ➡

CHAPTER 5 TASKS

| 1 • Summarize Your Plan | 2 • Make Final Preparations for Day 1 | 3 • Implement Your Plan on Day 1 |

Reproducible 5.1   *Classroom Management and Discipline Plan (p. 3 of 3)*

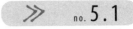

CLASSROOM MANAGEMENT AND DISCIPLINE PLAN (3 of 3)

Procedures for Managing Student Work

1. Procedures for assigning classwork and homework: At the start of each week, I provide an assignment sheet that specifies all the things that need to be completed and turned in for each day during that week. This specifies both class assignments and homework. It includes a place for students to check off each assignment after it is handed in.

   Students know that they have: (a) math homework every Mon., Tues., and Wed.; (b) a writing assignment assigned on Tues. and due on Thurs.; and (c) a spelling list assigned on Mon. with a test on Fri.

2. Procedures for collecting completed work: I collect homework during the Morning Starter activity by having students place their homework on their desks as I come around and collect it. Any student who does not have homework completes a Zero Slip and turns that in to me.

   Classwork is placed in the "Assignments Completed" basket by the windows. I conduct random checks of assignment sheets and students' records of what has been turned in.

3. Procedures for keeping records and providing feedback to students:

   I enter scores for all assignments as I grade them. My goal is to get graded work back to students the next day or, at the latest, two school days after completion.

   Each week, students get a printout that specifies their current grade averages and a list of any missing assignments or homework. They take this sheet home and have their family sign it.

4. Procedures and policies for dealing with late and missing assignments: Any late assignment (other than those late due to absences) immediately loses 10% of the possible point value.

   A student has up to one week to make up assignments; after that it becomes a zero in the grade book.

   A student who begins to exhibit a chronic pattern of late or missing assignments will have a student/teacher/family conference. If the conference does not solve the problem, the situation will be referred to the Problem-Solving Team to assist in setting up an intervention plan.

Procedures for Managing Independent Work Periods

On all but the easiest review assignments, we complete the first part of the task as a class (guided practice) to make sure students know what is expected. If a small group of students is likely to struggle with an assignment, I work directly with those students while the rest work independently. Independent work times are never scheduled for more than 30 minutes at a time, with teacher-directed or cooperative groups scheduled to create variety.

CHAMPS expectations for Independent Work are posted so if a student is not meeting expectations, I can simply point to the CHAMPS Chart.

Students can get assistance by quietly asking another student. If they have asked two students, they can come and join the small group I am working with. If I am circulating, they can put up their Please Help flag.

Figure 5.1 *Bulleted Points for Classroom Management and Discipline Plan (p. 1 of 3)*

PLAN WITH BULLETED POINTS (RUBRIC)

C H A M P S

BULLETED PLAN no. 5.1

CLASSROOM MANAGEMENT AND DISCIPLINE PLAN (1 of 3)

Teacher _____   School Year _____   Room No. _____   Grade Level _____

The level of structure I anticipate establishing is (check one): ❑ High   ❑ Medium   ❑ Low

Guidelines for Success (pp. 34–39)

Set of positive expectations—what students must do to be successful in school and in life:

- They don't need to be specific behaviors.
- They teach students how to be successful.
- Teacher must refer to them when teaching, encouraging, and correcting.

Posted Rules (pp. 115–119)

Objective descriptions of specific behaviors:

- They should address the most frequent misbehaviors.
- Three to six rules are preferred.
- Post the rules and refer to them when needed.
- Decide on consequences ahead of time.
- Teach and review them at the start of the year.
- Demonstrate and teach the rules at the start of the year and after major breaks.
- Deliver consequences calmly and consistently.

Attention Signal (pp. 76–78)

- The signal should immediately capture the students' attention. It should be both auditory and visual. An effective signal is to raise one arm from the side to over the head while saying, "Class, your attention please."
- Teach students to stop talking, stop working, and establish eye contact with you within five seconds of hearing and/or seeing the attention signal.
- Consistently use the attention signal in the classroom, hallway, bus, and auditorium. Also use it on field trips.

CHAMPS Expectations for Classroom Activities and Transitions

See your CHAMPS plans (Reproducible Forms 4.2 and 4.4).

Encouragement Procedures (see Ch. 7, Motivation, and Ch. 8, Classwide Motivation)

You need to do the following:

- Provide *noncontingent attention* (verbal and nonverbal) to each student throughout the day, regardless of behavior.
- Give *positive feedback* to the student and class when appropriate academic and/or behavioral performance is demonstrated. Feedback should be accurate, specific, descriptive, contingent, age-appropriate, and delivered in a manner consistent with your personal style.
- Provide *intermittent celebrations* by giving rewards when a student or the class demonstrates a particularly important behavior. Reward or celebration must be meaningful to the student(s) and delivered on an unpredictable schedule (not every day).
- Have 3 times more positive interactions with each student (either noncontingent attention or positive feedback) than corrective interactions as a result of misbehavior.

If you plan to use a reward-based system for a medium- or high-structure class, you need to:

- Determine the system's goal (i.e., what you want to accomplish).
- Choose a system that is appropriate for and interesting to students.
- Select rewards that are highly desirable to students.
- Set up a system so that student success is likely.
- Avoid systems with arbitrary time limits.
- Carefully organize the entire system before you begin implementation.
- Make sure that your expectations for student behavior are clear and that you have adequate procedures for monitoring student behavior.
- Teach students how the entire system works.

- Make sure you believe that the system will help improve student behavior.
- Keep your energy and enthusiasm about the system high.
- Keep your focus on the students' behavior rather than on the rewards they earn.
- Continue using other motivational strategies at a high level.
- Gradually make the rewards criteria more challenging when students have been consistently successful in the system.
- When students are ready, modify the system to be based on intermittent rewards.
- Talk with the class before making any changes to the system.

➡

CHAPTER 5 TASKS

| 1 • Summarize Your Plan | 2 • Make Final Preparations for Day 1 | 3 • Implement Your Plan on Day 1 |

Figure 5.1 *Bulleted Points for Classroom Management and Discipline Plan (p. 2 of 3)*

PLAN WITH BULLETED POINTS (RUBRIC)

C H A M P S

BULLETED PLAN no. **5.1**

CLASSROOM MANAGEMENT AND DISCIPLINE PLAN (2 of 3)

Correction Procedures for Misbehavior (see Ch. 3) (both early-stage corrections and rule violations consequences)

- Preplan mild consequences that you will deliver consistently, appropriately, and unemotionally when a rule is broken. Interact with the student only briefly at the time of the misbehavior, without arguing. Decide whether to use progressive or nonprogressive consequences.

- When responding to early-stage misbehavior, a preplanned response is not needed. Respond by using proximity management, gentle verbal reprimands, discussion, family contact, or praise of students who are behaving responsibly. Emotional reaction and humor can be used, but carefully and sparingly.

- When dealing with chronic misbehavior, preplan by using consequences like time owed, timeout from favorite object, timeout from small group, timeout at desk, timeout in classroom, timeout in another class, restitution, positive practice, response cost–loss of points, response cost lottery, detention, demerits, or having the student fill out a Behavior Improvement Form. For severe misbehavior, refer the student to the office.

Beginning and Ending Routines (pp. 78–89)

1. Routine for how students will enter the room:
   - Stand in hallway at the classroom door and greet the students.
   - If a student is upset or misbehaving, intervene before the student enters the classroom.
   - Have students go immediately to their assigned seats or desks where they have productive seatwork to do.
   - Decide whether students can talk, to whom, about what, how loud, and how long during this time. Also decide whether they can get out of their seats and if so, for what. Teach the expectations to your students.

2. Routine for how students will be instructionally engaged while attendance is taken and for how opening business is conducted:
   - During attendance, students need an assignment to work on displayed on the board or via the overhead projector.
   - Have students sit in assigned seats and take attendance by referring to the seating chart.

3. Routine for dealing with tardy students:
   - Track tardies by having a tardy student sign the tardy notebook.
   - Teach what you expect students to do when entering the class so they don't disturb the class.

4. Routine for dealing with students who come to class without necessary materials:
   - Make sure students know exactly what materials are needed each day.
   - Students need to have a procedure for getting materials without disrupting the teacher or the instruction. Options include having the student ask a neighbor, go to a specified spot in the room to borrow the materials (require the student to leave a "deposit" like a book bag so that the borrowed materials are returned), or return to his or her locker.
   - Establish a consequence if the student has to interrupt instruction to get materials from the teacher. Time owed is typically effective (e.g., owe the teacher a minute of lunch time) or assign a tardy if the student needs to go to his or her locker to get materials.

5. Routine for dealing with students returning after an absence:
   - Set up a system where a student collects work and assignments and delivers makeup work without taking your time.
   - One effective system is to use two baskets, one labeled "Absent, What You Missed" and the other, "Absent, Assignments In."
   - Decide how many days the student is allowed to make up the missed work. Consider giving the same number of days to complete missed work as the number of days the student was absent from school.

6. Routine for wrapping up at end of day/class:
   - Make sure students don't leave until they have organized their materials, cleaned up, and received appropriate positive and corrective feedback. End each class or day on a positive note.
   - For primary and elementary students, five to ten minutes may be needed to wrap up, while only a minute might be needed for a core class in middle school.

7. Routine for dismissal:
   - Establish the expectation that the teacher dismisses class when the room is quiet and the ending routine is done. Explain to the students that the bell does not dismiss the class.
   - Dismiss primary students by rows. If older students are rushing out, dismiss by rows.

Figure 5.1   *Bulleted Points for Classroom Management and Discipline Plan (p. 3 of 3)*

PLAN WITH BULLETED POINTS (RUBRIC)

CHAMPS

no. 5.1

BULLETED PLAN

CLASSROOM MANAGEMENT AND DISCIPLINE PLAN (3 of 3)

Procedures for Managing Student Work (pp. 90–99)

1. Procedures for assigning classwork and homework:
   - Design a permanent place where students can easily find information about work and assignments. Options include writing on board, overhead projector, or distributing an assignment sheet. Keep the assignment posted throughout the day.
   - Include daily reminders about short-term and long-term assignments (e.g., "Science project is due Monday, and you should have finished your first draft.").
   - Teach students how to write the assignments in their notebooks and to put them in a consistent location (e.g., three-ring binder or agenda book). Show examples of how their assignment sheet should look.
   - Place a copy of the daily assignment in "Absent, What You Missed" basket.

2. Procedures for collecting completed work:
   - Personally collect each student's work, if possible. This allows you to quietly provide positive feedback and to know immediately who hasn't done the work. While collecting the work, make sure students are doing something worthwhile.
   - For students who haven't completed their work, establish the procedure that they must talk to the teacher later about why the work isn't done.
   - An option for older students is to have them place their completed work in a basket and check off their name on an assignment sheet or a wall chart.

3. Procedures for keeping records and providing feedback to students:
   - Students need regular weekly feedback on their work completion (for all grades) and current grade status (for grades 3 through 12).
   - Options for keeping track of the student's work include using an accurate and complete grade book or a computer grade book. If a student is behind a specified number of assignments (e.g., three to five), send home a letter or call the family.
   - For classes that need high structure, maintain a chart illustrating the rate of work completion by the entire class. The chart provides daily feedback to the class. An intermittent class reward for improving or maintaining a certain rate of completion can be an effective reinforcement.

4. Procedures and policies for dealing with late/missing assignments:
   - Assign a mild penalty for late assignments (e.g., 10% off the grade).
   - Set a deadline for accepting late work (e.g., within one week of due date).
   - Establish how many late assignments will be accepted during a grading period or semester. Share policy with family.

Procedures for Managing Independent Work Periods (pp. 99–104)

- Make sure that students can complete the work independently. The work might need to be modified for lower performing students. Briefly work with selected students to make sure they can do the work.
- Maximize on-task behavior during independent work by avoiding long work periods (typically more than 30 minutes). Don't schedule independent work after an exciting activity, and do assign a shorter work period at the end of the day.
- Decide how you want the students to behave during the independent work. What should student behavior look like and sound like? Use the CHAMPS acronym to decide and then teach.
- Provide guided practice to make sure students know how to do the work. If needed, provide more instruction.
- Determine how students can ask for help during the independent work period. Options include a "Help" sign on their desk, standing in the question box, writing their name on the board, and asking a neighbor for help.

Task 2: Make Final Preparations for Day One

> *Make final preparations to ensure an orderly, respectful, and comfortable first day for you and your students.*

> " You have the opportunity to communicate to students that your classroom will be interesting, organized, and fun. "

On the first day of the school year, you have the opportunity to communicate to students that your classroom will be interesting, organized, and fun—although students will work hard, the work will be relevant and will help them to be successful students. In this task, you will work through suggestions to ensure that you are ready on day one to implement all of the work you have prepared.

DEVELOP A MODIFIED SCHEDULE FOR THE FIRST DAY OF SCHOOL

In Chapter 2, Task 1, you learned about developing a well-thought-out daily class schedule. That schedule should be modified for the first day of school to allow the inclusion of the unique tasks and activities that must occur on the first day. Your goal is to have the day be as representative of a typical day as possible, but also include activities that will accomplish these important first-day functions:

- Help students feel comfortable and settled.

- Communicate your classroom goals, rules, guidelines, and expectations.

- Communicate any schoolwide rules and expectations.

- Deal with logistics such as distributing textbooks.

Elementary teachers will probably want to plan get-acquainted activities for the first day to help the class begin to function as a group. Be careful not to fill the entire first day with games, however. Students should leave at the end of the day feeling that the class provides a welcoming and enjoyable environment and fully aware that they will be expected to work and study to the best of their abilities.

At the middle school level, get-acquainted activities can be included in advisory or homeroom periods, but should not be a part of every class period. Imagine how you would feel if you had to play the "Get to Know the Names" game in six different class periods on the first day of school!

Before you create your Day One Schedule, find out from your building administrator whether you need to take into account any schoolwide activities (assemblies or testing, for example). Be sure to schedule the first few minutes of the day to go over your goals, classroom rules, Guidelines for Success, and other essential information. Other activities to consider in your scheduling include how and when to pass out books, assign storage space, and otherwise get students settled. Plan to allow more time than usual for each activity on the first day in order to acquaint students with your procedures. For example, something as simple as having second-grade students line up at the door for recess, which should eventually take no more than thirty seconds, may take anywhere between two and five minutes on the first day of school.

Figure 5.2 shows two sample Day One Schedules as they might be posted—one for an elementary classroom and one for a middle school classroom.

take note

Chapter 4, Task 3, and Tasks 3 and 4 of this chapter present detailed information on how to introduce and communicate your expectations to students.

Figure 5.2 *Sample Day One Schedules*

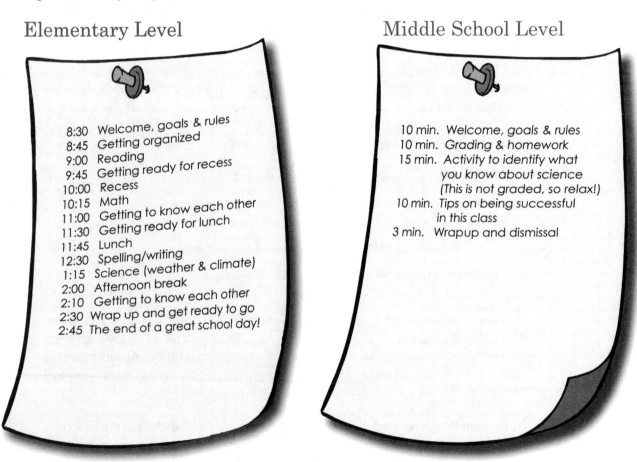

Elementary Level

8:30 Welcome, goals & rules
8:45 Getting organized
9:00 Reading
9:45 Getting ready for recess
10:00 Recess
10:15 Math
11:00 Getting to know each other
11:30 Getting ready for lunch
11:45 Lunch
12:30 Spelling/writing
1:15 Science (weather & climate)
2:00 Afternoon break
2:10 Getting to know each other
2:30 Wrap up and get ready to go
2:45 The end of a great school day!

Middle School Level

10 min. Welcome, goals & rules
10 min. Grading & homework
15 min. Activity to identify what you know about science (This is not graded, so relax!)
10 min. Tips on being successful in this class
3 min. Wrapup and dismissal

Make a sign for your room.

Create an easy-to-read sign that you can place in the hall on or near the classroom door to help your students find your room. Include your name, your grade level or subject, and the room number. Be sure to print large enough that students will be able to see the information from a distance. Remember, your students are likely to be self-conscious about looking lost—a nice clear sign will keep them from having to go door to door looking at small room numbers or teacher names.

 Prepare an initial activity for students to work on when they enter the room.

An initial activity serves several important functions. First, it gives students something to do while they wait for the bell to ring and for class to begin, reducing the self-consciousness that some students may feel about not having someone to talk to. In addition, having an activity to work on keeps students who do know each other from congregating and conversing in groups. Without an activity, groups of students may become so engrossed in conversations that when the bell rings, you must interrupt them or try to get them into their seats before you can begin class. If students have a task to work on when they enter the room, you can keep most of your attention on greeting all students as they arrive. Finally, an initial task communicates the expectation that when students are in your class, they will be actively engaged, not just sitting around (Ornstein & Lasley, 2004).

Choose any task that students can do independently—in other words, a task that will not require assistance from you. Ideally it should be reasonably short and somewhat open ended. Don't forget that students who enter the room first will have longer to work on the task than students who enter just before the final bell rings. Following are some suggestions for this initial first-day task.

At the kindergarten and first-grade levels, give students a coloring sheet and a couple of crayons.

At the second-grade level and beyond, have students fill out a general information form (name, phone number, address). Or have students write answers to one or two open-ended questions that will help you get to know them better.

For example, you might ask students in grades 2 through 5 to identify the two school activities or subjects they like most and why, and the two school activities they like the least and why. Middle school students could be asked to identify when (for what accomplishments) they like to receive public praise and when they prefer to get feedback in a more private manner.

Prepare a plan for dealing with families who want to take your time on the first day.

This is an especially important consideration for teachers of primary students, kindergartners in particular. Families of young students often want to spend time helping their student adjust or telling you about the unique needs or interests of their child. Spending five minutes with the families of just three students, however, would cost you the first 15 minutes of school.

One way to prevent this problem is to pick a day during the week prior to the first day of school and invite kindergarten (or primary) students and their families to visit the classroom and talk with you—something like an open house. These visits can be time consuming, but they can make the first day go much more smoothly. Another procedure is to hold conferences with families before school starts. Conferences can be even more time consuming but pay even bigger dividends in building relationships with your students and their families. You get to know each student as a unique individual and create a working relationship with the family; at the same time, you learn about the student's medical or behavioral issues, if any.

> *Conferences can be even more time consuming but pay even bigger dividends in building relationships with your students and their families.*

At the open house or conference, you can also explain how the first day of school will work, how the student will be dropped off by the family or arrive on the bus, how the student will get to the classroom, and other first-day details. In other words, you can work out how the child's care will be transferred from the family to you, the teacher. You can assure the family that the child will be supervised and supported in getting safely to class on the first day of school.

If time does not permit the suggestions above, and if families bring the student to your classroom, plan to have a prepared note that you can distribute to families who drop into the classroom on the first day.

If you know that the families of several of your students speak a language other than English, see if you can arrange to have the note written in English on one side and in that language on the other side. A sample Note to Families is shown in Figure 5.3.

If you are a kindergarten teacher, you may also want to ask the school counselor (or someone else who has a more flexible schedule on the first day of school) to assist you in getting families to leave their students behind. You can interact with the student while the counselor gently escorts the student's family into the hall. "Hi, Mrs. Thompson, I am Mr. Verner, the school counselor. While Mrs. Morales helps Joanie find her desk, let's you and I go out in the hall. I can give you some information about Mrs. Morales' program and how you can get in touch with her."

Figure 5.3 *Sample Note to Families*

ABC School
Anytown, USA 55555
(555) 555-1234

Dear Families,

Welcome! My name is Mrs. Morales and I will be your child's teacher this year. I want to get to know you and your child as soon as possible, but on this first day, I need to give all of my attention to helping the children adjust and feel comfortable in my classroom. It will probably be easier for your child to adjust if you are not here. If there are things I should know about your child right away (for example, he or she has allergies that are not on the school records), please go to the office and let the office staff know. They will inform me. If there is other information I should know, or if you just want to talk to me, please feel free to call me at 555-1111. The best time to reach me is between 3:00 and 3:45 p.m. on any day other than Tuesday.

I look forward to a great day with your child.

Mrs. Morales

Mrs. Morales

take note

Pages 6–9 in the Introduction contain suggestions on cultural competence—that is, how to work effectively with students and families who may come from a background that is different from yours. You may wish to review that section when considering plans for family contact.

You can plan a similar scenario with ELL families. They often have great and justifiable concerns about whether the first day of school will be difficult for their child because of language issues—especially if their son or daughter is the only one or one of few ELL students in the classroom. Teachers or their administrators should contact someone at the district level to help with orientation and translation. If your district does not have personnel who can do this, most communities have volunteers fluent in different languages who can provide translation services.

The procedures suggested in this task are designed to ensure that the first day of school goes smoothly and that students feel comfortable and know what you want them to do from the moment they arrive at your classroom. Implementing these procedures will help you head into the first day feeling confident, organized, and prepared to guide your students toward responsible, motivated behavior.

Task 3: Implement Your Plan on Day One

Be prepared to implement strategies that allow you to make a great impression on your students on the first day of school.

The first day of school is an important one for both you and the students. When the day is managed well, students leave thinking, "This teacher is organized and friendly, and expects a lot from us. This class will be a lot of work, but should be exciting and fun. The teacher really wants to help me be successful!" Your goal is to conduct the first day of school in a manner that will make students feel welcome and will help them learn to behave responsibly from the beginning (Moskowitz & Hayman, 1976). The following strategies can help you do just that.

 Write your Day One Schedule on the board, an overhead transparency, or a flip chart.

When students enter the room, they will want to know what the day or class period will be like. If students see a prepared schedule or agenda, they can get a sense for "what they are in for." In addition, a written schedule provides a subtle message that you are prepared and organized, and that you have a clear idea of how you want the day or period to go (Trussell, 2008). Middle school teachers who have different classes may want to put the first-day schedule information for each class on a separate page of a flip chart. Before class starts, flip to the appropriate page so students see only their class period schedule. (Obviously, for kindergarten and first-grade students, most of whom probably cannot read, it would be silly and even intimidating to have a written schedule.)

Greet the students individually as they enter your room.

Exactly how you greet students depends on the amount of time you have before the bell rings. If the time period for students to enter your classroom is less than ten minutes, arrange to be near the door so you can greet each student as he or she enters. Ask the students their names and introduce yourself. Then instruct (or help) them to take their seats and start on the task you prepared (coloring, filling out the information form, answering the questions). Then go back to greeting other entering students. By the time the bell rings, all students should be in their seats and quietly working on the task.

In schools where the building is open early, you may have some students enter the classroom up to 30 minutes before the opening bell rings. If this is the case, greet individual students as they enter the room, but realize that you probably cannot be at the door the entire time. Get the early arrivals seated and started on the initial task. Let the students know that if they complete the task, they can raise their hand and wait for you to give them something else to do. Decide in advance whether you will give these students other tasks to do quietly at their seats, chat with them in small groups, or have them assist you with last-minute classroom tasks. You may want to ask other teachers what they do to keep students occupied during a lengthy waiting period before the official beginning of the school day.

 Get students' attention as soon as the bell rings.

Use your attention signal to get students to focus on you (for example, raise your hand and say, "Class, your attention please"—see Chapter 2, Task 3). Even though students do not yet know your signal, it is likely to be effective because students will be working quietly at their seats. If students look at you, thank them for their attention and explain that regardless of whether they completed the task, they should put their pencils down and pay attention to you. If students fail to give you their attention, repeat the signal, but only one time. Wait with your hand up until everyone is quiet and looking at you. Even if this takes several minutes (it probably won't), simply maintain the visual aspect of the signal and wait quietly. Resist the urge to shout at the students to get their attention. If you start shouting for students' attention at the beginning of the year, you are likely to be shouting at them every day from then on.

 Communicate the essential classroom information in the first ten minutes.

Once you have the full attention of all students, introduce yourself and tell the students one or two personal or interesting things about yourself. Do not go into great detail. Then describe your long-range goals for the year, both academically and behaviorally.

Thank you for giving me your attention. Please put your pencils down for now; you will be able to complete the questions later in the period. My name is Mr. Younce (write it on the board). I will be your teacher this year. Over the year we will get to know each other better. For now I just want to tell you a couple of things about myself. I have two children of my own. They are both older than you—my daughter is 13 and my son is 17. My hobby is bicycling, and I sometimes bike as many as 100 miles in a day. We will have a chance to learn more about each other as the year goes on.

Next, explain to students what your Guidelines for Success and classroom rules are. As you share this information, involve the students in age-appropriate ways.

Raise your hand if you have an idea about why I might have a rule that says "Keep hands and feet and objects to yourself."

At the conclusion of the first ten minutes, students should have a preliminary sense of who you are, what will be expected of them, and what they will learn. Do not spend more than ten minutes on this orientation. If you talk too much or provide too many details, students may get overwhelmed or tune you out.

 ### Teach your attention signal.

Demonstrate the signal you will be using to get students' attention and tell them why the signal is important.

I appreciate how well all of you are keeping your attention on me while I am speaking. During class there will be times when I need you to stop what you are doing and look at and listen to me. At those times, I will say, "Class, your attention please," while I make this big circular motion with my arm. Then I will hold my hand in the air. When you hear me say those words or see me make that motion, stop whatever you are doing, stop talking or walking, look at me, and raise your own hand. When you raise your hand, it helps get the attention of other students who may not have seen or heard my signal.

> **"**
> *If you talk too much or provide too many details, students may get overwhelmed or tune you out.*
> **"**

Stopping immediately when I give that signal is important. There will be many times when we need to start an activity together. Even if everyone is doing something different, like working at your seats or in the learning centers, or sharpening a pencil, I can give the signal and everyone will be quiet and paying attention within five seconds. Then we can all be together for the next activity. I'm going to show you my signal one more time and show you how long five seconds is. This is how quickly I expect the whole class to be quiet and looking at me.

Demonstrate the signal and count the five seconds.

Orient students to the posted Day One Schedule and begin using the three-step process for communicating your expectations.

Start by giving students a clear idea of what the day or class period is going to be like. For students in second grade and higher, point out the schedule you posted for the day or class period. Then, for each activity, use the three-step process for communicating expectations. This cycle, which was introduced in Chapter 4, is summarized in Figure 5.4 and explained below.

Figure 5.4 *Three-Step Process for Communicating Expectations*

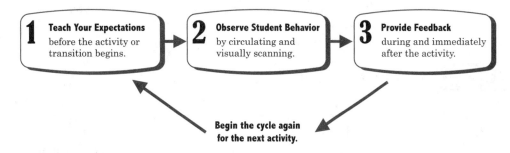

STEP 1   Teach your expectations.

The first step in this process is teaching students what your expectations are. Just before students engage in any activity or transition, use the lessons you have developed (see Chapter 4, Task 3) to prepare students to exhibit the proper behavior during that activity or transition. It's important to note that you should teach your lesson for each particular activity or transition immediately before the activity or transition occurs. You do not want to teach the expectations for all (or even several) activities or transitions at one time.

Be prepared to spend as much time as necessary at the beginning of an activity or transition to ensure that students understand what is expected of them. If the lesson you have prepared involves modeling or practicing a behavior, you need to allow for more time than if you simply describe your expectations to students.

For example, say you have scheduled a 15-minute teacher-directed instructional period. It is possible that, on the first day, five to seven of those 15 minutes will be spent explaining and modeling your expectations for student behavior during that activity. In other words, you should be prepared to spend anywhere from 20 to 50 percent of the time scheduled for a given activity on teaching your expectations for that activity during the first day(s) of school. If you think it likely that students will exhibit a particular misbehavior during the activity, you can precorrect and prompt desired behavior during the first week or so of school to minimize problem behaviors

(Colvin et al., 1993; Darch & Kame'enui, 2004). Correct the error before it happens by explaining the potential problem and then reclarifying the positive expectation.

Some of you may feel that you do not have enough time to teach expectations because there is so much academic content to cover. However, taking the time to thoroughly teach your expectations makes such a positive difference in student behavior that you actually save time in the long run—there will be fewer disruptions and better on-task behavior for the rest of the year (Sugai & Horner, 2002). As a result, students will likely learn more. An established relation exists between high rates of student problem behavior and low rates of student learning (Brophy & Good, 1986; Martella et al., 2003; Sutherland & Wehby, 2001).

> *You actually save time in the long run—there will be fewer disruptions and better on-task behavior for the rest of the year.*

STEP 2   Observe student behavior.

The only way to know how well students are meeting your behavioral expectations for classroom activities and transitions is for you to observe their behavior in some way—the second step in the three-step process for effectively communicating expectations. Two of the most useful and efficient ways to observe student behavior during an activity or transition are to circulate among students and to visually scan all parts of the classroom (Colvin et al., 1997; DePry & Sugai, 2002; Gettinger & Ball, 2008; Pedota, 2007; Schuldheisz & van der Mars, 2001; Shores et al., 1993).

Circulating and scanning are two basic (but absolutely essential) strategies that allow you to know exactly what is going on at all times. You can use the information you gain from observing your class to help you make sound decisions about the type and frequency of feedback you should provide to students about their behavior. Circulating has an additional benefit in that your physical presence tends to reduce student misbehavior (Evertson, 1989)—it's human nature. Just as most drivers are more likely to adhere to the speed limit when a police officer is present, so too are students more likely to follow classroom rules and procedures when the teacher is physically close to them.

While circulating, frequently look around at other parts of the classroom. This is called scanning. Also scan frequently during those times you cannot circulate, such as when you are helping an individual student or working with a small group. Chapter 6, Task 1, provides further explanations of and suggestions for the strategies of circulating and scanning.

Observing is an important component of communicating your expectations and is a critical tool regardless of the type of classroom structure your students need.

You have to know what is going on in your classroom. A classroom that needs high structure requires monitoring at all times. In fact, a line you sometimes hear from an experienced teacher with a class that needs high structure is, "This class is so tough you can't take your eyes off them for a second." This is a teacher who understands that continuous monitoring is absolutely essential with high-needs students.

STEP 3 Give students feedback on their implementation of expectations.

The third step in the process of effectively communicating your behavioral expectations involves giving students (individually and as a class) clear feedback about their behavior. Both during and after each activity or transition, give students information about the degree to which they are behaving (and have behaved) as expected. Provide positive feedback in the form of age-appropriate praise when students are meeting or have met your expectations. Provide corrective feedback—calmly, immediately, and consistently—when they are not meeting or have not met your expectations (Babkie, 2006; Emmer & Evertson, 1980; Greenwood et al., 1974; Mayer, 1995; Sugai & Tindal, 1993; Trussell, 2008). Positive feedback serves several vital functions—it gives students specific information about what they are doing correctly, and it gives them adult attention when they are behaving responsibly (Alberto & Troutman, 2006; Lewis & Sugai, 1999; Trussell, 2008). In addition, positive feedback serves as a prompt for misbehaving students and students who may be on the verge of misbehaving. Specific positive feedback to one or a few students provides a reminder to the class of the appropriate expected behavior.

Corrective feedback serves two vital functions—it lets students know that you are observing their behavior, and it communicates that you are serious and will be consistent about your expectations for student behavior (Barbetta et al., 2005).

PROVIDING FEEDBACK DURING AN ACTIVITY OR TRANSITION

As you observe students during an activity or transition, you are likely to notice examples of students who are meeting your expectations as well as examples of students who are not meeting your expectations. Both represent opportunities for you to continue to teach students how to meet your behavioral expectations by giving them positive and corrective feedback.

POSITIVE FEEDBACK

Following are a few quick tips on providing effective positive feedback (Alberto & Troutman, 2006; Cooper et al., 2007; Martella et al., 1995; O'Leary & O'Leary, 1977; Shores et al., 1993; Walker et al., 2004). More detailed information is provided in Chapter 7.

Give feedback that is accurate. Do not provide positive feedback unless the individual (or class) has actually exhibited the responsible behavior. If you tell a student that he has been responsible when he has not, you ruin your credibility and lead students to think (justifiably) that your positive feedback means nothing.

Give feedback that is specific and descriptive. Tell the student or the group exactly what they are doing that is responsible and important. "Alex, Maria, Travis, you are keeping your attention focused on your work. That is a very important part of being successful in this class." Avoid a rote phrase like, "Good job."

Give feedback that is contingent. Positive feedback provides useful information on important behaviors—that is, it is not simply a mindless compliment. For example, an experienced driver who receives a "Great right turn" compliment will probably be insulted. On the other hand, if this is the first time the driver has ever been behind the wheel, receiving a compliment like, "Great right turn—you signaled and checked your blind spot," is probably useful information. Inform students how the positive behaviors they are demonstrating will contribute to their success and the success of the class. Also, praise students for demonstrating behaviors that are new or difficult.

Give feedback that is age-appropriate. Feedback for a kindergarten student should be presented differently than feedback for an eighth grader. With older students, it is more appropriate to focus on advanced behaviors, and it is important to present the feedback without embarrassing the student. If feedback is presented too publicly or enthusiastically, your efforts to encourage good behavior may backfire—the student may do anything to avoid getting any more embarrassing praise. When giving praise to older students, use a quiet voice, be brief, be somewhat businesslike, and avoid pausing and looking at the student for a response after you praise.

Give positive feedback immediately. Immediacy is important because students need to know when they are doing something correctly. In addition, students who are starved for attention may start demanding attention through misbehavior if they get none for meeting expectations—they may feel that attention for behaving badly is better than none at all. Positive feedback is most effective when it occurs very soon after the behavior you are trying to encourage. With primary students in particular, waiting until later to give the feedback will not help to solidify the desired behaviors. By the time you praise them, the students will have forgotten exactly what it was they did.

CHAPTER 5 TASKS

Give positive feedback in a manner that fits your style. The specific manner in which you give positive feedback does not matter—what is important is that you are specific and sincere. Thus, if you are a bubbly, happy person, your positive feedback should take that form. On the other hand, if you are a more serious and businesslike person, your positive feedback should be given in a more serious, businesslike manner.

CORRECTIVE FEEDBACK

When students (one or more) exhibit behavior that does not meet your expectations for the activity, you must correct the inappropriate behavior. To give the most effective correction, consider each instance when a student does not meet expectations as an instructional opportunity (Alberto & Troutman, 2006; Barbetta et al., 2005; Colvin et al., 1993; Cooper et al., 2007; Kerr & Nelson, 2002; Rhode et al., 1992; Scheuermann & Hall, 2008; Simonsen et al., 2008). That is, consider the students' behavioral errors to be similar to errors they might make in math. Most math errors are a function of students not fully understanding a particular concept or all of the steps in a particular process. Effectively correcting those errors involves re-teaching the concept or steps. If students fail to meet your behavioral expectations, ask yourself, "Is it possible students did not understand what the expectations were? Is it possible they did not know how to meet the expectations?" If the answer to either of those questions is yes, you need to re-teach your expectations or how students can meet them (or both). If the answer is no, you need to provide corrective feedback.

> "Consider each instance when a student does not meet expectations as an instructional opportunity."

These two questions are especially important at the primary level, particularly with academically challenged, language delayed, and ELL students. It's difficult to put some rules or expectations into very simple words. Sometimes a picture is worth a thousand words! The primary icons in Appendix D may be especially helpful to primary-level teachers. Following are a few quick tips on providing effective corrective feedback. More detailed information on using corrective feedback is provided in Chapters 3 and 9.

Correct the misbehavior immediately. When students are not meeting behavioral expectations, let them know. Do not ignore the misbehavior and do not wait until the end of the activity, transition, or event to address it. Ignoring can be an effective strategy for responding to chronic misbehavior designed to elicit attention, but when you are trying to establish your expectations at the beginning of the year, students may interpret ignoring to mean, "She was not really serious about how she expects us to behave."

Correct the misbehavior calmly. Correcting calmly shows students that you are serious and have high expectations, but also that you are completely in control and will not be rattled by their misbehavior. Emotional corrections, on the other hand, are more likely to give power to the misbehavior and put you in a position of seeming somewhat out of control. Students may think, "When I do this, look how frustrated and angry I can make the teacher." Be calmly assertive, but not strident, emotional, or aggressive.

Correct misbehavior consistently. For the first several days of instruction, correct most misbehavior with mild verbal reprimands that focus on the behavior, not the person. Simply restate what the students should be doing at the time. Be direct. Communicate that you are firm and that the expectations are nonnegotiable. Saying something like, "Tina and Adam, you should be working quietly on your lab notebooks at this time," is more appropriate and effective than saying, "Tina and Adam, you are so immature. I should not have to remind you that this is a work period, not a time to socialize."

If it becomes necessary because of the severity or frequency of a misbehavior to use a prearranged corrective consequence, calmly state the misbehavior and the corrective consequence—and then follow through.

PROVIDING FEEDBACK AT THE END OF AN ACTIVITY, TRANSITION, OR EVENT

Early in the year, you should plan to end each activity or transition by giving students feedback about how well they collectively met your CHAMPS expectations. When an activity or transition is finished but before the next activity or transition begins, let the group know whether their behavior was appropriate. Did they behave as expected (the way they should for the rest of the year)? Or do they need to improve their behavior the next time that particular activity or transition occurs? When an activity goes perfectly, you have a wonderful opportunity to reinforce the class and begin establishing a sense of group pride.

> *Class, this work period went exactly the way a lab activity of this type should go. Everyone followed safe lab procedures. Conversations at the lab stations were quiet, and all the talking I heard as I was going around was focused on the lab activity. This is going to be a great class.*

If an activity does not go well, describe the specific behaviors that need to be different (without singling out individuals) and set a goal for the next time you have that activity.

> *Class, during the teacher-directed portion of the math lesson that we just completed, there were several times I had to remind people to raise their hand if they had something to say. Please remember that whenever anyone is presenting*

CHAPTER 5 TASKS

to the class, whether it is me or a student, there should be no side conversations. Later this afternoon we will be having a science lesson. During the time I am demonstrating an experiment, remember—no side conversations and keep your attention focused entirely on the person who is speaking.

Avoid statements such as, "Almost everyone remembered the expectation about talking only if you raise your hand and I call on you." A statement of this type is not positive feedback; it serves only to make students wonder, "Which students did not meet the expectations?"

Conclude the day or class period by orienting students to your end-of-day procedures (see Chapter 2, Task 4).

> " Put closure on this day in such a way that the students leave your classroom feeling comfortable and eager to return. "

On the first day of school, allow plenty of time for this activity. Remember that you may have to take time to help students identify their bus, review materials they need to bring the next day, and make sure they have any and all important papers to take home. You should put closure on this day in such a way that the students leave your classroom feeling comfortable and eager to return. They should leave with the sense that you are a teacher who will demand they do their best but is also concerned and interested in each of them as individuals.

The strategies presented in this task have been included because they will help you have a smooth first day of school, leading you and your class into a productive and rewarding school year. Remember, the information you present and the atmosphere you establish on Day One yields valuable dividends throughout the school year.

Task 4: Implement Your Plan on Days 2 Through 20 (The First Four Weeks)

During the first month of school, continue to implement the three-step process for communicating expectations, and take the time to verify that students understand what is expected of them.

No matter how clearly and carefully you communicate your CHAMPS expectations on the first day of school, few students will know exactly how they are supposed to behave after just one day. Students will truly learn your expectations only when you continue the three-step communication process for two or three weeks—begin each activity and transition with a lesson on the expectations, observe student performance of the behaviors during the activity or transition, and give positive and corrective feedback during and after the activity or transition to both individuals and the class as a whole.

If you are a middle school teacher, remember that your students will be hearing about expectations from four to six other teachers. They are likely to get tired of hearing about expectations, but they are also likely to be confused about details such as which teachers let them talk during independent work and which teachers do not. As you continue to present lessons on your CHAMPS expectations, be sure to vary the format of the lessons.

As the first month of school progresses, the lessons should become increasingly brief, and they should focus mainly on any specific expectations that have been problematic (students talking when the teacher is presenting, for example). You can also use the lesson time to set goals for student behavior. When students seem to fully understand and remember the expectation for an activity or transition, you can start to fade the lessons. For instance, you might introduce an activity by letting students know that because they have been so responsible, you do not need to review the expectation.

> *Class, next we have a 20-minute work period for you to get going on the math assignment. Since this type of work period has gone so well, I don't even need to review the expectations. Get started working on the assignment that is written on the board.*

Another option is to consider using an alternating pattern of lessons, or teaching different expectations on different days. For example, during a math lesson on Monday, you present CHAMPS lessons on the teacher-directed and cooperative group portions of the lesson, but not on the independent work period. On Tuesday, you present a brief CHAMPS lesson on independent work and cooperative group activities, but not on teacher-directed instruction. Whenever a particular activity or transition has not gone as smoothly as you would like, plan to use the three-step process to reassert your expectations. If more than three students have not been meeting the expectations, plan on re-teaching your expectations to the entire class. If only one, two, or three students are having problems, focus the re-teaching process on those individuals.

By gradually reducing the length and frequency of your CHAMPS lessons and by shifting your focus to individuals or small groups who may need more review than others, you gain more time for instruction. Before you cease all CHAMPS lessons for any given activity or transition, however, you should verify whether or not students fully understand your expectations for that activity or transition. The final part of this task provides suggestions for administering a quiz and conducting student interviews to determine the degree to which students understand your expectations.

> *If more than three students have not been meeting the expectations, plan on re-teaching your expectations to the entire class.*

The second step in the communication cycle for expectations—observing student behavior—should be maintained at a very high level. If a class requires only a low-structure management plan, you can get by with less direct monitoring than if the class needs medium or high structure. Whatever the degree of structure your students need, however, plan on continuing to circulate and visually scan during all activities and transitions throughout the year.

During the first several days of instruction, give students very frequent feedback on how they are (or are not) meeting your expectations—the third step in the communication process. In fact, you can consider feedback an ongoing monologue. With low-structure classes, you can begin to reduce the amount of positive feedback given to the class and to individual students as soon as any given activity or transition has gone well for several consecutive days. In addition, corrective feedback can be reduced to simply stating the name of a student who is not meeting your expectation. For example, if two students are talking when they should be listening to a lesson, you may be able to correct the error by saying the names of the two students, making brief eye contact, and getting on with your lesson. On the other hand, if your class needs medium or high structure, you should probably keep the frequency of positive feedback and the descriptive clarity of corrective feedback at a very high level for a long time—at least the entire first month of school.

EXAMPLES OF THE THREE-STEP COMMUNICATIONS CYCLE

Following are explanations of how you might implement the three-step process for communicating expectations during the first month of school with three different sets of expectations:

1. Expectations for student behavior in response to your attention signal

2. Expectations for student behavior during independent work periods when you are otherwise occupied

3. Expectations for student behavior when they are with specialists.

The basic processes described can be used as is, or modified as appropriate, for communicating any and all of your expectations.

Communicate expectations for student behavior in response to your attention signal.

For the first several days of school, frequently review with students your attention signal and your expectations for student behavior when you give the signal. Whenever you give the signal, check your watch or the clock. If the students respond with silence, stillness, and attention in less than five seconds (and every student raised his or her hand), thank them for their cooperation.

> *Class, that took only four seconds. Some of you who were moving toward the back of the room stopped, turned around, and looked at me immediately. That was exactly the way to respond to this signal. The reason I need your attention is to let you know that . . .*

If the students do not respond appropriately within five seconds, do not repeat the signal and do not say anything. Simply wait with your hand raised, and make it obvious that you are looking at the time. When the class is finally silent, provide corrective feedback.

> *Class, some students immediately stopped what they were doing and raised their hand. However, it took 18 seconds from the time I gave the signal until everyone stopped talking and looked at me. That is too long. By continuing to talk, you were being disrespectful to the students who gave me attention immediately because you wasted their time. Next time I give this signal, be respectful of your classmates and me. Stop what you are doing immediately. Now, the reason I need your attention is to let you know that . . .*

For several days, provide frequent positive feedback to students for following the signal. If students are taking too long to respond to the signal, provide additional instruction and practice opportunities. If, after a few days of this kind of positive and corrective feedback, students are still not responding quickly enough to your signal, inform the class that you are going to start implementing a consequence for not paying attention to the signal. If only two to four students are not responding to the signal, assign those individuals time owed off recess (for elementary level) or after class (for middle school). If more than four students are not responding to the signal, have the entire class owe time. Make the time owed equal to the number of seconds wasted (the number of seconds beyond five after you gave the signal).

For example, if it takes the class 18 seconds to be fully compliant, they owe 13 seconds. Then, when it is time for recess or a break between classes, the entire class must wait quietly for 13 seconds. This procedure usually quickly generates enough peer pressure that students start responding to the attention signal within the five-second limit.

CHAPTER 5 TASKS

| 1 • Summarize Your Plan | 2 • Make Final Preparations for Day 1 | 3 • Implement Your Plan on Day 1 |

For a class that is having a great deal of difficulty responding to the signal, you might consider adding a positive component. For example, you could let the class know that each time all students respond appropriately to the signal within the five-second time period, the class earns a point. When they earn 10 points, the class gets five extra minutes of recess.

 Communicate expectations for student behavior during independent work times when the teacher is otherwise engaged.

> *Working independently tends to be especially hard for young students when their teacher is engaged in another activity.*

Teaching students how to behave responsibly during independent work times can be difficult. Working independently tends to be especially hard for young students when their teacher is engaged in another activity, such as teaching a small reading group. If you have a teaching assistant, one solution is to have this person supervise students who are doing seatwork and working at learning centers while you are with a small group. If this is a possibility, you need to prepare the instructional assistant and the students. During the first few days of school, have your assistant watch as you supervise the whole class for the first ten minutes of an independent work period. Make a point of demonstrating how you answer questions, reinforce on-task behavior, and correct misbehavior. For the remainder of the work period, switch roles—have the assistant supervise students as you observe and give feedback to her. After a few days, you can start the small group work and have the assistant supervise the other students for the entire period. When you have a system like this, be sure to schedule time (at least once per week) for you and your assistant to discuss how things are going during these independent work periods. Encourage her to ask questions and raise concerns. "I am not quite sure how to respond to Barry. I think he is depending too much on my help. What do you think I should do?"

If you do not have an assistant to supervise students, you will have to teach your students how to function without direct supervision. Plan on spending at least three days rehearsing the scenario with students.

> *Class, each day at this time, I will be working with a group of students over here. Most of you will be at your seats working on the papers that I will give you. Every one of you has the papers we just went over, and you know what you are going to be working on. Today, I will be walking around and helping you if you need it. I will be commenting about how well you are working. Usually, I will not be able to do this because I'll be busy with the students in the small group, but today . . .*

Make a point of praising students frequently for keeping their attention focused on their work.

After three days of rehearsal, spend another two to four days training students how to implement the strategy of "Finish what you know, then come back to anything you are not sure of." During these work periods, modify the rehearsal so that students cannot get help from you (even though you are available). If a student asks for help, give a reminder about the strategy. "Todd, you need to ask someone at your table for help. Remember that on most days I'll be working over in the reading circle." Frequently praise students for keeping their attention on their work and for getting their questions answered without involving you.

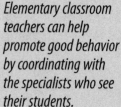

Elementary classroom teachers can help promote good behavior by coordinating with the specialists who see their students.

After a few days of this sort of rehearsal, you should be ready to begin conducting your small groups. When you first start working with small groups, you may want to modify your schedule just a bit. That is, if you will typically work with each group for 30 minutes, consider working with them for only 15 minutes initially and spending the remaining 15 minutes circulating among students working independently to give positive and corrective feedback. If you group students homogeneously by ability, you can probably work with your lowest group for the full 30 minutes from the beginning. These are the students who are likely to have the greatest difficulty staying on task. The students working independently while you are working with the lowest group may very well be academically able and mature enough to function independently for the full 30 minutes.

 Communicate expectations for behavior when students are with specialists.

Specialists in areas such as media, PE, computers, and music may be in a unique and difficult position in terms of teaching their behavioral expectations. In many cases, these specialists see all the students in a school, but only for one or two 20- to 30-minute period(s) per week. While a classroom teacher might be able to teach his expectations for math class every day for a week, a specialist needs five weeks for that same amount of teaching time. Furthermore, because students see the specialist only once or twice a week, they are more likely to forget many of this teacher's expectations from the first meeting to the second. Elementary classroom teachers can help promote good behavior by coordinating with the specialists who see their students. Following are some general suggestions for achieving efficient and effective coordination.

- Each specialist should provide all classroom teachers with a written explanation of how students should enter her setting (the gym or the computer room, for example) and a written list of two or three important rules for her class. To make this easy for the general education teachers, the specialists could each have their expectations on a different-colored (e.g., PE=red, media=blue, etc.), laminated 4" x 6" card. These can all be held together with a metal ring or spiral binding so the teacher does not have to keep track of loose cards.

- Immediately before students go to a particular specialist, the classroom teacher should tell the class where they are going and the name of that teacher. The classroom teacher should also go over the written expectations and make it very clear that he expects students to behave responsibly.

---

for example

Before the class goes to PE, the classroom teacher might prepare the class as follows:

Class Teacher: Class, the next thing we are going to do today is go to the gym for Physical Education class. The PE teacher this year is Ms. Simonson. When we go to the gym, we will go quietly in lines, just the way we go to the cafeteria. When we get to the gym, you need to stay in your lines and wait outside the gym with me until Ms. Simonson comes to tell you what you should do and where you should go. Ms. Simonson will go over her rules for safe and responsible gym behavior with you, but she asked me to let you know that her two most important rules are:

- Keep hands, feet, and objects to yourself.
- Freeze and listen for directions when you hear her blow the whistle.

During PE, Ms. Simonson is the teacher. I fully expect you to give her the same level of respect and cooperation you demonstrate in the classroom. Now I'll excuse you by tables to line up and wait quietly at the door. Everyone at Table 4 is waiting quietly. You may line up. Table . . .

- There should be a formal and public transfer of authority from the classroom teacher to the specialist. That is, students should see and hear an interaction between the classroom teacher and the specialist that sounds something like the following example:

- When the time with the specialist is over, the specialist should publicly hand authority back over to the classroom teacher and inform the teacher of how well the class did.

These procedures should be implemented for at least the first four times the students go to a particular specialist. Thus, if students see the specialist twice a week, do this for a minimum of two weeks. If they see the specialist once a week, do it for a minimum of four weeks.

 Verify that students understand the behaviors that are expected from them.

During the second or third week of school, take some time to systematically determine whether your students really understand your expectations for their behavior. This information will help you decide whether you need to continue actively teaching your CHAMPS expectations or eliminate the lessons because students have mastered the content. If most of your students are able to accurately answer specific

A written quiz is a relatively simple way to get information from all students on their knowledge of your expectations.

and detailed questions verbally or on paper about your CHAMPS expectations, you can rapidly fade the process of teaching and reviewing the expectations. However, if a significant percentage of students cannot answer your questions, or cannot answer them correctly, you should continue to conduct CHAMPS lessons on a reasonably regular basis.

Making the effort to determine students' understanding of your expectations by giving a quiz or conducting interviews (or both) does more than provide you with information on whether your students fully understand the expectations. By taking the time to give quizzes or conduct interviews, you further communicate to students the importance you place on their knowledge of the CHAMPS expectations. Two main procedures for verifying students' understanding (or lack of understanding) of expectations are:

- Give all students a short written quiz.

- Conduct one-on-one interviews with a few individual students.

You should use at least one of these procedures—and consider using both. On the following pages are directions and materials for giving a quiz and for conducting interviews on CHAMPS expectations.

GIVING A QUIZ

A written quiz is a relatively simple way to get information from all students in your class or classes on their knowledge of your expectations. A major advantage of the quiz (as opposed to individual interviews with a few students) is that you can get information from all students in a relatively short period of time. The major disadvantage is that some of the students who do poorly on the quiz may actually know the expectations perfectly well but have trouble with reading or writing. For this reason, a quiz is probably not suitable for grades 2 and lower or for ELL students who are just beginning to learn English.

DIRECTIONS

1. **Decide on the format of the quiz.**

    The format of the quiz may be true/false, multiple choice, fill in the blank, short essay, or some mix of these formats. Base your decision on both the type of format you typically use for academic purposes (a format your students are familiar with) and on the type of format you think will yield the most useful information.

2. **Determine the specific content of the quiz.**

    Choose one or two activities and one or two transitions to be the focus of your quiz. You may get the most useful information by targeting those activities and transitions that have the most complex expectations and those that seem to be giving students the most difficulty. Examine your written CHAMPS worksheets (see Chapter 4) for details to ask students about. Your questions should target issues such as whether students can talk during the activity or transition, what kind of movement (if any) is allowed, and so on. Keep the quiz fairly short so that students can complete it in approximately ten minutes.

3. **Prepare your students to take the quiz.**

    Explain to the students that the quiz will help you know whether the class understands some of your important expectations. Make sure they know they are not being graded, but the more errors there are on the quiz, the greater the likelihood that you will provide additional practice and explanation of expectations for student behavior.

Figure 5.5 is a sample quiz on expectations that might be used in a fifth-grade classroom.

INTERVIEWING STUDENTS

Student interviews can provide more detailed and slightly more reliable information than a written quiz. If, during an interview, you are unsure from a student's answer whether she really understands a particular expectation, you can ask additional questions. The interview format also allows students who struggle with written tests to provide more accurate information about what they really know. The major disadvantage of interviews is that they are more time consuming—you can only do one interview at a time. Because of the time issue, you should probably interview just a representative sample of about six students.

DIRECTIONS

1. **Identify two major classroom activities and two major transitions that occur daily (or at least three times per week) in your classroom.**

    Choose activities and transitions that are complex or seem to be particularly troublesome for students. Classroom activities might include, for example, opening activities, teacher-directed instruction (whole class and small group), independent seatwork, class discussions, cooperative groups, and work in learning centers or lab stations. Transitions might include coming into the room at the beginning of the day or period, handing in materials,

Figure 5.5 *Sample Quiz on Expectations*

SAMPLE QUIZ ON EXPECTATIONS

Name _Brandi C_   Date _10/2_

Circle the letter for the best answer to each of the questions below.

1. **When you enter the classroom first thing in the morning . . .**
   a. you should be completely silent from the moment you enter the room.
   b. you can talk quietly to other students about schoolwork, but must be silent when you get to your seat.
   c. you can talk quietly about anything, but when the bell rings you should be in your seat and can talk only about the challenge problem on the overhead projector.
   d. you can talk loudly about anything, and when the bell rings you should get to your seat within two minutes and then be quiet.

2. **In Room 9, you can use the pencil sharpener . . .**
   a. before and after class only.
   b. before and after class and during independent work periods.
   c. any time you need to.
   d. only with teacher permission.

3. **When the teacher gives the attention signal—"Class, your attention please"—you should . . .**
   a. be silent with eyes on the teacher within five seconds.
   b. be silent with eyes on the teacher within ten seconds.
   c. be silent with eyes on the teacher within 25 seconds.
   d. loudly tell other students to be quiet and pay attention to the teacher.

4. **During the time the teacher is presenting lessons and speaking to the class, you should . . .**
   a. talk quietly to someone near you and get out of your seat only to sharpen your pencil.
   b. talk quietly to someone near you and stay in your seat.
   c. talk only if the teacher calls on you and get out of your seat only if you need a drink of water or supplies.
   d. talk only if the teacher calls on you and stay in your seat (unless you have been given permission to get up).

5. **Active participation in class when the teacher is presenting lessons should look and sound a certain way. Circle any of the items that describe active participation. You should have six items circled when you are done with this question.**
   a. Sit up straight or lean forward.
   b. Raise your hand if you have something to say.
   c. Answer questions when the teacher calls on you.
   d. Write notes to your friends.
   e. Write notes that will help you study for tests.
   f. Tell people who are talking that they need to be quiet and listen.
   g. Have toys and other things on your desk that will entertain you during the lesson.
   h. Keep your eyes on the person speaking or on the class notes you are writing (notes to study for the test).
   i. Let your mind wander wherever it wishes to go.
   j. Talk while the teacher is talking.
   k. Speak and act respectfully toward the teacher and other students.

moving to and from small group work, going to the library, cleaning up the classroom, getting books out and open to a particular page, and getting ready for dismissal.

2. **Develop interview questions that address specific aspects of the CHAMPS expectations for the two classroom activities and two transitions that you have selected.**

You may wish to use Reproducible Form 5.2, found on the CD, to organize your interviews. A completed sample of this reproducible with one teacher's interview questions appears on the next page. As suggested for the quiz items, base your questions on the issues covered in the CHAMPS worksheets that you completed in Chapter 4.

3. **Identify a representative sample of students.**

Choose about six students to interview. Select three students who are academically average or higher and three who are academically lower or have demonstrated some misbehavior.

4. **Decide on a time and format for conducting the interviews.**

Identify a time when you will be free to conduct the interviews. If you cannot be completely free of supervising your class, plan to conduct the interviews while the class is doing independent work or working in cooperative groups. Because the interviews will take about five minutes per student, it may take more than one day to complete them. You may wish to work with a colleague and interview each other's students.

> *Because the interviews will take about five minutes per student, it may take more than one day to complete them.*

5. **Prepare students for the interviews.**

The whole class: Describe what you will be doing and why. Emphasize that no one is in trouble—rather, you want to see how clear you have been in communicating what students need to do to be successful. Let them know that you would like to be able to meet with all the students to talk about this, but because of time constraints, you can meet with only a few.

The individual students you are interviewing: Identify the activity or transition and then proceed with your questions.

Each day during math, I begin the lesson by presenting information on the overhead projector. I'm going to ask you some questions about what you and the other students should be doing during that time. Imagine we had a new student in class—what you would tell her about how we do things? For example, what should a student do when he has a question? What should a student do . . .

Reproducible 5.2 *Student Interview*

Print from CD

CHAMPS

sample

≫ no. 5.2

STUDENT INTERVIEW

Student _____ Period _____ Date _____

Classroom Activity _Teacher-directed work_

Questions	Student Responses
• Can you talk to another student while I am teaching? • What should you do if you have a question or don't understand something? • When I say, "Work on the problem," what should you do? • Can you get out of your seat for any reason? • How do you show that you are actively participating in the lesson?	

Classroom Activity _Independent seatwork in math_

Questions	Student Responses
• Can you talk to another student while you are working? About what? How loud a voice? • What should you do if you need help? • Can you get out of your seat for any reason? • How do you show that you are actively participating in this part of the lesson?	

Transition _Beginning class, before and after bell_

Questions	Student Responses
• What should you do when you come into the room and are waiting for the bell to ring? • Where should you be when the bell rings? • While we are going through calendar, sharing, etc.: -can you get out of your seat? -can you talk to people at your table? • What should you do if you want to say something to the class?	

Transition _Getting book out and open_

Questions	Student Responses
• When I say get your math book out and open, how do you know which page? • What should you do if you ever do not have your book? • How long should it take for everyone to have books open and ready? • Is it OK to talk to your neighbor as you are finding the page? Why not?	

Task 5: Prepare Your Students for Special Circumstances

Be prepared to teach your CHAMPS expectations to any new students who enter your class. Also be prepared to develop and teach all students your expectations for any unique events that may occur.

We have emphasized the importance of defining and teaching your expectations, observing student performance, and giving students feedback on your expectations for their behavior. In addition to the information presented thus far, you should address two other situations involving behavioral expectations:

- Students may enter your class after you have taught your expectations (students who enter your class after the first few weeks of school).

- Students may participate in unique events such as field trips, assemblies, and having a classroom guest speaker.

TEACHING EXPECTATIONS TO NEW STUDENTS

The first two weeks of school are the most important time for teaching behavioral expectations and classroom routines. However, most of you will experience some degree of flux in your student population over the course of the year. That is, you will have at least one student leave and at least one new student enter your class. Many

The more structured and well-managed your classroom is, the easier it will be for new students to learn expectations because the expectations will be consistently modeled by other students and reinforced by you. A student who enters a poorly managed class has more difficulty understanding the expectations because they are not clearly modeled or consistently enforced.

schools have such high student mobility rates that less than half of the students in a class at the beginning of the year are still there at the end of the year. When a new student enters your classroom, some form of orientation (similar to what you provide for all students during the first two weeks of school) will be essential to get the student off to a successful start. You should plan in advance how you will do this. In fact, the higher you expect your student mobility rate to be, the more prepared you need to be to teach your expectations to new students.

To help you develop a plan for teaching your expectations to new students, consider these four basic strategies that you can implement at a classroom level:

• Teach the New Student Individually

• Re-teach the Entire Class

• The Buddy System

• "Welcome to Our Class" Video

We have also included the description of a Newcomers Club, a schoolwide strategy for schools with high mobility—those likely to have several new students each week If you anticipate getting only one to three new students during the year, implementing the first two strategies is probably sufficient. On the other hand, if you are likely to have quite a few new students entering your class during the year, consider implementing at least three of the following strategies.

TEACH THE NEW STUDENT INDIVIDUALLY

The most common and basic method of orienting a new student to your class is to simply teach the new student your expectations yourself. For the first several days to a week, meet with the student for a couple of minutes immediately before each major activity and transition. Tell the student what will be happening and explain your CHAMPS behavioral expectations for that activity or transition. At the conclusion of the activity or transition, let the student know how he did and orient him to the next activity or transition.

> *The advantage of this approach is that it generates frequent contact between you and a new student.*

The advantage of this approach is that it generates frequent contact between you and a new student during the student's first week in class. The disadvantage is that it requires a great deal of your time. If you are likely to get only one to three new students during the year, pairing this approach with Re-teach the Entire Class is probably both reasonable and effective. However, if you have many new students during the year, it is impractical, and a disservice to the rest of the class, to take that much time with each new student.

RE-TEACH THE ENTIRE CLASS

If you have to orient a new student to your class, take the opportunity to go over the CHAMPS expectations for all activities and transitions with the entire class. For one day, immediately before each activity and each major transition, ask students to volunteer to share some information about expected behaviors and procedures with the new student. "Please raise your hand if you can tell Sandra one of the important expectations for independent work periods during math class." Call on students until all the important information has been reviewed. If students leave out something essential, add it yourself.

> *Having students present the information communicates that the expectations are shared by the class, not just the teacher.*

This procedure has several advantages. The new student gets important information, and the information is reviewed and reinforced for the other students. Having students present the information communicates that the expectations are shared by the class, not just by the teacher. Finally, taking a couple of minutes to do this before each activity and transition makes a statement that you believe that student knowledge of correct behavior is important enough that you will use class time to re-teach it.

The main disadvantage of re-teaching the entire class is that if you must do it more than once every four to six weeks, it takes too much class time. In addition, students may get tired of discussing the same expectations over and over. Therefore, if you re-teach for one new student and then get another new student two weeks later, do not repeat the procedure.

Another disadvantage is that when you use this procedure by itself, a new student gets only one day of orientation. You will not want to take the entire class's time to orient a new student for more than one day, but the typical class has so many expectations and routines that the student is not likely to remember all the details on the second day at a new school. So if you use this procedure, use one of the other procedures (Teach the New Student Individually or The Buddy System) as well.

THE BUDDY SYSTEM

With this procedure, you give individual class members the responsibility of orienting new students to the routines and procedures of the class.

> *Paul, this is Rico. Rico is a student who really understands and follows the procedures that will help you be successful in this class. Throughout the day (or class period), you two have permission to quietly talk—even at times when talking is usually not allowed. Paul, if you have a question about how we do things, you can ask me or quietly ask Rico. Rico, anytime during the next week that something is going on that may be new to Paul, please quietly explain what we are doing and why.*

CHAPTER 5 TASKS

| 1 • Summarize Your Plan | 2 • Make Final Preparations for Day 1 | 3 • Implement Your Plan on Day 1 |

If you plan to use this procedure and are likely to have a lot of new students during the year, take time in the second or third week of school to talk to the entire class about how you may call on them individually to help orient a new student. Be sure you don't always use the same student as the buddy—call on different students as the year progresses.

The advantage of this approach is that it takes pressure off you to spend class (instructional) time with a new student. In addition, it communicates your expectation and belief that your students fully understand and implement your expectations.

A possible disadvantage is that you won't have enough contact with a new student for that student to feel a real connection with you. If you use the Buddy System, make a point of frequently interacting with and getting to know any new student (checking on her work, asking how she is doing, seeing if she has any questions, and so on). The buddy concept also makes the class member who is orienting the new student feel very special—he or she becomes invested in the classroom rules.

"WELCOME TO OUR CLASS" VIDEO

If you anticipate a high rate of student mobility, it may be worth taking time to have your students develop an orientation video at the beginning of the year. The amount of time required to plan and direct this activity will vary depending on your own style and preferences. Some teachers may assign the task to a small group of students and give them only a broad outline of topics to cover. Other teachers may guide the entire process and involve class members only as actors to demonstrate procedures. If you think this might be a reasonable option for you, plan to produce the video in about the third week of school. By then, procedures and routines should be well established, and developing the video can help solidify and reinforce the important expectations for the class.

> *An advantage of this procedure is that it can help create a sense of class pride and unity.*

An advantage of this procedure is that it can help create a sense of class pride and unity—and it's also great fun to make and potentially very entertaining. New students can view the video at school (with a school counselor or a peer buddy) or take a video home to view it with their families. If your community has a significant number of families who speak a particular language other than English, see if you can get district personnel or a community volunteer to help you produce a version of your video in that language. A video can help families get a feel for your classroom rules and expectations and may serve to prevent miscommunication between school and home that may occur with written information, especially if the family is not literate or fluent in English.

The major disadvantage of an orientation video is that it can be time consuming to develop and, without monitoring and guidance, some students may get overly silly during the production process. Use your own judgment regarding the trade-off between time spent up front developing such a video and time saved later in welcoming and orienting new students.

NEWCOMERS CLUB (SCHOOLWIDE PLAN)

If your school has extremely high rates of student mobility, it may be worth proposing some form of orientation to the whole school. For example, at a large elementary school in California that gets between 3 and 20 new students every week, a highly skilled bilingual paraprofessional has been trained to run the Newcomers Club every morning. This paraprofessional (who has other responsibilities later in the day) spends the first two hours each morning with any new students and their families. When a new student and his family arrive, they are introduced to and greeted by the principal who, in turn, introduces them to this paraprofessional. They go to a classroom (decorated to be very bright and welcoming) that has been converted to serve as the Newcomers Club and Family Room.

> " The Newcomers Club has created an exceptionally inviting and relaxed introduction to the school. "

In this relaxed setting, the paraprofessional shows a video (in either English or Spanish) that greets and welcomes the student and his or her family. The paraprofessional then takes the student and his family on a walking tour of the school, including a brief visit to the classroom the student will go to later in the morning. After the tour, they go back to the Family Room to discuss expectations, play a couple of age-appropriate games, and resolve any questions the student and family may have. Both the student and the family are invited to come to the Family Room or to the principal with any questions or concerns that come up.

The Newcomers Club was very time consuming to develop initially. However, it has created an exceptionally inviting and relaxed introduction to the school. In schools with no designated welcoming personnel, a new student can feel as though she is being shuffled from person to person and just plopped into a new classroom! The teacher is still responsible for orienting the student to the classroom expectations and routines, but the overall responsibility for welcoming and orientation is taken care of at the schoolwide level.

In schools with a moderately high rate of student mobility (5 to 20 new students each month), a Newcomers Club might be run on a regular but less frequent basis (every other Thursday afternoon for an hour or more, for example). The school counselor or a well-trained paraprofessional can gather all students who have enrolled in the previous two weeks and spend time with them as a group, going over expectations, answering questions, touring the grounds, introducing them to the nurse, the custodian, the principal, and so on. The key to making this procedure work is that it be highly inviting and welcoming.

TEACHING EXPECTATIONS FOR UNIQUE EVENTS

In addition to knowing the behavioral expectations for major classroom activities and common transitions, students need to know how they are expected to behave during any unique events that occur, such as field trips. If you have not taught your class the expectations for a particular event, misbehavior may be likely—not because students are willfully disobedient, but because they do not have the knowledge and skills to behave in a manner that you consider responsible.

for example

Imagine taking your unprepared third-grade students to an assembly to hear a speaker. If your class is one of the first to arrive, students may have to wait five to ten minutes. Some students may start conversations with friends two or three rows away; others may get bored and start pushing and shoving each other. As the assembly begins, many of the students may continue their inappropriate behaviors. You try to get them to quiet down and listen to the speaker, but soon the situation feels out of control. Now imagine that one to two weeks before the assembly you defined and started teaching how you expected students to behave during the assembly. Students would then know that they are allowed to quietly converse only with someone no more than "a 12-inch voice" away and that they need to stop talking and pay attention once the principal walks to the microphone.

As soon as you know that your students will be participating in some special event that calls for new behavioral expectations, you need to start defining and then teaching your expectations.

Because each special event will be unique, at least in some ways, the first step should be to identify the specific types of situations students are likely to be engaged in during the event. You may need to do some advance research to find out about the nature of the event and the types of experiences students will encounter. Figure 5.6 on the next page shows the kind of event analyses you might come up with for two different events—an assembly and a field trip to a hydroelectric dam.

Once you identify the major situations for the special event, the next step is to use the CHAMPS acronym to define your behavioral expectations for each of those situations. Then start communicating your expectations to students. For each situation you have identified, teach students the CHAMPS expectations so that they know exactly what constitutes responsible behavior. Keep in mind that simply telling students your expectations is not as effective as modeling, role-playing, and discussion.

The greater the complexity of the event or the more problems that have been associated with that type of event, the more days you should rehearse the appropriate behavior for the event. For a simple situation—a guest speaker, for example—a brief orientation the day before and a short review immediately prior to the event is probably sufficient. However, if students had a problem the last time they were engaged in a similar event, plan on teaching and reviewing expectations for at least four or five consecutive days.

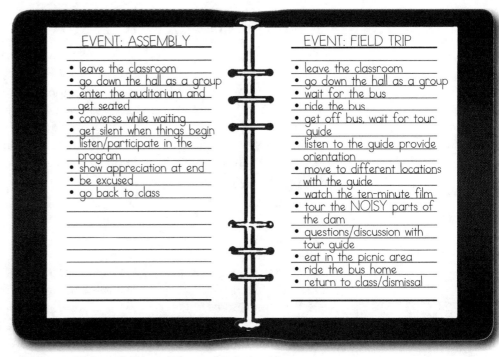

Figure 5.6   *Sample Special Events Analysis*

If the situation or your expectations are complex, if the event involves potential danger, or if there are many different components to the event (as in the field trip in Figure 5.6), you definitely should plan to teach your expectations for at least five days. Don't try to teach all your expectations every day; break them down so that each day you introduce a few of the expectations.

---

for example

Teaching expectations for an event like the field trip example in Figure 5.6 might be organized as follows:

Day 1: Take about ten minutes to discuss and practice the CHAMPS expectations for the following:
- Leaving the classroom
- Going down the hall as a group

- Waiting for the bus
- Riding the bus
- Getting off the bus and waiting for the tour guide

Day 2: Review content from the previous day and introduce expectations for:
- Being silent while the guide is providing orientation
- Moving to different locations with the guide
- Watching the ten-minute film

Day 3: Review the previous two lessons. Introduce and mentally prepare students for staying calm and keeping their voices down (no shouting) while:
- Touring the NOISY parts of the dam

Day 4: Review content covered in the three previous lessons and introduce expectations for:
- Asking questions and discussion with the tour guide
- Eating in the picnic area
- Riding the bus home
- Returning to class and dismissal

Day 5: Put all of the above information together and introduce the learning objectives for the event—that is, what you want students to learn from the trip.

Conclusion

This chapter offered suggestions for how you can implement your Classroom Management and Discipline Plan. The first month of school is an incredibly important time. It is essential to get students behaving responsibly right away because it can be very difficult to change negative behavior patterns later in the year.

The five tasks covered the final preparations you should make before school starts, what to do on the first day of school, procedures and considerations to deal with during the remainder of the first month, and preparations for special circumstances that may come up later.

Use the Self-Assessment Checklist shown on the following pages to keep track of the tasks you've completed and those that require further work. A fillable version of the Self-Assessment Checklist is available on the CD.

Print from CD

Launch Your Management Plan in the First Month of School

Chapter 5: Launch

Use the worksheet on the following pages to identify which (or which parts) of the tasks described in this chapter you have completed. For any item that has not been completed, note what needs to be done to complete it. As appropriate, translate your notes onto your planning calendar in the form of specific actions that you can take (e.g., August 20, make sign for classroom).

✓	TASK	NOTES & IMPLEMENTATION *Ideas*
TASK 1: SUMMARIZE YOUR CLASSROOM MANAGEMENT AND DISCIPLINE PLAN		
☐	I have summarized my vision, classroom organization, and discipline procedures into a concise document that can be used by my building administrator, substitute teachers, and me (see Reproducible 5.1, Classroom Management and Discipline Plan, on the CD).	
TASK 2: MAKE FINAL PREPARATIONS FOR DAY ONE		
☐	I have developed a modified daily or class schedule for the first day of school.	

✓	TASK	NOTES & IMPLEMENTATION *Ideas*
TASK 3: IMPLEMENT YOUR PLAN ON DAY ONE		

✓	TASK	NOTES & IMPLEMENTATION *Ideas*
☐	I have thought about how I will display my Day One Schedule—on the board, an overhead transparency, or flip chart.	
☐	I have thought about how I will greet students individually as they enter the room.	
☐	I have thought about how I will get students' attention as soon as the bell rings.	
☐	I have thought about how I will communicate essential classroom information in the first ten minutes of the day or class.	
☐	I have thought about how I will teach my attention signal.	
☐	I understand the three-step process for communicating my expectations.	
☐	I have thought about how ... expectatio...	
☐	I have thou... behavioral ... and visual ...	
☐	I have thoug... class positiv... transitions.	
☐	I have thoug... corrective fe... transitions.	

✓	TASK	NOTES & IMPLEMENTATION *Ideas*
TASK 4: IMPLEMENT YOUR PLAN ON DAYS 2 THROUGH 20 (THE FIRST FOUR WEEKS)		
☐	I have thought about how I will use the three-step process of teaching, observing behavior, and giving feedback to communicate my behavioral expectations during the first month of school.	
☐	If I am an elementary teacher, I have thought about how I will help students learn the behavioral expectations of the specialists with whom they will have classes.	
☐	I have thought about how I will verify that my students understand the behavioral expectations I have for them.	
☐	I have prepared a quiz that can be administered to all the students.	
☐	I have arranged to conduct interviews with a sample of students.	
TASK 5: PREPARE YOUR STUDENTS FOR SPECIAL CIRCUMSTANCES		
☐	I have thought about how I will teach behavioral expectations to students who enter my class. Possibilities include: • Teach the student individually. • Re-teach the entire class. • Use a buddy system. • Make a "Welcome to Our Class" video. • Establish a schoolwide Newcomers Club.	
☐	I have thought about how I will define and teach behavioral expectations for any unique events in which my students will participate (for example, field trips).	

STOIC

OBSERVE
student
behavior

Section *Three*

Section 3 addresses the O in STOIC—Observe student behavior. You have already Structured your room for success and set up a plan to Teach students to behave successfully. Now you will learn the importance of Observing student behavior as well as how to observe effectively. This section (which includes only one chapter) begins by providing information on how to circulate and scan, how to make judgments about when and how to provide positive Interactions and praise, and when to Correct student misbehavior. The chapter then goes on to suggest a range of tools for doing more objective observations of student behavior and observations to assess the effectiveness of your management plan so you can make adjustments to facilitate responsible behavior from your students.

*S*tructure Your Classroom for Success

*T*each Expectations

*O*bserve Student Behavior

*I*nteract Positively

*C*orrect Fluently

Section *Three*

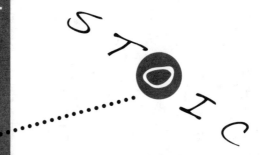

OBSERVE student behavior

Imagine...

You own a good car and live in an area with well-maintained roads, signage, and sensible laws. You received good driving instruction and drive defensively and courteously. You follow all the laws of your state. Most drivers are just like you in this respect. And yet, most drivers on interstate highways go faster than the speed limit (think about your own behavior!). Let's look at three different examples of situations where the act of observing can motivate the typical driver to adhere more closely to the speed limit.

When a police officer is visible, most people slow down to the speed limit because they do not want to get a ticket.

When your passenger is someone you highly respect (your pastor, an off-duty police officer, or just another citizen—but one you know places great value on following the law), you are more likely to travel below the speed limit because you do not want to disappoint this person.

Your state observes patterns of accident reports and realizes that a particular stretch of highway has more problems than others. Highway officials may modify the speed limit, post caution signs, and increase the frequency and visibility of officers on this particular stretch of road. They are using data to make judgments about revisions in the management plan.

The act of observing can affect the behavior of the person being observed and the observer. The three examples above translate easily into the classroom environment. You as a teacher will capitalize on these same ideas of observation as a tool to affect behavior in the classroom.

Use Data to Monitor and Adjust Your Management Plan

 # Observe

When you collect data, you are able to make adjustments to your Classroom Management and Discipline Plan.

Introduction

*T*he act of observing affects the behavior of the people being observed (Kazdin, 1977; Repp, Nieminen, Olinger, & Brusca, 1988). This is more true in the classroom than almost anywhere else. You probably remember a teacher who seemed to "have eyes in the back of her head." She never missed any rule violation, and there was very little misbehavior in her classroom. You also probably remember a teacher (maybe the same one with that multidirectional vision) who you liked and admired so much that you never wanted to disappoint her. Perhaps you also remember a classroom where large numbers of students misbehaved because the teacher was so oblivious he never noticed either positive or negative behavior—he just went through the motions of teaching as though students were not even in the room.

This chapter has two tasks:

Task 1: Circulate When Possible, and Scan All Sections of the Classroom Continuously • While teaching, observe students for behaviors to praise and misbehaviors to correct.

Task 2: Use Data to Monitor and Adjust Your Classroom Management and Discipline Plan • Once or twice a month, use observation tools to collect data that can help you adjust your management plan.

CHAPTER 6 TASKS

Task 1
Circulate When Possible, and Scan All Sections of the Classroom Continuously

Task 2
Use Data to Monitor and Adjust Your Classroom Management and Discipline Plan

The first task covers strategies and techniques for effectively observing your students' behavior. The second teaches you about the utility and benefits of periodic data collection to determine whether your management plan is working as well as you hope, with suggestions for modifications if it is not. This task includes a calendar plan with suggestions for times during the year to conduct these checkups. It also provides seven specific tools that can help you conduct these periodic objective observations of your classroom:

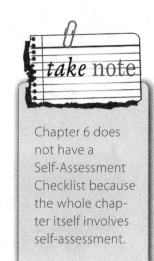

take note

Chapter 6 does not have a Self-Assessment Checklist because the whole chapter itself involves self-assessment.

Tool 1: CHAMPS Versus Daily Reality Rating Scale

Tool 2: Ratio of Interactions Monitoring Form

Tool 3: Misbehavior Recording Sheet

Tool 4: Grade Book Analysis Worksheet

Tool 5: On-Task Behavior Observation Sheet

Tool 6: Opportunities to Respond Observation Sheet

Tool 7: Family/Student Satisfaction Survey

Task 1: Circulate When Possible, and Scan All Sections of the Classroom Continuously

While teaching, observe students for behaviors to praise and misbehaviors to correct.

The importance of observing students by circulating and scanning was identified in the very early research on how effective teachers manage the classroom. Kounin (1970) described effective teachers as having both "with-it-ness" and "in-touch-ness." By circulating throughout the room as much as possible and by using visual and auditory scanning (fancy term for keeping your eyes and ears open) whether you are circulating or not, you can stay in touch with all parts of the classroom. "With-it-ness" really means that you are not just circulating, looking, and listening, but you are also mentally paying attention to that information.

for example

You are circulating around the room during a cooperative group activity. You notice (you get sound and visual cues) that a group across the room—Group A—is getting a bit agitated. You know the maturity level of the students, and you want to see if they can work out the problem by themselves, without your intervention. So rather than rushing over to Group A, you move to Group B about halfway across the room. You look as if you are listening and interacting with Group B (and you are), but part of your senses and mind are actually focused on Group A. If Group A solves the problem, you go over and give positive feedback on their ability to disagree, stay respectful, and resolve the difference in a mature and responsible manner. On the other hand, if while interacting with Group B you notice that the intensity of Group A's agitation is increasing, you leave Group B and go directly to Group A—not to scold them, because you arrive before there is any major problem, but rather to guide them through a process for resolving the difficulty in a respectful and responsible way. A teacher who does not scan may not notice that Group A is having a problem until it becomes a loud argument or fight, a situation that then requires the teacher to impose a corrective consequence.

Keep in mind that you are not just observing for problems, but also for opportunities to give the class and individuals positive feedback. When you scan early in an independent work period and notice a student working hard—someone who in the past has tended to get off task—go to that student immediately and provide a positive interaction, such as descriptive praise, in a manner that will not embarrass the student (more on this in Chapter 7). In other words, scan for problems, but also scan for opportunities to provide meaningful positive feedback.

CIRCULATING

Whenever possible, circulate throughout the classroom in unpredictable patterns. Do not spend the majority of your time in any one part of the room, and avoid a walking pattern that may let students know that you will not be near them for a significant amount of time. This is especially important during independent work periods and cooperative group activities. Your proximity communicates your concern for and interest in the students. It also communicates that if someone chooses to engage in misbehavior, you will likely notice it.

Obviously, there are times when circulating is difficult—for instance, when you are teaching a small group or presenting to the class using an overhead or digital visual presenter. However, whenever you can, try to move about the room. For example, in the middle of teaching a 30-minute small reading group, you might consider giving the students in the group a short task to perform independently while you quickly circulate among the other students. Then you can resume instruction with the small group. Or, while teaching a math lesson to the whole class with an overhead projector, you might give students a couple of problems to work on and then circulate through the room. After looking at students' work, you can return to the overhead and continue with the teacher-directed portion of the lesson.

Remember, as you circulate, give positive feedback to students who are meeting your expectations, answer any questions students may have, and provide gentle reprimands or consequences to students who are not meeting expectations (Colvin et al., 1997; De Pry & Sugai, 2002). And always try to avoid staying too long in any one place.

VISUAL SCANNING

Regardless of what you and the students are doing, you should have a clear line of sight to all students and visually scan all settings in the classroom frequently (Emmer et al., 1980; Scheuermann & Hall, 2008; Shores et al., 1993). For example, when you are circulating, don't just look at the students nearest to you—visually sweep any place students are present, even a learning center across the room. When you are conducting a whole-class activity, visually scan the back rows and the front corners. When you are helping an individual student with her work, plan to occasionally stand up and look around the room. When you are teaching a small group, look up from the group periodically and observe students who are working at their seats.

As you scan, look for any misbehavior that requires correction. If a student is engaged in a misbehavior, go to the student and issue a gentle reprimand or assign an appropriate consequence. Also look for opportunities to acknowledge and encourage responsible behavior. For example, if you notice that a particular student who often tends to be off task is working, go to that student at the next opportunity and give him age-appropriate positive feedback. Or, if a cooperative group is handling a conflict in a responsible way, go over to the group when there is a pause in their interactions and congratulate them on the mature way they are handling the situation.

> *Look for opportunities to acknowledge and encourage responsible behavior.*

Finally, use visual scanning to identify students who may have questions or otherwise need your assistance. During independent work periods especially (when you are not engaged with a small group), look for students who have signaled to you that they need assistance. If you ask students to use a flag or open book as a signal for help (see Chapter 2, Task 6), you need to show students that the signal actually works. If students find that you don't respond when they signal, they will stop using the signal and will come to you or call out to get your attention instead.

CHAPTER 6 TASKS

| 1 • Circulate and Scan All Sections of the Classroom | 2 • Use Data to Monitor and Adjust Your Plan |

AUDITORY SCANNING

In addition to looking to all parts of the classroom, you should listen to all parts of the classroom. Within your management plan there will emerge a baseline, or normal, level of background noise in your room—though this level may be quieter or louder than the normal level of other teachers in your building. Whenever you notice a change in the baseline level of background noise, turn up your level of "with-it-ness"—that is, analyze whether the change is a problem. The noise level may increase because students are very excited and engaged about the assigned cooperative task, and they may just need a gentle reminder to keep their conversations quiet enough so that the noise does not disturb the class next door. Or the noise level may suddenly decrease because students become aware of a conflict brewing between two students in the back of the room and stop what they are doing to see what is going to happen.

Actively observe your students by circulating in unpredictable patterns whenever possible and by using both visual and auditory scanning consistently. You will use the information from this continuous observation process to make judgments about when to prompt students to solve a problem before it has escalated (see the Group A example on p. 241), when to capitalize on reinforceable opportunities, and—whenever rule violations are observed—when to apply corrective consequences consistently, calmly, and immediately.

Task 2: Use Data to Monitor and Adjust Your Classroom Management and Discipline Plan

Once or twice a month, use observation tools to collect data that can help you adjust your management plan.

Periodically use some simple data collection tools to determine whether your management plan is working as effectively as you would like. You may use data to consider:

- Which aspects of your classroom management plan are going well and should be maintained as is.

- Whether there are one or more problem areas that indicate you need to make adjustments to your management plan.

- Whether the level of classroom structure you are currently using should be maintained or revised.

To help you with your decisions about these issues, this chapter includes a variety of tools for collecting and evaluating objective information (data) about what is actually occurring in your classroom. Without accurate information, your decisions are likely to be based on hunches, guesses, or whatever feels right at the moment. As a professional, you should be making informed decisions based on objective information (Alberto & Troutman, 2006; Scheuermann & Hall, 2008).

Another example from the medical profession illustrates the importance of objective data. When you have a routine physical examination, your doctor gathers a variety of information—pulse, respiration, blood pressure, urinalysis, cholesterol levels, and so on. Then your doctor evaluates the objective information she has gathered along with your subjective reports about how you feel, then makes a judgment about your overall health. She may decide that you are just fine, she may recommend that additional information be collected, or she may suggest that a treatment plan be implemented. Without the objective data, your doctor would be less able to accurately assess your overall health or make useful recommendations about your health care options.

> *These information-gathering tools give you objective information about the overall health of your current management plan.*

The information-gathering tools in this chapter are designed to give you objective information about the overall health of your current Classroom Management and Discipline Plan, essentially a snapshot of your class at a particular point in time. They include the following:

TOOL 1: CHAMPS VERSUS DAILY REALITY RATING SCALE

This tool allows you to look at each major activity and transition during your day and evaluate (on a five-point scale) how well students meet your CHAMPS expectations for that activity or transition. With the information you collect, you will be able to decide whether you need to re-teach your CHAMPS expectations or modify the level of structure you have selected as most appropriate for your students (or both). Monitor this particular aspect of your classroom management plan—the actual implementation of your CHAMPS expectations—several times per year.

TOOL 2: RATIO OF INTERACTIONS MONITORING FORM

There are actually three different versions of this tool for determining whether you have fallen into the Criticism Trap—that is, you are inadvertently paying so much attention to student misbehavior that you may actually be perpetuating some of it. The first version of this tool involves documenting your interactions with students during a particular period of time (approximately 30 minutes). You can use the supplementary forms to document interactions with a specific student or interactions relative to a specific behavior such as disrespect.

take note

These tools may seem complicated at first glance, but if you work on implementing only one tool at a time, you will find them relatively simple to use and very useful in making your classroom a better place for all students. In other words, don't be overwhelmed if you skim the remaining content of this chapter. Carefully read the directions for a particular tool only immediately before you use that tool.

TOOL 3: MISBEHAVIOR RECORDING SHEET

Keeping a systematic record of your students' misbehavior for one day (elementary teachers) or one week for a particular class period (middle school teachers) can help you determine whether your management plan's level of structure needs adjusting or whether one or more of your students or the whole class would benefit from a targeted behavior management plan or classwide motivation system. Four different versions of this tool are provided so that you can choose the one that allows you to most easily record misbehavior that occurs in your classroom.

TOOL 4: GRADE BOOK ANALYSIS WORKSHEET

An up-to-date grade book is a wealth of data. You can compile and analyze the existing data in your grade book to determine whether individual students are exhibiting chronic problems with absenteeism, tardiness, work completion, or assignment failure. If you are using a computerized grade book, you can simply call up reports for each of these considerations. Use the information from your analysis to make judgments about whether any individual student, or the class as a whole, would benefit from the implementation of a behavior management plan that targets one or more of these problems.

TOOL 5: ON-TASK BEHAVIOR OBSERVATION SHEET

This simple tool can be used to determine your class's average rate of on-task behavior during independent work times. If students are on task less than 80 percent of the time, you need to re-teach your CHAMPS expectations for work periods or implement some form of classwide incentive system that will encourage students to use class work times more productively.

TOOL 6: OPPORTUNITIES TO RESPOND OBSERVATION SHEET

This tool can be used to examine the degree to which you actively engage students in your lesson. How frequently do students have the opportunity to respond during instruction as opposed to being passive recipients of the lesson content? This tool involves observing yourself teaching a lesson on video, or having a colleague observe you. The results help you evaluate the effectiveness of your instructional presentations and lesson design.

TOOL 7: FAMILY/STUDENT SATISFACTION SURVEY

Just as many businesses find it worthwhile to look at customer satisfaction, you can benefit from knowing how satisfied your students and their families are with your classroom. Tool 7 is a short survey that can be given to families to discuss with their children at the end of the year or during the year (or both). The information will help you identify whether there are aspects of your classroom management plan that you need to communicate more clearly or do differently.

SCHEDULE FOR SUCCESS

You are much more likely to use these tools when you build their implementation into your schedule. Therefore, stop right now and write the prompts shown below in your planning calendar! Write each prompt on or near the suggested date. Make sure to avoid specific dates that are already scheduled for other major activities such as field trips or schoolwide testing. The Chapter references tell you where to find the specific task or strategy in the CHAMPS book.

As the year progresses and you come to a particular prompt on your calendar, go to the specified page or pages in this book and follow the directions for collecting and analyzing the data. For now, just skim the rest of this chapter to familiarize yourself with the included tools. At this point you need only a minimal familiarity with each tool. However, when it is time to actually use a particular tool, plan on carefully reviewing the specific instructions.

take note

A Teacher Planner designed specifically for use with CHAMPS is available from Pacific Northwest Publishing, www.pacificnwpublish.com.

Week 3	Student Interviews or Quiz **(Chapter 4, Task 3)**
Week 4 or 5	CHAMPS Versus Daily Reality Rating Scale **(Chapter 6, Tool 1)**
2nd Month	Ratio of Interactions Monitoring Form **(Chapter 6, Tool 2)**
3rd Month (early)	Misbehavior(s) Recording Sheet **(Chapter 6, Tool 3)**

3rd Month (late)	Grade Book Analysis Worksheet **(Chapter 6, Tool 4)**
4th Month	On-Task Behavior Observation Sheet **(Chapter 6, Tool 5)**
January (early)	CHAMPS Versus Daily Reality Rating Scale **(Chapter 6, Tool 1)**
January (late)	Opportunities to Respond Observation Sheet **(Chapter 6, Tool 6)**
February (early)	Ratio of Interactions Monitoring Form **(Chapter 6, Tool 2)**
February (late)	On-Task Behavior Observation Sheet **(Chapter 6, Tool 5)**
March (early)	Grade Book Analysis Worksheet **(Chapter 6, Tool 4)**
April (after spring break) ...	CHAMPS Versus Daily Reality Rating Scale **(Chapter 6, Tool 1)**
Last Two Weeks	Family/Student Satisfaction Survey **(Chapter 6, Tool 7)**

Even if you start the CHAMPS program during the school year, you can still use the preceding timeline. From today's date, identify the next recommended evaluation activity. Write it and all the activities suggested for the remainder of the year on your planning calendar. Implement those activities at the appropriate times.

TOOL 1   CHAMPS versus Daily Reality Rating Scale

Determine the degree to which student behavior during daily activities and transitions matches your CHAMPS expectations.

WHY

- To help you decide whether you need to re-teach your CHAMPS expectations

- To help you decide whether your current level of structure fits the needs of your class

- To help you decide whether you might need some kind of classwide system to increase students' motivation to behave responsibly

WHEN

- During the fourth or fifth week of school

- Shortly after major vacations (e.g., winter and spring breaks)

HOW

1. **Make a copy (or copies) of the appropriate reproducible form (Reproducible Forms 6.1a [Version 1] and 6.1b [Version 2] on the CD).**

2. **Identify activities and transitions.**

   Use your plan book, daily schedule, or the CHAMPS Classroom Activity and Transitions worksheets you filled out in Chapter 4 (Reproducibles 4.1 and 4.3) to identify the major activities and transitions that occur during a typical school day. Write each activity and transition on the "Activity" line in one of the form's rating boxes. (See Reproducible 6.1, Versions 1 and 2).

   - Elementary teachers may need several pages and may wish to spread this evaluation activity across several days. For example, one day evaluate the morning activities and transitions, and the next day evaluate the afternoon activities.

Reproducible 6.1b   *CHAMPS Versus Daily Reality Rating Scale, Version 2 (Version 1 is shown on the next page)*

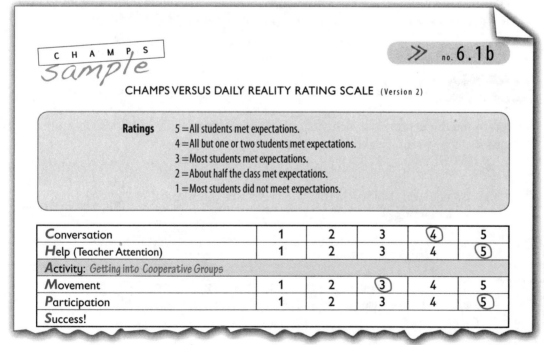

CHAMPS *sample*

≫ no. 6.1b

CHAMPS VERSUS DAILY REALITY RATING SCALE (Version 2)

Ratings
5 = All students met expectations.
4 = All but one or two students met expectations.
3 = Most students met expectations.
2 = About half the class met expectations.
1 = Most students did not meet expectations.

Conversation	1	2	3	(4)	5
Help (Teacher Attention)	1	2	3	4	(5)
Activity: *Getting into Cooperative Groups*					
Movement	1	2	(3)	4	5
Participation	1	2	3	4	(5)
Success!					

Print from CD

Reproducible 6.1a *CHAMPS Versus Daily Reality Rating Scale (Version 1)*

Print from CD

C H A M P S

sample

>> no. **6.1a**

CHAMPS VERSUS DAILY REALITY RATING SCALE (Version 1)

Teacher ___Mrs. McNally___   Date ___9/27___

Ratings
5 = All students met expectations.
4 = All but one or two students met expectations.
3 = Most students met expectations.
2 = About half the class met expectations.
1 = Most students did not meet expectations.

Conversation	1	2	3	4	**(5)**
Help (Teacher Attention)	1	2	3	4	**(5)**
Activity: Before the bell					
Movement	1	2	3	4	**(5)**
Participation	1	2	3	4	**(5)**
Success!					

Conversation	1	2	3	4	**(5)**
Help (Teacher Attention)	1	2	3	4	**(5)**
Activity: Getting ready for independent work (T)					
Movement	1	2	3	**(4)**	5
Participation	1	2	3	4	**(5)**
Success!					

Conversation	1	2	3	**(4)**	5
Help (Teacher Attention)	1	2	3	4	**(5)**
Activity: Attendance/Opening					
Movement	1	2	3	**(4)**	5
Participation	1	2	3	4	**(5)**
Success!					

Conversation	1	2	3	4	**(5)**
Help (Teacher Attention)	1	2	3	**(4)**	5
Activity: Independent work					
Movement	1	2	3	4	**(5)**
Participation	1	2	3	4	**(5)**
Success!					

Conversation	1	2	3	4	**(5)**
Help (Teacher Attention)	1	2	3	4	**(5)**
Activity: Teacher-directed instruction (math)					
Movement	1	2	3	**(4)**	5
Participation	1	2	3	**(4)**	5
Success!					

Conversation	1	2	3	4	5
Help (Teacher Attention)	1	2	3	4	5
Activity: Wrap-up/Closing					
Movement	1	2	3	4	5
Participation	1	2	3	4	5
Success!					

Conversation	1	2	**(3)**	4	5
Help (Teacher Attention)	1	2	3	4	**(5)**
Activity: Getting into cooperative groups					
Movement	1	2	3	4	**(5)**
Participation	1	2	3	**(4)**	5
Success!					

Conversation	1	2	3	4	5

Conversation	1	**(2)**	3	4	5
Help (Teacher Attention)	1	2	3	4	**(5)**
Activity: Cooperative groups					
Movement	1	2	3	4	**(5)**
Participation	1	2	3	**(4)**	5
Success!					

— Analysis and Plan of Action —

In this sample, only one activity (Cooperative Groups) and one transition (Getting into Cooperative Groups) have ratings that are lower than 4s and 5s. The teacher realizes that the main problem is students talking too loudly, making the noise level in the room excessive. Therefore, she decides to leave her classroom structure as it is—low structure. However, she also plans to re-teach her behavioral expectations, particularly emphasizing how students in each cooperative group can monitor and manage the voice levels within their own groups.

- Middle school teachers should complete a rating scale for each of their classes. You may want to spread this across several days. For example, one day conduct the evaluation for first and second periods; the next day, for third and fourth periods; and the third day, for fifth and sixth periods.

3. **Before each activity or transition, briefly review your CHAMPS expectations with students, if necessary. Then, immediately after completing the activity or transition, use the following scale to rate the degree to which students met your expectations:**

   5 = All students met expectations
   4 = All but one or two students met expectations
   3 = Most students met expectations
   2 = About half the class met expectations
   1 = Most students did not meet expectations

4. **Review the data you collected and determine which activities or transitions require re-teaching of expectations.**

   See Reproducible 6.1a (Version 1) on the previous page for an analysis of a sample completed form. In addition, consider the following as you interpret your data.

   - If all the activities and transitions rated a 4 or a 5, keep doing what you are doing. If you wish to give an extra boost to students, consider implementing one or more of the classroom motivational systems appropriate for a low-structure classroom (see Chapter 8). If one or two students' behavior concerns you, you may need to consider individual behavior management plans (see Chapter 9).

   - If at least 70 percent of activities and transitions rated a 4 or a 5, it may be a good idea to implement one or more of the classwide motivation systems appropriate for a medium-structure classroom (see Chapter 8). If one or two students' behavior concerns you, you may need to consider individual behavior management plans (see Chapter 9).

   - If fewer than 70 percent of activities and transitions rated a 4 or a 5, you should probably implement one or more of the classwide motivation systems appropriate for a high-structure classroom (see Chapter 8).

   - If fewer than 50 percent of activities and transitions rated a 4 or a 5, you should implement one of the classwide systems for a high-structure class and at least two systems appropriate for a medium-structure class (see Chapter 8).

Review the data you collected and determine which activities or transitions require re-teaching of expectations.

take note

Some teachers may want to involve students in the CHAMPS rating process. If you choose to do so, explain the purpose and procedures to students ahead of time. Be sure to tell students that their input should have no references to individual students who did not meet expectations. A reproducible master of an enlarged rating form is provided on the CD (Reproducible Form 6.1 Enlargement). It can be used as an overhead transparency if you plan to involve your class in the rating process.

TOOL 2   Ratio of Interactions Monitoring Form(s)

Determine whether you are interacting with students at least three times more often when they are behaving responsibly than when they are misbehaving.

WHY

- To help you evaluate whether you have fallen into the Criticism Trap—that is, whether you are responding so frequently to misbehavior that the behavior stops in the short run but is actually increasing over time

- To help you decide whether you need to increase the number of interactions you have with students when they are behaving appropriately

WHEN

- During the second month of school

- In early to mid-February

- Any time you sense that you are nagging a lot

HOW

1. **Make a copy (or copies) of the appropriate reproducible forms—choose one of these reproducible forms from the CD:**

   - Reproducible 6.2: Ratio of Interactions Monitoring Form (During a Particular Time of Day)

   - Reproducible 6.3: Ratio of Interactions Monitoring Form (With a Particular Student)

   - Reproducible 6.4: Ratio of Interactions Monitoring Form (For a Particular Behavior)

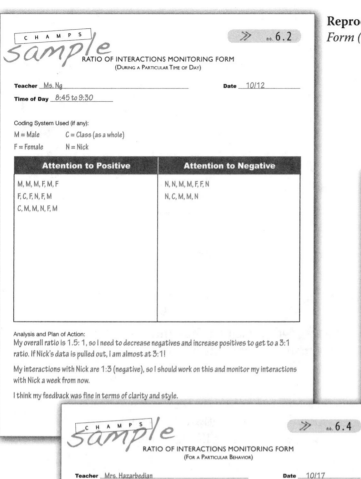

Reproducible 6.2 *Ratio of Interactions Monitoring Form (During a Particular Time of Day)*

Reproducible 6.3 *Ratio of Interactions Monitoring Form (With a Particular Student)*

CHAMPS

sample

RATIO OF INTERACTIONS MONITORING FORM
(DURING A PARTICULAR TIME OF DAY)

no. 6.2

Teacher Ms. Ng   Date 10/12

Time of Day 8:45 to 9:30

Coding System Used (if any):

M = Male   C = Class (as a whole)
F = Female   N = Nick

Attention to Positive	Attention to Negative
M, M, M, F, M, F F, C, F, N, F, M C, M, M, N, F, M	N, N, M, M, F, F, N N, C, M, M, N

Analysis and Plan of Action:
My overall ratio is 1.5: 1, so I need to decrease negatives and increase positives to get to a 3:1 ratio. If Nick's data is pulled out, I am almost at 3:1!

My interactions with Nick are 1:3 (negative), so I should work on this and monitor my interactions with Nick a week from now.

I think my feedback was fine in terms of clarity and style.

CHAMPS

sample

RATIO OF INTERACTIONS MONITORING FORM
(WITH A PARTICULAR STUDENT)

no. 6.3

Teacher Mr. Fleming   Date 10/15

Student Rasheef

Coding System Used (e.g., to indicate specific activities or transitions):

BC = Before class   L = Lining up   TI = Teacher-directed instruction
RG = Reading group   P = Partners   ED = End of day

Attention to Positive (Praise and/or noncontingent attention)	Attention to Negative
BC, TI, L, L, RG, ED	TI, RG, RG, RG, P, P, P, P

Analysis and Plan of Action:
Ratio for Rasheed is 0.75:1, so I definitely need to decrease negatives and increase positives. I will look for more opportunities for praise during reading group and partner work, where he tends to lose focus and make too much noise. I will also look for opportunities to priase when he is on task during lessons.

© 2009 Pacific Northwest Publishing | Reproducible Form

CHAMPS

sample

RATIO OF INTERACTIONS MONITORING FORM
(FOR A PARTICULAR BEHAVIOR)

no. 6.4

Teacher Mrs. Hazarbedian   Date 10/17

Behavior Respecting Others

Coding System Used (e.g., to indicate gender, activity):
M = Male   TI = Teacher-directed lesson   T = Transition (recess
F = Female   I = Independent work

Label the positive and negative behaviors that will be monitored (e.g., Attention to Respect and Attention to Disrespect).

Attention to Positive	Attention to Negative
Respect for Others (Behavior Label) M-TI, F-TI, F-TI, F-I, M-I	Disrespect (Behavior Label) M-I, M-TI, F-TI, M-I, F-I

Note: Decide if you will use a "Public Posting" (see Chapter 5) monitoring system, or if you wish to keep a less obtrusive record (e.g., marks made on a clipboard).

Analysis and Plan of Action:
Ratio is 1:1, so I need to find more opportunites to pay attention to respectful behavior, especially during class time.

© 2009 Pacific Northwest Publishing | Reproducible Form

Reproducible 6.4 *Ratio of Interactions Monitoring Form (For a Particular Behavior)*

CHAPTER 6 TASKS

1 · Circulate and Scan All Sections of the Classroom	2 · Use Data to Monitor and Adjust Your Plan

2. **Make sure you thoroughly understand the difference between positive interactions with students and negative interactions with students.**

Review the following:

- It is the student behavior that prompts the interaction (or the behavior that is occurring at the time the interaction is initiated), not the tone of the interaction, that determines whether an interaction is positive or negative. When you interact with a student who is or has just engaged in appropriate (or desirable) behavior, the interaction is counted as Attention to Positive.

---

for example

Praise: "Owen, you have been using this work time very efficiently and have accomplished a great deal.

Noncontingent attention: "Charlene, how are you today?"

Implementing a positive system: "Both Teresa and Ming earned a marble in the jar for the class. They worked out a disagreement without needing my help." (This example is counted as two positive interactions because the teacher gave attention to two different students.)

- When you interact with a student who is or has just exhibited an inappropriate (or undesirable) behavior, the interaction is recorded as Attention to Negative.

---

for example

Reminders: "Cody, you need to get back to work."

Reprimands: "Khadijah, you know that you should be keeping your hands to yourself."

Corrections: "Amar, I don't think you need to tell me about that because I think you can handle it on your own."

Warnings: "Jennifer, if I have to speak to you again about talking in class, I will have to call your mother."

Consequences: "Javier, that is disruptive. You owe 15 seconds off recess."

---

3. **Determine a time of day (approximately 30 minutes) when you seem to have the most trouble being positive with students. Arrange to record (either audio or video) that time period for one day.**

4. **Listen to (or watch) the recording and mark your interactions on the Ratio of Interactions Monitoring Form.**

   Make a tally mark under "Attention to Positive" for each interaction you had with a student (or the class) when the behavior was responsible. Make a tally mark under "Attention to Negative" for each interaction you had with a student (or the class) when the behavior was irresponsible. Do not mark instructions to the group—for example, "Class, open your books to page 133." However, do count an instruction to an individual student ("Beth, please turn out the lights") as positive if the student was behaving responsibly at the time and negative if the student was misbehaving.

   If you wish to get more detailed information, consider using codes instead of simple tally marks for each interaction.

take note

If you have an I-Pod, I-Phone or other MP3 player, you can purchase a low-cost microphone and record directly to that device.

---

for example

M or F	=	Brief attention to an individual male or female student
C	=	Brief attention to the class or a group
F/15	=	Attention to an individual female lasting approximately 15 seconds
NC	=	Noncontingent attention to an individual (for example, "Good morning!")
NV	=	Nonverbal attention (for example, a reassuring smile or a threatening look)

---

5. **Calculate your ratio of positive interactions with students to negative interactions with students.**

   If you coded your interactions—by gender, type of instructional activity, or type of attention, for example—calculate separate ratios for each category.

6. **Analyze your performance.**

   • Evaluate whether you achieved an overall 3:1 ratio of positives to negatives.

   • Evaluate whether your ratio of positives to negatives varies by category (for example, it's lower with females than males).

- Evaluate the overall style of your interactions (corrections too harsh, praise too friendly or insincere sounding) and whether or not you are comfortable with it.

- Evaluate the contingency of the positive feedback you give to individual students.

- Evaluate whether one or two individuals receive most of the negative interactions. If so, plan to use the Ratio of Interactions Monitoring Form (With a Particular Student).

- Evaluate whether you had to correct a particular category of behavior (for example, off-task talking) more frequently than other problems. If so, use the Ratio of Interactions Monitoring Form (For a Particular Behavior).

7. **Plan a course of action.**

   - If your overall interactions or any subset of interactions do not reflect a 3:1 (positive to negative) ratio, use the strategies suggested below and make an effort to both decrease attention to negative behavior and increase attention to positive behavior. After approximately two weeks, monitor your interactions again to see if you have achieved the desired 3:1 ratio.

   - Once you have successfully modified your ratios, check for an improvement in student behavior. If students are behaving better, congratulate yourself and keep up the good work. If they are not, plan to read and implement the suggestions about increasing motivation in Chapter 7 to see if there are any variables regarding student motivation that you have not implemented. In addition, read Chapter 8 to determine whether a classwide motivation system might be appropriate.

INCREASING POSITIVE INTERACTIONS

As necessary, implement one or more of the following strategies:

- Each time you have a negative interaction, remind yourself that you "owe" three positives.

- Identify specific times during each day that you will give individual students or the whole class positive feedback on some aspect of their behavior or class performance. For example, at the beginning of the math lesson, you might compliment five or six students.

- Use individual conference times, such as the first few minutes of periods during which the class is working on an independent assignment, to compliment individual students on their performance.

- Frequently scan the room and search for important reinforceable behaviors.

- Identify particular events that occur during the day—a student getting a drink of water, for example—that will serve as a prompt to observe the class and identify a reinforceable behavior.

- Reduce the amount of attention (time and intensity) the student receives for misbehavior. Increase the amount of attention (time and intensity) the student receives when not engaged in misbehavior.

- Interact with the student(s) frequently with noncontingent positives.

DECREASING NEGATIVE INTERACTIONS

As necessary, implement one or more of the following strategies.

- Identify whether you might modify aspects of the physical setting, schedule, organization, and so on to reduce the probability that students will misbehave. For example, if some students push others in the rush to get out the door, excuse the students by rows or table groups.

- Try precorrecting a misbehavior before it occurs (Colvin et al., 1993, 1997). For example, if you anticipate that students will push each other while leaving the classroom, give a prompt like, "Remember to keep your hands and feet to yourself as you are leaving the room when I excuse the class."

- Try praising someone who is behaving the "right way" and intervene only if the misbehaving student does not change the behavior.

Positive Negatives   ▨▨▨

Your goal is not to eliminate all negative interactions. Some are essential. For example, when a student does not know that a particular behavior is not acceptable, a gentle correction is the most direct and efficient way to provide the information the student needs to be successful. Or, if you have a preestablished corrective consequence for a particular behavior, you must intervene any time a student exhibits that behavior in order to maintain consistency.

CHAPTER 6 TASKS

TOOL 3 Misbehavior Recording Sheet

Determine whether you need to implement an intervention plan or plans to deal with specific types of student misbehavior.

WHY

- To help you identify how often and for what reason you are intervening with students regarding their inappropriate behaviors

- To help you detect any patterns to students' misbehavior (for example, times of day, day of week, individual students who never misbehave)

- To give you specific and objective information about the behavior of individual students that you can share with the students and their families, if necessary

- To help you decide whether you might need a classwide system to increase students' motivation to behave responsibly

WHEN

- During the early part of the third month of school

- In mid- to late January

HOW

1. **Choose one of the following four reproducible forms and print it from the CD. You may wish to design your own form:**

   - Reproducible 6.5: Misbehavior Recording Sheet (Daily by Student Name). This form is a daily record of misbehavior by hour, organized by student name. This form is appropriate for an elementary teacher. If you wish, you can change the headings (1st hour, 2nd hour) to reflect particular activities (math, reading). The idea is for the columns to reflect meaningful divisions in the school day so you can analyze whether certain times or subjects have a greater preponderance of misbehavior.

   - Reproducible 6.6: Misbehavior Recording Sheet (Weekly by Student Name). This is a weekly record of misbehavior by day, organized by student name. This form is probably most appropriate for a middle school teacher, who would need one form for each class that will be monitored. Note that the week runs from Friday through Thursday so that you don't have to wait over a weekend to give feedback. If you give students feedback about the previous five days on Friday, it is much more immediate, and they will see Friday as the beginning of a new chance to be successful.

take note

Some teachers use this tool every day as an integral part of their classroom management plan.

- Reproducible 6.7: Misbehavior Recording Sheet (Daily by Seating Chart)

- Reproducible 6.8: Misbehavior Recording Sheet (Weekly by Seating Chart)

The last two forms are daily and weekly records of misbehavior, organized by student seating when desks are arranged in rows. Each square represents a desk. Elementary teachers should use the daily form and note individual class activities on the horizontal lines within a square. Middle school teachers should use the weekly form (one form per class period for the week) and note the days of the week on the horizontal lines within a square. Create your own form if desks are arranged in clusters or a U-shape.

For Middle School Teachers and Elementary Specialists

Decide whether to use a Misbehavior Recording Sheet in one, two, or all of your classes. You should record misbehavior with all classes for at least one full week. However, you might try it initially for a week with just one class (probably the class with the most misbehavior). If you find the information useful, you can plan how and when to use the tool with the rest of your classes.

---

2. **Put the appropriate Misbehavior Recording Sheet on a clipboard.**

   Plan to keep the clipboard close by for the entire day if you are an elementary teacher or for five days of a particular class period if you are a middle school teacher.

3. **Explain to students that for the entire day or the next five class periods, you will be recording any time you have to speak to someone or the whole class about inappropriate behavior.**

4. **Whenever you speak to a student about a misbehavior, note the specific misbehavior on the form using a coding system.**

Reproducible 6.5 *Misbehavior Recording Sheet (Daily by Student Name)*

Reproducible 6.6 *Misbehavior Recording Sheet (Weekly by Student Name).*

Print from CD

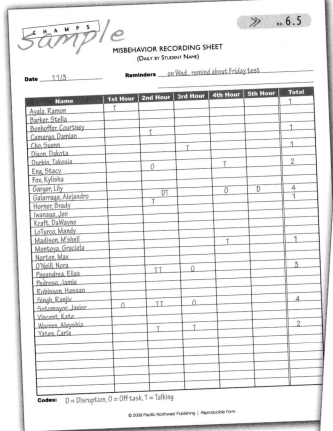

CHAMPS sample » no. 6.5

MISBEHAVIOR RECORDING SHEET
(DAILY BY STUDENT NAME)

Date 11/3   Reminders on Wed., remind about Friday test

Name	1st Hour	2nd Hour	3rd Hour	4th Hour	5th Hour	Total
Ayala, Ramon	T					1
Barker, Stella						
Bonhoffer, Courtney						1
Camargo, Damian		T				1
Cho, Suenn						
Dixon, Dakota			T			1
Durbin, Takesia		O		T		2
Eng, Stacy						
Fox, Kylisha						
Garger, Lily		DT		O	D	4
Galarraga, Alejandro		T				1
Horner, Brady						
Iwanaga, Jen						
Kraft, DaWayne						
LoTurco, Mandy						
Madison, M'shell				T		1
Montoya, Graciela						
Norton, Max						
O'Neill, Nora		TT	O			3
Papandrea, Elias						
Pedroso, Jamie						
Robinson, Hassan						
Singh, Ranjiv						
Sotomayor, Javier	O	TT	O			4
Vincent, Kate						
Warren, Aleyshia			T	T		2
Yates, Carla						

Codes: D = Disruption, O = Off task, T = Talking

© 2009 Pacific Northwest Publishing | Reproducible Form

CHAMPS sample » no. 6.6

MISBEHAVIOR RECORDING SHEET
(WEEKLY BY STUDENT NAME)

Date 11/4   Reminders on Wed., remind about Friday test

Name	Fri.	Mon.	Tue.	Wed.	Thu.	Total
Anderson, Chantel						
Baena, Ruben			T			1
Bell, Justin						0
Carraza, Melinda						0
Cummings, Teresa		T		T		2
Demalier, Lee						0
Diaz, Margo				T		1
Etienne, Jerry						0
Fujiyama, Kim		O				0
Grover, Matthew					T	2
Henry, Scott	DDT	DO		DT	T	8
Isaacson, Chris						0
Kaufman, Jamie				D		1
King, Mark						0
LaRouche, Janel						0
Morales, Maria		T				1
Nardon, Jamayla						0
Neely, Jakob	T		T			2
Nguyen, Trang						0
Ogren, Todd	TTD	D	OO	T	TT	9
Pallant, Jared						0
Piercey, Dawn		T	O	T		3
Reeves, Rashawn						0
Thomason, Rahsaan	TT		T	T	TT	6
Vandever, Aaron						0
Wong, Charlene						0
Yamamoto, Junko		T		T		2

Codes: D = Disruption, O = Off task, T = Talking

© 2009 Pacific Northwest Publishing | Reproducible Form

— Analysis and Plan of Action —

Scott Henry, Todd Ogren, and Rahsaan Thomason are the students with the most misbehaviors. Together they had a total of 23 misbehaviors this week (see Reprodudible 6.6). The total for the whole class (including the three) was 39. That means the misbehaviors of the three students accounted for approximately 59 percent of the total class misbehavior. This suggests that a medium level of structure is appropriate for the class, which is what the teacher currently has in place. The teacher decides that she needs a classwide motivation system, so she reviews the information and menu of systems in Chapter 8. She decides to implement the 100 Squares system. With this system, the teacher will be on the lookout for times when the class is behaving responsibly. At such times, she'll have a student draw a number from a jar (like Bingo), then cross out that number on the 100 Squares chart. When a row of the chart is filled in—across, up and down, or diagonally—the entire class gets a reward. The teacher will also teach the class strategies for gently correcting classmates who are engaging in a misbehavior.

---

for example

O = Off-task
H = Hands/feet/objects bothering others
T = Talking
D = Disruption
S = Out of seat at wrong time
A = Arguing

Build your code so that you have a different letter for each type of major misbehavior you think is likely to happen.

Reproducible 6.7   *Misbehavior Recording Sheet (Daily by Seating Chart)*

Reproducible 6.8   *Misbehavior Recording Sheet (Weekly by Seating Chart)*

5. **Analyze the data and determine a plan of action.**

- You may find that the behavior of some students improves simply because you are keeping records. If so, consider using the Misbehavior Recording Sheet on an ongoing basis. This data will be very useful for discussing behavior with students and their families, determining citizenship grades, and making decisions about your Classroom Management and Discipline Plan.

- Make a subjective decision regarding your level of concern about the amount of misbehavior that is occurring. If you are unconcerned (the amount of misbehavior is so low that it is not interfering with student learning), do not bother making any changes.

- If you are concerned about the amount of misbehavior in your class, analyze the data from the Misbehavior Recording Sheet further. First, determine how much of the misbehavior is exhibited by just a few students. Identify the three students who had the most frequent incidents of misbehavior and calculate the percentage of the total class misbehavior attributed to those students (divide the total number of misbehaviors exhibited by the three students by the total number of misbehaviors exhibited by the entire class). For example, if the three students' total for two days is 45 and the total for the entire class is 61, divide 45 by 61 to get 74 percent.

- Once you identify the percentage of misbehavior exhibited by the top three misbehaving students, use the following criteria to determine the most appropriate action.

  If more than 90 percent of the total classroom misbehavior can be attributed to the three individual students, keep your level of structure and procedures as they are. For the one, two, or three individuals with the most misbehavior, consider implementing individual behavior management plans.

  If 60 to 89 percent of the total classroom misbehavior can be attributed to the three individuals, review your level of classroom structure and implement one or more classroom motivation systems appropriate for medium structure (see Chapter 8). In addition, consider individual behavior management plans for the students whose behavior is the most problematic.

  If less than 60 percent of the misbehavior can be attributed to the three individuals (that is, the problem is classwide), review and implement all the suggestions for high-structure classrooms in Chapters 1, 2, 3, 4, 5, and 7. In addition, carefully read the information in Chapter 8 and arrange to implement one or more of the classwide systems appropriate for high-structure classrooms.

TOOL 4 Grade Book Analysis Worksheet

Determine whether student attendance, punctuality, in-class work completion, homework completion rates, and academic work are satisfactory.

WHY

- To help you decide whether you need to implement a plan to improve one or more area of concern with your class, a small group of students, or individuals
- To help you determine how the specified variables may interact

WHEN

- During the third month of school
- In early to mid-March
- Prior to the end of each grading period

HOW

1. **Gather relevant data.**

   If you use a computerized grade book, determine whether and how the program provides you data for:

   - Attendance rates (percentage)
   - Punctuality rates (percentage)
   - Percentage of in-class work completion
   - Percentage of homework assignments completed
   - Current grade status (to identify students who may need targeted academic assistance)

   If you do not have a computer grade book, calculate data for each student in your class.

   - Attendance: Divide the actual number of days each student has been at school by the total number of days school has been in session.

   - Punctuality: Divide the actual number of days the student arrived on time by the total number of days the student has been in attendance.

Reproducible 6.9 *Grade Book Analysis Worksheet*

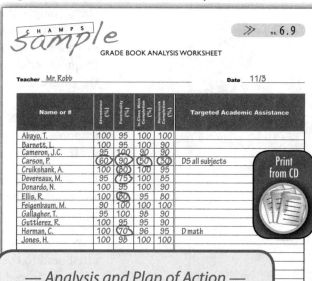

— Analysis and Plan of Action —

P. Carson falls below expectancies on all variables. As a first step, Mr. Robb will conference with the student and family to develop an attendance plan. He also notes that five students are below 95% for punctuality. He decides to post daily punctuality percentages and establish a whole class motivation system. Finally, Mr. Robb notes that C. Herman has a D in math, despite reasonable rates of work completion. He decides to have the student work with a small group on in-class math assignments. The student will also practice math homework with a cross-age tutor before repeating the assignment for homework.

- In-class work completion: Divide the actual number of in-class assignments the student has turned in by the total number of in-class assignments that have been due. Elementary teachers should make these calculations for students across all academic content areas.

- Homework completion: Divide the actual number of homework assignments the student has turned in by the total number of homework assignments that have been due. Elementary teachers should make these calculations for students across all academic content areas.

- Calculate grades for each student in your class in each graded subject area.

2. **Print a copy or copies of Reproducible Form 6.9, Grade Book Analysis Worksheet, from the CD and enter data for each student.**

3. **Under targeted academic assistance, record any unsatisfactory grade and the related subject.**

4. **Analyze your results. Does your data indicate a problem with your class or individuals?**

   - Attendance: Students should have at or above 95% attendance, missing no more than 2 or 3 days per quarter or 4 to 5 days per semester.

   - Punctuality: Students should be at or above 95% punctuality.

   - In-class work completion: Students should be at or above 95% in-class work completion.

   - Homework completion: Students should be at or above 95% homework completion.

   - Targeted academic assistance: Students should be passing all academic subjects.

   If three or more individuals fail to meet a goal, consider implementing a whole-class action plan.

   For individuals, examine the interrelationships among the data. A student may be failing due to poor attendance that results in an inability to complete in-class work. In this instance, the student needs a plan to improve attendance. Another student may need a homework plan. Yet another student may fail to complete homework due to a lack of skills and may need pre-teaching or modified homework assignments. Once problems have been identified, proactive plans can make a difference.

take note

Check school/district guidelines to determine when formal intervention is recommended or required.

---

for example

For individuals, you might select from the menu below:
- Schedule a discussion with the student.
- Schedule a discussion with the student and family members.
- Establish an individualized plan for the student.
- Discuss the problem with your principal, special education teacher, school counselor, school psychologist, or district behavior specialist.

---

for example

For whole-class interventions, you might select from the menu below:
- Revise and/or re-teach your CHAMPS expectations for independent work periods. See Chapter 4.
- Review and, if necessary, revise your procedures for managing work completion. See Chapter 2.
- Publicly post and discuss daily class percentages. See Chapter 2.
- Establish a classwide motivation system. See Chapter 8 for ways to directly motivate students to improve specific behaviors.

TOOL 5 On-Task Behavior Observation Sheet

Determine how effectively your students use independent work time.

WHY

- To help you decide whether you need to re-teach students your CHAMPS expectations for independent work periods

- To help you identify the possible cause of poor work completion rates and misbehavior during independent work periods

WHEN

- During the fourth month of school

- In mid- to late February

HOW

1. **Print a copy (or copies) of Reproducible Form 6.10 from the CD.**

2. **Identify the independent work period(s) that you wish to monitor. Middle school teachers should target any class or classes that are having trouble completing work or those with frequent misbehavior.**

3. **Determine whether you will conduct your own observation or have a colleague observe (you reciprocate at another time).**

   Having a colleague collect the data has several advantages. First, you will be available to do whatever you usually do during this work period—for example, teach a small group or circulate and help students who have questions. Second, a colleague is likely to be slightly more objective. You may have an unconscious tendency to make students look better or worse than they really are. Third, exchanging classroom observations with a colleague gives the two of you a great opportunity to share ideas about how to help students improve their overall rate of on-task behavior.

Reproducible 6.10   *On-Task Behavior Observation Sheet*

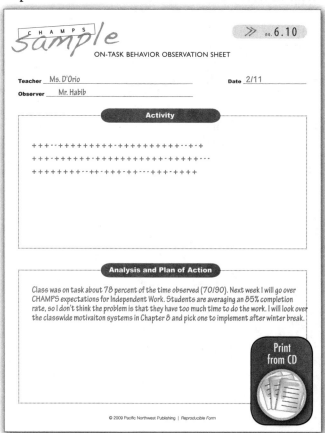

4. **During the observation period, whoever is collecting data should use the instantaneous time sampling method of observation.**

   This is a fancy name for the following easy method of data collection:

   • The observer is positioned away from high-traffic areas and in a place where he can easily see students working at their seats. He has a blank On-Task Behavior Observation Sheet (Reproducible 6.10) and a pen or pencil.

   • The observer chooses an observation pattern that allows him to observe each student in the class a minimum of three times. For example, if students are in rows, the observer might start with the student in the front row to the left. He then looks at the next front-row student to the right, and then the next student in the front row, and so on until he has observed each student in the front row. Then the observer goes to the students in the second row, moving from left to right; then the third row; and so on. After observing the last student in the back row, he repeats this pattern at least two more times. Note that it is important to keep a consistent, unchanging pattern—if you skip around, the data will be less accurate.

- When observing an individual student, the observer looks at that student for only an instant—almost like taking a mental snapshot. Then he looks down at the paper and asks himself whether the student was on- or off-task at the instant of observation. If the student was on task, the observer marks a + (plus). If the student was off task, he marks a − (minus). Repeat this for every student, following the pattern established in the step above. The idea is for the observer to set up a rhythm with a quick pace, spending no more than three to five seconds on each student. Look, think, mark. Next student: Look, think, mark. Note that the mark should reflect what the student is doing at the moment of being observed—not what he or she was doing a moment before the observation or what he or she does a moment after (even if he or she is off task).

- The observer should work through the whole pattern at least three times so that every student is observed a minimum of three times. When finished, the Observation Sheet should look something like sample Reproducible 6.10 on the previous page (from a class with 30 students).

- Notice that no effort is made to record which individual students were on or off task. The point of this tool is to look at a class average.

take note

If, as is possible, the process of monitoring seems to improve student behavior (that is, the act of observing motivates students to be more on task than usual) and if you are working with students in grades 4 and above, consider teaching the students how to record this kind of data. Then, periodically ask an individual student (not always the same person) to observe and record. Give the class feedback at the end of the work period. Use this procedure a couple of times per week until the class is consistently on task 90 percent or more of the time.

5. **Determine the percentage of on-task behavior by dividing the total number of on-task marks (pluses) by the total number of marks (pluses and minuses).**

   In the sample, this would be 70 divided by 90, meaning that during the observation period the class was on task approximately 78 percent of the time.

6. **Analyze the data and, if necessary, determine a plan of action.**

   - If the class had an on-task rate of 90 percent or more, provide positive feedback (including telling them how they did) and encourage them to keep up the good work. If you feel that the percentage does not accurately reflect their typical behavior (they were more on task because they knew they were being observed), let them know that you are pleased with what they demonstrated they could do and that you want them to strive to behave every day the way they did when observed. If you know that only one or two students exhibited all of the off-task behavior, arrange a private discussion with those individuals. Use the time to set improvement goals for the students and, if necessary, to develop individualized management plans to help them learn to manage work times more responsibly.

   - If the class had an on-task rate of between 80 and 89 percent, tell them what the percentage was and let them know that although they did well, there is room for improvement. Together with the students, identify strategies that individual students can use to monitor and improve their own on-task behavior. If you feel that the percentage does not accurately reflect their typical behavior (they were more on task because they knew they were being observed), let them know that you are pleased with what they demonstrated they could do and that you want them to strive to behave every day the way they did when observed. If you know that only one or two students exhibited all of the off-task behavior, arrange a private discussion with those individuals. Use the time to set improvement goals for the students and, if necessary, to develop individualized management plans to help them learn to manage work times more responsibly.

   - If the class had an on-task rate of less than 80 percent, tell them what the percentage was and explain that improvement needs to occur. Review your CHAMPS expectations for independent work periods, placing special emphasis on what constitutes appropriate participation. At a later time, examine your grade book. If, despite their high rates of off-task behavior, the class has high rates of work completion (above 95 percent), consider the possibility that you are giving students too much class time to do their assignments. If both on-task behavior and work completion are low, you may want to establish a classwide system to motivate students to improve both their work completion and on-task behavior (see Chapter 8). Remember, if students are on task less than 80 percent on average, too much valuable instructional time is being lost, and you need to intervene.

TOOL 6   Opportunities to Respond Observation Sheet

Determine the degree to which your students are engaged during teacher-directed instruction parts of your class.

WHY

- To help you decide whether you need to modify your instructional methods to create more active student involvement

- To help you identify the possible causes of poor work completion rates and misbehavior during teacher-directed lessons

WHEN

- During the fourth month of school

- In mid- to late February

HOW

1. **Make copies of Reproducible Form 6.11, found on the CD.**

2. **Identify the teacher-directed lessons that you wish to observe.**

   Target any class or classes that have trouble staying focused or those with frequent misbehavior during lessons.

3. **Determine whether you will observe yourself using video or whether a colleague will observe your lesson.**

   Analyzing your own lesson on video has several advantages. Taking video of the class is less threatening to your students than having someone else watch you teach. In addition, you will learn a great deal about your own teaching by observing students during your lesson. The major disadvantage is that students may behave differently when you film them than they would for a neutral party. Another disadvantage is that there may be restrictions on taping students without getting parental permission (check with your administrator).

Reproducible 6.11 *Opportunities to Respond Observation Sheet*

CHAMPS
Sample

≫ no. 6.11

OPPORTUNITIES TO RESPOND OBSERVATION SHEET

Teacher Ms. Montoya   **Date** 12/4

Observer Mrs. Nguyen   **Activity** Math class

Lesson Start Time 12:50   **Lesson End Time** 1:30   **Duration of Observation** 10
(# of minutes)

Student 1	Student 2	Student 3	Student 4
V, V, W, W, V, V, V V, V	W, W, W, W, V, V, V W, V, V, V	V, W, W, W, V, V, V, V W, W, V, V, V, V	V, V, V, W, W, V, V W, W, V, V, V, V, W

Mark a "V" for each verbal response. Mark a "W" for each written response.

Total number of responses 48   **divided by 4 equals** 12
(average # of responses)

Average number of responses divided by number of minutes equals 1.2
(average responses per minute)

Notes on subjective perception of the degree of student engagement in the lesson:

All but one student seemed attentive during presentation of new material. One student appeared to be reading a different assignment and did not respond to most group questions.

Analysis and Plan of Action:

Work on adding opportunities to respond when presenting new material to keep students engaged. Try to move around the classroom more during instruction to keep students focused on the lesson.

Having a colleague collect the data has several advantages. A colleague is more likely to be objective. You may have an unconscious tendency to make students look better or worse than they really are. Exchanging classroom observations with a colleague gives the two of you an opportunity to share ideas about how to create lessons that facilitate the active engagement of your students.

4. **During the observation period, plan to focus on three or four specific students.**

   If you are videotaping, set the camera to the side of the room toward the back. Inform students that you are filming your teaching so you can improve the quality of your lessons. Focus the camera on a group of four students, preferably four who represent different ability levels, so you can see them making written or verbal responses. If you are having a colleague observe, arrange for her to sit to one side of the room toward the back. Have her observe four students of different ability levels.

   Whoever does the observation—you or your colleague—should record the start time of the lesson, mark a V on the observation sheet each time any of the target students makes a verbal response, and mark a W each time any of the target students makes a written response.

   At the end of the teacher-directed portion of the lesson, record the stop time and the length of the lesson. If you have an observer who is not available for the entire class period, have her record the length of the observation.

5. **Determine the average number of responses per minute.**

   Determine the average response rate for the four students by adding the total Vs and Ws and dividing by four.

   Divide the average response rate by the number of minutes. This figure is the average responses per minute.

6. **Analyze the data and, if necessary, determine a plan of action.**

   Preliminary research with primary-level students determined that learning was maximized when students were responding between four and six times per minute with 80 percent accuracy during instruction on new material and between nine and twelve times per minute with 90 to 95 percent accuracy during drill and practice work (Council for Exceptional Children, 1987; Gunter et al., 2002; Gunter & Denny, 1998; Gunter, Hummel, & Venn, 1998; Rosenshine, 1983).

There is little research, however, on what represents optimal response rates for intermediate and middle school students with more complex tasks and with different types of activities such as discussion and lecture. Therefore, you (and your colleague if you had an observer) need to determine whether the number of student responses is optimal for your class. Recognize that the more students are doing something that engages them with the lesson content, the greater the chances are that they are learning the essential content (Brophy & Good, 1986; Englemann & Becker, 1978).

If students seemed overly passive during your lesson, explore with colleagues or instructional supervisors and department chairs how to get students to participate more actively. More active response methods could include whole-group choral responses, whole-group physical responses (for example, "Stand up if the statement is true. Stay seated if it's false."), copying notes, and quick ungraded quizzes.

TOOL 7 Family/Student Satisfaction Survey

Determine how your students and their families perceive various logistical and organizational features of your classroom.

WHY

- To help you identify those aspects of your classroom program that are working well and those that may need modification

- To help you identify whether there are aspects of your classroom program that you need to communicate more clearly to students and their families

WHEN

- Last two weeks of school

- (Optional) Midyear

take note

See "Cultural Competence" (Introduction, pp. 6–9) for suggestions on working effectively with students and families whose backgrounds are different from yours.

For Middle School Teachers

Discuss with colleagues whether to have a schoolwide survey that goes to all families as opposed to individual teachers doing their own surveys. If too many individual teachers give their own surveys, a family with two students in the school could end up having to complete up to twelve surveys!

Reproducible 6.12 *Family/Student Satisfaction Survey (page 1)*

FAMILY/STUDENT SATISFACTION SURVEY (1 of 2)

Dear Families,

As we approach our mid-winter break, I want to thank you all for your help and support. As a professional trying to meet the needs of all students, I am always looking for ways to improve. You can help by giving me feedback about the strengths and weaknesses you see in my program. Please take a few minutes to fill out the following survey. If possible, please discuss these questions with your child and come up with answers together.

Note that there is no place to put your name, so you will remain anonymous unless you wish to sign your name. Once it's completed, fold the survey in half and have your student return it to the box by my desk. As always, if you wish to talk to me personally, give me a call.

Sincerely,

Mr. Lincoln

HOMEWORK

1. **The amount of homework assigned has been:**
   ○ way too much   ☒ a bit too much   ○ about right   ○ not enough

2. **Homework has been:**
   ○ way too difficult   ○ a bit too difficult   ☒ about right   ○ not difficult enough

ASSIGNMENTS AND CLASSWORK

3. **The amount of in-class work assigned has been:**
   ○ way too much   ○ a bit too much   ☒ about right   ○ not enough

4. **In-class work has been:**
   ○ way too difficult   ○ a bit too difficult   ☒ about right   ○ not difficult enough

5. **Most of the time my child has felt that the work was:**
   ○ stupid
   ○ boring
   ☒ OK
   ○ interesting
   ○ fun

➡

Reproducible 6.12   *Family/Student Satisfaction Survey (page 2)*

C H A M P S   *sample*

≫ no. **6.12**

FAMILY/STUDENT SATISFACTION SURVEY (2 of 2)

ASSIGNMENTS AND CLASSWORK *(continued)*

6. **Circle the subject your child likes the most:** Reading / Spelling / Writing / (Math) / Science / Social Studies
Please explain why:
Elisa is good at it and enjoys it.

7. **Circle the subject your child likes the least:** Reading / (Spelling) / Writing / Math / Science / Social Studies
Please explain why:
Elisa finds it boring.

CLASSROOM ATMOSPHERE

8. **Most of the time, my student has:**
   ○ hated coming to school   ✗ felt that school is OK   ○ looked forward to coming to school
   Please explain why:

9. **My student feels that he or she has been treated with respect by the teacher:**
   ○ not often   ○ most of the time   ✗ all of the time
   Please explain why:

10. **What might have been (might be) done to make this year a more pleasant and productive experience for your child?**

HOW

1. **Make copies of the two-page Reproducible Form 6.12, found on the CD.**

2. **Determine how you will let families know they will be receiving the survey, and determine the logistics of how families will receive and return the survey.**

   For example, you could have students take the surveys home and return them to school. Or, if your school can budget for postage, send the surveys by mail with pre-addressed, postage-paid return envelopes enclosed.

3. **When all surveys have been returned, analyze the results.**

   Keep in mind that although the information is subjective opinion, it can help you identify aspects of your classroom that may require further review. For example, if 50 percent of the families respond that students do not have enough homework, you should carefully consider whether the amount of homework you assign is sufficient. On the other hand, if 60 percent say the amount of homework is about right, 20 percent say it's too much and 20 percent say it's not enough, you can probably assume that the amount of homework matches the average family's perception of what is appropriate.

Conclusion

In this chapter, you learned two techniques for effectively observing your students' behavior. By circulating throughout the room as much as possible and by keeping your eyes and ears open whether you are circulating or not, you can stay in touch with all parts of the classroom. You also have a set of tools that you can use to periodically collect data to help assess how well your Classroom Management and Discipline Plan is working.

take note

The survey can and should be modified to reflect your classroom program and any areas of concern that you may have.

Also note that giving a survey of this type can be very threatening. As you examine the results, remind yourself that you cannot take critical information personally. Rather, you are looking for patterns of information that will help you fine-tune your classroom program.

S T O I C

INTERACT positively

Structure Your Classroom for Success

Teach Expectations

Observe Student Behavior

Interact Positively

Correct Fluently

Section *Four*

This section includes two chapters about how to increase student motivation. While Observing student behavior, you are looking for opportunities to increase your students' motivation to continue behaving responsibly and to try to behave even better in the future. In Chapter 7, you will learn how to use attention and praise as a tool to increase motivation and how to avoid using your attention to unintentionally reinforce negative behavior. Chapter 8 provides information on using goal-setting strategies to increase the motivation of classes with low structure. It also discusses how you can use whole-class extrinsic reinforcement systems with classes that need medium or highly structured tools to increase motivation.

Section *Four*

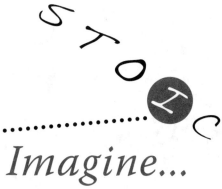

INTERACT positively

STOIC

Imagine...

You have a job where you are required to do a range of tasks each day. As soon as you master a task, you are given more difficult tasks. When you master those, you are given even more difficult tasks. For each of these tasks, you are graded. For many of the tasks, you have to take tests that are used to compare your performance with the performance of your co-workers. You do not have the option of quitting this job or getting a different job.

Imagine that your boss is impersonal He mainly points out what you do wrong. He says nothing about what you do correctly or about your focus, work habits, and ability to get along with co-workers. In fact, your boss takes pride in being tough. He truly believes that if he does not criticize your behavior or work output, you know that you are doing well. In addition, you do not particularly enjoy the tasks you have to do each day (that is, you lack intrinsic motivation for these tasks), and the pay is terrible.

Now imagine that you have a boss you respect, one who treats you with dignity and communicates that you are valued. This boss provides positive feedback on your performance in a manner that is respectful and does not embarrass you. You like this boss so much that you want to do your best for her and for your co-workers because you all take pride in the excellent quality of your work. At first you are motivated mostly by the pay, which is pretty good, rather than by any intrinsic motivation. Over time the pay becomes less important than the feeling of being part of a great team doing great work.

Which boss would you like to work for? Which boss would you rather be?

Motivation

chapter 7

Increase Student Motivation

When you build positive relationships and provide frequent positive feedback, you motivate students to demonstrate their best behavior.

Introduction

*I*n Chapter 1, we explored some concepts about motivation, including:

- If a person exhibits any behavior repeatedly, that person has motivation to exhibit the behavior.

- A person's motivation toward any particular behavior or task is probably a complex mix of both intrinsic and extrinsic factors.

- A person's level of motivation is a function of both expectancy of success and the degree to which the rewards that accompany success are valued.

Chapter 1 also explored variables that you can manipulate—particularly by providing effective instruction—to increase your students' expectancy of success. Remember that if a student perceives himself to be incapable of being successful, he is unlikely to be motivated, so your interventions will have to include instructional interventions.

This chapter includes four tasks that focus on increasing the Value factor in the Expectancy times Value equation. These are tasks you can implement to enhance students' motivation to follow your rules, strive toward your Guidelines for Success, and achieve your goals and instructional expectations.

At the end of this chapter is a Self-Assessment Checklist designed to help you determine which (or which parts) of the tasks you have done or are in the process of doing, and which you still need to do.

CHAPTER 7 TASKS

Task 1
Build Positive Relationships With Students

Task 2
Provide Positive Feedback

Task 3
Provide Intermittent Celebrations

Task 4
Strive to Provide a High Ratio of Positive Interactions

The four tasks presented and explained in this chapter are:

Task 1: Build Positive Relationships With Students • Students work harder when they like and respect their teacher and feel the teacher cares about them. Demonstrate to students that you value them as individuals by using greetings, nonverbal communication, and (when possible) conversations.

Task 2: Provide Positive Feedback • Give students a variety of positive feedback on their progress and success in meeting behavioral and academic goals.

Task 3: Provide Intermittent Celebrations • Periodically reward both individual students and the whole class with a celebration that acknowledges their progress and success in meeting behavioral and academic goals.

Task 4: Strive to Provide a High Ratio of Positive Interactions • Plan to interact at least three times more often with each student when he or she is behaving appropriately than when he or she is misbehaving (that is, at least a 3:1 ratio of positive to negative interactions).

Task 1: Build Positive Relationships With Students

Create a positive relationship with each student by using every opportunity possible to provide each student with noncontingent attention.

An increasing body of research literature indicates that students have higher achievement and engage in fewer behavior problems when they have a positive relationship with their teacher (Brophy, 1981; Cameron & Pierce, 1994; Chalk & Bizo, 2004; Reinke, Lewis-Palmer, & Martin, 2007; Stormont, Smith, & Lewis, 2007; Sutherland et al., 2000).

Studies have also shown that students tend to work more diligently when they receive higher rates of positive feedback than when they do not (Bain, Houghton, & Williams, 1991; Beaman & Wheldall, 2000; Ferguson & Houghton, 1992; Hall, Lund, & Jackson, 1968; Harrop & Swinson, 2000; Merrett & Wheldall, 1987; Nafpaktitis, Mayer, & Butterworth, 1985; Pergande & Thorkildsen, 1995). These findings have been consistent from preschool to high school. Over time, the importance of positive relationships with adults has become even more critical because lack of school connectedness has been correlated with high school dropouts and substance abuse (Bonny, Britto, Klostermann, Hornung, & Slap, 2000; Glover, Burns, Butler, & Patton, 1998; McNeely & Falci, 2004; Resnick et al., 1997; Sprick, Garrison et al., 2002; Yan, Beck, Howard, Shattuck, & Kerr, 2008).

While the research is impressive, you do not even need a research base to realize that this concept is true. From your own experience, you probably know that most people will work harder for a teacher or boss who is personable and respectful, and treats students or employees like a person—not like a number in the grade book.

> " *Most people will work harder for a teacher or boss who is personable and respectful.* "

Imagine three different students in a hypothetical classroom. The first is a highly talented, good-looking, socially adept student. The second student struggles academically and behaviorally, and is not particularly liked by peers. The third is an average student. Each of these students, and all the others in the room, should feel equally valued and respected by you not because of what they accomplish or how they behave, but just because they are one of your students. So, how do you give each of these students the kind of attention they need to feel valued and respected?

In this task, specific suggestions are offered for how to build relationships with students. The focus is on noncontingent attention—a fancy way of saying that you will give some time and attention to each student, regardless of how that student behaves or performs academically. Mike Booher, a *Safe & Civil Schools* trainer, refers to noncontingent attention as "reach outs," because you are in essence reaching out to make a connection with every student.

It is very important for you to make an effort to provide every student with attention that is not contingent on any specific accomplishment. Contingent positive attention (as described in Tasks 2 and 3) involves interacting with and giving feedback to students when they have accomplished or demonstrated improvement on important behavioral or academic goals (O'Leary & O'Leary, 1977; Sheuermann & Hall, 2008).

Noncontingent attention, on the other hand, involves giving students time and attention not because of anything they've done, but just because you notice and value them as people (Alberto & Troutman, 2006; Carr et al., 2000). Ways of giving noncontingent attention include greeting your students as they enter your room, calling on them during class, and showing an interest in the thoughts, feelings, and activities of each student.

The benefits of noncontingent attention are fairly obvious. Like all of us, students need to be noticed and valued. When they feel noticed and valued, they are more likely to be motivated to engage in appropriate behaviors. The benefits to you include the following:

- You will feel more connected to your students.

- Students will have a model of pleasant supportive social interactions—you!

- Student behavior will improve.

- Each day will be much more pleasant, resulting in an improved classroom climate for you and the students.

You may wonder how simply saying "hello" and making an effort to talk to students can improve their behavior. Dr. Vern Jones (1998), a leading expert on student discipline and motivation, explains noncontingent attention to students as akin to putting something in the bank. Each time you interact with a student and show an interest in him or her as a person, you make a deposit. When you have invested enough (had enough of the right type of interactions so that the student feels valued by you), the student is more likely to want to follow your rules and strive to achieve your Guidelines for Success. In addition, if you make enough deposits, there will be reserve capital for those times when you may have to make a withdrawal because of student misbehavior. Whether the withdrawal consists of a gentle reprimand, a discussion, or a consequence designed to help improve the student's behavior, the more you have invested in the student, the more likely she is to understand that you are trying to help her by correcting her.

"Mrs. Jacobsen cares so much about me that she is taking the time to help me learn to be responsible. I want to do what she is asking me to do." When nothing has been invested, the student may feel that you are simply trying to control her behavior. "Mrs. Jacobsen wants me to sit down and be quiet because she doesn't like me. Well, the heck with her. I'll do whatever I want, whenever I want. She can't make me sit down." Noncontingent attention helps you build a spirit of cooperation between yourself and your students. In addition, by building a relationship with your students, you increase the likelihood that they will feel connected to you and to their school. This connectedness has been shown to correlate with long-term student success (Glover et al., 1998; McNeely & Falci, 2004; Resnick et al., 1997; Sprick, Garrison et al., 2002).

Dr. Ruby Payne (1996), an expert on the mindset of poverty, stresses that the primary motivation for students and adults in poverty is relationships. For students in poverty, the deposits and withdrawals, however, are different. Payne outlines these in Figure 7.1, Deposits and Withdrawals Made to and from Individuals in Poverty.

Showing an interest in students and acting friendly does not mean you should try to be a friend or a peer. You are the teacher, and you do not want to be so friendly that you seem to be an equal. You are the person in authority and the one who needs to

take note

If you work with ELL students, be sure to make eye contact with them, mention their names during your presentations, and every so often stand near their desks. This way, you communicate that you are genuinely interested and have not forgotten them.

CHAPTER 7 TASKS

Figure 7.1 *Deposits and Withdrawals Made to and from Individuals in Poverty*

DEPOSITS	WITHDRAWALS
Acceptance for humor and entertainment provided by the individual	Put-downs or sarcasm about the humor of the individual
Acceptance of what the individual cannot say about a person or situation	Insistence and demands for full explanation about a person or situation
Respect for the demands and priorities of relationships	Insistence on the middle-class view of relationships
Using the adult voice	Using the parent voice
Assisting with goal setting	Telling the individual his or her goals
Identifying options related to available resources	Making judgments about the value and availability of resources
Understanding the importance of personal freedom, speech, and individual personality	Assigning pejorative character traits to the individual

Reprinted with permission. Excerpted from A Framework for Understanding Poverty *by Ruby K. Payne. Adapted from Stephen Covey's* The Seven Habits of Highly Effective People.

intervene if there are rule violations. However, as the person in authority, you want to communicate that you value and are interested in every one of your students as individual people. Following are more detailed explanations of some ways to give your students noncontingent attention.

 Greet students.

This is the simplest but perhaps most important way to provide noncontingent attention. As students enter your room first thing in the morning or at the beginning of class, provide a friendly greeting. "Hello, Jonathan. Good morning Wachera. Francine, how are you today? You know, I'm tired this morning, too. You and I may have to nudge each other to stay awake in class. Maria, Jacob, Tyrone, good to see you today." You may not be able to greet every student each day, but you should try to greet enough students each day so that over the course of a week every student has been greeted at least once.

Elementary teachers should continue to greet their students throughout the day—greet a few students when they come in from recess or after music class or when they return from lunch. Middle school teachers should attempt to greet at least five to eight students per class as students enter the room. You can also make a point of greeting your students when you see them in the hall. They may barely respond (some students will be self-conscious if they are with friends), but they will notice if you don't take the time to acknowledge them.

> *Taking a few seconds to look at what a student is doing demonstrates that you are interested in the student and his work.*

 ### *Show an interest in students' work.*

During independent work periods, when no one needs immediate assistance, go to individual students or cooperative learning groups and look at students' work. Taking a few seconds to look at what a student is doing demonstrates that you are interested in the student and his work. Sometimes you may offer praise in this context; other times you can simply say something like, "I am looking forward to reading this when you are finished, Tamai."

 ### *Invite students to ask for assistance.*

Occasionally ask individual students how they are doing in class. If anyone indicates that he or she is having trouble, arrange a time for that student to get some additional help from you. For those who say they are doing fine, let them know that if they ever have trouble, they should not hesitate to come see you. If you make an offer of assistance to every student in the first couple of months of school, you communicate that you are aware of them as individuals and that you are available to help them.

 ### *Whenever time permits, have a conversation with a student or a group of students.*

Having a conversation with students demonstrates (more so than just greeting them) that you are interested in them—in their experiences and their ideas. Brief social interactions create an emotional connection between you and your students, and they are not hard to do. For example, if three students enter your middle school classroom at the beginning of the passing period, you can casually chat with them as you stand at the door and greet other entering students. As you are escorting your second-grade class to lunch, you might talk quietly with a couple of students as you go down the hall (unless students are not supposed to converse in the halls). Find out your students' individual interests and ask about them—ask a student about his soccer game the previous evening, for example. Periodically share something about yourself. "My son played goalie for his team in college. What position do you like to play?"

Make a special effort to greet or talk to any student you've recently interacted with regarding a misbehavior.

This kind of gesture on your part communicates that past corrective interactions with the student are now just that—past—and that you do not hold a grudge. It also lets the student know that you are prepared for a fresh start. For example, if immediately before lunch you had to talk to a student about being disruptive, that student should definitely be one of the five or six students you greet when the class comes back after lunch. "Aaron, good to see you. How are you doing?" A greeting in these circumstances actually decreases the probability that the student will misbehave in the next instructional activity.

LEVEL OF STRUCTURE AND NONCONTINGENT ATTENTION

Task 1: Build Positive Relationships With Students is one of the few tasks in the CHAMPS approach in which the level of classroom structure makes absolutely no difference. Whether your students need high, medium, or low structure, you owe it to every individual to build a positive relationship by interacting with them as frequently as possible in a manner that is friendly, inviting, and personable.

Task 2: Provide Positive Feedback

Give students a variety of positive feedback on their progress and success in meeting behavioral and academic goals.

Among the most important practices of an effective teacher is giving feedback—letting students know about their behavioral and academic progress and success (Brophy, 1981; Brophy & Good, 1986; Burns, VanDerHeyden, & Boice, 2008; Evertson & Harris, 1992; Gettinger & Stoiber, 1998; Simonsen et al., 2008; Sugai & Tindal, 1993; Trussell, 2008). In Chapter 1, Task 1, we identified five major actions a teacher can take in an effort to improve student behavior. One of those is to implement procedures designed to encourage responsible behavior. Giving positive feedback is a powerful way to encourage responsible behavior. When done well, positive feedback confirms for students that they are on the right track and increases the probability that they will strive to demonstrate the same behaviors in the future (Kazdin, 1980; Skinner, 1953; Trussell, 2008).

In this task, we discuss six hallmarks of effective positive feedback. Feedback should be:

- Accurate

- Specific and descriptive

- Contingent

- Age-appropriate

- Given immediately

- Given in a manner that fits your style

If you incorporate these suggestions into the positive feedback you give your students, you can significantly increase the probability that your feedback will encourage and motivate students to behave more responsibly in the future.

 Feedback should be accurate.

Effective positive feedback is related to a behavior or set of behaviors that did in fact occur. When an individual receives positive feedback about something he or she did not actually do, the feedback is meaningless. If you comment verbally or in a note to a student that his accuracy in completing math assignments is improving, be sure that the student's accuracy really is improving. If you note that a student demonstrated improved self-control by staying in her seat during an entire instructional period, be sure that the student actually did stay in her seat. Students should receive a clear, consistent message about why they are receiving your positive attention (Alberto & Troutman, 2006; O'Leary & O'Leary, 1977). Your feedback should be especially frequent and immediate if the skill is new for the student or has been difficult in the past (Dishion & Stormshak, 2007; Scheuermann & Hall, 2008).

 Feedback should be specific and descriptive.

When giving positive feedback, be sure to tell students exactly what it was they did (Brophy, 1981; Martella et al., 1995). Feedback should be full of information—confirming for a student what the behavior or task was and what was important or useful about it. If you want to let a cooperative group know they have done well, describe the specific behaviors that were exhibited. When writing a note regarding a student's paper, identify the specific things the student did that contributed to the quality of the paper.

Specific descriptive feedback lets the student know which aspects of his or her behavior you are commenting on. Behavior-specific praise has been consistently shown to have a positive effect on on-task student behavior in general and special education (Bain et al., 1991; Cameron & Pierce, 1994; Ferguson & Houghton, 1992; Hall et al., 1968; Houghton, Wheldall, Jukes, & Sharpe, 1990; Sutherland et al., 2000). Simply writing "excellent" at the top of a paper, with no other notes, does not give the student any information about what aspects of the paper led to your positive reaction. Was it the effective use of figurative language? The organization? The creative use of the overall idea? The student has no idea what was particularly good about the paper, so he will not necessarily use those writing skills again. The next paper he writes may not include any of the good qualities of the first one because he doesn't know what those qualities are.

> When a particular phrase is overused, it becomes background noise, and students will cease to hear it.

Following are some common mistakes teachers make when providing positive feedback. All of them can be avoided by providing specific descriptions of student behavior.

THE "GOOD JOB" SYNDROME

It's easy for teachers to fall into a simple repetitive phrase that they use over and over and over to give positive feedback. There are two problems with this. First, most simple phrases such as "Good job," "Nice work," "Yes," and "Fantastic" provide no specific information—what exactly the student did that was useful or important. Second, when a particular phrase is overused, it becomes background noise, and students will cease to hear it.

MAKING JUDGMENTS OR DRAWING CONCLUSIONS ABOUT THE STUDENT

Be very cautious about reinforcing correct answers or praising positive behavior by stating or implying that a student is "good" or "smart" or "brilliant." When a student answers a difficult question, it can be tempting to say something like, "Allison, you are so smart." The problem is that a statement like this not only doesn't provide specific information about what the student did, but it may imply to the student that if she had not come up with that particular answer, you might not think of her as smart. It's far more effective to say, "Allison, you applied the formula, performed a series of computations, and came up with the correct answer."

Of course, you can still tell students they are smart—just don't use that type of judgmental phrase to reinforce particular answers or behaviors. Sometimes when you are talking individually to a student, feel free to use phrases like, "You are so smart!" If you make this a general comment rather than praise for a specific answer, you reduce the chances that the student will misunderstand you. He may feel that you think he is smart only when he answers correctly and that you think he is stupid when he answers incorrectly. Also, feel free to occasionally tell the entire class what a smart group of students they are. These broad statements about how smart and talented you consider students to be can counteract, at least to a small degree, the fact that some of your students have been told by other children or even their families that they are "dumb" or "no good." These students will benefit from hearing you tell them they are capable and smart. The difference is that you are not using this phrase to reinforce particular events or responses.

CALLING ATTENTION TO YOURSELF

Some teachers praise by saying, "I like the way you . . ." Even if you finish the sentence by specifically describing the student's behavior, a student may inadvertently take that initial phrase to mean that they should behave to please you. In fact, what you are working toward is for students to behave in particular ways because it will help them be successful learners. Another problem with an "I like the way you . . ." kind of phrase is that some students might get the idea that you like them when they are good, which in turn implies you don't like them when they are not good. Keep the focus of your feedback on the student and what he did, not on your likes and dislikes.

If you want to use a lead-in phrase when delivering your descriptive praise, consider using variations of "You should be proud of how well you . . ." This keeps the focus on the student, not on you. The one exception is when a student does something particularly helpful. In that circumstance, feel free to let the student know that you appreciate his help. For example, if you drop some papers and a student helps you pick them up, it is reasonable and logical to say something like, "Thank you for helping me pick those up. I appreciate having such a thoughtful student."

 Feedback should be contingent.

Contingent delivery of feedback allows the student to see a direct relationship between her behavior and your positive attention. You provide the positive attention only when the student demonstrates the target behavior that you want to increase or maintain (Alberto & Troutman, 2006; Cooper et al., 2007; O'Leary & O'Leary, 1977; Scheuermann & Hall, 2008). Contingent feedback has been successfully used to increase academic and social behaviors as well as to decrease problem behaviors (Merrett, 1981; Merrett & Wheldall, 1990; Simonsen et al., 2008; Wheldall & Merrett, 1984, 1989).

> "
> *If you are going to provide feedback to a student about a target behavior, be sure the behavior has some level of importance.*
> "

If you are going to provide feedback to a student about a target behavior, be sure the behavior has some level of importance. It should not be an overly simple behavior for the person who demonstrated it. To understand why, imagine that someone you know and respect (a favorite college professor, your minister, your boss) sees you drive into a parking lot. As you

> "Contingent feedback is also important when you want to increase a behavior that requires effort."

step out of your car, he comes over to you and says, "Excellent left turn into this parking lot. You used your turn signals, you checked your blind spot, and you controlled your speed as you pulled into the parking space to ensure that you did not scratch the car on either side of you." This feedback may be accurate and descriptive, but it is also at best meaningless and at worst insulting to you. It implies that these driving behaviors are something special when, to an experienced driver, making a left turn into a parking lot is really no big deal. You would probably wonder why the person was being so gushy and excited about something that you have done successfully many times. It's even possible that receiving this meaningless (or insulting) feedback reduces your respect for that person.

There are three major circumstances when using contingent positive feedback may be especially beneficial.

When learning a new skill. The first is when the feedback occurs while someone is learning a new skill or behavior. If you had a good teacher when you were first learning to drive, that person may have occasionally given you positive feedback similar to the statements in the previous paragraph. The difference is that because you may have driven only once or twice before, those statements were probably not at all insulting or meaningless because they provided specific and descriptive confirmation of what you did correctly.

When increasing a behavior that requires effort. Contingent feedback is also important when you want to increase a behavior that requires effort, whether or not it is a new behavior. For example, imagine you have been making a concerted effort to be more helpful around the house because your partner has been carrying more than his or her fair share. If your partner expresses gratitude for the extra help and shares his or her appreciation that the household chores are more equally divided, that positive feedback is unlikely to be meaningless or insulting to you. The behavior isn't new or particularly complex—after all, putting socks in the hamper is not exactly rocket science—but it does take effort to change a bad habit. Feedback that acknowledges effort is likely to be valued by the person receiving the feedback and can lead them to maintain or increase the frequency of the behavior in the future.

When taking pride in the behavior. Finally, positive contingent feedback is important when a person is proud of his or her behavior or set of behaviors. For example, think about a term paper you wrote—one you felt was especially well written. When you got the paper back, you probably looked at the grade and then went through the paper page by page to see if the instructor had written any comments. For most people, any positive comments received in these circumstances are not viewed as meaningless or insulting. In fact, it is quite likely that you will be pleased by the comments, particularly if the instructor described which parts of the paper were well thought out or well written.

Feedback should be age-appropriate.

It is important that feedback is sincere and meaningful (O'Leary & O'Leary, 1977; Scheuermann & Hall, 2008). The feedback you give to a kindergarten student will be presented somewhat differently from the feedback you give to an eighth-grade student. For example, with primary students and some classes of older students, you may find that they like public praise. Below are two examples of praise statements that may be very meaningful and highly reinforcing to younger students.

---

for example

Rosa, what beautiful handwriting! You did a great job using Theo Bear's guidelines. This is your personal best.

Everyone, look at Jamal. He is being polite and respectful. Jamal, you get to show the class how to be a good partner.

With older students, you can use more sophisticated vocabulary to describe behavior. And in terms of being contingent, with older students it is more appropriate to focus on advanced behaviors and combinations of behaviors. At the same time, be careful not to embarrass older students when you provide positive feedback. Middle school students, in particular, may feel a great deal of peer pressure to fit in and be cool. Think about the thousands of messages students get that suggest that being good is geeky. If you provide feedback in a way that embarrasses a student, it not only won't be positive or encouraging, it may actually discourage the student from behaving responsibly in the future. For example, many students avoid behaving responsibly when they are praised in a way that makes them look like a teacher's pet. If a student (or students) seems to be embarrassed when you give positive feedback, consider experimenting with one or more of these suggestions:

Use a quiet voice when providing feedback to individual students. If a student feels you are putting him on public display, it may increase the possibility that he will feel embarrassed in front of his friends.

Be brief. If you go on too long, accepting the praise graciously may be difficult.

Be somewhat businesslike. Simply state the positive behavior(s) the student exhibited. If you sound too excited or pleased when you praise, it can make a student think, "I pleased the teacher—goody, goody."

Avoid pausing and looking at the student after you praise. A pause can imply that you expect the student to respond, and this puts a student in an awkward position—"Should I smile? Should I say thank you?" Smiling or saying "thank you" in front of peers can be socially embarrassing, especially to a student who values her tough image. A tough student will often make a smart-aleck comment or engage in misbehavior to reassert her image to peers.

 Feedback should be given immediately.

Immediacy is important because students need to know when they are doing something correctly. In addition, students who are starved for attention may start demanding attention through misbehavior if they get none for meeting expectations—they may feel that attention for behaving badly is better than none at all. Positive feedback is most effective when it occurs very soon after the behavior you are trying to encourage. With primary students in particular, waiting until later to give the feedback does not help to solidify the desired behaviors. By the time you praise them, the students have forgotten exactly what it was they did.

 Feedback should fit your style.

> " *There is no one right way to give positive feedback.* "

There is no one right way to give positive feedback. You can incorporate these suggestions for giving effective positive feedback and still have plenty of room for your individual style. A teacher who has a businesslike personality can and should employ a more businesslike style of providing positive feedback. A teacher who tends to be excited and energetic may be more like a cheerleader when giving feedback. A soft-spoken teacher's feedback will probably be quieter than a boisterous teacher's feedback. In most cases, if you are comfortable with your style of giving feedback, your students are probably comfortable as well. Remember, it is important that praise is delivered and received sincerely (O'Leary & O'Leary, 1977), and this is difficult to do if you don't deliver praise in a manner that is comfortable for you and your students. If your students are responding to your current style with embarrassment, you should probably consider our suggestions about age-appropriate and nonembarrassing feedback.

LEVEL OF STRUCTURE AND POSITIVE FEEDBACK

Research has demonstrated that teachers of students with high rates of behavioral difficulties rarely use praise (Sutherland et al., 2000; Van Acker, Grant, & Henry, 1996) and often use more disapproval than approval (Jack et al., 1996). This tendency is shocking in that the students who most desperately need lots of positive feedback and encouragement are the least likely to receive it. With the strong research linking positive feedback and student-teacher relationships with improved outcomes, it is especially important that teachers of at-risk students work to provide a structured classroom with high rates of positive feedback for appropriate behavior (Stormont et al., 2007).

Within the CHAMPS approach, the more risk factors your class has, the more you need to manage student behavior with positive, not punitive, means. With a low-structure class, you may be able to get away with relatively low rates of positive feedback and still have students behave responsibly. We do not recommend this, but you can probably give relatively little positive feedback and students will be fine. If your students come from stable situations and their families give them encouragement to work hard and behave responsibly, they may work hard and behave well without getting much positive feedback from you, although they probably will not experience high levels of motivation.

> *The more risk factors your class has, the more you need to manage student behavior with positive, not punitive, means.*

However, when students need high structure (that is, the class has many risk factors), frequent positive feedback is essential. The many benefits (increased academic engagement, improved social behavior, decreased problem behavior) of positive feedback, especially feedback that is specific and contingent, have been well demonstrated in the literature (Broden, Bruce, Mitchell, Carter, & Hall, 1970; Brophy, 1981, 1983; Cameron & Pierce, 1994; Craft, Alber, & Heward, 1998; Espin & Yell, 1994; Ferguson & Houghton, 1992; Hall et al., 1968; Reinke et al., 2007; Roca & Gross, 1996; Sutherland et al., 2000; Wolford, Heward, & Alber, 2001).

Without feedback, some students will not know when they have met your expectations—when they have behaved or performed a task as you requested. Furthermore, when students try to meet your academic and behavioral expectations and do not receive any feedback—any indication that you notice their efforts—some of them will cease striving to meet the expectations (Dishion & Stormshak, 2007). "I try to do what she wants, and she never even notices. Why should I bother?" The greater the number of high-needs students, the greater the need for you to provide frequent positive feedback that follows the recommendations within this task (Barbetta et al., 2005; Beaman & Wheldall, 2000; Chalk & Bizo, 2004; Sutherland et al., 2000).

WHEN STUDENTS RESPOND NEGATIVELY TO POSITIVE FEEDBACK

Some students may respond negatively to a teacher's efforts to provide positive feedback. For example, shortly after being told that he is behaving in a mature and responsible manner, a student may exhibit his worst behavior, leading a teacher to decide that the student should no longer receive positive feedback or acknowledgment. The student who misbehaves after receiving positive feedback is a relatively common phenomenon with several possible explanations. Fortunately, there are techniques you can try to reduce the probability that a student will continue to react badly to positive feedback.

One reason a student may misbehave immediately after receiving positive feedback is that he is embarrassed by the feedback. If you suspect this is the case, try modifying your feedback as suggested earlier in this task. See whether making the feedback more private, stating it in a more businesslike or brief way, or eliminating pauses after you provide positive feedback results in the student reacting more positively. Think about whether the feedback is age-appropriate.

The other reasons a student may respond negatively tend be more complex and slightly harder to remedy. The student may have an image of himself as a tough guy and feels he has to uphold that image. The student may feel peer pressure to maintain his bad image. Or the student may have trouble handling success. When you provide feedback to someone who has one or more of these issues, the feedback won't fit her image of herself and can make her feel uncomfortable—terrified by her own success. Exhibiting misbehavior helps a student like this return to feeling like a troublemaker or a loser. She may believe she is incapable of being successful, and she must show you that the success was an aberration. In addition, the misbehavior takes some pressure off the student—"See? You can't expect me to be successful all the time." Regardless of the reason for a student's misbehavior after receiving positive recognition, you can try experimenting with one or more of the following suggestions:

 Treat the misbehavior (the downturn after receiving positive feedback) as a momentary interruption in the student's success.

You praise a second-grade student for the quality of an assignment he completed, and he then tears up the paper and throws it on the floor while you are handing papers to other students. You might say something like, "Jamie, please pick up that paper and put it in the trash before you go out to recess."

Try not to communicate anger or disappointment at this misbehavior. Keeping your emotions under wraps can be tough. When a student falls apart after you acknowledge his success, it is natural to feel angry or disappointed. You may want to say something like, "Jamie, you were doing so well and now you're throwing paper on the floor. I just don't understand, and I am very disappointed." Statements like these may feed into the student's need to feel like a tough guy or a loser, and they definitely take the pressure off the student to continue to succeed—it's clear the teacher has once again seen the worst the student has to offer.

At a neutral and reasonably private time, talk to the student about her tendency to misbehave after getting positive feedback.

See if the student can give you any insights into the reason for her misbehavior. Ask her if she has any suggestions for ways you can give positive feedback that will reduce the chance that she will misbehave afterwards. Try experimenting with any reasonable suggestions the student makes. If the student cannot come up with any strategies for you to try, ask her what she thinks about some of the suggestions included in this task, such as the one below about giving feedback more privately.

 Find a way to give the positive feedback more privately.

The student may prefer to get a note rather than public praise. He may prefer to have you give the feedback at the end of the period rather than during it. He may prefer that you use a signal that only he knows (scratch your forehead, for example) to tell him he is behaving responsibly.

 Switch from giving specific descriptive feedback to simply interacting with the student when she is behaving responsibly.

Say "hello" to the student as she enters class. If she is on task during independent work, don't specifically praise her, but do go over and ask if she has any questions or needs any help. If she has behaved responsibly throughout the morning, don't praise, but ask her if she would be willing to distribute handouts to the class. At the end of the day, tell her to have a nice evening. This contingent attention, given when she is behaving responsibly, may reinforce the appropriate behavior even though you are not providing specific descriptive positive feedback (Skinner, 1953).

If eliminating the positive feedback is successful (the student handles the attention as long as no praise is included), continue to withhold praise for a few weeks while continuing to provide attention to the student. If the student's behavior is improving, gradually introduce subtle praise. Once a day or so, make a matter-of-fact statement about something the student has done. Don't gush or be overly enthusiastic, just make a comment.

- *Thank you for getting that assignment in on time.*

- *That was a creative contribution you made to your cooperative group.*

If you see a downturn, back off and return to attention without praise. However, if the student is handling it, gradually increase the frequency of specific descriptive feedback.

> *If the student's behavior is improving, gradually introduce subtle praise.*

Task 3: Provide Intermittent Celebrations

Periodically reward both individual students and the whole class with a celebration that acknowledges their progress and success in meeting behavioral and academic goals.

An occasional celebration of progress and success can be especially useful for motivating immature students, students with a long history of behavior problems, and students who need to make major behavioral changes. In general, intermittent celebration means giving a reward on some, but not all, occasions when a student or group demonstrates a particularly important behavior. Those of you familiar with behavioral theory may recognize this concept as an intermittent reinforcement schedule (Skinner, 1953).

Rewarding behavior is not bribery, although some people equate the two. Bribery is the inducement to do something illegal, unethical, or immoral. Providing intermittent rewards for students who have exhibited desired behavior more accurately reflects an attempt by school personnel to recognize and celebrate students' progress and success. To understand the power of this kind of feedback, imagine a second-grade student who has written a story that really impresses the teacher. The teacher shows the story to the principal, who in turn calls the student into the office to congratulate him. The principal also calls the student's mother to let her know what a special skill the student demonstrated. This student will remember these events for the rest of his life. (*I know, because it happened to me. —RS*)

Use more frequent intermittent celebrations of success when students are in the early stages of learning a new skill or improving an existing skill, or whenever they are working on a behavior that is difficult for them (Scheuermann & Hall, 2008). For example, if you are trying to motivate students to increase their rates of work completion, you might occasionally (say, an average one out of three times—but be unpredictable) reward the class when 100 percent of the students complete their daily assignments by playing music during the next day's work period. As the level of work completion improves, you reduce how often you give a reward (for example, an average of one out of six times—remaining unpredictable). Please note that making the delivery of rewards unpredictable keeps them special and reduces the likelihood that students will become bored with them (Alberto & Troutman, 2006).

Rewards that are meaningful to your students will be most effective (Dishion & Stormshak, 2007; Scheuermann & Hall, 2008). The more academically successful or socially mature the students, the greater the chance that some sort of informational feedback will suffice. For example, most successful students in grades 4 and above appreciate a specific descriptive note on a paper. On the other hand, the younger the class or the less academically successful and socially mature the students, the more likely it is that they need a more extrinsically valuable reward in order to be excited about the celebration. And, of course, with primary students and even some secondary-level students, adding a sticker of some sort can make a note even more meaningful.

The essential idea behind intermittent celebrations is that when a student or a group of students makes a significant academic or behavioral improvement, you give them more than simple verbal praise. Provide some form of positive feedback that lets them know they have accomplished something special. Create a sense of celebration about what they accomplished. The key is to use these celebrations as sparingly as possible but as frequently as necessary (and always unpredictably!) to keep students proud and excited about their achievements.

> " Be creative about the kinds of intermittent celebrations you use in your classroom. "

Be creative about the kinds of intermittent celebrations you use in your classroom—have fun in a manner that fits your personality and your style. Some people may think that students will not respond well to intermittent reinforcement unless it has a monetary value or involves food. Not true! If you use intermittent rewards wisely and understand the concept, you can make almost anything work.

for example

Mike Booher shared the following examples from high school teachers. If high school students liked these rewards, elementary and middle school students will be sure to like them as well.

- My daughter's high school AP calculus teacher (65 years old) performs what the students called the Wally Wiggle. When the class grasps a new concept or does well on a particular concept, he does a quick John Travolta dance from *Saturday Night Fever*. The students love watching him dance. Getting him to do a Wally Wiggle is a big deal—and these are AP students!
- Gloria Bozeman from C.E. Byrd High School in Shreveport, Louisiana, says, "I blow a kiss with a smile for intermittent celebrations—the students love it!" This nonverbal reward would also work as a noncontingent reward.
- Another Shreveport high school teacher says that her students love it when she places stickers on their foreheads as an intermittent celebration.

The CD that accompanies this book includes a variety of reproducible awards, certificates, notes to students, and notes to parents (see examples on the next page).

Reproducible 7.1a–n   *Awards and Certificates (See Appendix D for more certificates.)*

Reproducible 7.2a–b   *Daily Report Cards*

Reproducible 7.3   *Badges and Buttons (See Appendix D for more badges and buttons.)*

You can print these reproducible forms and write in the student's information. You can also type the student's information directly into the electronic file for a more formal and professional appearance. Reproducible 7.1 shows a few examples of the reproducible awards and certificates. Reproducible 7.2 shows reproducible daily report cards that can be sent home, and Reproducible 7.3 shows examples of badges and buttons. See Appendix D for previews of more of the reproducible forms found on the CD.

Some of the badge examples can be printed on labels so they can be used as stickers and placed on student work, or as a badge the student can wear on clothing for the day. Use Avery Labels #5294 for printing badges.

Figure 7.2 shows a variety of ideas for intermittent celebrations of success. The suggestions in the left-hand column are most appropriate for younger students. Those in the middle column are appropriate for older students, though most will work with younger students as well. The suggestions in the right-hand column are appropriate for whole groups and classes. These lists are by no means comprehensive or complete. For additional ideas, talk to colleagues, read other books, and—the best idea of all—ask your students.

LEVEL OF STRUCTURE AND INTERMITTENT CELEBRATIONS OF SUCCESS

For students in a low-structure classroom (a class with few risk factors), you can probably maintain motivation primarily with noncontingent attention and positive feedback. If you wish, you can use intermittent celebrations for variety or for a sense of change—but do so sparingly. With a medium-structure classroom, occasional celebrations can be used as a way to keep students striving to be successful and to keep things interesting and exciting. If your students have many risk factors and need a high-structure management plan, it will probably be essential for you to use intermittent rewards regularly, along with noncontingent attention and positive feedback (Barbetta et al., 2005).

take note

For a class that needs high structure, even this combination of procedures may not be sufficient to keep students motivated. You may also need to implement one or more of the reinforcement systems suggested in Chapter 8: Classwide Motivation in order to maintain responsible behavior and high levels of enthusiasm.

CHAPTER 7 TASKS

1 • Build Positive Relationships   2 • Provide Positive Feedback

Figure 7.2 *Ideas for Intermittent Celebrations of Success*

IDEAS FOR YOUNGER STUDENTS (Grades Pre K–4)	IDEAS FOR OLDER STUDENTS (Grades 3–8)	IDEAS FOR THE GROUP
• Let student choose a story. • Let student be first in line. • Let student use piano, computer, etc. • Let student dictate a story that someone types and prints for the student to illustrate. • Let student earn extra minutes of recess for entire class. • Let student wear a sign or badge. • Let student work near a class pet or have hamster or other caged pet on desk for the day. • Let student sit in your chair. • Let student perform for the class. • Have class give student applause. • Identify student as "Special Student of the Day." • Allow student to keep a special trophy or stuffed animal on desk for the day. • Give student a gift certificate for free ice cream or french fries. • Congratulate student in front of class. • Take student's picture and post it. • Draw stars on back of student's hand. • Invite student to eat in room with you. • Give student a paper crown to wear. • Post banner or poster with student's name and accomplishment.	• Let student teach a portion of the lesson. • Let student tell a joke to the class. • Let student supervise or tutor younger students. • Let student repair a broken desk or replace batteries in a calculator. • Let student choose a modified or independent assignment. • Let student choose a peer with whom to play a board game or computer game. • Let student leave class a few minutes early. • Give student a Certificate of Achievement. • Publicly congratulate (but be careful not to embarrass) student. • Congratulate student in front of another adult. • Give or lend student a book that was special to you at the same age. • Give student a job or responsibility. • Give student a ticket to school dance or sporting event. • Ask the principal or counselor to call student in and congratulate student on classroom success. • Send student or family a letter via the mail. • Shake student's hand and congratulate in a very adult-to-adult manner. • Give student a Free Homework Pass. • Write a positive note to student. • Call student at home to congratulate for classroom success.	• Let class listen to recorded music during an independent work period. • Let class select a theme for one day, such as Talk-Like-a-Pirate Day, Dress-up Day, Backward Day, Opposite Day, Hat Day. • Let class invite someone to come to class to see completed projects or assignments. • Let class work outside. • Let class redecorate classroom. • Have a class party. • Give everyone in class food or a beverage, such as popcorn, fruit, crackers, juice. • Go to recess or lunch with class. • Have class applaud for themselves. • Tell a joke to class. • Give class a new freedom or more responsibility (for example, increased freedom to move about the room). • Give everyone in class a special pencil or other school supply item. • Read to class. • Give class additional recess or break time. • Invite parents to come and watch class demonstrate a particular skill or competency. • Set up a competition with another class. • Have a pizza delivered to classroom. • Teacher wears funny clothes to class. • Schedule a field trip.

Adapted from and used with permission from Sprick, 1995.

Task 4: Strive to Provide a High Ratio of Positive Interactions

Plan to interact at least three times more often with each student when he or she is behaving appropriately than when he or she is misbehaving (that is, at least a 3:1 ratio).

This behavior management strategy is one of the most essential but also one of the most difficult to implement. Providing a high ratio of positive interactions (RPI) means making the effort to interact with every student more frequently (at least three times more frequently) when the student is behaving appropriately than when he or she is behaving inappropriately (Good & Grouws, 1977; Shores et al., 1993; Trussell, 2008; Walker et al., 2004). To understand why this strategy is so essential yet so difficult, consider the following:

- Some students are starved for attention. Most teachers have direct experience with students who demand attention, and most have seen the desperate measures some students will take to get attention.

- For the student who is truly starved for attention, the form of attention may not matter. A reprimand for misbehaving may satisfy this student's desire for attention just as much as positive feedback for behaving responsibly (Alberto & Troutman, 2006). In fact, the scolding may be even more satisfying because it probably lasts longer and involves greater emotional intensity from the teacher.

- With students who are starved for attention, the behavior you reinforce with attention is the behavior that you will begin to see more often (Skinner, 1953). When you have more interactions with students when they are behaving appropriately (positive interactions), you will see an increase in positive behavior over time. On the other hand, when you have more interactions with students when they are behaving inappropriately (negative interactions), you will see an increase in negative behavior over time.

> " *Interactions with students are considered positive or negative based on the student's behavior at the time you attend to him or her.* "

Note that your interactions with students are considered positive or negative based on the student's behavior at the time you attend to him or her. For example, if a student is off task and you say, "Wanda, you need to get back to work or you will not complete your assignment," it is considered a negative interaction even if you made the request very pleasantly

> "
> *Just because an interaction is considered negative does not mean it is wrong.*
> "

and your intention was to help the student. It is a negative interaction because the student was engaged in a negative behavior (being off task) when you initiated the interaction. Some teachers mistakenly believe that when they are nice to a student, it is a positive interaction and when they are acting hostile or sounding angry, it is a negative interaction.

It's also important to realize that just because an interaction is considered negative does not mean it is wrong. It may, for example, be the most useful way to get the student back on task at the time. However, understand that unless you make an effort to interact with this same student when she is on task, she may learn that it is actually easier to get your attention (which may be what she wants) for being off task than for behaving well. Remember, each time you give attention to a student, you may be reinforcing the behavior you are paying attention to—whether the behavior is positive or negative (Alberto & Troutman, 2006; Carr et al., 2000; Skinner, 1953). Thus, you should pay at least three times more attention to students when they are exhibiting positive behavior than when they are exhibiting negative behavior.

Unfortunately, achieving this 3:1 positive to negative ratio is not always easy. In fact, observational studies regularly show that most teachers pay significantly more attention to students' misbehavior than to students' positive behavior (Alber, Heward, & Hippler, 1991; Brophy, 1981; Lewis et al., 2004; Matheson & Shriver, 2005; Sutherland, 2000; Sutherland et al., 2000; White, 1975). In 1986, Dr. Wes Becker wrote about studies he had conducted with teachers who were reprimanding and reminding students about out-of-seat behavior during work periods. He encouraged the teachers to reprimand students more immediately and more consistently—"Don't miss a single student who gets out-of-seat at the wrong time." The teachers assumed this would decrease the behavior. In fact, the number of students getting out of their seats at the wrong times actually increased.

Dr. Becker called this phenomenon the Criticism Trap. Although the teachers thought they were doing something effective (reprimanding or issuing a consequence for an inappropriate behavior), the students, who were starved for attention, were getting out of their seats at least in part to get their teachers to look at them and talk to them. The students' need for attention was satisfied when their teachers told them to get back in their seats—and they typically did sit down, at least initially. When students took their seats, the teachers were reinforced for reprimanding. "Ah, now I can teach." But before long the students realized, consciously or unconsciously, that they were not getting attention when they did what the teachers wanted, so they got out of their seats again. The teachers reprimanded again, giving the desired attention, and the students were again reinforced for getting out of their seats.

A scenario like the above example becomes a destructive pattern in which all parties involved get what they want in the short run. The students get attention when they violate the teacher's expectations. The teacher gets momentary compliance each time he reprimands. However, when this cycle is allowed to continue, no one gets what he or she wants in the long run. Over time, students behave less and less responsibly, and the teacher gets more frustrated and more negative. The only real way out of the Criticism Trap is to have more interactions with students when they are behaving responsibly than when they are misbehaving.

If you think you have fallen into the Criticism Trap, or if you believe that your RPI with students is less than 3:1, consider implementing one or more of the following suggestions for increasing positive interactions. See Chapter 9 for more information on how to reduce negative interactions.

- Each time you interact with a student engaged in negative behavior, tell yourself that you owe that student three positive interactions.

- Identify specific times during each day that you will give students positive feedback on some aspect of their individual behavior or class performance. For example, you might decide that at the beginning of each math period, you will compliment five or six students.

- Schedule individual conference times with students to compliment them on their behavioral or academic performances.

- Periodically scan your classroom, specifically searching for important reinforceable behaviors that you can acknowledge to students.

- Identify particular events that occur during the day (for example, a student getting a drink of water) that will prompt you to observe the class and identify a reinforceable behavior.

take note

Students often believe that if the teacher corrects their behavior, the teacher does not like them. Even high school teachers report that students have this misconception. By providing noncontingent attention or specific praise as soon as possible after correcting a student's misbehavior, you send the message that you still care for the student and dissolve the tension the student may feel.

CHAPTER 7 TASKS

- Reduce the amount of attention (that is, the time and intensity) a student receives for misbehavior and increase the amount of attention the student receives when not engaged in misbehavior.

- Engage in frequent noncontingent positive interactions with the students.

- Devote 15 seconds at the end of each day to identify one or two students who had a rough day—lots of negative interactions. Write their names on a sticky note and place the note in your plan book for the next day. Use that note as a reminder to pump up the RPI with those students. By focusing on positive attention, you can usually nip in the bud the likelihood of falling into a Criticism-Trap spiral. (*Thanks to a teacher in Guilford County Schools, North Carolina, for sharing this idea.*)

In Chapter 6: Observe, we provide suggestions for how you can periodically monitor your RPI by using Tool 2: Ratio of Interactions Monitoring Form (Reproducibles 6.2, 6.3, and 6.4) to determine if you have fallen into the Criticism Trap. For now, just be aware that the behaviors you pay the most attention to are the behaviors that are likely to occur with the most frequency as the year progresses. Consequently, we urge you to make a concerted effort to interact with every one of your students more frequently when the student is engaged in positive behavior than when he or she is engaged in negative behavior.

If you have an individual student with frequent misbehavior that you must correct, it can be very difficult to maintain a high RPI. In Chapter 9 we discuss chronic misbehavior and provide suggestions for setting up an organized plan to maintain a high RPI with a particular student.

LEVEL OF STRUCTURE AND RATIO OF POSITIVE TO NEGATIVE INTERACTIONS

The higher the level of structure necessary for your students, the greater the probability that at least some of the students are starved for attention. Students who are starved for attention are likely to try to get their attention needs met through misbehavior, potentially leading you into a pattern of frequent nagging and reprimanding—the classic spiral into the Criticism Trap. Therefore, the greater your class' need for structure, the more you need to make an effort to maintain positive interactions at a very high level. This task is absolutely essential for classes that need high structure. You may even need to strive for a 5:1 or, with a few of the more needy individual students, even a 9:1 RPI. Maintaining a 3:1 RPI is also important with low-structure classes, but it is generally easier to accomplish because there tends to be less misbehavior in these classes.

Conclusion

This chapter covered four strategies that can help improve students' motivation to follow your rules, strive toward your Guidelines for Success, and achieve your goals and instructional expectations.

- Demonstrate to students that you value them as individuals by using greetings, nonverbal communication, and (when possible) conversations.

- Give students positive feedback on their progress and success in meeting behavioral and academic goals.

- Intermittently reward individuals and the whole class with a celebration that acknowledges their progress and success.

- Strive for at least a 3:1 ratio of positive to negative interactions with all students.

Use the Self-Assessment Checklist shown on the following pages to keep track of the tasks you've completed and those that require further work. A fillable version of the Self-Assessment Checklist is available on the CD.

SELF-ASSESSMENT CHECKLIST pg. 1

Print from CD

Chapter 7: Motivation

Increase Student Motivation

Use the worksheet on the following pages to identify which (or which parts) of the tasks described in this chapter you have completed. For any item that has not been completed, note what needs to be done to complete it. Then translate your notes onto your planning calendar in the form of specific actions that you can take (e.g., December 2, take time to review my RPI with students).

✓	TASK	NOTES & IMPLEMENTATION *Ideas*
	TASK 1: BUILD POSITIVE RELATIONSHIPS WITH STUDENTS	
☐	I have considered how I will provide each of my students with noncontingent attention—including, but not limited to, the following:	

- Greet students.
- Show an interest in student work.
- Invite students to ask for assistance.
- Have conversations with students, when possible.

SELF-ASSESSMENT CHECKLIST pg. 2

✓	TASK	NOTES & IMPLEMENTATION *Ideas*
	TASK 2: PROVIDE POSITIVE FEEDBACK	
☐	I have made a plan to ensure that I am incorporating the following characteristics into the positive feedback I give students regarding their academic and/or behavioral performance. My feedback will be:	

- Accurate
- Specific and descriptive
- Contingent
- Age-appropriate
- Given immediately
- Given in a manner that fits my personal style

| ☐ | If any stu... increase ... the feedb... | |

SELF-ASSESSMENT CHECKLIST pg. 3

✓	TASK	NOTES & IMPLEMENTATION *Ideas*
	TASK 3: PROVIDE INTERMITTENT CELEBRATIONS	
☐	Based on the level of structure I have determined my students need, I will plan on using intermittent celebrations:	

- Rarely
- Occasionally
- Frequently

☐	I will watch for any tendency on my part to fall into the Criticism Trap.	
☐	I have identified (or have a plan for how I can identify) the kinds of rewards that are likely to be most useful with my students.	
	TASK 4: STRIVE TO PROVIDE A HIGH RATIO OF POSITIVE INTERACTIONS	
☐	I understand how important it is for me to interact with each of my students at least three times more when they are behaving responsibly than when they are misbehaving.	
☐	I will watch for any tendency on my part to fall into the Criticism Trap.	
☐	I will periodically assess my patterns of interactions using Tool 2: Ratio of Interactions Monitoring Form (Reproducibles 6.2, 6.3, and 6.4) from Chapter 6.	

Classwide Motivation

Classwide systems can increase students' motivation to behave responsibly and strive toward goals.

Consider Implementing a Classwide Motivation System

Introduction

*C*hapters 1 and 7 suggested basic strategies for promoting student motivation—using effective instructional practices and giving students meaningful and relevant positive feedback on their behavioral and academic progress. This chapter extends those suggestions by explaining when and how to implement an effective classwide system or systems to increase student motivation to behave responsibly and to strive to achieve goals such as your Guidelines for Success (see Chapter 1, Task 4). A *classwide system* is an organized and systematic set of procedures designed to have a positive impact on all the students in your class (Fairbanks et al., 2007; Farmer et al., 2006; Lohrmann & Talerico, 2004; Shores et al., 1993). Using a classwide system to enhance motivation is appropriate for many circumstances and may even be necessary in some circumstances, such as:

CHAPTER 8 TASK

Task 1
Effectively Employ a Classwide System or Systems to Increase Motivated and Responsible Student Behavior

- The behavior of many students in your class is challenging in many different ways—for example, not following directions, wasting class time, and showing disrespect.

- Students are for the most part responsible, but quite a few students have a problem with one specific behavior, such as work completion or talking during work periods.

- Your class behaves responsibly enough, but students have grown somewhat apathetic.

This chapter provides information on how to decide which basic kind of system (nonreward- or reward-based) to use. It also discusses how to implement, maintain, and fade a reward-based system. In addition, a menu of easy-to-implement classwide systems is provided—you can choose one or more most appropriate for your particular situation.

Unlike most of the previous chapters, this chapter contains only one task. It is:

Task 1: Effectively employ a classwide system or systems to increase motivated and responsible student behavior • Classwide systems can increase student motivation to behave responsibly and strive toward goals.

To help you accomplish this task, this chapter presents information and suggestions on the following topics, based on the three steps presented in Reproducible 8.1, Develop and/or Revise Your Classwide Motivation System:

Step 1. Identify problems, goals, level of structure needed, and the type of system you will use.

Step 2. Select a system (one or more) and prepare to implement it—effectively choosing, designing, and implementing a reward-based system.

Step 3. For reward-based systems, identify how you will effectively maintain, modify, and fade the system.

A sample Reproducible 8.1 appears on pp. 308–309. The CD contains a blank fillable version of Reproducible 8.1.

Following this how-to information are descriptions of different types of systems—what the system is designed to accomplish, the level of classroom structure (high, medium, or low) for which it is most appropriate, and the specifics on how to use it. This menu begins with the high-structure systems—these are the most powerful but also the most time consuming and difficult for the teacher to implement. The menu of classwide systems begins on p. 324.

for example

Mr. Harn's third-grade class was bordering on out of control. Before the year began, he thought a medium level of structure would be appropriate for his students. By the third week of school, it was clear that the initial procedures he had set up were not sufficient. He began using the daily Misbehavior Recording Sheet (see Chapter 6). From his data he determined that he needed to revise his level of classroom structure to high and implement a classwide motivation system appropriate for a high-structure class to further encourage students to behave responsibly. After reading the descriptions of the various systems in the menu, he decided that the Whole-Class Points (Time Interval) system would work well for his students and fit his own personal style.

With this system, Mr. Harn awarded one point to the class for each 15-minute period during which all the students behaved appropriately. For each point the class earned, Mr. Harn moved the rocket on the rocket chart up one space. When the class earned ten points (the rocket moved ten spaces), the students got five minutes of extra recess and the rocket was moved back down to the launch pad, ready for another blastoff. Once the system was implemented, Mr. Harn noticed significant improvement in the students' behavior. Periodically he would change the theme of the chart—going from a rocket theme to a race car theme to a speedboat theme. Over time, he also gradually added more spaces on the chart before students got their reward and increased the time students were required to behave appropriately. After the students had earned a number of rewards and were demonstrating consistent improvements in their behavior, Mr. Harn held a class meeting and together he and the class decided to switch to an intermittent type of system using Classroom Lottery Tickets.

STEP 1 Identify problems, goals, level of structure needed, and the type of system you will use.

Following are the issues and decisions to consider in Step 1 of Reproducible 8.1, Develop and/or Revise Your Classwide Motivation System:

WHAT PROBLEMS ARE YOU TRYING TO SOLVE?

Begin by thinking about behavioral and motivation concerns. Brainstorm a list of your concerns. Does it seem that a significant number of students do just enough to get by? What misbehaviors occur fairly frequently? These are the types of concerns you should list here. If you are addressing this question before the year begins but have taught in this school in the past, use the last couple of years as a guide to the types of problems you may encounter. If you have not taught in this school before, talk to your new colleagues who have taught this population of students. The issues you list will guide you toward the objectives of your system.

GOAL(S) OF YOUR SYSTEM

Based on your brainstormed list of concerns, decide what you want to achieve by implementing a classwide system. If you have many problems listed, you may need to limit the focus of the system. For example, you may prioritize and say that initially the system will focus on reducing disruptions (callouts, disrespect, name-calling) and later, after disruptions are under control, you will modify the system or build a new system that focuses on increasing work completion and quality of written work.

(continued on p. 310)

Reproducible 8.1 *Develop and/or Revise Your Classwide Motivation System (page 1)*

Print from CD

```
C H A M P S
sample
```

>> no. 8.1

DEVELOP AND/OR REVISE YOUR CLASSWIDE MOTIVATION SYSTEM (1 of 2)

Teacher Ms. Garcia **Grade** 5 **Room** 31 **School Year** _____

Step 1 Preparation

1. What problem(s) are you trying to solve?

   Call-outs, interruptions during instruction (jokes, burping noises), disrespectful comments, horseplay, poor-quality work, missing assignments, foul language

2. Describe the goal(s) of your system; limit your objective to one major category of behavior (e.g., reduce disruptions and name-calling, increase work completion, or decrease apathy—increase motivation).

   Decrease disruptions: call-outs, interruptions during instruction, disrespectful comments, horseplay, foul language

3. At the present time, the level of structure I need is: ☒ High ☐ Medium ☐ Low

4. Decide whether you need a nonreward-based or a reward-based system. (See pages 310–312 to help with this decision.) ☐ Nonreward-based ☒ Reward-based

Step 2 Select a system (one or more) and prepare to implement it

1. Read through the different systems to find one appropriate for the level of structure your class currently needs. The system I will implement (one from the CHAMPS book or something else) is:

   Whole-Class Points (Time Interval)

2. Describe the system.

   For each 20 minutes I will set the timer. When the timer goes off, I will award the class 0 to 3 points.
   3 = no disruptions/everyone worked hard
   2 = no disruptions
   1 = only a few disruptions
   0 = too many disruptions

3. Identify materials needed to monitor behavior and record progress (e.g., tickets, charts, Mystery Behavior Envelopes).

   I will use the CHAMPing the Way to Success charts. For the first chart, I will use the 20-point CHAMPS chart. I will also need a timer to remind me of the 20-minute intervals.

➡

CHAPTER 8 TASK

1 • Employ a Classwide System or Systems to Increase Motivated and Responsible Behavior

Reproducible 8.1 *Develop and/or Revise Your Classwide Motivation System (page 2)*

CHAMPS

DEVELOP AND/OR REVISE YOUR CLASSWIDE MOTIVATION SYSTEM (2 of 2)

≫ no. **8.1**

Step 2 (continued)

4. Identify the rewards to be used. If you will involve the students in generating the list of rewards, describe how.

Initially the reward will be 10 minutes for the whole class to play a game. I know they like this. After the class has earned this reward two or three times, I will conduct a brainstorming session to get additional ideas for rewards and activities to work toward.

5. Identify when and how you will explain the system to the students and the date for implementation.

During Friday morning welcome/announcement I will explain the chart, the reward, the timer, and the 0–3 points per interval. I will do practice runs during the day from 10:00 to 10:30 and at 2:00 to 2:30 (times the class typically does well). If they do well, I will put points on the chart. We will start the full system of Monday.

Step 3 **For reward-based systems, identify how you will maintain, modify, or fade the system**

1. How will you keep your energy and excitement about the system at a high level?

After each interval in which they do well (2 or 3 points), I will express how proud they should be and emphasize teamwork. If they do poorly (0 or 1 point), I will keep the focus on what they can do during the next interval to get to 3. I will stay focused on even small improvements.

2. How will you make the system more challenging as the class reaches a high level of consistent success?

I will continue at the 20-point level, using different themed charts until the class is getting 2 or 3 points at each interval. I will let the class know that the next chart will have 25 points, and the next will have 30 points. Then I will change the time interval to 30 minutes, but go back to the 20-point chart. Then I will make the interval 60 minutes and use a 15-point chart, eventually getting to half-day intervals and a 20-point chart.

3. Once the system is fairly lean, how will you move to increasingly intermittent rewards?

While still using the 20-point chart and a half-day interval, I will intermittently give other rewards and activities. After demonstrating this intermittent concept, I will encourage the class to realize that they do not need the time interval system any longer.

4. When appropriate, fade the system by having a discussion with the students about abandoning the system and/or switching to goal-setting systems.

After using the intermittent system for at least several weeks, and if positive behavior continues and students seem proud of their success, I will implement individual Goal Contracts. We will then have discussions about whether or not the class still needs the reinforcement system.

Print from CD

The following information and suggestions should also help you with the issues and decisions in Step 1.

LEVEL OF STRUCTURE

Think about your class's current need for structure. If you are thinking about class structure before the year begins, base this decision on the Management and Discipline Planning Questionnaire that you completed in Chapter 3 (Reproducible 3.1). If you are thinking about your class structure needs during the year, base this decision on your subjective perception of the behavior and motivation of the class. Also consider any objective data you have, such as one or more of the tools in Chapter 6: Observe. If there are rare or very few problems, low structure is probably fine. If many students misbehave on a very frequent basis, you probably need high structure.

REWARD- AND NONREWARD-BASED SYSTEMS

Classwide motivation systems generally fall into one of two categories:

- Nonreward-based systems potentially improve students' desire to behave responsibly and achieve goals by enhancing their intrinsic motivation.

- Reward-based systems use extrinsic reinforcers to increase student motivation to behave responsibly and strive for goals.

If your students are for the most part behaving responsibly, completing most of their work, and exhibiting cooperation, they do not need extrinsic rewards to be motivated. In a class that is functioning this well, students demonstrate daily that they are intrinsically motivated to meet classroom expectations. With such a class, a nonreward-based system such as goal setting is perfectly reasonable. In fact, goal setting can be a very effective strategy for not only maintaining but also enhancing already acceptable levels of motivation (Copeland & Hughes, 2002; Fuchs, Fuchs, & Deno, 1985; Johnson, Graham, & Harris, 1997; Troia & Graham, 2002). Goal-setting procedures are designed to give students something to strive for so they do not fall into patterns of "going through the motions" in the classroom. If you do not need a reward-based system for your students because the class is already behaving responsibly, go directly to the descriptions of various goal-setting systems in the menu (pp. 324–353) and select one that seems most appropriate for you and your class.

> *In a class that is functioning well, students demonstrate daily that they are intrinsically motivated to meet classroom expectations.*

On the other hand, if you are frustrated by the amount of student misbehavior or the lack of student productivity in your class, your students are demonstrating that they are not intrinsically motivated to behave responsibly. Implementing a system in which students can earn extrinsic rewards for

If you have any doubts, the data from one or more of the monitoring procedures in Chapter 6 (such as the CHAMPS v. Daily Reality Rating Scale or the Misbehavior Recording Sheet) can help you confirm the need for a motivation system based on extrinsic rewards.

responsible behavior may be just what is needed to encourage them (Cameron et al., 2001; Scheuermann & Hall, 2008). A reward-based system may provide the incentive needed to light a fire under students and get them moving in a more positive and productive direction.

Even if you determine that your class needs or would benefit from a reward-based motivation system, you may find yourself reluctant to implement a system that depends on extrinsic rewards. Some people have concerns about the use of rewards and reward-based systems to improve student behavior. Following are answers to some of the most commonly raised questions about using rewards. The information provided should help you understand how a reward-based system (or systems) can be incorporated usefully and effectively into your Classroom Management and Discipline Plan. After looking over the following questions and answers, read the sections on effectively choosing and implementing a reward-based system (Step 2) and maintaining, modifying, and fading a reward-based system (Step 3). Then review the menu (p. 324) and choose the system or systems that you want to use or modify.

Shouldn't students work without needing rewards?

Yes, they should, but some don't. When you can motivate students by making your expectations clear and your instruction effective, that's what you should do. If all your students seem to be working up to their fullest potential, you do not need and probably should not implement a reward-based system. However, if you have some (or many) students who are not working as hard or as well as you think they should and you have done what you can to make expectations clear and instruction compelling, your choices are limited. You can let the students fail, you can continue to try to increase their intrinsic motivation to behave, or you can experiment with rewards.

Keep in mind that using rewards effectively does not mean you use them forever. A reward-based system is meant to be used and gradually modified until students are intrinsically or naturally reinforced by the task. This concept is called behavioral momentum—once students start experiencing success, they are increasingly motivated to be successful and thus work harder, experiencing even greater levels of success. In other words, success breeds success.

Isn't rewarding behavior the same as bribery?

Emphatically not! A bribe is an offer of payment, usually monetary, to do something illegal, unethical, or immoral. For example, when a building contractor offers to pay a building inspector under the table to ignore inadequate or unsafe aspects of a construction project, that is a bribe. Establishing a system in which students are rewarded for improving their rates of schoolwork completion is not bribery. It is more analogous to someone getting points for successfully completing classes and eventually earning a diploma, or getting a paycheck for doing a job.

Won't students get hooked on the rewards?

Possibly. If you can sufficiently motivate your students without using rewards, you should do so. However, recent research reviews have found that concerns about children becoming dependent on extrinsic rewards are unwarranted (Akin-Little, Eckert, & Lovett, 2004) and that positive reinforcement may actually increase intrinsic motivation (Cameron et al., 2001). If you find that you need some form of reward system, always keep your focus and enthusiasm on what students are doing, not on what they are earning. Initially, the students may work mainly for the reward, but if you make a point of emphasizing their accomplishments, eventually most of them will begin to work for the enjoyment of the task and a sense of satisfaction with a job well done—whether they earn rewards or not (Skinner, 1982).

Isn't intrinsic motivation better?

Maybe. Nobody really knows. However, as noted in Chapter 1, most behaviors are the result of a complex mix of both intrinsic and extrinsic motivation. The basic rule for teachers is: If you can't motivate students intrinsically, use extrinsic rewards to get the desired behavior established. Once the desired behavior is established, you can fade back the extrinsic rewards because students will readily access the natural rewards, such as praise from you or the joy of mastering a new academic skill, associated with meeting expectations (O'Leary & Becker, 1967; Scheuermann & Hall, 2008; Skinner, 1982; Walker & Holland, 1979). Think about your own experience as a student—would you have done *all* of the assignments for *all* of your college classes if it weren't for the extrinsic reinforcement of the credits (points) toward the diploma?

Will giving students rewards reduce their intrinsic motivation?

Possibly. While there is evidence that positive reinforcement may increase intrinsic motivation (Cameron et al., 2001), it is likely that when students are already exhibiting desired behaviors, using high-powered rewards may slightly reduce their willingness to work without rewards. Therefore, as noted earlier, if students are intrinsically motivated to meet your expectations, do not use structured rewards—instead use goal-setting procedures and age-appropriate positive feedback. However, if less structured methods have failed or seem likely to fail to motivate students to behave responsibly, you should consider the use of structured rewards (Cameron et al., 2001; Scheuermann & Hall, 2008).

> " *If you can't motivate students intrinsically, use extrinsic rewards to get the desired behavior established.* "

CHAPTER 8 TASK

take note

If your class is made up of predominantly highly responsible students with one or two students who exhibit behavioral or motivational challenges, consider using goal-setting procedures as your whole-class approach to improving motivation and set up individualized extrinsic systems with those challenging students. Individualized approaches to behavior management are discussed in Chapter 9; one suggestion is to set up individual reward contracts. However, if you have three or more students with behavioral challenges, set up a reward-based classwide system. Managing too many individualized systems is much more work than managing one classwide system. The classwide system may improve the behavior of all but one student, and then you could work on an individualized intervention with that student.

STEP 2   Select a system and prepare to implement it.

The issues and decisions to consider in Step 2 of the Develop and/or Revise Your Classwide Motivation System form (Reproducible 8.1) relate to selecting and implemeting a classwide system.

To select a system, read through all of the systems described for the level of structure your class needs. Pick the one that you think will accomplish your goals, best fit your style, and meet the needs of your students. Describe a few of the essential components of the system on the form as a quick reminder to yourself so that you do not have to keep referring back to the book.

If you are planning to use a reward-based system, read the following information and suggestions to clarify the issues in Step 2.

USING A REWARD-BASED SYSTEM

If you decide that a reward-based system will be appropriate and helpful in improving your students' motivation, be aware that it's important to carefully choose, implement, maintain, and eventually fade the system or systems you use. In fact, the effectiveness of a reward-based system, like all other aspects of your management plan, is dependent on how well you facilitate it (Shores et al., 1993). Read through the following information on using a reward-based system before you read the menu of suggested systems. Then you will be prepared to choose or design a system that best fits the needs of your class and then implement, maintain, and fade it effectively.

As you choose your system, keep in mind that some systems are regular and highly systematic in terms of how students earn the rewards ("If you do ___, then you earn ___"), while others give students rewards intermittently and unpredictably. Intermittent systems are not so regular ("Sometimes when you do ___, you might earn ___"). Regular systems tend to be more appropriate when you are trying to motivate a class that needs high structure, but they can also be harder to maintain and fade than intermittent or unpredictable systems. Intermittent reward systems are often sufficient for medium-structure classes.

From a technical standpoint, intermittent systems are actually the most powerful (Alberto & Troutman, 2006; Cooper et al., 2007; Scheuermann & Hall, 2008; Skinner, 1953). All gambling is based on intermittent reward schedules. We are motivated to keep putting money in the slot machine because we never know when we are going to win. However, in the initial stages of teaching and motivating a high-structure class, you may need a systematic and regular system (Alberto & Troutman, 2006). The regular system is important for teaching and getting students to buy in because it encourages students to practice the skill regularly and allows them to receive a high rate of reinforcement (rewards, positive feedback).

> *Intermittent systems are actually the most powerful.*

Once students are consistently successful with a regular system, one step on the way to fading to intrinsic rewards is to switch to an intermittent system. Try to select the simplest system that seems likely to grab the interest of your students and get them to exert gentle peer pressure to succeed—for example, getting students to say to each other something like, "Allan, quit talking or you will make us lose a point."

All reward-based systems—regular and intermittent—require maintenance after they are up and running (Conroy, Sutherland, Snyder, & Marsh, 2008; Kazdin, 2001; Kerr & Nelson, 2002). It's like having a car. No matter how well engineered your vehicle is, you still have to put fuel in it and make sure it gets the occasional oil change, brake job, and tune-up. In fact, you wouldn't expect your car to run without gas and periodic mechanical work. Unfortunately, some teachers think that once a motivation system is in place, it should pretty much run by itself. It won't. Furthermore, in most cases a reward-based system should be a temporary measure that you employ to get the class into a pattern of successful behavior. Your eventual goal should be to fade it so that your students' intrinsic motivation maintains their responsible and enthusiastic behavior (Walker & Holland, 1979).

Following are tips on how you can effectively choose and implement a reward-based system, keep it running well, and eventually fade it altogether.

Make sure the system is appropriate for and interesting to students.

In addition to deciding whether students need a regular or an intermittent reward-based system, be sure the system is one that the students find compelling. For example, the Whole-Class Points (Time Interval) system described in the menu can be made visually stimulating (like the rocket chart example) and exciting to primary students, but it is probably too "babyish" for most middle school classes. Conversely, if you try to use the Behavioral Grading system with a first- or second-grade class, many of the students probably won't understand how the system works because grading is a somewhat abstract concept to them. The goal is to design a system that students are drawn to and find exciting.

 Make sure the rewards students will be working toward are highly motivating.

If students don't care about or don't want to earn the reward they are working toward, your system is not likely to be effective. You should use high-power rewards—rewards that students want so badly that they are motivated to try to meet your expectations to earn it. Therefore, you need to identify a range of rewards that the whole class will want to earn. Examples include free time, extra recess, getting out of class two minutes early, and a reduction in the number of problems or questions assigned for homework. You should also be prepared to vary the rewards so that students don't become bored or satiated with one reward (Hall & Hall, 1980).

Sometimes it can be useful to have students help you decide on the rewards for the class (Lerman et al., 1997; Northup, 2000; Thompson, Fisher, & Contrucci, 1998; Wheeler & Richey, 2005). For example, you might conduct a brainstorming session and ask students to identify rewards that they as a class can get or do when all students demonstrate responsible behavior. During a brainstorming session, write down any suggestion that any student makes, unless it is obscene or disrespectful. Continue the activity for at least five to ten minutes so that various ideas are generated. When the brainstorming session is complete, go back and eliminate any items that are too expensive or otherwise unrealistic—it is important that you select rewards that you can and will use (Hall & Hall, 1980). Some of the items on your final list will probably have more value than others. For example, some may cost money while others do not, some may cut into more class time than others, and some may require more time from school personnel than others. When you first implement your system, do not hesitate to start with rewards that have a fairly high value. The value of the reward should correlate with the effort involved to receive it (Hall & Hall, 1980; Walker & Holland, 1979). Bigger rewards should be used for behaviors that students are least motivated (possibly because of difficulty) to display. The system should be exciting enough that most of the students feel it is in their best interest to improve their behavior.

Set up the system so that student success is likely.

Students must believe that they have a high probability of achieving success. If students think their chances of earning a reward are low, they are not likely to change their behavior—even if they really want the reward. (Think about the concept of "Expectancy x Value = Motivation" that was discussed in Chapter 1, Task 2).

One way to increase the probability of student success is to ensure that any time limits involved are short enough that students can meet your criteria (Alberto & Troutman, 2006; Walker, Severson et al., 1998). For example, a fifth-grade teacher implements a system in which the class earns one point for each day the entire class behaves responsibly. Students may reasonably believe that they will never earn any points because the chances are slim that they will make it through a full day without someone messing up. This system is likely to fail because the students will never feel motivated enough to make it work. Remember the Expectancy Times Value formula discussed in Chapter 1. If expectancy of success is zero, it does not matter how valuable the reward is. Motivation will be zero. The system would be stronger and probably more effective if it were set up so that the class earns a point for each hour, or even each half hour, that all students behave responsibly.

> "Another way to make students believe that success is possible is to make the cost of earning the rewards relatively inexpensive."

Another way to make students believe that success is possible is to make the cost of earning the rewards relatively inexpensive for the students. In other words, students initially need to see that they will get a reward relatively quickly when they meet your expectations (Alberto & Troutman, 2006; Scheuermann & Hall, 2008). Say you establish a system where your second graders can earn extra recess time by accumulating 25 points, but the most points they can earn in a day is five. At best, the students will have to work for a whole week before they get extra recess time. For second-grade students, this may be too long to wait for any payoff. When you choose your system, remember that if the students believe that it will take too long to earn the reward, their attitude may be, "Why bother?" In the second-grade example, the extra recess is more likely to motivate students if it costs eight points rather than 25 points. The less mature your students are, the more immediately obtainable the rewards need to be for the system to be effective.

Once students are consistently behaving responsibly, you can and should make the time intervals longer or the rewards more expensive (or both) as part of the process of gradually fading the system. See Step 3 in this chapter for tips on effectively maintaining and fading a reward-based system.

Avoid systems with arbitrary time limits.

A weakness of many reward-based systems is that they include an unnecessary and arbitrary time limit—the points must be earned within a certain time period in order for students to receive the reward. For example, consider a system in which a class can earn 5 points per day if everything goes extremely well. If the class earns 15 points by Friday, the students get the last 15 minutes of class as earned time with snacks. The arbitrary time limit in this system creates several potential problems. First of all, if students have trouble behaving well early in the week, they may know by Wednesday morning that they cannot possibly earn the reward that week. If they know they won't get the reward, they have no incentive to behave well on Wednesday afternoon, Thursday, and Friday. Or students might do so well that they have 15 points by the end of the day Wednesday. At least some of them are going to realize that they can misbehave all they want on Thursday and Friday because the reward has already been earned. Still another potential problem with a time limit is the difficult decision you face if the class earns 14 points by Friday afternoon. If you give them the reward because they came so close, they learn that you do not follow through on what you say (they cannot really trust you). However, if you do not give them the reward, meaning they start back at zero points on Monday, they may feel so discouraged they won't even want to try at all.

All of these potential problems can be eliminated by simply removing the time limit. The system in the above example would be much stronger if, as soon as the class earns 15 points, students get the last 15 minutes of class as earned time with snacks. They may earn the points in three days, or it may take a couple of weeks, depending on how well students manage their own behavior.

 Carefully organize the entire system before you begin implementation.

Many teachers rush to implement a motivation system when faced with behavior problems. However, to implement an effective system, you need to think carefully about your goals for the class's behavior and then develop a preliminary implementation plan in your mind. Once you create your mental plan, put it into writing. The act of writing out the procedures can help you identify possible weaknesses with the system and issues that need to be addressed (Scheuermann & Hall, 2008). As you identify those problems or issues, resolve them—make decisions.

> *What will I do if one student repeatedly behaves in a way that prevents me from giving the point or reward to the entire group? Well, I will give that student a warning and tell him that his continued misbehavior will not prevent the group*

from earning points. At the same time, when the class earns the reward, he will not get to participate in the reward activities. If necessary, I will set up an individualized behavior management contract.

After you have a written plan that addresses all questions and issues you can think of, discuss the plan with a colleague. Speak to someone who is teaching or has taught the grade level you teach. Ask him or her to listen to your proposed plan with a critical ear. Encourage this person to identify any weaknesses and unanswered questions in your plan.

 Make sure your expectations for student behavior are clear and that you have adequate procedures for observing student behavior.

Even a well-designed reward system can fail when the expectations for student behavior within the system are unclear (Conroy et al., 2008; Scheuermann & Hall, 2008). Without clearly defined behavioral expectations, you may be inconsistent in determining whether students have met the criteria for earning their reward (Anderson, Evertson, & Emmer, 1980; Evertson & Emmer, 1982). That is, you may award points on a day when you are in a good mood, but the next day, when you are feeling more frustrated, you don't award any points, even though the students behaved the same way. This sort of inconsistency is very destructive to motivation because earning the reward is not contingent on the behavior students actually display. Students are likely to stop trying to meet expectations that are unclear and inconsistent (O'Leary & O'Leary, 1977).

> *Students are likely to stop trying to meet expectations that are unclear and inconsistent.*

In addition to clear expectations, you must have adequate procedures for observing student behavior (Conroy et al., 2008; Scheuermann & Hall, 2008). In fact, the only way you can reasonably implement a reward-based motivation system is if you can adequately observe student behavior. For example, if you have a system to address student behavior at recess—if everyone in the class follows the rules at recess, the class earns one point—you either need to be out with students during recess or have some way to get information from the playground supervisors at the conclusion of each recess. If there is some aspect of your students' behavior that you cannot adequately observe, that behavior should not be part of your system.

 Teach the students how the entire system works.

Before you implement any system, prepare one or more lessons to teach the students how the system works. When students don't understand all aspects of a system, there is very little chance it will motivate them—particularly the cognitively low or least mature students. If, when preparing the lessons, you find that the system seems too complicated for students to grasp, you should revise it. If you can't make it clear, concise, and easy to understand, you probably need a different system.

After you teach students how the reward system will work, verify that they understand. Make sure that any English Language Learners in your classroom understand your system. Ask questions to determine their level of understanding. If specific aspects of the system are confusing, re-teach those aspects. In addition, you may want to give students an opportunity to suggest refinements or modifications. If students make suggestions that would strengthen the system—for example, rewards that would increase their interest in the system—try to incorporate those suggestions.

 Make sure you believe the system will help improve student behavior.

Start with the assumption that your students will meet your expectations regarding the system. If you believe the system will work, the students will pick up on your optimism. Likewise, if you believe the system will probably fail, the students will sense that you do not expect them to be successful. It's in your best interest to be optimistic. Even if the system does not work initially, an optimistic attitude will lead you to try to identify refinements and modifications that will make the system work. On the other hand, with a pessimistic attitude you are likely to give up if the system does not produce immediate and drastic improvement in student behavior. Remember: Optimists are wrong just as often as pessimists; the big difference is optimists have a lot more fun.

STEP 3 Identify how you will maintain, modify, and fade a reward-based system.

The following information should help you maintain your system as long as necessary at one level as well as help you decide when and how to modify the system. If the system is not working, you should either modify it or select a new system. If the system is working well, you can make it incrementally more challenging for students and eventually fade it out altogether.

 Keep your energy and enthusiasm about the system high.

You are the fuel that keeps the system supplied with energy to run. If you don't "fill 'er up" with your excitement, interest, and support, students are very likely to lose interest, even if the rewards they are working toward are compelling.

Keep your focus on the students' behavior rather than the rewards they earn.

The energy and excitement you invest in the system and in acknowledging student successes should be concentrated on what students do to earn the reward, not the reward itself (Horcones, 1992). That is, say to students "Look at what you did!" rather than "Look at what you get." By keeping your focus on the students' improved growth, maturity, and progress, you increase the chances that the students will begin working less for the reward and more for their sense of satisfaction in meeting expectations successfully (Kazdin & Bootzin, 1972; O'Leary & Becker, 1967; Scheuermann & Hall, 2008; Skinner, 1982; Walker & Holland, 1979).

 Continue to use other motivational strategies at a high level.

In Chapters 1 and 7, a number of basic strategies for establishing and maintaining student motivation were presented. All the classwide systems for boosting motivation discussed in this chapter require that you maintain your use of the following basic strategies:

- Present activities and tasks in a manner that induces student motivation.

- Use effective instructional practices and present tasks in interesting ways.

- Provide frequent noncontingent attention.

- Provide frequent positive feedback that is contingent, specific, descriptive, and age-appropriate.

- Pay more attention to every student when he or she is engaged in responsible behavior than when he or she is engaged in misbehavior (minimally, a ratio of 3:1).

To increase the likelihood that students will continue to be successful, be prepared to increase your use of these strategies as you begin to fade back the use of the external reward system (Kazdin, 2001; O'Leary & Becker, 1967; Walker & Holland, 1979).

 When a system has been successful for a period of time, start making it more challenging.

Once student behavior improves to the point that your class is successfully meeting your expectations most of the time, modify the system to make it more challenging so students don't get bored with it. In addition, as students become more successful at meeting expectations, you will likely want to increase the standards for success.

for example

Let's say a third-grade class is implementing the Whole-Class Points (Time Interval) rocket chart system. Initially it is set up so that the timer goes off every 15 minutes. If students have met expectations for responsible behavior during the 15-minute interval, the class earns a point. When the class earns ten points, they get one of the rewards. If the class is regularly earning a point during most intervals (more than 80 percent of the time), you need to make things slightly more challenging. The next time the students earn a reward and the rocket is moved down to zero, inform the class that after the rocket gets to the moon again, the system will change. Instead of a rocket chart, it will be a race car chart. Instead of ten spaces to reach the goal, there will be 13 spaces before the race car reaches the finish line. By increasing the difficulty, you make earning the next reward slightly more challenging.

It's important to give students plenty of advance notice before making this kind of modification. As you explain the increased number of spaces, emphasize to students that you are making the change because they have been successful. Be careful not to sound apologetic about this change. If students complain, let them know that the system, like many things in life, is challenging and may increase in difficulty, but emphasize that they have the skills to still earn the reward quickly. Increasing the difficulty by requiring more points is the first of many steps you will take in fading the system.

Another way to make the system more challenging is to make the criteria for earning points harder.

for example

With the rocket chart system, you might go from monitoring in 15-minute intervals to monitoring in 20-minute intervals. Or you could increase the number of behaviors being monitored. For example, you could add the behavior "treating everyone with respect" as an additional criteria for determining whether the class earns a point for a given interval. The following chart shows how you can make gradual changes in something like the rocket chart system. These changes would be phased in over a period of several months.

continued

15-minute intervals	10 points required for reward
15-minute intervals	13 points required for reward
20-minute intervals	13 points required for reward
20-minute intervals	18 points required for reward

"Treating everyone with respect" added to expectation

30-minute intervals	18 points required for reward
30-minute intervals	25 points required for reward
45-minute intervals	25 points required for reward
45-minute intervals	35 points required for reward
60-minute intervals	35 points required for reward

Remember, don't increase a system's difficulty until students have been consistently successful. If you make things too difficult before students feel somewhat in control of their own success, they may be inclined to give up and stop trying to meet the expectations.

By making changes like these gradually, you make the system increasingly lean—students demonstrate highly responsible behavior for relatively small extrinsic rewards (Freeland & Noell, 1999). Notice that in the preceding example, students started out working in 15-minute intervals and needing ten points for a reward, so 150 minutes of responsible behavior earned students a reward. A few months later, the same class works in 45-minute intervals and needs 25 points for a reward—meaning 1,125 minutes of responsible behavior earns a reward.

 Once a system is fairly lean, modify it to be based on intermittent rewards.

Some of the systems in the menu that are identified as appropriate for medium-structure classrooms involve the use of intermittent rewards—rewards that are given only on some occasions rather than every time performance criteria are met. Even if your classroom is highly structured, you should eventually shift to intermittent rewards once the students have learned and are consistently displaying the skill or skills that are the focus of your classwide system. Moving to intermittent rewards is important for two reasons:

- It is not practical for you to deliver rewards at a high rate over a long period of time (Freeland & Noell, 1999).

- Intermittent schedules of reinforcement have been shown to be most effective in maintaining student behavior over time (Alberto & Troutman, 2006; Cooper et al., 2007; Scheuermann & Hall, 2008).

CHAPTER 8 TASK

Moving to intermittent rewards is another step in making your motivation system more challenging. For example, you could propose that the Whole-Class Points system be replaced by the 100 Squares system. With this change, you do not increase the time interval. Instead, when you feel the class is working well, you have a student draw a number, then you fill in the space for that number on the 100 Squares chart. When the class completes a line (across, up/down, or diagonally), they earn a reward. The intermittent nature of the system—no timer, you draw a number intermittently—moves the class even closer to the way rewards work in natural, less structured settings (Freeland & Noell, 1999).

 Once a class is working successfully for intermittent rewards, consider adding or switching to one of the goal-setting systems described in the menu.

Goal setting is one of the last steps in fading students from the support of extrinsic rewards to reliance on their intrinsic motivation. While you are still using a system of intermittent rewards, begin setting individual goals for each student (or have the students set their own goals) and help the class set a classwide goal. Then, make a point of providing frequent positive feedback to students for meeting the goals. Once you have motivated students to strive toward their individualized goals and you are maintaining high rates of positive feedback to individuals and the whole class, you will be very close to being able to abandon reward-based systems altogether (O'Leary & Becker, 1967; Skinner, 1982).

 When appropriate, have a class discussion about abandoning the use of the reward-based system.

When the class seems ready—most students seem to take pride in behaving responsibly—arrange to conduct a whole-class discussion about whether students feel they can continue to behave responsibly without getting rewards. If the tone of the discussion suggests that most students think they can maintain their responsible behavior without a reward system, set a classwide goal such as:

> *We, the students in Room 14, can behave responsibly and we will strive to meet our Guidelines for Success without needing a reward system.*

When students can agree to this kind of classwide goal, you can stop using a reward-based system. However, you do need to continue providing positive feedback and an occasional special treat when the class exhibits ongoing responsible behavior. (See Chapter 7, Task 3: Provide Intermittent Celebrations).

~~~~~~~~~~~~~~~~~~~~~~~~~~~~~~~~~~~~

MENU OF CLASSWIDE SYSTEMS

The rest of this chapter describes a variety of classwide systems for increasing student motivation—a menu of procedures. Those appropriate for high-structure classes are presented first, followed by those for medium- and then low-structure classes. Read through the systems that fit the level of structure your class needs (you will probably want to read others as well to gain some perspective), then choose the system or systems that you think will be practical to implement and will improve the motivation of your students. You can also use the ideas presented here as a basis for creating your own system, if you wish. Figure 8.1 lists the systems described in the menu in the order they appear.

Figure 8.1   *Motivation Systems by Level of Classroom Structure*

REWARD-BASED SYSTEMS APPROPRIATE FOR HIGH-STRUCTURE CLASSES	REWARD-BASED SYSTEMS APPROPRIATE FOR MEDIUM-STRUCTURE CLASSES	NONREWARD-BASED SYSTEMS APPROPRIATE FOR LOW-STRUCTURE CLASSES
• Whole-Class Points (Time Interval) • Economic Simulation • Reinforcement Based on Reducing Misbehavior • Good Behavior Game • Behavioral Grading	• 100 Squares • Group Response Cost • Lottery Tickets • Mystery Behavior of the Day • Public Posting (Classwide) • Public Posting (Individual) • Self-Evaluation of On- and Off-Task Behavior • Target and Reward a Specific Behavior • Mystery Motivators • Team Competition with Response Cost Lottery • Whole-Class Points (Intermittent)	**GOAL-SETTING PROCEDURES** • Teacher sets goals for students • Teacher guides students in setting goals • Teacher guides students in setting a classwide goal

REWARD-BASED SYSTEMS APPROPRIATE FOR HIGH-STRUCTURE CLASSES

WHOLE-CLASS POINTS (TIME INTERVAL)

In this system you provide feedback, both positive and corrective, to the entire class at regular intervals. For each interval during which the behavior of the class meets your expectations, the group earns a point, or if you prefer, a range of points (for example, zero to three points). Once the group earns a predetermined number of

Several of the systems listed in Figure 8.1 have been taken or adapted from *The Tough Kid Book* (2nd ed.), by Rhode, Reavis, & Jenson (available 2010). This excellent book and its corresponding *Tough Kid Tool Box* are filled with many useful ideas for managing the behavior of difficult students. See the Pacific Northwest Publishing website (www.pacificnwpublish.com) for more information.

points, the entire class gets a reward. This is an excellent system to use when you have quite a few immature students in the class. However, it is not a good choice when most of your class behaves well and one or two students are responsible for most of the misbehavior.

The first thing to determine when using this system is the duration of the interval—each hour, each half hour, or each quarter hour, for example. The less mature your class, regardless of grade level, the shorter the intervals should be. For example, with a relatively immature group of students, you may need intervals as short as 15 minutes. You also need to determine how to keep track of the duration—what will prompt you that it's time to evaluate behavior. Possibilities include an alarm on your watch, a kitchen timer, or a preprogrammed classroom computer.

Next, have a class brainstorming session to identify possible rewards. Eliminate unreasonable suggestions and then set prices for how many points it will take to earn various reward items and activities. Your prices should be based in part on the length of the interval you are using—if you use 15-minute intervals, the rewards should cost more than if you use 60-minute intervals. Prices should also be based on the monetary, instructional, and personnel costs (the time that school personnel will spend providing the rewards) the various rewards entail. Thus, a two-hour movie with popcorn will be more expensive than five minutes of extra recess.

The last consideration is how you will keep track of the points. With most elementary classes, some kind of graphic representation on a bulletin board or flip chart is very effective. The CD has a variety of reproducible forms (Reproducibles 8.2a–q) that can be used for Whole-Class Point systems. The version you choose depends on how many points you plan to award and how quickly you want the class to receive the rewards. Note that if you start with a low number, students can earn the reward quickly and start a new chart. Then, once they become highly successful (they earn points on 90 percent of the intervals), you can move to a version of the chart with a different theme and more required points. The CD includes full-color point charts for 5, 10, 15, 20, 25, 50, and 100 points, each with a different theme, which you can resize for an 11" x 17" poster.

Print from CD

Reproducible 8.2   *Whole-Class Point Charts (17 Versions)*

Figure 8.2 *Oregon Trail Point Chart*

The examples to the left show how you can use the CHAMPS icons provided on the CD to create your own CHAMPS-themed point charts. There are also blank templates (Reproducible 8.3a–h) on the CD for you to start with. The templates are preprinted with 5, 10, 15, 20, 25, 30, 50, and 100 stars to fill in as points are earned, with space for you to add your own slogan and artwork.

Instead of using the reproducibles from the CD, you could make a bulletin board display that relates the reward system to a subject the class is currently studying. For example, you might track points using a covered wagon on the way to Oregon or a whale migrating to Baja. Figure 8.2 shows this system with an Oregon Trail motif.

Figure 8.3 shows another graphic representation idea that might be appropriate for an intermediate or middle school science class. This chart shows a picture of the parts of a cell. Each part is labeled as soon as the class earns the specified number of points. The various labels cost different amounts—the cell wall costs five points, the chromosomes ten points, the cytoplasts three points, for example. When the entire cell has been labeled, the group earns the reward.

Figure 8.3   *Parts of a Cell Point Chart*

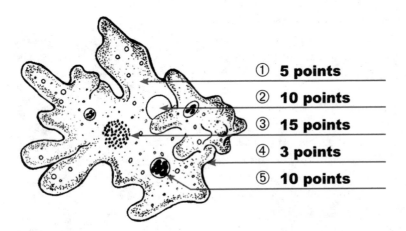

①	**5 points**
②	**10 points**
③	**15 points**
④	**3 points**
⑤	**10 points**

If you are a middle school teacher, use your own judgment about whether your students will be motivated by this kind of graphical point tracking. If you don't think they will be, simply devote a small corner of the chalkboard to recording the points (for example, "4th period: 6 points").

Once these decisions are made, implementation is fairly simple. At the conclusion of each interval (when the timer goes off after 30 minutes, for example), review the behavior of the entire class for the preceding 30-minute period. If students met your expectations, the group earns two points. If all but one or two students met your expectations, the group earns one point. If more than one or two students failed to meet expectations, the group earns zero points. If the group earns anything less than two points, describe the inappropriate behaviors that led to your assessment, but do not name the students who misbehaved. "Because I had to give several of you reminders about talking during quiet study time, the group does not get any points for this time period. However, I am resetting the timer, and I am sure that in the next 30 minutes you will be able to earn two points."

If student behavior does not improve, increase the amount of positive feedback you give to individual students and to the class during each interval. If improvement is still insufficient, consider using shorter intervals (15 minutes rather than 30). When the class earns a reward, begin the system again by having the class vote on the next reward. You can keep the system interesting for students by changing the theme periodically—you do not want to use a cell motif or rocket motif for more than a couple of weeks at a time.

A variation of this system is the Whole-Class Points (Intermittent) system, appropriate for high- or medium-structure classes. The intermittent system is described on p. 347.

ECONOMIC SIMULATION

In an Economic Simulation system, you use pretend money and create a mini-economy in your classroom. Students are paid for their good behavior and can use the money to purchase a variety of items. This can be a useful system in grades 2 through 8 for reducing frequent but minor misbehavior such as off-task behavior, talking in class, put-downs, and so on.

You can make this type of system simple or complex. In its simplest form, it functions as a response cost type of system. Every student starts the week with a certain amount of money in the bank. During the week, you use a Misbehavior Recording Sheet (see Chapter 6, Tool 3) to observe the inappropriate behavior of individual students. Each misbehavior costs the student who misbehaved one dollar. At the end of the week, you determine each student's payout. Any student who has had no recorded misbehaviors receives ten dollars.

CHAMPS Bucks in one-, five-, and ten-dollar amounts are shown on the next page. These printable sheets of CHAMPS bucks are found on the CD. Reproducible 8.4a–c uses primary-level icons, Reproducible 8.5a–c uses intermediate-level icons, and and Reproducible 8.6a–c uses graphic icons. You can use these reproducible masters to mint your class money, or you may prefer to design your own money.

A student who misbehaved six times receives four dollars, and a student who misbehaved once receives nine dollars. Students can spend the money on items in a student store, such as pencils, stickers, erasers, and certificates for computer time. Plan to give bonuses (one or two extra dollars, for example) to individual students who have been following rules and striving toward the Guidelines for Success. Be careful not to be inadvertently discriminatory, though. Every student should get a bonus every now and then.

> "Every student should get a bonus every now and then.

In a slightly more sophisticated version of this system, students can also be paid for completing academic work or demonstrating responsible behavior. For example, you might pay students two dollars for each assignment completed (more for major projects). If you want to incorporate something like this, you need to record the positive feedback you give students in addition to recording their misbehavior. See the information in the Behavioral Grading system for suggestions on how to manage this kind of recording. Then have each student start each day with a certain number of dollars (say five). Throughout the day, they add one dollar for each positive behavior and subtract one dollar for each negative behavior. To start, students might be paid daily, but as they get familiar with the system, this can be modified to a weekly payday.

Reproducibles 8.4a-c, 8.5a-c, and 8.6a-c   *CHAMPS Bucks (One, Five, and Ten Dollars)*

Grades 1–2

Grades 3–8

Graphic

If you wish, once the basic system is running smoothly and showing positive effects, you can use it to teach students about how the real economy works. Every two weeks, add one of the following features:

- Establish savings accounts for students.

- Establish checking accounts for students.

- Charge students rent for their desks.

- Require students to buy certain supplies (e.g., pencils, art paper).

- Have students purchase certain privileges.

- Arrange to pay students extra for special projects (extra-credit assignments).

- Establish charitable foundations to which students can contribute.

- Assess taxes on the money students are paid.

- Give every student a class job for which he or she is paid. Examples include:

  Managers of student store
  Accountants (help you compute payments)
  Bankers (manage savings accounts)
  City council (paid from taxes collected)
  Supply managers
  Tutors or helpers who assist in kindergarten
  Real estate agents (determine and collect rents for desks)
  Zoologists (care for class animals)
  Computer maintenance
  Graphic artists (prepare bulletin boards and displays)

REINFORCEMENT BASED ON REDUCING MISBEHAVIOR

This system is designed to reward an entire class for significant reductions in the total number of misbehaviors that occur on any given day. It is particularly effective when many different students in the class exhibit a wide variety of misbehavior.

To implement the system, use either a daily or weekly Misbehavior Recording Sheet (see Chapter 6, Tool 3) and keep data on class misbehavior for at least five days. Design a chart with spaces to record the data from those five days along with at least another 20 or 30 days. Then determine the average number of misbehaviors per day that occurred during your five-day baseline period (add the total number of misbehaviors you recorded and divide by five).

From the average number of incidents per day, build a sliding scale for awarding points. Create the scale so that if the average number of incidents (or more) occurs, students earn no points, but as progressively fewer incidents occur, they earn an increasing number of points that can be applied toward a reward.

for example

If the average number of incidents for the five days was 33 (obviously this hypothetical class has a lot of misbehavior), your point scale might look like this:

More than 32 incidents = 0 points
22–32 incidents = 1 point
15–21 incidents = 2 points
7–14 incidents = 3 points
3–6 incidents = 4 points
1–2 incidents = 5 points
0 incidents = 6 points

Post the chart and point out to students the number of incidents that occurred over
the preceding five days. Explain your concern and inform students that you are willing to provide the class with some rewards if they work on reducing the amount
of misbehavior that occurs each day. Then show students your scale of number of
incidents and corresponding points. Next, have students brainstorm a list of class
reward ideas.

Once you have a reasonable list, set prices for each of the possible rewards in terms of
how many points will be required to get it. The prices need to be set by you, and you
should base the prices on the instructional, personnel, and/or monetary costs of the
items. Monetary cost is clear—the more expensive the item, the more points should
be required to earn it. Instructional cost refers to the amount of instructional time
lost or interrupted as the result of a particular reward—for example, an extra ten
minutes of recess means ten minutes taken from instructional time. Any reward that
results in the class missing academic instruction should cost more points than one
that does not result in missed instruction, such as a reward the class can do during
recess time. Personnel cost refers to the time required for you or other staff to give
the reward. An extra recess that requires arranging for extra supervision costs
more than playing music for students during an independent work period.

Have the class vote on the rewards. Students will work for the winning
reward first. The items that come in second and third in the voting will
be the second and third rewards that students have a chance to win.

> *You should base the prices
> on the instructional,
> personnel, and/or
> monetary costs of the
> items.*

Each day, keep a careful count of the number of incidents of misbehavior.
At the end of the day, record the total number of misbehavior incidents
and tell the class how many points they earned that day. Also let students
know each day the total number of points they have accumulated to date.
When the class has enough points, they get the designated reward. Then the

system starts again, and they have zero points. Remind the class of the next reward they are working toward (the item that got the second most votes).

GOOD BEHAVIOR GAME

The Good Behavior Game (Barrish, Saunders, & Wolf, 1969) is a simple but effective system that has been used successfully in elementary classrooms. Divide the class into two teams and list each team on the board. Tell students that every time they misbehave (be sure to specify the behavior you are looking for), you will place a mark next to their team name on the board. The team with the fewest marks at the end of the day, or both teams if they each stay under five marks, receives a reward such as first to line up or a couple of minutes of extra recess. In the original 1969 study, the Good Behavior Game was implemented in a fourth-grade classroom. The intervention resulted in decreases in disruptive behavior and was well liked by both the implementing teacher and the students. Since the 1969 study, versions of the game have been implemented in a variety of general and special education settings, primarily with students in first through sixth grade. Although the exact procedures implemented across studies vary, the core components include:

- Specifically teach expected and unacceptable behaviors.

- Divide the class into two or more teams to use peer influence to increase appropriate behavior and minimize problem behaviors.

- Reinforce appropriate behaviors by acknowledging social behavior successes and allowing students to earn rewards (Barrish, Saunders, & Wolf, 1969).

The Good Behavior Game has resulted in decreased disruptive behaviors and increases in appropriate social behaviors (Darch & Thorpe, 1977; Patrick, Ward, & Crouch, 1998; Robertshaw & Hiebert, 1973; Swiezy, Matson, & Box, 1992; Tingstrom, Sterling-Turner, & Wilczynski, 2006). It has also resulted in improvements in students' work completion rates (Darveaux, 1984; Harris & Sherman, 1973; Maloney & Hopkins, 1973; Robertshaw & Hiebert, 1973).

BEHAVIORAL GRADING

Behavioral Grading involves keeping records on each individual student's behavior and translating those records into grades. It is a classwide system in that every student is graded on the same behaviors, but it is individualized in that each student receives his or her own grades. This is an especially useful system with middle school students. It may also be effective with fourth- and fifth-grade students, but is likely to be less effective with primary students than some of the other systems in this menu, such as Whole-Class Points. The behavioral grades may be incorporated as part of students' academic grades, or they may stand alone as something like citizenship

Figure 8.4   *Sample of Codes for Behavioral Grading*

Misbehavior	Code	Positive Trait	Code
off task	o	do your best (effort)	E
talking (at wrong time)	t	be responsible	B
swearing	s	respect/cooperation	R

grades. For middle school students, the behavior grade may be included as a percentage of the student's overall grade (for example, 20 percent of the science grade or 50 percent of the PE grade).

This system depends on accurate and systematic record-keeping. A Misbehavior Recording Sheet (see Chapter 6, Tool 3) is a very effective tool to use with this system, though you will be recording both positive and negative behavior. First, identify the three or four particular misbehaviors that you wish to reduce or eliminate at a classwide level. Then identify three or four positive traits or behaviors you wish to encourage at a classwide level (the positive traits may correspond directly to your Guidelines for Success). For each positive and each negative behavior, assign a code that you will use to record occurrences of those behaviors on your recording sheet. Figure 8.4 shows a sample of a code.

Elementary teachers can use a Daily Misbehavior Recording Sheet (Reproducible 6.5 or 6.7), and middle school teachers can use a Weekly Misbehavior Recording Sheet (Reproducible 6.6 or 6.8). These forms are discussed in Chapter 6, pp. 257–261, and provided on the CD.

Then, each time you speak to a student about a misbehavior, mark the appropriate code next to that student's name in the appropriate column. Whenever you provide positive feedback to a student, identify the positive trait his or her behavior demonstrated—for example, on-task behavior might be an example of "doing one's best" —then mark the appropriate code. See the example in Figure 8.5.

As an option, elementary teachers who use this system might create a weekly recording form that corresponds to the Daily Misbehavior Recording Sheet and put one on each student's desk.

Whenever you mark a positive or negative behavior on your record sheet, have the student put a tally mark in the appropriate column on her form. You can send this sheet home with the student at the end of the week so her family can see how much positive and corrective feedback she received during the week. Figure 8.5 shows a sample of the form for students' desks—keep in mind that you will label the columns with the specific positive and negative behaviors you are monitoring. Also, you may want to start your week on Friday and run it through Thursday of the following week—then you can send the sheets home every Friday.

At the end of each week, enter the total number of points for the week in the last column of the Misbehavior Recording Sheet. For middle school students, enter a score of between 0 and 20 points based on their behavior. To determine each student's weekly points, assume that each student starts each new week with 15 points, which

Figure 8.5   *Misbehavior Recording Sheets for Individual Students (top) and Teacher (below)*

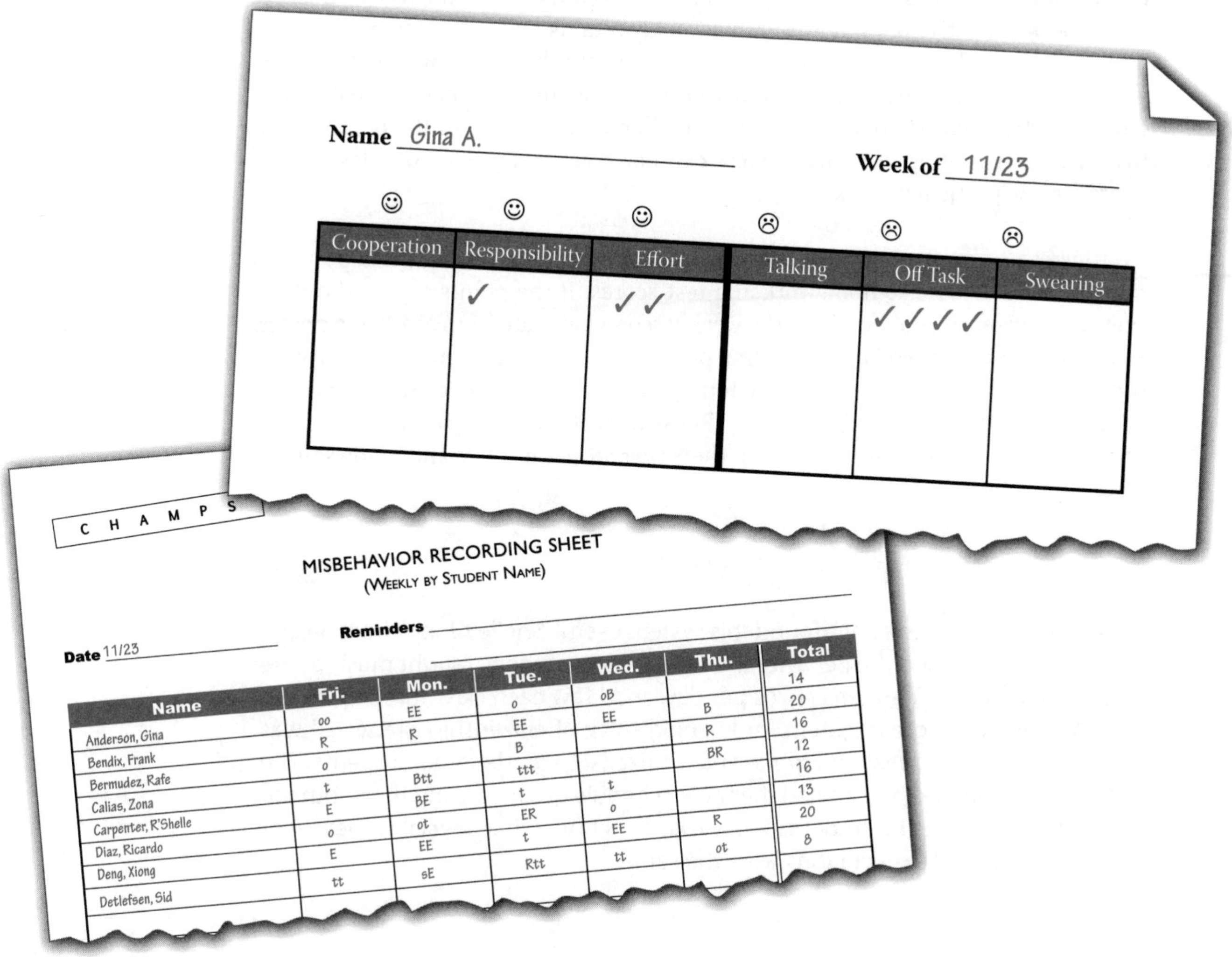

Name   Gina A.   Week of   11/23

☺ Cooperation	☺ Responsibility	☺ Effort	☹ Talking	☹ Off Task	☹ Swearing
	✓	✓ ✓		✓ ✓ ✓ ✓	

C H A M P S

MISBEHAVIOR RECORDING SHEET
(Weekly by Student Name)

Date 11/23   Reminders _____

Name	Fri.	Mon.	Tue.	Wed.	Thu.	Total
Anderson, Gina	oo	EE	o	oB	B	14
Bendix, Frank	R	R	EE	EE	R	20
Bermudez, Rafe	o		B		BR	16
Calias, Zona	t	Btt	ttt	t		12
Carpenter, R'Shelle	E	BE	t	o		16
Diaz, Ricardo	o	ot	ER	EE	R	13
Deng, Xiong	E	EE	t			20
Detlefsen, Sid	tt	sE	Rtt	tt	ot	8

is 75 percent of the total possible for the week (20), or roughly a grade of C. During the week, students lose one point for each misbehavior and gain one point for each positive behavior that you notice and comment on. There may be some days when nothing is coded for a student, and other days when several things are coded. Only record the times you talk directly to a student about one of the targeted (positive or negative) behaviors.

At the end of the week, figure each student's total by adding and subtracting points to and from the student's baseline of 15, based on your records of the student's behavior for the week. Notice that in the sample in Figure 8.5, the week begins on a Friday. If you compute students' point totals on Thursday evening, they get the results on Friday, thus reducing the delay in giving them feedback.

The teacher's Weekly Misbehavior Recording Sheet in Figure 8.5 uses the code described earlier (see Figure 8.4). An E stands for effort, a T for talking, and so on. Note that the first student, Gina, has three positive comments and four negative ones, so her total for the week is 14 ($15 - 4 + 3 = 14$). The next student, Frank, has six positive codes and no negative ones; however, his weekly total is only 20 points rather than 21 ($15 + 6 = 21$). This score makes sense when you think about how most teachers grade an essay worth 100 points. No matter how good an individual student's essay is, if only 100 points are possible, the student will not get more than 100 points. With this behavioral grading system, a student can never get more than 20 or less than 0 points for any particular week.

If you use this system as part of students' academic grades, record these points in your grade book just like homework and test scores. If the points are used only to determine citizenship grades, keep the weekly scores separate from academic grades. Then total them at the end of the grading period and determine percentages. That is, students who earned 90 percent of the total possible points receive an A, those who earned 80 percent receive a B, and so on. Regardless of how you use the system, students should get weekly information on their current point totals and grade status.

Recommended

Elementary specialists have found this system useful. Shelley Jones from Salem, Oregon, says, "I used the Behavioral Grading system when I taught music at the elementary level. I had ten classes per day, and I saw each class three times per week. This was a great system for keeping track of citizenship grades—I was required to give both a class grade and a citizenship grade for all students. The PE teacher and the librarian had the same schedule of classes, and they both adopted this system. The students knew that no matter what specialist they went to, the behavioral expectations were the same."

This type of motivation system has several advantages. First, you can monitor the nature of your interactions with students simply by scanning your completed daily or weekly recording sheet. Are you paying more attention to positive behavior or negative behavior? Are there some students with whom you rarely interact? Are there some students you interact with only in a corrective capacity? Every week you can quickly consider these issues as you review the data, then plan any necessary adjustments in your behavior for the following week.

Another advantage to this type of system is that it provides you with a lot of specific and objective data that you can share with families during conferences or when speaking with them about reoccurring behavioral problems. Finally, you will probably find that students tend to take your praise and your corrections more seriously when they know you are keeping a record of their behaviors—appropriate and inappropriate—and that the record will be reflected in their grades.

REWARD-BASED SYSTEMS APPROPRIATE FOR MEDIUM-STRUCTURE CLASSES

100 SQUARES

100 Squares is a combination of tic-tac-toe and bingo. It uses intermittent rewards to acknowledge the behavior of the entire class. 100 Squares is especially useful when trying to improve student behavior regarding a specific rule ("work during all work times," for example).

Figure 8.6 *100 Squares Tokens and Chart*

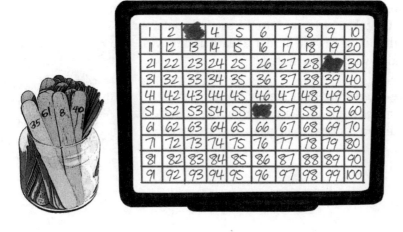

Draw a large 10-square by 10-square grid (100 spaces total) on a white board or flip chart. Number each square from 1 to 100 (see Figure 8.6). Place the chart in a prominent place in the room. Get two containers (bowls or hats, for example) and 100 small tokens such as poker chips, small tag board squares, or Popsicle sticks. On each token, write a number from 1 to 100. Place all of them into one of the two containers.

On *some* occasions when the entire class is working well, stop what is going on and have a student draw one of the tokens from the full container. Identify the number written on the token, then fill in—initial or color—the space on the chart that has the same number. Put the token into the empty (second) container. When ten squares in a row—horizontally, vertically, or diagonally—have been filled in, the entire class gets one of the group rewards identified by you or by the class during a brainstorming session. Once a full line has been completed and a reward given, erase the filled-in squares or put up a new grid on the flip chart, and return all the drawn tokens to the original container. Identify the next reward students will work toward (you choose or have the class vote) and begin the system again.

Have a different student draw the number each time so that eventually every student has a chance. In the early stages of using the system, try to have at least ten drawings per day, but *do not* have a drawing unless everyone in the class is doing well at that particular moment.

> *Class, right now everyone is seated, with eyes on the overhead, and anyone who wants to talk is waiting for me to call on them. Micah, please draw a number from the bowl and tell me the numbered space that we will fill in.*

After the class has earned at least six or more rewards, modify the system to make the chart an 11 x 11 grid with 121 spaces and add the additional tokens. This allows you to continue to hold frequent drawings, but it also means that it takes longer for students to earn a reward. As time goes on, if the system continues to have a positive effect on student behavior, you can make the chart a 12 x 12 grid with 144 spaces and eventually even a 15 x 15 grid with 225 spaces.

At some point, plan to have a class discussion to see whether students want to continue the system. If they think they can continue to behave responsibly without the system, let them know that you will periodically give them free time or other favorite rewards. If students want to continue the system, double the number of tokens in the container—so that there are two tokens for each number. If a number is drawn and its space is already filled in, the token just goes into the second container. This doubling of tokens makes the actual reward harder to earn and moves students one step closer to working without the system.

Students find this system more interesting than simply filling in successive boxes because there is an element of chance—they hope, but can't be sure, that the number drawn is one that brings a row closer to completion.

take note

Be sure to clarify that the students who draw the numbers are doing so for a class, not an individual, reward.

> *Students find this system more interesting than simply filling in successive boxes because there is an element of chance.*

GROUP RESPONSE COST

Group Response Cost is a simple system that can be used very effectively to reduce one specific misbehavior that tends to be exhibited by several different students in the class. It is also effective in improving a group's behavior in terms of following directions and being efficient during transitions.

> *Too much focus on a negative behavior without frequent positive interactions can backfire on you.*

To use this system to reduce a common group misbehavior (for example, use of profanity), first set up a special time in the afternoon for a fun group activity—an extra ten minutes of recess, for instance. On index cards write times in 30-second intervals from zero to ten minutes—on one card write zero seconds, on the next 30 seconds, on the next one minute, then one and one-half minutes, and so on until you reach ten minutes. Tell students that each day the class will start out with ten minutes of extra recess, but if at any time you hear profanity, they will lose 30 seconds of that extra recess. Take your stack of cards (with the "ten minutes" card on top) and demonstrate how when you hear profanity, you will take the top card and move it to the bottom of the stack, leaving the "nine and one-half minutes" card on top. The time on the top card at recess time will show how much extra recess the class gets that afternoon.

When using this system to improve behaviors such as following directions and being efficient during transitions, make cards for ten extra minutes of recess as described above. Let students know that when you give a directive for a transition ("Everyone get out your math books and a blank piece of paper"), they have a reasonable amount of time, say one minute, to complete the transition. Tell students that if it takes them more than one minute to complete the transition, that additional time will come off the ten minutes of extra recess time. Then, after you give your first directive in a day, wait for one minute. If the class is ready, thank students for their efficiency. If students are not ready, hold up the stack of cards with the "ten minutes" card showing. Every 30 seconds, move the top card to the back of the stack. Continue this process, without saying a word, until all students are ready. After you give the next directive for a transition, wait the allotted time, and then pick up the stack of cards. After 30 seconds, move the top card (which now may say "nine minutes") to the back of the stack. Over the course of a day, each block of 30 seconds that students waste will cost them 30 seconds off the extra recess period.

Because Group Response Cost is predominately punitive (taking time away from the extra recess), you really need to make a concerted effort to provide students with frequent positive attention, positive feedback, and even intermittent rewards (see Chapter 7) when they behave appropriately. Too much focus on a negative behavior without frequent positive interactions can backfire on you—students may try to lose the ten minutes quickly just to frustrate you and see what you will do next.

This system is most likely to work when more than three or four students exhibit one specific misbehavior. If only one, two, or three students are causing the problem, you are better off setting up individualized plans (both positive and corrective) with those students. The system is also unlikely to be powerful enough to be effective if your class frequently exhibits many different misbehaviors.

LOTTERY TICKETS

A relatively simple but highly effective way to specifically encourage appropriate behavior or a specific positive behavior is to use an intermittent weekly lottery reward system.

Each week on an unpredictable basis, present individual students who are following the rules or demonstrating responsible behavior with lottery tickets for a weekly drawing. Reproducibles 8.7a and 8.7b, shown below, are reproducible sheets of multiple lottery tickets available on the CD.

When you give a ticket, have the student write her name and the date on it. Be sure to tell the student exactly why she is getting the ticket so she can write a brief description (such as "completed all homework"). Have the student put the completed ticket into a container for a drawing that will occur at the end of the week. Each Friday before the drawing, identify two rewards you think students would like, perhaps a coupon for free ice cream or 15 minutes of computer time. At the time of the drawing, announce the first reward and draw a lottery ticket from the container. The student whose name is on that ticket receives the reward. Repeat the process for the second reward. Throw away or recycle the tickets that remain in the container. The next Monday, start giving out tickets for that week's drawing.

take note

This is a difficult system to use with very young primary students—they don't understand why one or two people get a reward and they don't.

Reproducible 8.7a, 8.7b *Lottery Tickets (Version 1) and CHAMPS Tickets (Version 2)*

Print from CD

With a Lottery Ticket system, it is important to watch that you are not being discriminatory. For example, it would be easy to inadvertently harbor a grudge toward individual students who have been especially troublesome during the current week or in the past, and so not notice their positive behavior. It can also be easy to fall into the trap of noticing the small improvements of your more difficult students and the great leaps of your high achievers but not recognizing or acknowledging the ongoing, sustained effort of your average students.

MYSTERY BEHAVIOR OF THE DAY

This simple and creative intermittent reward-based system was developed by Pat Gagnon, a fourth-grade teacher in Springfield, Oregon. Each morning Pat decides on a particular positive behavior or trait that she will look for that day—helping others, for example. The students know that she will be watching for some behavior, but she does not tell them what the day's behavior or trait is. During the day, she watches for and notes to herself examples of students exhibiting the Mystery Behavior. Toward the end of the day, she puts a small treat on the desks of the students she caught exhibiting the behavior. After the rewards are given, the class spends a few minutes guessing what the day's Mystery Behavior is. Whether or not students guess correctly, Pat tells them the behavior and lets them know that she will be looking for a different Mystery Behavior the next day.

You can add to the level of interest in this system by having a large envelope with the words Mystery Behavior of the Day prominently displayed in the room. Before the students arrive each morning, write the behavior or trait you will look for that day on a piece of paper and place it in the envelope. At the end of the day, after students discuss what they think the Mystery Behavior is, have one of the students who earned a treat that day draw the piece of paper from the envelope and announce the behavior. You might even want to encourage the student to add a bit of fanfare—like an Academy Awards ceremony: "And, the Mystery Behavior for today is . . ."

When using this system, be sure to vary the Mystery Behavior so that every student gets recognized periodically. That is, be very careful that no student goes too long without being caught exhibiting one of the Mystery Behaviors.

take note

For teachers struggling with transitions or clean-up, a variation on the Mystery Behavior system is Mystery Items. In this system, the teacher secretly names an item in the classroom as the Mystery Item, and then sets a timer for students' clean-up time. The student who puts that item in its place within the time frame gets a prize.

PUBLIC POSTING (CLASSWIDE)

When there is one specific behavior you want to increase (homework completion, for example) or decrease (use of student-to-student put-downs during class), you can overtly chart that behavior in a place and in a way that all students can see it. This is especially useful when quite a few students in the class exhibit a specific problem as opposed to a problem that only a couple of students exhibit. Public posting makes everyone aware of how pervasive a problem is and gives the entire group positive feedback when the situation improves.

for example

If a middle school class has trouble with frequent name-calling, laughing at peers' mistakes, and other forms of student-to-student disrespect, you could start by keeping a simple tally of the total number of disrespectful actions that occur each day for three days. Then post a chart with the data from those three days. Posting the chart serves as the impetus for holding a class discussion about the problem, the benefits of reducing the negative behavior, and strategies that individual students might employ to help reduce the problem. In this example, one strategy that you could share is that individuals should avoid laughing when someone calls someone else a name or otherwise puts somebody down. Each day, keep a simple count of the number of disrespectful incidents. At the end of the day, record that data on the chart. At least twice a week when you post the data, initiate a short discussion about whether the problem is getting better, getting worse, or staying about the same. If the situation is staying the same or getting worse, have students discuss other actions they can take to help reduce the problem.

As noted before, public posting can also be effective in helping you increase a positive behavior—daily work completion, for example. To use the system for this purpose, start by determining the class's daily percentage of completed work turned in on time for a period of one week. You can do this by simply counting the number of assignments turned in each day and dividing that number by the total number of assignments that should have been turned in that day. This figure is the class's percentage of work completion for that day. Record a week's worth of daily work completion percentages on a chart placed prominently in the room.

Use the initial record to prompt a discussion of the importance of work completion, the benefits to each individual of completing his or her work, and strategies individuals can use to help increase their own work completion. Then compute the class's daily percentage of work completion and plan to record it on the chart the next day. At least twice a week, preferably daily, discuss the data on the chart and whether the percentage of work completion is increasing, decreasing, or staying about the same.

PUBLIC POSTING (INDIVIDUAL)

Publicly posting student performance may be an effective way to improve performance in academic areas such as math, reading, and language arts. Research has shown public posting to be effective in decreasing specific problem behaviors (Brantley & Webster, 1993) and increasing desired social and academic behaviors (on-task, reading, spelling, writing) (Kastelen, Nickel, & McLaughlin, 1984; Van Houten & McKillop, 1977).

> *The lowest 50 percent of your students are likely to make the most significant gains in achievement.*

To use this system, create a large chart with each student's name on it and with places to record scores. For example, you might create a chart to record each individual student's best score every week on a timed math exercise. At the end of the week, have each student enter his or her best score for that week in the correct space on the chart. Have individual students compare their best score for the current week to their best scores from previous weeks. When using public posting of individual data, it is important to emphasize and to keep emphasizing that the purpose of the system is not for students to compete with each other but for each student to compete against his or her own personal best.

Some of you may be concerned that this type of system will humiliate those students who are struggling academically. The fact is that the lowest 50 percent of your students are likely to make the most significant gains in achievement. Nonetheless, if you are considering this system, discuss it with your administrator first to determine whether it is an acceptable practice in your school district.

SELF-EVALUATION OF ON- AND OFF-TASK BEHAVIOR

In this system, students observe and record their own behavior (Mace, Belfiore, & Shea, 2001), and you monitor their on-task and off-task behavior during instructional activities to determine whether the students' and your evaluations match. This system is particularly appropriate when your students do not exhibit a great deal of overt misbehavior but also do not use their work time well. That is, quite a few students in the class tend to sit and do nothing or converse instead of doing their work or participating actively in instructional activities.

Before you use this system, it's important to have already provided lessons on your CHAMPS expectations for teacher-directed instruction, independent work periods, and cooperative groups (see Chapters 4 and 5). Once you have thoroughly taught students what on-task behavior looks and sounds like, which may take several weeks, make copies of Reproducible 8.8, Self-Evaluation of On- and Off-Task Behavior, for each student. With clear instruction and feedback, self-monitoring has been successfully used to improve academic and social behaviors (Dalton, Martella, & Marchand-Martella, 1999; Freeman & Dexter-Mazza, 2004; Harris, Friedlander, Saddler, Frizzelle, & Graham, 2005; Hughes & Hendrickson, 1987; Hughes et al., 2002; Koegel, Harrower, & Koegel, 1999; Reid, Trout, & Schartz, 2005).

Reproducible 8.8   *Self-Evaluation of On- and Off-Task Behavior*

sample

Self-Evaluation of On- and Off-Task Behavior ✓

Name _Tranh_   Date _10/27_

ON TASK

①②③④⑤⑥⑦⑧ 9 10
11 12 13 14 15 16 17 18 19 20

OFF TASK

①②3 4 5 6 7 8 9 10
11 12 13 14 15 16 17 18 19 20

Print from CD

My percentage of on-task behavior for today was _80_ **%**

To use the system, set a timer at the beginning of each work period for anywhere from one to 30 minutes. When the timer goes off, each student evaluates whether he or she was on task or off task at that moment and then fill in the circle for the next number in the appropriate column of the recording sheet. After you give students an opportunity to do their recording, instruct them to get back to work and reset the timer. Vary the length of the timed period so that students never know exactly when they will be evaluating their behavior next.

Before you implement the system, be sure to explain to students how it works. Teach them how to evaluate whether they were on-task or off-task and how to accurately fill out the form. Then, each time the timer goes off, monitor a few students (not always the same ones!) to see if they are recording accurately. When you are monitoring, if you disagree with a student's rating, discuss your assessment of the situation with the student. Never argue, but do encourage students to be honest with themselves in their ratings. You can teach students in grades 5 and above how to calculate their own daily percentage (divide the total on-task numbers filled in by the total of both on-task and off-task numbers filled in). With younger students, you will probably have to calculate the percentage for them. Have each student keep a graph of his or her daily on-task percentage and encourage students to try to improve their performance from one day to the next. Use the procedure for a couple of weeks.

> *Never argue, but do encourage students to be honest with themselves in their ratings.*

Timing Intervals

A class prompter for your computer is a convenient tool for many of these systems that use timed periods. They allow you to program your computer to beep at various intervals. Class prompters are readily available at a very moderate cost. A simple kitchen timer also makes a good low-tech prompter. Another way to time intervals is to use beeper tapes. These are audiotapes, usually 30 minutes in length, that are blank except for 2 to 15 randomly recorded beeps. You can make your own beeper tapes using an audio cassette recorder, a clock with a second hand, and some means of making a noise—a doorbell, hitting a chime, or hitting an empty glass with a spoon. You may want to have a variety of tapes on hand. For example, you could have two tapes with beeps that occur at regular intervals (one with beeps every five minutes and one with beeps every 12 minutes) and two or three tapes with beeps that occur at irregular intervals (one with two beeps, one with eight beeps, and one with 12 beeps, for example).

This procedure can be used with kindergarten and first-grade students by making the focus on "Being in the Right Place" versus "Being in the Wrong Place" and evaluating whether students are in their seats during seatwork time, on the rug during story time, in line when it is time to line up, and so on. With young students, however, it may be better to set the system up as a group count—how many students are in the right place when the timer goes off?

The group earns a point if everyone is in the right place when the beeper goes off. Reserve a place on a chalkboard or flip chart to record the students' accumulated point total. When the class earns a predetermined number of points, they get a treat or a special activity.

TARGET AND REWARD A SPECIFIC BEHAVIOR

This simple classwide behavior management system is useful when quite a few different students exhibit one specific behavioral problem, such as name-calling or put-downs. For a couple of days, count the number of times the targeted behavior occurs. Don't bother to count how many incidents any individual student has, just the total number of incidents for the class during the day or class period.

After two days, share the information you have collected with students and tell them they need to reduce the frequency of this misbehavior. Guide the class in the process of setting a realistic improvement goal —reducing the number of daily incidents from 40 to 32, for example. Students may be tempted to set an unrealistic goal such as reducing the number of incidents from 40 per day to zero. Explain that if they set an unreasonable goal, it will be very difficult to achieve that goal. Explain that a realistic goal—say, no more than 32 incidents—increases their chances of success. Also tell them that once they achieve their initial (reasonable) goal, they can start setting more challenging goals for themselves.

Have the class generate a list of classwide rewards. Create a Grab Bag—write each reward on a small card and put all the cards in a container. On any day that the class meets the goal, one of the students gets to draw a card from the container. The class receives the reward written on the card. When you are ready to start fading the system, let students know that you have put some cards into the container that say, "Congratulations! Today you have the satisfaction of having attained your goal." Explain that when one of these cards is drawn, students will not get an actual reward that day. Instead, it will give them the opportunity to learn that people do many things in life not for any reward but simply for the satisfaction of doing something well. The more of these cards you add, the closer you move students toward eliminating the system completely.

MYSTERY MOTIVATORS: A VARIATION OF "TARGET AND REWARD A SPECIFIC BEHAVIOR"

A variation of the previous system is called Mystery Motivators. This variation makes the system even more of a gamble, which may mean that it is more interesting and compelling for some classes. On a calendar for the next month, use an invisible-ink pen to mark an X on approximately 60 percent of the school days. (Invisible-ink pens are available at novelty stores.) *The Tough Kid Tool Box*, available from Pacific Northwest Publishing, has many reproducible samples of Mystery Motivator forms that are fun and interesting.

Choose one of the rewards from the list generated by the class, write it on a card, then place the card in an envelope labeled Mystery Motivator. Do not tell students what reward is written on the card. On days when the class meets its behavior goal, one student gets to color in that day on the calendar to see if there is an X (previously invisible) in the square.

If there is an X, have another student open the Mystery Motivator envelope and announce which Mystery Motivator the class has earned. If there is no X when the calendar square is colored in, enthusiastically congratulate students on meeting their goal, but don't award or reveal the Mystery Motivator. On days when the class does not meet the goal because there were too many incidents of the misbehavior, students do not get to check to see whether there is an X. If the system is effective, you can begin fading it during the second month by putting fewer Xs on the calendar, thereby creating fewer chances to get an extrinsic reward.

TEAM COMPETITION WITH RESPONSE COST LOTTERY

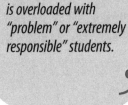

A system that involves team competition (groups of students competing against each other) can be useful for reducing a minor but annoying behavior such as students blurting out or disruptions. Of course, whenever you do anything with teams—especially when the competition involves academic or behavioral performance—it's important to ensure that the teams themselves are as comparable as possible. Thus, you should assign students to teams rather than letting them self-select their teams, and you should make sure that no team is overloaded with "problem" or "extremely responsible" students.

> *Make sure that no team is overloaded with "problem" or "extremely responsible" students.*

To use this system, divide students into four to six teams. Have each team give itself a team name. At the beginning of each day, every team receives a certain number of tickets, perhaps ten. Have the students write their team's name on their tickets. Then, whenever a student misbehaves, take a ticket from his or her team. At the end of the day, collect the remaining tickets from each team and put them in a container for a lottery drawing. The team whose name is on the winning ticket earns the reward for the day. (The class can generate a list of desired rewards.) Start the system over again the following day.

WHOLE-CLASS POINTS (INTERMITTENT)

An alternative to using whole-class points based on time intervals (see p. 324) is to intermittently catch the class when everyone is behaving well and award one or more points. Use the time interval concept and time interval reinforcement graphic on the CD and have the class brainstorm various reward items and activities. You set the prices. Then whenever you notice that everyone in the class is meeting expectations, you can announce that you are awarding one (or any number you wish) points.

Whole-Class Points (Intermittent) may be used with both medium- and high-structure classes.

The advantage to this variation is that the system is entirely under your control—you decide when to award points. You can make it a high-structure system if you award points frequently. The disadvantage is that without a specific interval (as marked by the timer going off or by the end of a work period), it is easy to forget about the system. Ironically, this is especially true if the students are behaving really well. So if you are going to use this system intermittently, keep reminding yourself to catch the class and award points. If you do this well and student behavior responds quickly, an easy way to begin fading this system is to use longer intervals (on average, because this is an intermittent system) between the times you award points. For example, during the early days of using the system, you might catch the class ten or fifteen times a day. Later in the year, you catch the class only once or twice per day.

NONREWARD-BASED SYSTEMS APPROPRIATE FOR LOW-STRUCTURE CLASSES

Goal setting involves helping students learn to strive for positive goals they can achieve (Rader, 2005). Goals can be academic, behavioral, or a mix of both. Because the focus tends to be on increasing desired behaviors as opposed to reducing negative ones, goal-setting systems are generally most appropriate for students who need only a low-structure management plan. If a class exhibits frequent misbehavior, there may not be sufficient intrinsic motivation among the students for goal-setting procedures to have much of an impact. On the other hand, if a class is for the most part behaving responsibly, by definition a significant amount of intrinsic motivation is being demonstrated. When this is the case, use of goal-setting procedures can often extend and channel that intrinsic motivation in productive directions.

A goal-setting system such as setting goals for each student and sharing them with the individual students represents a first level of implementation. Once students understand the concept of striving to achieve a goal and are motivated to do so, you can teach them to set their own goals and goals for the class as a whole.

You should work with a class for at least one full month before implementing any goal-setting system. Following are descriptions of three effective goal-setting procedures.

TEACHER SETS GOALS FOR STUDENTS

To use this procedure, go through your class list student by student and think about each one—what attitude, behavior, or trait would help each individual student be more successful? Examples of goals you might identify for different students include:

- Complete more work.

- Write more neatly.

- Follow directions without arguing.

- Get along better with other students (be less bossy).

- Be willing to take more risks—accept more challenges.

- Have a more positive attitude—complain less.

- Accept and learn from mistakes.

- Stay focused on work during class.

- Talk only at appropriate times.

- Demonstrate more self-control (anger management).

- Master basic multiplication and division facts.

- Become more independent and self reliant.

- Interact more with other students (be less shy).

- Be more creative.

- Be willing to try new things.

You can use Reproducible 8.9 to record goals for each student in your class. Write the name of each student on the form. Then take 15 to 30 seconds per student and think about what that student most needs to learn. Think about the lasting legacy you want to leave with this student. "If I could help her learn only one thing, it would be . . ." Leave the Priority column blank for now. If you can't think of a goal for a particular student, skip that student and come back to him later. When you go back to that student, try to identify why you could not come up with a goal. Perhaps the student is already hard working and responsible—if this is the case, you could set the goal that the student continue to be highly motivated ("Continue to do your best and continue to be a hard-working, creative, and cooperative student"). If you do not know a student well enough to identify a goal, do not set a goal for the student, but set one for yourself to get to know that student better. This task of identifying a goal for each student (and going back to the students who require more thought) should take between 15 and 30 minutes for an entire class.

Reproducible 8.9 *Goal-Setting Form*

CHAMPS
sample
GOAL-SETTING FORM
≫ no. **8.9**

Student Name	Goal	Priority 1+, 1, 2, 3
Allison, Keith	Keep up good work!	3
Bhatt, Vang	Participate more	1
Cedeno, Rosa	Manage her temper	1+
Draper, Melissa	Neatness	2
Erlandsen, Joe	No more late work	2
Foley, Trent	Stop bullying	1+
Green, Jamaya	Keep up good work!	3
Houzedah, Ashraf	Stay focused in groups.	2
Jackson, Rainbow	Finishing work	1
Katayan, Jazmin	Neatness	2
Lachowicz, Peter	No talking during class	2
Moreno, Nando	Keep up good work!	3
	Participate more	2
	Use quiet voice in groups	2
	Raise hand to speak	2

Print from CD

© 2009 Pacific Northwest Publishing | *Reproducible Form*

Once you identify a goal for each student, you can set priorities. You need to determine which of the students' goals have an element of urgency to them and which represent goals that are merely desirable. You should plan on committing greater time and attention to helping the students who may not be successful in school and life if they do not achieve their goal or learn the skill or trait. If a goal is less urgent (the student will probably do fine whether or not he improves in this particular skill or trait), it will not require as much time or attention from you. This step of prioritizing students' goals is essential because even the best teacher cannot do everything at once.

Figure 8.7   *Guide for Setting Goal Priorities*

	Urgency for the Student	Action by the Teacher
1+	This student must immediately learn to meet this goal in order to succeed in my classroom and in the future.	I will meet with the student and family, fill out a goal contract, provide frequent positive feedback, and may set up an individualized contract.
1	This student would benefit greatly from learning to meet this goal.	I will meet with the student, fill out a goal contract and provide frequent positive feedback when the student strives to meet the goal.
2	This student might benefit from learning to meet this goal.	I will provide frequent positive feedback when the student strives to meet the goal.
3	This student is going to be fine whether she/he learns to meet goal or not.	I will provide occasional positive feedback when the student strives to meet the goal.

You will notice that the Priority column on the Goal-Setting Form calls for rating each student's goal with a priority of 1+, 1, 2, or 3.

Figure 8.7 is a guide for determining which rating is most appropriate and identifying the corresponding action you should take to help the student achieve the goal.

Be careful about identifying too many goals as priority 1+. For goals with priority 1+, arrange to have a student/family conference concerning the goal. If you identify eight or more students with priority 1+ goals, the class probably needs a reward-based motivation system.

Once you identify a goal for each student and specify priorities for all the goals, determine how to make students aware of the goals you hope they will achieve (Fuchs, et al., 1985; Johnson, et al., 1997). One way is to have a conference with each student to discuss the goal and provide the student with a written description of the goal. With very young students, use a pictorial description. Many readers are probably now thinking (or shouting!), "I don't have time to meet with every student! I have 30 students!" Prioritizing will help the potentially overwhelmed teacher through this procedure. You should definitely plan to meet with the students who have the highest

Reproducible 8.10 *Goal Contract*

Keep your filled-out Goal-Setting Form handy and review it a couple of times each week. This will remind you of what specific behaviors you are looking for with each of the students in the class.

sample **GOAL CONTRACT**

Name ___Rosa C_____   Date ___11/16_____

A goal for you to work toward is ___to control your temper in class when you are angry___
___or frustrated.___

You can show you are working toward this goal by:

A. ___Going to the reading station to calm down when you feel angry or frustrated.___

B. ___Decreasing the number of times I send you to the timeout seat to calm down.___

C. ___Learning new ways let others know when you are angry or frustrated --for example, to say___
___that you are angry because . . . or you are frustrated about . . .___

___Rosa Cedeno___   ___Mr. Tsai___
Student's Signature   Teacher's Signature

priority goals, the 1+s. In fact, for students with 1+ goals, you should try to meet with the individual student and his or her family. For students who have priority 1 goals, you should also meet with the student, but you do not need to involve the family. You can hold off scheduling meetings for the students who have priority 2 and 3 goals. In fact, it's fine if you meet with these students only if you can find the time.

When you meet with a student or the student and his or her family, complete a Goal Contract (see Reproducible 8.10). To fill out a Goal Contract, first identify the overall goal—it will probably be what you wrote for the student on the Goal-Setting Form. However, if your goal for the student is framed in terms of something the student should *not* do, transform the goal into a positive statement of what the student *should* do (for example, "stop being disruptive" becomes "participate responsibly in lessons and study times"). Then list *three specific ways* the student can demonstrate that he or she is striving to achieve the goal. It is very important to tell the student that he can exhibit tangible, objective behaviors to show you he is working toward his goal. You should also have a rationale in mind that you can present to the student about how striving to achieve this goal will help him. Communicate all of this information to the student during your conference.

Another way you can share your goals with students is by having mini-conferences—take time during independent work periods to briefly inform individual students of the goals you hope to see them strive to achieve. You might use mini-conferences with students who have priority 2 and 3 goals.

Finally, you can communicate your goals for students somewhat indirectly by looking for and capitalizing on opportunities to give each student positive feedback related to the behavior or trait that you hope to help him or her achieve. This method of communication works even if you have not yet had a goal conference or a mini-conference with the student. When a student exhibits behavior that reflects the identified goal, comment on it.

---

for example

Your goal for a student is for him to "talk only at appropriate times" and he participates appropriately while a guest speaker is in the room. You might say, "Jamal, while our guest artist was here this morning, I noticed that you gave him your full attention. You talked only during the times that he wanted you to discuss things at your table and when you raised your hand to be recognized. That demonstrated a great deal of respect for the speaker."

Whether or not you've had a goal discussion or completed a Goal Contract with a student, feedback of this nature will help the student realize that this is a behavior that you are monitoring and that you feel is important for him to learn. Providing this type of contingent, descriptive, and immediate positive feedback is also extremely valuable after you have conducted a goal conference with a student.

Elementary teachers should go through this entire goal-setting process once a month. Middle school teachers should also plan to use the process once a month, but for a different class each month so that you end up thinking about goals for each of your classes once or twice a year. Remember, whether you are a middle school or elementary teacher, wait to use goal setting as a classwide motivation system until you have worked with your students for at least a month. As you repeat the goal-setting process, your goal for a particular student may vary from time to time. If a student has not made progress on the goal or has made some progress but still has more to go, maintain the same goal. If the student has met your goal, consider setting a new goal. Each time you go through the process, you should restate the priorities and conduct conferences with students who have priority 1+ and 1 goals and mini conferences with students who have priority 2 and 3 goals. For all students, give positive feedback when you see them taking steps toward their goals.

TEACHER GUIDES STUDENTS IN SETTING GOALS

Once students understand the concept of striving to achieve a goal, you can conduct one or more lessons to teach students how to set their own goals. If students are involved in their own goal setting as opposed to the teacher setting goals for them,

> " Setting goals in areas outside of school such as sports and hobbies can also be very useful. "

they may be more likely to work harder (Fuchs, Bahr, & Rieth, 1989). Begin by discussing the importance of goal setting. Remind students that they have been working hard to achieve the goals that you set for them. Then explain that learning to set goals and striving to meet them is a beneficial skill that can help them succeed in school, in work situations, and in life.

Have students identify and discuss some short-term goals they want to achieve for themselves. Encourage students to focus on school-based goals—however, let them know that setting goals in areas outside of school such as sports and hobbies can also be very useful. You may want to put some sample goals on the board to provide ideas for students who have trouble coming up with goals of their own. Pass out copies of the Goal Contract. Have each student write an overall goal and three ways to demonstrate that he or she is trying to achieve the goal. If you complete a Goal Contract for yourself as students do the activity, you validate the students for their efforts. Once students complete their Goal Contracts, tell them to keep a copy of their goal on their desk or on the front cover of a notebook so they will be reminded frequently of the goals they are striving to achieve.

For a couple of days after this session, try to meet with each student to discuss his or her Goal Contract. If a student has set an unreachable goal, help her to make the goal more realistic. Record each student's goal on a blank version of the Goal-Setting Form so that you have a summary of all the students' goals on one or two pages. Once you sign all the contracts and summarize all of the students' goals, watch for any opportunity to give students positive feedback on their efforts to achieve their goals (as you did when you set the goals for students).

If this process proves useful—behavior is improving, motivation is increasing—repeat the activity once each month.

TEACHER GUIDES STUDENTS IN SETTING A CLASSWIDE GOAL

Consider guiding your students in the process of setting a classwide goal. The goal might involve reducing a classwide problem (eliminate teasing), increasing a positive behavior (improve classroom climate through increased positive interactions), or participating in a service project (make regular visits to a retirement home). Put a reasonable time limit on achieving the goal so that you and the class will have a specific date to evaluate their success.

Establishing and actively working toward a common goal as a group is a powerful way to increase students' sense of purpose and belonging (Rader, 2005). It can build classroom pride and create a powerful sense of community.

Conclusion

This chapter covered the nuts and bolts of classwide motivation systems. It discussed how to choose between a nonreward- and a reward-based system, then explained how to implement, maintain, and fade a reward-based system. Finally, a menu of classwide systems was provided to help you choose an effective and easy-to-implement system for your particular situation.

Use the Self-Assessment Checklist shown below to keep track of the tasks you've completed and those that require further work. A fillable version of the Self-Assessment Checklist is available on the CD.

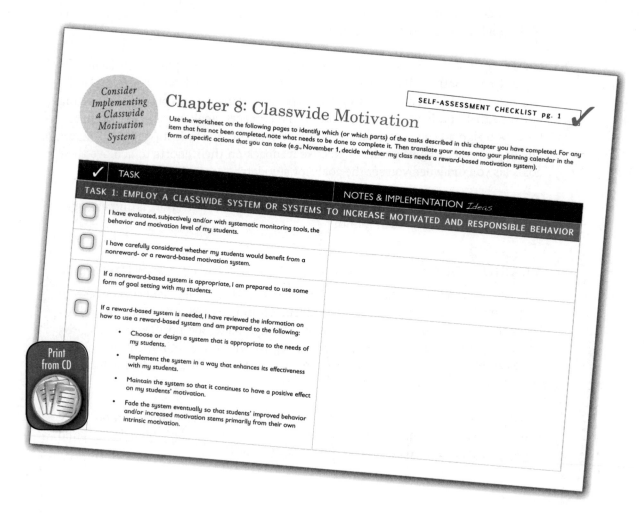

Consider Implementing a Classwide Motivation System

Chapter 8: Classwide Motivation

SELF-ASSESSMENT CHECKLIST pg. 1 ✓

Use the worksheet on the following pages to identify which (or which parts) of the tasks described in this chapter you have completed. For any item that has not been completed, note what needs to be done to complete it. Then translate your notes onto your planning calendar in the form of specific actions that you can take (e.g., November 1, decide whether my class needs a reward-based motivation system).

✓	TASK	NOTES & IMPLEMENTATION *Ideas*
	TASK 1: EMPLOY A CLASSWIDE SYSTEM OR SYSTEMS TO INCREASE MOTIVATED AND RESPONSIBLE BEHAVIOR	
☐	I have evaluated, subjectively and/or with systematic monitoring tools, the behavior and motivation level of my students.	
☐	I have carefully considered whether my students would benefit from a nonreward- or a reward-based motivation system.	
☐	If a nonreward-based system is appropriate, I am prepared to use some form of goal setting with my students.	
☐	If a reward-based system is needed, I have reviewed the information on how to use a reward-based system and am prepared to the following: • Choose or design a system that is appropriate to the needs of my students. • Implement the system in a way that enhances its effectiveness with my students. • Maintain the system so that it continues to have a positive effect on my students' motivation. • Fade the system eventually so that students' improved behavior and/or increased motivation stems primarily from their own intrinsic motivation.	

Print from CD

CORRECT fluently

STOIC

Structure Your Classroom for Success

Teach Expectations

Observe Student Behavior

Interact Positively

Correct Fluently

Section *Five*

As a teacher, you will observe misbehavior: one student does not follow your classroom expectations about when to use the pencil sharpener, another makes disruptive noises during a lesson, two students are caught cheating on a test, and one student is chronically disrespectful and insubordinate directly to you.

This section includes one chapter about how to Correct student misbehavior in a way that reduces the probability that the misbehavior will occur in the future. This skill may sound simple, but in fact it's one of the most difficult teaching techniques to master. When you "Correct Fluently"—the title of this section—you respond to misbehavior in a manner that does not disrupt other students or the flow of instructional activities. You enforce routines and rules in a way that reduces the chance that the misbehaving student, or any other student, exhibits the misbehavior in the future. You also correct in a way that does not have side effects—you don't harm the relationship you have established with the misbehaving student or reduce that student's motivation to do her best in your classroom.

Section *Five*

CORRECT *fluently*

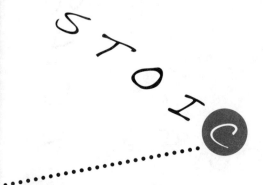

Imagine...

People in certain circumstances have some level of authority over you (even if that authority is only temporary):

- Airport security staff
- An umpire or referee when you are playing a sport
- An IRS auditor, if you have been selected
- Your boss at work
- A police officer who pulls you over for a driving violation
- College professors when you are working toward a degree
- A judge, if you are in court

Now imagine that these people are fair, competent, consistent, unemotional, and even helpful as they enforce the rules as their job requires them to do. How do you react to their authority over you?

Now imagine an authority figure, let's say a basketball referee, who is unfair, incompetent, arbitrary, and mean-spirited in his enforcement of the rules. How would you react to the referee if he called a wrongful foul on you, or even several fouls, during a game? What if you were stuck with this referee for every game the whole season? At best, you would be unhappy and unmotivated to play; at worst, you might want to quit the team.

Teachers need to be very skillful in how they correct students who are engaged in misbehavior. When in a position of authority, one must enforce the rules. This section is about how you as a teacher can enforce rules skillfully in a way that provides maximum benefit for everyone—you, the student who misbehaved, and the other students in the classroom.

Correcting Severe and Chronic Misbehavior

Correcting

When you treat student misbehavior as an instructional opportunity, you give students the chance to learn from their mistakes.

Introduction

A certain amount of misbehavior is bound to occur in your classroom, no matter how well you organize your room or how effectively you communicate your behavioral expectations to students. (Though if you have followed our suggestions in Chapters 1 through 8, you have minimized the misbehavior.) Unfortunately, teachers may tend to react, rather than respond, to student misbehavior in ways that actually lead to more, rather than less, of the inappropriate behavior (Dreikurs et al., 1998; Lewis & Sugai, 1999). This chapter is based on the idea that when you can regard misbehavior as an opportunity to help students learn, you will be more likely to respond to the misbehavior effectively (Colvin, et al., 1993; Sprick, et al., 2002).

Correcting student misbehavior effectively is surprisingly difficult to do well for a variety of reasons. A fundamental question to consider is: What is an effective correction?

What correction strategies are effective is a debatable topic. If the teacher reacts by communicating how angry he is to the student, he may feel better and think he has conveyed an effective correction. However, imagine that in this case the emotional reaction is actually reinforcing to this student. The student delights in demonstrating to the other students his ability to press the teacher's buttons and make the teacher upset. The teacher's emotional reaction makes the teacher feel better in the short run, but it is not really an effective correction because it increases the chance that the student will exhibit this behavior again. In fact, this attempt to punish the student is more closely analogous to giving the child a paycheck for misbehaving.

CHAPTER 9 TASKS

Task 1
Analyze and Adjust the Implementation of Your Basic Management Plan

Task 2
Analyze and Adjust the Strategies You Are Using to Build a Positive Relationship with the Student

Task 3
Analyze the Misbehavior and Develop a Function-Based Intervention

Who This Chapter Is For

The information in Chapter 9 is most useful for classrooms where student behavior is basically under control, but one or two students misbehave frequently enough to annoy or concern you. If your class has more than one or two students who chronically misbehave, consider holding off on this chapter for now. Instead, do one or more of the following to refocus your efforts on increasing the level of classroom structure:

- Organize your classroom routines and procedures (Chapters 1 and 2).

- Design and implement your Classroom Management & Discipline Plan (Chapter 3).

- Define and then communicate your behavioral expectations (Chapters 4 and 5).

- Observe and supervise systematically (Chapter 6).

- Build positive relationships with your students (Chapter 7).

- Implement a high-structure extrinsic classwide motivation system (Chapter 8).

In other words, the content of this chapter may be overwhelming and the ideas probably ineffective if the totality of your management plan is not effective.

Some teachers may think removing a disruptive student from the classroom is an effective corrective strategy, and in some cases it may be. Of course, the best way to ensure that the student never misbehaves again at school is to remove the student from the school! While removing every disruptive student from the classroom may at first glance seem compelling, it is not a realistic option in our society. We are under pressure to try to keep students in class because they cannot learn when they are out of the room. Besides, even the most tough-minded teachers would agree that expulsion is an excessive consequence for a student who, for example, gets out of his seat during a classroom activity when the expectation is to stay seated. Not to say that such a disruption will be tolerated—just that removal, in this case, does not fit the crime. Some misbehavior is very minor, similar to a parking violation; some is moderate, similar to a speeding violation; and some behavior, although infrequent, is very serious—such as a threat of violence or an attack.

Does the Student Already Have a BIP?

Check with your school counselor, administrator, or special education staff to determine whether the student already has a behavior intervention plan (BIP) designed as part of a special education intervention. If she does, work with the special education department to assist in implementing that plan. If the student does not currently have a BIP, proceed with the suggestions in this chapter.

As a teacher, you need to be prepared to deal with this full range of behaviors, and your corrective strategies need to match the severity of the infraction (Barbetta et al., 2005; Conroy et al., 2008; Lewis & Sugai, 1999; Simonsen et al., 2008).

In the CHAMPS approach, an effective correction is one that:

- Changes the future occurrence of the behavior. The correction reduces the chance that the student will exhibit that behavior in that situation in the future.

- Does not disrupt other students. In other words, the correction is fluent. The teacher's response does not stop the flow of instruction and does not distract other students from the work they are doing at the time the student misbehaved.

- Treats the student who misbehaved with dignity and respect. As stated in the introduction to this book, teachers should never belittle their students.

- Does not reduce the student's motivation to exhibit positive behaviors. Imagine a high school coach who corrects athletes in a manner that makes students want to quit the team, as opposed to a coach whose corrections inspire all players to want to work even harder in the future.

- Does not jeopardize the positive relationship you have worked to establish with the student. The student should still perceive that the teacher likes her and has high expectations for her—both academically and behaviorally.

The difficulty in effectively correcting misbehavior is further compounded by the myriad of things the teacher is required to do at any given moment. While teaching lessons the teacher has to be thinking about making them interesting, differentiating instruction for different ability levels, keeping the students safe, staying on schedule, and so on. When a student misbehaves, the teacher must enforce the rules, but in what manner? Does she take on the role of umpire, cop, judge, boss, or . . . ? It depends on the type and severity of the misbehavior. But the teacher cannot stop teaching for an hour, or even for three minutes, to decide how to handle the situation.

It is difficult to correct effectively, but it is absolutely essential—if there were no rules of the road, or enforcement of those rules, driving would be extremely dangerous. In some authority/subordinate relationships, the absence of feedback when there is a behavioral problem is highly problematic.

Imagine you have a job as a low-level manager in a corporation with multiple layers of management between you and the president. You like this job and are highly moti-vated to work your way up the ladder. However, your immediate supervisor has some concerns about your job performance. He is a friendly and supportive manager, and likes people to think he is a nice guy, so he never tells you his concerns—you receive no corrective feedback. Years go by, and you find yourself being passed over for both salary increases and promotions—and you don't know why. If the manager had told you his concerns, you could have tried to correct your shortcomings. This absence of corrective feedback is negligent at best and perhaps even discriminatory.

So it is to everyone's advantage that you correct misbehavior when it occurs. The suggestions in this chapter can help you correct in a manner that helps the student whose behavior is chronically problematic, reduces the degree to which that stu-dent's behavior interferes with the learning of others, and makes it easier for you to have a sense of efficacy about your role as a teacher. This chapter has three major tasks designed to help you implement corrective consequences effectively. Task 1 is the easiest suggestion—try implementing the ideas in this task first. If there are still problems move on to the suggestions in Task 2 and then, if necessary, Task 3.

> **Task 1: Analyze and, if needed, adjust the implementation of your basic management plan** • This task provides a fillable form you can use to evaluate whether the basics of your management plan are fully in place, along with suggestions for minor adjustments you can make to your plan to help the student improve his behavior.

> **Task 2: Analyze and, if needed, adjust the strategies you are using to build a positive relationship with this student** • This task provides a fillable form you can use to evaluate whether there are minor adjustments you can make in your interactions with this student that may increase the student's motivation to engage in positive behaviors and thus reduce the frequency and severity of the chronic misbehavior.

> **Task 3: Analyze the misbehavior and develop a function-based intervention** • This task provides information on how to analyze the function of the misbehavior— why is the student chronically engaging in this misbehavior? It then covers how to design an individu-alized management plan that corrects the misbehavior and also teaches and motivates the

take note

This chapter is lengthy and may at first glance seem overwhelm-ing to the reader new to these con-cepts. However, keep in mind that the process is se-quential and step-by-step. As stated in the introduc-tion, try Task 1 first, then—only if necessary—Task 2. Go on to Task 3 only if the plan you designed in Task 2 is ineffec-tive after several weeks. In other words, you don't need to read this whole chapter at one time—use this information in bite-size chunks.

student to meet his needs in positive ways. For example, if the function of the misbehavior is to get attention, you can help her learn how to get attention in pro-social instead of antisocial ways.

Task 3 is by no means an easy fix. It requires careful thought and more work on your part than making the minor tweaks suggested in Tasks 1 and 2. So, for your own sake and sanity, make a concerted effort to implement Task 1 first. Run that plan for about ten teaching days. If the behavior improves, carry on with that plan until the problem has disappeared. If the behavior does not improve, or improves for a while but then stabilizes at a still-unacceptable level, or gets worse, implement the suggestions in Task 2. If that plan does not work after implementing it for a couple of weeks, work through the suggestions in Task 3.

Task 1: Analyze and, if Needed, Adjust the Implementation of Your Basic Management Plan

Minor changes to your Classroom Management and Discipline Plan may be enough to help students improve their behavior.

In some cases, making some minor adjustments to your management plan for the individual student who exhibits chronic misbehavior may be enough to help the student improve her behavior (Lewis & Sugai, 1999; Scheuermann & Hall, 2008). For example, moving the student's desk to a different location or being even more explicit with the student about your expectations may help improve the situation. To work through this task, carefully consider the questions and suggestions on the Classroom Management and Discipline Plan—Reflection/Implementation form (Reproducible 9.1). The CD includes a fillable version of this form. On the next page is a completed sample of Reproducible 9.1, followed by a version with bullet points for you to consider as you fill out your own form. Note that the ideas and suggestions in this task have been covered earlier in the book, but you are now exploring how you might adjust the suggestions to help an individual student.

Try the easy thing first. Make some minor tweaks to your management plan or how you implement your management plan. If you are successful, you can turn a chronic problem into no problem. Be sure to keep your positive feedback at a very high level with this student and tell the student's family that improvement is taking place. If these adjustments in your plan prove ineffective after a couple of weeks, try implementing the procedures in Task 2.

(continued on p. 366)

Reproducible 9.1   *Classroom Management and Discipline Plan—Reflection/Implementation (page 1)*

 **C H A M P S**
Sample

 >> no. **9.1**

CLASSROOM MANAGEMENT AND DISCIPLINE PLAN (1 of 2)
(REFLECTION/IMPLEMENTATION)

Student Eleana   **Teacher** Mr. Torres   **Date** 10/16

As you reflect on these questions, make notes about adjustments you can make in how you implement your plan with this student.

1. **Do classroom variables such as physical setting, schedule, and beginning/ending routines affect the student's inappropriate behavior?**

   I am going to try moving her desk location from the middle of the class to the front center where she will be closer to me. I will be able to observe, praise, and correct her more easily. I am going to require that she get permission to leave her seat during class because she bothers other students when she has the freedom to get up without permission.

2. **Does this student fully understand your behavioral expectations and your concerns about the misbehavior? If not, or if you are unsure, implement a Planned Discussion to further clarify your expectations.**

   I think she understands what is expected, but I am going to make an appointment to sit down with her and her mother and go over my concerns and the positive behaviors she should exhibit. I will see if her mother can come in tomorrow after school for this conference.

3. **Are your classroom rules clear? Does this student fully understand the rules? If not, or if you are unsure, schedule a Planned Discussion and lesson to clarify your rules and consequences.**

   During the discussion with Eleana and her mother, I will clarify the rules and let them know that at least for a while, Eleana has an extra rule that does not apply to the other students—"Ask permission from Mr. Torres before leaving your seat." I will explain that when she can successfully follow this rule and show that she no longer bothers other students while they are working or I am presenting lessons, she will earn the privilege of leaving her seat without permission to hand in work, pick up supplies, and so on.

4. **Is your enforcement of these rules:**
   a. **Consistent? (e.g., day to day or hour to hour, relative to your mood)**

   No, I need to work on this. When I am feeling good, I probably do not correct her. When I am stressed, I probably do correct her. I will have to work on correcting her for bothering others even if it does not concern me at that moment.

   b. **Fair? (Are other students who violate these rules corrected?)**

   Yes, I try to correct any student who is bothering others. However, while Eleana's new rule is in place, I will correct her for getting out of her seat without permission even though other students have the right to leave their seats. In explaining this concept to the student, I will use the example of a driver who gets his license suspended for six months because he has too many speeding tickets.

Reproducible 9.1 *Classroom Management and Discipline Plan—Reflection/Implementation (page 2)*

CHAMPS
sample

» no. **9.1**

CLASSROOM MANAGEMENT AND DISCIPLINE PLAN (2 of 2)
(REFLECTION/IMPLEMENTATION)

4. **Is your reinforcement of these rules (*continued*):**
   c. **Brief? (Does the student receive five seconds or less of attention at the time of the misbehavior?)**

   I probably talk too much. I will try to correct by giving a quick reminder. If Eleana does not immediately stop bothering others and go back to her seat, I will calmly let her know that she is owing time until she does get back to her seat. Time owed will come off of recess time and/or Choice Time activity at the end of the day.

   d. **Calm? (Are you emotionally neutral when correcting this student's behavior?)**

   For the most part, yes. I never act really angry, but I may show exasperation or frustration. I will work a bit more to be completely neutral when I correct her.

   e. **Respectful? (Are you correcting objectively, not judgmentally, and as privately as possible?)**

   Yes.

5. **Is this student misbehaving to cover some learning problem and/or an inability to understand or complete the work?**

   No—her work is very high quality and she gets it all done. However, maybe I should have some fun enrichment assignments or cushion assignments that she can do when she completes the basic class work. Maybe I should talk to the special ed teachers about whether she is eligible for the Talented/Gifted program.

6. **Does this student have an "expectancy of success"?**

   Yes—at least academically. Maybe I should put more emphasis on how I know she can be responsible and helpful in the classroom so I build up her expectancy of behavioral success.

Figure 9.1 *Classroom Management and Discipline Plan—Reflection/Implementation Template (page 1)*

C H A M P S

PLAN WITH BULLETED POINTS (RUBRIC)

BULLETED PLAN 9.1

CLASSROOM MANAGEMENT AND DISCIPLINE PLAN (1 of 2)
(REFLECTION/IMPLEMENTATION)

Student _____ Teacher _____ Date _____

As you reflect on these questions, make notes about adjustments you can make in how you implement your plan with this student.

1. **Do classroom variables such as physical setting, schedule, and beginning/ending routines affect the student's inappropriate behavior?**
   - Consider whether the student would be less distracted or disruptive in a different part of the room.
   - Consider whether you can observe more frequently and easily if the student is in a different part of the room.
   - Giving Stand up and Stretch breaks during long work periods may help this and other students stay focused.
   - Giving the student a job assisting with some part of your beginning and ending routines may help the student stay focused and cooperative.
   - Skim Chapters 1 and 2 to see if other variables of this type may help this student.

2. **Does this student fully understand your behavioral expectations and your concerns about the misbehavior? If not, or if you are unsure, implement a Planned Discussion to further clarify your expectations.**
   - Consider whether the student is aware that the misbehavior of concern is an example of not meeting the expectations.
   - Schedule a neutral time to discuss the misbehavior with the student—a time when there will not be an audience of other students.
   - Keep the focus on the positive expectation, then refer specifically to the problem, then re-emphasize the positive expectation. End with high expectations—say that you know the student will make an effort to meet your expectations and be successful in the classroom.
   - Consider inviting the family to participate in this Planned Discussion, especially with a severe problem or a minor problem where you have seen no improvement after discussing it with the student only.
   - Examine your CHAMPS expectation sheets (or reread Chapter 4).

3. **Are your classroom rules clear? Does this student fully understand the rules? If not, or if you are unsure, schedule a Planned Discussion and lesson to clarify your rules and consequences.**
   - Schedule a time to meet with the student to discuss your rules and consequences .This can be added to the discussion above when rule violations are part of the problem.
   - For a younger student, model or use pictures to communicate examples of following the rule and not following the rule.
   - Clarify that enforcing the rules is part of your job as the teacher and that this enforcement has nothing to do with liking or disliking the student.
   - Clarify that the student is not bad. When he or she breaks a rule, it is the behavior at that moment that is a problem, not the student.

4. **Is your enforcement of these rules:**
   a. **Consistent?** (e.g., day to day or hour to hour, relative to your mood)
      Do not let the student get away with misbehavior when you are in a good mood if you would correct that same misbehavior when you are in a bad mood. Using a sports metaphor, offside in football should be called whether the referee is in a good mood or a bad mood.

   b. **Fair?** (Are other students who violate these rules corrected?)
      - Be cautious about any bias—even unconscious—wherein you hold one group of students (e.g., based on gender, race, academic ability) to one standard of rule following, and another group to a different standard.
      - Note that on some occasions you may adapt an expectation or rule (as shown in the sample Reproducible 9.1). This is analogous to a driver getting her license suspended for a period of time. Be very careful about doing this so you don't have to keep track of too many exceptions to your management plan.

Figure 9.1 *Classroom Management and Discipline Plan—Reflection/Implementation Template (page 2)*

CHAMPS

CLASSROOM MANAGEMENT AND DISCIPLINE PLAN (2 of 2)
(Reflection/Implementation)

4. **Is your reinforcement of these rules** (*continued*):

   c. **Brief? (Does the student receive five seconds or less of attention at the time of the misbehavior?)**

   • Don't talk too much—take action.

   • In the early stages of correcting a misbehavior, you may use that opportunity as a teachable moment, which will take longer than five seconds. However, once a problem is chronic, your reprimand or consequence should take five seconds or less so you can immediately return to the flow of instruction and give positive feedback to students who are following the rules.

   • If you think the student needs a "lesson," schedule a planned discussion. Do not have that discussion at the time of the misbehavior.

   • If the student tries to argue, say, "You can make an appointment to speak to me later about this, but right now I must go on with the lesson." Then ignore any further attempts by the student to suck you into a power struggle.

   d. **Calm? (Are you emotionally neutral when correcting this student's behavior?)**

   • Some students love having the power to upset a teacher.

   • When you stay calm as you are correcting misbehavior, you do not give these students any power.

   • Staying calm also reduces the chance that in the heat of the moment you may say something insensitive, embarrassing, or hurtful.

   • Remember that you do not necessarily have to be calm—you just have to act calm.

   • There is a great quote about staying calm that middle school teachers will appreciate: "Arguing with an adolescent is like mud-wrestling a pig—you both get dirty and the pig loves it."

   e. **Respectful? (Are you correcting objectively, not judgmentally, and as privately as possible?)**

   • Remember that the only absolute rule in the CHAMPS approach is that students must be treated with dignity and respect.

   • It is easy to get frustrated with a student and then put the student in his place. Try to avoid this.

   • Correct as privately as the immediate situation allows.

   • Comment on the behavior, not the person.

   • Provide an objective description about the behavior, not a label. Don't resort to name-calling.

   • Avoid sarcasm in your words, tone of voice, and even body language (e.g., rolling eyes).

   • Try to treat students as you would like to be treated. If your principal was concerned about some aspects of your job performance, how would you like her to provide corrective feedback or enforce district rules? (reasonably private, objective descriptions of the problem, etc.).

5. **Is this student misbehaving to cover some learning problem and/or an inability to understand and/or complete the work?**

   • Can the student read assigned work fluently and accurately?

   • Does the student comprehend when reading?

   • Can the student do handwriting easily, or does she hold the pencil in a death grip?

   • Can the student complete independent assignments independently, or does she need lots of assistance?

   If the answer to any of these questions is no, make academic adaptations (differentiation). If you are unfamiliar with how to differentiate, talk to colleagues in special education for ideas.

6. **Does this student have an "expectancy of success"?**

   • Re-examine the "Expectancy x Value" theory of motivation in Chapter 1.

   • Sometimes a student can do the work, but does not see himself as capable. You may need to "pump up" the student so he believes he will be able to be successful.

Task 2: Analyze and, if Needed, Adjust the Strategies You Are Using to Build a Positive Relationship with this Student

A positive relationship with a teacher can motivate students to behave appropriately.

Research suggests that students are more likely to behave well and work hard to meet a teacher's expectations when the student-teacher relationship is positive and respectful (Borich, 2004; Brophy, 1983; Cameron & Pierce, 1994; Gettinger & Stoiber, 1998; Hall et al., 1968; Marzanno, 2003; Niebuhr, 1999; Pianta, Hamre, & Stuhlman, 2003). Negative interactions are associated with poorer academic and social behavior outcomes (Murray & Greenberg, 2006; Murray & Murray, 2004).

Any adult is also more likely to be highly motivated when he works for a great boss than when he feels used, abused, and disrespected by his boss. If they have an abusive boss, most people do only the minimum amount of work required to stay out of trouble, and some may even take great delight in subtly sabotaging or embarrassing that boss (yes, even adults sometimes engage in misbehavior). In this task, you will explore how to build a plan to try to improve your connection with an individual student and increase the student's motivation to behave appropriately and be academically successful.

To work through Task 2, carefully consider the questions and suggestions on the Connect/Motivation Plan—Reflection/Implementation form (Reproducible 9.2). This task uses the fillable Reproducible 9.2: Connect/Motivation Plan on the CD in the Chapter 9 folder. A completed sample of Reproducible 9.2 appears on the next two pages, followed by Figure 9.2, a version with bullet points for you to consider as you fill out your own form.

If you implement a Connect/Motivate Plan for at least two weeks and it is not effective, you have learned at least one important thing—this is really a chronic problem. How do you know? Because the problem has been resistant to your basic management plan that works for most students, this student did not respond successfully to some individualized adjustments to that plan (Task 1), and she did not respond to your organized plan to enhance your relationship with the student (Task 2). So, it's time to move on to the hard work of Task 3.

(continued on p. 371)

take note

Special thanks to Mike Booher for developing the Connect/Motivation Plan concept and form.

Reproducible 9.2 *Connect/Motivation Plan—Reflection/Implementation (page 1)*

Print from CD

CHAMPS
sample

≫ no. **9.2**

CONNECT/MOTIVATION PLAN—REFLECTION/IMPLEMENTATION (1 of 2)
(QUESTIONS TO ASK WHEN AN INDIVIDUAL STUDENT IS NOT MOTIVATED TO SUCCEED IN YOUR CLASS)

Student Sally   **Teacher** Mrs. Bradford   **Date** 11/13

Targeted Activities (activities in which the student is unmotivated and/or unsuccessful)	List the student's strengths
• Coming to school regularly	• Gets along well with others
• Completing assignments in class	• Easily redirected
• Completing homework	• Enjoys nonacademic activities

1. List three strategies you will use to provide *noncontingent attention* to the student every day.

A. I will give her a smile and/or a compliment (e.g., "You look sharp this morning" or "My daughter has a pair of shoes like yours") every day as she enters the classroom.

B. When I see her exhibiting appropriate social behaviors when interacting with other students, I will establish eye contact and wink, smile, give a thumbs up, etc.

C. Every time she is absent, I will say to her on the day of her return something like, "I'm so glad you're back. It's just not the same without you here."

2. For which targeted activities will you provide *positive verbal feedback* to the student?

A. Beginning an assignment on time

B. Following a direction or responding to a redirection

C. Turning in her homework

➡

Reproducible 9.2 *Connect/Motivation Plan—Reflection/Implementation (page 1)*

no. 9.2

CONNECT/MOTIVATION PLAN—REFLECTION/IMPLEMENTATION (2 of 2)
(QUESTIONS TO ASK WHEN AN INDIVIDUAL STUDENT IS NOT MOTIVATED TO SUCCEED IN YOUR CLASS)

3. **What will you do if he or she doesn't respond well to positive feedback?**
    Try a different method of providing the feedback, such as writing her a private note.

4. **Identify two strategies for increasing your ratio of interactions with the student and describe how and when you will use them.**

    A. I will make a point to greet her every morning when she enters the room and will tell her at dismissal that I'm looking forward to seeing her the next morning.

    B. I will provide both positive feedback and noncontingent attention when she is appropriately interacting with other students.

5. **Which intermittment celebration(s) will you use to reinforce the student for showing appropriate behaviors and/or progress on the targeted activities? How will you select the celebration and when will you deliver it?**

    A. I will have her use a prepared checklist to identify her top five choices for celebrations.

    B. I will randomly provide the celebrations once or twice a week when she comes to school and when she submits her homework.

CHAPTER 9 TASKS

1 · Analyze and Adjust Plan Implementation   2 · Analyze and Adjust Strategies for Building Positive Relationships

Figure 9.2 *Bulleted Points for Connect/Motivation Plan—Reflection/Implementation (page 1)*

CHAMPS

PLAN WITH BULLETED POINTS (RUBRIC)

BULLETED PLAN 9.2

CONNECT/MOTIVATION PLAN—REFLECTION/IMPLEMENTATION (1 of 2)
(QUESTIONS TO ASK WHEN AN INDIVIDUAL STUDENT IS NOT MOTIVATED TO SUCCEED IN YOUR CLASS)

Student _____ Teacher _____ Date _____

Targeted Activities (activities in which the student is unmotivated and/or unsuccessful)	**List the student's strengths**
• Give specific examples; do not say "everything" • Identify each academic area • Consider study skills and work habits • Don't forget nonacademic activities (e.g., sports, singing, peer relationships, drawing)	Consider: • Academic strengths • Behavioral strengths • Social strengths • Interests

1. **List three strategies you will use to provide *noncontingent attention* to the student every day.**

   These strategies should be specific (e.g., verbal greetings, hand gestures like thumbs up or handshake, facial expressions like smile, head nod, or wink) that are delivered at specific times of the day (e.g., entering or leaving the classroom, during small group work) *and* whenever appropriate (e.g., seeing student in the hallway).

2. **For which targeted activities will you provide *positive verbal feedback* to the student?**

   • Look at the student's strengths and consider using some of them as opportunities for providing positive feedback.

   • Positive feedback should also be given for behaviors that are new, difficult, or a source of pride for the student.

   • Remember to deliver verbal positive feedback calmly and quietly, and within 3 to 4 feet of student. Be brief, specific, and descriptive.

➡

Figure 9.2 *Bulleted Points for Connect/Motivation Plan—Reflection/Implementation (page 2)*

C H A M P S

PLAN WITH BULLETED POINTS (RUBRIC)

BULLETED PLAN 9.2

CONNECT/MOTIVATION PLAN—REFLECTION/IMPLEMENTATION (2 of 2)
(QUESTIONS TO ASK WHEN AN INDIVIDUAL STUDENT IS NOT MOTIVATED TO SUCCEED IN YOUR CLASS)

3. What will you do if he or she doesn't respond well to positive feedback?

- Does the student feel embarrassed by the public display of positive feedback or not know how to accept positive feedback?
- Ask yourself if you are being too public or too dramatic with the feedback.
- Are you pausing expectantly after giving feedback so that the student feels compelled to respond verbally?
- Adjust feedback delivery accordingly and revert to giving only noncontingent attention for several weeks if the student continues to reject positive feedback.

4. Identify two strategies for increasing your ratio of interactions with the student and describe how and when you will use them.

The goal is to provide a ratio of at least three positive interactions when the student is behaving appropriately to one negative interaction when the student is engaged in inappropriate behavior. Here are some ways to increase the ratio:

- Identify the times of day when the student often behaves appropriately.
- Schedule individual conference times.
- Scan the room to identify reinforceable behaviors.
- Give the student plenty of noncontingent attention when entering the room, at lunch, on playground, and so on.
- Use gestures (e.g., thumbs up, head nod, OK sign) to acknowledge appropriate behavior.
- Post visual reminders to praise students on your plan book, wall, desk, or overhead.
- Give students more opportunities to respond.
- Publicly post examples of positive work by students.
- After praising one student, find and praise another student who is displaying the same behavior.
- Provide pre-corrections (quick reminders of how to behave appropriately when you anticipate students might have problems behaving appropriately).
- Emphasize attending to positive behaviors after responding to misbehavior.

5. Which intermittent celebration(s) will you use to reinforce the student for showing appropriate behaviors and/or progress on the targeted activities? How will you select the celebration and when will you deliver it?

- Provide a concrete reward or celebration when the student shows an important appropriate behavior. The reward or celebration must be meaningful to the student. Ask the student to identify rewards.
- While delivering, make sure to provide specific positive feedback on what the student has done well. Also keep up the noncontingent attention.
- Deliver on an unpredictable schedule so that the student won't know the celebration is coming. Deliver it more often at first.

Task 3: Analyze the Misbehavior and Develop a Function-Based Intervention

Analyze the function of the chronic misbehavior and design a comprehensive individualized intervention based on that analysis.

The good news is that you have ruled out certain interventions—you tried them and they did not work, so you know you have a fairly complex problem. The bad news is that it's not likely that a complex problem can be solved by a simple solution. This task introduces some basic concepts about these more complex chronic misbehaviors, explains why you need data and how to use it to make decisions, and describes how you might build an intervention plan for major categories of chronic misbehavior.

Because most chronic misbehavior serves a function, or purpose, for the student (the behavior is happening for a reason), and because there are many different reasons why students misbehave, correction efforts for specific misbehaviors are more effective when they address the underlying reasons for those behaviors (Crone & Horner, 2000, 2002; Lewis & Sugai, 1996a, 1996b; Martella et al., 2003; O'Neill et al., 1997). In addition, we can often reliably identify specific activities or contexts that increase the likelihood that one or more students may misbehave. Some of these contexts may be internal to the student (being hungry, sleepy, or sick) or external (working on independent seatwork tasks, participating in large group instruction). Following is a list of common reasons why students misbehave, including situations that may be resistant to simpler interventions:

 Students are not aware of their behavior.

- They do not know precisely what the teacher expects (Brophy & Good, 1986; Emmer et al., 1980). For example, the teacher views a student as disruptive because she gets up to sharpen her pencil while the teacher is speaking, but the student's previous teachers did not mind if students did this.

- They are unaware of when or how much they exhibit an inappropriate behavior. A student doesn't realize that he complains every time the teacher asks him to do something, for example.

Students are unable to, or do not know how to, exhibit the desired behavior.

Students may not be physically able to perform a task or don't have the knowledge to exhibit the appropriate behavior (Carr & Durand, 1985; Gresham, 1998). A first-grade student has never learned to stay seated and bring a task to completion, for example.

> *Students generally feel powerless and have discovered they get a sense of power by making adults frustrated and angry.*

 Students are seeking attention.

They are starved for attention and have found it easier or more effective to get attention through reprimands than through praise (Gunter & Jack, 1993; Sutherland, 2000). An example is a student who frequently gets out of her seat and wanders around, so the teacher is continually giving corrections such as, "Allison, how many times do I have to tell you to get back to your seat?"

 The behavior serves some other purpose for the student.

- Students generally feel powerless and have discovered they get a sense of power by making adults frustrated and angry (Cole & Kupersmidt, 1983; Walker et al., 2004). A student talks back and argues with adults, for example, and finds that some peers look up to him as bad or tough.

- They want the teacher to send them out of class in order to avoid the task or looking stupid at attempting a task (Carr, Newsom, & Binkoff, 1980; Chandler & Dahlquist, 2002). A student who is disrespectful to the teacher gets sent out of class and suspended for a week, and so escapes school work.

Correcting chronic misbehavior requires more time and effort than most classroom misbehavior. In fact, with chronic misbehavior you should be prepared to analyze the nature—the reason and purpose—for the behavior and to develop and implement a comprehensive intervention plan that is directly linked to your assessment (Crone & Horner, 2002; O'Neill et al., 1997). These six steps represent the overall approach recommended for addressing any misbehavior that you identify as chronic.

Step 1: Identify the target (problem) behavior and collect objective data. Use that data as you proceed to Step 2.

Step 2: Develop a hypothesis (educated guess) about the function of the misbehavior.

Step 3: Identify any specific contexts and conditions (time, locations, tasks) when the target behavior typically occurs or does not occur.

Step 4: Identify a preliminary behavior change (intervention) plan based on your hypothesis about the function of the misbehavior and your understanding of when (under what conditions) the behavior typically occurs.

Step 5: Discuss your preliminary intervention plan with the student and, if appropriate, the student's family.

Step 6: Implement the intervention plan for at least two weeks. Continue to collect data on the target behavior to evaluate the plan's effectiveness.

Reproducible 9.3 is a form that guides you through designing a function-based intervention plan. Consider printing this form from the CD and using it to take notes as you read the following directions and suggestions for each step of the planning process.

INTERVENTION PLANNING STEPS

STEP 1 Identify the target (problem) behavior and collect objective data. Use that data as you proceed to Step 2.

It's important to collect information about a behavior that concerns you before you develop an intervention plan (Alberto & Troutman, 2006). Identify a specific behavior or category of behavior that is the target of your concerns and will be the target of your intervention plan. The student may have multiple problems, but pick one behavior (disrespectful comments) or one category of behavior (classroom disruptions such as callouts, noise-making, use of obscenity, bothering other students by not keeping hands to self).

If the target problem is unclear—you are not sure exactly why the behavior bothers you or how to collect data on it—keep anecdotal notes for a few days. Anecdotal notes are brief descriptions of specific situations that trouble you. With notes from several incidents over a few days, you can usually clarify the nature of the problem behavior. Then you can collect more objective data on the frequency or duration of the behavior.

If you have identified the target behavior or category of behavior, plan to immediately start collecting data on the frequency, duration, and intensity of the behavior.

Reproducible 9.3 *Function-Based Intervention Plan*

C H A M P S
sample

≫ no. 9.3

FUNCTION-BASED INTERVENTION PLAN

Student Courtney Driver   **Teacher** Ms. Fang   **Date** 10/19

Step 1

The target behavior is: complaining

I collect data on this behavior by: frequency count. I will mark a tracking sheet each time Courtney complains about an assignment or direction.

Step 2

My hypothesis about the function of this target behavior is:

____ Lack of awareness   ____ Lack of ability or skill

__X__ Attention-seeking   ____ Habitual/Purposeful

Step 3

Identify any specific contexts or conditions (times, locations, tasks) when the target behavior typically occurs (or does not occur).

Courtney usually complains when I assign independent work and homework. She will complain during independent work about how hard it is or how there's too much to finish in the time allotted. She doesn't complain when I am presenting or when working in small groups.

Step 4

Develop a preliminary behavior change (intervention) plan based on your hypothesis about the function of the misbehavior.

I will announce to the class that I am going to ignore all complaints about their assignments. I will answer any questions about the work. Then I will ignore Courtney's (and any other student's) complaints and praise her when she works without complaining.

Step 5

Discuss your preliminary intervention plan with the student and, if appropriate, the student's family.
I will talk with Courtney after class on Friday.

Step 6

Implement the intervention plan for at least two weeks. Continue to collect data on the target behavior so that you can evaluate the plan's effectiveness.

CHAPTER 9 TASKS

1 • Analyze and Adjust Plan Implementation   2 • Analyze and Adjust Strategies for Building Positive Relationships

Then, instead of relying on your instincts, you will have objective data available to help you make decisions about what to do next (Hintze, Volpe, & Shapiro, 2002; Sugai & Tindal, 1993). Data can be systematic, clear, and concise—but it can also be unsystematic, unclear, and of little use. To make sure you collect relevant, useful data, use the following common methods of data collection. This information about frequency data, duration data, latency data, and rating magnitude or quality is adapted from RIDE (Responding to Individual Differences in Education), published by Sopris West Publishing.

FREQUENCY DATA

Frequency data records the number of occurrences of a given behavior within a specific time period. For example, use of obscenity can be recorded as the total times profanity is used within a class period. Frequency data can be recorded using any one of the following techniques:

- **Tally sheet kept on a clipboard or an index card.** Make a mark each time the target behavior occurs. If you are tracking several different behaviors, you can easily divide the card into sections. For example, you could have a card with the name Joshua and two headings below the name—one for disruptive noises and one for negative comments.

- **Wrist or golf counter.** Each time the target behavior occurs, advance the counter. The counter can easily be kept in a pocket if you want to be unobtrusive.

- **Paper clips in a pocket.** Keep a supply of small objects (beads, beans, paper clips, buttons) in one pocket. Each time the target behavior occurs, move one of the objects to another pocket or a container. The number of objects collected at the end of the time period is the number to record. This technique lets you track only one behavior at a time, but it is very effective and simple to use.

- **Pages in a book.** Keep a book on your desk open to page one. Each time the target behavior occurs, turn a page. Note that you can count the pages turned or look at the page number at the end of the day and divide by two.

Frequency data can be displayed on a simple graph like the one shown in Figure 9.3.

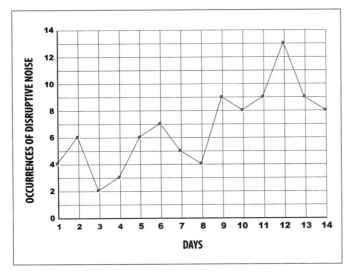

Figure 9.3 *Frequency Data Graph*

DURATION DATA

Duration data expresses the total amount of time a student engages in a given behavior. For example, off-task behavior can be expressed as the number of minutes a student is off-task during a 50-minute class period.

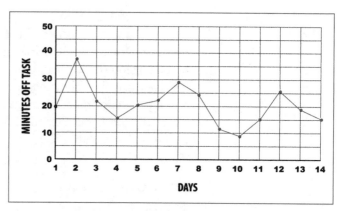

Figure 9.4   *Duration Data Graph*

This information can be useful when a student engages in a behavior for extended periods of time. A student may technically be off-task only one time during the class, but it may be for the entire length of the class. In such a case, tracking the total number of incidents would not be useful. To record duration, you simply need a stopwatch. Start the watch when the target behavior begins and stop it when the target behavior stops. Start it again if necessary. The total minutes on the watch when class is over tells you how much time the student spent misbehaving. The time can then be recorded on a graph like the one shown in Figure 9.4.

LATENCY DATA

Latency data expresses how much time passes between a directive and the student's response. Latency data is almost always used in the context of tracking compliance and following directions. To track this information for a student who is frequently noncompliant, you need a stopwatch. Each time you give a direction, start the timer. Stop it when your instructions are carried out. If you do this during the entire class, you will have a latency total by the end of the class. Figure 9.5 shows an example of a latency graph.

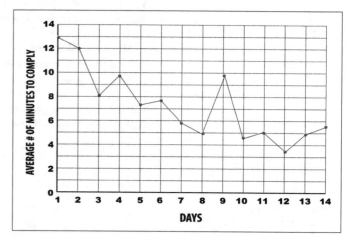

Figure 9.5   *Latency Graph*

RATING MAGNITUDE OR QUALITY

Rating magnitude or quality is a way to record data that rates a student's behavior during a specified time period using a scale—for example, from one to five. At the end of each class period, you and the target student rate the degree of cooperation and respect the student demonstrated toward you. A rating of one means that the student was disrespectful and uncooperative the entire time, while a rating of five represents that the student was respectful and cooperative during the entire class period.

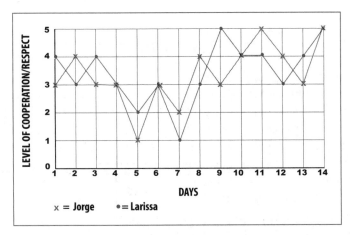

Figure 9.6 *Rating Magnitude or Quality Graph*

Although this method is subjective, discussing and determining the rating standards with your student before you implement it can make this method an accurate and helpful way to record data. Because each rating is a numerical value, the information can be graphed easily for quick reference. You can also track information on more than one student at a time. See Figure 9.6 for an example.

COLLECTION PROCESS

Meet with the student or students you plan to track before you begin collecting this data. Inform them of your plan and emphasize that you are collecting this information to determine if there is a problem. Then, meet with the student for a few minutes each day (when you are elementary level) or week (when you have the student only one period a day) to discuss the data on your graph.

Just the act of collecting data in a systematic way sometimes serves to improve a problem situation (Scheuermann & Hall, 2008; Sprick, Booher, et al., 2009). Perhaps this is because the student becomes aware of how serious you are about the problem or because the student receives increased attention from you. It may be that by collecting data, you are communicating that you value the student enough to have expectations that the situation will improve. It may simply be the placebo effect—a sugar pill sometimes helps a person's health improve just because he thinks he is receiving helpful treatment. Regardless of the reason, the phenomenon is frequent enough that regular data collection and debriefing with the student is a reasonable strategy when a simple intervention, like those described in Tasks 1 and 2, was not sufficient.

In addition, the data itself helps you decide whether the situation is improving, staying the same, or getting worse. Without data, you will have subjective perceptions about progress or the lack of progress. A busy teacher focusing on many different students may form inaccurate subjective perceptions.

> ## *for* example
>
> Let's say that you have collected data on the frequency of a student's sarcastic and disrespectful comments toward you. The data shows that the frequency has decreased from an average of ten comments per week to six per week over a period of three weeks. The six comments per week may be so aggravating that you think the situation is not improving. However, the data indicates a 40% reduction—from ten per week to six—in the frequency of the problem, so you know you actually implemented a very successful intervention and should continue it without modification. Conversely, let's say that over four weeks you find that the comments continue to average about ten per week. With data in hand, you know with confidence that the current intervention plan is not sufficient and a more carefully planned intervention is warranted—and that it is probably time to ask for assistance from a school psychologist or behavior specialist.

STEP 2   Develop a hypothesis (educated guess) about the function of the misbehavior.

With the target behavior in mind, look at the data you have collected and reflect on why this problem might be occurring. Knowing the function (reason and purpose) of a misbehavior is important because correction procedures that are effective with behaviors that serve one particular purpose for the student may not be effective with other behaviors that serve a different purpose for the student (Iwata, Dorsey, Slifer, Bauman, & Richman, 1994). For example, if a student is misbehaving because she wants attention, giving that student corrective consequences each time she misbehaves is not likely to work because she is getting what she wants—attention. Using planned ignoring will be far more effective in this case. On the other hand, if a student continually gets out of her seat because she does not realize that it is inappropriate or because she does not know how to stay in her seat, ignoring her out-of-seat behavior is not likely to change that behavior. This student needs information—she needs to be taught what the appropriate behavior is and how she can exhibit it.

As stated previously, the four subcategories of chronic misbehavior are:

- Misbehaviors due to lack of awareness

- Misbehaviors due to lack of ability or skill

- Attention-seeking misbehavior

- Purposeful/habitual misbehavior

> *Look at the data you have collected and reflect on why this problem might be occurring.*

Think about the function of your student's target behavior—it probably falls into one of these subcategories. To help you decide, read the following descriptions of the four subcategories. Specific suggestions for how to effectively intervene with misbehavior in each of these subcategories are presented in Step 4.

MISBEHAVIORS DUE TO LACK OF AWARENESS

Sometimes when a student seems to be willfully misbehaving, the student is actually unaware of the behavior he is exhibiting. An example of a misbehavior caused by a lack of awareness is a seventh-grade student who always responds argumentatively to corrective feedback—at school for behavioral and academic performance and, according to his family, at home as well. The teacher tries the early-stage correction strategy of discussing the problem with the student but sees no improvement in his behavior. Because this student responds negatively every time he is given corrective feedback, and because initial efforts to correct the behavior with information have been ineffective, it is reasonable to assume that the student may not be aware of how negatively he reacts when he is given corrective feedback.

When a student engages in ongoing misbehavior because of a lack of awareness, the intervention plan needs to include the following:

- Make expectations clear.
- Help the student become aware of his or her behavior.
- If necessary, provide incentives to encourage the student to change his or her behavior.

MISBEHAVIORS DUE TO LACK OF ABILITY OR SKILL

Sometimes a student misbehaves because he or she is unable to or does not know how to exhibit the desired behavior (Carr & Durand, 1985; Gresham, 1998; McGinnis & Goldstein, 1994; Ostrosky, Drasgow, & Halle, 1999). The case study on the next page describes a student whose misbehavior may be related to an inability to exhibit the desired behavior.

> *Taking Action to Improve Irresponsible Behavior*
>
> A very active first-grade student is rarely able to stay in one place for more than two or three minutes at a time, regardless of the activity. A physician evaluates him and suggests that implementing effective behavioral interventions would be the best way to determine whether medication may be necessary or helpful. Because the student's misbehavior is pervasive across a range of activities, it is reasonable to assume that the student may lack the knowledge and skill to be able to stay in one place for a longer period of time.

When students misbehave due to issues of ability, you must first ascertain whether the student is physiologically capable of exhibiting the desired behavior by reviewing the student's records. If he or she is capable, the intervention plan needs to include giving the student the necessary skills and knowledge. If the student is not physiologically capable of exhibiting the behavior, modifications need to be made to the student's environment or adjustments made to the expectations (or both).

ATTENTION-SEEKING MISBEHAVIOR

Attention-seeking misbehaviors are behaviors that a student engages in to satisfy his or her (often unconscious) need for attention. Chronic blurting out, excessive helplessness, tattling, and minor disruptions are examples of behaviors that may be attention-seeking in nature. When a student is seeking attention through misbehavior, any intervention effort that involves giving the student attention when he is misbehaving is likely to actually reinforce the inappropriate behavior (Gunter & Jack, 1993; Sutherland, 2000).

Planned ignoring is designed to reduce or eliminate the attention the student receives for engaging in misbehavior (at the same time giving the student frequent attention when he is not engaged in misbehavior) and should be part of any intervention plan for this category of misbehavior. Planned ignoring has been shown to increase appropriate behaviors when used in conjunction with other strategies such as re-teaching rules and praising appropriate behavior (Hall et al., 1968; Madsen, Becker & Thomas, 1968; Yawkey, 1971)

PURPOSEFUL/HABITUAL MISBEHAVIOR

When chronic misbehavior does not stem from a student's lack of awareness or ability and is not being exhibited because the student wants attention, you need to assume that it is serving some other purpose for the student. Some students misbehave to escape something aversive—for example, they would rather get sent to the office for misbehaving than take a test they believe they will fail. Other students use misbehavior to demonstrate and achieve a sense of power and control—talking back and arguing with adults to look tough in front of friends.

> *With truly purposeful and/or habitual misbehavior, you will probably need to include the use of corrective consequences.*

Still other students may engage in misbehaviors that provide competing reinforcement, such as reading during instructional lessons, because they find it more enjoyable than participating in the lesson. For some students, misbehavior has become so habitual that the original purpose of the misbehavior is unclear or no longer relevant. For example, a student who has successfully engaged in attention-seeking behaviors for years may continue to misbehave even when planned ignoring is implemented because the inappropriate behaviors are firmly established in her behavioral repertoire.

With truly purposeful and/or habitual misbehavior, you will probably need to include the use of corrective consequences for the misbehavior as part of your intervention plan. In Step 4 of this task, information is provided on developing an effective intervention plan for this category of misbehavior.

STEP 3 Identify any specific contexts or conditions (time, locations, tasks) when the target behavior typically occurs (or does not occur).

In what context or under what conditions does the target behavior occur? Are there times when it does not occur? Understanding what typically happens before and after the target behavior occurs may give you a better idea about the purpose of the misbehavior for the student. In addition, this information is useful for building your intervention plan. If the student typically has difficulty during independent work times, for example, your support plan probably won't need to include large group instruction.

STEP 4 Develop a preliminary behavior change (intervention) plan based on your hypothesis about the function of the misbehavior and your understanding of when (under what conditions) the behavior typically occurs.

Once you develop a hypothesis about why the target behavior may be occurring, review the decision-making chart shown in Figure 9.7. Think about the target misbehavior as you examine the chart. Information about each category of misbehavior and suggested interventions is presented in the following pages. Figure 9.7 is designed to guide you to the appropriate procedures that will fit the nature of the target problem.

Use the suggestions in the following pages or modify them as necessary to develop a preliminary plan for improving the target behavior. Although the specific procedures for intervening within each subcategory of chronic misbehavior (awareness, ability, attention-seeking, and purposeful/habitual) are different from each other, there are several critical features to include in any plan (Crone & Horner, 2002; O'Neill et al., 1997; Scheuermann & Hall, 2008; Sugai, Horner, et al., 2000).

First, think about strategies you can put into place to prevent the problem behavior from occurring in the first place.

Second, plan for possible skill-building or teaching strategies. Even if there is no skill deficit, it is likely that you will have to teach some components of the support plan to the student.

Lastly, two fundamental types of consequence procedures should be included in all intervention plans. First, include procedures for encouraging the positive opposite of the misbehavior. For example, if the target misbehavior is disrespect, the intervention plan should identify how you will encourage and increase demonstrations of respectful behavior by the student. Second, your plan needs to specify exactly how you will respond to instances of the misbehavior in ways that allow you to be calm, consistent, and brief. Once you develop a preliminary plan using the information about each of these subcategories presented in this chapter, you can continue with the remaining planning steps.

Figure 9.7 *Analysis of Chronic Misbehavior and Suggested Interventions*

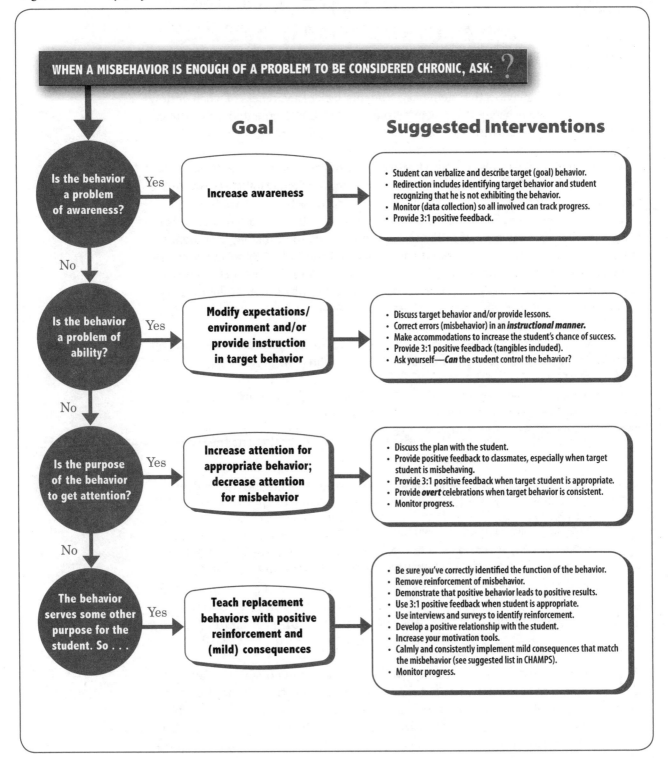

ANALYSIS OF AND INTERVENTIONS FOR MISBEHAVIORS DUE TO LACK OF AWARENESS

For ongoing misbehaviors that stem from students' lack of awareness of when or how much they are misbehaving, be prepared to develop and implement an intervention plan that includes increasing their awareness of their behavior.

When a student misbehaves because he isn't aware of when or how often he is engaging in an irresponsible behavior, your intervention plan should focus on increasing the student's awareness of his behavior. It is not appropriate to use traditional corrective consequences ("punishers") in this situation. In fact, using corrective consequences for this category of misbehavior is analogous to punishing a student for making mistakes on a math assignment without telling him that he made errors. When a student lacks awareness of his misbehavior, ensure that he understands the expectations for how he is supposed to behave and then help the student learn to recognize when he is misbehaving (Colvin et al., 1993).

If you determine that a student's misbehavior stems from a lack of awareness, you should develop and implement a four-phase intervention plan.

1. Make sure the student knows what behavior you expect him to exhibit (the target or goal behavior).

2. Respond to instances of the misbehavior in a manner that lets the student know he is not meeting the goal.

3. Monitor the student's behavior so that you, the student, and the student's family have an objective basis for discussing progress.

4. Provide positive feedback when the student is successful or makes improvements. If positive feedback doesn't seem sufficient to motivate the student to stop exhibiting the behavior, consider using some kind of incentive (reward).

 Make sure the student knows what behavior you expect him to exhibit (the target or goal behavior).

When you meet to discuss the situation with the student and possibly the family, be sure to explain the behavior you want the student to demonstrate. It may be helpful to demonstrate examples and non-examples of both the expected and the problem behaviors to make sure the student clearly understands the difference and is able to discriminate between them (Kame'enui & Simmons, 1990). See Chapter 4 for more details on teaching expected behaviors. Emphasize, in age-appropriate ways, the benefits to the student of demonstrating this new behavior. Be prepared to identify actions you will take to help the student learn the new behavior. Also consider writing the behavioral goal into an informal contract, using something like Reproducible 8.10, Goal Contract (see p. 351). Information on goal-setting procedures you can use with all your students is provided in Chapter 8.

TIME-PREDICTION SELF-MONITORING

An example of a way to help students become aware of your expectations is a time-prediction self-monitoring strategy. This simple strategy can be effective with students who have a difficult time completing assignments or staying on task. It is also appropriate for students who lose focus when given open-ended time for individual work. Essentially, you give the student an opportunity to predict how long it will take him to complete an assignment. When the student has a personal target in mind, the framework becomes based on the student's intrinsic motivation rather than an extrinsic factor.

Write the following on the top of the student's paper:

Time Started: *Time Predicted:*   *Time Completed:*

1. Say to the student, "It is now [8:15]."

2. Ask, "What time do you think you will complete the assignment?" If possible, have the student write his or her response.

3. Say, "When you are finished with your task, please come up and show me so we can see if you reached your goal!"

   a. You may have the student write down the time of completion to reinforce his ownership of the goal.

   b. If the student simply rushes through assignments to reach the goal, have him predict his percentage of correct answers as a second goal.

If the assignment is to be completed in a specific amount of time, the following variation is useful.

Time Available: *Predicted Number of Completed Questions:*   *Completed Questions:*

1. Say to the student, "You have ten minutes to complete this assignment."

2. Ask, "How many questions do you think you can complete in ten minutes?" Have the student write his prediction.

3. Say, "When you're done with your work, please let me know."

The time-prediction self-monitoring strategy allows students to set small personal goals and monitor their own progress. It reinforces the importance of staying on task. Students may even enjoy the "beat the clock" aspect or the notion of competing against themselves to see their work potential. (*Submitted by and used with permission from professional school counselor Anthony Pearson, Ed.S., author of* Guidance with Good Measure *from Youthlight Books.*)

 Respond to instances of the misbehavior.

Respond to instances of the misbehavior in a manner that lets the student know she is not meeting the goal. As stated earlier, students should not be punished for behavioral mistakes that are related to a lack of awareness or ability. Instead, each time an error occurs, give the student corrective feedback that includes neutral information about the inappropriate behavior and a direction about what she should do instead (Acker & O'Leary, 1988; Burns et al., 2008; Colvin et al., 1993; McAllister et al., 1969; O'Leary & Becker, 1968; Winett & Vachon, 1974). Following are descriptions of several information-based correction strategies. Use one or more to provide the student with information that will help her be more successful in the future. Remember, just like a student learning to correct errors in math, a student learning a new behavior may make frequent errors and need to be corrected each time.

GENTLE VERBAL REPRIMANDS

Remember that effective reprimands are brief, proximate (close), respectful, clear, and reasonably private. They should provide a verbal description of what the student is expected to be doing (Abramowitz, O'Leary, & Futtersak, 1988; Acker & O'Leary, 1988; McAllister et al., 1969; O'Leary & Becker, 1968; Winett & Vachon, 1974). When students make errors in math, one of the most effective correction procedures is to tell them what they should have done: "You need to remember to carry the ten from the ones column over to the tens column." Use a similar tone when giving a correction. Reprimands are discussed in detail in Chapter 3, Task 3.

REDIRECTION

Redirection involves guiding the student back to what she should be doing instead of misbehaving. Instead of verbally reminding the student, you literally direct the student to the desired activity (Karen, 1974). For example, if a young student is not where she should be, go to her and guide her back to her seat while complimenting other students for showing self-control by staying in their work areas. If you have a low-functioning special education student who tends to wave his hands in front of his face or engage in some other sort of self-stimulatory behavior, you might simply take one of his hands, put a pencil in it, and then redirect him to the work on his desk. All of this can and should be done without giving the student much attention.

> " *Instead of verbally reminding the student, you literally direct the student to the desired activity.* "

CHAPTER 9 TASKS

SIGNAL

If a student seems truly unaware that he is engaging in a misbehavior, it can be very helpful to use a verbal or nonverbal signal to cue the student. For example, if you have a student who hums while doing seatwork, the signal might be to say his name and subtly shake your head "no." Tell the student that whenever he notices you using that signal, it means that he is humming and needs to stop. You may have the student help you identify an appropriate signal when you first meet to discuss the situation. For example, let's say a child has a problem of humming while doing just about anything—in a way that bothers her family, teachers, and other students. The family and teachers puzzle over this for some time, and finally realize this is how she eases the stress of a situation or assignment. Once they understand the underlying reason for the humming, all they have to do is ask the student to hum more quietly so she doesn't disturb her neighbors. That request (conveyed by a signal) solves the immediate problem. Over time, the child will learn to manage this behavior in a way that no longer bothers others.

PRECORRECTION

When there seems to be a good chance based on prior history that a student will exhibit the misbehavior in a particular situation, consider using a precorrection to help the student be successful. Before the student has a chance to exhibit the misbehavior in a typically problematic situation, give her information that increases the probability that she will exhibit a responsible behavior (De Pry & Sugai, 2002; Lampi, Fenty, & Beaunae, 2005; Walker et al., 2004).

> *for* example
>
> If a student has trouble accepting corrective feedback, just before you return papers precorrect by saying something like, "Sheila, I am about to hand back some papers I have graded. You solved most of the problems correctly, but you do have a couple of errors that need to be fixed. Give some thought to the neutral or positive ways of reacting to corrections we discussed. I am sure you will be able to manage your reaction in a responsible way."

 Monitor the student's behavior.

Monitor the student's particular behavior so that you, the student, and the student's family will have an objective basis for discussing progress.

When a student tends to be unaware that he is engaging in a misbehavior, an important part of increasing the student's awareness is objectively discussing his progress or lack of progress. Thus, if a student is not aware of how frequently he engages in a behavior, you should keep a continuous record of the number of incidents that occur each day. You can graph each day's total and arrange to periodically review the graph with the student. In some cases, it can be beneficial to give the student a recording sheet and have him mark each incident. However, if the student is unlikely to keep an accurate record or is embarrassed to record his behavior in front of peers, you should do the recording. Arrange to meet with the student at the end of each day to graph the incidents and discuss progress.

For more ideas on this type of recording and for a sample of a recording sheet, see Chapter 6, Tool 3. Sometimes it can be useful to track a positive and a negative behavior concurrently. Reproducible 9.4 is a monitoring sheet that you can print from the CD to use to record both appropriate and inappropriate reactions to corrective feedback.

> *Set the system up so that the student has a good chance of earning a high rating most of the time.*

When a student's behavior problem involves qualitative rather than quantitative issues (how well rather than how much), it can be useful to have the student use some kind of self-evaluation monitoring form. The student rates the quality of a given behavior at particular times during the day or just at the end of the day. Reproducible 9.5 is a self-evaluation sheet appropriate for a student who is learning to keep his desk and work area neat and organized. Reproducible 9.6 shows a form used by a student who is learning to participate more actively in class. Both forms are provided on the CD.

If you decide to incorporate student self-evaluation into your intervention plan, set the system up so that the student has a good chance of earning a high rating most of the time. For example, if a student who is rating himself on how well he uses in-class work times gets to evaluate himself only once for the whole day, he may have to give himself an overall poor rating. However, if it is set up so that he evaluates his behavior for each thirty-minute work period throughout the day, he is likely to feel more successful overall. Although there may be some time periods when he has to rate himself low, there should also be several work times during the day when he can give himself a high rating.

Get Help

Shelley Jones, a teacher in Salem, Oregon, notes, "Our school counselor was very visible—often spending time in classrooms observing students. I occasionally asked him to record a particular student's behavior for me. This was really helpful, as it allowed me to concentrate on my teaching and still get objective data. He was also able to record my interactions with the students."

Reproducible 9.4 *Monitoring Reactions to Correction*

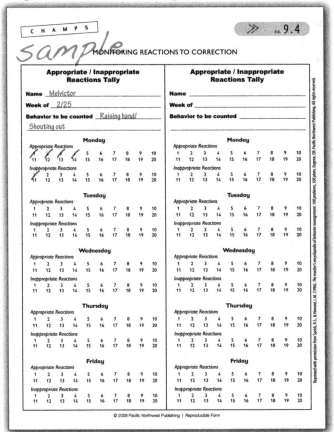

Reproducible 9.6 *Class Participation Self-Evaluation*

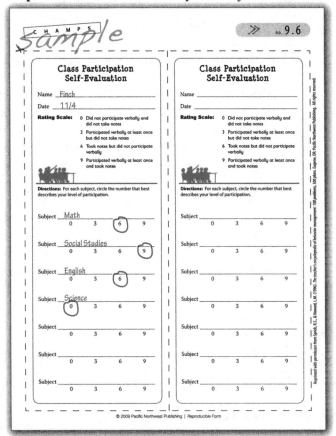

Print from CD

Reproducible 9.5 *Desk Neatness Self-Evaluation*

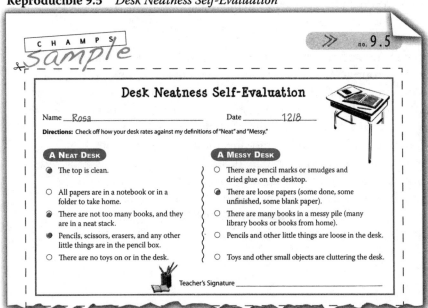

Give feedback.

Provide positive feedback when the student is successful or makes improvements. If positive feedback doesn't seem sufficient to motivate the student to stop exhibiting the behavior, consider using some kind of incentive (reward).

Throughout the day, as the student demonstrates success or takes steps toward success, provide positive verbal feedback (Hall et al., 1968; Madsen et al., 1968; O'Leary & Becker, 1967; Stormont et al., 2007). Increased awareness requires that the student know when she is doing well. Furthermore, without positive feedback, the corrective feedback you provide when she makes an error may discourage the student.

If you do not see progress (that is, the misbehavior decreases as the goal behavior increases) within a couple of weeks, consider establishing a simple system of reward-type incentives. For example, a student who is learning to keep a work area organized and materials neat can be given a point for each day that her area is neat. When she accumulates a certain number of points, she gets a predetermined reward.

ANALYSIS OF AND INTERVENTIONS FOR MISBEHAVIORS DUE TO LACK OF ABILITY OR SKILL

For ongoing misbehaviors that stem from students' lack of ability or skill, be prepared to develop and implement an intervention plan that includes modifying the expectations or environment for physiological inability and/or providing instruction in the goal behavior for lack of skill.

Sometimes a student misbehaves because he or she is either physiologically unable to exhibit the appropriate (goal) behaviors or does not know how to do so. The most effective intervention plans in these situations include a reasonable response to the underlying cause of the situation. That is, if a student is physically or neurologically not able to exhibit the desired behavior, your intervention must involve making modifications to the student's environment or adjusting your expectations, or both. If the student is capable of the behavior but does not know how to exhibit it, your intervention must involve teaching the student (Colvin et al., 1993; Elliott & Gresham, 1991; Walker et al., 2004). In both cases, implementing corrective consequences for this category of misbehavior is inappropriate at best and inhumane at worst.

> " *The most effective intervention plans in these situations include a reasonable response to the underlying cause of the situation.* "

CHAPTER 9 TASKS

1 • Analyze and Adjust Plan Implementation   2 • Analyze and Adjust Strategies for Building Positive Relationships

Children with ADD or ADHD   %%%

Unlike individuals with Tourette syndrome, children identified as having Attention Deficit Disorder (ADD)—with or without Hyperactivity (ADHD)—are capable of learning to control their behavior. Although a student with this diagnosis may have some ability-type problems, those problems can be treated using some of the strategies outlined in this section.

When you believe that a student's misbehavior stems from a lack of ability, the first thing you need to ascertain is whether or not the student is capable of learning to exhibit the goal behavior. This is essential because if a student is not physiologically capable of exhibiting the goal behavior, establishing a plan, even a positive plan, to change the student's behavior would be cruel. Instead, you need to adjust your rules and expectations.

Consider the following two examples. Imagine you have a student in your class who is permanently confined to a wheelchair due to a spinal cord injury. Your school probably has a rule to the effect of "Students will walk in the halls." It is obviously completely inappropriate for you to expect this student to walk in the halls. It makes no sense to think that you could use either corrective consequences or positive incentives to get the student to walk rather than wheel himself through the halls. In fact, the idea of trying to change this student's behavior is inhumane. Instead, you adjust the rule to fit this student's capabilities. That is, you learn to live with the situation regarding this student.

A more difficult example involves a student with Tourette syndrome. When reviewing this student's records, you see the notation that teachers are supposed to "ignore his outbursts such as barking, snorting, and swearing." Your first thought may be that such a recommendation is ridiculous. However, the only way a student with Tourette syndrome can control these kinds of behaviors is through the use of medication—and in some cases, medication does not completely eliminate them. Therefore, you must learn to live with this student and his disability.

If you are unsure whether a desired behavior is within a student's physiological capability, check with your special education staff, school psychologist, or the student's physician. Students who are incapable of doing their assigned work because of skill deficits often behave in a manner that makes the teacher think the student is misbehaving because he simply does not want to do his work. In reality, he cannot do the work no matter how hard he tries. In this case, the intervention plan must involve academic remediation or adaptation in addition to behavioral intervention.

This task presents a four-phase process for helping students who exhibit misbehavior that is related to a lack of ability but who are physiologically capable of exhibiting the desired behavior.

1. At a neutral time, have a discussion and/or provide lessons on the goal behavior(s).

2. Correct errors in a manner that provides instruction.

3. Make accommodations to increase the student's chance of success.

4. Provide positive feedback when the student is successful or makes improvements. Set up reward-type incentives if simple positive feedback seems insufficient to motivate the student.

 At a neutral time, have a discussion and/or provide lessons on the goal behavior(s).

At least three days per week, conduct lessons with the student. Use the lessons to model and have the student practice the goal behavior. Keep in mind that when a student lacks the ability to demonstrate a particular behavior, just talking about it will not be enough for the student to really learn it (Elliott & Gresham, 1991; McGinnis & Goldstein, 1994; Walker et al., 2004).

Sports coaches know this. The coach who wants a beginning basketball team to learn about free throws not only provides step-by-step demonstrations of the process but actually has the players use a ball and practice the skill. And, the coach does not do this just one time. He or she provides repetition and practice daily across a period of weeks.

If it does not seem possible for you to provide the instruction yourself, talk to your administrator. Ask if an instructional aide can cover your class for ten minutes a day, or if the school counselor can conduct the lessons with the student. In fact, if several students in the building have the same ability-type problem, the counselor might even run a small group session.

For example, if one or two students in each of three first-grade classes have trouble staying on task and in their seats, the counselor or another skilled person could arrange to provide a daily twenty-minute lesson specifically on "staying on task" for all of these students.

> Use the lessons to model and have the student practice the goal behavior.

Correct errors in a manner that provides instruction.

Punishing students for exhibiting misbehaviors when they have not yet learned to exhibit a positive alternative is silly and potentially cruel. You are far more likely to improve the behavior when you respond to instances of misbehavior with a correction strategy such as gentle reprimands, a cueing signal, or redirection (all described earlier in this chapter). For example, if you have a student labeled ADD who tends to drum on his desk, prearrange a signal to give him each time he starts to drum. Teach him that when he sees you give the signal, he needs to stop drumming.

 Make accommodations to increase the student's chance of success.

Determine whether there are modifications you might make in terms of the daily schedule, class structure, behavioral expectations, classroom physical arrangements, or your interactions with the student that would make it easier for the student to be successful (Babkie, 2006; Barbetta et al., 2005; Scheuermann & Hall, 2008; Trussell, 2008). For example, with a first grader who has trouble staying in one place for more than a few minutes at a time, make a masking tape box on the floor around the student's desk. Tell the student that the box is his office. If he feels the need to move around or get out of his seat, he can do so as long as he stays in his office. In effect, you are expanding the range of what is acceptable behavior for the student, yet keeping parameters that reduce the possibility the student will disturb others.

 Provide feedback.

Provide positive feedback when the student is successful or makes improvements. Set up reward-type incentives when simple positive feedback seems insufficient to motivate the student.

Throughout the day as the student demonstrates success or takes steps toward success, give him or her positive verbal feedback. Students who exhibit this category of misbehavior need information that lets them know when and what they are doing well (Brophy, 1981; Cameron & Pierce, 1994; Gottfried, 1983).

Without a positive feedback component, these students may feel overwhelmed and discouraged by the corrective feedback they receive when they make errors. If the student fails to make progress within a couple of weeks (the misbehavior is not decreasing and the goal behavior is not increasing), consider establishing a simple reward-type incentive system. For example, have the first-grade student with the masking-tape office earn one point for each hour that he stays in his office (unless you give him permission to go outside the boundary). He can accumulate points and then spend them on activities he particularly enjoys.

ANALYSIS OF AND INTERVENTIONS FOR ATTENTION-SEEKING MISBEHAVIORS

For ongoing but mild attention-seeking misbehaviors, be prepared to develop and implement an intervention plan that includes maximal attention for appropriate behaviors and planned ignoring of problem behavior.

An attention-seeking misbehavior is a mild, recurring behavior that a student knows is unacceptable but engages in nonetheless as a way to get teacher or peer attention. Chronic blurting out, excessive helplessness, tattling, and minor disruptions are examples of behaviors that may be attention-seeking in nature. When a student is seeking attention through misbehavior, responding with a correction strategy or corrective consequence will necessarily give the student attention and may actually reinforce the student for misbehaving (Alberto & Troutman, 2006; Barbetta et al., 2005; Gunter & Jack, 1993; Newcomer & Lewis, 2004; Sutherland, 2000). The strategy that is most likely to correct attention-seeking misbehavior is planned ignoring. Note that planned ignoring is not appropriate for early-stage attention-seeking behavior. In the early stage, give the student information to try to stop the behavior before it becomes chronic.

> *Planned ignoring is not the same as tolerating a student's misbehavior.*

By implementing planned ignoring, you reduce or eliminate the attention a student receives for engaging in misbehavior while concurrently giving the student frequent attention when he or she is behaving appropriately. The goal is for the student to learn that using misbehavior to get attention is ineffective and that behaving responsibly results in frequent and very satisfying attention. Planned ignoring is not the same as tolerating a student's misbehavior. Tolerating misbehavior implies that one has given up expecting a change and has decided to live with the misbehavior. Planned ignoring is a conscious strategy applied by the teacher in an effort to change the misbehavior. Following are suggested steps for implementing planned ignoring as part of an intervention plan designed to help a student learn to get his or her attention needs met without engaging in misbehavior.

1. Ascertain whether ignoring is an appropriate response.

2. Discuss the proposed plan with the student.

3. When the misbehavior occurs, continue what you are doing and provide positive feedback to other students.

4. When the attention-seeking misbehavior ceases, give the student attention.

5. Maintain frequent interactions with the student when he is not misbehaving.

6. Monitor the student's behavior to determine whether progress is being made.

 Ascertain whether ignoring is an appropriate response.

To determine whether planned ignoring is the best strategy for the problem behavior, ask yourself the following questions:

Is the misbehavior really attention-seeking in nature?

If the student's misbehavior is due to a lack of ability or awareness, ignoring will not work and can even be somewhat cruel. Not paying attention to a misbehavior caused by lack of awareness or ability is as inappropriate as ignoring math mistakes made by students. Without correction, students assume they are behaving correctly. If a student tattles on other students because he is trying to help, he needs lessons and feedback about the difference between tattling and social responsibility. On the other hand, if the student fully understands that a behavior is not acceptable but uses the misbehavior as a way to seek or demand attention from teacher or peers, planned ignoring is likely to be effective.

Is the behavior itself acceptable, but the problem is with the amount (frequency or duration) of the behavior?

> *Without correction, students assume they are behaving correctly.*

Sometimes the issue with attention-seeking behavior is not that the behavior itself is inappropriate, but rather that the frequency or duration of the behavior is problematic. For example, you have a student who asks a lot of questions and is always seeking teacher assistance. Though you do not want to discourage the student from asking questions or seeking assistance when necessary, if he asks for help more often than he really needs to, that is learned helplessness.

You cannot ignore a student's questions or requests for assistance. You could not justify such action to the student, his family, or your building principal. However, with a problem of excess you can specify a reasonable amount of the behavior. Using the previous example of the student with learned helplessness, first determine how much this student asks for help compared with other students at a similar developmental level. For a couple of days, keep a record of how many times the target student asks for help and how many times one or two similar students ask for help. At the end of the second day, you have a record that looks something like the following:

	MARK	OLIVIA	ROSE
Mon.	19	3	4
Tues.	19	4	2

This objective information shows you that your concern is warranted. It also tells you that your goal should be to get Mark to ask for help no more than five times during a day. One technique to help Mark is to set up a system where each day you give Mark fifteen tickets. Every time he asks for help, he has to give you one of the tickets. When all his tickets are gone, you cannot help him—you ignore requests for assistance that are in excess of the current limit. Conversely, each ticket he has left over at the end of the day is worth one minute of time to help you after school or during recess. Once he is consistently staying below 10 requests in a day, you can modify the system so that he will get only ten tickets per day. Continue the system until the student gets only five tickets each day.

Is the misbehavior so severe (hitting, for example) that ignoring is not an appropriate strategy?

Sometimes a behavior that is attention-seeking in nature is so severe that you cannot responsibly ignore it. For example, when a student is hitting other students, you must intervene. Or if a student's disruptive behavior is so severe that lessons cannot

Important!   %%%

During the first several days of using planned ignoring, you should expect the behavior to get worse before it begins to get better. This is commonly referred to as an extinction burst (Lerman, Iwata, & Wallace, 1999; Watson, 1967). Believe it or not, when a behavior gets worse it is a sign that the strategy will eventually work. Remember, the student has received attention for exhibiting this behavior in the past, and that attention has been very satisfying. Now when the student exhibits the behavior, she is not getting attention. The logical response from the student is to try harder to get your attention using the behavior that was so successful in the past. If you continue to ignore, eventually the student will learn that if she really wants attention, she needs to behave responsibly.

continue, you must intervene. When an attention-seeking misbehavior is very severe, you need to treat it as a purposeful or habitual misbehavior and include the use of corrective consequences (see pp. 400–408). However, remember that the student wants attention, so when you assign a consequence make every effort to do so in a manner that gives the student as little attention as possible. In addition, be sure to make a concerted effort to give the student frequent attention when he is not engaged in misbehavior. The goal is for the student to learn that although he will get attention for misbehavior, it is less attention and less satisfying attention than what he can easily get for behaving responsibly.

Will you ignore the behavior from all students or just from the target student?

When one or two students exhibit the behavior chronically and several other students exhibit it intermittently, you should ignore any student who exhibits it. For example, if blurting out without raising a hand is a problem for quite a few students, make a classwide announcement that you are going to ignore blurting out and call on only those students who remember to raise their hands. However, when the behavior is exhibited primarily by one student, plan to ignore that student when she engages in the misbehavior but give verbal reprimands to any other student who exhibits the misbehavior.

Once you determine that a behavior is attention-seeking and that ignoring is an appropriate correction strategy, the next step is to develop an intervention that includes using planned ignoring. To develop an effective plan, give careful thought to and specify for yourself exactly which behaviors you will ignore, which you will assign corrective consequences to, and which you will encourage. For example, you might end up with a list like that in Figure 9.8.

BEHAVIOR TO IGNORE	BEHAVIOR THAT REQUIRES A CONSEQUENCE	BEHAVIOR TO ENCOURAGE
• Blurting out • Silly noises • Tapping pencil	• Bothering other students • Hitting • Kicking	• Raising hand • Hands/feet to self • Working quietly • On-task • Getting to work immediately • Following directions

Figure 9.8 *List of Behaviors and Responses*

Discuss the proposed plan with the student.

When the problem involves only one student, arrange to meet with that student (and, if appropriate, with the student's family). During the meeting, describe the problem behavior and your proposed plan to ignore it. Make it clear that your intent is not to ignore the student as a person, but rather to ignore the student's behavior because he should be managing it without attention from you. Explain that because you have such high expectations for the student's ability to manage this behavior, you are not going to give reminders or assign consequences. Inform the student that if he engages in more severe misbehaviors that cannot be ignored (bothering others, hitting, and kicking), you will assign corrective consequences. Finally, let the student know that you will be looking for opportunities to give him your time and attention when he is behaving responsibly.

Decide whether or not to discuss the planned ignoring with the entire class. If you believe a class discussion is necessary, inform the student during your initial meeting. Make sure the student knows that you will present the plan in a way that communicates to the class that everyone has behaviors to work on, and his behavior is getting attention in positive ways. If you discussed ignoring as a strategy during your first two weeks of school, review the key concepts you taught the students—most notably that ignoring is a strategy used to help a student learn to manage his or her own behavior.

If the situation involves a behavior exhibited by many students, inform the entire class that you will use ignoring as a strategy. Emphasize that ignoring does not mean the behavior is acceptable. Rather, explain that you are using ignoring because this particular behavior is so clearly unacceptable that you should not have to take your valuable time to tell students not to do something they know they should not do. Keep the tone of this discussion complimentary rather than accusatory—that is, communicate high expectations.

 When the misbehavior occurs, continue what you are doing and provide positive feedback to other students.

Once you have informed the student of your plan to ignore, give no attention to the misbehavior. Some teachers feel a need to tell the student each time, "I am ignoring you now." DO NOT DO THIS! Telling a student that you are ignoring him is giving him attention. Give no attention to the student at the time of the misbehavior (Alberto & Troutman, 2006). Do not shrug, sigh, or act exasperated. Teach. Present lessons. Give your attention to students who are doing the responsible thing at that moment. With primary-age students, you can even overtly praise students who are behaving appropriately. "Ashanti, you are keeping your attention focused on your work and you are working quietly without making any unnecessary noise."

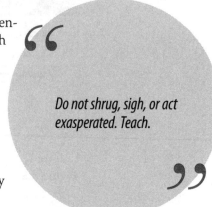

Do not shrug, sigh, or act exasperated. Teach.

If a number of students in your class exhibit chronic misbehavior, you should plan to use one or more of the corrective consequences described in Chapter 3, Task 4, and to implement one or more of the classwide motivation systems described in Chapter 8.

If other students pay attention to the student engaged in misbehavior, give a gentle verbal reprimand. "Julio, Adam can take care of himself, and the most helpful thing you can do right now is mind your own business and do your own work." If another student laughs at the target student, you might say something like, "Yasmin, please don't laugh. Your laughter might encourage Carla to continue clowning around and that would not be helpful to Carla. Mind your own business and do your own work."

Be consistent. Remember that intermittent reinforcement is the schedule that is most resistant to extinction (Alberto & Troutman, 2006; Cooper et al., 2007; Scheuermann & Hall, 2008; Skinner, 1953). Therefore, ignoring intermittently is worse than not ignoring at all. For example, if you have decided to ignore blurting out, ignore all blurting out. If you ignore it the first five times it happens, then get frustrated and assign a consequence the sixth time, you simply teach the student to be more persistent—"The teacher will eventually give me attention if I misbehave long enough."

A common question regarding ignoring is "What if I am ignoring a student's noises and blurting out, and then he hits someone?" The answer is that, under those circumstances, you should implement your consequence for hitting. This is not inconsistent. In fact, it is the reason you should develop lists of behaviors to ignore, behaviors that require consequences, and behaviors to encourage. You need to be prepared to consistently ignore the behaviors that will benefit from ignoring. However, if the student exhibits a behavior that you previously decided would require consequences, you need to stop ignoring and implement the consequence. When the attention-seeking misbehavior ceases, give the student attention.

Demonstrate to the student that responsible behavior results in attention. Shortly after the student begins behaving responsibly, give the student attention. For primary students, the attention should be given within a minute or two; for intermediate and middle school students, within five minutes. Either praise the responsible behavior or just go over and talk to the student for a few moments. "Carla, you are working so quietly, I thought I would come over and see if you had any questions or needed any help. No? Well, OK, but if you need anything, raise your hand and I'll be right over."

 Maintain frequent interactions with the student when he is not misbehaving.

Chapter 7: Motivation explained the importance of providing at least three times more attention to positive behavior than to negative behavior. This strategy is essential whenever you are using planned ignoring. If the student does not experience lots of attention when behaving responsibly, he will simply increase the severity of misbehavior until you cannot possibly ignore him—he will start hitting other students, for example. You must praise this student frequently and give him lots of noncontingent attention.

Monitor the student's behavior to determine whether progress is being made.

At least once per week, count the frequency or record the duration of this behavior. After two weeks of using planned ignoring, evaluate whether the situation is improving. If it is not, continue the ignoring and increase the amount and intensity of attention you provide when the student is not misbehaving. If there is still no improvement after another two weeks, abandon planned ignoring as a strategy and treat this misbehavior as purposeful/habitual (see the following section).

ANALYSIS OF AND INTERVENTIONS FOR PURPOSEFUL/HABITUAL MISBEHAVIORS

For ongoing misbehaviors that are habitual and/or serve a purpose other than getting attention, be prepared to develop and implement an intervention plan that includes the use of corrective consequences.

Chronic misbehavior may occur for reasons other than a lack of awareness or ability, or a need for attention. Chronic misbehavior may help a student avoid something aversive or help him demonstrate and achieve a sense of power and control. Sometimes the original purpose of a student's misbehavior is no longer relevant—she misbehaves just because the inappropriate behaviors have become firmly established in her behavioral repertoire.

When ongoing misbehavior is truly purposeful and/or habitual, it is probably necessary to use corrective consequences (punishers) to help the student learn that the misbehavior has negative costs. Because the student is not responding to your classwide management plan, the use of corrective consequences alone is not likely to be sufficient to change a student's behavior (Mayer, 1995). Therefore, in addition to using corrective consequences, an intervention plan for purposeful/habitual misbehaviors needs to include efforts to remove any positive or satisfying aspects of engaging in the misbehavior as well as efforts to continually demonstrate that positive behavior leads to positive results (O'Neill et al., 1997; Sugai, Horner, et al., 2000).

> *"Chronic misbehavior may help a student avoid something aversive or help him demonstrate and achieve a sense of power and control.*

The remainder of this task describes intervention planning guidelines for purposeful/habitual misbehavior. This information addresses the three important components of an intervention plan for this type of misbehavior:

1. Remove any positive or satisfying aspects of demonstrating the misbehavior.

2. Demonstrate to the student that positive behavior leads to positive results.

3. Respond to the misbehavior by assigning appropriate corrective consequences.

 Remove any positive or satisfying aspects of demonstrating the misbehavior.

Remember that the misbehavior you want to change serves a purpose for the student. She may misbehave in order to be removed from class and escape doing the academic work, or she may not participate in class because she enjoys reading a book more than listening to the lesson. As you develop your intervention plan, you need to ensure that the student will no longer be rewarded or get satisfaction from the misbehavior—making the misbehavior ineffective. If a student has gained power by engaging in arguments with you, your plan should address how you will avoid engaging in arguments with this student. If a student has been using misbehavior to escape from doing his work, ensure that the corrective consequence included in your intervention plan does not result in the student getting out of doing work. If a student does not complete work because he plays with toys at his desk, part of your plan must be that there are no toys at his desk. If a student enjoys hurting other people's feelings with mean comments, you need to train yourself and the other students not to take his critical comments personally ("Sticks and stones can. . .").

 Demonstrate to the student that positive behavior leads to positive results.

In addition to making sure that the student does not benefit from the misbehavior, your intervention plan should also specifically address how you can continually demonstrate to the student that responsible behavior is worthwhile. This can include efforts to meet the student's needs in positive ways and increase the student's motivation to behave responsibly. It is important that you consider ways to make the appropriate behavior more efficient than the problem behavior at gaining positive results for the student.

MEET THE STUDENT'S NEEDS IN A POSITIVE WAY

Once you identify the purpose served by a student's misbehavior, try to find some positive way of satisfying that purpose. For example, if a fourth-grade student talks back to adults as a means of seeking power, ask the student if he would be willing to be a positive help around the school and use his power to help the school be a better and safer place. Give the student a choice among several different jobs (being a tutor for a younger student, teaching and refereeing soccer games during the primary recess, or serving as a fire drill assistant to the principal, for example). Job options such as refereeing soccer games during recess have other potential benefits because a counselor may use the time as an opportunity to train the student how to be a positive leader for the younger students. Along with the use of appropriate corrective consequences if the student does talk back, having a positive position of power can solve this kind of problem behavior in a couple of months.

> *If a student is seeking to escape academic work, ask yourself whether the student is capable of doing the work successfully.*

If a student is seeking to escape academic work, ask yourself whether the student is capable of doing the work successfully. If not, modify his assignments or get some kind of help for the student so he will begin to experience success.

When a misbehavior involves competing reinforcers, arrange for the student to have access to the desired reinforcer when he has met your expectations. For example, if the student likes to read novels instead of doing his work, allow him to read when his other work is completed, or occasionally give the student an alternative assignment that involves reading a novel and giving a report to the class.

INCREASE THE STUDENT'S MOTIVATION TO BEHAVE RESPONSIBLY

For some students, a change in the type or frequency of your positive feedback may be sufficient to increase the student's motivation to behave responsibly (see Chapter 7: Motivation). In other cases, it may be necessary to establish some form of positive feedback system where the student earns rewards for exhibiting positive behavior. For ideas on classwide systems, see Chapter 8: Classwide Motivation. For ideas on individual contracts and systems, see Sprick and Howard (1995). An example of an individual system (for increasing homework completion) from this resource is shown in Figure 9.9.

 Implement corrective consequences that are appropriate to the problem behavior.

When misbehavior is purposeful or habitual, carefully plan how you will respond to specific instances of the behavior. If you do not preplan your response, there is a high probability that you will inadvertently reinforce the misbehavior. The following suggestions can help you choose and implement an effective corrective consequence—one that helps the student learn that when he engages in misbehavior, there is a logical cost. See Chapter 3, Task 4, for a descriptive menu of corrective consequences you may implement in your classroom.

Figure 9.9 *Individual System to Increase Homework Completion*

When a student is not concerned about the designated consequences for failing to turn in completed homework and/or does not value the sense of satisfaction that comes from completing and turning in required work, you may need to implement a system of external incentives (i.e., rewards and consequences) to motivate him to turn in completed homework on time.

1. **Establish a structured system for reinforcing appropriate behavior and providing a consequence for inappropriate behavior.**

   a. With the student, create a list of rewards he would like to earn. The rewards may need to be relatively high in perceived value in order to create a powerful incentive to motivate the student to get his homework completed on a regular basis. To get some ideas for the list, watch what the student does during less structured times in class—what does he do when he has choices? Or you can ask the student for his preferences.

   You might also have the student read through the list of your ideas and then discuss the possibilities together. If the student's family will be working with you and the student on the plan, maybe some of the reinforcers could be things that the family provides at home (for example, having a friend spend the night, a later curfew, additional money for clothing, etc.).

   b. Assign prices (in points) for each reward on the list and have the student select the reward he would like to earn first.

   The prices should be based on the instructional, personnel, and/or monetary cost of the items. Monetary cost is clear—the more expensive the item, the more points required to earn it. Instructional cost refers to the amount of instructional time lost or interfered with by a particular reward. Thus, an activity that causes the student to miss part of academic instruction should require more points than one the student can do on his own free time. Personnel cost refers to the time required by you and/or other staff to fulfill the reinforcer. Having lunch with the principal, therefore, would cost more points than spending five minutes of free time with a friend.

   The prices must be low enough that the student will think, for example, "You mean all I have to do is _____, and I can earn _____!" If the desired reinforcers are priced too high and would take too long to earn (from the student's perspective), he may not be any more motivated to complete his homework than he was without the system.

   c. Develop a homework completion self-monitoring form and establish a system to translate each successfully filled-in space into points. For example, the student might earn one point each for accurately recording the assignment, the due date, and the necessary materials (three points total). When the assignment is completed and turned in, the student might earn another five points, making each homework assignment worth a total of eight points.

   Larger assignments or projects, such as writing a report, can be broken down into steps, each with its own line and due date on the monitoring form. For example, the outline, the note cards, the rough draft, and the final draft could be treated as separate assignments, each worth eight points—making the whole report worth a possible 32 reinforcement points.

   d. When the student has accumulated enough points to earn the reward he has chosen, he spends the points necessary and the system begins again. That is, he selects another reward to earn and begins with zero points.

2. **Respond consistently to the inappropriate behavior.**

   a. Gently correct the student when he fails to turn in his homework.

   b. Establish consequences (in addition to any predetermined classwide consequences) for not being responsible for his homework. The most obvious consequence would be that if the student does not turn in the work, he fails that assignment. However, that consequence alone may be too abstract and delayed to affect the student's behavior in the short run. Another, and more immediate, consequence will probably be necessary (for example, the student must stay in from recess/ breaks and/or stay after school until the work is caught up).

   If the family is working with you on the reinforcement portion of the plan, you can consider asking them to implement a consequence at home as well, such as grounding the student until he is caught up with his work. However, this is appropriate only if the family is also reinforcing the student; the family's role should never be punitive.

   c. When neither home-based nor school-based consequences are possible, it puts more pressure on the positive aspects of the intervention to ensure that the plan is powerful enough to motivate the student to complete the homework, despite the lack of consequences for not turning it in.

3. **Use reinforcement to encourage appropriate behavior.**

   a. Give the student increased praise and attention for turning in completed homework on time.

   b. In addition, show interest and enthusiasm about how the student is doing on the system. "Salvador, every day this week you have earned all eight points for every assignment. Congratulations! You should be proud of your organizational skill."

Reprinted with permission from Sprick. R.S., & Howard, L.M. (1996). The teacher's encyclopedia of behavior management: 100 problems, 500 plans. *Eugene, OR: Pacific Northwest Publishing.*

PLAN TO IMPLEMENT THE CORRECTIVE CONSEQUENCE CONSISTENTLY

For corrective consequences to reduce or eliminate purposeful and habitual misbehavior, they must be implemented consistently (Acker & O'Leary, 1988). If you implement a corrective consequence only some of the times the student exhibits the misbehavior, the consequence, no matter how severe, is not likely to change the behavior. In fact, inconsistent consequences may even make the situation worse than if there were no consequences at all (Barbetta et al., 2005). Any time a student is able to engage in a misbehavior and not receive the designated consequence, he is likely to feel a sense of satisfaction. Getting away with it can be great fun, and the student may find he likes playing games to see how frequently he can engage in the behavior without getting caught.

> "Inconsistent consequences may even make the situation worse than if there were no consequences at all."

Teachers tend to implement corrective consequences based on an accumulation of misbehavior. Thus, teacher emotion ends up controlling the use of consequences. The student gets away with a misbehavior the first five times, but when he misbehaves a sixth time, the teacher gets mad and implements a consequence. The first several times the behavior does not bother the teacher, but by the sixth time the teacher is fed up. Though understandable, this leads to grossly inconsistent responses. To change purposeful and habitual misbehavior, you need to define specific behaviors that are not acceptable and then implement corrective consequences for those behaviors each time they occur, regardless of how you feel about the behavior at the time.

Your goal is to develop clear expectations of what behaviors are unacceptable so you can be consistent in implementing consequences. If you are concerned about disruptions, specify the precise behaviors you consider disruptive. Also be sure to identify examples of noise and class participation that are not disruptive. If your concern is a student who is disrespectful, describe specific ways the student has been disrespectful and ways the student could behave respectfully in the same situations. Creating a T-chart that specifies responsible and irresponsible behavior can help. Use the chart when discussing your expectations and consequences with the student. Figure 9.10 is a sample T-chart for a student who makes disruptive noises.

Once you develop a T-chart and discuss what constitutes responsible and irresponsible behavior with the student, be sure to implement the designated corrective consequence every time the student exhibits one of the irresponsible behaviors on the list. Be aware that your greatest tendency to be inconsistent will not occur on a bad day when you are tired, but rather on a good day when you are feeling relaxed and refreshed. On good days, disruptive behavior may not bother you and so you may be inclined to ignore it. DO NOT DO THIS. The student needs to know that each time he engages in the misbehavior, the consequence will be implemented regardless of whether the behavior bothers you at a particular moment.

CHAPTER 9 TASKS

MAKE SURE THE CORRECTIVE CONSEQUENCE FITS THE SEVERITY AND FREQUENCY OF THE MISBEHAVIOR

When deciding on the corrective consequence to implement, choose one that matches the severity of the problem (Simonsen et al., 2008; Wolfgang & Glickman, 1986). Start by examining the irresponsible behaviors listed on your T-chart. Choose a consequence that fits even the mildest example of the unacceptable behavior. All too often, teachers pick a consequence that is so harsh they are unwilling to implement it when the occasion arises. "Vanita, stop that because I do not want to have to give you a detention." This leads to inconsistency. The consequence should be mild enough that you will be comfortable implementing it every time the student exhibits one of the irresponsible behaviors. As you think about your choice of a consequence, look at each example of the misbehavior listed on your T-chart. If the consequence seems too harsh for any of those examples of irresponsible behavior, you may need to select a milder consequence. When determining the severity of consequences, err on the side of making consequences too mild—because you may not follow through on consequences that are overly harsh.

Whatever corrective consequence you choose, plan to implement the consequence in the same way for all of the behaviors within that category. In other words, if you decide to use demerits, all disruptive acts should result in one demerit. Do not create a situation in which some disruptive acts get one demerit and some get three. If you do, every time the student is disruptive you will have to explain why you are assigning one demerit or three demerits. If you decide to use time owed as a consequence for a student who tends to be disrespectful, have each infraction equal the

Figure 9.10   *Sample T-chart for Disruptive Behavior*

RESPONSIBLE NOISE	DISRUPTIVE NOISE
Putting paper in the trash	Wadding up paper
Getting paper out	Tearing up paper
Quietly opening/closing notebook rings	Snapping open/closed notebook rings or slamming notebook on desk
Writing, sharpening pencil at breaks	Tapping pencil
Raising hand, waiting to be called on, using an appropriate volume level	Blurting out without raising hand or waiting to be called on
Working quietly	Humming, making "clicking" noises with tongue
Once or twice per work period, asking a neighbor a work-related question	Talking about anything other than work during work periods

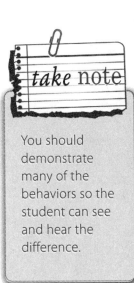

take note

You should demonstrate many of the behaviors so the student can see and hear the difference.

same amount of time owed—one minute, for example. Do not set it up so that some instances of disrespect cost one minute while others cost five minutes. Don't put yourself in the position of having to explain why one misbehavior equals one minute owed and another equals five minutes owed. Again, if you err on the side of consequences that are too mild, you are more likely to follow through than if the consequences are too harsh.

In addition to matching the corrective consequence to the severity of the infraction, you also need to consider the frequency of the infraction.

for example

At first glance it might seem reasonable to say that every time a student is disruptive the student loses five minutes from recess. However, if the student is likely to be disruptive seven times in a day and you have only one fifteen-minute recess, that student will not have to pay for each infraction. In fact, by the middle of the morning, the student may well have already lost her entire recess and so justifiably conclude that there is no reason to even bother to behave.

Furthermore, when consequence severity does not match misbehavior frequency, you may be more inclined to be inconsistent in implementing your consequences. For example, by the second infraction you start thinking that you'll ignore some misbehaviors because you don't want the student to lose her entire recess too soon. Overly harsh consequences make consistency difficult for most teachers. You are better off planning for the student to lose one minute of recess for each infraction. This way, even when the student has a bad day, you will be likely to consistently implement the consequence. "Joanie, that is disruptive. You owe another minute."

PLAN TO IMPLEMENT THE CONSEQUENCE UNEMOTIONALLY

With purposeful and habitual misbehavior, there is a high probability that the student has learned that he can make adults frustrated, hurt, or angry. If you get angry when correcting the student, your anger may actually reinforce the student's misbehavior. When a student feels hostility toward adults, seeing the adult frustrated or exasperated can be highly satisfying. For a student who feels powerless, making an adult angry on a regular basis provides a huge sense of power and control. Strive to implement corrective consequences unemotionally so your reactions do not give the student the idea that misbehavior is a way to achieve power over you (Dreikurs et al., 1998).

> *If you get angry when correcting the student, your anger may actually reinforce the student's misbehavior.*

PLAN TO INTERACT WITH THE STUDENT BRIEFLY AT THE TIME OF A MISBEHAVIOR—NEVER ARGUE

When a student misbehaves, your interaction with that student should last less than five seconds. Simply state the misbehavior and the consequence (Abramowitz et al., 1988; McAllister et al., 1969). A common mistake is to explain and justify. All explanations should be done in your initial discussion with the student or in a regularly scheduled follow-up meeting.

If the student has a tendency to argue or deny that he exhibited the misbehavior, tell the student during your initial discussion that at the time of an incident you will not argue or negotiate and that you will ignore any attempts on his part to do so. At the same time, let the student know that if he ever wants to speak to you about something he thinks is unfair, he can make an appointment to see you before or after school. Once you have made this clear, if the student tries to argue, simply remind him that he can make an appointment to see you. Then resume teaching.

Although keeping interactions brief may be a difficult habit to develop, you will find that it allows you to keep your focus where it belongs—on teaching and on providing positive feedback to all students when they are meeting your expectations. Think about the consequence you are planning to use for a misbehavior. If you cannot imagine implementing that consequence without lengthy explanations or negotiations at the time of the misbehavior, you should select a different consequence.

 Implement the intervention plan for purposeful/habitual misbehavior.

The preceding pages addressed the three important components of an intervention plan for purposeful and/or habitual misbehavior:

1. Remove any positive or satisfying aspects of demonstrating the misbehavior.

2. Demonstrate to the student that positive behavior leads to positive results.

3. Respond to the misbehavior by assigning appropriate corrective consequences.

Reminder:
A menu and descriptions of different consequences for misbehavior are included in Chapter 3, Task 4.

Once you define the behaviors (positive and negative) and consequences, ask yourself some "what-if" questions. What if the student objects? What if the family objects? Will my administrator support me if there are objections? What if the behavior increases for a few days—can I still follow through with this consequence? Do I need to explain this consequence to the entire class? Will I apply the consequence to anyone who exhibits this behavior or just to the target student?

The more issues you can identify and address, the greater the likelihood that your intervention plan will be effective—that is, help reduce and eventually eliminate the misbehavior. Discuss any "what-if" questions you cannot answer with your school administrator or building counselor. Do not implement any intervention plan until you know you can follow through on all aspects of the plan. Remember that your plan needs to address these two questions:

> *Make sure the student knows the cost of choosing to exhibit the misbehavior.*

- How will you eliminate or reduce the probability that the student will get positive benefits from engaging in the misbehavior?

- How will you see that the student experiences positive benefits from exhibiting responsible behavior?

Once all aspects of your plan have been developed and all potential difficulties resolved, meet with the student (or class, if the consequence will be implemented class-wide) to explain what will happen each time he or she engages in the misbehavior. Make sure the student knows the cost of choosing to exhibit the misbehavior in the future, but keep the tone of this discussion positive.

Remember, you should implement an intervention plan consistently for at least two weeks. Collect data on the behavior during this two-week period to determine if the behavior is getting better or worse. Even if things seem to get worse for a few days, do not switch to a different consequence right away. After two weeks, if the behavior is about the same or getting worse, go through the planning steps again and make necessary modifications. Monitor the behavior for two more weeks. If the behavior improves, continue what you are doing. If the behavior still has not improved, consider trying a new corrective consequence and implementing a motivation system to encourage the student to improve his or her behavior.

STEP 5 Discuss your preliminary intervention plan with the student and, if appropriate, the student's family.

Prior to implementing an intervention plan for any chronic misbehavior, schedule a time to discuss your concerns about the target behavior and your proposed plan with the student or the entire class, if many students are exhibiting the behavior. Decide whether or not to include the student's family in the discussion. If the behavior involved is quite serious (for example, the student is hitting other students or is verbally abusive), the family should definitely be asked to participate. On the other hand, if the behavior is a relatively minor one (the student is restless and overuses the pencil sharpener and the drinking fountain), it may not be necessary to include

See "Cultural Competence" (Introduction, pp. 6–9) for suggestions on working effectively with students and families whose backgrounds are different from yours.

the family. If you are not sure whether to involve the family, you should probably include them (Dishion & Stormshak, 2007; Gortmaker et al., 2004; Henderson & Mapp, 2002; Miller & Kraft, 2008; Ysseldyke et al., 2006).

During the discussion, define the target behavior for the student as clearly as you can. Whenever possible, describe the behavior in observable terms and share any objective data about the behavior that you have collected. ("Troy, you have hit, poked, or kicked someone eight times in two days.") Avoid making statements that imply judgments. ("Tamika, you are so bad most of the time that something has to be done.")

After you explain the nature of the problem, present your proposed plan. Ensure that the student and the family, if present, understand all aspects of the proposed plan. You should invite ideas for improving the plan from the student and family. Incorporating reasonable suggestions will give the student and family a sense of ownership in the plan and demonstrate that you want them to be active partners in efforts to improve the student's behavior (Esler et al., 2008; Freer & Watson, 1999; Gortmaker et al., 2004; Keith et al., 1998; Rones & Hoagwood, 2000; Sheridan et al., 1996).

Reproducible 9.7 on the next page is a template for structuring a phone conversation with a student's family about joining you and the student for a discussion. A fillable version of the form is provided on the CD.

STEP 6 Implement the intervention plan for at least two weeks. Continue to collect data on the target behavior to evaluate the plan's effectiveness.

Once you have analyzed the behavior, developed a preliminary plan, and discussed the plan with the student and family, you are ready to implement the plan. Keep your plan in effect for at least two weeks—you should collect daily data for about two weeks before you can make a reliable decision about the student's progress (Farlow & Snell, 1994). Objective data about the frequency or duration of the behavior allows you to determine whether or not the problem is improving. Do not be alarmed if the behavior gets worse during the first week—a phenomenon known as an extinction burst. This sometimes happens, even with a plan that eventually will be successful (Lerman et al., 1999; Watson, 1967).

For example, when you first begin ignoring an attention-getting behavior, the student is likely to try even harder to get attention by misbehaving more frequently. If you persist in ignoring the behavior, the student eventually learns that responsible behavior leads to more attention than misbehavior. However, if you eventually give

Reproducible 9.7   *Chronic Problems—Request for Conference*

 CHAMPS *Sample*

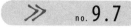 >> no. **9.7**

Print from CD

CHRONIC PROBLEMS—REQUEST FOR CONFERENCE

1. **Introduce yourself and provide an appropriate greeting:**
    Hello, Mr. Houser? This is Ms. Grier, Toby's teacher. May I take just a moment of your time?

2. **Inform the family that you are calling about a problem:**
    I am calling because I want to speak with you about something that happened at school today.

3. **Describe the problem (avoid labeling or passing judgment on the child):**
    Today during science class, Toby was working with a group of other students. They got into a disagreement that led to Toby getting quite angry at one of the female students in the group, a student named Melissa. Now, there is nothing wrong with disagreements and even anger. But Toby called Melissa some very inappropriate names that can not be tolerated in school. He threatened to hurt her. Although this incident was the worst, Toby has gotten angry on a couple of other occasions as well.

4. **Describe why the behavior is a problem (keep the focus on the student, not yourself or the other students):**

    Even though he is only in second grade, he needs to learn that when he is angry, calling names and threatening others is not acceptable school behavior.

5. **Explain why you think a conference would be useful and specify whether the student should attend the conference:**

    I think it would help Toby to realize how serious this behavior is if you and/or Mrs. Houser would come to school to meet with Toby and me. Together we can decide on a plan for helping Toby behave more responsibly.

6. **Inform the family if other school personnel (or other agency personnel) will be in attendance:**
    Because making threats is so serious, I feel we need to ask Ms. Nestor, the principal, to join us.

Date of this contact: 1/14, 11:50 a.m.

Time and place for the conference: Ms. Nestor's office at 2 p.m.

CHAPTER 9 TASKS

1 • Analyze and Adjust Plan Implementation   2 • Analyze and Adjust Strategies for Building Positive Relationships

in to the student's increased attempts to get your attention, you may reinforce the misbehavior at the new intensity and the misbehavior may remain at the elevated level (Alberto & Troutman, 2006).

> *Remember that most successful behavior changes occur gradually, improving a little each week.*

After two weeks, evaluate the situation. If the behavior is getting better, continue to implement your plan. It is very important to remember that most successful behavior changes occur gradually, improving a little each week. For more information on fading a structured reinforcement system, see pp. 319–323 of Chapter 8. The suggestions in that chapter for fading group-based reward systems can be easily adapted to reward systems for individual students. However, if you see no behavioral improvement after two weeks, try modifying one or more aspects of your plan. Ask the student for ideas on what would make the plan more effective. Whenever you make a change in your intervention plan, implement the new plan for a minimum of two weeks and continue to evaluate effectiveness.

Conclusion

Chronic misbehavior presents one of the greatest frustrations and challenges to classroom teachers (Elements of an effective discipline strategy, 1995-96; Lewis & Sugai, 1999; Walker et al., 1995). In designing an intervention plan, always try the easiest strategy first. Try to use the strategy that is likely to have the biggest impact on the student's behavior. If more than one or two students are chronically misbehaving, work on the implementation of your overall management plan—trying to implement multiple individualized interventions while also teaching a class with 20 to 30 other students is too challenging for even the most skilled teacher. If one or two students are chronically misbehaving, first try an intervention that makes minor adjustments, tailored for that student or students, to your management plan.

If that is ineffective, design an intervention that specifically focuses on building a positive relationship with the target student. If that is ineffective, begin collecting objective data and design a function-based intervention plan. Although a function-based intervention plan is a great deal of work, a well-designed and implemented individualized intervention has the potential to bring about life-altering behavior change for an at-risk student.

Use the Self-Assessment Checklist shown on the following pages to keep track of the tasks you've completed and those that require further work. A fillable version of the Self-Assessment Checklist is available on the CD.

Print from CD

Correcting Chronic and Severe Misbehavior

Chapter 9: Correcting

Use the worksheet on the following pages to identify which (or which parts) of the tasks described in this chapter you have completed. For any item that has not been completed, note what needs to be done to complete it. Then translate your notes onto your planning calendar in the form of specific actions that you can take (e.g., January 22, begin planned ignoring intervention for Paulo).

✓	TASK	NOTES & IMPLEMENTATION *Ideas*

TASK 1: ANALYZE AND, IF NEEDED, ADJUST THE IMPLEMENTATION OF YOUR BASIC MANAGEMENT PLAN

☐ I have evaluated my Classroom Management and Discipline Plan and have worked through the Reflection/Implementation form (Reproducible 9.1). I have considered the questions and suggestions and will make some minor adjustments to my management plan or its implementation that may help my student improve his behavior.

If no improvement is noted after two weeks, I will proceed to Task 2.

TASK 2: ANALYZE AND, IF NEEDED, ADJUST THE STRATEGIES YOU ARE USING TO BUILD A POSITIVE RELATIONSHIP WITH THIS STUDENT

☐ I have evaluated my relationship with the student and have worked through the Connect/Motivation Plan—Reflection/Implementation form (Reproducible 9.2). I have considered the questions and suggestions and will make some minor adjustments in my interactions with the student that may increase the student's motivation to engage in positive behaviors and decrease the frequency and severity of the chronic misbehavior.

If no improvement is noted after two weeks, I will proceed to Task 3.

✓	TASK	NOTES & IMPLEMENTATION *Ideas*

TASK 3: ANALYZE THE MISBEHAVIOR AND DEVELOP A FUNCTION-BASED INTERVENTION

☐ I understand the common reasons students misbehave:

- Misbehaviors due to lack of awareness
- Misbehaviors due to lack of ability or skill
- Attention-seeking misbehaviors
- Purposeful/habitual misbehaviors

☐ I have worked through the Function-Based Intervention Plan form (Reproducible 9.3), which incorporates the six steps recommended for addressing chronic misbehavior:

Step 1: Identify the target (problem) behavior and collect objective data. Use that data as you proceed to Step 2.

Step 2: Develop a hypothesis (educated guess) about the function of the misbehavior.

Step 3: Identify any specific contexts and conditions (time, locations, tasks) when the target behavior typically occurs (or does not occur).

Step 4: Identify a preliminary behavior change (intervention) plan based on your hypothesis about the function of the misbehavior and your understanding of when (under what conditions) the behavior typically occurs.

Step 5: Discuss your preliminary intervention plan with the student and, if appropriate, the student's family.

Step 6: Implement the intervention plan for at least two weeks. Continue to collect data on the target behavior to evaluate the plan's effectiveness.

SELF-ASSESSMENT CHECKLIST pg. 3

✓	TASK	NOTES & IMPLEMENTATION *Ideas*
☐	For misbehaviors due to lack of awareness, I understand the four-phase intervention process: 1. Make sure the student knows what behavior you expect him to exhibit (the target or goal behavior). 2. Respond to instances of the misbehavior in a manner that lets the student know he is not meeting the goal. 3. Monitor the student's behavior so that you, the student, and the student's family have an objective basis for discussing progress. 4. Provide positive feedback when the student is successful or makes improvements. If positive feedback doesn't seem sufficient to motivate the student to stop exhibiting the behavior, consider using some kind of incentive (reward).	
☐	For misbehaviors due to lack of ability or skill, I understand the four-phase intervention process: 1. At a neutral time, have a discussion and/or provide lessons on the goal behavior(s). 2. Correct errors in a manner that provides instruction. 3. Make accommodations to increase the student's chance of success. 4. Provide positive feedback when the student is successful or makes improvements. Set up reward-type incentives if simple positive feedback seems insufficient to motivate the student.	

SELF-ASSESSMENT CHECKLIST pg. 4

✓	TASK	NOTES & IMPLEMENTATION *Ideas*
☐	For attention-seeking misbehaviors, I understand the steps to take to implement the intervention of planned ignoring: 1. Ascertain whether ignoring is an appropriate response. 2. Discuss the proposed plan with the student. 3. When the misbehavior occurs, continue what you are doing and provide positive feedback to other students. 4. When the attention-seeking misbehavior ceases, give the student attention. 5. Maintain frequent interactions with the student when he is not misbehaving. 6. Monitor the student's behavior to determine whether progress is being made.	
☐	For purposeful/habitual misbehaviors, I understand the three components of an intervention plan: 1. Remove any positive or satisfying aspects of demonstrating the misbehavior. 2. Demonstrate to the student that positive behavior leads to positive results. 3. Respond to the misbehavior by assigning appropriate corrective consequences.	

Professionalism

FOR THE FIRST-YEAR TEACHER

INTRODUCTION

This appendix provides suggestions for how to look, think, and behave like a professional. A professional can be defined as one who works in a position that requires specialized knowledge and often long academic preparation and who exhibits a courteous, conscientious, and generally business-like manner in the workplace.

Special thanks to Maureen Gale for her contributions to this Appendix!

Congratulations on embarking on an exciting adventure! Your first year of teaching will hold many rewarding and memorable experiences. The CHAMPS text and its many suggestions, activities, and reflective tools will assist you in proactively planning your classroom management and organizational strategies. However, your first year as a teacher can also include many intimidating moments. You'll encounter some of the most challenging situations of your career because many situations will be new to you. There is so much to learn and so much to do—learning your district's expectations about insurance, curricular expectations, and paperwork; understanding and fitting into your grade-level team and school campus; and trying to meet the needs of all your students.

You are beginning your career as a professional. Effective teachers understand that it's important to behave in a manner that communicates professionalism. Imagine you go to see a professional—a physician, architect, or attorney—and find he is sloppily dressed and acts hesitant and unsure, or arrogant and condescending. During your discussion he does not actively listen to you or make eye contact. He appears distracted by other responsibilities. Later you discover he talked about your personal issues with members of your community. How would you feel about engaging this person's services? What opinion would you form about his level of expertise? Would you trust this person? Would you feel a rapport with him? It is doubtful that you would have much confidence in him. Consequently, he probably wouldn't be very effective in helping you, nor would you willingly seek his advice when you needed it. An effective teacher is a professional who works to assist all staff, students, and students' families in a manner that leaves them informed, reassured, and hopeful. An effective teacher goes the extra mile in building relationships with students and everyone who has a vested interest in the students.

This appendix provides suggestions for how to look, think, and behave like a professional. A professional can be defined as one who works in a position that requires specialized knowledge and often long academic preparation and who exhibits a courteous, conscientious, and generally businesslike manner in the workplace. Teachers who fail to demonstrate characteristics of professionalism tend to have more difficulty managing the behavior of their students, so it is appropriate to include tips on professionalism in a book about classroom management. Of course, professionalism alone will not ensure that your students don't misbehave—it's not that simple. However, there is no doubt that if you lack professionalism, you can cause behavioral situations to be worse. You, your students, their families, and your colleagues will benefit if you maintain a vision of yourself as a professional and demonstrate professionalism at all times. For additional information on how to manage your classroom in your first year of teaching, see *The Tough Kid New Teacher Book* (Sopris West, 2003; Pacific Northwest Publishing, available 2010).

Read the suggestions below, discuss them with your mentors, and reflect on whether you are exhibiting professional qualities. Keep this information in mind as you work through the tasks in this book.

 Build a professional relationship with each of your students.

Students need to believe that you have their best interests at heart and that you will do everything in your power to help them succeed in your class and throughout the school. Building positive relationships with your students is an important component of any successful classroom management plan. There are many strategies you can use to achieve this goal. The first step in building this relationship is to learn students' names and use their names to greet them each day. Greeting each student by name demonstrates that you are aware of and interested in each student as an individual.

Beyond this first easy step of using students' names, the concept of building relationships gets a little less clear-cut. Building a relationship with your students is like being a great tour guide. Imagine that you arrange a group tour in a foreign country where you cannot speak or read the language and the culture is very different from your own. Your ideal tour guide will have enough leadership ability and organizational skill to keep the group together and safe and to take you where you want to go, ensuring that everyone has a good time in the process. This tour guide's main responsibility is to be a leader, not a friend. She will make sure you feel that she is interested in you, that she enjoys your company, and that she has your best interests at heart. So, be a good tour guide—be a leader. Organize your classroom, orchestrate student behavior, and let every student know that he or she is important to you. Avoid any effort to be a friend or peer, to be cool or trendy. The students need you to be their professional guide on this journey you take together.

Building positive relationships with students does not mean that you should cut them a break by being lenient with your rules and consequences. Always enforce the rules in a consistent, calm, pleasant, professional, and nonnegotiable manner. Students need the structure and safety of your organized and consistent Classroom Management and Discipline Plan. See Chapter 3 for details on creating this plan.

To build and maintain a positive relationship with students, avoid shutting down on a student who has misbehaved or been disrespectful to you—no matter how badly or how often. Don't take student behavior personally! Some students may even actively strive to push you away. Remember that you are the adult in this daily adventure. Even the student who seriously misbehaved on Tuesday needs a friendly greeting and a fresh start on Wednesday morning.

Keep in mind that you are modeling how to build positive relationships for your students. As an educator, you are not only building and maintaining your relationships, but you are also showing your students how to build relationships with their peers and the adults on campus. If you find you are struggling to either build or maintain a positive relationship with one student or perhaps several students, try these suggestions:

- Sponsor after-school activities.

- Take a walk and have a conversation with a group of students.

- Implement class meetings.

- Find out more about your students through the use of interest inventories or reinforcement menus.

- Celebrate the good times.

- Ask a colleague to join you for a home visit.

- Invite a small group of students to have lunch with you.

- Read a book recommended by students and then share your opinion of the book with them.

- Greet students verbally, with handshakes, or with high fives.

- At dismissal, use specific praise with students' names for a job well done!

Remember the "I" in STOIC—positive interactions build positive relationships! See Chapter 1, Task 5: Maintain Positive Expectations for more tips on how to keep your relationships positive. Also see pp. 6–9 in the Introduction for suggestions on cultural competence—that is, how to work effectively with students and families from backgrounds that are different from yours.

 Build professional relationships with your students' families.

Plan ahead to build a professional relationship with each student's family. This is discussed in more detail in Chapter 1, Task 7: Initiate and Maintain Family Contacts. Families do not want you to be their friend or their child's friend. They want you to guide their child on her journey, to use the metaphor from above, to successfully learn the essential skills and competencies of your grade level or subject. They expect you to keep the child's best interests at heart. Keep families informed about their child's progress on this journey.

Building relationships and connecting with families supports not only them but also your students, your class, and your school community. To collaborate with and support the families of your students, keep these strategies in mind:

- Establish a rapport and positive communication.

- Respect the confidentiality of the information you have regarding their children.

- Provide reassurance.

- Be open to family input.

- Be compassionate and communicate with families often.

If you have to talk to the family about a misbehavior their child has exhibited, keep the focus of the discussion on how the behavior is interfering with their child's academic and behavioral progress. When you focus on the child, the family will be far more responsive to supporting you than if you talk about how the child's behavior affects you or the other students in the class. Avoid getting defensive if the family is critical of you. Ask a colleague or mentor to join you for a family conference if you are unsure how to proceed. Remember that you are the professional—keep the focus on what can be done to help the child be successful.

Build professional and collaborative relationships with your colleagues.

As a first-year teacher, you are entering a preexisting social structure. There are formal relationships such as grade-level or departmental colleagues as well as informal structures of friends and other alliances. In some schools you may find cliques or groups who do not like or respect other groups. Until you have been on staff for a period of time, be careful not to get caught up in these alliances. Administrative teams and principals also have their own styles and strategies to get the job done. It's vitally important that you are aware of their preferred methods and the tone of their professional relationships with colleagues. Treat everyone with dignity and respect: teachers, administrators, and clerical, custodial, and food service staff. You are the new kid on the block and need to act with humility while you learn the systems and structures of the school.

Ask questions, volunteer to assist committees, and be flexible, cooperative, prompt, and optimistic—all professional qualities. If you work toward building positive relationships with colleagues, they will be more open to planning with you and you will learn more from each other. Avoid criticizing institutional traditions that you don't understand or that existed before you began teaching. Avoid gossip, and don't get pulled into negative, unproductive groups.

As you get to know the staff, seek out mentors—people you feel comfortable going to for advice and assistance. For example, if you have a student who consistently misbehaves and your attempts to help her improve her behavior have been ineffective, you should not hesitate to ask a fellow teacher for additional ideas. Seeking collegial assistance is a sign of professional strength, not weakness. This may be most clearly demonstrated by professionals in the field of medicine. When faced with a puzzling situation, most physicians discuss the case with other physicians. Teachers can and should exhibit this same level of collegial problem-solving.

> *Seek out mentors—people you feel comfortable going to for advice and assistance.*

Be an active problem-solver. When faced with a problem—for example, a student is not behaving responsibly or is not making adequate academic progress—the teacher who is demonstrating professionalism analyzes the problem and takes responsibility for seeking and implementing a solution. On the other hand, a teacher who is not acting professionally tends to blame the problem on someone else or feels that someone else should solve the problem (or both). The teacher who is demonstrating professionalism continues to try various strategies until a solution is found—he or she never gives up. Keep Eleanor Roosevelt's words in mind: "We have never failed unless we have ceased to try."

(continued on p. 422)

Tips for the First-Year Teacher

Shelley Jones, co-author of the *Read Well* curriculum, offers these tips on collaboration for first-year teachers:

Most of the young or first-year teachers that I've worked with as a mentor or as a supervising teacher expressed great appreciation for my support, help, and collaboration with both the details of running a classroom and big issues such as discipline and lesson plans. Some of the questions these young teachers asked were:

→   How and where do I get posters and decorations to put up on my walls?

→   How do I use the district computer system for reporting grades?

→   What do I do at staff meetings? (Is it OK to grade papers at the meeting?)

→   Do I have a budget for printing?

→   How do I get copies of assignments for my students?

→   What do I do when my students have no materials?

→   What do I do when my students need counseling?

→   What do I do if I think a student is being abused?

As a result of my experiences, I would say the following five things are really important for a first-year teacher:

1. **Request (or find your own) mentor.**

    A mentor is another teacher or someone else in the educational field who can help you plan for your class, offer tips and advice, answer questions, and provide you with supplemental materials. Ideally, your mentor teaches in your school at your grade level.

    Trading observations and evaluations with your mentor can be valuable training. Your mentor can observe you teach and write an evaluation, and you should be asked to do the same for your mentor. Observe, evaluate, and talk with each other as often as possible—perhaps weekly to begin with, and then monthly.

A small number of new teachers seem to think they know it all. I've found they can be the most difficult to help, and yet they often need the most assistance. More than anything they need a strong mentor presence.

2. **Attend a CHAMPS training.**

Attend a CHAMPS training prior to the start of the school year. If it's not offered in your district, actively seek out a training opportunity. Take your mentor along with you. If you are unable to attend a training, create your own—ask your mentor to guide you through the CHAMPS book and encourage the less experienced teachers (or other first-year teachers) in your building to form a CHAMPS work group. Use the Peer Discussion questions in Appendix B as a guide to working through each chapter.

3. **Invite your principal into your classroom on a regular basis.**

Tell your principal that you welcome his or her informal and formal observations. Most inexperienced teachers think I'm crazy when I make this suggestion. However, frequent visits to your classroom allow your principal to become familiar with your teaching style and to know what kinds of training she or he can offer privately or during staff meetings to meet your needs. It's a wonderful feeling to know that your principal is invested in your future and wants you to succeed as a teacher! Also, your comfort level with being observed will increase at every visit.

4. **Get out of your classroom and observe.**

Whenever possible, take the time (yes, even your prep time) to get out of your own classroom and observe other teachers. There is nothing more powerful than seeing a master teacher at work! Once again, involve your mentor and principal. They should be able to identify master teachers in both your building and your district.

5. **Ask questions. Ask for help.**

ASK, ASK, ASK! No one knows you need help unless you ask. No question is too silly or dumb. Every question is an opportunity to learn. You will undoubtedly make mistakes in your first year of teaching—turn every one of those mistakes into a learning opportunity. Ask your mentor how you can improve and constantly strive for success.

Your professional and collaborative relationships will also benefit if you respect the confidentiality of both students and colleagues. You should not discuss your students outside of school, especially if you live in the community where you teach. In addition, unless you are participating in a school-sponsored problem-solving procedure, avoid talking about school business or the concerns of your co-workers.

For example, imagine that another teacher is not giving you the help and support you need regarding a student who both of you teach. The most professional response is to go directly to this person, discuss your concerns, and ask for more assistance. It would be highly unprofessional to discuss the problem with other teachers or talk about the problem during a family-teacher conference. Again, look at the medical profession as an example. A physician can and should discuss cases confidentially with colleagues at work. However, it is inappropriate and unprofessional for her to talk about a patient or colleagues at a dinner party. As a teaching professional, you owe your students and fellow staff members the same level of professionalism that they expect and deserve from their doctors. Be aware that in some schools, discussions in the faculty room may border on being unprofessional—you may hear teachers discussing students in a hostile, rude, or sarcastic manner. If this happens in your school, just be sure that you are not a contributor. Regardless of the behavior of others, maintain your high level of professional behavior.

> A teacher should try to project a relaxed and confident manner.

 Act in a professional manner.

The definition of how to act in a professional manner is somewhat subjective, but a good model for professional behavior is, for example, a physician or an attorney. Think about the demeanor you want and expect from your doctor or lawyer. Most of us probably prefer someone who seems knowledgeable, confident, and comfortable—but not haughty and arrogant. We are generally uncomfortable with someone who seems hesitant or insecure, doesn't seem to like her job, or complains about her working conditions. We may not trust someone who doesn't make eye contact, and we may find it hard to interact with someone who mumbles when he talks to us.

A teacher should try to project a relaxed and confident manner. You do not need to be relaxed and confident at all times (very few of us are capable of this!), but you should act relaxed and confident. In fact, there will probably be times when you are unsure of yourself or unsure of how to handle a situation. While it's not necessary to give the impression that you know what to do when you really don't, do keep in mind that you are a professional, you provide a valuable service to your students and the community, and you can solve any problem—eventually. Ask yourself whether you would rather go to a physician who bluffs and blusters when he is unsure or one who confidently says, "I am unsure what is the best course of action, but I will find out."

FOR MORE INFORMATION

Survival Guide for the First-Year Special Education Teacher by Mary Kemper Cohen, Maureen Gale, and Joyce M. Meyer (1994). This book is a great resource for all teachers—special educators, general education teachers, and paraprofessionals—working in traditional or inclusive school settings. It provides easy-to-use suggestions for organizing classrooms, planning and record-keeping, getting lessons ready for substitute teachers, building collaborative partnerships, managing stress, and working with parents, administrators, and fellow teachers. Published by Council for Exceptional Children, http://www.cec.sped.org.

Survive and Thrive! A Laminated Reference Card for Special Education Teachers by Maureen Gale, M.Ed. This two-sided card covers topics such as organizing your classroom, ways to improve your delivery of instruction, collaborating with colleagues and parents, and tips on data collection. Published by DayOne Publishing, http://dayonepublishing.com/Educational/S_and_T/index.html.

The Tough Kid New Teacher Book, by Ginger Rhode, William R. Jenson, and Daniel P. Morgan (2003, 2009). Easy-to-use manual chock-full of tips, suggestions, and proven tactics to help the first-year teacher thrive. Available Dec. 2009 from Pacific Northwest Publishing, www.pacificnwpublish.com.

Professionalism also includes dependability. As a professional, you need to arrive at work on time, fulfill your various duties (for example, supervising a bus loading area for two weeks) without needing reminders, attend staff meetings and give your full attention to the proceedings, and complete attendance and grade reports on time.

 Present a professional appearance.

Your appearance affects the impression others have of you—perhaps even more than you realize. In addition to making sure that you dress neatly and cleanly, consider the degree of formality most appropriate for your work attire. Although wearing high-powered business suits is not necessary for most teachers, a teacher who is dressed in baggy sweat pants and a holey, coffee-stained sweater definitely gives the wrong impression—to students, students' families, other teachers, and administrators.

Susan Isaacs, a *Safe & Civil Schools* trainer, shared a tip she received from a principal: "If you don't change your clothes when you get home from work, you weren't dressed for work."

> *If you don't change your clothes when you get home from work, you weren't dressed for work.*

Carefully select an appropriate level of formality for your school attire. For a PE teacher who frequently provides demonstrations to students, wearing nice workout clothing is probably perfectly reasonable. However, workout clothes are probably not appropriate for classroom teachers. Specific questions like "Should men always wear a tie?" and "Are casual pants acceptable?" should be answered within the context of your particular school and the community's standards. As a general rule, dress with a level of formality that is typical of the most professional staff in your district. If you are unsure about what attire is considered appropriate, ask your administrator.

 Engage in ongoing professional development, including reflecting on your own teaching practices.

Professionals are expected to continually learn and grow in their chosen fields. For example, most physicians do some things differently today than when they first started practicing. Professional development requires both keeping up to date on new information in your field and being willing to look at your own behavior with a critical eye. "What am I doing that is working effectively? What is not working effectively?" After identifying strategies and techniques that are not working effectively, the true professional is always looking for a better way—from peers, from staff development, from professional books, and from the research literature.

The information in this book, along with the Self-Assessment Checklists, will help you examine and, as necessary, modify your behavior management practices. In addition, you should work with and learn from colleagues. The Peer Discussion Worksheets in Appendix B help facilitate a collaborative approach to professional development. The questions from these worksheets can guide a whole staff, a small study group, or even just you and a partner in discussing the skills and procedures suggested in this book. In these discussions, recognize that there are no dumb questions. Ask—be a lifelong learner and enjoy the adventure you're about to begin!

Schoolwide
IMPLEMENTATION OF CHAMPS

INTRODUCTION

This appendix clarifies the concept of what CHAMPS is—and is not—and then suggests three major considerations for schoolwide implementation:

1. Create clear expectations from administrators regarding the outcome of teachers' implementation of CHAMPS in the classroom.

2. Develop staff agreement regarding which procedures will be schoolwide and which will be unique to each classroom.

3. Create a continuous improvement cycle for schoolwide implementation.

Special thanks to Maureen Gale for her contributions to this Appendix!

CHAMPS is an *approach*, not a program.

CHAMPS is an approach. It's a way of thinking, not a fixed program, so the process of implementing CHAMPS schoolwide is difficult to describe in precise terms. If CHAMPS were a canned program, it would be easy to describe implementation: "All staff should follow steps A, B, and C . . ." These fixed steps would be easy to train, and the program would be easy to monitor because all teachers would essentially be doing the same thing. The problem is that no set of simple steps can help manage and motivate all, or even most, students. As the introduction to this book states, CHAMPS is designed to help the classroom teacher develop (or fine-tune) an effective classroom management plan that is proactive, positive, and instructional. CHAMPS guides the teacher in how to be effective in making decisions about managing behavior—everything from how the physical setting is organized to the teaching of expectations to when and how to provide positive feedback. The CHAMPS approach guides the teacher in making research and data-based decisions about classroom management; however, final decisions about managing the behavior of their students are left up to the teacher. This approach allows the teacher to reap the benefits of research-based strategies and also provides the teacher the opportunity to feel comfortable including his or her individual personality and style choices when designing a Classroom Management and Discipline Plan.

Making those initial decisions and then implementing a unique classroom management plan is the beginning of a yearlong process. Any time a student, a group of students, or a whole class is misbehaving or is not fully motivated, the CHAMPS approach dictates that the teacher modify some aspect or aspects of his management plan to try to solve that behavioral or motivational problem. If his management plan works, he can target another behavioral or motivational concern and tweak his plan to have a positive effect on that problem. If those tweaks are ineffective, he should experiment with different variables of his plan to seek a positive effect on the target concern. Those trained in behavior analysis will notice that CHAMPS is simply a user-friendly how-to manual for implementing behavior analysis in the classroom. When the CHAMPS approach is used effectively, the result is the implementation of a proactive, positive, and instructional classroom management plan.

One implication of this "uncanned" approach to student behavior and motivation is that you can never say, "I tried CHAMPS and it didn't work." You can legitimately say, "The things I have implemented to date have not worked"—and within the CHAMPS approach, the logical response to that statement would be, "So the next things that I am going to focus on are . . ."

A second implication of the uncanned nature of CHAMPS is that when implementing the approach schoolwide, school administrators need to be very careful to avoid inadvertently implying to staff that they must follow steps A, B, and C. For example, some schools and districts have told teachers that they must post CHAMPS expectations in the classroom. Though there may be a compelling reason to consider doing this (discussed later in this Appendix), some teachers may consequently think that all there is to CHAMPS is putting up some posters. Using a visual display of the CHAMPS acronym has many benefits; however, the careful reader of this book will recognize that whether or not to use visual displays of CHAMPS expectations is only one of many decisions that the teacher needs to make when defining her Classroom Management and Discipline Plan.

So, truly implementing CHAMPS schoolwide requires that the entire school staff (both professional and noncertified employees) engage in proactive thinking about how to manage behavior and also in active problem-solving—including analyzing data and designing and implementing positive strategies to solve behavior and motivational problems. Staff will work together to manipulate the STOIC variables (Structure, Teach, Observe, Interact, Correct) to continuously refine and improve the strategies used to help students—both individuals and whole classes—learn to behave responsibly and be academically successful.

> *Truly implementing CHAMPS schoolwide requires that the entire school staff engage in proactive thinking about how to manage behavior.*

SCHOOLWIDE *1*
CONSIDERATION

Create clear expectations from administrators regarding the outcome of teachers' implementation of CHAMPS in the classroom

When implementing CHAMPS on a schoolwide basis, develop agreements between administrators and teachers regarding the expected outcomes of effective implementation. To do this, faculty and staff must believe that any change in student behavior starts with the adults in the school changing their approach to behavior management. Everyone must understand: "If we want good student behavior, we must teach it!"

The outcomes of an effective management plan are threefold:

- *High rates of academic engagement.* When a teacher's management plan is working well, students should be on task and academically focused at least 90 percent of the time or more. If engagement is less than 90 percent, the teacher should work to solve the problem.

- *Consistently respectful interactions.* When a teacher's management plan is working, students should be treating each other and the teacher with respect, and the teacher should be treating the students with respect. If interactions are not consistently respectful, the teacher should work to solve the problem.

- *The teacher's posted expectations and observed student behavior should match.* The classroom teacher or a visitor to the classroom should be able to observe students behaving in a manner that demonstrates compliance with the teacher's expectations—that is, students should be doing what the teacher expects of them. If there is not a match, the teacher needs to work to solve this problem. Note that this is a great reason for teachers to post expectations when CHAMPS is implemented schoolwide—if the rules and behavioral expectations are clearly displayed for all to see, teachers will find it easier to teach and enforce the expectations and students will find it hard to argue that they are not breaking the rules or violating an expectation.

This focus on the outcomes of effective management has several implications. *First and foremost, if it isn't broken, don't try to fix it!* If student behavior is engaged and respectful, and meets the teacher's expectations, no one should tell that teacher he needs to do something different. Second, no administrator should be visiting teacher's rooms with a "21-Point CHAMPS Checklist" to determine whether teachers are implementing the CHAMPS approach. Rather, use the decision-making strategies to tweak what the teacher believes she needs to improve based on the data collection tools included in Chapter 6. Third, if any of the problems exist—low levels of engagement, disrespectful interactions, or students not following the teacher's expectations—the teacher needs to do something differently. In other words, if it is broken, you have to try to fix it. This third concept means that a teacher cannot say, "I implemented CHAMPS and it did not work." If student behavior is unacceptable, the teacher needs to experiment with the STOIC variables until he finds a strategy that solves the problem.

SCHOOLWIDE CONSIDERATION 2

Develop staff agreements about which procedures will be schoolwide and which will be unique to each classroom

If your school or district is considering implementing CHAMPS on a systemwide basis, a leadership team should be organized that includes the building administrator and representative classroom teachers and support staff. The team should work together to determine what will be standard procedures, routines, and expectations throughout the school and what will be left to each teacher to decide for her own classroom.

As the author of the program, I strongly urge administrators to leave most decisions about expectations for classroom behavior to each individual classroom teacher. For example, each teacher should be able to decide expectations such as whether students can talk to each other during independent work, whether students are to raise their hand to speak during discussion activities, and when students can sharpen their pencils. Teachers need to make these decisions based on their professional judgment about what works best given their personal style, the needs of the students, and the nature of the subject being taught. Do not, in the name of consistency or clarity, take away teachers' ability to create their unique classroom.

However, the leadership team may want to discuss and make some decisions regarding schoolwide implementation of the CHAMPS approach. Some suggested topics for discussion are:

Organization for communicating expectations to students.
Chapter 4 introduces the CHAMPS acronym along with some alternatives—TEAM, MAC, and ACHIEVE. In addition, this chapter suggests ways to communicate expectations to students—for example, T-charts, table display boards, and icons. Consider developing agreements about whether T-charts

or an acronym will be used, and if an acronym, which one. For example, an elementary school that encompasses prekindergarten through fifth grade might decide to use the TEAM acronym with icons for prekindergarten and kindergarten, and the CHAMPS acronym with descriptive words for grades 1 through 5.

Required posting of visual displays. Some schools have required that all teachers post CHAMPS expectations for teacher-directed instruction, independent seatwork, cooperative groups, and tests. There are three potential advantages to this. First, if students have several different teachers during the day, as in most middle schools, the visual displays (using icons or words) make it easy for students to learn the unique expectations of each teacher. If they forget, they can easily look at the display and determine, for example, "Is it OK for me to get up and sharpen my pencil now, or do I need to ask permission?" A second advantage to posted displays of basic expectations is that administrators or other observers can easily see that student behavior matches the teacher's expectations—that is, the student was not rude or disrespectful by getting up to sharpen her pencil because in this teacher's room, during this activity, that is the teacher's expectation. Third, posted expectations can make the substitute teacher's job much easier and can decrease the degree to which students play games with substitutes by saying, "Our teacher doesn't do it that way." See below for more information about CHAMPS for substitute teachers.

Behavior in common areas. Teachers should have great flexibility to design their own expectations for classroom behaviors. However, schoolwide consistency is essential on the playground and in hallways, restrooms, and cafeterias. Although this strategy is not specifically addressed in this book, some schools have used the CHAMPS acronym to clarify expectations for behavior in these areas. Though clear and consistent expectations are important, they are only part of the picture. *Safe & Civil Schools* has designed specific programs to address behavior management issues related to common areas. These comprehensive programs suggest ways to examine structural considerations in common areas, provide detailed lessons on expectations, examine patterns of adult supervision, and provide training for supervisors.

Consider using *Foundations: Establishing Positive Discipline Policies* to guide a comprehensive process for improving your common areas. The process also includes designing schoolwide Guidelines for Success that can be used as an acronym to teach common area expectations to all students. Also note that *Safe & Civil Schools* offers specific programs for managing bus behavior, behavior on the playground and in the cafeteria, and hallway, restroom, and tardiness issues:

Cafeteria Discipline: Positive Techniques for Lunchroom Supervision (Video) by R. S. Sprick (1995). Eugene, OR: Pacific Northwest Publishing. For grades K–8.

In the Driver's Seat: A Roadmap to Managing Student Behavior on the Bus (CD-ROM and DVD program) by R. S. Sprick, L. Swartz, and A. Glang (2007). Eugene, OR: Pacific Northwest Publishing and Oregon Center for Applied Sciences. For grades K–12.

On the Playground: A Guide to Playground Management (CD-ROM) by R. S. Sprick, L. Swartz, and A. Glang (2005). Eugene, OR: Pacific Northwest Publishing and Oregon Center for Applied Sciences. For grades K–6.

START on Time! Safe Transitions and Reduced Tardies (CD-ROM) by R. S. Sprick (2003). Eugene, OR: Pacific Northwest Publishing. For grades 6–12.

STUDENT EXPECTATIONS WITH SUBSTITUTE TEACHERS

By creating an environment where expectations are consistent schoolwide, you can make life much easier for substitutes. Include expectations for student behavior with substitute teachers in your schoolwide plan. Student behavior will be more consistent when a substitute is present, and teachers will return from their days off to more peaceful classrooms. When students clearly understand that the behavior expectations are the same whether you are the teacher that day or not, everyone benefits. If substitutes know what the general expectations are, they will be more confident in their interactions with students and will be able to teach and maintain the expectations. They can spend more time teaching and less time dealing with misbehaving students. On average, students will spend more than a full year of their K–12 school experience with substitute teachers (Sykes, 2002). That year should and could be a productive and rewarding time for both students and substitutes.

For more information on organizing a school to provide effective support for substitute teachers and on training your cadre of substitutes in the CHAMPS approach, see *Behavior Management for Substitutes* (2009), available from Pacific Northwest Publishing.

POLICIES ENFORCED BY MULTIPLE ADULTS

Another component of schoolwide discipline to consider is ensuring that all adults are consistent in implementing your school's policies for dress code, truancy, tardiness, and other code-of-conduct violations. CHAMPS does not specifically address these issues, but whether or not you are implementing CHAMPS schoolwide, all staff must strive to be consistent in implementing these kinds of schoolwide policies and procedures. In addition, schoolwide consistency is essential for routines and procedures such as assemblies, arrival, dismissal, and transitions (passing between classes or changing schoolwide activities).

ATTENTION SIGNAL

Chapter 2 discussed the importance of an attention signal in the classroom. If CHAMPS is being implemented schoolwide, consider addressing this with your leadership team and faculty. In order to monitor all students, all faculty and staff should agree to use the same signal. If everyone uses the same signal, that signal can be used consistently in the cafeteria, auditorium, and any other school location.

SCHOOLWIDE *3*
CONSIDERATION

Create a continuous improvement cycle for CHAMPS implementation

Because CHAMPS is an approach, not a program, and because a good management plan is fluid (for example, more highly structured in the last month of school than in the second-to-last month of school), teachers should develop a mindset that emphasizes continuous improvement. Any professional, such as the physician you trust with your health, should be a lifelong learner of her craft. No matter how skilled the teacher, every classroom has some students who can learn to behave more responsibly or increase their motivation, so every teacher should periodically reflect on his or her classroom management plan and the needs of individual students. Below are some suggestions for creating an ongoing dialogue with faculty and staff about CHAMPS implementation. Note that these different suggestions can be combined in creative ways to keep staff thinking and talking about using CHAMPS as a vehicle for developing a "continuous improvement model."

> ***Create initial inservice training opportunities at the building or district level.*** The schoolwide implementation of CHAMPS can be enhanced if all the teachers receive engaging, practical, and entertaining inservice. Initial training is best when conducted during the summer months, with additional refresher sessions conducted at least quarterly where people can discuss what is and is not working. If training begins during the school year, ideally plan to devote a three-hour class to each of the nine chapters. Most class time should be spent discussing each chapter using the Peer Discussion Worksheets provided in the following pages. Note that there is no Peer Discussion Worksheet for Chapter 6 because most of that chapter is about specific data collection tools. Discussion on this chapter should be about the tools and when and how to use them.

Inservice provided by groups within the school. Some schools that have implemented CHAMPS by grade level or schoolwide have a system wherein different groups—grade levels, departments, teams, or professional learning communities within the school—are assigned to review and lead a discussion about each chapter for the entire staff. For example, each month one grade level is responsible for reviewing the content and facilitating a staff discussion about a particular chapter (in December, the third-grade team will present and facilitate discussion of Chapter 4). Note that the Peer Discussion Worksheets can be used to create these professional exchanges of ideas.

New staff trained by experienced teachers. One problem with a schoolwide approach is how to train new teachers and staff who join the school two or three years after the initial training and follow-up sessions. Some schools appoint individuals or teams of experienced CHAMPS teachers to be "in charge" of particular chapters. Not only does this allow the trainers to develop a level of expertise with their chapters, it also prepares the training team for when a member of the team leaves the school. The team member can then be replaced the following year by a new trainer who will benefit from assisting the remaining trainer. This process helps to ensure the sustainability of schoolwide CHAMPS implementation. With this training model, each person is responsible for meeting with new teachers and experienced teachers new to the school sometime during the first half of the school year to introduce the content, assign the reading, and then facilitate the Peer Discussion questions.

Data collection assignments. Chapter 6 includes a variety of data collection tools. At left is the suggested calendar plan for using these tools. The building administrator can assign staff to conduct these data collection tasks and schedule opportunities to discuss what teachers learned from the experience. Depending on other priorities, the principal may decide to implement the entire plan or only one or a few of these data collection tasks.

Suggested data collection calendar

Week 3	Student Interviews or Quiz (Chapter 4, Task 3)
Week 4 or 5	CHAMPS versus Daily Reality Rating (Chapter 6, Tool 1)
2nd Month	Ratio of Interactions Monitoring (Chapter 6, Tool 2)
3rd Month (early)	Misbehavior(s) Recording (Chapter 6, Tool 3)
3rd Month (late)	Grade Book Analysis (Chapter 6, Tool 4)
4th month	On-Task Behavior Recording (Chapter 6, Tool 5)
January (early)	CHAMPS versus Daily Reality Rating (Chapter 6, Tool 1)
January (late)	Opportunities to Respond (Chapter 6, Tool 6)
February (early)	Ratio of Interactions Monitoring (Chapter 6, Tool 2)
February (late)	On-Task Behavior Recording (Chapter 6, Tool 5)
March (early)	Grade Book Analysis (Chapter 6, Tool 4)
April (after spring break)	CHAMPS versus Daily Reality Rating (Chapter 6, Tool 1)
Last two weeks	Family/Student Satisfaction Survey (Chapter 6, Tool 7)

ADDITIONAL TRAINING TIPS

- Administrative support for schoolwide CHAMPS training should be visible, positive, and documented.
- Establish a site coordinator and CHAMPS training team.
- Identify willing and "able" trainers.
- Define your schoolwide vision.
- Identify who will facilitate training.
- Identify who will be trained first.
- Identify where training takes place.
- Identify when training will begin.
- Define expectations for participants after training.
- Establish a budget for substitutes, materials, and snacks.
- Continually reflect on your training. Is it meeting the needs of your staff?
- Use data to support continuous training and identify focus.
- Improve sustainability by training new trainers each year and provide refresher trainings for staff.

Because CHAMPS is an approach, not a progam, teachers should develop a mindset that emphasizes continuous improvement.

There is no Peer Discussion Worksheet for Chapter 6 because most of that chapter is about data collection. Discussion on this chapter should be about the tools and when and how to implement them.

PEER DISCUSSION WORKSHEETS

On the following pages are suggested topics for peer discussion that correspond to each of the tasks within each chapter. These worksheets can be used for the following:

- College credit class
- Full faculty study as suggested above
- Small study group of interested professionals
- Pair of interested professionals
- Within a mentor/mentee relationship
- Homework assignments for a staff development opportunity offered within a school district

Peer Discussion Worksheet

CHAPTER 1
Develop a Specific Vision for Your Class

Schedule one to two hours with one to five colleagues. Each participant should have read Chapter 1 and worked through the Self-Assessment activities in advance of this discussion time. By discussing each participant's policies, procedures, and questions regarding the tasks in Chapter 1, each participant will gain a deeper understanding of the chapter and learn tips and techniques from colleagues. Begin the discussion by prioritizing the seven tasks. Which task interests participants most? Which task is the next highest priority? This way, if there is not adequate time to discuss all seven tasks, the discussion will focus on the tasks of greatest interest or value to you and the other participants. Work through the prioritized tasks by discussing the questions or topics within that task. Then go on to the next highest priority. Continue this process and complete as many of the tasks as possible within the scheduled time.

TASK 1: UNDERSTAND HOW TO SHAPE BEHAVIOR

A. Identify the three major categories of teacher-based actions for promoting responsible behavior.

B. Identify the three major categories of teacher-based actions to take into account once you have identified the reason a chronic misbehavior may be occurring (for example, the student loves getting attention from other students by making rude comments in class).

C. Have group members discuss whether this organization for categorizing behavior management strategies is useful. Ask them to share specific examples.

TASK 2: UNDERSTAND MOTIVATION

As a group, discuss the classroom implications and examples of the following four concepts related to motivation:

- When a particular behavior occurs repeatedly, it demonstrates a person's level of motivation to engage in that behavior. When a particular behavior does not occur, it demonstrates a person's lack of motivation to engage in that behavior.

- In most cases, when a person engages in a particular behavior, a mix of intrinsic and extrinsic motivational factors prompts it.

- A person's motivation to engage in a particular behavior is affected by the person's proficiency at that behavior.

- A person's level of motivation can be explained as a function of the formula: *Expectancy x Value = Motivation.*

TASK 3: IDENTIFY LONG-RANGE CLASSROOM GOALS

A. Have each group member share his or her goals and explain why he or she chose those goals.

B. As a group, examine each member's goals individually, giving positive and constructive feedback on the content and language.

C. Have each group member share how he or she plans to communicate long-range goals to students, students' families, and school administration.

TASK 4: DEVELOP GUIDELINES FOR SUCCESS

A. If your school does not have schoolwide Guidelines for Success, have each group member share his or her guidelines with the other group members. Brainstorm at least six different strategies, other than those identified in the text, for helping students understand and internalize the Guidelines for Success.

B. If your school does not have schoolwide Guidelines for Success, discuss:

- Whether it would be worth trying to develop schoolwide agreement so that all staff emphasize the same set of attitudes, characteristics, and traits.

- What actions would be necessary to get a schoolwide development process started.

TASK 5: MAINTAIN POSITIVE EXPECTATIONS

A. Have group members share what they do to avoid developing low expectations for a student who is chronically behaviorally challenging.

B. Objectively consider whether the atmosphere at your school is one of positive expectations for students (for example, evaluate the comments about students that are made in the faculty room). If it is not, identify things group members might do to help your whole staff develop more positive expectations.

TASK 6: IMPLEMENT EFFECTIVE INSTRUCTIONAL PRACTICES

A. Have each group member give a specific example of how he or she will use each of the following strategies to generate student enthusiasm and increase students' intrinsic motivation to engage in desired tasks and behaviors.

- • Explain the task or behavior clearly.

- • Explain how the task or behavior will be useful to students.

- • Give the students a vision of what they will be able to do eventually.

- • Relate the new task or behavior to previously learned skills.

- • Rally student enthusiasm and energy for the task or behavior.

B. Have each group member identify one or two aspects of his or her presentational style that he or she intends to work to improve over the course of the year.

C. As a group, create a list of ideas beyond those suggested in this program for actively involving students in lessons and increasing Opportunities to Respond.

D. As a group, discuss the relationship among course content, course objectives, and course evaluation.

E. Have each group member describe what he or she will do to ensure high rates of student success.

F. Have each group member share the ways he or she gives students timely performance feedback.

TASK 7: INITIATE AND MAINTAIN FAMILY CONTACTS

A. Have each group member share his or her strategy for making initial contact with families.

   • Discuss the advantages and feasibility of contacting all students' families before the school year begins.

   • Discuss the advantages and feasibility of contacting only the families of behaviorally challenged and high-needs students.

   • Have group members share any orientation letters they have used.

   • Discuss the advantages and feasibility of making a "Welcome to My Classroom" CD or DVD.

B. Have each group member share his or her strategies for maintaining ongoing contact with families.

   • Have group members share samples of any newsletters they have used.

   • Discuss how a Contact Log might be used to keep records of family contacts.

C. If relevant, discuss strategies for improving communication with families that speak little or no English.

Peer Discussion Worksheet

CHAPTER 2
Organization

With one or more of your colleagues, work through the following discussion topics and activities related to the tasks in Chapter 2. If necessary, refer back to the text for additional ideas or clarification. See the Chapter 1 Peer Discussion Worksheet for suggestions on structuring effective discussion sessions.

TASK 1: ARRANGE AN EFFICIENT DAILY SCHEDULE

A. Have each group member share his or her daily schedule and explain the balance he or she has established among teacher-directed instruction, independent student work, and cooperative group activities.

B. As a group, identify those times and events during the day or class period that are likely to produce more misbehavior. Discuss how you each might proactively address those times or events to reduce the specific misbehavior you have observed.

TASK 2: CREATE A POSITIVE PHYSICAL SPACE

Arrange for the group to visit each group member's room one at a time. Have group members give feedback on the arrangement of desks, the use of bulletin board space, and the general effectiveness of or potential problems with the way each room is arranged.

TASK 3: USE AN ATTENTION SIGNAL

A. Have each group member share what he or she has decided to use for an attention signal and get feedback from the other group members.

B. As a group, discuss how you will provide positive and corrective feedback to students regarding how they respond or don't respond to the signal.

TASK 4: DESIGN EFFECTIVE BEGINNING AND ENDING ROUTINES

For each of the following times or issues, have each group member explain his or her procedures. Provide feedback and help each other solve any problems teachers may be having with a time of the day or a specific activity, transition, procedure, or routine.

- Arrival (immediately before entering the classroom)

- Entering class (before and immediately after the bell rings)

- Opening activities (middle school: taking attendance, dealing with tardy students)

- Opening activities (elementary school)

- Dealing with students who are not prepared with materials

- Dealing with students who are returning after an absence

- End-of-day or end-of-class procedures

- Dismissal (procedures for leaving the classroom)

TASK 5: MANAGE STUDENT ASSIGNMENTS

Have group members explain the procedures they use for managing these aspects of student work. Give each other feedback.

- Assigning classwork and homework

- Collecting completed work

- Keeping records and giving feedback about students' performance and progress

- Dealing with late and missing assignments

TASK 6: MANAGE INDEPENDENT WORK PERIODS

Have group members explain their procedures for managing these aspects of scheduling and monitoring independent work periods. Give each other feedback.

- Assigning work that can be done independently by students

- Scheduling independent work times in a way that maximizes on-task behavior

- Developing a clear vision of what student behavior should look and sound like during work times

- Providing guided practice on tasks and assignments during the first part of the work period

- Developing a specific system for students to ask questions and get help

Peer Discussion Worksheet

CHAPTER 3
Management Plan

With one or more of your colleagues, work through the following discussion topics and activities related to the tasks in Chapter 3. If necessary, refer back to the text for additional ideas or clarification. See the Chapter 1 Peer Discussion Worksheet for suggestions on structuring effective discussion sessions.

TASK 1: DETERMINE THE LEVEL OF CLASSROOM STRUCTURE

A. Have each group member share his or her completed Management and Discipline Planning Questionnaires, both the teacher's and students' versions.

B. Have group members discuss how the level of structure they have identified will affect their Classroom Management and Discipline Plan.

C. Briefly discuss why you should periodically reevaluate the level of structure required for your class. Have each group member identify when he or she will reevaluate the level of structure necessary for his or her class throughout the school year.

TASK 2: DEVELOP AND DISPLAY CLASSROOM RULES

Have each group member share the classroom rules he or she has developed. As a group, give feedback to each person. Discuss the following aspects of classroom rules:

*   Rules should be stated positively.

*   Rules should be specific and refer to observable behaviors.

*   Teachers should plan to teach the rules using positive and negative examples. Plan on ending your lesson with a positive example.

*   Rules should be applicable throughout the class period.

*   Rules should be posted in a prominent, visible location.

TASK 3: CORRECT RULE VIOLATIONS DURING THE FIRST WEEK OF SCHOOL

As a group, discuss the pros and cons of the following instructional correction strategies. Have each group member identify those strategies he or she will plan to use during the first week of school.

- Proximity

- Gentle verbal reprimand

- Discussion

- Family contact

- Humor

- Praise students who are behaving responsibly

- Restitution

- Emotional reaction

TASK 4: ESTABLISH CORRECTIVE CONSEQUENCES FOR RULE VIOLATIONS

A. Have each group member identify whether he or she will use progressive or nonprogressive consequences.

B. As a group, discuss the possible corrective consequences that are reasonable to assign for various infractions of classroom rules.

- Time owed

- Timeout

- Restitution

- Positive practice

- Response cost—loss of points

- Response cost lottery

- Detention

- Demerits

- Behavior Improvement Form

TASK 5: KNOW WHEN AND WHEN NOT TO USE DISCIPLINARY REFERRAL

- Discuss your school's policy regarding office disciplinary referrals.

- Ask your building administrator to share trends and patterns of classroom referrals, such as type of offense or time of day, to determine if there are proactive strategies or interventions that can be implemented to reduce these trends. For example, if insubordination is a frequent problem in many classrooms, all teachers could provide more detailed CHAMPS lessons (see Chapter 4) to teach students how to interact respectfully with people in authority.

Peer Discussion Worksheet

CHAPTER 4

Expectations

With one or more of your colleagues, work through the following discussion topics and activities related to the tasks in Chapter 4. If necessary, refer back to the text for additional ideas or clarification. See the Chapter 1 Peer Discussion Worksheet for suggestions on structuring effective discussion sessions.

INTRODUCTION

A.   Identify the six issues represented by the acronym CHAMPS.

B.   Identify the three steps in the process for communicating expectations.

TASK 1: CLARIFY CHAMPS EXPECTATIONS FOR INSTRUCTIONAL ACTIVITIES

A.   Have each group member share his or her list of major classroom activities or categories of classroom activities. As a group, help each person identify whether he or she has omitted any important activities from the list.

B.   Have group members share their CHAMPS Classroom Activity Worksheets. As a group, give each person feedback on the clarity and thoroughness of his or her expectations. Remember, group members do not have to agree with each other's expectations—their feedback should focus on whether the expectations are specific and detailed enough to be clearly taught to students and consistently monitored and enforced.

TASK 2: CLARIFY CHAMPS EXPECTATIONS FOR TRANSITIONS

A.   Have each group member share his or her list of common transitions or categories of transitions. As a group, help each person identify whether any important transitions were left off the list.

B.   Have group members share their CHAMPS Transition Worksheets. As a group, give each person feedback on the clarity and thoroughness of his or her expectations. Remember, group members do not have to agree with each other's expectations—their feedback should focus on whether the expectations are specific and detailed enough to be clearly taught to students and consistently monitored and enforced.

TASK 3: PREPARE LESSONS TO COMMUNICATE YOUR EXPECTATIONS

A.   Have each group member share his or her ideas for lessons on communicating expectations. In particular, discuss your answers to the following questions about your lessons:

- Do you plan to use the CHAMPS acronym or some other acronym (MAC, TEAM, ACHIEVE) with your students?

- Will you use visual displays within your lessons on expectations?

- Will you use modeling and role-playing within your lessons?

- Will you have students actually practice some of the expectations?

- Will you verify students' understanding of expectations prior to beginning activities?

B.   Discuss how group members may use the icons provided on the CD. Share samples of other visual displays, ideas for modeling and role-playing, and any other ideas.

C.   Have each group member identify how he or she will adapt the teaching of expectations to fit the level of structure his or her class needs. Make a note of additional times throughout the school year when you will re-teach your expectations—after long weekends, holidays, and vacations, and during the last six weeks of school, for example.

D.   Discuss how many days you anticipate teaching these lessons at the beginning of the school year. Identify strategies to reduce the probability that students will get bored with whatever repetition is likely to be required.

Peer Discussion Worksheet

CHAPTER 5
Launch

With one or more of your colleagues, work through the following discussion topics and activities related to the tasks in Chapter 5. If necessary, refer back to the text for additional ideas or clarification. See the Chapter 1 Peer Discussion Worksheet for suggestions on structuring effective discussion sessions.

TASK 1: SUMMARIZE YOUR CLASSROOM MANAGEMENT AND DISCIPLINE PLAN

Have each group member share his or her completed Classroom Management and Discipline Plan form. As a group, give feedback and problem-solve any areas that are giving anyone difficulty.

TASK 2: MAKE FINAL PREPARATIONS FOR DAY ONE

ONLY IF YOU HAVE TIME, have group members share what they have done in terms of final preparations for the first day of school. Specifically, individual members may want to share ideas for an initial activity that students can work on when they arrive and for how they plan to address families who want to take their time on the first day.

TASK 3: IMPLEMENT YOUR PLAN ON DAY ONE

A. ONLY IF YOU HAVE TIME, have group members share ideas and plans for displaying their schedule for the first day of school, greeting students as they arrive, getting students' attention when the bell rings, communicating essential information in the first 10 minutes, and teaching their attention signal.

B. Have group members discuss how they will begin to use the three-step process (teaching, observing behavior, and giving feedback) to communicate behavioral expectations.

TASK 4: IMPLEMENT YOUR PLAN ON DAYS 2 THROUGH 20 (THE FIRST FOUR WEEKS)

A. Have group members who are elementary teachers share suggestions for helping their students learn the behavioral expectations of specialists such as music, PE, and computer teachers.

B. Have individual group members share any quizzes and interview protocols they have developed to verify student understanding of behavioral expectations. Group members should give each other feedback. If applicable, work in pairs and arrange to interview each other's students.

TASK 5: PREPARE YOUR STUDENTS FOR SPECIAL CIRCUMSTANCES

Have group members share ideas on how they can teach their behavioral expectations to new students who enter their classrooms. In particular, discuss the viability and logistics of creating an individual "Welcome to Our Class" video and a schoolwide Newcomers Club. Have individual group members share any behavioral expectations they have developed for unique events.

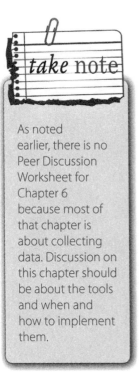

take note

As noted earlier, there is no Peer Discussion Worksheet for Chapter 6 because most of that chapter is about collecting data. Discussion on this chapter should be about the tools and when and how to implement them.

Peer Discussion Worksheet

CHAPTER 7
Motivation

With one or more of your colleagues, work through the following discussion topics and activities related to the tasks in Chapter 7. If necessary, refer back to the text for additional ideas or clarification. See Chapter 1 Peer Discussion Worksheet for suggestions on structuring effective discussion sessions.

TASK 1: BUILD POSITIVE RELATIONSHIPS WITH STUDENTS

A. Have each group member identify situations (times of day or types of activities) when he or she provides noncontingent attention to several or many students.

B. Consider having group members pair up and observe each other for part of a day (the first ten minutes of the day as students arrive, for example) in order to give each other feedback on the quantity and quality of the noncontingent attention they provide their students.

C. Discuss the feasibility and logistics of encouraging all staff members to make an effort to give individual students as much noncontingent attention as possible.

TASK 2: PROVIDE POSITIVE FEEDBACK

A. Have each group member give specific correct and incorrect examples of positive feedback that reflects each of the following statements:

  • Feedback should be accurate.

  • Feedback should be specific and descriptive.

  • Feedback should be contingent.

  • Feedback should be age-appropriate.

- Feedback should be given immediately

- Feedback should be given in a manner that fits your own style.

B. Have one group member describe a student who reacts badly to positive feedback. As a group, discuss possible strategies.

TASK 3: PROVIDE INTERMITTENT CELEBRATIONS

Have each group member identify whether his or her class is likely to require the rare, moderate, or frequent use of intermittent celebrations to keep students motivated and enthusiastic. Have each person identify two or three reward ideas appropriate for individual students in their class and two or three reward ideas appropriate for the class as a whole.

TASK 4: STRIVE TO PROVIDE A HIGH RATIO OF POSITIVE INTERACTIONS

- As a group, discuss the concept of the Criticism Trap. Have group members come up with specific examples from their experience.

- Have each group member identify the specific strategies he or she will employ to ensure that he or she interacts at least three times more often with each student when the student is behaving responsibly than when the student is misbehaving.

Peer Discussion Worksheet

CHAPTER 8
Classwide Motivation

With one or more of your colleagues, work through the following discussion topics and activities related to the tasks in Chapter 8. If necessary, refer back to the text for additional ideas or clarification. See the Chapter 1 Peer Discussion Worksheet for suggestions on structuring effective discussion sessions.

TASK: EFFECTIVELY EMPLOY A CLASSWIDE SYSTEM OR SYSTEMS TO INCREASE MOTIVATED AND RESPONSIBLE STUDENT BEHAVIOR

A. Have each group member share whether his or her class needs or could benefit from a nonreward- or reward-based motivation system and explain how he or she reached that decision. Other group members should provide feedback.

B. All group members who have decided that goal setting is appropriate for their students should explain how they plan to implement the system, including how they will conduct conferences with students.

C. All group members who have decided that a reward-based system is needed for their students should share the specifics of any system or systems that they plan to use, including how they will implement, modify, maintain, and fade the system. Other group members should provide feedback.

MENU OF CLASSWIDE SYSTEMS

A. As a group, review the various systems presented in the menu. Discuss how they could be implemented in your individual classrooms and how you could address any issues and problems that may arise.

B. Have individual group members share other "system" ideas they have found to be effective.

Peer Discussion Worksheet

CHAPTER 9
Correcting

With one or more of your colleagues, work through the following discussion topics and activities related to the tasks in Chapter 9. If necessary, refer back to the text for additional ideas or clarification. See Chapter 1 Peer Discussion Worksheet for suggestions on structuring effective discussion sessions.

TASK 1: ANALYZE AND, IF NEEDED, ADJUST THE IMPLEMENTATION OF YOUR BASIC MANAGEMENT PLAN

Have each member of the group bring a completed Classroom Management and Discipline Plan—Reflection/Implementation form (Reproducible 9.1). Have each person describe the student's behavior, explain his or her hypotheses as to why the student is misbehaving, and discuss how he or she may adjust the management plan to help the student with his behavior. Have the rest of the group give feedback.

TASK 2: ANALYZE AND, IF NEEDED, ADJUST THE STRATEGIES YOU ARE USING TO BUILD A POSITIVE RELATIONSHIP WITH THIS STUDENT

Have each member of the group bring a completed Connect/Motivation—Reflection/Implementation form (Reproducible 9.2). Have each person describe the student's behavior, explain his or her diagnosis of why the student is unmotivated, and describe how he or she may begin to implement relationship-building strategies to motivate the student. Have the rest of the group give feedback.

TASK 3: ANALYZE THE MISBEHAVIOR AND DEVELOP A FUNCTION-BASED INTERVENTION

Have each group member bring a completed Function-Based Intervention Plan form (Reproducible 9.3). Have each person describe the student's behavior and the data collected about the behavior, explain how and why he or she labeled the behavior (Lack of Awareness, Lack of Ability or Skill, Attention-Seeking, or Purposeful/Habitual), and describe the preliminary intervention plan. Have the group give feedback.

Is CHAMPS

Evidence Based?

by Billie Jo Rodriguez

CONCLUSION

Based on the most recent recommendations set forth by researchers and the U. S. Department of Education, CHAMPS is an evidence-based approach to classroom behavior management. CHAMPS is not a curriculum or program, but instead is a collection of recommendations that are based on more than 30 years of research in the fields of education and psychology. *Safe and Civil Schools* has many examples of district-based studies where CHAMPS has been implemented with remarkable results. Improvements include reductions in classroom disruptions, office referrals, and in-school and out-of school suspensions, along with corresponding increases in teachers' perceptions of efficacy and student motivation and behavior.

The field of education has been particularly vulnerable to adopting unproven interventions based on current fads, whims, or material attractiveness (Scheuermann & Evans, 1997). However, the political and societal expectations that schools face have dramatically shifted over the past twenty years. For example, today's entry-level jobs require reading skills that are more advanced than the reading level of approximately half of current high school students (Fielding, Kerr, & Rosier, 2007). To meet these heightened expectations and combat fad-based educational approaches, federal mandates such as No Child Left Behind (NCLB, 2001) and the Individuals with Disabilities Education Act (IDEA, 2004) have shifted from suggesting that most children be successful to mandating that every child is successful. Both NCLB and IDEA legislation focus on the use of evidence-based practices ("scientifically based research"—Report on Scientifically Based Research Supported by the United States Department of Education, 2002) and documenting the progress of each child's learning. This age of educational accountability comes at a time when the resources to support students are declining (Walker & Sprague, 2006) and the composition of the student population is expanding in its diversity of needs, skills, and expectations (Merrell, Ervin, & Gimple, 2005; Ortiz & Flannagan, 2002).

Though the field of education has not come to complete agreement on the definition of evidence-based practice, we have received some guidance. The United States Department of Education (2002) defines scientifically based evidence as "research that involves the application of rigorous, systematic, and objective procedures to obtain reliable and valid knowledge relevant to education activities and programs" (p. 2). More recently, Lembke and Stormont (2005) define research-based practices as those that "are supported by rigorous substantiation of effectiveness." They clarify that research-based (proven or promising) practices are those that "have been demonstrated to be effective for a group of students as compared to a group of students that did not get the intervention" and have generalized results when "examined in a variety of settings, replicated over time, utilized with a variety of learners" (Lembke & Stormont, p. 271).

> *The research should document whether the independent variables of interest produce changes in the dependent variables.*

The research should document whether the independent variables of interest produce changes in the dependent variables through the use of a group or single-subject design. Single-subject designs have been recommended for use in research focusing on special populations (Scientifically Based Evaluation Methods, 2005). Horner, Carr, et al. (2005) offer further guidance for determining the rigorousness of single-subject designs. Schools receiving federal funds to implement the Reading First Program (U.S. Department of Education Policy Guidance 2002, www.ed.gov/programs/readingfirst/guidance.doc) have also received guidance on the types of research that constitute evidence-based practice. Recommended research includes:

- Systematic, empirical methods that draw on observation or experiment.

- Rigorous data analyses that are adequate to test the stated hypotheses and justify the conclusions drawn.

- The use of measurements or observational methods that provide reliable and valid data across multiple evaluators or observers, across multiple measurements and observations, and across studies by the same or different investigators.

- Evaluation using experimental or quasi-experimental designs with control groups to evaluate the effectiveness of the conditions, with a preference for random assignment designs or other designs that contain within-condition or across-condition controls.

- Acceptance in a peer-reviewed journal or approved by a panel of independent experts through a comparably rigorous, objective, and scientific review.

- Experimental studies that are presented in sufficient detail and clarity to allow replication or systematic expansion of the findings.

The reason for this shift from access to outcomes may lie in the compelling and compounding evidence documenting the long-term stability and poor outcome trajectories for students who demonstrate early academic and social behavior difficulties (Kazdin, 1987; Walker & Severson, 1992; Walker et al., 1996).

It is often the case that students who need the most support receive the least. The interaction between learning and social behavior is reciprocal. Typically, high-achieving students experience greater social and academic success, while low-achieving students experience increased social and academic failure (Caprara et al., 2000; Catalano, Loeber, & McKinney, 1999).

Academically successful students often assume responsibility for learning (e.g., use self-regulation and goal orientation, exhibit positive social behaviors) and are intrinsically motivated (Caprara, Barbaranelli, Pastorelli, Bandura, & Zimbardo, 2000; Ellis, 1992; Ellis & Worthington, 1994; Grimes, 1981; Swift & Swift, 1968, 1969a, 1969b, 1973), while students with high needs often engage in behaviors that interfere with learning (McKinney, Mason, Clifford, & Perkeson, 1975; Shinn, Ramsey, Walker, Stieber, & O'Neill, 1987; Walker & McConnell, 1988; Walker et al., 2004).

Some school factors have been correlated with increased risk of failure for at-risk students. These factors include inconsistent management of behavior, inappropriate use of reinforcement contingencies, and ineffective instruction (Kauffman, 2005; Keogh, 2003; Walker et al., 2004). Research has shown that teachers may provide less instruction to students who exhibit high levels of problem behaviors (Carr, Taylor, & Robinson, 1991; Wehby, Symons, Canale, & Go, 1998) and that teachers of students with high rates of behavioral difficulties rarely use praise (Sutherland et al., 2000; Van Acker et al., 1996) and often use more disapproval than approval (Jack et al., 1996; White, 1975). Teacher praise has been shown to result in many benefits, including:

- Decreased problem behavior (Madsen et al., 1968; O'Leary & Becker, 1967; Ward & Baker, 1968).

- Increased appropriate behavior and instructional time (Broden et al., 1970; Ferguson & Houghton, 1992; Hall et al., 1968).

- Increased student intrinsic motivation (Cameron & Pierce, 1994)

- Competence development for the student (Brophy, 1981; Gottfried, 1983; Swann & Pittman, 1977).

Negative interactions are associated with poorer academic and social behavior outcomes (Murray & Greenberg, 2006; Murray & Murray, 2004). Research also suggests that students are more likely to behave well and work hard to meet a teacher's expectations when the student-teacher relationship is positive and respectful (Borich, 2004; Brophy, 1981; Cameron & Pierce, 1994; Hall et al., 1968; Marzanno, 2003; Niebuhr, 1999; Pianta et al., 2003; Reinke et al., 2007; Sutherland et al., 2000).

Students achieve more when teachers have high expectations for them (Brophy & Good, 1986; Fuchs et al., 1989). When teachers implement effective behavior management techniques, they can simultaneously increase student engagement and improve academic achievement (Brophy, 1996; 1980; Brophy & Good, 1986; Christenson et al., 2008; Gettinger & Ball, 2008; Luiselli et al., 2005; Scheuermann & Hall, 2008; Smith, 2000). With the increase in diverse student needs and the strong research that links classroom structure, positive feedback, and student-teacher relationships with improved outcomes, it is especially important that teachers of at-risk students work to provide a structured classroom with high rates of positive feedback for appropriate behavior (Stormont et al., 2007).

> *CHAMPS is not a program, but rather a compilation of how-to strategies.*

CHAMPS is not a program, but rather a compilation of how-to strategies that support teachers in the very skills that have been associated with student success. CHAMPS is a systematic, prevention-oriented approach that guides teachers in providing universal classroom supports that are likely to promote appropriate behavior and reduce disruptive behavior in the classroom. Once the teacher has implemented the core supports, there is guidance for how to structure supports that target smaller groups or individual students who need additional supports. Systemic models like the one utilized in CHAMPS were initially implemented in public health and now span the fields of medicine, welfare, and education (Walker et al., 1996). Educational research has shown that when these levels of support are in place and incorporate meaningful involvement of relevant parties (e.g., teachers, parents, peers), positive student outcomes can be achieved (Horner et al., 2005; Nelson, Martella, & Marchand-Martella, 2002; Walker et al., 1996; Walker & Shinn, 2002).

The foundational principle of CHAMPS—the idea that behavior occurs for a reason and can be taught and changed—is also well supported in the literature (Alberto & Troutman, 2006; Baer et al., 1968; Carr, 1993; Cooper et al., 2007; Gresham et al., 2001; Johnston & Pennypacker, 1993; Langland et al., 1998; Skinner, 1953). In addition, the core features of CHAMPS are organized around the STOIC acronym:

S *Structure your classroom*

T *Teach expectations*

O *Observe and supervise*

I *Interact positively*

C *Correct fluently*

Each core recommendation is directly linked to studies that document its effectiveness.

S **Structure your classroom for success.** The way the classroom is organized (physical setting, schedule, routines and procedures, quality of instruction, and so on) has a huge impact on student behavior; therefore, effective teachers carefully structure their classrooms in ways that prompt responsible student behavior (Baer, 1998; Evans & Lowell, 1979; Gettinger & Ball, 2008; Good & Brophy, 2000; Scheuermann & Hall, 2008; Udvari-Solner, 1996; Walker & Bullis, 1990; Weinstein, 1979). Well-designed physical space prevents a wide array of potential behavioral problems (Evans & Lowell, 1979; Simonsen et al., 2008; Weinstein, 1977). Research suggests the physical arrangement should allow the teacher to visually scan all parts of the room from any other part of the room (Pedota, 2007; Shores et al., 1993) and allow for movement that minimizes distractions for students who are working at their seats (Evertson et al., 2003; Jenson et al., 1994).

T **Teach behavioral expectations to students.** Effective teachers overtly teach students how to behave responsibly and respectfully in every classroom situation and during all major transitions (Brophy & Good, 1986; Emmer et al., 1980; Evertson et al., 2003; Lewis & Sugai, 1999). The research supports the effectiveness of teaching rules (Brophy & Good, 1986; Mendler & Curwin, 2002) using positive and negative examples (Gresham, 1998; Kame'enui & Simmons, 1990; Sugai & Lewis, 1996) with a focus on what teachers expect students to do. This ensures that students know the expected behavior and sets the stage for student success (Barbetta et al., 2005; Colvin et al., 1993; Darch & Kame'enui, 2004; Emmer et al., 1980; Greenwood et al., 1974; Lewis & Sugai, 1999; Marshall, 2001; Mayer, 1995; Simonsen et al., 2008; Walker et al., 1996).

O **Observe and supervise.** Effective teachers monitor student behavior by physically circulating whenever possible and visually scanning all parts of the classroom frequently. One of the most effective behavior management strategies a teacher can implement is to circulate throughout the room as much and as unpredictably as possible (Colvin et al., 1997; DePry & Sugai, 2002; Gettinger & Ball, 2008; Schuldheisz & van der Mars, 2001). In addition, effective teachers use meaningful data to observe student behavior (particularly chronic misbehavior) in objective ways and monitor trends across time (Alberto & Troutman, 2006; Evertson et al., 2003; Scheuermann & Hall, 2008; Shores et al., 1993).

I **Interact positively with students.** Teachers should focus more time, attention, and energy on promoting and acknowledging responsible behavior than on responding to misbehavior (Beaman & Wheldall, 2000; Brophy & Good, 1986; Martella et al., 2003; Rosenshine, 1971; Sprick, 2006; Thompson et al., 1968; Walker et al., 2004). Increased positive interactions between teachers and students have been shown to decrease misbehavior and lead to increases in on-task behavior (Beaman & Wheldall, 2000; Brophy & Good, 1986; Thomas et al., 1968; Walker et al., 2004).

> *Increased positive interactions between teachers and students have been shown to decrease misbehavior.*

C **Correct fluently.** Teachers are encouraged to preplan their responses to misbehavior to increase the likelihood they will respond in a brief, calm, and consistent manner. This practice helps ensure that the flow of instruction is maintained (Brophy & Good, 1986; Lewis & Sugai, 1999). Research has consistently shown that students learn more efficiently when they receive immediate feedback about their behavior (Gettinger & Ball, 2008; Good & Brophy, 2000; Hudson & Miller, 2006; Kame'enui & Simmons, 1990). The research supports correcting misbehavior by providing instruction about the rule and how to follow the rule (Darch & Kame'enui, 2004; Emmer et al., 1980, 2003; Evertson et al., 2003) in a direct, brief, and explicit manner (Abramowitz et al., 1988; McAllister et al., 1969). There is a focus on implementing corrective consequences consistently (Acker & O'Leary, 1988; Alberto & Troutman, 2006; Scheuermann & Hall, 2008) and matching consequences to the severity of the problem (Simonsen et al., 2008; Wolfgang & Glickman, 1986). In addition, with chronic and severe misbehavior, the teacher is prompted to consider the function of the misbehavior and build a corresponding plan to help the student learn and exhibit the appropriate behavior (Alberto & Troutman, 2006; Crone & Horner, 2003; O'Neill et al., 1997).

Simonsen and colleagues (2008) conducted a systematic review of the literature. They identified 20 practices that, in general, are supported by the research and have sufficient evidence to recommend adoption to support classroom behavior. The practices were then grouped into five evidence-based critical features of classroom management:

a. Maximize structure and predictability (including using a physical arrangement that minimizes distraction).

b. Post, teach, review, monitor, and reinforce expectations (and provide active supervision).

c. Actively engage students in observable ways.

d. Use a continuum of strategies to respond to appropriate behaviors (including specific and/or contingent praise, classwide group contingencies, behavioral contracting, and token economy strategies).

e. Use a continuum of strategies to respond to inappropriate behaviors (including error corrections, performance feedback, differential reinforcement, planned ignoring plus praise and/or instruction of classroom rules, response cost, and timeout from reinforcement strategies).

These recommendations directly align with the practices incorporated into the STOIC model, providing additional evidence for the use of CHAMPS to guide classroom behavior support.

Based on the most recent recommendations set forth by researchers and the U. S. Department of Education, CHAMPS is an evidence-based approach to classroom behavior management. CHAMPS is not a curriculum or program, but instead is a collection of recommendations that are based on more than 30 years of research in the fields of education and psychology. *Safe and Civil Schools* has many examples of district-based studies where CHAMPS has been implemented with remarkable results. Improvements include reductions in classroom disruptions, office referrals, and in-school and out-of school suspensions, along with corresponding increases in teachers' perceptions of efficacy and student motivation and behavior.

For information on efficacy data, contact *Safe & Civil Schools* (800/323-8819) or visit www.safeandcivilschools.com.

Guide to
CHAMPS ICONS AND
REPRODUCIBLE FORMS

INTRODUCTION

The CD provided with this book contains a wealth of materials to help you implement the CHAMPS approach to classroom management and discipline. All of the Reproducible Forms shown in the text are available as PDFs that you can fill in electronically using Adobe Reader. In addition, the CD contains six sets of CHAMPS icons that you can use to teach and display your expectations for classroom activities and transitions.

The Print from CD icon indicates that a blank version of a form shown in this book is available on the accompanying CD. The CD also contains six sets of icons that can be used to teach CHAMPS expectations. See pp. 178–184 for more details on how these icons can be used.

The reproducible forms on the CD are provided in PDF format. They can be printed and filled out by hand. They are also enabled so they can be filled out and saved electronically when opened in Adobe Reader version 6 or above. See the Readme file on the CD for more detailed instructions on how to fill out forms using Adobe Reader.

Following is a list of all materials included on the CD. If a form is not shown in the book, we have provided a thumbnail preview version here.

 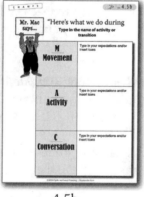 

4.5a   4.5b   4.5c

Note: There are two certificates on each reproducible form. Print in full color or black and white.

7.1a   7.1b   7.1c   7.1d

7.1e   7.1f   7.1g   7.1h

7.1i   7.1j   7.1k   7.1l

7.1m   7.1n

Reproducible 7.2a–b   Daily Report Cards
Note: There are two certificates on each reproducible form.
Reproducible 7.3   Badges and Buttons
Note: There are twelve different badges on this reproducible.
Print in full color or black and white. Use Avery #5294 labels.

7.2a   7.2b   7.3

Chapter 7 Self-Assessment Checklist

CHAPTER 8

Reproducible 8.1   Develop and/or Revise Your Classwide Motivation System
                        (2 pages)
Reproducible 8.2a–q   Whole-Class Point Charts
Note: Print in full color or black and white.

8.2a (5 points)   8.2b (10 points)   8.2c (15 points)

8.2d (20 points)   8.2e (25 points)   8.2f (50 points)

8.2g (100 points)

8.2h (5 points)

8.2i (10 points)

8.2j (15 points)

8.2k (20 points)

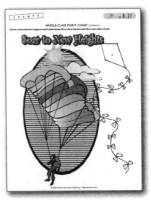

8.2l (25 points)

8.2m (50 points)

8.2n (50 points)

8.2o (100 points)

8.2p (30 points)

8.2q (30 points)

Reproducible 8.3a–h   Whole-Class Point Chart Templates

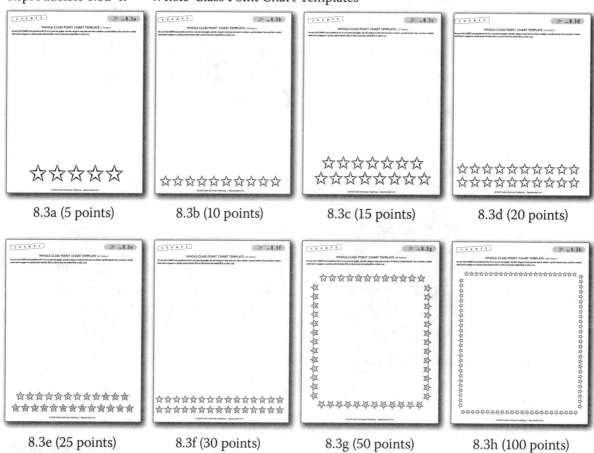

| 8.3a (5 points) | 8.3b (10 points) | 8.3c (15 points) | 8.3d (20 points) |

| 8.3e (25 points) | 8.3f (30 points) | 8.3g (50 points) | 8.3h (100 points) |

CHAMPS ICONS

This revised edition of CHAMPS comes with six sets of icons you can use to display and teach your classroom expectations. The sets are:

Version 1:   Primary (B/W). Line drawings that young students (K–2) can color.

Version 2:   Primary (Color). Full-color illustrations aimed at young students (K–2). Note that thumbnails are shown in grayscale, but the images on the CD are in full color.

Version 3:   Intermediate. Grayscale drawings aimed at older students (3–8).

Version 4:   Graphic. Black-and-white graphic symbols depict expectations.

Version 5:   Sentence Strip. Text-only icons.

Version 6:   Road Sign. Text-based street signs in different shapes and colors.

Thumbnail views of each icon appear on the following pages to help you determine which ones are most appropriate for your classroom. See Chapter 4 for ideas on how to use the icons. Note that the actual icons for versions 2 and 6 are in color, which is not reflected in the thumbnail versions.

Each set of icons is stored in a separate folder. Each icon file is numbered to match the CHAMPS expectations listed in the tables that follow.

Icons are provided in PDF format. You can print them out on 8.5" x 11" sheets of paper. You can also use the free Adobe Reader to resize them and print on 11" x 17" paper, if your printer accommodates that size sheet. To do this, open the icon file in Adobe Reader. From the File menu select Page Setup. Select your desired paper size from the pull-down list in the Paper Size window. Then start the Print command. Set Page Scaling to Fit to Printable window. This will enlarge or reduce the icon sheet to fit your selected paper size.

You can also use Adobe Reader to copy the icons to insert into a CHAMPS Template (Reproducibles 4.5a–c and 8.3a–h) or a Word or PowerPoint file. Select the Snapshot tool from the Select & Zoom menu in the Tools menu. The Snapshot tool lets you draw a window with your cursor around the part of the PDF file you want to copy and paste. As soon as you complete the window, Adobe Reader automatically copies its contents. You can then paste into your file and resize. Note that if you paste icons into a CHAMPS PDF template, you will need to have Print Documents and Markups selected in the Print dialog box for the icons to appear on the print.

See the "Using the CHAMPS CD" file on the CD for more tips on working with the icons.

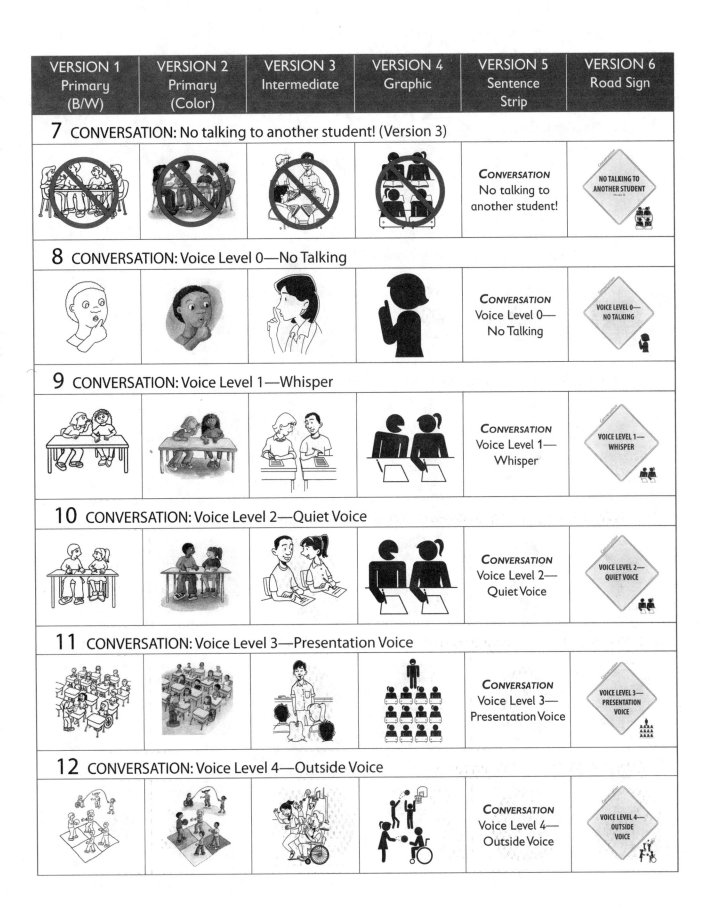

VERSION 1 Primary (B/W)	VERSION 2 Primary (Color)	VERSION 3 Intermediate	VERSION 4 Graphic	VERSION 5 Sentence Strip	VERSION 6 Road Sign
7 CONVERSATION: No talking to another student! (Version 3)					
				CONVERSATION No talking to another student!	NO TALKING TO ANOTHER STUDENT
8 CONVERSATION: Voice Level 0—No Talking					
				CONVERSATION Voice Level 0— No Talking	VOICE LEVEL 0— NO TALKING
9 CONVERSATION: Voice Level 1—Whisper					
				CONVERSATION Voice Level 1— Whisper	VOICE LEVEL 1— WHISPER
10 CONVERSATION: Voice Level 2—Quiet Voice					
				CONVERSATION Voice Level 2— Quiet Voice	VOICE LEVEL 2— QUIET VOICE
11 CONVERSATION: Voice Level 3—Presentation Voice					
				CONVERSATION Voice Level 3— Presentation Voice	VOICE LEVEL 3— PRESENTATION VOICE
12 CONVERSATION: Voice Level 4—Outside Voice					
				CONVERSATION Voice Level 4— Outside Voice	VOICE LEVEL 4— OUTSIDE VOICE

VERSION 1 Primary (B/W)	VERSION 2 Primary (Color)	VERSION 3 Intermediate	VERSION 4 Graphic	VERSION 5 Sentence Strip	VERSION 6 Road Sign

13 HELP: Raise hand.

HELP Raise hand.

RAISE HAND

14 HELP: Do not raise hand (no help available except in emergency).

HELP Do not raise hand (no help available except in emergency).

DO NOT RAISE HAND

15 HELP: Put up "Please Help" flag.

HELP Put up "Please Help" flag.

PUT UP "PLEASE HELP" FLAG

16 HELP: Do not put up "Please Help" flag (no help available except in emergency).

HELP Do not put up "Please Help" flag (no help available except in emergency).

DO NOT PUT UP "PLEASE HELP" FLAG

17 HELP: Do not talk to any other student.

HELP Do not talk to any other student.

DO NOT TALK TO ANY OTHER STUDENT

18 HELP: Ask one person next to you.

HELP Ask one person next to you.

ASK ONE PERSON NEXT TO YOU

VERSION 1 Primary (B/W)	VERSION 2 Primary (Color)	VERSION 3 Intermediate	VERSION 4 Graphic	VERSION 5 Sentence Strip	VERSION 6 Road Sign
19 HELP: Ask any student in your group or cluster.					
				HELP Ask any student in your group or cluster.	ASK ANY STUDENT IN YOUR GROUP OR CLUSTER *Help*
20 HELP: If your group has a question, at least two people raise their hand.					
				ACTIVITY If your group has a question, at least two people raise their hand.	IF YOUR GROUP HAS A QUESTION, AT LEAST TWO PEOPLE RAISE THEIR HAND *Help*
21 ACTIVITY: Small-Group Instruction					
				ACTIVITY Small-Group Instruction	SMALL GROUP INSTRUCTION *Activity*
22 ACTIVITY: Whole-Class Instruction (students at desks)					
				ACTIVITY Whole-Class Instruction (students at desks)	WHOLE-CLASS INSTRUCTION (STUDENTS AT DESKS) *Activity*
23 ACTIVITY: Whole-Class Discussion Circle					
				ACTIVITY Whole-Class Discussion Circle	WHOLE-CLASS DISCUSSION CIRCLE *Activity*
24 ACTIVITY: Whole Class at Rug					
				ACTIVITY Whole Class at Rug	WHOLE-CLASS AT RUG *Activity*

VERSION 1 Primary (B/W)	VERSION 2 Primary (Color)	VERSION 3 Intermediate	VERSION 4 Graphic	VERSION 5 Sentence Strip	VERSION 6 Road Sign
25 ACTIVITY: Independent Seatwork (teacher available to help)					
				ACTIVITY Independent Seatwork (teacher available to help)	
26 ACTIVITY: Independent Seatwork (teacher not available to help)					
				ACTIVITY Independent Seatwork (teacher not available to help)	
27 ACTIVITY: Test					
				ACTIVITY Test	
28 ACTIVITY: Cooperative Groups					
				ACTIVITY Cooperative Groups	
29 ACTIVITY: Silent Reading					
				ACTIVITY Silent Reading	
30 ACTIVITY: Clean Up					
				ACTIVITY Clean Up	

VERSION 1 Primary (B/W)	VERSION 2 Primary (Color)	VERSION 3 Intermediate	VERSION 4 Graphic	VERSION 5 Sentence Strip	VERSION 6 Road Sign
31 ACTIVITY: Choice Time/Free Play					
				ACTIVITY Choice Time/ Free Play	CHOICE TIME/ FREE PLAY
32 ACTIVITY: Centers/Stations					
				ACTIVITY Centers/Stations	CENTER/ STATIONS
33 ACTIVITY: Snack					
				ACTIVITY Snack	SNACK
34 ACTIVITY: PE/Gym					
				ACTIVITY PE/Gym	PE/ GYM
35 ACTIVITY: Library/Media					
				ACTIVITY Library/Media	LIBRARY/ MEDIA
36 ACTIVITY: Computer Lab or Computer Station					
				ACTIVITY Computer Lab/ Computer Station	COMPUTER LAB/ COMPUTER STATIONS

VERSION 1 Primary (B/W)	VERSION 2 Primary (Color)	VERSION 3 Intermediate	VERSION 4 Graphic	VERSION 5 Sentence Strip	VERSION 6 Road Sign
37 ACTIVITY: Music					
				ACTIVITY Music	MUSIC
38 ACTIVITY: Fire Drill					
				ACTIVITY Fire Drill	FIRE DRILL
39 ACTIVITY: Lock-Down Drill					
				ACTIVITY Lock-Down Drill	LOCK-DOWN DRILL
40 ACTIVITY: Pair Practice					
				ACTIVITY Pair Practice	PAIR PRACTICE
41 MOVEMENT: Hand in completed assignments.					
				MOVEMENT Hand in completed assignments.	HAND IN COMPLETED ASSIGNMENTS
42 MOVEMENT: Do not get up to hand in completed assignments.					
				MOVEMENT Do not get up to hand in completed assignments	DO NOT GET UP TO HAND IN COMPLETED ASSIGNMENTS

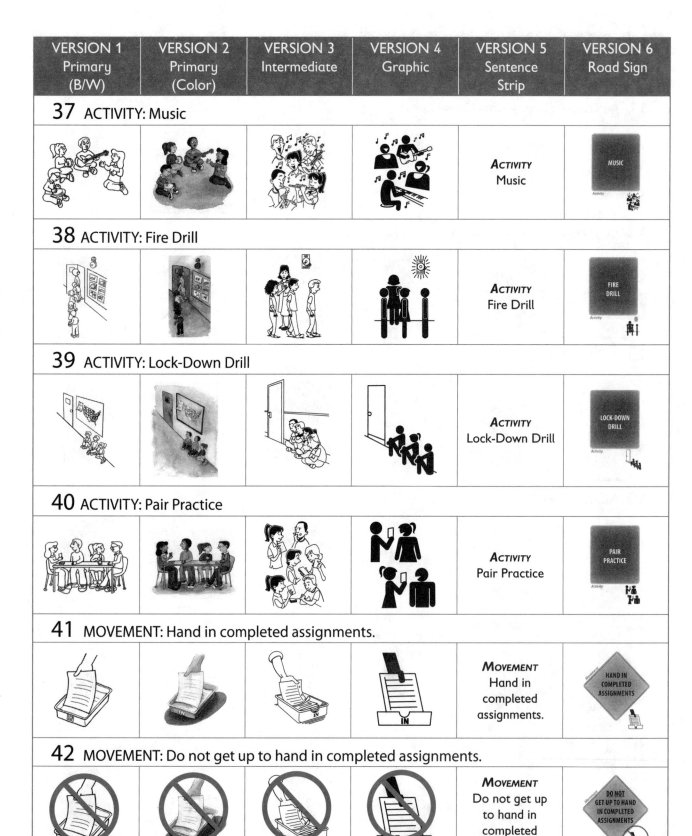

VERSION 1 Primary (B/W)	VERSION 2 Primary (Color)	VERSION 3 Intermediate	VERSION 4 Graphic	VERSION 5 Sentence Strip	VERSION 6 Road Sign
43 MOVEMENT: Sharpen pencil.					
				MOVEMENT Sharpen pencil.	
44 MOVEMENT: Do not get up to sharpen pencil.					
				MOVEMENT Do not get up to sharpen pencil.	
45 MOVEMENT: Get supplies.					
				MOVEMENT Get supplies.	
46 MOVEMENT: Do not get up to get supplies.					
				MOVEMENT Do not get up to get supplies.	
47 MOVEMENT: Get a drink of water.					
				MOVEMENT Get a drink of water.	
48 MOVEMENT: Do not get up to get a drink of water.					
				MOVEMENT Do not get up to get a drink of water.	

VERSION 1 Primary (B/W)	VERSION 2 Primary (Color)	VERSION 3 Intermediate	VERSION 4 Graphic	VERSION 5 Sentence Strip	VERSION 6 Road Sign

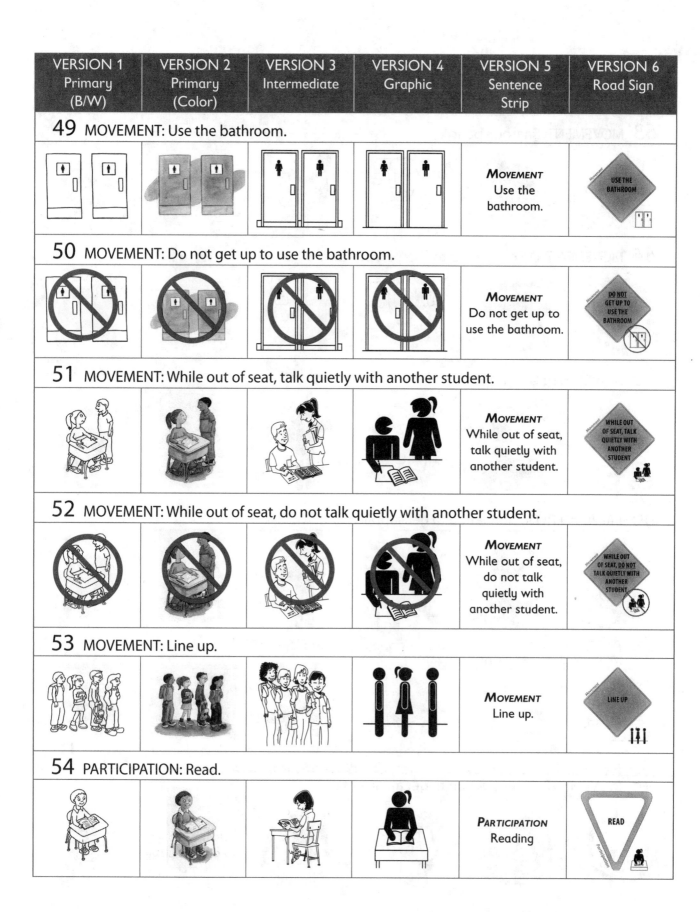

49 MOVEMENT: Use the bathroom.

Movement Use the bathroom.

50 MOVEMENT: Do not get up to use the bathroom.

Movement Do not get up to use the bathroom.

51 MOVEMENT: While out of seat, talk quietly with another student.

Movement While out of seat, talk quietly with another student.

52 MOVEMENT: While out of seat, do not talk quietly with another student.

Movement While out of seat, do not talk quietly with another student.

53 MOVEMENT: Line up.

Movement Line up.

54 PARTICIPATION: Read.

Participation Reading

VERSION 1 Primary (B/W)	VERSION 2 Primary (Color)	VERSION 3 Intermediate	VERSION 4 Graphic	VERSION 5 Sentence Strip	VERSION 6 Road Sign
55 PARTICIPATION: Write.					
				PARTICIPATION Write.	WRITE
56 PARTICIPATION: Write (eyes only on your own work).					
				PARTICIPATION Write (eyes only on your own work).	WRITE (EYES ONLY ON YOUR OWN WORK)
57 PARTICIPATION: Listen.					
				PARTICIPATION Listen.	LISTEN
58 PARTICIPATION: Listen and take notes.					
				PARTICIPATION Listen and take notes.	LISTEN & TAKE NOTES
59 PARTICIPATION: Listen, answer, ask questions, and/or share.					
				PARTICIPATION Listen, answer, ask questions, and/or share.	LISTEN, ANSWER, ASK QUESTIONS, AND/OR SHARE
60 PARTICIPATION: Talk quietly and respectfully with one other student. Listen when that person talks.					
				PARTICIPATION Talk quietly and respectfully with one other student. Listen when that person talks.	TALK QUIETLY AND RESPECTFULLY WITH OTHER STUDENTS IN YOUR GROUP. LISTEN WHEN ANOTHER PERSON TALKS.

VERSION 1 Primary (B/W)	VERSION 2 Primary (Color)	VERSION 3 Intermediate	VERSION 4 Graphic	VERSION 5 Sentence Strip	VERSION 6 Road Sign
61 PARTICIPATION: Talk quietly and respectfully with other students in your group. Listen when another person talks.					
				CONVERSATION Talk quietly and respectfuly with other students in your group. Listen when another person talks.	
62 SUCCESS: Great job!					
				SUCCESS Great job!	
63 SUCCESS: Great job, class!					
				SUCCESS Great job, class!	
64 SUCCESS): Excellent work!					
				SUCCESS Excellent work!	
65 SUCCESS: Well done!					
				SUCCESS Well done!	
66 SUCCESS: Thumbs up!					
				SUCCESS Thumbs up!	

Abramowitz, A. J., O'Leary, S. G., & Futtersak, M. W. (1988). The relative impact of long and short reprimands on children's off-task behavior in the classroom. *Behavior Therapy, 29*(2), 243–247.

Acker, M. M., & O'Leary, S. G. (1988). Effects of consistent and inconsistent feedback on inappropriate child behavior. *Behavior Therapy, 19*(4), 619–624.

Akin-Little, K., Eckert, T., & Lovett, B. (2004). Extrinsic reinforcement in the classroom: Bribery or best practice. *School Psychology Review, 33,* 344–362.

Alber, S., Heward, W., & Hippler, B. (1999). Teaching middle school students with learning disabilities to recruit positive teacher attention. *Exceptional Children, 65,* 253–270.

Alberto, P., & Troutman, A. (2006). *Applied behavior analysis for teachers* (7th ed.). Upper Saddle River, NJ: Merrill/Prentice-Hall.

Anderson, L., Evertson, C., & Emmer, E. (1980). Dimensions in classroom management derived from recent research. *Journal of Curriculum Studies, 12,* 343–356.

Archer, A., & Gleason, M. (1989). *Skills for school success.* North Billerica, MA: Curriculum Associates.

Arlin, M. (1979). Teacher transitions can disrupt time flow in classrooms. *American Educational Research Journal, 16,* 42–56.

Azrin, N., & Foxx, R. (1971). A rapid method of toilet training the institutionalized retarded. *Journal of Applied Behavior Analysis, 4,* 89–99.

Babkie, A. (2006). 20 ways to be proactive in managing classroom behavior. *Intervention in School and Clinic, 41,* 184–187.

Baer, G. (1998). School discipline in the United States: Prevention, correction, and long-term social development. *School Psychology Review, 27,* 14–32.

Baer, D. M., Wolf, M. M., & Risley, T. R. (1968). Some current dimensions of applied behavior analysis. *Journal of Applied Behavior Analysis, 1*(1), 91–97.

Bain, A., Houghton, S., & Williams, S. (1991). The effects of a school-wide behaviour management programme on teachers' use of encouragement in the classroom. *Educational Studies, 17*(3), 249–260.

Bandura, A. (1977). *Social learning theory.* Upper Saddle River, NJ: Prentice Hall.

Barbetta, P., Norona, K., & Bicard, D. (2005). Classroom behavior management: A dozen common mistakes and what to do instead. *Preventing School Failure, 49,* 11–19.

Barrish, H. H., Saunders, M., & Wolf, M. M. (1969). Good behavior game: Effects of individual contingencies for group consequences on disruptive behavior in a classroom. *Journal of Applied Behavior Analysis, 2,* 119–124.

Beaman, R., & Wheldall, K. (2000). Teachers' use of approval and disapproval in the classroom. *Educational Psychology, 20,* 431–446.

Becker, W. C. (1986). *Applied psychology for teachers—A behavioral cognitive approach.* New York: Macmillan.

Berliner, D. (1978). *Changing academic learning time: Clinical interventions in four classrooms.* San Francisco: Far West Laboratory for Educational Research and Development.

Beyda, S., Zentall, S., & Ferko, D. (2002). The relationship between teacher practices and the task-appropriate and social behavior of students with behavioral disorders. *Behavioral Disorders, 27,* 236–255.

Bonny, A. E., Britto, M. T., Klostermann, B. K., Hornung, R. W., & Slap, G. B. (2000). School disconnectedness: Identifying adolescents at risk. *Pediatrics, 106,* 1017–1021.

Borich, G. (2004). *Effective teaching methods* (5th ed.). Upper Saddle River, NJ: Pearson/Merrill/Prentice Hall.

Brantley, D., & Webster, R. (1993). Use of an independent group contingency management system in a regular classroom setting. *Psychology in the Schools, 30,* 60–66.

Broden, M., Bruce, C., Mitchell, M., Carter, V., & Hall, R. (1970). Effects of teacher attention on attending behavior of two boys at adjacent desks. *Journal of Applied Behavior Analysis, 3,* 199–203.

Brophy, J. (1981). Teacher praise: A functional analysis. *Review of Educational Research, 51,* 5–32.

Brophy, J. (1983). Classroom management techniques. *Education and Urban Society, 18,* 182–194.

Brophy, J. (1986). Teacher influences on student achievement. *American Psychologist, 41,* 1069–1077.

Brophy, J. E. (1987). *Educating teachers about managing classrooms and students.* (Occasional Paper No. 115). East Lansing: Michigan State University, Institute for Research on Teaching. (ERIC Document Reproduction Service No. ED285844)

Brophy, J. (1996). *Teaching problem students.* New York: Guilford Press.

Brophy, J., & Evertson, C. (1976). *Learning from teaching: A developmental perspective.* New York: Longman.

Brophy, J. E., & Good, T. L. (1986). Teacher behavior and student achievement. In M. C. Wittrock (Ed.), *Handbook of research on teaching* (3rd ed., pp. 328–375). New York: Macmillan.

Brown, T. (1998). Effective school research and student behavior. *Southeast/South Central Education Cooperative Fourth Retreat: Making a difference in student behavior.* Lexington, KY.

Burns, M., VanDerHeyden, A., & Boice, C. (2008). Best practices in delivery of intensive academic interventions. In A. Thomas & J. Grimes (Eds.), *Best practices in school psychology V* (pp. 1151–1162). Bethesda, MD: National Association of School Psychologists.

Cameron, J., Banko, K., & Pierce, W. (2001). Pervasive negative effects of rewards on intrinsic motivation: The myth continues. *The Behavior Analyst, 24,* 1–44.

Cameron, J., & Pierce, W. (1994). Reinforcement, reward, and intrinsic motivation: A meta-analysis. *Review of Educational Research, 64,* 363–423.

Caprara, G., Barbaranelli, C., Pastorelli, C., Bandura, A., & Zimbardo, P. (2000). Prosocial foundations of children's academic achievement. *Psychological Science, 11,* 302–306.

Carnine, D., Silbert, J., Kame'enui, E., & Tarver, S. (2004). *Direct instruction reading* (4th ed.). Upper Saddle River, NJ: Pearson.

Carr, E. (1993). Behavior analysis is not ultimately about behavior. *The Behavior Analyst, 16,* 47–49.

Carr, E., & Durand, V. (1985). Reducing behavior problems through functional communication training. *Journal of Applied Behavior Analysis, 18,* 111–126.

Carr, E., Newsom, C., & Binkoff, J. (1980). Escape as a factor in the aggressive behavior of two retarded children. *Journal of Applied Behavior Analysis, 13,* 101–117.

Carr, E., Taylor, J., & Robinson, S. (1991). The effects of severe behavior problems in children on the teaching behavior of adults. *Journal of Applied Behavior Analysis, 3,* 523–535.

Carr, J., Coriaty, S., Wilder, D., Gaunt, B., Dozier, C., Britton, L., et al. (2000). A review of "noncontingent" reinforcement as treatment for the aberrant behavior of individuals with developmental disabilities. *Research in Developmental Disabilities, 21,* 377–391.

Catalano, R., Loeber, R., & McKinney, K. (1999). *School and community interventions to prevent serious and violent offending.* Juvenile Justice Bulletin. Washington, DC: U. S. Department of Justice, Office of Juvenile Justice and Delinquency Prevention.

Chalk, K., & Bizo, L. (2004). Specific praise improves on-task behavior and numeracy enjoyment: A study of year four pupils engaged in the numeracy hour. *Educational Psychology in Practice, 20,* 335–351.

Chandler, L., & Dahlquist, C. (2002). *Functional assessment.* Upper Saddle River, NJ: Merrill/Prentice Hall.

Christenson, S., & Godber, Y. (2001). Enhancing constructive family-school connections. In J. N. Hughes, A. M. LaGreca, & J. C. Conoley (Eds.), *Handbook of psychological services for children and adolescents* (pp. 455–476). New York: Oxford University Press.

Christenson, S., Reschly, A., Appleton, J., Berman-Young, S., Spanjers, D., & Varro, P. (2008). Best practices in fostering student engagement. In A. Thomas & J. Grimes (Eds.). *Best practices in school psychology V* (pp. 1099–1119). Bethesda, MD: National Association of School Psychologists.

Clarfield, J., & Stoner, G. (2005). The effects of computerized reading instruction on the academic performance of students identified with ADHD. *School Psychology Review, 34,* 246–254.

Cole, J., & Kupersmidt, J. (1983). A behavioral analysis of emerging social status in boys' groups. *Child Development, 54,* 1400–1416.

Colvin, G., & Sugai, G. (1988). Proactive strategies for managing social behavior problems: An instructional approach. *Education and Treatment of Children, 11,* 341–348.

Colvin, G., Sugai, G., Good, R.H., III, & Lee, Y. (1997). Using active supervision and precorrection to improve transition behaviors in an elementary school. *School Psychology Quarterly, 12,* 344–361.

Colvin, G., Sugai, G., & Patching, B. (1993). Pre-correction: An instructional approach for managing predictable problem behaviors. *Intervention in School and Clinic, 28,* 143–150.

Conroy, M., Sutherland, K., Snyder, A., & Marsh, S. (2008). Classwide interventions: Effective instruction makes a difference. *Teaching Exceptional Children, July/Aug.,* 24–30.

Cooper, J. O., Heron, T. E., & Heward, W. L. (2007). *Applied behavior analysis* (2nd ed.). Upper Saddle River, NJ: Pearson.

Copeland, S., & Hughes, C. (2002). Effects of goal setting on task performance of persons with mental retardation. *Education and Training in Mental Retardation and Developmental Disabilities, 37,* 40–54.

Council for Exceptional Children (1987). *Academy for effective instruction: Working with mildly handicapped students.* Reston, VA: Author.

Craft, M. A., Alber, S. R., & Heward, W. L. Training elementary students with developmental disabilities to recruit teacher attention in a general education classroom: Effects on teacher praise and academic productivity. *Journal of Applied Behavior Analysis, 31,* 399–415.

Crone, D., & Horner, R. (2003). *Building positive behavior support systems in schools: Functional Behavioral Assessment.* New York: Guilford.

Dalton, T., Martella, R., & Marchand-Martella, N. (1999). The effects of a self-management program in reducing off-task behavior. *Journal of Behavioral Education, 9,* 157–176.

Darch, C., & Kame'enui, E. (2004). *Instructional classroom management: A proactive approach to behavior management.* Upper Saddle River, NJ: Pearson/Prentice Hall.

Darch, C. B., & Thorpe, H. W. (1977). The principle game: A group consequence procedure to increase classroom on-task behavior. *Psychology in the Schools 14,* 341–347.

Darveaux, D. (1984). The Good Behavior Game plus merit: Controlling disruptive behavior and improving student motivation. *School Psychology Review, 13*(4), 510-514.

Delpit, L. (2006). *Other people's children: Cultural conflict in the classroom* (2nd ed.). New York: New Press.

Delquadri, J., Greenwood, C., Whorton, D., Carta, J., & Hall, R. (1986). Classwide peer tutoring. *Exceptional Children, 52,* 535–542.

De Pry, R.L., & Sugai, G. (2002). The effect of active supervision and pre-correction on minor behavioral incidents in a sixth grade general education classroom. *Journal of Behavioral Education, 11,* 255–264.

Dishion, T. J., & Stormshak, E. A. (2007). *Intervening in children's lives: An ecological, family-centered approach to mental health care.* Washington, DC: American Psychological Association.

Dreikurs, R., Grunwald, B., & Pepper, C. (1998). *Maintaining sanity in the classroom: Classroom management techniques* (2nd ed.). Washington, DC: Taylor and Francis.

Elements of an effective discipline strategy (1995–96). *American Education, 19*(4), 24–27.

Elliott, S., & Gresham, F. (1991). *Social skills intervention guide: Practical strategies for social skills training.* Circle Pines, MN: American Guidance Service.

Ellis, E. (1992). Perspective on adolescents with learning disabilities. In E. S. Ellis (Ed.), *Teaching the learning disabled adolescent: Strategies and methods.* Denver: Love Publishing Co.

Ellis, E., & Worthington, L. (1994). *Technical Report No. 5: Research synthesis on effective teaching principles and the design of quality tools for educators.* National Center to Improve the Tools of Educators, University of Oregon.

Emmer, E., & Evertson, C. (1980). *Effective classroom management at the beginning of the year in junior high school classrooms* (Report No. 6107). Austin, TX: The Research and Development Center for Teacher Education.

Emmer, E., & Evertson, C. (1981). Synthesis of research on classroom management. *Educational Leadership, January,* 342–347.

Emmer, E., Evertson, C., & Anderson, L. (1980). Effective classroom management at the beginning of the school year. *The Elementary School Journal, 80,* 219–231.

Emmer, E., Evertson, C., & Worsham, M. (2003). *Classroom management for secondary teachers*. Boston: Allyn and Bacon.

Englemann, S., & Becker, W. (1978). Systems for basic instruction: Theory and applications. In A. C. Catania and T. A. Brigham (Eds.), *Handbook of applied behavior analysis* (pp. 326–377). New York: Irvington.

Esler, A., Godber, Y., & Christenson, S. (2008). Best practices in supporting school-family partnerships. In A. Thomas & J. Grimes (Eds.). *Best practices in school psychology V* (pp. 917–936). Bethesda, MD: National Association of School Psychologists.

Espin, C. A., & Yell, M. L. (1994). Critical indicators of effective teaching for preservice teachers: Relationship between teaching behaviors and ratings of teacher effectiveness. *Teacher Education and Special Education, 17,* 154–169.

Evans, G., & Lowell, B. (1979). Design modification in an open-plan school. *Journal of Educational Psychology, 71,* 41–49.

Evertson, C. M. (1989). Classroom organization and management. In M. C. Reynolds (Ed.), *Knowledge base for the beginning teacher.* Oxford, UK: Pergamon Press.

Evertson, C., & Anderson, L. (1979). Beginning school. *Educational Horizons, 57,* 164–168.

Evertson, C., & Emmer, E. (1982). Effective management at the beginning of the school year in junior high classes. *Journal of Educational Psychology, 74,* 485–498.

Evertson, C., Emmer, E., & Worsham, M. (2003). *Classroom management for elementary teachers* (6th ed.). Boston: Allyn & Bacon.

Evertson, C. M., & Harris, A. H. (1992). What we know about managing classrooms. *Educational Leadership, 49*(7), 74.

Fairbanks, S., Sugai, G., Guardino, D., & Lathrop, M. (2007). Response to intervention: Examining classroom behavior supports in second grade. *Council for Exceptional Children, 73,* 288–310.

Farlow, L., & Snell, M. (1994). *Making the most of student performance data.* Washington, DC: American Association on Mental Retardation.

Farmer, T. W., Goforth, J., Hives. J., Aaron, A., Hunter, R., & Sigmatto, A. (2006). Competence enhancement behavior management. *Preventing School Failure, 50,* 39–44.

Feather, N. T. (1982). *Expectations and actions: Expectancy-value theories in psychology.* Hillsdale, NJ: Erlbaum.

Ferguson, E., & Houghton, S. (1992). The effects of contingent teacher praise, as specified by Canter's assertive discipline programme, on children's on-task behaviour. *Educational Studies, 18,* 83–93.

Fielding, L., Kerr, N., & Rosier, P. (2007). *Annual growth for all students, catch-up growth for those who are behind.* Kennewick, WA: The New Foundation Press.

Fisher, C., Fibly, N., Marliave, R., Cahen, L., Dishaw, M., More, J., & Berliner, D. (1978). *Teaching behaviors, academic learning time, and student achievement* (Report of Phase III-B, Beginning Teacher Evaluation Study. Tech. Rep. V-1). San Francisco: Far West Laboratory for Educational Research and Development.

Foxx, R., & Bechtel, D. (1982). Overcorrection. In M. Hersen, R. Eisler, & P. Miller (Eds.), *Progress in behavior modification* (pp. 227–288). New York: Academic Press.

Freeland, J., & Noell, G. (1999). Maintaining accurate math responses in elementary school students: The effects of delayed intermittent reinforcement and programming common stimuli. *Journal of Applied Behavior Analysis, 32,* 211–215.

Freeman, K., & Dexter-Mazza, E. (2004). Using self-monitoring with an adolescent with disruptive classroom behavior. *Behavior Modification, 28,* 402–419.

Freer, P., & Watson, T. S. (1999). A comparison of parent and teacher acceptability ratings of behavioral and conjoint behavioral consultation. *School Psychology Review, 28,* 672–684.

Fuchs, D., Fuchs, L., Dailey, A., & Power, M. (1985). The effect of examiner's personal familiarity and professional experience on handicapped children's test performance. *Journal of Educational Research, 78,* 141–146.

Fuchs, L., & Fuchs, D. (1986). Linking assessment to instructional interventions: An overview. *School Psychology Review, 15,* 318–323.

Fuchs, L., Fuchs, D., & Hamlett, C. (1989). Effects of alternative goal structures within curriculum based measurement. *Exceptional Children, 55,* 429–438.

Fuchs, L. S., Bahr, C. M., & Rieth, H. J. (1989). Effects of goal structures and performance contingencies on the math performance of adolescents with learning disabilities. *Journal of Learning Disabilities, 22,* 554–560.

Fuchs, L. S., Fuchs, D., & Deno, S. L. (1985). Importance of goal ambitiousness and goal mastery to student achievement. *Exceptional Children, 52,* 63–71.

Gathercoal, F. (1997). *Judicious discipline* (4th ed.). San Francisco: Caddo Gap Press.

Gersten, R., & Baker, S. (2000). *Practices for English language learners: An overview of instructional practices for English language learners: Prominent themes and future directions.* Denver: National Institute for Urban School Improvement.

Gersten, R., & Brengelman, S. (1996). The quest to translate research into classroom practice: The emerging knowledge base. *Remedial and Special Education, 17,* 67–74.

Gersten, R., & Jimenez, R. (2002). Modulating instruction for English-language learners. In E. J. Kame'enui, D. Carnine, R. Dixon, D. Simmons, & M. Coyne (Eds.), *Effective teaching strategies that accommodate diverse learners* (2nd ed.). Columbus, OH: Merrill/Prentice Hall.

Gettinger, M., & Ball, C. (2008). Best practices in increasing academic engaged time. In A. Thomas & J. Grimes (Eds.), *Best practices in school psychology V* (pp. 1043–1058). Bethesda, MD: National Association of School Psychologists.

Gettinger, M., & Stoiber, K. (1998). Excellence in teaching: Review of instructional and environmental variables. In C. Reynolds & T. Gutkin (Eds.), *Handbook of school psychology* (3rd ed., pp. 933–958). New York: Wiley.

Glover, S., Burns, J., Butler, H., & Patton, G. (1998). Social environments and the emotional wellbeing of young people. *Family Matters, 49,* 11–16.

Good, R., & Brophy, J. (2000). *Looking in classrooms* (8th ed.). New York: Longman.

Good, T., & Beckerman, T. (1978). Time on task: A naturalistic study in sixth-grade classrooms. *The Elementary School Journal, 78,* 193–201.

Good, T., & Grouws, D. (1977). Teaching effects: A process-product study in fourth grade mathematics classrooms. *Journal of Teacher Education, 28,* 49–54.

Gortmaker, V., Warnes, E. D., & Sheridan, S. M. (2004). Conjoint behavioral consultation: Involving parents and teachers in the treatment of a child with selective mutism. *Proven Practice, 5,* 66–72.

Gottfried, A. E. (1983). Intrinsic motivation in young children. *Young Children, 39,* 64–73.

Greenwood, C. R., Hops, H., Delquadri, J., & Guild, J. (1974). Group contingencies for group consequences in classroom management: A further analysis. *Journal of Applied Behavior Analysis, 7,* 413–425.

Gresham, F. M. (1998). Social skills training with children. In T. S. Watson & F. M. Gresham (Eds.), *Handbook of child behavior therapy* (pp. 475–497). New York: Plenum.

Gresham, F. M. (2002). Teaching social skills to high-risk children and youth: Preventive and remedial strategies. In M. R. Shinn, H. M. Walker, & G. Stoner (Eds.), *Interventions for academic and behavior problems II: Preventive and remedial approaches* (pp. 403–432). Bethesda: National Association of School Psychologists.

Gresham, F. M., Watson, S. T., & Skinner, C. H. (2001). Functional behavioral assessment: Principles, procedures, and future directions. *School Psychology Review, 30,* 156–172.

Grimes, L. (1981). Learned helplessness and attribution theory: Redefining children's learning problems. *Learning Disability Quarterly, 4,* 92–100.

Gunter, P., Coutinho, M., & Cade, T. (2002). Classroom factors linked with academic gains among students with emotional and behavior problems. *Preventing School Failure, 46,* 126–132.

Gunter, P., & Denny, R. (1998). Trends, issues, and research needs regarding academic instruction of students with emotional and behavioral disorders. *Behavioral Disorders, 24,* 44–50.

Gunter, P. L., Hummel, J. H., & Venn, M. L. (1999). Are effective academic instructional practices used to teach students with behavior disorders? *Beyond Behavior, 9*(3), 5–11.

Gunter, P. L., & Jack, S. L. (1993). Lag sequential analysis as a tool for functional analysis of student disruptive behavior in classrooms. *Journal of Emotional and Behavioral Disorders, 1,* 138–149.

Hall, R. V., & Hall, M. C. (1980). *How to select reinforcers.* Lawrence, KS: H&H Enterprises.

Hall, R. V., Lund, D., & Jackson, D. (1968). Effects of teacher attention on study behavior. *Journal of Applied Behavior Analysis, 1,* 1–12.

Haring, T., Roger, B., Lee, M., Breen, C., & Gaylord-Ross, R. (1986). Teaching social language to moderately handicapped students. *Journal of Applied Behavior Analysis, 19,* 159–171.

Harris, K., Friedlander, B., Saddler, B., Frizzelle, R., & Graham, S. (2005). Self-monitoring of attention versus self-monitoring of academic performance: Effects among students with ADHD in the general education classroom. *Journal of Special Education, 39,* 145–156.

Harris, V. W., & Sherman, J. A. (1973). Use and analysis of the "Good Behavior Game" to reduce disruptive classroom behavior. *Journal of Applied Behavior Analysis, 6,* 405–417.

Harrop, A., & Swinson, J. (2003). Teachers' questions in the infant, junior and secondary school. *Educational Studies, 29*(1), 49–57.

Henderson, A., & Mapp, K. (2002). *A new wave of evidence: The impact of school, family, and community connections on student achievement.* Austin, TX: National Center for Family and Community Connections with Schools, Southwest Educational Development Laboratory.

Hintze, J. M., Volpe, R. J., & Shapiro, E. S. (2002). Best practices in the systematic direct observation of student behavior. In A. Thomas & J. Grimes (Eds.), *Best practices in school psychology IV* (pp. 993–1006). Bethesda, MD: National Association of School Psychologists.

Hofmeister, A., & Lubke, M. (1990). *Research into practice: Implementing effective teaching strategies.* Boston: Allyn & Bacon.

Horcones, R. (1992). Natural reinforcements: A way to improve education. *Journal of Applied Behavior Analysis, 25,* 71–75.

Horner, R., Carr, E., Halle, J., McGee, G., Odom, S., & Wolery, M. (2005). The use of single-subject research to identify evidence-based practice in special education. *Exceptional Children, 71,* 165–179.

Horner, R., Dunlap, G., Koegel, R. L., Carr, E. G., Sailor, W., Anderson, J., et al. (1990). Toward a technology of "nonaversive" behavior support. *Journal of the Association for Persons with Severe Handicaps, 15,* 125–132.

Horner, R. H., Sugai, G., Todd, A. W., & Lewis-Palmer, T. (2005). Schoolwide positive behavior support. In L. M. Bambara & L. Kern (Eds.), *Individualized supports for students with problem behaviors: Designing positive behavior plans* (pp. 359–390). New York: The Guilford Press.

Horner, R. H., Vaughn, B. J., Day, H. M., & Ard, W. R. (1996). The relationship between setting events and problem behavior: Expanding our understanding of behavioral support. In L. Koegel, R. L. Koegel, & G. Dunlap (Eds.), *Community, school, family, and social inclusion through positive behavioral support* (pp. 381–402). Baltimore: Paul H. Brookes.

Houghton, S., Wheldall, K., Jukes, R., & Sharpe, A. (1990). The effects of limited private reprimands and increased private praise on classroom behaviour in four British secondary school classes. *British Journal of Educational Psychology, 60,* 255–265.

Howell, K. W., & Nolet, V. (2000). *Curriculum-based evaluation: Teaching and decision making.* Belmont, CA: Wadsworth/Thomason Learning.

Hudson, P., & Miller, S. P. (2006). *Designing and implementing mathematics instruction for students with diverse learning needs.* Boston: Allyn and Bacon.

Hughes, C., Copeland, S., Wehmeyer, M., Agran, M., Rodi, M., & Presley, J. (2002). Using self-monitoring to improve performance in general education high school classes. *Education and Training in Mental Retardation and Developmental Disabilities, 37,* 262–272.

Hughes, C., & Hendrickson, J. (1987). Self-monitoring with at-risk students in the regular class setting. *Education and Treatment of Children, 10,* 225–236.

Huston-Stein, A., Friedrich-Cofer, L., & Susman, E. J. (1977). The relation of classroom structure to social behavior, imaginative plan, and self-regulation of economically disadvantaged children. *Child Development, 48,* 908–916.

Individuals with Disabilities Education Improvement Act, 20 U.S.C. § 1400 (2004).

Iwata, B., Dorsey, M., Slifer, K., Bauman, K., & Richman, G. (1994). Toward a functional analysis of self-injury. *Journal of Applied Behavior Analysis, 27,* 197–209.

Jack, S., Shores, R., Denny, R., Gunter, P., DeBriere, T., & DePaepe, P. (1996). An analysis of the relationship of teachers' reported use of classroom management strategies on types of classroom interactions. *The Journal of Behavioral Education, 6,* 67–87.

Jackson, R. R. (2009). *Never work harder than your students and other principles of great teaching.* Alexandria, VA: ACSD.

Jacobsen, B., Lowery, B., & Ducette, J. (1986). Attributions of learning-disabled children. *Journal of Educational Psychology, 78,* 59–64.

Jenson, W. R, Rhode, G., & Reavis, H. K. (in press). *The tough kid toolbox.* Eugene, OR: Pacific Northwest Publishing.

Johnson, L., Graham, S., & Harris, K. (1997). The effects of goal setting and self-instruction on learning a reading comprehension strategy: A study of students with learning disabilities. *Journal of Learning Disabilities, 30,* 80–91.

Johnson, T. C., Stoner, G., & Green, S. K. (1996). Demonstrating the experimenting society model with classwide behavior management interventions. *School Psychology Review, 25,* 199–214.

Johnston, J., & Pennypacker, H. (1993). *Strategies for human behavioral research.* Hillsdale, NJ: Lawrence Erlbaum.

Jones, V., & Jones, L. (2007). *Comprehensive classroom management: Creating positive learning environments* (8th ed.). Boston: Allyn & Bacon.

Kame'enui, E., & Carnine, D. (1998). *Effective teaching strategies that accommodate diverse learners.* Upper Saddle River, NJ: Merrill/Prentice Hall.

Kame'enui, E., & Simmons, D. (1990). *Designing instructional strategies: The prevention of academic learning problems.* Englewood Cliffs, NJ: Macmillan Publishing Co.

Kame'enui, E., & Simmons, D. (1999). *Toward successful inclusion of students with disabilities: The architecture of instruction.* Reston, VA: Council for Exceptional Children.

Karen, R. (1974). *An introduction to behavior theory and its applications.* New York: Harper & Row.

Kastelen, L., Nickel, M., & McLaughlin, T. F. (1984). Performance feedback system: Generalization of effects across tasks and time with eighth-grade English students. *Education & Treatment of Children, 7*(2), 141–155.

Katzell, R., & Thompson, D. (1990). Work motivation: Theory and practice. *American Psychologist, 45,* 144–153.

Kauffman, J. (2005). *Characteristics of emotional and behavioral disorders of children and youth* (8th ed.). Upper Saddle River, NJ: Merrill/Prentice Hall.

Kazdin, A. (1977). Assessing the clinical or applied importance of behavior change through social validation. *Behavior Modification, 1,* 427–451.

Kazdin, A. (1987). *Conduct disorders in childhood and adolescence.* London: Sage.

Kazdin, A. (2001). *Behavior modification in applied settings* (6th ed.). Belmont, CA: Wadsworth.

Kazdin, A., & Bootzin, R. (1972). The token economy: An evaluative review. *Journal of Applied Behavior Analysis, 5,* 343–372.

Keith, T., Keith, P., Quirk, K., Sperduto, J., Santillo, S., & Killings, S. (1998). Longitudinal effects of parent involvement on high school grades: Similarities and differences across gender and ethnic groups. *Journal of School Psychology, 36,* 335–363.

Keogh, B. (2003). Temperament in the classroom: Understanding individual differences. Baltimore: Brooks.

Kerr, J., & Nelson, C. (2002). *Strategies for addressing behavior problems in the classroom* (4th ed.). Englewood Cliffs, NJ: Merrill/Prentice Hall.

Koegel, L. K., Koegel, R. L., & Dunlap, G. (1996). *Positive behavioral support.* Baltimore: Brookes.

Koegel, R., Harrower, J., & Koegel, L. (1999). Support for children with developmental disabilities in full inclusion classrooms through class management. *Journal of Positive Behavior Interventions, 1,* 26–34.

Kounin, J. (1970). *Discipline and group management in classrooms.* New York: Holt, Rinehart, & Winston.

Lalli, J., Vollmer, T., Progar, P., Wright, C., Borrero, J., Daniel, D., et al. (1999). Competition between positive and negative reinforcement in the treatment of escape behavior. *Journal of Applied Behavior Analysis, 32,* 285–296.

Lampi, A., Fenty, N., & Beaunae, C. (2005). Making the three Ps easier: Praise, proximity, and precorrection. *Beyond Behavior, 15,* 8–12.

Langland, S., Lewis-Palmer, T., & Sugai, G. (1998). Teaching respect in the classroom: An instructional approach. *Journal of Behavioral Education, 8*(2), 245–262.

Lembke, E., & Stormont, M. (2005). Using research-based practices to support students with diverse needs in general education settings. *Psychology in the Schools, 42,* 761–763.

Lerman, D., Iwata, B., Rainville, B., Adelinis, J., Crosland, K., & Kogan, J. (1997). Effects of reinforcement choice on task responding in individuals with developmental disabilities. *Journal of Applied Behavior Analysis, 30,* 411–422.

Lerman, D., Iwata, B., & Wallace, M. (1999). Side effects of extinction: Prevalence of bursting and aggression during the treatment of self-injurious behavior. *Journal of Applied Behavior Analysis, 32,* 1–8.

Lewis, T. J., Hudson, S., Richter, M., & Johnson, N. (2004). Scientifically supported practices in emotional and behavioral disorders: A proposed approach and brief review of current practices. *Behavioral Disorders, 29,* 247–259.

Lewis, T., & Sugai, G. (1996a). Functional assessment of problem behavior: A pilot investigation of the comparative and interactive effects of teacher and peer social attention on students in general education settings. *School Psychology Quarterly, 11,* 1–19.

Lewis, T., & Sugai, G. (1996b). Descriptive and experimental analysis of teacher and peer attention and the use of assessment based intervention to improve pro-social behavior of a student in general education setting. *Journal of Behavioral Education, 6,* 7–24.

Lewis, T. J., & Sugai, G. (1999). Effective behavior support: A systems approach to proactive school-wide management. *Focus on Exceptional Children, 31*(6), 1–24.

Lloyd, J., Forness, S., & Kavale, K. (1998). Some methods are more effective than others. *Intervention in School and Clinic, 33,* 195–200.

Lohrmann, S., & Talerico, J. (2004). Anchor the boat: A classwide intervention to reduce problem behavior. *Journal of Positive Behavior Interventions, 6,* 113–120.

Lovitt, T. C. (1978). Applied behavior analysis and learning disabilities—specific research recommendations and suggestions for practitioners. *Journal of Learning Disabilities. No. 8,* 504–518.

Luiselli, J. K., Putnam, R. F., Handler, M. W., & Feinberg, A. B. (2005). Whole-school positive behavior support: Effects on student discipline problems and academic performance. *Educational Psychology, 25*(2–3), 183–198.

Mace, F., Belfiore, P., & Shea, M. (2001). Operant theory and research on self-regulation. In B. Zimmerman and D. Schunk (Eds.), *Learning and academic achievement: Theoretical perspectives* (pp. 39–65). Mahwah, NJ: Lawrence Erlbaum.

Madsen, C. H., Jr., Becker, W. C. , & Thomas, D. R. (1968). Rules, praise, and ignoring: Elements of elementary classroom control. *Journal of Applied Behavior Analysis, 1,* 139–150.

Ma, X., & Willms, J. D. (2004). School disciplinary climate: Characteristics and effects on eighth grade achievement. *Alberta Journal of Educational Research, 50,* 169–189.

Malone, B. G., & Tietjens, C. L. (2000). Re-examination of classroom rules: The need for clarity and specified behaviors. *Special Services in the Schools, 16*(1–2), 159–170.

Maloney, K. B., & Hopkins, B. L. (1973). The modification of sentence structure and its relationship to subjective judgments of creativity in writing. *Journal of Applied Behavior Analysis, 6,* 425–433.

Marshall, M. (2001). *Discipline without stress, punishments or rewards: How teachers and parents promote responsibility and learning.* Los Alamitos, CA: Piper.

Martella, R., Marchand-Martella, N., Miller, T., Young, K., & Macfarlane, C. (1995). Teaching instructional aides and peer tutors to decrease problem behaviors in the classroom. *Teaching Exceptional Children, 27,* 53–56.

Martella, R. C., Nelson, J. R., & Marchand-Martella, N. E. (2003). *Managing disruptive behaviors in the schools.* Boston: Allyn & Bacon.

Marzanno, R. (2003). *Classroom management that works.* Alexandria, VA: ASCD.

Matheson, A., & Shriver, M. (2005). Training teachers to give effective commands: Effects on student compliance and academic behaviors. *School Psychology Review, 34,* 202–219.

Mayer, G. (1995). Preventing antisocial behavior in the schools. *Journal of Applied Behavior Analysis, 28,* 467–478.

McAllister, L., Stachowiak, J., Baer, D., & Conderman, L. (1969). The application of operant conditioning techniques in a secondary school classroom. *Journal of Applied Behavior Analysis, 2,* 277–285.

McGinnis, E., & Goldstein, A. (1994). *Skillstreaming the elementary school child* (Rev. ed.). Champaign, IL: Research Press.

McKinney, J., Mason, J., Clifford, M., & Perkerson, K. (1975). Relationship between classroom behavior and academic achievement. *Journal of Educational Psychology, 67,* 198–203.

McLeod, J., Fisher, J., & Hoover, G. (2003). *The key elements of classroom management: Managing time and space, student behavior, and instructional strategies.* Alexandria, VA: ASCD.

McNamara, E., Evans, M., & Hill, W. (1986). The reduction of disruptive behaviour in two secondary school classes. *British Journal of Educational Psychology, 56,* 209–215.

McNeely, C., & Falci, C. (2004). School connectedness and the transition into and out of health-risk behavior among adolescents: A comparison of social belonging and teacher support. *Journal of School Health, 74*(7), 284–292.

Mendler, A. N., & Curwin, R. L. (2007). *Discipline with dignity for challenging youth.* Bloomington, IN: Solution Tree.

Merrell, K. W., Ervin, R. A., & Gimple, G. A. (2005). *School psychology in the 21st Century: Introduction, principles, and practices.* New York: Guilford Press.

Merrett, F. (1981). Studies in behaviour modification in British educational settings. *Educational Psychology, 2,* 147–157.

Merrett, F., & Wheldall, K. (1990). *Positive teaching in the primary school.* London: Paul Chapman.

Miller, D., & Kraft, N. (2008). Best practices in communicating with and involving parents. In A. Thomas & J. Grimes (Eds.), *Best practices in school psychology V* (pp. 937–951). Bethesda, MD: National Association of School Psychologists.

Miller, K., Gunter, P., Venn, M., Hummel, J., & Wiley, L. (2003). Effects of curricular materials modifications on academic performance and task engagement of three students with emotional or behavioral disorders. *Behavioral Disorders, 28,* 130–149.

Moskowitz, G., & Hayman, M. (1976). Success strategies of inner-city teachers: A year long study. *Journal of Educational Research, 69,* 283–389.

Murray, C., & Greenberg, M. (2006). Examining the importance of social relationships and social contexts in the lives of children with high-incidence disabilities. *The Journal of Special Education, 39,* 220–233.

Murray, C., & Murray, T. (2004). Child level correlates of teacher-student relationships: An examination of demographic characteristics, academic orientations, and behavioral orientations. *Psychology in the Schools, 41,* 751–762.

Nafpaktitis, M., Mayer, G. R., & Butterworth, T. (1985). Natural rates of teacher approval and disapproval and their relation to student behavior in intermediate school classrooms. *Journal of Educational Psychology, 77,* 362–367.

Nelson, J. R., Martella, R. M., & Marchand-Martella, N. (2002). Maximizing student learning: The effects of a comprehensive school-based program for preventing problem behaviors. *Journal of Emotional and Behavioral Disorders, 10,* 136–148.

Newcomer, L., & Lewis, T. (2004). Functional behavioral assessment: An investigation of assessment reliability and effectiveness of function-based interventions. *Journal of Emotional and Behavioral Disorders, 12,* 168–181.

Niebuhr, K. (1999). An empirical study of student relationships and academic achievement. *Education, 9,* 679–681.

No Child Left Behind Act of 2001, U.S.C. 115 Stat. 1426. PL. 107-110 (2002).

Northup, J. (2000). Further evaluation of the accuracy of reinforce surveys: A systematic replication. *Journal of Applied Behavior Analysis, 29,* 201–212.

O'Leary, K., & Becker, W. (1967). Behavior modification of an adjustment class. *Exceptional Children, 33,* 637–642.

O'Leary, K., & O'Leary, S. (Eds.). (1977). *Classroom management: The successful use of behavior modification* (2nd ed.). New York: Pergamon Press.

O'Neill, R. E., Horner, R. H., Albin, R. W., Sprague, J. R., Storey, K., & Newton, J. S. (1997). *Functional assessment and program development for problem behavior: A practical handbook.* Pacific Grove, CA: Brooks/Cole.

Ornstein, A., & Lasley, T. (2004). *Strategies for effective teaching* (4th ed.). Boston: McGraw Hill.

Ortiz, S. O., & Flanagan, D. P. (2002). Best practices in working with culturally diverse children and families. In A. Thomas & Grimes, J. (Eds.), *Best practices in school psychology IV* (pp. 337–351). Bethesda, MD: National Association of School Psychologists.

Ostrosky, M., Drasgow, E., & Halle, J. (1999). How can I help you get what you want? A communication strategy for students with severe disabilities. *Teaching Exceptional Children, 31,* 56–61.

Paine, S., Radicchi, J., Rosellini, L., Deutchman, L., & Darch, C. (1983). *Structuring your classroom for academic success.* Champaign, IL: Research Press.

Patrick, C., Ward, P., & Crouch, D. (1998). Effects of holding students accountable for social behaviors during volleyball games in elementary physical education. *Journal of Teaching in Physical Education, 17*(2), 143–156.

Payne, R. (1995). *A framework for understanding poverty.* Highlands, TX: Aha! Process.

Pedota, P. (2007). Strategies for effective classroom management in the secondary setting. *The Clearing House, 80,* 163–166.

Pergande, K., & Thorkildsen, T. A. (1995). From teachers as experimental researchers to teaching as moral inquiry. In J. G. Nicholls & T. A. Thorkildsen (Eds.), *Reasons for learning: Expanding the conversation on student-teacher collaboration* (pp. 21–35). New York: Teachers College Press.

Phelan, P., Yu, H., & Davidson, A. (1994). Navigating the psychosocial pressures of adolescence: The voices and experiences of high school youth. *American Educational Research Journal, 31,* 415–447.

Pianta, R., Hamre, B., & Stuhlman, M. (2003). Relationships between teachers and children. In W. M. Reynolds & G. E. Miller (Eds.), *Handbook of child psychology: Vol. 7. Educational psychology.* Hoboken, NJ: Wiley.

Rader, L. (2005). Goal setting for students and teachers. *Clearing House, 78,* 123–126.

Reid, R., Trout, A., & Schartz, M. (2005). Self-regulation interventions for children with attention deficit/hyperactivity disorder. *Exceptional Children, 71,* 361–376.

Reinke, W., Lewis-Palmer, T., & Martin, E. (2007). The effect of visual performance feedback on teacher behavior-specific praise. *Behavior Modification, 31,* 247–263.

Report on Scientifically Based Research Supported by U.S. Department of Education (Press Release, November 18, 2002). Retrieved from: www.ed.gov/news/pressreleases/2002/11/11182002b.html

Repp, A., Nieminen, G., Olinger, E., & Brusca, R. (1988). Direct observation: Factors affecting the accuracy of observers. *Exceptional Children, 55,* 29–36.

Resnick, M. D., Bearman, P. S., Blum, R. W., Bauman, K. E., Harris, K. M., Jones, J., et al. (1997). Protecting adolescents from harm: Findings from the national longitudinal study on adolescent health. *Journal of the American Medical Association, 278,* 823–832.

Rhode, G., Jenson, W., & Reavis, H. (1992). *The tough kid book.* Longmont, CO: Sopris West.

Rhodes, R., Ochoa, S., & Ortiz, S. (2005). *Assessing culturally and linguistically diverse students: A practical guide.* New York: Guilford Press.

Robertshaw, C. S., & Hiebert, H. D. (1973). The astronaut game: A group contingency applied to a first grade classroom. *School Applications of Learning and Theory, 6,* 28–33.

Roca, J. V., & Gross, A. M. (1996). Report-Do-Report: Promoting setting and setting-time generalization. *Education and Treatment of Children, 19,* 408–424.

Rones, M., & Hoagwood, K. (2000). School-based mental health services: A research review. *Clinical Child and Family Psychology Review, 3*(4), 223–241.

Rosenshine, B. (1971). *Teaching behaviours and student achievement.* London: National Foundation for Educational Research.

Rosenshine, B. (1983). Teaching functions in instructional programs. *Elementary School Journal, 83,* 335–351.

Rosenshine, B. (1986). Synthesis of research on explicit teaching. *Educational Leadership, 43,* 60–69.

Rosenshine, B. (1997). Advances in research on instruction. In J. W. Lloyd, E. J. Kame'enui, & D. Chard (Eds.), *Issues in education students with disabilities.* Mahwah, NJ: Lawrence Erlbaum.

Rusch, F., & Close, D. (1976). Overcorrection: A procedural evaluation. *AAESPH Review, 1,* 32–45.

Salend, S., & Sylvestre, S. (2005). Understanding and addressing oppositional and defiant classroom behaviors. *Teaching Exceptional Children, 37,* 32–39.

Scheuermann, B., & Evans, W. (1997). Hippocrates was right: Do no harm. A case for ethics in the selection of interventions. *Beyond Behavior, 8*(3), 18–22.

Scheuermann, B., & Hall, J. A. (2008). *Positive behavioral supports for the classroom.* Upper Saddle River, NJ: Pearson Education, Inc.

Schuldheisz, J. M., & van der Mars, H. (2001). Active supervision and students' physical activity in middle school physical education. *Journal of Teaching in Physical Education, 21,* 75–90.

Scientifically Based Evaluation Methods (January 25, 2005). Federal Register, Notices, 70(15), 3586–3589.

Sharpe, T., Brown, M., & Crider, K. (1995). The effects of a sportsmanship curriculum intervention on generalized positive social behavior or urban elementary school students. *Journal of Applied Behavior Analysis, 28,* 401–416.

Sheridan, S. M., Kratochwill, T. R., & Bergan, J. R. (1996). *Conjoint behavioral consultation: A procedural manual.* New York: Plenum Press.

Shinn, M., & Bamonto, S. (1998). Advanced applications of curriculum-based measurement: "Big ideas" and avoiding confusion. In M. R. Shinn (Ed.), *Advanced Applications of Curriculum-Based Measurement* (pp. 1–31). New York: Guilford Press.

Shinn, M., Ramsey, E., Walker, H., Stieber, S., & O'Neill, R. (1987). Antisocial behavior in school settings: Initial differences in an at-risk and normal population. *Journal of Special Education, 21,* 69–84.

Shores, R., Gunter, P., & Jack, S. (1993). Classroom management strategies: Are they setting events for coercion? *Behavioral Disorders, 18,* 92–102.

Silver-Pacuilla, H., & Fleischman, S. (2006). Technology to help struggling students. *Educational Leadership, 63,* 84–85.

Simmons, D. C., Fuchs, L. S., & Fuchs, D. (1995). Effects of explicit teaching and peer tutoring on the reading achievement of learning disabled and low-performing students in regular classrooms. *Elementary School Journal, 95,* 387–408.

Simonsen, B., Fairbanks, S., Briesch, A., Myers, D., & Sugai, G. (2008). Evidence-based practices in classroom management: Considerations for Research to Practice. *Education and Treatment of Children, 31,* 351–380.

Skinner, B. F. (1953). *Science and human behavior.* New York: Basic Books.

Skinner, B. F. (1982). Contrived reinforcement. *The Behavior Analyst, 5,* 3–8.

Smith, B. (2000). Quantity matters: Annual instruction time in an urban school system. *Educational Administration Quarterly, 35*, 652–682.

Spencer, V. G. (2006). Peer tutoring and students with emotional or behavioral disorders: A review of the literature. *Behavioral Disorders, 31*(2), 204–222.

Sprick, R. S. (1995). *Cafeteria discipline: Positive techniques for lunchroom supervision* [videotape]. Eugene, OR: Pacific Northwest Publishing.

Sprick, R. S. (2003). *START on time! Safe transitions and reduced tardies.* Eugene, OR: Pacific Northwest Publishing.

Sprick, R. S. (2006). *Discipline in the secondary classroom: A positive approach to behavior management* (2nd ed). San Francisco: Jossey–Bass.

Sprick, R. S., & Booher, M. (2006). Behavior support and response to intervention: a systematic approach to meeting the social/emotional needs of students. *Communique, 35*(4), 34–36.

Sprick, R. S., Booher, M., & Garrison, M. (2009). *Behavioral response to intervention; Creating a continuum of problem-solving and support.* Eugene, OR: Pacific Northwest Publishing.

Sprick, R. S., & Garrison, M. (2008). *Interventions: Evidence-based behavior strategies for individual students* (2nd ed.). Eugene, OR: Pacific Northwest Publishing.

Sprick, R. S., Garrison, M., & Howard, L. (1998). *CHAMPs: A proactive and positive approach to classroom management.* Eugene, OR: Pacific Northwest Publishing.

Sprick, R. S., Garrison, M., & Howard, L. (2002). *Foundations: Establishing positive discipline and schoolwide behavior support* (2nd ed.). Eugene, OR: Pacific Northwest Publishing.

Sprick, R. S., & Howard, L. (2009). *Stepping In: A Substitute's Guide to Behavior and Instruction.* Eugene, OR: Pacific Northwest Publishing.

Sprick, R. S., Howard, L., Wise, B. J., Marcum, K., & Haykin, M. (1998). *Administrator's desk reference of behavior management (Vols. 1–3).* Eugene, OR: Pacific Northwest Publishing.

Sprick, R. S., Knight, J., Reinke, W., & McKale, T. (2007). *Coaching classroom management: Strategies and tools for administrators and coaches.* Eugene, OR: Pacific Northwest Publishing.

Sprick, R. S., Swartz, L., & Glang, A. (2005). *On the playground: A guide to playground management.* Eugene, OR: Pacific Northwest Publishing and Oregon Center for Applied Sciences.

Sprick, R. S., Swartz, L., & Glang, A. (2007). *In the driver's seat: A roadmap to managing student behavior on the bus.* Eugene, OR: Pacific Northwest Publishing and Oregon Center for Applied Sciences.

Stichter, J., Lewis, T., Johnson, N., & Trussell, P. (2004). Toward a structural assessment: Analyzing the merits of an assessment tool for a student with E/BD. *Assessment for Effective Intervention, 30*, 25–40.

Stokes, T., & Baer, D. (1977). An implicit technology of generalization. *Journal of Applied Behavior Analysis, 7*, 599–610.

Stormont, M., Smith, S., & Lewis, T. (2007). Teacher implementation of precorrection and praise statements in Head Start classrooms as a component of a program-wide system of positive behavior support. *Journal of Behavioral Education, 16*, 280–290.

Sugai, G., & Horner, R. H. (2002). The evolution of discipline practices: School-wide positive behavior supports. *Child and Family Behavior Therapy, 24*, 23–50.

Sugai, G., Horner, R. H., Dunlap, G., Hieneman, M., Lewis, T., Nelson, C. M., et al. (2000). Applying positive behavior support and functional behavioral assessment in schools. *Journal of Positive Behavioral Interventions, 2,* 131–143.

Sugai, G., & Lewis, T. (1996). Preferred and promising practices for social skill instruction. *Focus on Exceptional Children, 29,* 1–16.

Sugai, G., & Tindal, G. (1993). *Effective school consultation: An interactive approach.* Pacific Grove, CA: Brooks/Cole.

Sulzer-Azaroff, B., & Mayer, G. R. (1991). *Behavior analysis for lasting change.* Fort Worth, TX: Holt, Rinehart, & Winston.

Sutherland, K. (2000). Promoting positive interactions between teachers and students with emotional/behavioral disorders. *Preventing School Failure, 44,* 110–116.

Sutherland, K., & Wehby, J. (2001). Exploring the relationship between increased opportunities to respond to academic requests and the academic and behavioral outcomes of students with EBD. *Journal of Emotional and Behavioral Disorders, 22,* 113–121.

Sutherland, K. S., Wehby, J., & Copeland, S. (2000). Effect of varying rates of behavior-specific praise on the on-task behavior of students with EBD. *Journal of Applied Behavior Analysis, 8,* 2–8.

Swann, W., & Pittman, T. (1977). Initiating play activity of children: The moderating influence of verbal cues on intrinsic motivation. *Child Development, 48,* 1128–1132.

Sweeney, W., Ehrhardt, A., Gardner, R., Jones, L., Greenfield, R., & Fribley, S. (1999). Using guided notes with academically at-risk high school students during a remedial summer social studies class. *Psychology in the Schools, 36,* 305–318.

Swiezy, N. B., Matson, J. L., & Box, P. (1992). The good behavior game: A token reinforcement system for preschoolers. *Child and Family Behavior Therapy, 14,* 21–32.

Swift, M., & Swift, G. (1968). The assessment of achievement related classroom behavior: Normative, reliability, and validity data. *Journal of Special Education, 2,* 137–153.

Swift, M., & Swift, G. (1969a). Achievement related classroom behavior of secondary school normal and disturbed students. *Exceptional Children, 35,* 677–684.

Swift, M., & Swift, G. (1969b). Clarifying the relationship between academic success and overt classroom behavior. *Exceptional Children, 36,* 99–104.

Swift, M., & Swift, G. (1973). Academic success and classroom behavior in secondary school. *Exceptional Children, 39,* 392–399.

Sykes, S. (October 24, 2002). *Substitutes Teach 6.4 Percent of Classroom Time.* The Salt Lake Tribune, p. B3.

Thomas, D., Becker, W., & Armstrong, M. (1968). Production and elimination of disruptive classroom behavior by systematically varying teacher's behavior. *Journal of Applied Behavior Analysis, 1,* 35–45.

Thompson, R., Fisher, W., & Contrucci, S. (1998). Evaluating the reinforcing effects of choice in comparison to reinforcement rate. *Research in Developmental Disabilities, 19,* 181–187.

Tingstrom, D. H., Sterling-Turner, H. E., & Wilczynski, S. M. (2006). The good behavior game: 1969-2002. *Behavior Modification, 30*(2), 225–253.

Troia, G., & Graham, S. (2002). The effectiveness of a highly explicit, teacher-directed strategy instruction routine: Changing the writing performance of students with learning disabilities. *Journal of Learning Disabilities, 35,* 290–305.

Trussell, R. (2008). Classroom universals to prevent problem behaviors. *Intervention in School and Clinic, 43,* 179–185.

Udvari-Solner, A. (1996). Examining teacher thinking: Constructing a process to designing curricular adaptations. *Remedial and Special Education, 17,* 245–254.

U. S. Department of Education (2002). *Guidance for the Reading First Program.* Retrieved from: www.ed.gov/programs/readingfirst/guidance.doc.

U.S. Department of Education (2002). *No Child Left Behind executive summary.* Washington DC: Author.

Van Acker, R., Grant, S., & Henry, D. (1996). Teacher and student behavior as a function of risk for aggression. *Education and Treatment of Children, 19,* 316–334.

Van Houten, R., & McKillop, C. (1977). An extension of the effects of the performance feedback system with secondary school students. *Psychology in the Schools, 14,* 480–484.

Walker, H., & Bullis, M. (1990). Behavior disorders and the social context of regular class integration: A conceptual dilemma. In J. W. Lloyd, N. N. Singh, & A. C. Repp (Eds.), *The regular education initiative: Alternative perspectives on concepts, issues, and models* (pp. 75–93). Sycamore, IL: Sycamore Publishing.

Walker, H., Colvin, G., & Ramsey, E. (1995). *Antisocial behavior in school: Strategies and best practices.* Pacific Grove, CA: Brooks/Cole.

Walker, H., Horner, R., Sugai, G., Bullis, M., Sprague, J., et al. (1996). Integrated approaches to preventing antisocial behavior patterns among school-age youth. *Journal of Emotional and Behavioral Disorders, 4,* 193–256.

Walker, H., & McConnell, S. (1988). *The Walker-McConnell scale of social competence and school adjustment: A social skills rating scale for teachers.* Austin, TX: Pro–Ed.

Walker, H., Ramsey, E., & Gresham, F. (2004). *Antisocial behavior in schools: Evidence–based practices* (2nd ed.). Belmont, CA: Wadsworth.

Walker, H. M., & Severson, H. H. (1992). *Systematic screening for behavior disorders* (2nd ed.). Longmont, CO: Sopris West.

Walker, H. M., Severson, H. H., Feil, E. G., Stiller, B., & Golly, A. (1998). First step to success: Intervention at the point of school entry to prevent antisocial behavior patterns. *Psychology in the Schools, 35,* 259–269.

Walker, H. M., & Shinn, M. R. (2002). Structuring school-based interventions to achieve integrated primary, secondary, and tertiary prevention goals for safe and effective schools. In M. R. Shinn, G. Stoner, & H. M. Walker (Eds.), *Interventions for academic and behavior problems: Preventive and remedial approaches* (pp. 1–26). Silver Spring, MD: National Association of School Psychologists.

Walker, H. M. & Sprague, J. (2007). Early, evidence-based intervention with school-related behavior disorders: Key issues, continuing challenges, and promising practices. In Crocket, J. B., Gerber, M. M., & Landrum, T. J. (Eds), *Achieving the radical reform of special education: Essays in honor of James M. Kauffman.* New York: Lawrence Erlbaum Associates.

Ward, M., & Baker, B. (1968). Reinforcement therapy in the classroom. *Journal of Applied Behavior Analysis, 1,* 323–328.

Warger, C. (1999). *Positive behavior support and functional assessment.* Arlington, VA: ERIC Clearinghouse on Disabilities and Gifted Education.

Watkins, C. L., & Slocum, T. A. (2004). The components of direct instruction. *Journal of Direct Instruction, 3,* 75–110.

Watson, L. (1967). Application of operant conditioning techniques to institutionalized severely and profoundly retarded children. *Mental Retardation Abstracts, 4,* 1–18.

Wehby, J., Symons, F., Canale, J., & Go, F. (1998). Teaching practices in classrooms for students with emotional and behavioral disorders: Discrepancies between recommendations and observation. *Behavioral Disorders, 24,* 52–57.

Weinstein, C. (1977). Modifying student behavior in an open classroom through changes in the physical design. *American Educational Research Journal, 14,* 249–262.

Wheeler, J., & Richey, D. (2005). *Behavior management.* Upper Saddle River, NJ: Merrill/Prentice-Hall.

Wheldall, K., & Merrett, F. (1984). *Positive teaching: The behavioural approach.* London: Allen and Unwin.

Wheldall, K., & Merrett, F. (1989). *Positive teaching in the secondary school.* London: Paul Chapman Publishing Ltd.

Winett, R. A., & Vachon, E. M. (1974). Group feedback and group contingencies in modifying behavior of fifth graders. *Psychological Reports, 34*(3), 1283–1292.

Wolfgang, C. H., & Glickman, C. D. (l986). *Solving discipline problems: Strategies for classroom teachers* (2nd ed.). Boston: Allyn & Bacon.

Wolford, P. L., Heward, W. L., & Alber, S. R. (2001). Teaching middle school students with learning disabilities to recruit peer assistance during cooperative learning group activities. *Learning Disabilities Research & Practice, 16,* 161–173.

Yan, F., Beck, K., Howard, D., Shattuck, T., & Kerr, M. (2008). A structural model of alcohol use pathways among Latino youth. *American Journal of Health Behavior, 32,* 209–219.

Yawkey, T.D. (1971). Conditioning independent work behavior in reading with seven-year-old children in a regular early childhood classroom. *Child Study Journal, 2*(1), 23.

Ysseldyke, J., & Christenson, S. L. (1988). Linking assessment to intervention. In J. Graden, J. Zins, & M. Curtis (Eds.), *Alternative educational delivery systems* (pp. 91–110). Washington, DC: National Association of School Psychologists.

Ysseldyke, J., Murns, M., Dawson, P., Kelley, B., Morrison, D., Ortiz, S., et al. (2006). *School psychology: A blueprint for training and practice III.* Bethesda, MD: National Association of School Psychologists.

Ysseldyke, J., Thurlow, M., Wotruba, J., & Nania, P. (1990). Instructional arrangements: Perceptions from general education. *Teaching Exceptional Children, 22,* 4–8.

Index